Advanced Assembler Language and MVS Interfaces for IBM Systems and Application Programmers

Advanced Assembler Language and MVS Interfaces for IBM Systems and Application Programmers

Carmine A. Cannatello

John Wiley & Sons, Inc.
New York • Chichester • Brisbane • Toronto • Singapore

Library of Congress Cataloging-in-Publication Data

Cannatello, Carmine, 1943-

Advanced Assembler language and MVS interfaces for IBM systems and application programmers / by Carmine Cannatello.

p. cm.

Includes bibliographical references.

ISBN 0-471-50435-1 (alk. paper)

1. Assembler language (Computer program language) 2. MVS (Computer system) 3. IBM computers--Programming. I. Title.

QA76.73.ABC36 1991

005.2'25--dc20 90-24395

Printed in the United States of America

91 92 10 9 8 7 6 5 4 3 2 1

To all Assembler language programmers—
may we continue to exist and enjoy what
we do.

About the Author

Carmine A. Cannatello has been in the EDP profession for about 20 years and has been an independent computer consultant since 1980. Over the years, he has presented many classes and seminars and is currently teaching evenings at the School of Continuing Education at NYU. His expertise is in systems programming in the areas of MVS, CICS, VTAM/NCP, and of course Assembler Language. Mr. Cannatello has a B.S. in Mathematics from Manhattan College and has studied Electrical/Computer Engineering at New York Polytechnic Institute. Carmine lives in Manhattan and enjoys various athletic activities and flying his Cessna Skyhawk. He holds a commercial pilots license and an instrument rating.

Contents

CHAPTER 2 Assembler Language Programming Development and Structure 28

CHAPTER 3 The Macro Facility and Conditional Assembler Language 54

Index of Coding Examples, Figures, and Tables

Coding Examples

Figures

Tables

Trademarks

The following are trademarks of International Business Machines Corporation.

MVS/370
MVS/XA
MVS/ESA
ESA/370
Hiperspace

Preface

The idea for this book came from the Advanced Assembler Language course which I have been teaching at NYU's School of Continuing Education since 1987. During the first year of teaching that course with IBM manuals and various handouts based upon my own experience, I felt that a text book would be very useful. So, after some consideration, I decided to write one. That decision has been continually reinforced by students taking the course. They have repeatedly asked me to recommend a text book for the course since they have been unable to find any dealing with advanced Assembler.

When I designed the book I decided upon certain goals that it should have. The goals that I selected and how I satisfied them are listed below:

To provide, in one book, a number of useful advanced Assembler language topics. The topics that I selected include explanations and examples of various assembler coding techniques that would not normally appear in elementary assembler language books, and the programming of a number of MVS facilities. The presentation of the MVS facilities include a description and use of the facility, the required program interface, and actual programming examples.

Realizing that technical books and manuals tend to be difficult and confusing to read and understand, I attempted to write an easy to read and understand book with detailed and "bug-free" examples. I provided background information wherever it appeared to be necessary and tried to avoid any complex, confusing or ambiguous language in the explanations. Of course, the book does assume a certain level of experience and competency since it is an advanced book. Coding examples are presented for most explanations and most of those coding examples were actually executed on a IBM mainframe computer. After they were debugged and executed properly, they were down-loaded to a PC and then, from there, incorporated into the book.

To provide information concerning how to code comprehendable, good Assembler language. Most of the Assembler language programs which I have examined (including some of my earlier ones) and/or attempted to modify, during my years in the profession, have been very poorly structured and documented and; therefore, difficult to read and understand. In fact, looking at some of them gave cerebral nausea. Some Assembler language programmers are under the false impression that there is something macho, glamorous or esoteric about programs that are difficult to understand (regardless of their function). For some of the smaller and sloppier programs, which I had to modify, I opted to rewrite them (properly) instead of laboring over them and modifying them.

I firmly believe (despite what some high level language programmers and DP managers may think) that Assembler language programs need not be difficult to comprehend. Therefore, I devoted two chapters (Chapters 1 and 2) to present and explain the concept of good

Assembler language and to describe how an Assembler language program should be designed, structured and commented in order to be easy to read, understand and maintain. I emphasize structured programming and top-down programming together with some of my own ideas on how an Assembler language program should be coded. I consider the first two chapters to be among the most important chapters in the book and strongly recommend that they be read and that at least some of the information presented be incorporated into your own programming styles.

After I decided upon the general content of the book, I then had the difficult task of selecting which coding techniques and which MVS facilities to include. The coding techniques, which I selected, are useful and practical and have application for industry related projects. I did not select any coding techniques that are esoteric and have limited practical value, except in the classroom. Since part of advanced Assembler language programming deals with interfacing with the operating system to use the various facilities provided, I tried to select a cross section of the existing MVS facilities that would be of use and/or of interest to a large portion of the readers of this book. Therefore, I selected the common facilities; and a number of uncommon and restricted facilities, which should be known to prospective advanced Assembler language programmers (who may or may not have aspirations of becoming system programmers and/or software developers). I did not select the facilities that are so esoteric that they have very limited use and then only in very special applications.

The chapters are not in any stringent sequence; however, the chapters containing the more basic information, such as the common IBM supplied macro instructions and Assembler language coding techniques, are at the beginning of the book; and the chapters that contain the more advanced information, such as the use of the less common and restricted macro instructions, inter-address space communication, etc., are at the end of the book. The chapters are basically self contained (however, some chapters do make an occasional reference to other chapters) and may be read in any sequence; but the recommendation is to read the chapters in the approximate sequence presented.

This book is not intended to replace the IBM manuals. One dramatic indication of this is Chapter 4, which discusses a number of supervisor services macro instructions. That chapter explains the facilities provided by those macros, discusses their use, and provides coding examples. However, that chapter does not: document the actual syntax; describes all the possible parameters; or tabulates every possible return code of those macro instructions discussed. That information is readily available in the appropriate IBM manuals. Another good example is Chapter 7, which discusses Dynamic Allocation. The numerous error and information codes returned by Dynamic Allocation are not tabulated either since that information is also readily available in the appropriate IBM manuals. My philosophy concerning that matter is that to include such information would be a waste of valuable book space which could be better used to provide and explain other information not directly found in IBM manuals; and it is also good practice and professional for programmers to reference the manuals provided by the manufacturer. This book will actually assist the reader to better understand the IBM manuals because, besides attempting to simplify and in some cases enhance the explanations contained in the IBM manuals, the book also provides detailed and practical coding examples for the various MVS interfaces and facilities presented.

The back of each chapter (except Chapter 1) contains a bibliography of IBM manuals that contain reference information pertinent to that chapter. There is also a bibliography at the end of the book which contains a list of books which provide prerequisite information and a list of IBM manuals which also provide prerequisite information and other reference information pertinent to most of the chapters of the book.

The Assembler language presented in this book is for the IBM System/370 instruction set. That means that it is for the old System/360, System/370 and 303x series mainframe computers; the current 43xx, 308x and 3090 series mainframe computers; and the newly announced System/390 series of mainframe computers. The macro instructions and facilities presented are available for the MVS/370 (non-XA version), the MVS/XA and the MVS/ESA Operating Systems. Where there is a difference among those operating systems, an attempt is made to mention it. Most of the macro instructions and facilities presented in this book are also available in the VS1 operating system, but no attempt is made to mention which ones are not available or function differently. This book will be of some value to DOS/VSE Assembler language programmers. The sections of Chapter 5, (Advanced Assembler Language Techniques), that deal only with Assembler language coding techniques, exclusive of operating system facilities, would also apply to DOS/VSE since the instgruction set is the same. Also, Chapters 1 and 2, which deal with good Assembler language characteristics and program structure and design; and Chapter 3, which deals with conditional assembler and macro writing, would also relate to DOS/VSE. The other chapters, which deal with programming the MVS facilities, would be of limited use to DOS/VSE Assembler language programmers; however, DOS/VSE does have some facilities which are similiar to the ones provided by MVS.

This book is intended primarily for individuals who are currently employed in the EDP profession, and who have a working knowledge of basic Assembler language for the IBM System/370 instruction set and who also have at least a conceptual knowledge of the MVS Operating System. However, the book is also suitable for graduate and undergraduate students who are studying advanced Assembler language. By virtue of the explanations and numerous coding examples, this book may be used for both study and as a reference guide.

The Coding Examples (over 150) in this book are available on a PC diskette (the contents can be uploaded to a mainframe). The information is available on 5 1/4 or 3 1/2 inch diskettes for IBM or IBM compatible personal computers. The price is $50, see last page of book for order form. For additional information or purchase (specify which diskette size), write to:

CAC, Inc.
JAF Station
P.O. Box 8585
New York, NY 10116

The information in the book is intended to enable the reader to improve his/her Assembler language ability, and to provide him/her with a better understanding of the MVS facilities that are available and the programming interfaces required to use those facilities. This book should appeal to application programmers, system programmers and software developers.

I hope that you find the book both enjoyable to read and useful for your professional pursuits.

Carmine A. Cannatello

Acknowledgments

As with any other involved, time consuming venture, the writing of a book requires the assistance of others. I wish to express my thanks and indebtedness to the following individuals.

Dr. Stuart Fink, former director of the Information Technologies Institute section of the School of Continuing Education at NYU. Dr. Fink felt the the book was a good idea when I mentioned it to him. He suggested that I write an outline and sample table of contents; which he read, critiqued and then put me in touch with some of the major book publishers.

Bruce Savell, friend and colleague. He introduced me to Dr. Fink for a teaching assignment at NYU. Bruce expressed encouragement, support and confidence for me when the book was only a though; and read the original outline and offered suggestions.

Marcia Meikle, close friend. Marcia expressed encouragement and support for me during the early stages of the development of the book.

Former students. A number of my former students at NYU expressed anticipation and support for the book during its developement.

Harry Morrison. My special thanks to Harry, a former "A" student of mine who was one of the two proofreaders (other than myself). Harry read nearly every word of the book and offered suggestions and caugh errors which myself and the other proofreader missed. Harry also verified most of the coding examples.

Collene McClintock. My very special thanks to Collene, also a former "A" student of mine and the other proofreader. Collene literally read every word of the book almost twice. She offered useful suggestions including: making the coding examples in the book available to the readers on a PC diskette (see the end of the PREFACE); and caugth errors which myself and the other proofreader missed including some subtle ones in the coding examples. Collene showed more enthusiasm than I did during the final stages of the development of the book.

Acknowledgments

1

Assembler Language Programming Style and Content

1.1 CHARACTERISTICS OF GOOD ASSEMBLER LANGUAGE

Before we can even begin to discuss advanced Assembler language, we must first have a thorough understanding of the characteristics of *good Assembler language*.

The IBM System/370 Instruction Set is very powerful and versatile and may be used to write very sophisticated and very efficient programs. However, as with anything that is powerful and complex, it could easily be misused to create programs that are difficult to understand, next to impossible to debug, inefficient, abnormally terminate with the slightest provocation, and so on, and so on.

IBM provides an Assembler (currently the F-level and the H-level) for their System/370 instruction set, which (besides the obvious functions of providing mnemonics for the machine instructions, assembling the programs, and issuing diagnostic messages) is augmented by a very powerful macro library and provides various features and facilities that, when properly used, facilitate the writing of good Assembler language.

A program written in good Assembler language has at least, but is not limited to, the following characteristics:

- Has simple, easy-to-understand logic;
- Uses mostly simple instructions;
- Has no relative addressing;
- Uses subroutines;
- Uses DSECTs;
- Has efficient code;
- Does not modify instructions;
- Does not abnormally terminate (ABEND) due to user error;
- Requests and checks feedback from macro instructions;
- Internal tables have the capability of expanding;
- Provides meaningful error messages;
- Uses only standard interfaces;
- Lets the Assembler determine lengths;
- Has op-codes, operands and comments aligned;
- Contains meaningful comments;
- Uses meaningful labels;

- Has meaningful DS instructions; and
- Does not specify BLKSIZE for files.

1.1.1 Has Simple, Easy-to-Understand Logic

Programs should be written in easy-to-understand, well-structured logic. There is no valid reason for sloppy, difficult-to-understand logic. The most complex piece of code can usually be reduced into simple logic, with some creative thought and planning.

When a complicated problem is broken into its simpler component parts and structured properly, it is easier to understand and, therefore, requires less time for programming, debugging, and modifying by both the original programmer and the maintenance programmer in the future.

The objective of programming is to direct a computer system to perform a specific task(s) and to provide a technical document (code and comments) for other programmers to understand and modify, if required, in the future. It is not to impress friends, co-workers, and other colleagues with how difficult a program is to understand. A program that is difficult to understand because of excessive and exotic instructions, sloppy logic, poor structure, and inadequate comments is *not* an advanced, sophisticated program written by a senior programmer. It is a sloppy, difficult-to-maintain program written by an inconsiderate (and perhaps insecure) programmer. The real challenge for a true senior programmer and professional is to write difficult program code, and structure and document it in such a way as to make it understandable to other programmers with comparable or, in particular, less experience and ability.

The remainder of this chapter and Chapter 2 provide guidelines and suggestions for writing efficient, well-structured Assembler language programs.

1.1.2 Uses Mostly Simple Instructions

Exotic instructions should not be used just for the sake of using them or to impress one's friends and colleagues. They should be used only when necessary. Most of the program should contain simple instructions. This makes the program easy to understand and maintain and eliminates the need for the original programmer and other programmers to refer constantly to IBM's *Principles of Operation* manual to learn the operation of the instructions whenever a program is examined.

For example, let us say that one of the tasks of a program is to convert all input bytes of binary zeros (X'00') and blanks (X'40') to zoned decimal zeros (X'F0'). One way of doing this is to use the TR (Translate) instruction and set up a 256-byte translate table. In the translation table, X'00' and X'40' are equated to X'F0' and all other characters are equated to themselves. Then, the TR instruction is executed. This task could also be performed by using two sets of CLI and BE instructions.

Using the translate table method, the programmer would have to create and examine it during debugging (if the translate task does not work properly). During maintainence in the future, the original programmer (or the maintenance programmer) would need to examine the table to determine what the TR instruction is doing. Reading the comments (if any exist) would not necessarily be reliable because they may not be accurate or complete, and if the programmer forgot how the TR instruction operates, then he/she would have to locate a copy of the *Principles of Operation* manual and read about the TR instruction.

Using two sets of CLI and BE instructions would be quicker and easier to write, and when examined in the future its meaning would be obvious.

The guideline in this case as to which method to use would be the following. If the programmer knows or strongly suspects that, in the future, there will be numerous other bytes to translate, then by all means he/she should use the translate table method. It would be easier to change one byte in an existing translate table than to modify existing logic in the program by inserting additional sets of CLI and BE instructions and their corresponding subroutines. If, however, the programmer is 90 percent sure that the program has no future requirement for additional characters to be translated, then use the CLI and BE instructions.

Another example is the use of the MVCL (move long) instruction to move 256 bytes or less. Besides being less efficient, the MVCL instruction requires the use of four registers. But more importantly, the contents of the operand of the MVCL instruction are not as obvious as in a MVC instruction. Most programmers do not know (or readily remember) the contents of the four registers, which means that the maintenance programmer would probably have to refer to the *Principles of Operation* if and when he/she locates one.

1.1.3 Has No Relative Addressing

Relative addressing refers to the use of a plus or minus value with a symbolic address. The symbolic address may be a label or the location counter. Some examples of relative addressing are VALIDATE+4, *-12, and *+22. Relative addressing should never (well, almost never) be used in an Assembler language program because of its potential for causing an error while developing the code and when modifying it in the future. Also, the instructions for its use are difficult to follow. Let us consider the following coding example:

```
SUBRTN01 LA      R15,0
         CLI     SW1,C'0'
         BE      SUBRTN02+8                (1)
         CLI     SW2,C'1'
         BE      *+24                      (2)
         MVI     SW2,C'1'
         MVC     LINE1,ERRMSG1
         MVC     LINE2,ERRMSG2
         B       SUBRTN02
         MVI     SW1,C'0'                  (3)
         MVI     SW2,C'0'
         MVC     LINE1,INFOMSG1
         MVC     LINE2,INFOMSG2
         BR      R6
*
*
SUBRTN02 MVI     SW1,C'1'                  (4)
         LA      R15,4
         MVC     FIELD1,INFO1              (5)
         MVC     FIELD2,INFO2
         BR      R6
```

There are a number of problems with the above code. Comment (2) has a BE to address *+24. Where is *+24? If you are looking at an Assembler listing, you would look to the left of that instruction and locate the value of the operand and then examine the instruction addresses down the left side of the listing until you find a match. If there is no match, then the programmer, who coded that instruction, made a mistake with the value after the plus sign. If you find a match, then the instruction at that address is the one that will receive control on the compare equal condition. If you are looking at a listing of the source, then you would have to add the lengths of the BE instruction and all of the instructions that follow until you reach the total of 24 in order to locate the instruction that the BE operand address references. If you do not know the length of the instructions, you would have to refer to either the System/370 Reference Summary card or the *Principles Of Operation* manual. You can also calculate the length of each instruction by referring to the first 2 bits of each instruction (00 indicates 2 bytes, 01 or 10 indicates 4 bytes, and 11 indicates 6 bytes). After you do all this, you will notice (assuming that you did not make a mistake) that BE *+24 refers to the instruction MVI SW1,C'0' at comment (3). If the instruction at comment (2) used a label to refer to the instruction at comment (3) instead of a relative address, then the task of locating the instruction would have been trivial.

Let us suppose that the subroutine SUBRTN01 is to be modified. If any instructions between the instructions at comments (2) and (3) are inserted, deleted, or changed to an instruction of a different length, the relative address *+24 will no longer refer to the intended instruction. It will be the responsibility of the maintenance programmer to change the *+24 to the proper value. If the maintenance programmer did not notice the BE *+24 instruction in the subroutine or changed it incorrectly, then the program will not function properly. The manifestation of this error will depend on what bit configuation is now at *+24. If there happens to be the beginning of another instruction at that location, then the program will execute but will not provide the proper results. Depending on how subtle the logic error is, the error may not be immediately noticed. If *+24 points to the middle of an instruction, then the results are unpredictable. It could, perhaps, result in an 0C1, 0C4, 0C6 (or any other program check) ABEND, or it could actually execute (if the bit configuation at that location is executable) and ABEND later into the program. What may have been a simple modification could now cause unnecessary problems. The use of a symbol at comment (2) (instead of a relative address) and a corresponding label at comment (3) would eliminate the potential problems described above because the Assembler will calculate the new address correctly and automatically when the program is reassembled, instead of the maintenance programmer having that responsibility.

Now let us look at the instruction at comment (1). This condition is worse and presents more of a potential problem than the one described above because it is making a reference to a different subroutine. The branch is to the address, which is eight bytes past the beginning of the subroutine SUBRTN02, which is the instruction at comment (5). When the time comes to modify SUBRTN02, the maintenance programmer would have no reason to suspect that this subroutine is receiving control somewhere in the middle from another part of the program. If you look at the logic of SUBRTN01 and SUBRTN02, you would notice that the value in general register 15 appears to be a return code that is being inspected elsewhere in the program. The value (return code) in general register 15 is being set to 4 if SUBRTN02 is entered at the beginning and the return code is left at 0 if the subroutine is entered at eight bytes into it. Also, the value of the switch SW1 would be different, depending on where SUBRTN02 receives control. If a future modification consisted of inserting additional instructions at the beginning of the subroutine, then it is conceivable that the instructions that were to be bypassed (if the subroutine were entered at eight bytes into it) could now be executed. If the modifications caused either or both of the first two instructions to be located eight or more bytes into the subroutine SUBRTN02 and if the beginning of an instruction is located at eight bytes into SUBRTN02, then when the new version of the program is executed, the value of the switch and/or the value of the return code will not have the intended values. When the other code in the program (which depends on the setting of SW1 and/or the value of the return code) executes, it may either cause a very obvious problem that will be noticed immediately or cause a very subtle error that may require days or even weeks before it is noticed.

In summary, avoid relative addressing. After the relative addresses are replaced with symbols and labels are added, the code will appear as follows:

```
SUBRTN01 LA       R15,0
         CLI      SW1,C'0'
```

```
         BE       SUBRTN2X              (1)
         CLI      SW2,C'1'
         BE       SUBRTN1X              (2)
         MVI      SW2,C'1'
         MVC      LINE1,ERRMSG1
         MVC      LINE2,ERRMSG2
         B        SUBRTN02
SUBRTN1X MVI      SW1,C'0'              (3)
         MVI      SW2,C'0'
         MVC      LINE1,INFOMSG1
         MVC      LINE2,INFOMSG2
         BR       R6
*
*
SUBRTN02 MVI      SW1,C'1'              (4)
         LA       R15,4
SUBRTN2X MVC      FIELD1,INFO1          (5)
         MVC      FIELD2,INFO2
         BR       R6
```

The above code will not have the potential problems with relative addressing as the original code (discussed earlier) would.

There are two valid cases for using relative addressing. The first is the loading of base registers at the beginning of the program. Some programmers prefer loading their base registers in the following way:

```
PROGRAM  CSECT
         BALR     R3,0
         USING    HERE,R3,R4,R5
HERE     LM       R4,R5,BASES
         B        BEGIN
BASES    DC       A(HERE+4096,HERE+8192)
BEGIN    DS       0H
```

This method of loading base registers is fairly common. I personally do not like it and prefer using only CPU instructions, with no reference to storage and with no need to manually multiply 4096 by the number of base registers. The following method is my preference:

```
PROGRAM  CSECT
         BALR     R3,0
         USING    *,R3,R4,R5
         LA       R4,4095
         LA       R4,1(R3,R4)
         LA       R5,4095
         LA       R5,1(R4,R5)
```

This method requires no manual calculations, and it is easier to add or delete base registers.

The other exception is when a subroutine consists of a large number of in-line compare instruction groups, causing the branch instructions, which are using relative addressing, to always branch to the next compare instruction group. The subroutine would look something like the following:

```
FINDOPT  CLC      OPTION,AAA
         BNE      *+12
         MVC      MESSAGE,MSGA
         BR       R6
         CLC      OPTION,BBB
```

```
         BNE      *+12
         MVC      MESSAGE,MSGB
         BR       R6
         ...
         CLC      OPTION,ZZZ
         BNE      *+12
         MVC      MESSAGE,MSGZ
         BR       R6
```

As you can see, the BNE instruction always has the same relative addressing expression of *+12 and branches to the next CLC instruction on a compare not equal condition. There are other ways of coding the above subroutine to eliminate the relative addressing. Each CLC instruction could have a label, and the previous BNE instruction could use that symbol for its operand. Admittedly, this could be very burdensome and tedious if the subroutine contained a few hundred CLC instructions, but that should not be an issue. The task of writing the labels may be difficult, but the task of selecting them is not. A good naming convention would be to use the same prefix for each label, with the suffix being a character string that described the option. Using labels in this case would have additional value if they were ordered in some logical sequence. This would make it easier for the programmer to locate the CLC group for a particular option, and it would also be easier to verify that the code for a particular option was not inadvertently omitted. This subroutine could also be coded as follows:

```
FINDOPT  CLC      OPTION,AAA
         BE       SETMSGA
         CLC      OPTION,BBB
         BE       SETMSGB
         ...
         CLC      OPTION,ZZZ
         BE       SETMSGZ
         ...
SETMSGA  MVC      MESSAGE,MSGA
         BR       R6
SETMSGB  MVC      MESSAGE,MSGB
         BR       R6
         ...
SETMSGZ  MVC      MESSAGE,MSGZ
         BR       R6
```

The above example would actually be a better method of coding this subroutine. However, if the subroutine contained a few hundred CLC instructions, then this method could become very inconvient because the programmer would then be continually flipping pages of a listing or scrolling frames of a display terminal to determine what processing occurs for each option. In this case, the *first* coding example of this subroutine would be more practicable because all the coding for each option is together.

The two valid cases of using relative addressing, as described above, have alternative ways of being coded to avoid relative addressing, but relative addressing in those cases is tolerable.

1.1.4 Uses Subroutines

A program is easier to develop, debug, and modify if it is divided into its elementary functions and/or tasks. After these functions are determined, they can then be coded into small pieces of self-contained logic called subroutines (or modules or segments). These subroutines can be thought of as building blocks of the program. The program is then constructed from these building blocks as they receive control in the proper sequence.

The use of subroutines provides a program with better structure and makes it easier to understand. It is much easier to examine a program that has a mainstream that consists of calls to subroutines that perform specific functions than to have the mainstream cluttered up with the code.

Also, the use of subroutines saves the effort required to write and maintain redundant code. If different points in a program require the same function to be performed (a certain calculation, I/O to a file, etc.), then that point in the program calls the appropriate subroutine to perform the function instead of having the code duplicated.

The physical size of a subroutine should be small if possible, so that one will not be overwhelmed by a large number of instructions and complex logic while viewing it. There is absolutely nothing wrong with a subroutine that contains as little as two instructions. If it was determined that a specific function requires a subroutine that can be coded in only two instructions, that is fine. Do not feel obliged to put those two instructions into another subroutine if they are logical and functional by themselves. One example is a subroutine that reads a record from a master file and is called from a number of different points in the program. The subroutine may look something like the following:

```
READMSTR    GET        MSTRFILE,IOAREA
            BR         R6
```

One exception to the guideline of a subroutine being physically small would be if the subroutine contained many Move or Compare instructions that logically belonged together. An example would be a subroutine that builds a report line or a record of a file that contains many fields. This subroutine would look something like the following:

```
BLDREC      MVC        $FIELD1,FIELD1
            MVC        $FIELD2,FIELD2
            MVC        $FIELD3,FIELD3
            ...
            MVC        $FIELD70,FIELD70
            BR         R6
```

Another example would be a subroutine that examines a Control statement or PARM Value and looks for a number of different verbs in order to pass control to the proper subroutine to process that verb (request). This subroutine would look something like the following:

```
FINDVERB    CLC        PARM,VERB1
            BE         PROCVB1
            CLC        PARM,VERB2
            BE         PROCVB2
            CLC        PARM,VERB3
            BE         PROCVB3
            ...
            CLC        PARM,VERB40
            BE         PROCVB40
            BR         R6
```

Most programs are developed, viewed, and modified from a display terminal; therefore, the ideal number of lines for a subroutine would be no more than the maximum size of the screen (usually 24 lines) of the display terminal, which is about a half-page on a hardcopy listing. It is understandable that some subroutines would logically require more than 24 lines of code to perform the desired result. The integrity of a subroutine should never be compromised in order to make its size fit into a guideline. However, there are valid cases in which a subroutine can be made smaller by having it call other subroutines to assist in its overall function, if it could be divided into smaller functions. For example, let us say that a specific subroutine has the function of doing very complex calculations involving a number of different numeric fields. Let us further say that the numeric fields are in zoned decimal format, the calculations will be done in binary for performance reasons, and the results are to be edited in order to be displayed. This subroutine could actually be divided into smaller functions. Besides the complex calculation, the numbers would first need to be converted into binary format and then, after the calculation, the results would need to be edited. After dividing the subroutine into smaller functions, it would look something like the following:

```
CALCRTN1  BAL   R7,CONVBIN1
          BAL   R7,DOCALC1
          BAL   R7,EDIT1
          BR    R6
*
*
CONVBIN1  DS    0H
          ...
          BR    R7
*
*
DOCALC1   DS    0H
          ...
          BR    R7
*
*
EDIT1     DS    0H
          ...
          BR    R7
```

If the subroutines CONVBIN1, DOCALC1, and EDIT1 were coded in the same subroutine, they would still work and provide the desired result, but it would be cumbersome to view them and to follow their logic on a display terminal or on a hardcopy since the one subroutine would be cluttered with a lot of instructions, each having a different function. By coding three separate subroutines, the program now has three manageable, easy to view subroutines, each with a different function, which together produce the desired result of the higher level subroutine that calls them.

After a subroutine is coded, debugged, and verified to work properly, it could then be used by a programmer with the same convenience and confidence as he/she would use a machine instruction. Since subroutines are designed to perform a specific task and usually require certain information passed to them (data, parameter, etc.), the programmer simply needs to set up the required input and pass control to the subroutine. Upon return from it, he/she has every reason to have the utmost confidence that the task was performed correctly.

1.1.5 Uses DSECTs

I/O areas and work areas that are defined in a program should have their individual fields defined via DS instructions with meaningful labels. However, if an I/O area is not defined in a program, such as when the address of a logical record is returned by QSAM (used in locate mode) then that area cannot directly have its fields defined by DS instructions since it is not in the program. The same situation is true when an area of virtual storage is obtained via the GETMAIN macro instruction (discussed in Chapter 4) for use as a work area or for creating a table, and so forth. However, those storage areas that are not defined in the program can still have their individual fields mapped via DS instructions by using DSECTs. Storage areas that contain multiple fields should always have the individual fields defined via DS instructions with meaningful labels and comments. Using, setting up and implementing DSECTs is discussed in Chapter 5.

1.1.6 Has Efficient Code

One of the advantages of writing programs in Assembler language is that they can be more efficient and, therefore, execute more quickly than programs written in high level languages such as COBOL. Writing efficient programs in Assembler language comes with increasing knowledge and experience. The knowledge should eventually include an understanding of the functions and uses of *all* the available machine instructions. The experience should provide the knowledge of which instructions and/or set of instructions and which coding techniques are best suited for certain types of tasks, such as searching an array, validating data, performing complex calculations, manipulating data, and so on.

The knowledge is obtained by reading IBM's *Principles of Operation* manual (and/or other similar publications) and experimenting with the use of the instructions in a test program until the instructions are thoroughly understood. The experience comes from writing programs and then analyzing the coding logic and "playing computer" to determine if the various subroutines are written as efficiently as possible. The writing of programs does not mean the mechanical copying of code from another program (your's or a coworker's) because one learns nothing from that. However, that does not necessarily mean that code should not be copied from another program if the code is efficient and understood.

It is difficult to teach efficient Assembler language programming. One method is to provide pages and pages and pages of boring, mechanical guidelines. Another method is by example. The coding examples provided in this book are written in efficient, well-structured Assembler language. However, there is one important guideline that should be mentioned. The fastest executing program is not necessarily the best structured or easiest to read program. In general, a well-structured program written efficiently will have excellent performance; however, there are times when an unstructured program written efficiently, to perform the same task, may execute slightly faster (because it may have fewer instructions (no or fewer BAL, BR instruction pairs) or not save and restore registers as often). However, performance is only one consideration when writing a program. It is more important to write a well-structured program rather than a sloppy one that executes a few seconds or a few minutes quicker.

If you are having a contest with a colleague to determine who can write a program to execute the fastest, then writing an unstructured program may be the way to win the contest. However, if you are having a contest to determine which program (one that has never been seen before) can be modified or debugged the quickest, then the well-structured program will usually win and still provide excellent performance.

If you want to be a fanatic about writing efficient programs, you can obtain the hardware manuals for the various CPU models and determine and compare the execution times of the various instructions. But that is probably not necessary because the modern IBM computers have such fast cycle times that the amount of time saved by using one instruction over another instruction is usually not very significant. Efficient code really implies writing whole routines that execute quickly and structuring a program to mimimize the amount of code used to perform the various functions required, as opposed to using one instruction over another. However, knowing which instructions or group of instructions perform a particular task quicker is useful. The following contains some general information on instruction timings.

- The fastest way to clear a register to binary zeros is with the XR instruction, as follows:

```
         XR    R15,R15
```

However, using either the LA or SR instruction is more descriptive:

```
         LA    R15,0
```

or

```
         SR    R15,R15
```

Since the time difference is slight, the LA or SR instructions are the preferred way to clear a register.

- Fullword instructions execute faster than halfword instructions. In the following example, the significant data is contained in the last two bytes of the area FULLWORD:

```
         LH    R10,FULLWORD+2      SLOWER
         L     R10,FULLWORD        FASTER
         AH    R10,FULLWORD+2      SLOWER
         A     R10,FULLWORD        FASTER
```

- The quickest and most descriptive way to increment the value of a register is with the LA instruction. In the following example, register 10 is incremented by four:

```
         LA    R10,4(0,R10)        (1)
```

The LA instruction executes exclusively in the CPU; there is no reference to virtual storage.

Some programmers use the above instruction in the following way:

```
         LA    R10,4(R10)          (2)
```

Both versions of the instruction perform the task successfully, but incrementing a register with the second LA instruction is both inefficient and illogical.

The first value after the open parenthesis of an LA instruction specifies the index register. The second LA instruction is inefficient; since the index register is not indicated as omitted by specifying a 0 value (register 0 cannot be used as an index register) or a comma, register 10 is used as the index register instead of the base register. The CPU requires additional time to process an index register.

The second LA instruction is also illogical because it indicates (on purpose or by ignorance) an index register when an index function is not being logically performed. One valid use of an index register is to increment through a table containing variable length entries. Such a coding technique is presented in Chapter 5.

Admittedly, the difference in CPU time for the two versions of the LA instructions above is insignificant since it would be in the order of microseconds or nanoseconds, depending upon the model CPU on which the instruction is executed. But instructions should be coded efficiently and properly regardless of the CPU's cycle time. It is more professional, and also one of the indications of a senior Assembler language programmer, to have an in-depth understanding of the instruction set and to code accordingly. Also, the destination between the index register and base register becomes significant in MVS/ESA if the access register facility is used for inter-address space communications.

A register could also be incremented by using the A instruction as follows:

```
         A     R10,=F'4'
```

The above instruction makes a reference to storage, which is slower than an instruction that executes exclusively in the CPU. Also, if the virtual storage page that contains the literal is not in real storage, then there is an additional delay to resolve the page fault.

A register may also be incremented with the following CPU instructions:

```
         LA    R11,4
         AR    R10,R11
```

Even though the above instructions make no reference to storage, the two instructions together are slower that the one LA instruction. Also, an additional register is required.

- Exotic instructions such as TR, MVCL, and so forth, require involved microcode to implement and therefore execute slowly. These instructions are efficient only if they are used properly. If one or two bytes are to be translated, it would be more efficient to code a CLI, BE, and MVI group of instructions than a single TR instruction with its required table. The following example shows how to translate a blank to a zoned decimal zero without using the translate instruction.

```
          CLI   ARGBYTE,X'40'
          BE    MAKEZERO
          ...
MAKEZERO  MVI   ARGBYTE,X'F0'
```

  The execution time is faster if an MVC instruction, instead of an MVCL instruction, is used to move a small amount of data. In fact, the break-even point is about 2K bytes of data. The exection time is faster for looping through an MVC instruction (with maximum length of 256 bytes) eight times together with the address increment instructions than it is for a single MVCL instruction for the same amount of data. Also, an MVCL instruction requires the use of four registers. However, an MVCL instruction will execute faster if more than 2K bytes of data are to be moved.

- Performing complex mathematical calculations is quicker when done in registers using binary data than when using packed data contained in virtual storage areas. When the calculations are complete, then the CVD instruction can be used to convert the binary numbers to packed decimal numbers.

Poor program performance may not always be caused by the combination of machine instructions used in a program. One example is in the performing of I/O operations. Allocating datasets efficiently may be considered to be in the realm of MVS tuning, but the programmer should be aware of any conditions that may cause his/her programs to perform inefficiently.

The datasets that reside on DASD or magnetic tape should have an optimal block size or the data transfer will be slow causing the program performance to be poor. This may give the impression that the program code is inefficient.

If the datasets reside on DASD, they should be contained in a single extent as opposed to multiple extents that are scattered all over the DASD volume. DASD datasets that go into multiple extents should be reorganized into a single extent periodically to avoid excessive DASD arm movement when reading/writing data. VSAM datasets that have excessive control interval and control area splits should also be periodically reorganized.

Also, if a program references datasets that reside on DASD volumes containing high activity datasets that are referenced during the same time interval as the program executes, then the program would appear to be coded inefficiently due to the excessive I/O time, which is due to excessive DASD arm movement required to service the high activity datasets. The solution in this case is to move the datasets to a lower activity DASD volume, if possible, or to rearrange the scheduling of the execution of the jobs to mimimize or eliminate the overlapping of the DASD usage.

Also, the access to datasets that reside on DASD or magnetic tape could also be slow due to excessive traffic across the channels and control units. The solution to that is the same as above: rearrange the DASD allocation and/or job execution schedule. Additional hardware, if planned properly, would also help.

Another example of poor program performance due to conditions other than the combination of machine instructions is poor paging performance. Like I/O allocations, paging performance is in the realm of MVS tuning. Most modern computer systems contain such a large amount of real storage that paging is usually not a performance issue. However, there are coding techniques and MVS facilities available to programmers that will enable a program to be paged more efficiently whether or not the system paging rate is high. These techniques and facilities are discussed in Chapter 9.

A final example is poor planning of dynamic load module calls in a dynamic structure program. The sections "Program Management" and "The LOAD Macro Instruction" in Chapter 4 discuss the techniques and facilities that can be used to cause better dynamic load module call performance.

1.1.7 Does Not Modify Instructions

Do not modify Assembler machine instructions by any means other than the EX (Execute) instruction. Programs that modify their instructions, or, more specifically, overlay them to create different ones, by any other means are difficult to follow. When one examines a program for the purpose of debugging or maintenance, one would normally look at specific parts of the program and determine the logic by the instructions that appear in the source or assembly listing. If instructions are being dynamically changed during execution, the programmer who is examining the code may not know or even suspect that this is being done. All he/she would see are the instructions (before they are modified) that appear in the source or assembly listing. Even if this is documented in the program, the programmer would still require the extra time and effort to go through the logic of the program to determine if the instructions were modified and to what, at the point of the execution in which he/she is interested. He/She may also determine this by looking at a storage dump (if one is available) and comparing instruction by instruction between the assembly listing and the dump to determine if the instructions are the same. This method may not be very reliable because the dump may not have been invoked at the proper time during the execution or the instructions may be modified at different times during the execution, which would require multiple dumps invoked at the proper times to indicate how the instructions are being modified.

All of this is very cumbersome, prone to error, a potential nightmare to debug, and unnecessary. It would be easier for the original programmer and for the maintenance programmer if a logic switch was used instead. The setting of the switch would indicate which set of unmodified instructions would execute, and the logic flow would be easier to understand and document.

There are valid situations when part of an instruction is required to be modified to provide efficient and/or flexible code. The guideline would be to use the EX instruction to do the modification. If the modification cannot be accomplished with the EX instruction, then a switch should be used, as described above. When the EX instruction is used to modify an instruction, a descriptive label should be used for the subject instruction (the instruction that is to be modified), as follows:

```
EXMVC  MVC    0(0,R10),0(R11)  MODIFY LENGTH OF MOVE INTO XYZ TABLE
```

or

```
EXCLC  CLC    0(0,R10),0(R11)  MODIFY LENGTH OF SEARCH ARGUMENT
```

Some programmers like to no-op certain instructions after the program is initialized because those instructions are required to execute only once during the initialization process and are not required after that. Also, based upon user specified parameters, some programmers choose to no-op certain instructions, which are not required for the services requested by the user, at the beginning of the program instead of logically bypassing them. *The argument is that since it is only a simple no-op at the beginning of the program, it is okay to modify the instructions.* The recommendation is that modifying any instructions to any degree is a bad habit to develop and the preferred method is to use either the EX instruction or a switch as mentioned above.

The following is a coding example of no-oping an instruction because it is not required due to a user specified parameter:

```
CHKCTR1   CLI   PARM,CTR1OPT      CHK PARM TO DETM IF CTR1 REQUIRED
          BNE   SETXCTR1          IF NOT REQ, SET NO-OP
          BAL   R7,ACCUM          INCREMENT COUNTERS
          BR    R6                RETURN TO CALLING RTN
SETXCTR1  MVC   ACCUM(L'APCTR1),NOOP  NO-OP AP INSTR FOR CTR1
          BAL   R7,ACCUM          INCREMENT COUNTERS
          BR    R6                RETURN TO CALLING RTN
*
*
ACCUM     DS    0H
APCTR1    AP    CTR1,VALUE1       INCREMENT COUNTER 1 (THIS INTR IS NO-OP'ED)
          AP    CTR2,VALUE2       INCREMENT COUNTER 2
          AP    CTR3,VALUE3       INCREMENT COUNTER 3
          ...
          BR    R7                RETURN TO CALLING RTN
*
*
CTR1OPT   EQU  1
NOOP      DC   3XL2'0700'
```

NOTES:

- NOOP is defined as three sets of X'0700'. Defining it this way is more flexible because this one DC may be used to No-Op a 2-, 4- or 6-byte instruction.
- Notice the length attribute at the label SETXCTR1. The length attribute of a label that contains an Op-Code is the length of the actual instruction. Coding it this way eliminates the need to know the length of the instruction that is being No-Oped.

The following is the same program except for using a logic switch instead of dynamically No-Oping an instruction.

```
CHKCTR1   CLI   PARM,CTR1         CHK PARM TO DETM IF CTR1 REQUIRED
          BNE   SETXCTR1          IF NOT REQ, SET NO CTR1 SWITCH
          BAL   R7,ACCUM          INCREMENT COUNTERS
          BR    R6                RETURN TO CALLING RTN
SETXCTR1  MVI   XCTR1SW,C'1'      SET SWITCH TO INDICATE CTR1 NOT REQ
          BAL   R7,ACCUM          INCREMENT COUNTERS
          BR    R6                RETURN TO CALLING RTN
*
*
ACCUM     CLI   XCTR1SW,C'1'      CHK IF CTR1 REQUIRED
          BE    BYPASS1           IF NO, BYPASS CTR1 INCREMENT
          AP    CTR1,VALUE1       INCREMENT COUNTER 1
BYPASS1   AP    CTR2,VALUE2       INCREMENT COUNTER 2
          AP    CTR3,VALUE3       INCREMENT COUNTER 3
          ...
          BR    R7                RETURN TO CALLING RTN
*
*
CTR1      EQU   1
XCTR1SW   DC    C'0'
```

NOTES:

- In the above example, the ACCUM subroutine could have checked the PARM value instead of using a switch. However, this example contains the better, more general technique of using a switch because in some cases the parameter value may not be available to other subroutines or the decision algorithm may be very complex.

1.1.8 Does Not Abnormally Terminate (ABEND) Due to User Error

A good program does not ABEND due to a user error. Instead, it should have the proper logic coded to check for at least the common error conditions that can be caused by a user that will result in an ABEND. These conditions can be handled in a number of different ways depending on the application and the policies of the data center. Some solutions would be:

- Ignore the error or log it and continue processing; or
- Correct the error with some predetermined default actions; or
- Issue a meaningful error message and terminate the program; or
- Issue a message and wait for a reply to indicate what action to take.

Probably the most common program ABEND due to a user error occurs when invalid data is submitted to the program. This invalid data is usually alphanumeric data or blanks and occurs when numeric data is expected, and packed decimal arithmetic instructions are used with the data. This results in an S0C7 ABEND. This ABEND can be eliminated easily by simply verifying the data before using it. Input numeric data to a program should never be used with packed decimal instruction without first verifying it because the exposure to an S0C7 ABEND is so great. If the program is unable to recover from the invalid data, then a meaningful error message and normal termination is much more professional and desirable than an S0C7 ABEND. The coding of validation routines for zoned decimal and packed decimal is illustrated in Chapter 5.

Another common problem occurs while attempting to access a file. If the block size specified in the program does not agree with the actual block size in the file or if other I/O errors are encountered, then the result is an S001 ABEND. The block size problem may be eliminated with the procedure discussed later in this chapter (Section 1.1.18). The other I/O errors can be intercepted by specifying in the DCB macro that a SYNAD (error analysis routine) be given control after an I/O error is encountered. In the SYNAD routine, the programmer has the option of coding the logic to analyze the problem and to print a customized error message or of using the SYNADAF macro and printing the error message generated by it. In either case, a meaningful message is preferred to an S001 ABEND. The coding of a SYNAD routine is illustrated in Chapter 14.

All file OPENs should be checked for successful completion. Certain OPEN failures will not cause an ABEND. Among these is an omitted JCL DD statement that is suppose to point to the file that is to be OPENed, or a misspelled ddname. When I/O is attempted to a file that has not been OPENed, the program will ABEND with an S0C1, S0C4 or other error code. The success of the OPEN may be verified by testing one of the bits in the Open Flags byte of the DCB. The following coding example illustrates this:

```
         OPEN  FILE1            OPEN FILE
         TM    FILE1+48,X'10'   CHECK FOR SUCCESSFUL OPEN
         BO    OPEN1OK          OPEN SUCCESSFUL
         B     OPEN1BAD         OPEN NOT SUCCESSFUL
         ...
FILE1    DCB   ...
```

A better way to code the above is to use the IBM-supplied DCB mapping DSECT named DCBD. The code will then look like the following:

```
         OPEN  FILE1            OPEN FILE
         TM    DCBOFLGS,DCBOFOPN CHECK FOR SUCCESSFUL OPEN
         BO    OPEN1OK          OPEN SUCCESSFUL
         B     OPEN1BAD         OPEN NOT SUCCESSFUL
         ...
FILE1    DCB   ...
```

The DCBOFOPN label is an EQU for X'10' and is defined by the DCBD DSECT. The use of DSECTs is discussed in Chapter 5.

Another potential problem occurs when the end-of-file (EOF) routine is not initialized before the first input reference (via READ or GET macros) is made to the file. If the file contains no data, the first attempt to read it will cause the EOF (specified via EODAD parameter of the DCB macro) routine to receive control. All counters used by the EOF routine for printing totals and so forth should be initialized to zero before the first read of the file is attempted. The EOF routine should never assume that a particular piece of code was executed if that code depends upon the successful retrieval of data from a file in order to execute. This would include actions such as priming an I/O area with data from a file, setting up addressability for a DSECT, OPENing another file, loading a register with a meaningful address, and so on. A simple programming technique can be used to assure that a particular file contains data. After the first (or all) successful read(s), a switch is set on (or off). If the file is empty, control is passed to the EOF routine and the instruction setting the switch will not execute. Then the EOF routine checks the setting of the switch to determine if the file contains any data. If it is determined that the file is empty, then the EOF routine could generate an appropriate error or warning message and will also "know" whether certain code has been executed. The following coding example illustrates how to code this:

```
READFILE   GET    FILE1
           MVI    NODATASW,C'0'
           BR     R8
           ...
DATAEND    CLI    NODATASW,C'1'
           BE     FILEMPTY
           ...
NODATASW   DC     C'1'
FILE1      DCB    EODAD=DATAEND,...
```

Uninitialized counters could cause an S0C7 ABEND and other assumptions could cause unpredictable results.

Sometimes a program may have a requirement to build an internal table to hold control statements or data that need to be manipulated in storage before they can be processed or that the program may need to access continually. If the user inputs an inordinate amount of data and causes the program to read more data than was planned and if the proper precautions are not taken, then the data will overflow the storage that was defined for the table and overlay portions of the program. This will cause unpredictable results. This problem could be eliminated by the procedure discussed later in this chapter (Section 1.1.10).

Potential user errors that can cause a program to ABEND will not necessarily be the same for all programs. The programmer should code logic for the ones that he/she is aware for that particular program. The programmer should consider using the SPIE/ESPIE and/or ESTAE macro instructions (discussed in Chapter 6) if it is vital that the program does not ABEND under any conditions.

1.1.9 Requests and Checks Feedback from Macro Instructions

The code generated by some IBM-supplied macro instructions issues a return code to indicate whether the requested service was successful. Other macro instructions provide the option of requesting services conditionally and provide feedback that indicate the results of the conditional request. Whenever a macro instruction provides the facility of requesting a service unconditionally or conditionally, it is good practice to request the service conditionally because this will avert a potential ABEND and enable the program to terminate normally or attempt a recovery.

If the macro feedback code is not checked for successful completion, then the program will experience erroneous results or even an ABEND if the requested service was not provided and the program made the assumption that is was. In this case, the ABEND will not be caused by a user error, as discussed in Section 1.1.8 above, but by careless programming.

One example would be the use of the GETMAIN macro instruction (discussed in Chapter 4). A GETMAIN request for virtual storage may be unconditional or conditional. An unconditional request that is not satisfied results in an S804 or S80A ABEND. A conditional request for storage that is not satisfied is indicated by a non-zero return code in register 15, and it does not cause an ABEND. The program then has the opportunity of:

- Either generating a meaningful error message and terminating normally or of attempting a recovery by issuing a GETMAIN macro instruction for a smaller amount of storage;
- Using DASD storage instead, if applicable; or
- Issuing a FREEMAIN macro instruction (discussed in Chapter 4) to release storage that is no longer required, which was previously obtained by a GETMAIN macro instruction, and then reissuing the GETMAIN macro instruction.

Another example would be the use of the LOAD macro instruction (discussed in Chapter 4). The LOAD macro instruction is used to request the loading of a program or table into virtual storage. Two of the ABENDs that can occur if the LOAD macro instruction does not function properly are S106-C and S806-4. An S106-C occurs when there is insufficient storage to contain the load module. An S806-4 occurs when the requested load module cannot be located in any of the specified load libraries. These ABENDs can be suppressed by specifying the ERRET operand of the macro instruction. In this case, the program has the opportunity to print a meaningful error message and terminate normally or to attempt a recovery. A possible recovery scenario for the S106-C ABEND would be to attempt to release sufficient storage by issuing a DELETE macro instruction (discussed in Chapter 4) for each load module that may no longer be required, which was previously loaded by a LOAD macro instruction, and/or issuing a FREEMAIN macro instruction to release storage that is no longer required, which was previously obtained via a GETMAIN macro instruction. Then, the LOAD macro instruction can be reissued.

1.1.10 Internal Tables Have the Capability of Expanding

When a program has the requirement to build an internal table in virtual storage to contain selected data from an external source (file, user input, etc.), the program should be designed to have the facility to dynamically expand the size of the table to accommodate any size input. If the data is coming from a file whose size may vary from execution to execution or from a user submitting varying amounts of control statements to request various services, and so forth, then the amount of input data used to create the table cannot be accurately predicted. If the amount of storage allocated for the table is a fixed length and if the input data for a particular execution exceeds the table capacity, then either the data could overflow the table, causing unpredictable results or the program could sense this condition, print an error message, and terminate. In either case, the user's needs will not be satisfied if the additional data is required to be processed for that particular execution of the program.

The solution to this problem is to initially allocate a fixed amount of storage for the table. The length of the fixed portion of the table should be large enough to hold the amount of data that would satisfy most situations. In addition, logic should be coded to sense when the capacity of the fixed portion of the table has been exceeded. At that point, additional storage is obtained via the GETMAIN macro instruction (discussed in

Chapter 4). The last entry in the fixed storage portion of the table is a pointer to the GETMAINed storage area containing some indication that it is a pointer and not data. From that point, the additional data is stored into the GETMAINed area until that area is exhausted. When this occurs, additional storage is obtained via GETMAIN and its pointer is stored in the last entry of the previous GETMAINed storage area and so on until the table is completely built. Also, some indication is required to indicate the logical end of the table. One convention is to use binary ones to indicate an entry containing a pointer to the next GETMAINed storage area and binary zeros to indicate end-of-data. Only conditional GETMAIN requests should be issued. If any GETMAIN request fails due to insufficient available virtual storage, then the program should generate a meaningful error message and terminate normally. When this condition occurs, the program is not failing due to its own inability to handle the request from the user, but due to an external condition, such as a System constraint or the user's failure to specify a large enough REGION size in the JCL JOB or EXEC statement. The error message, generated by the program, should indicate that the user should increase the size of the REGION parameter. A program designed with the expandable table facility could handle any amount of data if there is sufficient storage available. A detailed coding example illustrating this technique is presented in Chapter 5.

1.1.11 Provides Meaningful Error Messages

From time to time, a program is required to intentionally terminate prematurely due to a user induced error (invalid data, invalid PARM value, etc.) that makes it impossible for the program to continue to execute and provide meaningful results. A large number of programmers choose to do this with a User ABEND code via the ABEND macro instruction (discussed in Chapter 4). Other programmers may simply terminate the program normally after issuing either a very general or "catch-all" error message or a vague error message to the system console via the WTO macro instruction (discussed in Chapter 4).

A message issued by a program, whether it is an error message, warning message, or instructions, has to be meaningful to its intended audience. This message may be intended for the computer operator, the user, or another programmer.

Certain guidelines should be followed when a program is required to be terminated prematurely. The first and most important guideline is that it generates a message indicating the reason for the premature termination.

The messages should not necessarily be displayed on the operator/system consoles because the consoles should not be cluttered with user messages. This would distract the operators from performing their task of controlling the system. Except for important jobs, the messages should be directed only to the hardcopy log of the job. This is accomplished by coding the ROUTCDE=11 parameter with the WTO macro instruction.

If the audience is the user, or some other non-technical group, then the message should be quite explicit and technical terms should be avoided, if possible. If the user specified an incorrect parameter, had a syntax error in a control statement specified invalid data, and so forth, then the error message should indicate this as clearly as possible. If the message is intended for the production control or technical support personnel (the personnel responsible for preparing the jobs for the operators and for fixing simple problems like JCL errors), then the message may be technical but must still be understandable. For instance, let us say that a program creates an expandable internal table based upon the amount of input data or requires DASD work space defined by the JCL statement //WORK01 and whose allocation size is dependent upon the amount of certain types (let us say XYZ) of input data. Do *not* generate an error message that says the following:

```
GETMAIN MACRO FAILED, PROGRAM TERMINATED
```

or

```
TOO MUCH XYZ DATA, PROGRAM TERMINATED
```

The above messages really say "nothing." Better error messages would be the following:

```
INTERNAL TABLE CANNOT BE EXPANDED---INSUFFICIENT STORAGE
INCREASE THE VALUE OF THE JCL REGION PARAMETER
```

or

```
INSUFFICIENT WORK SPACE TO PROCESS XYZ DATA---INCREASE
SIZE OF JCL SPACE PARAMETER IN //WORK01 DD STATEMENT
```

The second set of error messages are much more meaningful and usable. The technical support person seeing those messages will know exactly what the problem is and how to fix it. If the program is "intelligent" enough to determine the problem and "knows" what is required in order to continue to execute, then why not share that information with the maintenance personnel? Also, do not be afraid to display multiple lines for the error message if required to generate a meaningful message.

The practice of terminating a program prematurely by means of a User ABEND code has a potential problem. If the termination is serious or occurs in an important program, then the programmer may choose to terminate the program with an ABEND macro instruction. This will provide the impact of an ABEND, as opposed to a normal termination with an error message, and will be more noticable to the computer operator. This is a good idea when the situation warrants it. However, since the number of the ABEND is a user number (a number that the programmer made up) as opposed to a system number (a number selected by IBM), it will not be documented in the IBM manuals. If a programmer chooses to terminate a program with User ABEND codes, then he/she must provide documentation for them. The normal convention is to document them in an "in-house" document, such as the Operations Procedures manual, the Run Book for that particular Application, or a separate User's Utility manual. In-house documents have a tendency of getting lost, being misplaced, and updated slowly or not at all. It is strongly recommended that when a program is terminated with a User ABEND code, a meaningful error message also accompany it. This technique would have both effects: a meaningful error message to assist the support personnel without the need to scramble around looking for the in-house document containing the User ABEND codes and the impact of an ABEND to notify the computer operator that the program terminated prematurely.

If the message is required to be displayed on the operator/system console, there is no guarantee that the computer operator will notice the error message or the ABEND message. The WTO macro instruction can be coded to highlight the error message and also to mark it non-deletable (discussed in Chapter 4) in order to make it more noticable to the computer operator. However, the computer operator may explicitly delete the error message from the operator/system console before he/she completely reads or understands it, or it may be inadvertently deleted by other staff members before the computer operator had the opportunity to notice it.

If the job executing the program is extremely important and it is vital that it executes to completion, and if the computer operator must notify the appropriate personnel immediately if the job fails, then the following technique can be used to assure that the operator notices the ABEND message. Display a meaningful error message as discussed above. After the error message, display, via the WTOR macro instruction (discussed in Chapter 4), a message that requires a reply from the computer operator to verify that he/she noticed the error message and that he/she is taking the appropriate action. The message may look something like the following:

```
nn          *** OPERATIONS, REPLY "ACK" TO ACKNOWLEDGE THAT JOB jjjjjjjj
            HAS ABENDED ***
```

The nn is the number of the reply (generated by the operating system) and the jjjjjjj is the name of the job, which may be determined by using the EXTRACT macro instruction (discussed in Chapter 4). After the computer operator notices the above message and replies "ACK", then the program may still terminate with a User ABEND code if desired. The advantage of using this technique for very important jobs is that even if the computer operator does not notice the error message or ABEND message, he/she would have to notice this message because the reply number (nn) of the messsage will remain outstanding until it is answered. Additionally, the program may monitor the amount of time that the reply is outstanding via the STIMER macro instruction (discussed in Chapter 4) and reissue the message after a predetermined amount of time has elapsed with no reply. A coding example showing how to do this is presented in Chapter 4.

1.1.12 Uses Only Standard Interfaces

When one interfaces with the operating system to use various services and facilities, one should use only standard interfaces. These interfaces consist of IBM-supplied macros and IBM-supplied exit points, such as the ones provided by JES2, SMF, and so on. In general, one should not modify system control blocks directly or use unpublished interfaces because the format of the control blocks or the interface may not be the same or may not exist in future releases of the operating system. If a program or a system modification is required to provide a certain facility for the computer installation or for a user and there is no published standard interface to accomodate that requirement, then the standard interface rule would have to be violated. The programmer is cautioned that, before an unsupported interface is used, thorough research should be performed to determine if that new in-house provided facility is really required and whether it can be implemented differently in order to make use of one of the available standard interfaces.

The use of nonstandard interfaces will make a program release dependent. These programs should be provided with complete and accurate documentation. Each time a new release of the operating system is implemented, these programs are required to be examined and tested thoroughly to determine if they still function properly. If they do not, then the code needs to be modified. The modification may be very simple, such as a different displacement into a system control block, or may be quite complex, such as locating a new place in the operating system to "hook" since the old one either does not exist anymore or has been modified to the point that it is no longer usable. The impact of referencing or modifying control blocks directly could be eliminated or minimized if IBM-supplied DSECTs are used whenever available.

1.1.13 Lets the Assembler Determine Lengths

Lengths of items such as tables, table entries, parameter-lists, and so forth should be calculated by the Assembler rather than by the programmer. The advantages of letting the Assembler calculate the lengths are as follows:

- The Assembler will not make a mistake when the lengths are initially defined or change due to modifications, additions, and so on;
- The lengths, if changed, are adjusted automatically when the program is reassembled;

■ If the lengths are defined as EQU symbols (as they should be), then the instructions that reference those lengths (EQU symbols) need not be modified, since that is also done by the Assembler; and
■ It removes the burden of these tasks from the programmer.

The following coding example illustrates how the Assembler will calculate lengths using EQUs and how to reference them:

```
SEARCH    LA   R0,TBLSIZE          LOAD NUMB OF TBL ENTRIES INTO REG 0
          LA   R10,TABLE           LOAD BEG OF TBL ADR INTO REG 10
NEXTENTY  CLC  ENTRYID,ARGID       CHECK TBL FOR ENTRY WITH SPEC ID
          BE   IDFOUND             IF FOUND, INDICATE IT
          LA   R10,ENTRYLEN(0,R10) INCREMENT TO NEXT ENTRY
          BCT  R0,NEXTENTY         CHECK FOR END OF TABLE
          LA   R15,4               TABLE END, INDICATE ENTRY NOT FOUND
          BR   R8                  RETURN TO CALLING RTN
IDFOUND   LA   R14,ENTYDATA        LOAD REG 14 WITH ADR OF ENTRY DATA
          LA   R15,0               INDICATE ENTRY FOUND
          BR   R8                  RETURN TO CALLING RTN
          ...
TABLE     DS   0H
          DC   C'01'
ENTIDEND  EQU  *
          DC   C'THIS IS THE ENTRY DATA FOR ID=01'
ENTRYEND  EQU  *
          DC   C'02',C'THIS IS THE ENTRY DATA FOR ID=02'
          DC   C'06',C'THIS IS THE ENTRY DATA FOR ID=06'
          DC   C'09',C'THIS IS THE ENTRY DATA FOR ID=09'
          DC   C'12',C'THIS IS THE ENTRY DATA FOR ID=12'
          DC   C'19',C'THIS IS THE ENTRY DATA FOR ID=19'
TBLEND    EQU  *
ENTIDLEN  EQU  ENTIDEND-TABLE            ENTRY ID LENGTH
ENTRYLEN  EQU  ENTRYEND-TABLE            ENTRY LENGTH
TBLSIZE   EQU  (TBLEND-TABLE)/ENTRYLEN   NUMBER OF ENTRIES IN TABLE
          ...
ARGID     DS   CL2
          ...
TBLMAP    DSECT
ENTRYID   DS   CL(ENTIDLEN)
ENTYDATA  DS   CL(ENTRYLEN-ENTIDLEN)
```

NOTES:

- The table contains fixed length entries, and the first two bytes of each entry contain the id or key of that entry.
- The length of the ID portion of each entry, the length of the entire entry, and the number of entries in the table are calculated automatically by the Assembler by using the EQU symbols ENTIDLEN, ENTRYLEN, and TBLSIZE, respectively.
- The program will continue to function properly with no coding changes being required if any new entries are added to the table, if any existing entries are deleted from the table, or if the lengths of the entries are changed.
- The DSECT TBLMAP is used to map each entry of the table.

As another example, let us say that a validation program, which validates the data of the records of a file, is being developed. It requires control statements, as input, to request the various services that the program offers. The program will validate the control statements for proper syntax and content, read the appropriate file and validate the specified fields of each record based upon the parameters specified by the control statements, and perform any other services requested by them.

The program is designed to generate error messages for each error that is found in the control statements and for each field of the records of the file that does not correspond to the specifications indicated by the control statements.

After the initial design, let us say that there are 90 error messages defined, with lengths that vary from 9 bytes to 110 bytes, the average being about 35 bytes.

There are a few ways of designing the actual error messages. One way is to define each error message with a length equal to the actual print line minus any prefix (such as record number or id for which the error message pertains). Assuming an 8-byte record id prefix, each error message would be defined with a length of 124 (132 - 8) and padded with low order blanks. This would appear to be convenient because the program would simply move the error message into the print I/O area without being concerned about the length. There are, however, a few problems with this method. One is that it is inefficient since the average length of the error messages is 35 and the maximum length is 110, there will be many low order blanks moved into the print I/O area each time an error message is required to be printed. Also the total number of bytes required to define all of the error messages is 11,160 (124 x 90). This will require nearly three base registers for addressability. To eliminate the potential base register shortage problem, the error messages could be defined in another CSECT of the program and mapped with a DSECT, but that would make the program needlessly more involved and that will not solve the performance inefficiency of moving all those low order blanks.

Another method would be to define each error message with a length equal to the largest error message, which in this case is 110. This would require 9,900 bytes (110 x 90), which would require over two base registers and still be inefficient because, as in the previous method, many low order blanks would be moved into the print I/O area. Also, if another error message is added with a longer length than the current maximum, then additional modifications would be required to the program.

The best method of all would be to define each error message with its actual length. This would be efficient because no low order blanks would be moved into the print I/O area and the total number of bytes required to define all the error messages would be only 3150 (35 x 90), which would require less than one base register. In this case, the error messages are defined with a DC instruction, with no length specified. This will direct the Assembler to calculate the actual length of each error message. Also, the length attribute (L') is used by the MVC instruction to direct the Assembler to move only the actual length of each error message. The following are some examples of typical error messages for this program:

```
ERR001        DC        C'INVALID CONTROL STATEMENT'
ERR002        DC        C'CONTROL STATEMENT OUT OF SEQUENCE'
ERR003        DC        C'NUMERIC VALUE TOO HIGH FOR CONTROL STMT ABC'
ERR004        DC        C'INVALID OPTION SPECIFIED FOR CONTROL STMT XYZ'
              ...
ERR020        DC        C'FIELD F1 OF RECORD IS MISSING'
ERR021        DC        C'FIELD F2 OF RECORD IS NOT NUMERIC'
              ...
ERR090        DC        C'RECORD TOO LONG'
```

The following coding example shows how to reference the above error messages using the length attribute.

```
VALDT001      DS        0H
              ...
              BAL       R9,SETER001
              BAL       R9,PRINT
              BR        R8
              ...
SETER001      MVC       #ERRMSG(L'ERR001),ERR001
              BR        R9
```

```
SETER002    MVC     #ERRMSG(L'ERR002),ERR002
            BR      R9
            ...
SETER090    MVC     #ERRMSG(L'ERR090),ERR090
            BR      R9
            ...
PRINT       DS      0H
            ...
            PUT     SYSPRINT,LINE
            BR      R9
            ...
            DC      C' '
LINE        DS      0CL133
#CNTLCD     DS      CL1
#RECID      DS      CL7
            DS      CL1
#ERRMSG     DS      CL124
```

1.1.14 Has Op-Codes, Operands, and Comments Aligned

The fields of the instructions of an Assembler language program should be aligned for readability. The normal *convention* is that the label starts in position 1, the Op-code starts in position 10, the operand starts in position 16, the comments start at least one blank past the operand, the continuation indicator is in position 72, and the continuation line starts in position 16. However, all that the default format indicates is that the label must start in position 1, the Op-code must start at least one blank past the label, the operand must start at least one blank past the Op-code, the comments must start at least one blank past the operand, the continuation indicator must be in position 72, and the continuation line must start in position 16. As you can see, the default format gives the programmer a lot of freedom as to where to place the various fields of each instruction. Therefore, a programmer could write a very unaesthetic, sloppy looking program with unaligned instruction fields that would still be acceptable to the Assembler But a program written like this, even if it does work, is very difficult to read and not something that the original programmer or maintenance programmer would enjoy reading in order to debug or modify.

The ICTL Assembler instruction is provided to change the default format. In most cases, it is not a good idea to use it since Assembler programmers are accustomed to a certain format. One valid use of the ICTL instruction would be while assembling the Stage I of an MVS SYSGEN. Most of the Stage I macro instructions exceed five chacters; therefore, it is impossible to start the operand in position 16 every time, but the continuation must still start in position 16 due to the default format. This would misalign the operand(s) of the first line with the operand(s) on the continuation lines. An ICTL operand of 1,71,19 would work nicely. This would indicate that continuation lines must start in position 19, which would align with the first line operand location (allowing a maximum length of eight for the macro instruction names).

The above example indicates that one valid use of the ICTL Assembler instruction for changing the instruction format would be when the source program contains numerous macros that exceed five characters and contain enough operands to require a continuation line(s).

1.1.15 Contains Meaningful Comments

A program should be well documented. Theoretically, the original prorammer or any other programmer or even a nonprogrammer should be able to know the function and understand the logic of an Assembler language program (or any other language program) just by reading the comments. Writing good comments is an art and requires experience. Comments should not be verbose nor should they be so concise that they become meaningless. The comments throughout this book are good examples of how comments should be written. The following guidelines and suggestions for writing good comments are offered.

Before each subroutine, add Comment statements to describe that particular subroutine. The description should include: the function of the subroutine; any fancy logic that may be used; expected input to (if applicable) and output from (if applicable) the subroutine including the contents, format, and so on of the specific registers used, storage area names used, and so on; and anything else that the programmer believes is pertinent. If the subroutine is called by one or a few major routines, then this may be mentioned. If, however, the subroutine is called from many places in the program, then this information is probably not required in the comment.

From day one, all or most programmers were told that each line of code *must* have a comment. This decree or advice is nonsense. Consider the following instruction and comment:

```
MVC      F1,F2      COPY THE CONTENTS OF F2 INTO F1
```

When a programmer sees this comment for this instruction, he/she should have an uncontrollable urge to say: NO KIDDING!!! Any Assembler language programmer knows that this is what an MVC instruction does. Would removing that comment from that instruction tell you anything less about the instruction? The answer is obviously NO! When a programmer has this kind of situation in his/her program, he/she should either provide no comment or, if applicable, provide a more meaningful comment. *A comment for an instruction should not mimic the IBM's Principles of Operation manual. The comment should not describe what the instruction does within the scope of the CPU, but should describe what the instruction does within the scope of the program.* Let us consider the same instruction with a different comment:

```
MVC      F1,F2      COPY EMPLOYEE ID FROM DATABASE TO PRINT LINE
```

If the comment is now removed, would you know less about the instruction? In this case, the answer is obviously YES!

Let us now consider setting up a meaningful naming convention since a meaningful naming convention is, in effect, part of the documentation. Let us say that the names of all fields that form the print line are preceded by the special character "pound sign" (#), the names of all fields of a record from the database are preceded by the special character "dollar sign" ($), and the names of all fields that are calculated are preceded by the special character "at sign" (@). This convention should be documented somewhere in the program. Let us further say that the other seven characters of the field name are used to form a meaningful, descriptive name. Now, let us consider the following two instructions and their corresponding comments:

```
         MVC     #EMPLYID,$EMPLYID      COPY EMPLOYEE ID FROM DATABASE
*                                       TO PRINT LINE
         MVC     #EMPSLRY,@EMPSLRY      COPY CALCULATED EMPLOYEE SALARY
*                                       TO PRINT LINE
```

If the comments were removed from the above instructions, would you know anything less about the function of these instructions within the scope of the program? Suppose that these two instructions were part of a subroutine, with other similar instructions using the same naming convention. Let us also say that the function of the subroutine is to build a print line which is documented via Comment statements in front of the subroutine. Would the comments be required for each instruction in this case? Would comments on each instruction line add any more meaning to the documentation of this subroutine? I am sure that most of you would agree that the answer is NO!

One must remember that the purpose of comments is to assist the original programmer and the maintenance programmers with understanding the function and logic of the program, not to decorate a page of code with redundant or obvious comments that may also be distracting. Also be aware that in some situations eight characters may not be enough to create a meaningful name to describe the contents of a field. In that case, you may consider putting a comment only on those lines.

The DS instructions that define the print I/O and database record I/O areas (or DSECTs that map them) should be fully documented.

Subroutines that perform arithmetical operations, manipulate addresses, or do complex logic operations will usually require a comment on each instruction line. Note that the H-level Assembler provides the option of defining labels up to 63 characters. However, this may be excessive and could cause the program op-codes to become misaligned. But, a useful convention could be to select a practical maximum length such as 10 or 12 and code the beginning of all the op-codes in a new position that will allow for the maximum length label. The ICTL Assembler instruction could also be used to define a new starting position for continuation statements.

A useful technique that may be used to write meaningful comments is to put yourself in the position of the maintenance programmer and pretend that you have never seen the program before. Be as objective as possible and ask yourself if the comments that you have just written are adequate to easily understand the function and logic of the program. If you cannot honestly answer YES, then review and enhance the comments.

1.1.16 Uses Meaningful Labels

Using meaningful labels contributes to the overall documentation of a program. The names of subroutines would be more descriptive if they were verbs (or the beginning of them were verbs) that indicated what the subroutine did (e.g., GETREC, VALIDATE, SETLINE), and the names of storage areas would be more descriptive if they were nouns that indicated their contents (e.g. EMPLNAME, VOLSER, TBL1ADR). If the storage area has a special purpose, such as being a switch, counter, edit mask, and so forth, then indicate this with a meaningful suffix (e.g., NWPAGESW, LINECTR, EDMASK1). Storage area names that are a logical part of a larger group (such as all the fields of a record for a specific file, all the fields of a mapping DSECT for a GETMAINed area, etc.) should have a common prefix. The common prefix should be no more than three characters, in order to leave enough characters available to attempt to form a meaningful label for the field. Besides an alpha character (A–Z), a label may also begin with one of the national characters (@, #, $). You may consider using one of them as a prefix. I like using the pound sign (#) as the prefix for all the fields of the print line (both start with the letter "P"). Since you are allowed only eight characters for labels with the F-level Assembler or if you elect not to exceed eight characters while using the H-level Assembler, you need to be resourceful at times to form a meaningful label. If you could use only one position as a prefix instead of three, you would have that many more available to form a meaningful label.

Do not use (as some programmers have been known to do) proper nouns or sequence numbers for labels (e.g., JOHN, MARY, NEWYORK, RTN006, RTN241, etc.) because they indicate absolutely nothing about the function of the subroutine or the contents of the storage area.

Since comments are used for subroutines, you may be wondering about all the concern over label names. If a programmer (the original or maintenance) could equate a comment with a meaningful label, then he/she would not need to continually refer to the comments in order to know what a particular subroutine does or what a particular storage area contains. The program also looks more professional if meaningful labels are used instead of silly, meaningless ones. If a program had a subroutine that read a master file, would you prefer to see that subroutine labeled READMSTR, or labeled HARRY or RTN049?

Also, use EQUs for all general registers. This is set up with the following group of Assembler instructions:

```
R0     EQU    0
R1     EQU    1
       ...
R15    EQU    15
```

When the general registers are represented by the numbers 0 through 15 and appear in machine instructions, their use will not be indicated in the Assembler cross-reference. However, if the symbols R0 through R15 (or any other symbols of the programmers choosing) are used in lieu of the numbers 1 through 15 to represent the general registers, then their use will appear in the Assembler cross-reference. This information is particularly useful for a number of reasons such as searching for a general register that has not been used yet, during debugging to determine all the uses of a particular register that may be getting modified incorrectly, and so forth.

1.1.17 Has Meaningful DS Instructions

As previuously mentioned, when storage is allocated in an Assembler language program via the DS Assembler instruction, it should be specified in a descriptive manner. This means more than just selecting a meaningful label. For example, if storage is being allocated for a fixed length table containing 10 25-byte entries, it should be specified as follows:

```
TABLE     DS     10CL25
```

When one looks at this instruction, it is obvious that the storage that is being allocated is for 10 25-byte items. Some may argue that it would be just as easy to define the same table as:

```
TABLE     DS     CL250
```

and indicate the entry size and number of entries via comments. There are a number a reasons why this is not a good technique. Let us say that instead of a table that is composed of 10 25-byte entries, it is composed of 27 89-byte entries or 53 36-byte entries, and so on. Now the multiplication is not as simple and the programmer could make an error doing the calculation. If the specifications of the table should change, the programmer would then have to do another calculation and again risk an error. It would be easier to let the Assembler do the multiplication. By using a descriptive DS instruction, there would be no need to comment the entry size and number of entries since that information would be inherent and obvious in the DS instruction. The comment could be used to document only the contents and use of the table. If the size of the table should change, only the DS instruction need be changed. The comment would remain as is. This would also eliminate the potential problem of neglecting to change the table size in the comment and then having a DS instruction and the corresponding comment indicating different sizes.

1.1.18 Does Not Specify BLKSIZE for Files

The BLKSIZE parameter of the DCB macro should be omitted for input and output files. This provides flexibility for the user by enabling him/her to change the block size of the files (when required) without necessitating a program modification. When the block size is not specified in the program for an input file, it is taken from the file's JCL or label (if not found in JCL). Using this method, all the user needs to do to process an input file, with a different block size, is to execute the program as is. The new block size will be specified in either the file's standard label or in the JCL, for an unlabeled file. The program will pick up this new block size automatically when the file is opened.

For an output file, this method is more involved. If the block size is not specified in the program, it must be specified in the JCL since the standard label has not been created as yet. A valid argument against this would be: *"Why burden the user to specify the block size value in the JCL?"* The answer is that the block size value is specified in the JCL during the implementation of the program and there is no need for it to be removed or changed after that, unless the user has a valid need to change it. Another valid argument against this would be: *"What if the DCB=BLKSIZE= parameter is somehow removed from the JCL and is not replaced? If the block size value is not hard coded in the program and omitted from the JCL, the program will ABEND with an S013. One of the characteristics of a good Assembler language program, mentioned above, is one that it does not ABEND due to a user error."* When the block size is hard coded in the program, the operating system will ignore the value specified in the JCL—this is not the objective. To eliminate this problem, the program uses the technique described in Chapter 7 to check if a block size value was specified in the JCL. If not, the program will provide a default block size in the DCB before it is opened. If a value is specified in the JCL, the program will use it instead. While the program is checking if the value was specified in the JCL by the user, it could also check to determine if the specified value adheres to certain criteria (if required), adjusting or ignoring it if it does not. This technique will satisfy both requirements. It provides the user with the flexibility to change the block size of his/her output file easily, and it will provide a default block size if the user neglects to specify one or specifies it incorrectly. This technique may also be used for input files.

Why would the user need to change the block size? There are a number of reasons. The block size may be increased to provide better I/O performance; the block size may be adjusted up or down when the file is moved to a new model DASD volume to accommodate the difference in the new track capacity more efficiently; the file may have been created at another data center using a nonstandard block size; and so forth.

1.2 WHAT IS ADVANCED ASSEMBLER LANGUAGE?

What is advanced Assembler language? There is a vague boundary between an ordinary Assembler language program and an advanced Assembler language program. If one were to conduct an informal survey among ten senior Assembler language programmers at random and ask: "What is advanced Assembler language?", one would probably receive at least two and perhaps as many as ten different answers.

Before I offer my answer, I would first like to reiterate and emphasize what advanced Assembler language is not. Advanced Assembler language is *not* writing complex, unstructured code using numerous exotic instructions (that may not all be justified) with no, little, or very poor comments. Advanced Assembler language is *not* writing difficult-to-understand programs to impress our friends, colleagues, and management.

An advanced Assembler language program has all of the characteristics of good Assembler language and may be either an Application program or a Systems program. In addition, it has some of the following characteristics, but is not necessarily limited to them:

- Contains one or more advanced coding techniques like the ones presented in Chapter 5;
- Uses exotic instructions when justified and uses them correctly and efficiently;
- Uses Conditional Assembler language and/or its own user-written macro instructions;

- Has very efficient code; and
- Interfaces with the operating system to use system facilities (other than basic data management) via macro instructions and/or system exits.

The above "definition" or characteristics of an advanced Assembler language program should be taken very loosely. They are not hard and fast rules, just generalities to describe what an advanced Assembler language program would probably contain.

SUMMARY OF CHAPTER 1

Chapter 1 emphasized the concept of good Assembler language programming. Basically, good Assembler language programming means the practice of writing Assembler language programs that:

- Are easy to follow and maintain;
- Are well documented;
- Function correctly and efficiently;
- Protect themselves from user errors; and
- Anticipate future requirements and modifications.

This chapter mentioned and delevoped a number of characteristics of good Assembler language programming. A program written in good Assembler language has at least the following characteristics, but is not limited to them:

- Has simple, easy-to-understand logic;
- Uses mostly simple instructions;
- Has no relative addressing;
- Uses subroutines;
- Uses DSECTs;
- Has efficient code;
- Does not modify instructions;
- Does not abnormally terminate (ABEND) due to user error;
- Requests and checks feedback from macro instructions;
- Internal tables have the capability of expanding;
- Provides meaningful error messages;
- Uses only standard interfaces;
- Lets the Assembler determine lengths;
- Has Op-Codes, operands and comments aligned
- Contains meaningful comments;
- Uses meaningful labels;
- Has meaningful DS instructions; and
- Does not specify BLKSIZE for files.

The reader is encouraged to think of additional good Assembler language programming characteristics.

Before one writes advanced Assembler language programs, one should master the writing of good Assembler language programs.

2

Assembler Language Program Development and Structure

In Chapter 1, we discussed the characteristics of *good Assembler language* and briefly mentioned proper structure. In this chapter, we will discuss in detail, the techniques and guidelines for developing well-structured, easy-to-maintain programs. A program could have all the characteristics that were mentioned in Chapter 1, but if it is poorly structured, it will still be difficult to read, modify, and debug.

2.1 STRUCTURED PROGRAMMING

Structured programming (sometimes called segmented programming) is a programming style or technique that improves the design and understandability of a program. In general, structured programs are easier to design, write, understand, modify, and debug. Unstructured programs are characterized by multiple entry and exit points, numerous unconditional branch instructions throughout, and code for various and/or numerous functions that appear to run together. All this causes an unstructured program to be difficult to understand and maintain.

A typical structured program is made up of building blocks called routines or subroutines (as described in Chapter 1), each with its own function, whether it be a major or minor one. The beginning of a structured program contains the mainstream of the program. This is a series of BAL instructions (and possibly some B instructions) that call all the main routines, which perform the major functions of the program, in the proper sequence. The mainstream should not contain any imbedded instructions between the BAL instructions that perform such functions as setting or testing switches, maintaining counters, and so on. If these functions are required, then they should also be coded as a main routine or subroutine and called via BAL. The mainstream should not be cluttered with stand-alone instructions because that would compromise the modular concept of structured programming and would also cause the mainstream to be needlessly larger. Besides being a router to all the main routines, the mainstream should also be a concise summary of what the program does.

The function of certain major routines may be so complex that multiple tasks are required to be performed in order to fulfill that function. The code required to perform some or all of the required tasks is placed into separate subroutines, each called by the major routine. If the task of any subroutine is also complex and can be logically divided into elementary or common tasks that are required by other suboutines, then that code is placed into separate (minor) subroutines and called by the (upper-level) subroutines that require that task. The ultimate objective is to reduce the code into simple, easy-to-code, easy-to-maintain subroutines.

Section 2.5 below illustrates the step-by-step development of a structured program.

2.2 TOP-DOWN PROGRAMMING

Top-down programming is another useful and productive programming technique and is used with structured programming. Basically, top-down programming involves sequencing: the sequencing of the development of code and the sequencing of the positioning of code. This means that the subroutines are developed at certain times relative to each other and are placed in the program at certain positions relative to each other.

The main routines, which perform the major functions of the program, are designed and coded first. Then the subroutines, which are called by the major routines to assist in their function, are designed and coded next. Minor subroutines, which are called from higher-level subroutines, are designed and coded next, and so on.

As an example, all the subroutines that are responsible for the data extraction and manipulation and for the calculations for a report are designed and coded before the subroutine that produces the actual report. The actual report may be designed first on print layout paper since this is one of the objectives (and part of the specs) of the program, but the actual code to produce the report should be coded after the coding of the subroutines that obtain the information required by the report subroutine.

As another example, the subroutine that extracts specific data from a file based upon specified parameters or predetermined conditions and determines what calculations need to be performed is designed and coded before the subroutine that performs the actual calculations and editing.

The advantage of this sequence of coding is that it is consistent with the actual thought process sequence that occurs when a program is being developed. Also, the subroutines, requiring information from the higher-level subroutines, are coded when that information is available, and its format is designed and finalized by the subroutines that produce it. This may save valuable recoding time.

In the actual program, the major routines are physically placed before the subroutines that they call, and the higher-level subroutines are physically placed before the minor subroutines which they call, and so on. The major routines are placed in the sequence in which they will execute. Therefore, the structure of a program, that uses the top-down programming technique will have the major routine, which will execute first, placed after the mainstream. That major routine is followed by its called subroutines, followed by their called minor subroutines. They are followed by the next major routine, which will receive control from the mainstream, followed by its called subroutines, and so on. The subroutines that are called by more than one subroutine may be placed after the first subroutine that calls them or may be placed near the end of the program in a section with all the other common subroutines that are called by multiple subroutines.

The advantage of this placement scheme is that it is easier to locate all the code that functions together, and the subroutines are in a logical sequence. If the program source is being viewed from a display terminal, fewer scrolls and less search time are required to locate specific pieces of code. If a hard copy listing or assembly of the program source is being examined, there would be fewer nonproductive, annoying page flips needed to locate specific pieces of code.

Section 2.5 below illustrates the development of a structured program using the top-down programming technique.

2.3 WRITING MEANINGFUL COMMENTS

In Chapter 1, we discussed writing meaningful comments for machine instructions, DC/DS instructions, DSECTs, and subroutines. In addition, it is also a good practice to write comments for the program as a whole (Prologue comments). These comments should be physically located at the begining of the program and be about a page or two or more in length, depending on the length and/or complexity of the program. They should contain the following:

- Program name;
- Programmer name;
- Date and description of last modification (or all modifications);
- Special assembly and/or linkedit instructions (if any), such as additional macro libraries, linkedit attributes, or additional load and/or object libraries;
- Names of any nonstandard macro instructions used, such as user-written macros, vendor-supplied macros, or the ones that IBM supplies, but that are not located in the standard macro library;
- Special load library requirements (if any) during execution;
- Names of other programs (if any) that may be called or referenced during execution and a description of them;
- Description of the input to the program;
- Description of the output from the program;
- Description of the function of the program;
- Format and use of any control information the program may accept via the PARM parameter of the JCL EXEC statement or via SYSIN control statements; and
- Anything else that the original programmer or the maintenance programmer may believe to be pertinent.

If the program optionally accepts or requires JCL PARM value or control statements in order to execute, then also document the format, syntax, and content of them, as well as the processing that the program performs for each corresponding PARM/control value.

When a program is well documented and structured with subroutines, it may still be difficult to read if everything (instructions and comments) is cluttered together. Part of good structure is to make a program pleasing to the eye. This will enable the eyes to locate sections of the program with less effort. Readability will be greatly increased if blank comment statements are inserted between subroutines. This method is better that using the Assembler SPACE instruction because that takes effect only when the program is actually assembled. If one examines a hardcopy listing of the program source or views it on a display terminal, there will be no spacing between subroutines if the SPACE instruction is used. Using blank comment lines will provide spacing for either a source listing or an assembly listing of the program. The spacing convention that I prefer to use is four blank comment lines between subroutines and one or two blank comment lines between the heading comments and the subroutine that follows it. Some programmers like to frame each subroutine with a whole line of asterisks (*). The spacing convention is usually a matter of personal taste. The important thing is that it be present and has the effect of improving readability. The following contains three examples of the same excerpt from a mythical program. The only difference is the spacing between subroutines. Look at all three and decide which one you would prefer to look at if you were looking at a hardcopy listing or viewing it on a display terminal.

Coding Example 2.3.1

```
LABEL1     DS      0H
           (Previous Subroutine)
           ...
           BR      R6            RETURN TO CALLER
*     THIS SUBROUTINE READS A LOGICAL RECORD FROM THE EMPLOYEE MASTER
*     FILE USING A QSAM GET IN LOCATE MODE. REGISTER 10 IS LOADED WITH
*     THE POINTER OF THE RECORD TO SET THE PROPER ADDRESSABILITY FOR
*     THE MAPPING DSECT.
READEREC   GET     EMPLMSTR      READ EMPLOYEE MASTER FILE
           LR      R10,R1        LOAD DSECT REG WITH LOGICAL REC ADDRESS
           BR      R6            RETURN TO CALLER
*     COMMENTS FOR NEXT SUBROUTINE
LABEL2     DS      0H
           (Next Subroutine)
           ...
           BR      R6            RETURN TO CALLER
```

Coding Example 2.3.2

```
LABEL1     DS      0H
           (Previous Subroutine)
           ...
           BR      R6            RETURN TO CALLER
           SPACE   4
*     THIS SUBROUTINE READS A LOGICAL RECORD FROM THE EMPLOYEE MASTER
*     FILE USING A QSAM GET IN LOCATE MODE. REGISTER 10 IS LOADED WITH
*     THE POINTER OF THE RECORD TO SET THE PROPER ADDRESSABILITY FOR
*     THE MAPPING DSECT.
           SPACE   2
READEREC   GET     EMPLMSTR   READ EMPLOYEE MASTER FILE
           LR      R10,R1     LOAD DSECT REG WITH LOGICAL REC ADDRESS
           BR      R6         RETURN TO CALLER
           SPACE   4
*     COMMENTS FOR NEXT SUBROUTINE
           SPACE   2
LABEL2     DS      0H
           (Next Subroutine)
           ...
           BR      R6         RETURN TO CALLER
           SPACE   4
```

Coding Example 2.3.3

```
LABEL1     DS      0H
           (Previous Subroutine)
           ...
           BR      R6         RETURN TO CALLER
*
*
*
*
*     THIS SUBROUTINE READS A LOGICAL RECORD FROM THE EMPLOYEE MASTER
*     FILE USING A QSAM GET IN LOCATE MODE. REGISTER 10 IS LOADED WITH
*     THE POINTER OF THE RECORD TO SET THE PROPER ADDRESSABILITY FOR
*     THE MAPPING DSECT.
*
```

```
*
READEREC  GET    EMPLMSTR   READ EMPLOYEE MASTER FILE
          LR     R10,R1     LOAD DSECT REG WITH LOGICAL REC ADDRESS
          BR     R6         RETURN TO CALLER
*
*
*
*
*     COMMENTS FOR NEXT SUBROUTINE
*
*
LABEL2    DS     0H
          (Next Subroutine)
          ...
          BR     R6         RETURN TO CALLER
*
*
*
*
```

I am sure that all of you would select Coding Example 2.3.3 since it is the one that is the most legible.

2.4 CONVENTIONS FOR GENERAL PURPOSE REGISTER USAGE

It is a good idea to set up a usage convention for general purpose registers even though it is not absolutely necessary for a well-structured program. Having such a convention does offer some convenience. By knowing in advance which general purpose register will be used for which types of functions, you could realize a number of benefits, some of which are mentioned below.

In this section and throughout the book, the terms general purpose register and register will be used interchangeably.

When the time comes to select a register to use in the coding of a particular function, the programmer will already know which one(s) to use and will not need to search the cross-reference listing (assuming that EQUs were used for the register numbers) to determine which ones are available.

By allocating certain registers to be used only for functions that do not require their values to be preserved after the end of the execution of the subroutine that uses them, you would automatically know which register to use for those functions, without the need to be concerned if there is a conflict with that register in another piece of code elsewhere in the program.

A general purpose register usage convention is, in effect, the same as managing them. This has the benefit of not wasting registers by using different ones for duplicate functions. For example, let us say that you require the use of two registers to perform binary arithmetic in a certain subroutine and their contents are not required after the end of the execution of the subroutine. When you code another subroutine with a similar register requirement, you may, if you do not have a general register usage convention, select two other registers if the same two from the previous subroutine could have been used. If you now require the use of a register, whose value must be preserved across subroutines, you would then search the cross-reference listing and determine which registers have not been used as yet. Since you, in effect, wasted two registers in the previous subroutine, that list of available registers is now two less than it should be. This could be very important in a large and/or complex program when you are on the verge of exhausting the available registers. There are 16 general purpose registers available for use by programmers, which may seem to be a lot.

But, if they are used wastefully or sloppily, that number can dwindle quite rapidly. This situation may eventually require the time and effort to review the register usage within the entire program and to restructure their use.

If registers, with consecutive higher numbers, are used as the link registers for nested subroutines, then it would be easier to see the logic flow of the program because you would know if a certain subroutine was called by the mainstream or by a higher-level subroutine. This would also assist in managing your subroutines and could, possibly, even assist in debugging efforts.

The following is a discussion for guidelines and considerations for a general purpose register usage convention and also describes the one that is used throughout this book.

Registers 0, 1, 14, and 15 cannot be used as base registers for obvious reasons. Using register 0 as a base register will permit access to only the first 4K of storage. Unless you are writing a stand-alone program, IPL TEXT or really need to reference only the first 4K of storage, this would not be applicable. Registers 0 and 1 are used in most IBM macro expansions, and registers 14 and 15 are used in some IBM macro expansions. It would also be impracticable to use register 2 as a base register because the TRT (Translate and Test) instruction requires it. Register 3 would be a good choice as the first base register, with registers 4 and 5 held in reserve as additional base registers, if required.

Some registers should be reserved as link registers for calling subroutines. Register 6 is used as the main link register for all subroutines called from the mainstream. Registers 7, 8, and 9 are used as additional link registers for nested subroutines. If subroutines are not nested or not nested too deeply, then at least one extra register should be reserved in the event that a future modification of the program requires that one of the existing subroutines call another one.

Certain registers should be reserved for usage in subroutines that require the contents of one or more registers to be initialized and used in the subroutine but not preserved after the subroutine returns control to the caller. This would include binary arithmetic, setting up and manipulating pointers for tables defined by DS instructions or GETMAINed areas, or addressability for DSECTs. It is strongly recommended that registers containing address pointers be initialized in the subroutine that uses that information. This will prevent the problem of the register being inadvertently modified before the subroutine receives control and will also make that register available for other uses outside of the subroutine. The address could simply be stored into a storage area (defined with a descriptive name) and loaded back into the register when required. Registers 10, 11, and 12 are reserved for this purpose. An example of this is presented in Coding Example 2.4.1.

Coding Example 2.4.1

This coding example illustrates how a register, which is used to contain a running pointer in a table, can be restored upon entry into the subroutine, which requires it, and saved when the subroutine returns control.

```
BLDTBL   L     R10,TBLPTR              LOAD ADR OF CUR TBL SLOT
         MVC   0(ENTLEN,R10),ENTRY     MOVE ENTRY INTO TABLE
         LA    10,ENTLEN(0,R10)        INCR TO NEXT TABLE SLOT
         ST    R10,TBLPTR              STORE ADR OF NEXT TBL SLOT
         BR    R8                      RETURN TO CALLER
         ...
ENTLEN   EQU   25
TBLPTR   DS    F
ENTRY    DS    CL25
```

In Coding Example 2.4.1, an in-storage table is being built with 25-byte entries. The field TBLPTR is initially loaded with the address of the beginning of the table (by another subroutine). Each time an entry is inserted into the table, register 10 is loaded with the address of the current available slot in the table. After the entry is inserted into the table, register 10 is incremented to the address of the next available slot in the table and then is stored into the field TBLPTR.

Register 0 is a good choice for use with the BCT instruction for controlling logic loops since it is usually not used for any other purpose and its use there will save a register, which may then be used for other functions. If the loop contains IBM macro instructions, then general registers 10, 11, or 12 should be used for the BCT instruction.

Registers 1, 14, and 15 may be used anytime in a subroutine if the contents of those registers are not required to be preserved after the subroutine returns control back to caller and if those registers do not conflict with any macro expansions. Possible uses for these registers would be the same as registers 10, 11, and 12, above.

For instructions, such as MR and DR, that require the specification of an even/odd pair of registers for the first operand, a good choice would be registers 14 and 15. For the MVCL and CLCL instructions, which require the specification of an even/odd pair of registers for both operands, a good choice would be registers 0 and 1 for the first operand and registers 14 and 15 for the second operand. Using these registers for those functions provide the following advantages:

- Since they are used infrequently, they will usually be available;
- An even/odd pair of registers is automically available—0/1 and 14/15;
- The other registers can be used in the subroutine for other tasks without the need to hold those registers in reserve or to save and restore them in order to use them for those instructions which require an even/odd pair.
- There is no need to scramble around seeking two (or four) available registers that are also consecutively numbered, starting with an even number.

Another register may be designated for passing internal return codes between subroutines. A good selection would be register 15, because this would be consistent with IBM's use of register 15 for passing return codes between job steps and programs and because it is usually not used for very much else besides macro expansions.

One example of using internal return codes would be for a subroutine to call another subroutine to validate data before it is processed. Such a validation may be to verify that a numeric field really contains numeric data. The validation subroutine would contain the actual logic to do the verification for the calling subroutine and then return to the calling subroutine with a return code in register 15, indicating the results of the verification. The normal convention would be a zero in register 15 for a success indication and a non-zero in register 15 for a failure indication.

Register 13, of course, points to the savearea required by the operating system. Incidentally, the savearea is required only if your program calls another program, is called by another program, or uses MVS Data Management macro instructions, which do not include a SVC instruction in the expansion. If none of those are performed, then all that is required is that register 14 be saved and then restored just before exiting. However, the savearea should always be set up because a future enhancement of the program may require that it perform one of the functions that requires a savearea. Also, you have no way of knowing if another program should require to call your program, and therefore, your program should be prepared for it.

If the program should become so large that registers 3, 4, and 5 are not sufficient to define all of the base registers required and there are no other registers available, then there are other solutions. Set up a multiple CSECT program or repackage some of the code into another progran and LINK to it. If that is impractical due to the way the program is structured or due to a time constraint for completing the enhancement, then there is one solution before the program would need to be divided into smaller pieces—use register 13 as a base register. No, that is not impssible! The trick is to have register 13 simultaneously point to the savearea and to the first 4K (it is easier if its the first 4K) of storage that requires addressability. Chapter 5 has a coding example showing how to initialize an Assembler language program using register 13 as a base register.

So far we have not allocated any general purpose registers to be used as "live" registers. Those are registers that contain information that needs to be preserved throughout portions of the program during execution. Such information may include addresses, data, parameters, results from binary calculations, logic switches, and so forth. Besides the base registers, the savearea address pointer register and subroutine link registers (when they are active); the use of "live" registers should be avoided whenever possible.

In general, the use of "live" registers has the following potential problems:

- Required information in these registers may be inadvertently overlayed by other logic in the progarm either during original development or during future enhancements;
- It causes a program to be more difficult to maintain due to the previous reason; and
- It decreases the pool of available registers.

There are some acceptable situations when a register may be used to contain information across subroutines. One such situation would be when one or more different subroutines call a common lower-level subroutine to perform a particular task, such as a complex binary arithmetic calculation or to determine an address into an array or table. This kind of information may be conveniently passed back to the calling subroutine via a register. The guideline would be to use a register to hold the information if it is required only by the calling subroutine. If the information is required to be preserved beyond that, then it is recommended that a storage area be used instead of a register to hold the information.

Another situation would be to dedicate a register to provide the addressability for a DSECT, which mapes out a storage area such as an I/O area, control block, an array of data, and so on, and which is referenced throughout the program by many different subroutines. The guideline would be that if the DSECT is referenced by only 1 or 2 subroutines, then it would be better to initialize the value of the register in the subroutines that reference the DSECT. (DSECTs are discussed in Chapter 5).

There are other situations where the use of a "live" register would be acceptable. These vary from program to program and should be determined by the programmer's own good judgment.

Whenever the programmer determines that the value in a register should be preserved throughout portions of the execution of a program, it should be very carefully documented in the appropriate places in the program. In the case of a common subroutine passing back information to the calling subroutine, the comment should be in the heading comments of both the common subroutine and the subroutine(s) that call it. In the case of one or more registers providing addressability for DSECTs to be used throughout the execution of the program, the comment should be at the beginning of the program with the other general comments (prologue comments) for the entire program.

2.5 STEP-BY-STEP DEVELOPMENT OF A WELL-STRUCTURED PROGRAM

This section illustrates the step-by-step development of a structured program using the techniques, suggestions, and philosophy presented in this chapter.

Coding Example 2.5.1 at the end of this section shows the entire program as a structured program using the top-down programming technique. The coding example shows the mainstream, the major routines, and the subroutines positioned in the proper places in the program, with suggested routine header comments.

Let us suppose that our project manager asked us to write a program with the following specifications:

Read the monthly cumulative SMF tape (SMF is System Management Facilities, a component of the operating system, whose function is to monitor system activity and report it via different record-types written into the system SMF datasets) and process all type 14 records (input non-VSAM datasets) and type 15 records (output non-VSAM datasets) and create a report showing the names of all non-VSAM datasets accesssed, the names of the jobs that referenced them, the date and time that the job was submitted (The SMF type 14 and type 15 records include the jobname and time-stamp) and whether the dataset access was Input or Output.

We start by analyzing the requirements of the program and then decide what major functions will be performed by the main routines. After the analysis, we may come up with the following list of major functions:

- Open the SMF and the report files;
- Read all SMF records and select only the required ones;
- Process the selected records;
- Set up a print line containing dataset name, jobname, type of access, and date and time job submitted;
- Print each line of the report;
- Print totals on the report, if applicable, at end-of-data;
- Close the files;
- Return to the operating system.

Considering the above analysis, the mainstream of the program will probably look something like the following:

```
         TITLE ...
*
*   PROGRAM PROLOGUE COMMENTS
*
REPORT   CSECT
         INITL 3,EQU=R        INITIALIZE PROGRAM
*
*
         BAL    R6,OPEN       OPEN SMF AND REPORT FILES
NEXTREC  BAL    R6,READSMF    READ AND SELECT REQUIRED SMF RECS
         BAL    R6,PROCREC    PROCESS THE SELECTED SMF RECORDS
         BAL    R6,SETLINE    SETUP REPORT LINE
         BAL    R6,DOREPORT   PRINT REPORT LINE
         B      NEXTREC       READ NEXT SMF RECORD
SMFEND   BAL    R6,DOTOTALS   AT EOD, PRINT TOTALS LINE ON REPORT
         BAL    R6,CLOSE      CLOSE SMF AND REPORT FILES
         B      RETURN        RETURN TO MVS OR CALLING PROG
*
*   ROUTINES, SUBROUTINES AND NON-EXECUTABLE CODE
*
         END
```

As you can see, all the major functions of the program have been made into separate routines. The major processing loop is defined in the mainstream of the program. By looking at the few lines of the mainstream, one is able to see the general logic flow of the program and have a good understanding of what the program does.

The INITL macro is a user-written macro that initializes the program. The first parameter, 3, defines the base register number, and the second parameter, (EQU=R), sets up an

EQU table for the general purpose register numbers using the letter "R" as a prefix. The macro definition for INITL is presented in Chapter 3.

The next step is to code the major routines that are called from the mainstream of the program. The first two major routines, OPEN and READSMF are very straightforward and would be coded as follows:

```
OPEN     OPEN   (SMFDATA,,REPORT,(OUTPUT))
         ...                   CHECK FOR GOOD OPENS
         BR     R6             RETURN TO CALLING RTN
*
*
READSMF  GET    SMFDATA        READ A SMF RECORD
         LR     R10,R1         LD REC ADR IN R10 FOR DSECT ADRBLTY
         BAL    R7,SELREC      SELECT ONLY THE REQUIRED RECORDS
         LTR    R15,R15        CHECK INDICATOR FROM SELREC
         BZR    R6             IF REC OK, RET TO CALLING RTN
         B      READSMF        IF NOT, READ NEXT RECORD
```

Notice that these routines contain only a few instructions (not counting macro expansions). As was indicated earlier in Chapter 1, the length of a routine/subroutine is not an issue. What matters is the function of the routine and how it relates to the rest of the program. If the programmer determines that OPEN and READSMF are separate functions that should be isolated in their own routines, then they should be coded as such, regardless of the number of instructions required to build them.

Now let us look at the SELREC routine. The function of this routine is to select type 14 and type 15 records. At this point, there may be some debate concerning where to place the SELREC routine. Should it really be called by READSMF as a subroutine or should it be called by the mainstream as a major routine? If the mainstream calls SELREC, it would be coded as follows:

```
SELREC   CLI    $SMFID,X'0E'       CHECK IF SMF TYPE 14 RECORD
         BER    R6                 IF YES, RET TO CALLING RTN
         CLI    $SMFID,X'0F'       CHECK IF SMF TYPE 15 RECORD
         BER    R6                 IF YES, RET TO CALLING RTN
         B      NEXTREC            NOT A REQRD REC, RD NEXT SMF REC
```

Notice that in this case SELREC will have two exit points. One will be a return back to the caller (via R6) if the record is either a type 14 or type 15. This will cause the next sequential instruction of the mainstream to execute. The other exit point will be a branch back to the beginning of the loop of the mainstream (via NEXTREC) if the record is not a type 14 or type 15. This will have the effect of ignoring the record and causing the next SMF record to be read. However, two exit points in a routine is a poor design and a violation of strict structured programming.

By having READSMF call SELREC, it could pass back a return code, indicating if the record satisfies the search criteria. Then READSMF, based upon the return code, will either read another record (until one satisfies the search criteria) or return to the mainstream. In this case, both READSMF and SELREC have only one exit point.

The function of SELREC is more that just to verify that the SMF record just read is a type 14 or type 15 record. Its name implies and its position in the program indicates that, in general, this subroutine will select or ignore SMF records for processing, based upon predetermined selection criteria. The current specifications of the program specify that the only selection criterion is record-type.

However, in the future the specifications may be enhanced to include other selection criteria such as the date that the dataset was referenced, the name of the job(s) that referenced the dataset, and so forth. Considering this possibility, the subroutine SELREC would contain the following:

```
SELREC   BAL   R8,CHKRECID      CHECK IF THIS SMF REC TYPE IS REQRD
         BR    R7               RETURN TO CALLING RTN
```

This would appear to be a better way to structure the logic for this subroutine. The subroutine CHKRECID would be coded as follows:

```
CHKRECID CLI   $SMFID,X'0E'     CHECK IF SMF TYPE 14 REC
         BE    SMFRECOK         IF YES, INDICATE IT
         CLI   $SMFID,X'0F'     CHECK IF SMF TYPE 15 REC
         BE    SMFRECOK         IF YES, INDICATE IT
         LA    R15,4            INDICATE NO REQRD REC TYPE FOUND
         BR    R8               RETURN TO CALLING RTN
SMFRECOK LA    R15,0            INDICATE A REQRD REC TYPE FOUND
         BR    R8               RETURN TO CALLING RTN
```

All labels prefixed with a "$" are part of the DSECT that maps out the SMF records.

The subroutine SELREC is set up to call another subroutine to check the record-types. This may appear to be excessive subroutine calls for this function. However, if additional selection criteria were required in the future, then the structure is already set up for those enhancements.

The function of the PROCREC routine is to determine the record-type selected and perform whatever processing that is required for that record-type. There are probably two different approaches to coding this routine. One approach follows:

```
PROCREC  CLI   $SMFID,X'0E'     REC TYPE 14?
         BE    PROC14           IF YES, PROCESS IT
         CLI   $SMFID,X'0F'     REC TYPE 15?
         BE    PROC15           IF YES, PROCESS IT
         B     INVSMFID         PROGRAM BUG
PROC14   DS    0H
         ...
         BR    R6               RETURN TO CALLING RTN
PROC15   DS    0H
         ...
         BR    R6               RETURN TO CALLING RTN
INVSMFID ...
```

This method is fine and would work properly. It uses one routine to process all the selected record-types. However, a potential problem exists with it from a structural point of view. If the processing requirements of record-types 14 and 15 are very long and/or complex or become that way due to future enhancements or if additional record-types are required to be processed, then this routine will become quite large and cumbersome to view. The other way to code this subroutine would be as follows:

```
PROCREC  CLI   $SMFID,X'0E'     REC TYPE 14?
         BE    SMF14            IF YES, PROCESS IT
         CLI   $SMFID,X'0F'     REC TYPE 15?
         BE    SMF15            IF YES, PROCESS IT
         B     INVSMFID         PROGRAM BUG
SMF14    BAL   R7,PROC14        CALL SUBR TO PROCESS REC TYPE 14
         BR    R6               RETURN TO CALLING RTN
SMF15    BAL   R7,PROC15        CALL SUBR TO PROCESS REC TYPE 15
         BR    R6               RETURN TO CALLING RTN
INVSMFID WTO   '*** LOGIC ERROR-CONTACT SYS/PROGM DEPT ***', ROUTCDE=11
         ABEND 901,DUMP
*
*
PROC14   DS       0H
         ...
         BR       R7            RETURN TO CALLING RTN
*
*
```

```
PROC15   DS       0H
         ...
         BR       R7                  RETURN TO CALLING RTN
```

This implementation of PROCREC, although logically equivalent to the previous implementation, is easier to view from either a hard copy listing or from a display terminal. Futhermore, it is set up for future enhancements. If additional processing is required for record-types 14 and 15, such as extracting and/or manipulating other fields from the records, then those changes are made only in the isolated subroutines PROC14 and PROC15. The routine PROCREC need not be modified and will remain a manageable size. If additional record-types are required to be processed in the future, then only a hook (a CLI and BE instruction) would need to be placed into PROCREC for that record-type. The actual code to process that record-type would be written and isolated as a separate subroutine. The routine PROCREC will remain a small, easy-to-view piece of code and will, in effect, function as a router to the actual subroutines that process the particular record-types.

The PROC14 and PROC15 subroutines have some processing in common. The Date in SMF records is stored in packed decimal format and must be edited before it is printed. The Time in SMF records is stored as binary seconds since midnight. That value needs to be converted into hours, minutes, and seconds and edited before it is printed. These two requirements are excellent candidates for separate subroutines. If any other SMF records must be processed in the future, the subroutines that process them can also call the GETDATE and GETTIME subroutines to obtain the edited Date and the converted and edited Time. The PROC14 and PROC15 subroutines will now be coded as follows:

```
PROC14   BAL      R8,GETDATE          GET EDITED DATE
         BAL      R8,GETTIME          GET CONV/EDITED TIME
         ...
         BR       R7                  RETURN TO CALLING RTN
*
*
PROC15   BAL      R8,GETDATE          GET EDITED DATE
         BAL      R8,GETTIME          GET CONV/EDITED TIME
         ...
         BR       R7                  RETURN TO CALLING RTN
```

Notice the INVSMFID label and associated code in the PROCREC routine. The function of PROCREC is to route the selected SMF records to the proper subroutines for processing. The required records were already selected by the SELREC routine. If the PROCREC routine receives a record that is not one of the required records, then there must be a logic error somewhere. This code generates an error message and supplements it with a User ABEND code. This ABEND indicates an internal logic error in the program and should be used for debugging purposes only (preferably during development). The ABEND code should be unique for each predetermined logic error to pinpoint the exact location in the program where the problem is occurring and should start with the same unique high order digit (a "9" in this case) to identify the ABEND code as an indication of an internal logic error. The ABEND and the WTO macro instructions are discussed in Chapter 4.

The SETLINE routine builds the detail report lines from the information it receives from the PROC14 and PROC15 subroutines. As an alternate design, the SETLINE routine can be omitted and the detail report line built by the PROC14 and PROC15 subroutines.

The DOREPORT routine "prints" the detail line; maintains the line counter; and passes control to the NEWPAGE subroutine (not shown), when required, whose function is to print headers for each new page, reset the line counter to zero, and increment the page number.

Now, let us suppose that we receive additional specifications for the program. The user wishes the report to contain VSAM datasets and EXCP (I/O) counts for all the datasets. Also, the user wants the facility of being able to optionally select two search criteria. One is to select datasets that were referenced by jobs that were submitted at or after a specified date and time. The second selection criterion is to select datasets with names that have a specified high-level index. Since the program was structured well, these new enhancements are relatively easy to incorporate.

The VSAM dataset information is included in the SMF type 64 records. To include VSAM dataset information in the report requires additions to the subroutine CHKRECID and the routine PROCREC, as well as the writing of the new subroutine PROC64. The CHKRECID and PROCREC routines will look as follows after the additions:

```
CHKRECID  CLI    $SMFID,X'0E'
          BE     SMFRECOK
          CLI    $SMFID,X'0F'
          BE     SMFRECOK
          CLI    $SMFID,X'40'        *NEW*
          BE     SMFRECOK            *NEW*
          LA     R15,4
          BR     R8
SMFRECOK  LA     R15,0
          BR     R8
*
*
PROCREC   CLI    $SMFID,X'0E'
          BE     SMF14
          CLI    $SMFID,X'0F'
          BE     SMF15
          CLI    $SMFID,X'40'        *NEW*
          BE     SMF64               *NEW*
          B      INVSMFID
SMF14     BAL    R7,PROC14
          BR     R6
SMF15     BAL    R7,PROC15
          BR     R6
SMF64     BAL    R7,PROC64           *NEW*
          BR     R6                  *NEW*
INVSMFID  WTO    '*** LOGIC ERROR—CONTACT SYS/PROG DEPT ***',ROUTCDE=11
          ABEND  901,DUMP
```

The EXCP count in SMF records is stored as a 4-byte binary number. Since the EXCP count is required for all datasets (VSAM and non-VSAM), the code required to convert the EXCP count to decimal and to edit it will be common to the PROC14, PROC15, and the PROC64 subroutines and should therefore be coded as a separate subroutine. The EXCP count is not stored in the same location in each SMF record-type as is the Date and Time. Therefore, to keep the GETEXCP subroutine generalized and simple, the EXCP count is loaded into register 10 before the GETEXCP subroutine is called. This puts the responsibility of determining the proper location of the EXCP count field in the subroutine that processes the respective SMF record-type. The following shows how the PROC14, PROC15, and PROC64 subroutines will be coded after the new enhancement:

```
PROC14    BAL    R8,GETDATE
          BAL    R8,GETTIME
          L      R10,$NVSIOCT        *NEW*
          BAL    R8,GETEXCP          *NEW*
          ...
          BR     R7
          ...
PROC15    BAL    R8,GETDATE
          BAL    R8,GETTIME
          L      R10,$NVSIOCT        *NEW*
          BAL    R8,GETEXCP          *NEW*
```

```
                ...
                BR        R7
                ...
PROC64          BAL       R8,GETDATE          *NEW*
                BAL       R8,GETTIME          *NEW*
                L         R10,$VSIOCT         *NEW*
                BAL       R8,GETEXCP          *NEW*
                ...                           *NEW*
                BR        R7                  *NEW*
```

The implementation of the two new search criteria requires an addition to the SELREC subroutine and the writing of the three new subroutines— CHKDATE, CHKTIME, and CHKINDEX. It appears that the existing SELREC subroutine should be modified as follows:

```
SELREC          BAL       R8,CHEKRECID
                BAL       R8,CHKDATE       *NEW*
                BAL       R8,CHKTIME       *NEW*
                BAL       R8,CHKINDEX      *NEW*
                BR        R7
```

But this would not provide the desired result. All the search criteria are a logical AND relation, which means that *all* the search criteria must be satisfied for the record to be selected. The above SELREC subroutine passes only the return code from the CHKINDEX back to READSMF. Instead, SELREC must examine the return codes from each called subroutine. If any of those subroutines issue a non-zero return code, then the other subroutines are not called and that non-zero return code is passed back to READSMF to indicate that the current record is not selected. The SELREC subroutine should be coded as follows:

```
SELREC        BAL      R8,CHKRECID
              LTR      R15,R15             *NEW*
              BNZR     R7                  *NEW*
              BAL      R8,CHKDATE          *NEW*
              LTR      R15,R15             *NEW*
              BNZR     R7                  *NEW*
              BAL      R8,CHKTIME          *NEW*
              LTR      R15,R15             *NEW*
              BNZR     R7                  *NEW*
              BAL      R8,CHKINDEX         *NEW*
              BR       R7
```

Since the SELREC subroutine was designed to accommodate additional search criteria, their incorporation is a very simple task.

It is the responsibility of the CHKDATA, CHKTIME, and CHKINDEX subroutines to determine if the record satisfies the selection criteria specified by the user and then set a return code to indicate the result of the test. If the search criteria is satisfied, then a return code of zero is set; otherwise, a return code of non-zero is set.

Since the Date, Time, and Dataset Index may be specified by the user, there must be some code in the program to receive this input. The input may be specified via the PARM parameter of the JCL EXEC statement (retrieving information from the PARM parameter is discussed in Chapter 5) or as control statements via an input card-image file, or both. This would be considered a major function and, therefore, would be in the mainstream as follows:

```
REPORT        CSECT
              INITL    R3,EQU=R
*
```

```
*
               BAL      R6,GETPARM      *NEW*
               BAL      R6,OPEN
               BAL      R6,GETCNTL      *NEW*
NEXTREC        BAL      R6,READSMF
               BAL      R6,PROCREC
               BAL      R6,SETLINE
               BAL      R6,DOREPORT
               B        NEXTREC
SMFEND         BAL      R6,DOTOTALS
               BAL      R6,CLOSE
               B        RETURN
*
               ...      REST OF PROGRAM
*
               END
```

Either the GETPARM or the GETCNTL routine is required, depending on the source of the input. The GETPARM routine should precede the OPEN routine because the contents of register 1 is destroyed by OPEN and the address in register 1 is required by GETPARM. The GETCNTL may follow the OPEN routine, in which case the OPEN routine will also OPEN the input file containing the control statements.

Coding Example 2.5.1

This coding example illustrates how the entire program would appear as a structured program, using the top-down programming technique. This coding example shows the mainstream, the major routines, and the subroutines positioned in the proper places in the program, with suggested routine header comments.

```
          TITLE ...
*
*
*****************************************************************
*
*    PROGRAM PROLOGUE COMMENTS GO HERE
*
*****************************************************************
*
*
REPORT       CSECT
*
*
*****************************************************************
*    INITIALIZATION
*****************************************************************
*
             INITL   3,EQU=R
*
*
*****************************************************************
*    MAINSTREAM OF PROGRAM
*****************************************************************
*
             BAL     R6,GETPARM
             BAL     R6,OPEN
             BAL     R6,GETCNTL
NEXTREC      BAL     R6,READSMF
             BAL     R6,PROCREC
             BAL     R6,SETLINE
```

```
            BAL     R6,DOREPORT
            B       NEXTREC
SMFEND      BAL     R6,DOTOTALS
            BAL     R6,CLOSE
            B       RETURN
*
*
*****************************************************************
*****************************************************************
*    MAJOR ROUTINES AND SUBROUTINES
*****************************************************************
*****************************************************************
*
*****************************************************************
*    THIS ROUTINE OBTAINS THE CONTROL INFORMATION SPECIFIED VIA
*    THE PARM PARAMETER OF THE JCL EXEC STATEMENT.
*****************************************************************
*
GETPARM     DS      OH
            ...
            BR      R6
*
*
*****************************************************************
*    THIS ROUTINE OPENS ALL THE DCBS.
*****************************************************************
*
OPEN        DS      OH
            ...
            BR      R6
*
*
*****************************************************************
*    THIS ROUTINE OBTAINS THE CONTROL INFORMATION SPECIFIED VIA
*    THE SYSIN DATASET.
*****************************************************************
*
GETCNTL     DS      OH
            ...
            BR      R6
*
*
*****************************************************************
*    THIS ROUTINE READS SMF RECORDS AND RETURNS ONLY THE ONES
*    THAT FULFILL THE SPECIFIED REQUIREMENTS. THIS ROUTINE
*    BRANCHES AND LINKS TO THE SELREC SUBROUTINE, WHICH DETERMINES
*    WHICH RECORDS ARE TO BE PROCESSED BY RETURNING A RC IN
*    REGISTER 15. RC=0 INDICATES THAT THE RECORD SATISFIES ALL THE
*    SPECIFIED SELECTION CRITERIA AND SHOULD BE PROCESSED AND A
*    NON-ZERO RC INDICATES THAT THE RECORD IS TO BE BYPASSED AND
*    THE NEXT SMF RECORD IS TO BE READ.
*****************************************************************
*
READSMF     DS      OH
            ...
            BAL     R7,SELREC
            ...
            B       READSMF
*
*
*****************************************************************
*    THIS SUBROUTINE SELECTS THE APPROPRIATE SMF RECORDS FOR
*    PROCESSING. IT BRANCHES AND LINKS TO A SEPARATE SUBROUTINE
*    TO CHECK FOR EACH SELECTION CRITERION. IF THE CALLED SUBROUTINE
```

```
*    RETURNS CONTROL WITH RC=0 SET IN REGISTER 15, THEN THE SELECTION
*    CRITERION WAS SATISFIED AND THE NEXT SUBROUTINE IS CALLED. IF
*    THE CALLED SUBROUTINE RETURNS CONTROL WITH A NON-ZERO RC SET IN
*    REGISTER 15, THEN THE SELECTION CRITERION WAS NOT SATISFIED AND
*    THAT PARTICULAR SMF RECORD IS TO BE IGNORED, INDICATED BY
*    RETURNING CONTROL TO THE CALLING ROUTINE WITH A NON-ZERO RC IN
*    REGISTER 15. IF ALL THE SELECTION CRITERIA ARE SATISFIED, THEN
*    THIS SUBROUTINE RETURNS CONTROL TO THE CALLING ROUTINE, WITH
*    RC=0 SET IN REGISTER 15 TO INDICATE THAT THE RECORD SHOULD BE
*    PROCESSED.
****************************************************************
*
SELREC      BAL      R8,CHKRECID
            ...
            BAL      R8,CHKDATE
            ...
            BAL      R8,CHKTIME
            ...
            BAL      R8,CHKINDEX
            ...
            BR       R7
*
*
****************************************************************
*    THIS SUBROUTINE CHECKS THE RECORD-TYPE ID OF EACH SMF RECORD
*    READ AND SETS RC=0 IN REGISTER 15 IF THE RECORD-TYPE ID IS ONE
*    OF THE REQUIRED ONES.
****************************************************************
*
CHKRECID    DS       0H
            ...
            BR       R8
*
*
********************************************************************
*    THIS SUBROUTINE CHECKS THE JOB-SUBMITTED-DATE FIELD OF THE SMF
*    RECORDS. SETS RC=0 IN REGISTER 15 IF THE DATE IS WITHIN THE
*    SPECIFIED RANGE.
********************************************************************
*
CHKDATE     DS       0H
            ...
            BR       R8
*
*
********************************************************************
*    THIS SUBROUTINE CHECKS THE JOB-SUBMITTED-TIME FIELD OF THE SMF
*    RECORDS. SETS RC=0 IN REGISTER 15 IF THE TIME IS WITHIN THE
*    SPECIFIED RANGE.
********************************************************************
*
CHKTIME     DS       0H
            ...
            BR       R8
*
*
********************************************************************
*    THIS SUBROUTINE CHECKS THE HIGH LEVEL INDEX OF THE DATASET-NAME
*    FIELD OF THE SMF RECORDS. SETS RC=0 IN REGISTER 15 IF THE
*    HIGH LEVEL INDEX IS ONE OF THE SPECIFIED ONES.
********************************************************************
*
CHKINDEX    DS       0H
            ...
```

```
            BR      R8
*
*
**********************************************************************
*    THIS ROUTINE PROCESSES THE SELECTED SMF RECORDS.
**********************************************************************
*
PROCREC     DS      0H
            ...
            BAL     R7,PROC14
            ...
            BAL     R7,PROC15
            ...
            BAL     R7,PROC64
            ...
            BR      R6
*
*
**********************************************************************
*    THIS SUBROUTINE PROCESSES THE SMF TYPE-14 RECORDS.
**********************************************************************
*
PROC14      BAL     R8,GETDATE
            BAL     R8,GETTIME
            ...
            BAL     R8,GETEXCP
            ...
            BR      R7
*
*
**********************************************************************
*    THIS SUBROUTINE PROCESSES THE SMF TYPE-15 RECORDS.
**********************************************************************
*
PROC15      BAL     R8,GETDATE
            BAL     R8,GETTIME
            ...
            BAL     R8,GETEXCP
            ...
            BR      R7
*
*
**********************************************************************
*    THIS SUBROUTINE PROCESSES THE SMF TYPE-64 RECORDS.
**********************************************************************
*
PROC64      BAL     R8,GETDATE
            BAL     R8,GETTIME
            ...
            BAL     R8,GETEXCP
            ...
            BR      R7
*
*
**********************************************************************
*     THIS ROUTINE SETS UP THE DETAIL PRINT LINE FOR THE REPORT.
**********************************************************************
*
SETLINE     DS      0H
            ...
            BR      R6
*
*
**********************************************************************
```

```
*    THIS ROUTINE PRINTS EACH DETAIL LINE OF THE REPORT AND CHECKS
*    THE LINE COUNTER TO DETERMINE WHEN A NEW PAGE IS REQUIRED.
*******************************************************************
*
DOREPORT    DS     0H
            ...
            BAL    R7,NEWPAGE
            ...
            BR     R6
*
*
*******************************************************************
*    THIS SUBROUTINE PRINTS THE HEADERS FOR THE FIRST PAGE AND EACH
*    NEW PAGE OF THE REPORT, RESETS THE LINE COUNTER TO ZERO AND
*    INCREMENTS THE PAGE NUMBER.
*******************************************************************
*
NEWPAGE     DS     0H
            ...
            BR     R7
*
*
*******************************************************************
*    THIS ROUTINE PRINTS THE TOTALS LINE ON THE REPORT AT SMF
*    END-OF-DATA.
*******************************************************************
*
DOTOTALS    DS     0H
            ...
            BR     R6
*
*
*******************************************************************
*    THIS ROUTINE CLOSES ALL THE DCBS.
*******************************************************************
*
CLOSE       DS     0H
            ...
            BR     R6
*
*
*******************************************************************
*******************************************************************
*    COMMON SUBROUTINES
*******************************************************************
*******************************************************************
*
*******************************************************************
*    THIS SUBROUTINE EXTRACTS THE JOB-SUBMITTED-DATE FROM THE SMF
*    RECORDS AND EDITS IT IN THE FORMAT YY.DDD.
*******************************************************************
*
GETDATE     DS     0H
            ...
            BR     R8
*
*
*******************************************************************
*    THIS SUBROUTINE EXTRACTS THE JOB-SUBMITTED-TIME FROM THE SMF
*    RECORDS AND EDITS IT IN THE FORMAT HH/MM/SS.
*******************************************************************
*
GETTIME     DS     0H
            ...
```

```
            BR      R8
*
*
*****************************************************************
*    THIS SUBROUTINE EXTRACTS THE EXCP COUNT FROM THE SMF RECORDS
*    AND EDITS IT IN THE FORMAT NN,NNN,NNN.
*****************************************************************
*
GETEXCP     DS      0H
            ...
            BR      R8
*
*
*****************************************************************
*    THIS ROUTINE RESTORES THE REGISTERS AND RETURNS CONTROL.
*****************************************************************
*
RETURN      ...
*
*
*****************************************************************
*    CONSTANTS AND WORK AREAS
*****************************************************************
*
ZERO        DC      P'0'
ONE         DC      P'1'
MAXLINES    DC      PL2'55'
LINECTR     DC      PL2'55'
PAGECTR     DC      PL2'0'
EDWORK01    DS      CL4
EDMASK01    DC      X'40202020'
            ...
*
*
*****************************************************************
*    DCB MACROS
*****************************************************************
*
SYSIN       DCB     ...
SMFDATA     DCB     ...
REPORT      DCB     ...
*
*
*****************************************************************
*    DSECTS
*****************************************************************
*
$SMF14      DSECT
*
$SMF15      DSECT
*
$SMF64      DSECT
*
#LINE       DSECT
*
*
*****************************************************************
*    END OF PROGRAM
*****************************************************************
*
*
            END
```

2.6 SUGGESTIONS FOR DEBUGGING DIFFICULT PROBLEMS

The purpose of this section is to provide some useful general techniques for resolving difficult programming problems. It is expected that the readers of this book have at least some basic dump reading and debugging experience; therefore, detailed dump reading procedures will not be discussed. What will be discussed are methodologies that will augment the basic problem determination techniques.

When a program ABENDs due to a relatively simple programming problem, such as an S0C7 due to invalid formatted data in a field, the resolution is usually straightforward. It is a matter of examining the dump, locating the failing instruction, and correcting the situation that caused the problem.

However, not all programming problems are so simple to resolve. How does one approach the very difficult problems? Some examples of such problems are ABENDs that occur at locations outside the program (or any of its called programs), ABENDs that occur at some time after the actual programming error was performed and then for some completely unrelated reason, or (not involving an ABEND at all) continuous loops or erroneous outputs.

The following subsections describe problem determination techniques that may be effective in the resolution of difficult programming problems.

2.6.1 Setting up a Trace

If the ABEND occurs at an address outside of the program or at nonexecutable code within the program, then the first objective is to determine the place in the program where control was passed to that address. The address in the PSW is not helpful because it contains the address of the location of the ABEND (actually, the instruction passed the failing one), not the location from where control was passed. The contents of register 14 may be helpful (if a Data Management call was made, a branch was made to another program, and so on) but usually not. Sometimes the setting in a switch, the value in a counter, or the contents in an I/O buffer may be helpful to determine where the bad branch was made. These methods may be helpful but are usually not reliable and would normally lead to just an educated guess of where the bad branch occurred.

If the program was designed using the structure and philosphy presented in this chapter, then there already exists a built-in trace facility in the contents of the link registers. This trace is useful if the problem involves the program making a bad branch either to an address outside of the program, thus causing an ABEND (because the code at that location is nonexecutable, is fetch-protected, and so on) or to an address within the program that should not receive control, such as a DC/DS instruction.

Let us say that the mainstream of a program is the following:

```
         BAL    R6,RTN01      (1)
         BAL    R6,RTN02      (2)
         BAL    R6,RTN03      (3)
         B      RETURN        (4)
```

By examining the contents of the high-level link register (in this case, register 6), it can be determined which routine caused the bad branch. Let us say that the contents of register 6 points to instruction (3). This indicates that RTN02 never returned control and, therefore, the bad branch was caused somewhere in the code contained in or called by RTN02. RTN02 may call other subroutines as follows:

```
RTN02    ...
         BAL    R7,RTN02A
         ...
         BAL    R7,RTN02B
```

```
         ...
         BR      R6
```

If that is the situation, then it is a matter of examining the contents of the next link register (in this case, register 7) and so on until the subroutine that caused the bad branch is located. Once that subroutine is located, then it is just a matter of examining it to determine how the bad branch occurred.

This trace is also useful if the program goes into a continuous loop. In this case, the instruction address in the PSW (after the job is cancelled with a dump) points to one of the loop addresses, but the appropriate link register indicates from where the looping code received control, which may be significant if that code is called from multiple places in the program.

If the program does not ABEND or go into a continuous loop, but provides incorrect results instead, then a finer, active trace is required. (The contents of the link registers is a passive trace and is useful only if there is a dump due to a program ABEND or CANCEL.) This can be accomplised by setting up a quick and crude (but effective) trace by coding the WTO macro instruction in strategic locations in the program. The WTO macro instruction is discussed in Chapter 4.

After the WTO macro instructions are coded, the mainstream may look something like the following:

```
         WTO     '*** MS-01 ***',ROUTCDE=11
         BAL     R6,RTN01
         WTO     '*** MS-02 ***',ROUTCDE=11
         BAL     R6,RTN02
         WTO     '*** MS-03 ***',ROUTCDE=11
         BAL     R6,RTN03
         WTO     '*** MS-04 ***',ROUTCDE=11
         B       RETURN
```

The ROUTCDE=11 parameter in the operand of the WTO macro instruction causes the message to appear only in the program's job listing (if the console route codes were defined properly by the operator or the systems programmer); otherwise the diagnostic WTO messages would appear on the operator/system consoles, cluttering it with unnecessary messages. Specifying multiple WTOs in a routine would be necessary to trace the execution flow if the routine contains internal branches or branches to other subroutines based upon switch settings, the contents of an I/O buffer, and so forth. RTN02 may look something like the following after the WTOs are coded:

```
RTN02    WTO     '*** RTN02-01 ***',ROUTCDE=11
         ...
         BAL     R7,RTN2A
         WTO     '*** RTN02-02 ***',ROUTCDE=11
         ...
         BAL     R7,RTN2B
         WTO     '*** RTN02-03 ***',ROUTCDE=11
         ...
         WTO     '*** RTN02-04 ***',ROUTCDE=11
         ...
         BR      R6
```

If applicable, the text of the WTO macro instruction may contain something descriptive about its location or the routine that contains it.

After the program terminates normally or is CANCELed either manually or via the ABEND macro instruction (placed in the proper location in the program to permit a meaningful trace), then the sequence of the messages issued by the WTOs should be examined to determine the execution flow of the program.

2.6.2 Using the SNAP Macro Instruction

After the execution flow of the program is determined by examining the link registers and/or the output from the WTO macro instructions, additional information may be required to resolve the problem. If the execution flow is determined to be incorrect or if the execution flow is correct but the output is incorrect and the reason cannot be determined just by examining the code, then the contents of switches, counters, I/O buffers, and any other indicators that may influence the execution path and/or the output are required while the program is executing, to determine how the execution flow becomes distorted. This can be accomplished by placing the SNAP macro instruction in strategic places along the path of the execution flow. The SNAP macro instruction is discussed in Chapter 4.

To minimize the amount of storage dumped by SNAP, a good idea would be to place all the areas, that are to be dumped next to each other in the program. Also, registers could be used to point to the more important items in the dump by loading the addresses of those items into available registers before issuing the SNAP macro instruction. This would eliminate the need to constantly subtract the entry point of the program from the offset of the areas in the program whose contents are to be examined in the dump. If only one or a few small values are required to be examined (such as the value in a switch, a counter, or a field in an I/O record) then they can be loaded into a register(s) before the SNAP macro instruction is issued. This will save the work required to examine the actual storage portion of the dump. If registers are used, then it is recommended to start with register 8 (then 9 and 10), if available. If the dump is viewed on a display terminal with an 80-character width, then the use of those registers will eliminate the need to shift to the right to view the other registers.

After the program terminates normally or is CANCELed either manually or via the ABEND macro instruction (placed in the proper location in the program to permit meaningful output from the SNAP macro instruction(s)), then the contents of the SNAP dumps should be examined to determine how the data is being changed during various stages of the program execution. The objective is to determine if the areas that influence the execution path and/or the output are getting set properly. If it is discovered that those areas are not being set properly, then the code and/or the input data, if applicable, should be examined to determine how the affected areas are being incorrectly changed. It is possible that the first set of SNAP macro instructions may not obtain all the required information to resolve the program problem. If that is the case, then the SNAP macro instructions may be required to dump additional areas of virtual storage and/or be placed in different locations of the program to dump those areas at different stages of the program execution. The contents of the various areas dumped by the SNAP macro instructions and the code responsible for changing those areas are examined until the program problem is resolved.

2.6.3 Diagnostic Traps

If the problem occurs only sporadically with no apparent pattern or if the ABEND occurs some time after the actual programming error was performed, then traces and SNAP dumps may not provide enough information to resolve the problem, may not provide the information at the proper time during the program execution or may provide so much information as to detract from the problem determination effort. In this case, a diagnostic trap is required. A diagnostic trap is a piece of user-written code which is placed in the execution path of the program and monitors the program for the symptoms of the problem or for the execution timing when the problem is expected to have occurred. The symptoms may be a certain record-type being processed, a certain value in a register, an area in the program being overlayed with a certain string of "garbage," and so forth. The symptoms themselves may not necessarily be causing the problem, but are present when the problem occurs.

When the conditions that satisfy the trap occur, then the trap performs some type of diagnostic action, such as issuing a SNAP dump of one or more areas of virtual storage, examining and verifying that a string of pointers are okay, and so on.

Before a trap is effective in resolving the problem, it may have to be enhanced a few times. Normally, each version of the trap provides more insight about the problem by uncovering other symptoms or apparent patterns. Therefore, additional information may be required to be examined or a better set of conditions may be determined to be more effective to activate the trap. The enhancements of the trap and the re-execution of the program continues until the condition causing the program problem is discovered and fixed.

2.6.4 TSO TEST Facility

Difficult problems can also be solved by using the TEST facility of TSO. The TEST facility provides an interactive problem determination environment.

TSO TEST can be used to establish breakpoints at instructions in the program where execution is to be interrupted. At the breakpoints, interim results can be examined similar to taking a snapshot via the SNAP macro instruction. Defining breakpoints at strategic locations in the program can function as a trace.

When execution is interrupted at a breakpoint, the following can be done:

- Display the contents of the registers and virtual storage;
- Display the PSW;
- Dump the contents of selected control blocks;
- Modify the contents of the registers and virtual storage;
- Start execution at the instruction after the breakpoint or at another instruction.

The general procedures followed for problem determination and resolution are the same with TSO TEST as they would be in a batch testing environment. TSO TEST can be used in lieu of the techniques mentioned in Sections 2.6.1 (WTO trace) and 2.6.2 (SNAP dumps) and in conjunction with the technique (diagnostic traps) mentioned in Section 2.6.3.

SUMMARY OF CHAPTER 2

Proper programming structure was briefly mentioned in Chapter 1. This chapter discussed, in detail, the techniques and guidelines for developing well-structured, easy-to-maintain programs. The terms "structured programming" and "top-down programming" were introduced and developed. A program can have all the characteristics that were mentioned in Chapter 1, but if the program is poorly structured, it will still be difficult to read, modify, and debug.

Structured programming is a programming style or technique that improves the design and understandability of a program. In general, structured programs are easier to design, write, understand, modify, and debug. Unstructured programs are characterized by multiple entry and exit points, numerous unconditional branch instructions throughout, and code for various and/or numerous functions that appear to run together. All this causes an unstructured program to be difficult to understand and maintain.

A typical structured program is made up of building blocks called routines or subroutines, each with its own function whether it be a major one or a minor one. The beginning of a structured program contains the mainstream of the program. This is a series of BAL instructions (and possibly some B instructions), which call all of the main routines that perform the major functions of the program in the proper sequence. Besides being a router to all the main routines, the mainstream is also a concise summary of what the program does.

Top-down programming is a programming technique used with structured programming. Basically, top-down programming involves sequencing: the sequencing of the development of code and the sequencing of the positioning of code. This means that the subroutines are developed at certain times relative to each other and are placed in the program at certain positions relative to each other.

The main routines, which perform the major functions of the program, are designed and coded first. Then the subroutines, which are called by the major routines to assist in their function, are designed and coded next. Minor subroutines, which are called from higher-level subroutines, are designed and coded next, and so on.

In the actual program, the major routines are physically placed before the subroutines that they call, and the higher-level subroutines are physically placed before the minor subroutines that they call, and so on. Also, the major routines are placed in the sequence in which they will execute. The advantage of this placement scheme is that it is easier to locate all the code that functions together and it places the subroutines in a logical sequence.

Besides writing meaningful comments for machine instructions, DC/DS instructions, DSECTs, and subroutines (as was discussed in Chapter 1), it is also good practice to write comments for the program as a whole (Prologue Comments). These comments should be physically located at the beginning of the program and be about a page or two or more in length depending on the length and/or complexity of the program. The proloque comments should contain the following:

- Program name;
- Programmer name;
- Date and description of last modification (or all modifications);
- Special assembly and/or linkedit instructions (if any), such as additional macro libraries, linkedit attributes, or additional load and/or object libraries;
- Names of any nonstandard macro instructions used, such as user-written macros, vendor-supplied macros, or the ones that IBM supplies, but that are not located in the standard macro library;
- Special load library requirements (if any) during execution;
- Names of other programs (if any) that may be called or referenced during execution and a description of them;
- Description of the input to the program;
- Description of the output from the program;
- Description of the function of the program;
- Format and use of any control information the program may accept via the PARM parameter of the JCL EXEC statement or via SYSIN control statements; and
- Anything else that the original programmer or the maintenance programmer may believe to be pertinent.

A general purpose register usage convention was described. A general register usage convention is, in effect, the same as managing them. This has the benefit of not wasting registers by using different ones for duplicate functions. Another benefit is that when a register is required to be used in the coding of a particular function, the programmer already knows which one(s) to use and will not need to search the cross-reference listing (assuming that EQUs were used for the register numbers) to determine which ones are available.

The summary of that convention, which is also used for the examples in this book, is the following:

Register 0	Same as register 10 if the routine does not contain any IBM macros. May be used with register 1 for instructions that require an even/odd pair of registers.
Register 1	Same as register 0.
Register 2	For TRT instruction and same as register 10 if the routine/subroutine does not contain a TRT instruction.
Register 3	First base register.
Register 4	Second base register, if required. Should be held in reserve if not immediately required.
Register 5	Third base register, if required. Should be held in reserve if not immediately required.
Register 6	First link register (for routines called via BAL from mainstream).
Register 7	Second link register (for nested subroutine calls).
Register 8	Third link register, if required. Same as register 10 if not required as a link register.
Register 9	Fourth link register, if required. Same as register 10 if not required as a link register.
Register 10	Work register used in routines/subroutines where the value is not required to be saved when the routine/ subroutine returns control to the caller. Some uses may include the following: • Perform binary arithmetic; • Contain a pointer into a table, array, and so on; • Calculate addresses; and • DSECT addressability. May also be used for DSECTs that require addressability for the life or the program.
Register 11	Same as register 10.
Register 12	Same as register 10.
Register 13	Pointer to savearea. Can also be used as a base register, if required.
Register 14	Same as register 10 if the routine does not contain any IBM macros. May be used with register 15 for instructions which require an even/odd pair of registers.
Register 15	For passing return codes between routines/subroutines. Same as register 14.

BIBLIOGRAPHY FOR CHAPTER 2

The following IBM manuals contain reference material for the topics discussed in this chapter.

ID	TITLE
GC28-0646	*OS/VS2 TSO Command Language Reference*
GC28-0646 (with GD23-0259)	*MVS/XA TSO Command Language Reference*
SC28-1881	*MVS/ESA TSO Extensions Version 2 Command Reference*

3

The Macro Facility and Conditional Assembler Language

The chapter discusses the concepts, facilities, and structure of macros, as well as writing and using them to facilitate the development of programs.

Conditional Assembler language is also discussed in this chapter because the development of macros and the use of Conditional Assembler language is so intimately related. Using Conditional Assembler within macro definitions provides the macro with sophisticated processing capability and enables the macro developer to provide additional function and flexibility for the users of the macros. Using Conditional Assembler in open code is also discussed.

Numerous coding examples of macro definitions are provided, both with and without Conditional Assembler, to illustrate the many functions that can be performed by both simple and complex macros.

3.1 INTRODUCTION TO THE MACRO FACILITY

This section discusses the structure of a macro and introduces the terminology used and the facilities available in macro development.

3.1.1 What Is a Macro?

A macro (macro definition) is a named group of statements in a specific sequence, similar to an actual program, that generates Assembler language statements into an Assembler language source program at pre-assembly time.

A macro definition may be optionally defined with processing logic and an operand. The user may specify parameters via the operand to influence which Assembler statements are generated and to alter the Assembler statements that are generated.

The processing logic is accomplished via Conditional Assembler (discussed in Section 3.4) and the generated Assembler statements are altered via variable symbols (discussed in Sections 3.1.3 and 3.2).

A macro definition is called by the programmer by specifying the name of the macro definition in the operation-code field of an Assembler statement. The Assembler statement that calls the macro definition is called a macro call statement or macro instruction. The macro definition is processed by the Assembler, and the generated Assembler statements are placed into the source program, immediately after the Assembler statement that calls the macro definition.

The word macro and phrase macro definition will be used interchangeably in this chapter. In the chapters that follow, the word macro and the phrase macro instruction will be used interchangeably.

3.1.2 Structure of a Macro Definition

A macro definition is composed of four sections: the header, the prototype, the body and the trailer.

THE HEADER SECTION

The header section indicates the physical beginning of the macro definition and is indicated by a single statement—the header statement. The header statement is simply the word MACRO in the operation-code field and must be the first statement in the macro definition. The MACRO statement has no operand, and its name field must be blank.

THE PROTOTYPE SECTION

The prototype section indicates the actual format of the statement that calls the macro. It is composed of one statement (but may occupy multiple lines) and must follow the header statement in the macro definition. The prototype statement provides the name of the macro by which it is called, defines its operand (if any), indicates if the operand contains positional parameters or keyword parameters, optionally provides default values for keyword parameters, and indicates if the macro will accept a label. The following is an example of a prototype statement:

```
&LABEL    MOVE    &TO,&FROM
```

The name of the macro is MOVE, and the names preceded by an ampersand are called symbolic parameters. Symbolic parameters are variable symbols that are declared in the prototype statement. Statements in the body of the macro definition contain the same named symbolic parameters. The purpose of the symbolic parameters is to enable the user to pass parameters to the generated Assembler statements. The user specifies values for the symbolic parameters in the operand field of the macro call statement. These values replace the same named symbolic parameters in the body of the macro definition. The &LABEL symbolic parameter indicates that the macro will accept a label. If the user specifies a value for &LABEL, then the generated Assembler statement, which contains &LABEL in the name field, will be generated with the user-specified label. The symbolic parameters &TO and &FROM comprise the operand of the macro. In this example, the operand contains positional parameters. Positional and keyword parameters are discussed in Section 3.1.3.

The prototype statement may also be coded in an alternate way. Each symbolic parameter may be coded on a separate line. In this case, the syntax is a comma at the end of each symbolic parameter except the one on the last line, a non-blank character to indicate a continuation line in the column following the end column of the statement (standard is 72) on every line except the last, and the symbolic parameters on the second and subsequent lines, starting in the continuation column (standard is 16).

The advantage of using this method is reading clarity and ease of maintenance (individual symbolic parameters may be changed without changing the entire statement) when many symbolic parameters are specified. Also, this method enables the macro developer to document the use of each symbolic parameter. The following is the MOVE macro prototype statement from above, recoded using the alternate method.

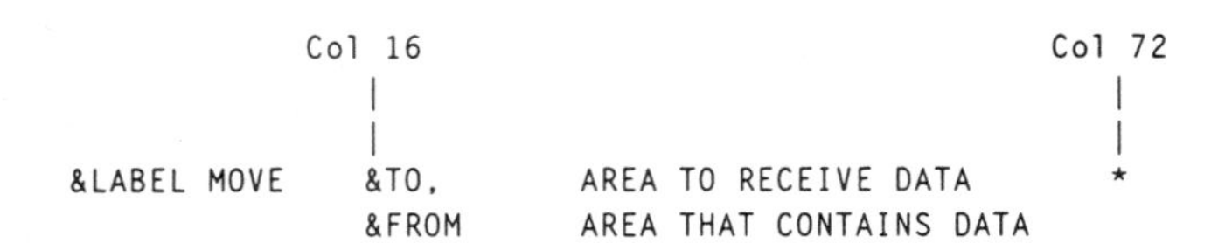

Col 16
Col 72
&LABEL MOVE &TO, AREA TO RECEIVE DATA *
&FROM AREA THAT CONTAINS DATA

It is good practice to code the prototype statement using the alternate method when defining complex macro definitions or macro definitions that have many symbolic parameters.

THE BODY SECTION

The body section of the macro follows the prototype statement and contains the actual processing logic of the macro and the Assembler statements that are to be generated. Using the values of the parameters specified by the user via the operand and/or the values of system parameters (discussed in section 3.2.2), it determines which Assembler language statements are generated and which ones are not; as well as what values are substituted in the generated statements. It also has the capability of performing validity checking against the specified parameters and issuing warning and/or error messages to the user (via MNOTEs, discussed in Section 3.5.2). The body section may contain one or more statements. The statements may be model statements and/or macro definition processing statements. Macro definition processing statements include Conditional Assembler instructions and the COPY, MEXIT, and MNOTE instructions.

The model statements are statements from which the Assembler language statements are generated at pre-Assembler time. They may be Assembler instructions, machine instructions, or other macros (called inner macros). A model statement may or may not contain imbedded variables symbols. If it does not contain any variable symbols, then it is generated as is. The following is an example of a model statement:

```
MVC       &TO,&FROM
```

The machine instruction MVC contains two variable symbols &TO and &FROM. When the macro expands, the values specified by the user for the variable symbols &TO and &FROM will replace the corresponding variable symbols in the model statement. The following example illustrates this:

```
MOVE      AREA1,AREA2         MACRO CALL WITH USER-SPECIFIED VALUES
MVC       AREA1,AREA2         MODEL STATEMENT AFTER SUBSTITUTION
```

Conditional Assembler statements are optional in the body section of a macro definition. They are used to perform the actual logic in the macro definition, if such logic is required, to control how Assembler statements are generated. They may be used to perform logical and arithmetic compares and branching, perform arithmetic operations, set values used to influence Assembler statement generation, and so forth. If no conditional Assembler statements are included in the macro definition, then all the model statements are processed sequentially and generated. Conditional Assembler is discussed in detail in Section 3.4.

The COPY instruction is used to copy Assembler source statements, as is, into a program. When used in a macro definition, the source statements become part of the body of the macro before the macro definition is processed. If the COPY instruction is used to copy whole macro definitions, then it must appear at the beginning of the program where source macro definitions are allowed as discussed in Section 3.1.6.

The MEXIT instruction is used to indicate the logical end of a macro. The MEXIT statement is simply the word MEXIT in the operation-code field. Multiple MEXIT instructions may be used throughout the body section of a macro definition to provide exit points from the macro. The statements in the body section of the macro definition are processed sequentially until a branch is indicated via Conditional Assembler (similar to the way a program is executed). If a MEXIT instruction is encountered, the macro stops generating Assembler statements and the Assembler will then start processing the next sequential instruction after the macro call statement.

The MNOTE instruction is used to generate information, warning, and/or error messages to the programmer. It is discussed in detail in Section 3.5.2.

THE TRAILER SECTION

The trailer section indicates the physical end of the macro definition and is indicated by a single statement, the trailer statement. The trailer statement is simply the word MEND in the operation-code field and must be the last statement in the macro definition. When the MEND statement is encountered, the Assembler stops processing the macro definition and processes the next sequential instructions which follow the macro call statement. The MEND statement has no operand, but may contain a sequence symbol in its name field. Sequence symbols are discussed in Section 3.4.2.

MACRO DEFINITION EXAMPLE

The following is a sample macro definition. The name of the macro is ADD. It accepts two positional parameters, which must be numbers with a value less than 4,096. The sum of the two numbers will be placed into register 14 by the code generated by the macro expansion. The macro will also accept a label. If the user specifies a label, it will be placed into the name field of the first generated Assembler statement.

```
         MACRO                  HEADER STATEMENT
&LABEL   ADD    &NUMB1,&NUMB2   PROTOTYPE STATEMENT
&LABEL   LA     R14,&NUMB1      MODEL STATEMENT WITH VARIABLE SYMBOLS
         LA     R15,&NUMB2      MODEL STATEMENT WITH A VARIABLE SYMBOL
         AR     R14,R15         MODEL STATEMENT WITH NO VARIABLE SYMBOLS
         MEND                   TRAILER STATEMENT
```

If the user specifies the following macro call statement:

```
COMPUTE  ADD    25,99
```

The following code will be generated by the macro expansion:

```
COMPUTE  LA     R14,25
         LA     R15,99
         AR     R14,R15
```

The above is an illustration showing how a simple macro definition is coded and functions. However, since this macro definition is straight-forward and simple, it does no validity checking and, therefore, would be susceptible to user errors and could generate erroneous code. The following are some of the errors that a user could make when calling this macro:

- Specify a label that exceeds eight characters;
- Specify alpha data instead of numeric data;
- Specify a number greater than 4,095;
- Specify only one number; and
- Specify no numbers.

More involved macro definitions that provide additional functions could introduce even more potential error situations.

Other sections that follow in this chapter will introduce facilities that will enable the macro developer to code complex macro definitions that will provide sophisticated and elaborate functions and also enable the macro developer to test for the above error conditions as well as others. In addition, macro definition coding examples will be provided to illustrate how to code and use those facilities. In addition, suggestions will be provided to indicate what actions to take when error conditions are encountered.

3.1.3 Symbolic Parameters

There two types of symbolic parameters that may appear in the operand field of the prototype statement of a macro definition. They are called positional parameters and keyword parameters. Both types of parameters may also be combined in the same macro definition. Symbolic parameters are separated by commas. Blanks are not allowed between them because the blank is used to delimit the entire operand. The number of symbolic parameters that may be declared in the prototype statement of the macro definition is, in effect, limitless to the Assembler. The maximum is actually limited by the amount of storage that is made available to the Assembler Section 3.1.4 discusses the syntax of the values that may be specified in the macro call statement for the symbolic parameters.

POSITIONAL PARAMETERS

Positional parameters are assigned values by coding these values in the operand field of the macro call statement in the same sequence as the positional parameters to which they refer appear in the prototype statement. The value of the first positional parameter is always in the first position of the operand, the value of the second positional parameter is always in the second position, and so on. The macro definition refers to the positional parameters by their symbolic names, but if their intended values are not specified in the correct sequence, then the macro definition will not receive the proper values for the specific positional parameters. Consider the following prototype statement for the macro MAC01:

```
MAC01       &P1,&P2,&P3
```

The positional parameters are &P1, &P2, and &P3. If a user desires to specify the values XYZ for &P1, 35 for &P2, and E11 for &P3, then the macro call statement would be coded as follows:

```
MAC01       XYZ,35,E11
```

If the value for any positional parameter is to be omitted during a macro call, then its omission must be indicated by a comma. For example, let us say that the value of &P2 is to be omitted. The macro call statement would then be coded as follows:

```
MAC01       XYZ,,E11
```

If the macro call statement were coded as:

```
MAC01       XYZ,E11
```

then the value of &P2 would be interpreted as E11 and the value of &P3 would be interpreted as omitted since only position is considered when the values of positional parameters are extracted from the operand of the macro call statement.

KEYWORD PARAMETERS

A keyword parameter is a symbolic parameter followed by an equal sign. Keyword parameters are assigned values by coding the actual keyword name in the operand field of the macro call statement and by specifying the value after the equal sign. However, unlike positional parameters, keyword parameters may be specified in any sequence. Consider the following prototype statement for the macro MAC02:

```
MAC02       &KW1=,&KW2=
```

The keyword parameters are &KW1 and &KW2. If a user desires to specify the value ABC for &KW1 and the value 922X for &KW2, then the macro call statement would be coded as follows:

```
MAC02       KW1=ABC,KW2=922X
```

or

```
MAC02       KW2=922X,KW1=ABC
```

Notice that the values may be specified in any sequence because the Assembler knows which values are intended for which symbolic parameters because the keywords are coded with their user-specified values. Also, notice that the lead ampersand is not included in the macro call statement for the keyword parameter names.

Besides having their values specified in any sequence, keyword parameters also have another useful facility. Default values may be specified for them in the prototype statement. Consider the following prototype statement for the macro MAC03:

```
MAC03       &KW4=,&KW5=DEFG,&KW6=V19
```

In the above prototype statement, the keyword parameter &KW4 has no default, but the keyword parameters &KW5 and &KW6 have defaults of DEFG and V19, respectively. The following macro call statement:

```
MAC03       KW5=PQ
```

would provide to the macro definition named MAC03 a null value (discussed in Section 3.1.4) for symbolic parameter &KW4, a value of PQ for the symbolic parameter &KW5 and a value of V19 for symbolic parameter &KW6.

COMBINING POSITIONAL AND KEYWORD PARAMETERS

Positional parameters and keyword parameters may be mixed in the same macro definition. When positional parameters and keyword parameters are both used, the declarations of each type may be interspersed with each other in the prototype statement of the macro definition. The specifications of the values of the positional parameters and keyword parameters may also be interspersed with each other in the macro call statement, but the relative sequence of the positional parameters must correspond to the same relative sequence in which they are declared in the prototype statement. In this chapter and the ones that follow, for macro definitions and macro call statements that require both positional parameters and keyword parameters, the positional parameters will be grouped together and specified before the keyword parameters. Consider the following prototype statement for the macro MAC04:

```
MAC04       &P1,&P2,&P3,&KW1=,&KW2=
```

Using the same values that were specified above, the macro call statement would be coded as follows:

```
MAC04       XYZ,35,E11,KW1=ABC,KW2=922X
```

or

```
MAC04     XYZ,35,E11,KW2=922X,KW1=ABC
```

If the values of &P1, &P2, and &KW1 were omitted, the macro call statement would be coded as follows:

```
MAC04     ,,E11,KW2=922X
```

The first two commas in the operand field indicate the absence of the values for the positional parameters &P1 and &P2. Unlike a positional parameter value, no special indication is required for an omitted keyword parameter value.

If all three positional parameters are omitted, would the macro call statement be coded as follows?

```
MAC04     ,,,KW1=ABC,KW2=922X
```

Are the three lead commas required to indicate the omission of the three positional parameters? The answer is no because the commas are required only to maintain position in order to enable the Assembler to assign the proper values for their intended positional parameters. In the above example, since no values for the positional parameters are specified, position is not required to be maintained. Therefore, the proper way to code the macro call statement for the above example would be as follows:

```
MAC04     KW1=ABC,KW2=922X
```

or

```
MAC04     KW2=922X,KW1=ABC
```

Another situation when commas are not required to maintain position is when the last or last group of positional parameters are omitted. Since no positional parameters are following the omitted ones, maintaining position serves no purpose. Consider the macro MAC01 from above. If the positional parameters &P2 and &P3 are omitted, then the last two commas are not required to indicate the absence of those parameters, and the macro call statement would be coded as follows:

```
MAC01     XYZ
```

Of course, if the values of all positional parameters are omitted, then the operand of the macro call statement would be blank as follows:

```
MAC01
```

GUIDELINES FOR SELECTING POSITIONAL AND KEYWORD PARAMETERS

When does a macro developer design a macro with only positional parameters, with only keyword parameters, or with a combination of both? The following are guidelines that will assist in that decision.

Positional parameters may be used effectively when:

- A macro requires very few parameters. An example would be the ADD macro described above.

- A macro requires many parameters that are repetitious. An example would be a macro that builds a table (the BLDTBL macro, coded in Section 3.5.3). The value of each parameter in the operand would be an entry in the table. Another example would be a macro that loads the base registers and sets up the savearea and linkage for an Assembler language program (the INITL macro, coded in Section 3.6). The value of each parameter would be a register number that is to be used as a base register.

Keyword parameters may be used effectively when:

- A macro requires many parameters. In this case, the use of positional parameters would require that the positions of all parameters be either memorized or looked up in a reference manual each time the macro is used. Also, if some or many parameters are not required for any given use of the macro, then numerous groups of consecutive commas would be required throughout the operand to indicate the missing parameters. The coding of the macro with positional parameters would be cumbersome and error prone. The use of keyword parameters with meaningful names would be easier to use because the user could equate the parameter values to specific keyword names and not be concerned with sequence or missing parameter indicators. An example would be the IBM DCB macro.
- A macro requires only a few parameters, but the same values are usually used for those parameters. In this case, keyword parameters could be used, and the frequently used values could be set as the defaults in the prototype statement.

  An example would be a macro that generates code to scan a character string containing groups of variable length characters separated by a certain delimiter, create a table of fixed length entries containing the character groups from the string, and provide a high order or low order pad character to each entry that is less than the length of the table entry.

  Let us say that the macro will normally be used to scan a character string containing numbers, the delimiter is usually a comma, the length of the table entries (and therefore the maximum length of a number in the character string) will usually be eight, and the padding, since they are numbers, will be high order zeros.

  Let us also say that the macro will assume that the character string will always end with a blank and that register 1 will be loaded with the address of the beginning of the character string.

  Consider the following prototype statement:

```
GETDATA  &DELIM=',',&MAXLEN=8,&HIGHPAD=0,&LOWPAD=
```

  The macro requires only four parameters (two of which are mutually exclusive). If positional parameters were used, three parameters would always need to be specified, with possibly an indication of an omitted one. This is not really cumbersome or error prone, but, since the same values are usually used, a better choice would be keyword parameters so that the default facility can be used. By defining the macro prototype statement as above, only the macro name would need to be coded in most cases. Since this macro would usually be coded with no operand, it would be a good idea to generate comments (via MNOTEs) before the generated code to document what the code will do.

Mixed parameters may be used effectively when:

- Some of the parameters of a macro satisfy the guidelines for selecting positional parameters and some of them satisfy the guidelines for selecting keyword parameters. An example would be the INITL macro mentioned above. Let us say that the macro also generates an EQU table for the registers and provides the user with the option of specifying the prefix. The default is R, that is, R0 EQU 0; R1 EQU 1; R2 EQU 2; and so on. Assuming that the user is usually satisfied with the prefix R, that parameter should be selected to be a keyword parameter because it is not specified often, the meaningful keyword name makes it easy to remember when it is used, and a default for the value can be defined. If the user desired to specify that registers 3, 4, and 5 be used as base registers and wanted R as the prefix (usual case) for the EQU table, then the macro call statement would be coded as follows:

```
INITL    3,4,5
```

- If the user wanted to use register 13 as a base register and required the prefix REG (unusual case) for the EQU table, then the macro call statement would be coded as follows:

```
INITL    13,EQU=REG
```

- A macro uses a variable number of repetitive positional parameters (like the BLDTBL and INITL macros mentioned above) and also requires additional information such as the register EQU table prefix (INITL macro). If a positional parameter is used for the additional information, then the number of repetitive parameters that may be specified must be fixed in order for the operand to have a specific position for the additional information. This technique reduces flexibility of the macro (must have fixed number of parameters instead of variable number) and makes it more difficult to code (discussed below). In addition, numerous consecutive commas would be required whenever the maximum number of values are not specified in order to preserve the position for the additional information. Let us say that the INITL macro is modified and the &EQU parameter is now a positional parameter and the maximum number of registers that may be specified is six. The macro definition prototype statement would be coded as follows:

```
INITL    &R1,&R2,&R3,&R4,&R5,&R6,&EQU
```

If registers 3, 4, and 5 and the prefix R are required, the macro call statement would be coded as follows:

```
INITL    3,4,5,,,R
```

The commas are required to indicate the omission of the fourth through sixth parameters in order to preserve the position for the value of the &EQU parameter. This could become more cumbersome with the BLDTBL or similar macros where the maximum number of parameters required may be in the hundreds or thousands.

Also, the requirement for a fixed number of repetitive positional parameters in order to have a specific position for the additional information makes the prototype statement unwieldy because each positional parameter must be defined. If a variable number of positional parameters were used, followed by one or more keyword parameters, then only the keyword parameters need be defined in the prototype statement as follows:

```
INITL    &EQU=R
```

The positional parameters would then be processed by using the system variable symbol &SYSLIST (discussed in Sections 3.2.2).

SUBLIST NOTATION

Individual positional and keyword parameters may have multiple values called sub-values or a sublist. Multiple values are specified by enclosing all the values for an individual symbolic parameter in parentheses and separating them by commas. Consider the following example:

```
MAC05    &P1,&P2,&KW1=                          PROTOTYPE STATEMENT
MAC05    (ABC,VAL2,XYZ),BBB,KW1=(K11,K22)       MACRO CALL STATEMENT
```

The positional parameter &P1 has a sublist of three. The sub-values are ABC, VAL2 and XYZ. The positional parameter &P2 has a sublist of one (or no sublist). The one and only value is BBB. The keyword parameter &KW1 has a sublist of two. The sub-values are K11 and K22.

Individual values of the sublist may be referenced by subcripting the symbolic parameter. The subcript is a number equal to the sequential position of the sub-value. The following illustrates the subcripts that are required to reference the various sub-values of the example above:

```
&P1(1) - ABC
&P1(2) - VAL2
&P1(3) - XYZ
&P2(1) or &P2 = BBB
&KW1(1) - K11
&KW1(2) - K22
```

If a sublist is specified and if it is referenced with an unsubcripted symbolic parameter, then the entire value (including the parentheses and the commas) is substituted. The following indicates the values that are substituted for the above example when no subscripts are used:

```
&P1 - (ABC,VAL2,XYZ)
&P2 - BBB
&P3 - (K11,K22)
```

The subscripts may be absolute numbers (like above) or SETA symbols, which are one of the types of variable symbols. SETA symbols are discussed in Section 3.2.3. The sublist may also be referenced with the system variable symbol &SYSLIST (for positional parameters only), mentioned above and discussed in Section 3.2.2.

3.1.4 Macro Operand Syntax

The operand of a macro call statement (macro instruction) is used to pass values into the macro definition. The following two types of values can be passed:

- Explicit value—This is an actual character string specified in the macro operand.
- Implicit value—This is the attribute inherent in the data specified by the explicit value. Attibutes are discussed in Section 3.4.3.

The rules for defining symbolic parameter names that are declared on the prototype statement of the macro definition are the following:

- The first character must be an ampersand (&) followed by from one to seven characters.
- The second character must be an alpha character (A–Z) or a national character (@, #, $).
- The third through eighth characters may be alhpameric characters (A–Z, 0–9) or national characters.

The values specified in the operand of the macro call statement for the symbolic parameters must be separated by commas. A blank is used to delimit the entire operand.

The syntax of the values that may be specified for the symbolic parameters are itemized below.

- The value may be a character string from 1 to 255 characters or a variable symbol. If a variable symbol (or, via concatenation, multiple variable symbols or a combination of a character string and variable symbols) is specified, the Assembler substitutes the value of the variable symbol. The resultant character string may not exceed 255 characters. When a variable symbol is specified in the operand of the macro call statement, its value must be set before the variable symbol is processed by the Assembler. A variable symbol would be used as a value for a symbolic parameter for inner macros (discussed in Section 3.1.7) or when the values for macro operands are determined by Conditional Assembler in open code. The value of a variable symbol is set by the conditional Assembler SETx statement (discussed in Section 3.2.3), which may be specified in a macro definition or in open code.

- The value may contain any of the 256 characters of the System/370 character set. However, the following characters require special consideration:

  - Ampersands. An ampersand indicates the presence of a variable symbol. The Assembler substitutes the value of the variable symbol for the symbolic parameter. This value is passed into the macro definition for that particular symbolic parameter. If the user wants to specify an ampersand as data, then the ampersand must be doubled, in which case only a single ampersand is passed into the macro definition. Consider the following example:

```
MACRO                                HEADER
MACO6       &P1,&P2,&P3              PROTOTYPE STATEMENT
...                                  BODY
MEND                                 TRAILER

MACO6       &V1,ABC&V2,&&CHARS       MACRO CALL STATEMENT
```

  - Let us say that the variable symbols &V1 and &V2 have been previously set to 123 and XYZ respectively. Then, the values that are passed into the macro definition for symbolic parameter &P1 would be 123 and for symbolic parameter &P2 would be ABCXYZ. The value ABC&V2 is a concatenation of the character string ABC with the value of the variable symbol &V2. Concatenation of variable symbols is discussed in Section 3.2.4. The value specified for the symbolic parameter &P3 is the character string &&CHARS. This is not a variable symbol because of the double ampersand. The value passed into the macro definition for symbolic parameter &P3 is &CHARS. Notice that only one ampersand is passed as data.
  - Apostrophes—An apostrophe is used to indicate the beginning and end of a quoted string and in a length attribute notation that is not within a quoted string.
    - Quoted String—A quoted string is any sequence of characters that begins and ends with an apostrophe. A quoted string may be used to pass certain characters that have special significance (such as a blank, comma, and parenthesis) into a macro definition as data (as themselves).

    - Length Attribute Notation is discussed in Section 3.4.3.

  - Blanks—A blank delimits the entire operand unless it is within a quoted string, in which case it is passed as a blank into the macro definition. Consider the following example:

```
MACO8       &P1,&P2                  PROTOTYPE STATEMENT
MACO8       ' '                      MACRO CALL STATEMENT
```

  The value passed into the macro definition for the symbolic parameter &P1 is a blank. The blank after the value specified for &P1 delimits the entire operand and, therefore, indicates that no value is specified for &P2.
  - Commas—A comma delimits symbolic parameter values; unless it is within a quoted string or within paired parentheses, which do not enclose a sublist, in which case it is passed as a comma into the macro definition. Consider the following example:

```
MACO9       &P1,&P2                  PROTOTYPE STATEMENT
MACO9       ',',A(,)B                MACRO CALL STATEMENT
```

The values passed into the macro definition for the symbolic parameter &P1 is a comma and for &P2 is A(,)B. The comma between the values for &P1 and &P2 separates them.

- Equal Signs—An equal sign may appear anywhere in a character string, inside or outside of a quoted string, and may be passed into the macro definition as data. The only precaution is that it must not appear immediately after a character string that is identical to a keyword name that is declared in the prototype statement if the equal sign is to be passed into the macro definition as an equal sign. Consider the following example:

```
MAC09      &P1,&P2,&KW1=,&KW2=        PROTOTYPE STATEMENT
MAC09      A=B,KW1=10                 MACRO CALL STATEMENT
```

The value passed into the macro definition for the symbolic parameter &P1 is A=B. However, the value passed into the macro definition for &P2 is not KW1=10 because the first three characters (KW1) are identical to the name of one of the keyword parameters that are declared in the prototype statement. Instead, the value of &P2 is considered to be omitted and the value of 10 is passed into the macro definition for the symbolic parameter &KW1.

- Parentheses—Parentheses are used to indicate a sublist and must be paired; that is, there must be an equal number of left and right parentheses. Unpaired parentheses may be specified only within a quoted string, in which case they do not define a sublist. A sublist is a method of specifying multiple values to a single symbolic parameter. Sublists were discussed in Section 3.1.3. Consider the following example:

```
MAC10      &P1,&P2                   PROTOTYPE STATEMENT
MAC10      (ABC,XYZ,123),'PQR(6'     MACRO CALL STATEMENT
```

The value passed into the macro definition for the symbolic parameter &P1 is the character string (ABC,XYZ,123), but it may also be interpreted as a sublist with the values of ABC, XYZ, and 123, depending on the logic within the macro definition. The value passed into the macro definition for the symbolic parameter &P2 is 'PQR(6'.

- Periods. A period may appear anywhere in a character string, inside or outside of a quoted string, and may be passed into the macro definition as data. The only precaution is that it must not appear immediately after a variable symbol because it then becomes the concatenation character. In this case, if the period is to be passed as a period, then it must be doubled. Concatenation of variable symbols is discussed in Section 3.2.4. Consider the following example:

```
MAC11      &P1,&P2,&P3                    PROTOTYPE STATEMENT
MAC11      &V1.DATA,N.Y..,&V2..SRCLIB     MACRO CALL STATEMENT
```

Let us say that the variable symbols &V1 and &V2 have been previously set to VAR and XYZ, respectively. Then, the values that are passed into the macro definition for symbolic parameter &P1 would be VARDATA, for &P2 would be N.Y., and for &P3 would be XYZ.SRCLIB.

- If the value is omitted, then a null value is passed into the macro definition. A null value is neither a blank nor binary zeros. It is the absence of a character. To illustrate this, consider the ADD macro, from Section 3.1.2 above, and the MAKEDC macro below:

```
               MACRO
&LABEL         ADD          &NUMB1,&NUMB2
               LA           R14,&NUMB1
               LA           R15,&NUMB2
               AR           R14,R15
               MEND
Coded:         ADD          16
Generated:     LA           R14,16
```

```
                LA         R15,         *** Null Value ***
                AR         R14,R15

                MACRO
                MAKEDC     &DATA
                DC         C'&DATA'
                MEND
Coded:          MAKEDC
Generated:      DC         C''          *** Null Value ***
```

3.1.5 Comments in Macro Definitions

Comments may be provided in a macro definition by use of the Assembler statement comment field, an ordinary comment statement, an internal macro comment statement, and the MNOTE instruction. Using the MNOTE instruction to generate comments is discussed in Section 3.5.2.

ASSEMBLER STATEMENT COMMENT FIELD

Comments may be provided on Conditional Assembler statements to document the internal processing of the macro and on model statements to indicate what the generated code does. The comments on Conditional Assembler statements are not generated and the comments on model statements are generated only if the model statements, which contain the comments, are generated.

ORDINARY COMMENT STATEMENT

An ordinary comment statement is indicated by an asterisk in position 1 of an Assembler statement. When ordinary comment statements appear in a macro definition, they are used to provide documentation for the generated code and should be generated with the code that they are documenting. Ordinary comment statements will be generated only if either the macro definition contains no Conditional Assembler or if the ordinary comment statements are in the path of the Conditional Assembler execution. Values are not substituted for any variable symbols that appear in ordinary comment statements.

INTERNAL MACRO COMMENT STATEMENT

An internal macro comment statement is indicated by a period in position 1 and an asterisk in position 2 of an Assembler statement. Internal macro comment statements are used to document the pre-Assembler processing that is performed when a macro definition is processed, and are never generated. Values are not substituted for any variable symbols that appear in internal macro comment statements.

3.1.6 Placement of Macro Definitions

Macro definitons may be placed into any of two locations. They may be placed at the beginning of the program that calls them or they may be placed in a library (a partitioned dataset). A macro definition that is placed at the beginning of a program is called a source macro definition and one that is placed in a library is called a library macro definition.

A source macro definition must be placed at the beginning of a program before the START or CSECT Assembler instruction. If multiple source macro definitions are included, then they must appear one behind the other. Comments and certain Assembler instructions (ISEQ, TITLE, PRINT, SPACE, and EJECT) may appear before or between the source macro definitions. The Assembler instructions ICTL and OPSYN, if used, must appear before the first source macro definition. If a START or CSECT Assembler instruction is not used, then all the source macro definitions must appear before the first Assembler statement that is not one of the Assembler instructions mentioned above. The following shows how source macro definitions are coded and called in a program.

```
              {Allowable Assembler statements may be Comments, ICTL,
              {OPSYN, ISEQ, TITLE, PRINT, SPACE, and EJECT
          MACRO
          MAC1
          ...
          MEND
              {Allowable Assembler statements may be Comments, ISEQ,
              {TITLE, PRINT, SPACE, and EJECT
          MACRO
          MAC2
          ...
          MEND
              {Allowable Assembler statements may be Comments, ISEQ,
              {TITLE, PRINT, SPACE, and EJECT
          MACRO
          MAC3
          ...
          MEND
              {Allowable Assembler statements may be Comments, ISEQ,
              {TITLE, PRINT, SPACE, and EJECT
PROG01    CSECT
          ...
          MAC1
          ...
          MAC2
          ...
          MAC3
          ...
          END
```

Source macro definitions may be called only by the program that contains the definitions. If a macro definition with the same name appears as both a source and a library macro, then the source macro definition is processed when the macro call is made.

Library macro definitions reside in a library as a member of a partitioned dataset (PDS). The macro name that appears on the prototype statement of the macro definition and the member name of the PDS must be the same. The Assembler automatically searches the macro library to resolve a macro call statement if the macro library is pointed to by the //SYSLIB DD JCL statement and the source program does not contain a source macro definition with the same name.

A macro definition may be placed into a library by executing a batch job using the IBM utility program IEBUPDTE or some other program with similar function, or by using an interactive editor, such as IBM's TSO/ISPF/PDF.

The normal procedure in developing a macro is to test and debug it as a source macro definition. When it functions properly, it may then be placed into a macro library and made available for all who require it.

3.1.7 Outer and Inner Macros

Macros may be nested, which means that one macro may call another macro. Macros called from the source program (open code) are called outer macros. Macros called from the body of other macros are called inner macros. A macro could be both an outer macro and an inner macro. An inner macro that calls another macro is an outer to the called macro. A macro is processed in the same way whether it is an outer macro or an inner macro. When an inner macro is encountered in the body of an outer macro, the inner macro is processed and expands. The expansion is inserted immediately after the inner macro call statement. Then, processing of the outer macro resumes with the first outer macro instruction after the inner macro call.

The operand of an inner macro may be hard-coded or may contain variable symbols. The variable symbols may be the symbolic parameters of the outer macro operand, SET symbols declared in the outer macro, or system variable symbols. For system variable symbols that have a local scope such as &SYSNDX, the value is adjusted to reflect the position of the inner macro. When control is passed back to the outer macro, the value of the system variable symbol is restored.

3.1.8 Open Code

Open code is source code that lies outside of any macro definitions. It starts with the first Assembler statement (except comments, ICTL, OPSYN, ISEQ, TITLE, PRINT, SPACE, and EJECT) that appears outside of a macro definition.

The importance of distinguishing between open code and macro definition code is because certain Assembler statements are not permitted in both types of code and certain other Assembler statements, which are permitted in both types, function differently in each type of code.

Throughout this chapter, Assembler statements that are not permitted in both types of code or that function differently in each type will be noted.

The Assembler statements MACRO, MEXIT, MNOTE, and MEND, which were discussed above, may be used only in a macro definition.

3.1.9 Uses of Macros

User developed macros are very useful. Some of those uses are itemized below:

- To generate routines that are used often. Such routines may be the same each time used or may have slight variations depending upon the differences in the data being processed or the way the parameters are specified (register versus a label, etc.). Such routines might include calculations, conversions, tables, I/O record layouts, DSECTs, and so on. By having a set of macros that generate involved, tedious or lengthy code to perform common tasks enables the programming effort to be more efficient.
- To generate difficult, complex, and efficient code for performing special tasks that only the senior programmers are capable of writing. This enables the less experienced programmers to have access to coding techniques, which they may not be able to develop themselves, to perform required tasks within their programs. This also saves the senior programmers the time and effort of rewriting the code or copying it from another program.
- To enforce certain coding standards and to provide an easy method of using standard user interfaces. IBM macros are excellent examples of macros that provide the user with an easy way of using standard system interfaces.
- To provide, in effect, a high-level programming language that provides an assortment of services and facilities, which the programmer tailors by specifying the proper parameters. This could be accomplished by developing a group of related macros (which also communicate with each other (via global SET symbols)), that generate in-line code, tables, parameter-lists used for communicating with called programs, and whatever else is required to provide the requested services.

3.2 VARIABLE SYMBOLS

In the System/370 Assembler there are three types of symbols: ordinary symbols, sequence symbols, and variable symbols. Ordinary symbols are used in the name and operand fields of Assembler instructions and machine instructions. Sequence symbols are used for branching during pre-assembly time and are discussed in Section 3.4.2.

Variable Symbols are symbols that have values associated with them. These values are substitued for the variable symbols that appear in Conditional Assembler statements and in the name, operation, operand, and comments fields of model statements. The values may be user-assigned or system (Assembler) assigned, may be read only or read/modify, and may change or remain the same during the life of an assembly. Variable symbols are set, referenced, and changed during pre-assembly time and may influence which model statements get generated and/or may alter the model statements that are generated. There are three types of variable symbols: Symbolic Parameters, System Variable Symbols, and SET Symbols.

3.2.1 Symbolic Parameters

Symbolic parameters are declared in the macro definition prototype statement and are used to pass values into the macro definition. Values are assigned to them in the operand of the macro call statement. These values are read-only, which means that the user cannot change them in the macro definition. The same symbolic parameter names appear in the body of the macro definition and are replaced by the values assigned to them. Symbolic parameters were discussed in detail above in Sections 3.1.3 and 3.1.4.

3.2.2 System Variable Symbols

System variable symbols are variable symbols whose values are assigned by the Assembler according to specific rules. Like symbolic parameters, system variable symbols can be used as points of substitution in model statements and Conditional Assembler statements. The system variable symbols are &SYSDATE, &SYSTIME, &SYSPARM, &SYSECT, &SYSNDX, and &SYSLIST and are assigned a read-only value, which means that the user cannot change it. The system variable symbols require no declaration in order to be used.

The system variable symbols &SYSDATE, &SYSTIME and &SYSPARM can be used as points of substitution both in a macro definition and in open code, and have a global scope. A global scope means that they are assigned a value by the Assembler that is the same throughout the entire assembly.

The system variable symbols &SYSECT, &SYSNDX, and &SYSLIST can be used as points of substitution only in a macro definition and have a local scope. A local scope means that they are assigned a value by the Assembler each time a macro is called and have that value only within the expansion of the macro call.

The system variable symbols have reserved names; therefore, the symbolic parameters, which are declared in the prototype statement, and the SET symbols (discussed below), which are declared by the LCLx or GBLx Conditional Assembler instructions, must not have the same names.

THE &SYSDATE VARIABLE SYMBOL

The global system variable symbol &SYSDATE provides the date of the assembly in the format mm/dd/yy.

The date could be displayed in the assembly listing by specifying this system variable symbol in the TITLE or DC Assembler instruction, as indicated below. Let us say that the date is February 25, 1991.

```
Coded:          TITLE 'THE DATE OF THIS ASSEMBLY IS &SYSDATE'
Generated:      THE DATE OF THIS ASSEMBLY IS 02/25/91
Coded:          ASMDATE     DC      C'&SYSDATE'
Generated:      ASMDATE     DC      C'02/25/91'
```

THE &SYSTIME VARIABLE SYMBOL

The global system variable symbol &SYSTIME provides the time of the assembly in the format hh.mm.

The time could be displayed in the assembly listing by specifying this system variable symbol in the TITLE or DC Assembler instruction, as indicated below. Let us say that the time is 7 minutes past 3 PM.

```
Coded:          TITLE 'THE TIME OF THIS ASSEMBLY IS &SYSTIME'
Generated:      THE TIME OF THIS ASSEMBLY IS 15.07
Coded:          ASMTIME     DC      C'&SYSTIME'
Generated:      ASMTIME     DC      C'15.07'
```

THE &SYSPARM VARIABLE SYMBOL

The global system variable symbol &SYSPARM is assigned a value from the PARM parameter of the JCL EXEC statement or from the equivalent field setup by a program that dynamically invokes the Assembler.

When the value is assigned via JCL, the following format is used:

```
//STEP      EXEC        ASMFC,PARM=(SYSPARM(ppp))
```

Where: ppp is the actual data that is specified.

When assigned by JCL, due to length restrictions and syntax, the maximum length of &SYSPARM is 52 characters. However, when assigned by a program invoking the Assembler, the maximum length is 255 characters.

The value assigned to &SYSPARM could be examined at pre-assembly time with the use of Conditional Assembler, and its value may be used to influence which model statements are generated.

THE &SYSECT VARIABLE SYMBOL

The local system variable symbol &SYSECT is assigned the name of the currect control section (CSECT) each time a macro definition is called. If the macro initiates a new CSECT or continues an existing one, then the value of &SYSECT is not changed for the macro definition. It remains the name of the CSECT from which the macro was called. However, the value of &SYSECT will change to the new CSECT name for any inner macros that are called from the outer macro after the CSECT name is changed. When the outer macro receives control back from the inner macro, the value of &SYSECT will revert back to the name of the CSECT that was in force when the outer macro was called.

THE &SYSNDX VARIABLE SYMBOL

The local system variable parameter &SYSNDX is assigned a 4-digit number (a 7-digit number for the H-level Assembler) starting with 0001 and incrementing by 1 each time a macro is called. If an outer macro calls an inner macro, then &SYSNDX is incremented for the inner macro; but reverts back to the previous number when the outer macro receives control back from the inner macro. The following illustrates how the value of &SYSNDX is assigned in outer macros and nested inner macros.

```
Outer macro MACXXX called                                 &SYSNDX=0001
    MACXXX calls inner macro MACYYY                       &SYSNDX=0002
       MACYYY calls inner macro MACZZZ                    &SYSNDX=0003
    MACYYY receives control back from MACZZZ              &SYSNDX=0002
MACXXX receives control back from MACYYY                  &SYSNDX=0001
Outer macro MACAAA called                                 &SYSNDX=0004
```

The &SYSNDX system variable symbol could be used to enable a macro definition to generate unique labels by appending all or part of the value of &SYSNDX to a base label. Generating unique labels is discussed in more detail in Section 3.5.1.

THE &SYSLIST VARIABLE SYMBOL

The local system variable symbol &SYSLIST refers to the entire list of positional parameters specified in the operand of the macro call statement. &SYSLIST may be used to:

- Indicate the total number of positional parameters specified in a macro call statement;
- Reference the value of any positional parameter;
- Indicate the total number of sub-values or entries (sublist notation) specified for any positional parameter; and
- Reference the sub-values of any positional parameter. &SYSLIST cannot be used to reference keyword parameters.

&SYSLIST may be coded with one or two subscripts: &SYSLIST(n) or &SYSLIST(n,m). The subcript n indicates the sequential position of the positional parameters of the operand of the macro call statememt and the subscript m indicates the sequential position of the entries of the sublist of the n'th positional parameter. Consider the following example:

```
MAC12       &P1,&P2,&P3                   PROTOTYPE STATEMENT
MAC12       (AAA,222,C33),XYZ,(123)       MACRO CALL STATEMENT
```

The following illustrates the required subscipts of &SYSLIST to reference the various positional parameters and entries of their sublists from the example above:

```
&SYSLIST(1) = (AAA,222,C33)
&SYSLIST(1,1) = AAA
&SYSLIST(1,2) = 222
&SYSLIST(1,3) = C33
&SYSLIST(2) or &SYSLIST(2,1) = XYZ
&SYSLIST(3) = (123)
&SYSLIST(3,1) = 123
```

The subscripts may be absolute numbers (like above) or SETA symbols, which are one of the types of variable symbols. SETA symbols are discussed in Section 3.2.3.

The total number of positional parameters that are specified in the operand field of the macro call statement and the total number of entries in the sublist of any positional parameter may be determined by using the Number attribute (N') with &SYSLIST. Attributes are discussed in Section 3.4.3. The following examples indicate how to obtain this information for the macro call statement for MAC12 above.

```
N'&SYSLIST = 3          Total number of positional parameters specified
                        in macro call statement.
N'&SYSLIST(1) = 3       Total number of entries in sublist of first
                        positional parameter.
N'&SYSLIST(2) = 1       Total number of entries in sublist of second
                        positional parameter.
N'&SYSLIST(3) = 1       Total number of entries in sublist of third
                        positional parameter.
```

&SYSLIST may be used to reference the values of positional parameters when symbolic parameter names are not defined for them in the prototype statement of the macro definition. This would be particularly useful when a large amount and/or variable amount of positional parameters are required. The prototype statement from the above example may also be coded with no symbolic parameters as follows:

```
         MAC12                        PROTOTYPE STATEMENT
```

3.2.3 SET Symbols

SET symbols are variable symbols that are declared by the LCLx or GBLx Conditional Assembler instructions and are assigned values by the SETx Conditional Assembler instructions. SET symbols may have arithmetic values (SETA), character string values (SETC), or binary bit values (SETB). The rules for defining SET symbol names is exactly the same as symbolic parameter names which were discussed in Section 3.1.4.

SET symbols may be used in macro definitions and in open code and have many uses. The following are some of those uses:

- All SET symbol types may be used in Conditional Assembler statements.
- All SET symbol types may be used to provide values for substitution in model statements.
- All SET symbol types may be used as switches to control which group of Conditional Assembler statements get executed and/or which model statements get generated.
- SETA symbols may be used as counters to control Conditional Assembler loops.
- SETA symbols may be used as subscripts for &SYSLIST to reference positional parameters and their sublists; and as subscripts for SET symbols that define arrays.
- SETC symbols may be used to manipulate character strings to create labels and other character strings for examination and/or for substitution in model statements.
- SETB symbols may be used to simplify logic decisions, which influence Conditional Assembler processing, by setting a binary (boolean) bit if a group of arithmetic and/or logic relations are all true or if one of more of those relations are true.

SCOPE OF SET SYMBOLS

The scope of a SET symbol is that part of a program for which the SET symbol is declared. The parts of a program, for SET symbol scope purposes, are individual macro definitions and open code. Set symbols may have local scope or global scope.

A local scope means that the value of the SET symbol may be used (set, referenced, and changed) only in individual macro definitions or only in open code. Local SET symbols must be declared in each part of the program where they are to be used. Local SET symbols with the same names in different parts of a program will be reinitialized each time they are declared. The values will not be saved across macro definitions or between a macro definition and open code.

A global scope means that the value of the SET symbol may be used across macro definitions and open code. Like local SET symbols, global SET symbols must also be declared in the parts of a program where they are to be used, but the values of global symbols with the same names will be saved across macro definitions and open code.

DECLARING SET SYMBOLS

A SET symbol cannot be used unless it is declared. Local SET symbols are declared with the LCLx Conditional Assembler instruction and global SET symbols are declared with the GBLx Conditional Assembler instruction.

Local SET symbols are initialized each time they are declared. Global SET symbols are initialized only during the first declaration. All other declarations of global symbols use the current value of the SET symbol. Arithmetic SET symbols are initialized to zero, character string SET symbols are initialized to a null character, and binary bit SET symbols are initialized to zero.

The SET symbols that have arithmetic values are declared by the LCLA or GBLA Conditional Assembler instructions and are assigned values by the SETA Conditional Assembler instruction. The SET symbols that have character string values are declared by the LCLC or GBLC Conditional Assembler instructions and are assigned values by the SETC Conditional Assembler instruction. The SET symbols that have a binary bit value are declared by the LCLB or GBLB Conditional Assembler instructions and are assigned values by the SETB Conditional Assembler instruction.

The LCLx and GBLx Conditional Assembler instructions may be placed anywhere between the prototype and MEND statements in a macro definition and anywhere in open code. However, for documentation and maintainability, it is a good idea to place them immediately after the prototype statement in a macro definition and at the beginning of open code.

The syntax for the declaration statements is a blank in the name field, LCLx or GBLx in the operation field, and the SET symbol names that are to be declared in the operand field, separated by commas. The LCLx and GBLx Conditional Assembler instructions may not be continued, but as many as needed may be coded to declare all the required SET symbols. Consider the following example:

```
         MACRO                        HEADER
         MAC13    &P1,&P2             PROTOTYPE STATEMENT
         GBLB     &SW                 GLOBAL SET SYMBOL DECLARATION
         LCLA     &NUMB1,NUMB2        LOCAL SET SYMBOL DECLARATION
         LCLA     &NUMB3              LOCAL SET SYMBOL DECLARATION
         LCLC     &NAME               LOCAL SET SYMBOL DECLARATION
         ...                          BODY
         MEND                         TRAILER
```

In the above example, MAC13 declares the following SET symbols:

- The global SET symbol &SW, which will contain a previously set binary bit unless this is the first declaration of &SW (in which case, it is initialized to zero);
- Three local SET symbols &NUMB1, &NUMB2, and &NUMB3, which are to contain arithmetic values, and are initialized to zero; and
- The local SET symbol &NAME, which is to contain a character string value and is initialized to a null character.

ASSIGNING VALUES TO ARITHMETIC SET SYMBOLS

Local and global arithmetic SET (SETA) symbols are assigned values with the SETA Conditional Assembler instruction. The value may vary from a single self-defining term to a complex arithmetic expression from which the Assembler will compute the value. Arithmetic expressions are discussed below. The value of SETA symbols may be changed as often as is required throughout the macro definition by specifying multiple SETA instructions with different values for the same SETA symbols. The format of a SETA instruction is as follows:

Name	Operation	Operand
An arithmetic SET symbol	SETA	An arithmetic expression

The allowable range of the value of the arithmetic expression is from -2^{31} through $2^{31}-1$.

An arithmetic expression consists of terms and operators. Terms are discussed below. Operators may be unary (operating on one value) or may be binary (operating on two values). The unary operators are plus and minus (represented by + and -, respectively), and the binary operators are addition, subtraction, multiplication, and division (represented by +, -, *, and /, respectively). An arithemtic expression may contain only one term or a combination of terms separated by binary operators.

The following are the rules for coding arithmetic expressions:

- The terms that may be contained in an arithmetic expression are the following, within the allowable range:
  - A self-defining term;
  - An arithmetic SET symbol;
  - A binary bit SET symbol;
  - A symbolic parameter, only if it contains an unsigned self-defining term;
  - A character string SET symbol, only if it contains an unsigned self-defining term;
  - The system variable symbol &SYSPARM, only if it contains an unsigned self-defining term;
  - The system variable parameter &SYSLIST, only if the value that it references is an unsigned self-defining term;
  - The system variable parameter &SYSNDX; and
  - A length, count, number, integer, and scaling attribute reference.
- An arithmetic expression may contain both unary and binary operators.
- Terms may be preceded by one or more unary operators, but must not be preceded by a binary operator.

```
+&A        Valid.
-16        Valid.
+-+&B      Valid, same as -&B.
*&C        Invalid, binary operator precedes term.
```

- Terms must be separated by binary operators.

```
&A+19      Valid.
&A&B       Invalid, terms not separated by binary operator.
```

- Binary operators in succession are not allowed, but an unary operator may follow a binary operator.

```
&A-&B       Valid.
&C*+25      Valid, unary operator follows binary operator.
&D/*&E      Invalid, successive binary operators.
```

- A blank must not be imbedded within an arithmetic expression since a blank is used to delimit the expression.

```
&X/&Y        Valid.
&A+ &B / &C  Invalid, blanks between terms and operators.
```

The Assembler evaluates arithmetic expressions at pre-assembly time. A certain hierarchy and conventions are used during evaluation. The following lists those rules:

- Individual terms are evaluated first.
- Arithmetic operations are performed from left to right except for following exceptions:
  - Unary operations are performed before binary operations.
  - Binary operations of multiplication and division are performed before binary operations of addition and subtraction.

```
8/2-3+5*6/2 = 4 - 3 + 15 = 16
```

- The use of parentheses overrides the above mentioned sequence. Operations within parentheses are performed first. In a nested parenthetical expression, the operations proceed from in the inner most parentheses to the outermost parentheses.

```
6+2*5 = 16
(6+2)*5 = 40
```

■ In division, the remainder is dropped and only the integer result is used.

```
7/2 = 3
5/3+4/5 = 1 + 0 = 1
3*3/2+5*(7/4) = 9/2 + 5*1 = 4 + 5 = 9
```

■ Division by zero gives a result of 0.

The following shows some examples of the assignment of values to arithmetic SET symbols via SETA instructions, the values of the symbols after evaluation, and the required LCLA instruction to declare the arithmetic SET symbols:

```
         LCLA  &CTR,&NUMB1,&NUMB2,&NUMB3,&NUMB4
&CTR     SETA  &CTR+1                        Value of &CTR = 1
&CTR     SETA  &CTR+1                        Value of &CTR = 2
&NUMB1   SETA  27                            Value of &NUMB1 = 27
&NUMB2   SETA  X'0A'                         Value of &NUMB2 = 10
&NUMB3   SETA  &NUMB1/&NUMB2+3               Value of &NUMB3 = 5
&NUMB4   SETA  &NUMB1*((11-&NUMB2)/4)-6      Value of &NUMB4 = -6
```

ASSIGNING VALUES TO CHARACTER SET SYMBOLS

Local and global character string SET (SETC) symbols are assigned values with the SETC Conditional Assembler instruction. The value specified may be a character expression or a type attribute reference. Character expressions are discussed below and type attributes are discussed in Section 3.4.3. The value of SETC symbols may be changed as often as is required throughout the macro definition by specifying multiple SETC instructions with different values for the same SETC symbols. The format of the SETC instruction is as follows:

Name	Operation	Operand
A character SET Symbol	SETC	A character expression or a type attribute reference

Character expressions consist of any combination of characters enclosed in apostrophes. Variable symbols are allowed in the expression, and their values are substituted as character strings before the entire expression is evaluated. A maximum of 255 characters are allowed within the apostrophes.

A character string expression may contain the following:

■ Any of the 256 characters of the System/370 character set. The characters ampersand, apostrophe, and period require special consideration, which is discussed below.
■ SETA symbols. The sign and high order zeros are suppressed, but a stand-alone zero is kept.
■ SETB symbols.
■ SETC symbols.

- Symbolic parameters.
- System variable symbols. The high order zeros of &SYSNDX are not suppressed.
- Substring notation, discussed in Section 3.4.4.
- Concatenation of character strings and variable symbols with each other or themselves, discussed in Section 3.2.4.
- A type attribute reference, discussed in Section 3.4.3.

The Assembler evaluates character expressions at pre-assembly time according to the following rules:

- The value of the character expression is the character string within the enclosed apostrophes after the values for variable symbols are substituted.
- A double apostrophe must be specified in order to generate a single apostrophe as part of the value of the character expression.

```
'DON''T DO IT' = DON'T DO IT
```

- A double ampersand, unlike when specified for a symbolic parameter, will generate a double ampersand as part of the value of the character expression. In order to generate a single ampersand, substring notation must be used.

```
'&&'(1,1) = &
```

- The operand of a SETC instruction may contain a concatenation of any combinations of terms that are allowed for a SETC operand. The concatenation may occur within the apostrophes, (in which case, the rules presented in Section 3.2.4 are used), or each expression within apostrophes may be concatenated to other expressions within apostrophes, using the concatenation character.

The following shows some examples of the assignment of values to character string SET symbols via SETC instructions, the values of the symbols after evaluation, and the required LCLC instruction to declare the character string SET symbols:

```
         LCLC    &CHAR1,&CHAR2,&CHAR3,&CHAR4
&CHAR1   SETC    'A'                     Value of &CHAR1 = A
&CHAR2   SETC    &CHAR1'.'&CHAR3.BC'     Value of &CHAR2 = ABC
&CHAR1   SETC    '04'                    Value of &CHAR1 = 4
&CHAR4   SETC    '123'.'&CHAR1.&CHAR2'   Value of &CHAR4 = 1234ABC
```

ASSIGNING VALUES TO BINARY SET SYMBOLS

Local and global binary bit SET (SETB) symbols are assigned values with the SETB Conditional Assembler instruction. The allowable values that can be assigned to a SETB symbol are the bit values, zero or one. The value of SETB symbols may be changed as often as is required throughout the macro definition by specifying multiple SETB instructions with different values for the same SETB symbols. The format of the SETB instruction is as follows:

Name	Operation	Operand
A binary SET symbol	SETB	One of the following: 1. A self-defining Term 2. A variable symbol 3. A logical expression

A self-defining term, when used as an operand of a SETB instruction, must be the value zero or one and may optionally be enclosed in parentheses.

When a variable symbol is used as the operand, it must be enclosed in parentheses and may be one of the following:

- An arithmetic SET symbol;
- A binary bit SET symbol;
- A character string SET symbol, only if it contains an unsigned self-defining term;
- A symbolic parameter, only if it contains an unsigned self-defining term;
- The system variable parameter &SYSLIST, only if the value that it references is an unsigned self-defining term;
- The system variable parameter &SYSNDX; and
- The system variable symbol &SYSPARM only if it contains an unsigned self-defining term.

The Assembler assigns a value of zero to the SETB symbol if the value of the variable symbol is zero. If the value of the variable symbol is non-zero, then the Assembler assigns a value of one to the SETB symbol.

A logical expression is evaluated by the Assembler to determine whether it is true or false and then it assigns the values one or zero, respectively, to the SETB symbol. A logical expression consists of one or more logical terms separated by logical operators. A logical term consists of a self-defining term and/or a variable symbol separated by a relational operator. The logical (boolean) operators are OR (addition), AND (multiplication), and NOT (negation). The relational operators are EQ (equal), NE (not equal), LE (less than or equal), LT (less than), GE (greater than or equal), and GT (greater than).

The following are the rules for coding logical expressions:

- The terms of a logical expression may consist of self-defining terms and any of the variable symbols mentioned above. Terms may be by themselves (free-standing) or combined with others and separated by a relational operator.

```
(&A)                         Valid, free standing term.
(&A GT &B)                   Valid, logical relation.
```

- A logical expression may contain any valid arithmetic relation or character string relation.

```
(&NUMB1 GT &A)               Valid, arithmetic relation.
(&NUMB2 LE 16)               Valid, arithmetic relation.
('&CHARS1' EQ '&NAME')       Valid, character relation.
('&CHARS2' EQ 'ABC')         Valid, character relation.
```

- A logical expression may contain multiple logical terms. Logical terms must be separated by logical operators.

```
(&N1 EQ &X OR &N2 LE 10)     Valid.
(&N3 GT &Z &N4 EQ &A)        Invalid, logical terms not separated
                               by logical operator.
```

- A logical expression must be enclosed in parentheses.

```
(&X GT 10 AND &Z EQ 5)       Valid.
&B LE &C                     Invalid, no enclosing parentheses.
```

- Logical and relational operators must be immediately preceded and followed by one or more blanks or other special characters, such as apostrophes.

```
(&A GT 5)                    Valid.
('&B'EQ'XYZ')                Valid.
(&C LE500)                   Invalid, no blank after operator LE.
```

- A logical expression must not contain terms in succession. They must be separated by logical or relational operators.

```
(&A GE &X)          Valid.
(&M&N)              Invalid, no operator between terms.
```

- A logical expression must not begin with a logical or relational operator except for the logical operator NOT.

```
(NOT &A OR &B)      Valid.
(GT &A OR &B)       Invalid, operator precedes expression.
```

- A logical expression must not contain logical or relational operators in succession except for the combination OR NOT or AND NOT. Those operators must be separated from each other by one or more blanks.

```
(&A OR NOT &B)      Valid.
(&A GT EQ &B)       Invalid, operators in succession.
```

- Any free-standing term, relation, or inner logical expression may be optionaly enclosed in parentheses. This option will improve readability.

```
(NOT (&C) OR (&A GT &X) OR (&B EQ &Z))     Valid, easy to read.
(NOT &C OR &A GT &X OR &B EQ &Z)           Valid, but harder to
                                             read.
(&A EQ 5 OR (&B GT 6 AND &B LE 25))        Valid.
```

The Assembler evaluates logical expressions at pre-assembly time according to the following rules:

- Each logical term is evaluated first. It is given a binary value of one if it is true or a binary value of zero if it is false.
- Arithmetic and character relations are performed in the following sequence:
  - The actual values of the variable symbols are substituted.
  - The indicated relation between the actual values is then determined to be true or false.
    - For a character relation: if the two comparands have character strings of unequal lengths, then the character string with the shortest length is considered to be LT the character string with the longer length.

```
('Z' LT 'ABC')        Value is 1
```

    - For a character relation: if the two comparands have character strings of equal lengths, then the collating sequence of the first character is used to resolve GT and LT relations.

```
('AX' LT 'CA')        Value is 1
('2A' GT 'PZ')        Value is 1
```

  - The logical term is replaced with a binary value of one if the relation is true or with a binary value of zero if the relation is false.

```
(10 GT 5)             Value is 1
(16 EQ 11)            Value is 0
('123' EQ 'XYZ')      Value is 0
('Z' LT 'ABC')        Value is 1
```

- The Assembler performs logical operations from left to right, except for the following exceptions:
  - Logical NOT's are performed before logical AND's and OR's.

```
(6 GT 4 OR NOT 10)
```

is evaluated as follows:

```
(6 GT 4 OR (NOT 10))
(    6 GT 4 OR 0    )
(      1 OR 0       )
(        1          )
```

- Logical AND's are performed before logical OR's.

```
(11 NE 6 OR 4 EQ 4 AND 9 LE 2)
```

is evaluated as follows:

```
(11 NE 6 OR (4 EQ 4 AND 9 LE 2))
(11 NE 6 OR    1     AND   0    )
(11 NE 6 OR          0          )
(    1   OR          0          )
(              1                )
```

- The use of parentheses overrides the above mentioned sequence. The innermost nested logical expression is evaluated first and is given a binary value of one or zero. Then, this value is used as a logical term in the next outer level logical expression and that one is evaluated. This continues until the outermost logical expression is evaluated.

The following shows some examples of the assignment of values to binary bit SET symbols via SETB instructions, the values of the symbols after evaluation, and the required LCLB instruction to declare the binary bit SET symbols:

```
              Assume: Symbolic parameter &P=5
                      SETA symbols &N1=10 and &N2=14
                      SETC symbols &C1=ABC and &C2=XYZ

         LCLB    &B1,&B2,&B3,&B4,&B5,&B6
&B1      SETB    1                                 Value of &B1 = 1
&B2      SETB    (&P)                              Value of &B2 = 1
&B3      SETB    ((&N1 LE 10) AND ('&C1' EQ '&C2')) Value of &B3 = 0
&B4      SETB    ((&N1 GT &N2) OR ('&C1' EQ 'ABC')) Value of &B4 = 1
&B5      SETB    (&B3 EQ 0)                        Value of &B5 = 1
&B6      SETB    ('&C1' GT '&C2')                  Value of &B6 = 0
```

DEFINING SET SYMBOLS AS ARRAYS

A SET symbol may be defined as an array. This is accomplished by declaring the SET symbol with a dimension. The dimension defines the number of elements that may be in the array and is specified as a decimal number enclosed within parentheses following the SET symbol in the declaration statement.

The following shows how to declare a local character string array called &GROUP, which may contain up to 10 elements:

```
         LCLC    &GROUP(10)
```

When the array is declared, the elements of the array are initialized as zero, null, and zero for arrays defined as SETA, SETC, and SETB symbols, respectively.

The individual elements are referenced by specifying a subscript for the SET symbol, starting with the number one (a subscript of zero is not allowed). The subscript number corresponds to the position of the element in the array. The subscript may be specified as a SETA symbol or as any expression that is valid in the operand of a SETA instruction.

A subscripted SET symbol may be used anywhere in a macro definition or in open code where an unscripted SET symbol is allowed.

The following code shows how to place the character string ABC into element position 2 of the array &GROUP:

```
         LCLC    &ELEMENT,&GROUP(10)
```

```
                   ...
&GROUP(2)          SETC 'ABC'
```

The following code shows how to select the n'th element of &GROUP and assign that value to the SETC symbol &ELEMENT:

```
                   LCLA          &N
                   LCLC          &ELEMENT,&GROUP(10)
                   ...
&ELEMENT           SETC          '&GROUP(&N)'
```

3.2.4 Concatenating Variable Symbols

Variable symbols may be concatenated to each other or to ordinary character strings. However, certain concatenation combinations may produce ambiguity. For example, let us say that the character K is to be concatenated after the contents of the variable symbol &SIZE. If the concatenation was coded as follows:

```
&SIZEK
```

then it would mean the variable symbol with the name &SIZEK instead of the concatenation of the contents of &SIZE with K. However, if the concatenation was reversed and the variable symbol &SIZE was concatenated after the character K as follows:

```
K&SIZE
```

then there would be no doubt as to the intent of the concatenation.

To avoid such ambiguity in concatenation, the concatenation character (period) is used. The concatenation character must be used when:

- An ordinary alphameric character string follows a variable symbol.

```
&SIZE.K
```

- A left parenthesis, which does not enclose a subscript value, follows a variable symbol.

```
&DISP.(R10)
```

The concatenation character is not necessary (if specified, it is ignored, except were noted) when:

- An ordinary alphameric character string precedes a variable symbol. In this case, if the period is specified, then it will be generated.

```
Assume &VS contains XYZ:

ABC&VS will generate ABCXYZ
ABC.&VS will generate ABC.XYZ
```

- A special character, other than a left parenthesis or period, follows a variable symbol. If the left parenthesis precedes a subcript value, then the concatenation character must not be specified because it would change the meaning of the left parenthesis.

```
&SCORE% will generate the same as &SCORE.%
```

- A variable symbol follows or precedes another variable symbol.

```
&VS1&VS2 will generate the same as &VS1.&VS2
```

If a period is to be generated between the concatenation of two terms, then it must be doubled except when an ordinary alphameric character string is the first term.

```
PROD.&DSNAME      will generate one period
PROD..&DSNAME     will generate two periods
&INDEX..&DSNAME   will generate one period
```

3.3 CODING SIMPLE MACRO DEFINITIONS

This section will discuss the coding of macro definitions that do not contain any Conditional Assembler statements. A macro definition that does not use Conditional Assembler is limited but is still useful for certain applications. All the model statements that are in the body of this type of macro definition must be generated since there would be no logic available to decide which model statements are to be generated and which ones are to be bypassed. But, numerous other functions would not be available. However, macros of this type still have some flexibility because the fields of the model statements may be altered without the use of Conditional Assembler This type of macro would be useful to generate tables or to generate the same group of instructions, during each invocation, such as subroutines to perform specific functions. A macro of this type would be similar to the COPY instruction except that the macro would have the option and flexibility to alter the fields of the generated statements, while a COPY instruction would not. Section 3.5 below discusses the coding of complex macro definitions, using Conditional Assembler.

3.3.1 Simple Macros that Generate Tables

The two macro definitions below generate tables. The first one, HEXTBL, generates a fixed content table, and the second one, TRTBL, generates a variable content table based upon user input specified via symbolic parameters.

The macro definition, HEXTBL, is an example of a macro definition that generates a table that cannot be altered by the user. Such tables should have no requirements to be altered; therefore, the macro definition need not provide a facility for making alterations. This particular table is used as a translation table in conjunction with the TR instruction for converting hexadecimal into character. Chapter 5 describes the actual processing required to translate hexadecimal into character for printing and/or displaying and the use of this tranlation table. Coding Example 3.3.1 contains macro definition of HEXTBL.

Coding Example 3.3.1

The following coding example contains the macro defintion for HEXTBL.

```
          MACRO
&TBLNAME  HEXTBL
&TBLNAME  DC    X'F0F1F2F3F4F5F6F7F8F9C1C2C3C4C5C6'    00-0F
          DC    X'F1',X15'00'                           10-1F
          DC    X'F2',X15'00'                           20-2F
          DC    X'F3',X15'00'                           30-3F
          DC    X'F4',X15'00'                           40-4F
          DC    X'F5',X15'00'                           50-5F
          DC    X'F6',X15'00'                           60-6F
          DC    X'F7',X15'00'                           70-7F
          DC    X'F8',X15'00'                           80-8F
          DC    X'F9',X15'00'                           90-9F
          DC    X'C1',X15'00'                           A0-AF
          DC    X'C2',X15'00'                           B0-BF
          DC    X'C3',X15'00'                           C0-CF
          DC    X'C4',X15'00'                           D0-DF
          DC    X'C5',X15'00'                           E0-EF
          DC    X'C6',X15'00'                           F0-FF
          MEND
```

The macro definition, TRTBL, is an example of a macro definition that generates a table that may be altered by the user. Such tables may be customized for specific applications;

therefore, the macro definition provides a facility for customization. This particular table is used as a translation table in conjunction with the TR instruction for translating certain characters to other characters. The characters that are supported are the asterisk, hyphen, percent sign, plus sign, and question mark. Other characters may be supported with minor enhancements to the macro definition. Keyword parameters are used because:

- They are easier to remember due to the descriptive keyword name and less cumbersome to use than positional parameters when many parameters are required (no need to use commas to indicate omitted parameters).
- It is easier to process a variable number of keyword parameters than it is to process a variable number of positional parameters (no requirement to use &SYSLIST).
- Default values may be specified.

This macro provides the user with the flexibility of being able to generate a different translation table based upon specific needs. In this particular version of the macro, the default translation value of each character supported is itself. This means that the translation table that is generated will not cause a character to be translated unless it is explicitly specified in the macro call statement operand with a different translation value. Coding Example 3.3.2 contains the macro definition of TRTBL.

Coding Example 3.3.2

The following coding example contains the macro definition for TRTBL.

```
          MACRO
&TBLNAME  TRTBL   &ASTERIK=*,&HYPHEN=-,&PERCENT=%,&PLUS=+,&QUES=?
&TBLNAME  DC      256AL1(*-&TBLNAME)  GEN 256-BYTE TBL OF X'00' TO X'FF'
          ORG     &TBLNAME+C'*'       SET TBL PTR TO ASTERISK POS
          DC      C'&ASTERIK'         ASTERISK TRANS CHAR
          ORG     &TBLNAME+C'-'       SET TBL PTR TO HYPEN POS
          DC      C'&HYPHEN'          HYPHEN TRANS CHAR
          ORG     &TBLNAME+C'%'       SET TBL PTR TO PERCENT SIGN POS
          DC      C'&PERCENT'         PERCENT SIGN TRANS CHAR
          ORG     &TBLNAME+C'+'       SET TBL PTR TO PLUS SIGN POS
          DC      C'&PLUS'            PLUS SIGN TRANS CHAR
          ORG     &TBLNAME+C'?'       SET TBL PTR TO QUESTION MARK POS
          DC      C'&QUES'            QUESTION MARK TRANS CHAR
          ORG     &TBLNAME+256        ADJ LOC CTR PASSED END-OF-TBL
          MEND
```

3.3.2 Simple Macros that Generate Executable Code

The two macro definitions below generate code to perform specific tasks. The macro GETPARM generates the same code with each invocation of the macro, and the macro PUTTBL generates the same set of instructions, but allows the user the flexibility of altering the fields of the generated instructions.

The macro definition GETPARM is an example of a macro that generates code to perform a specific task. In this particular case, the task is so specific that providing the user with the option of altering the fields (other than label names) of the generated instructions is not applicable. The code generated from the macro extracts the data specified via the PARM parameter of the JCL EXEC statement (discussed in Chapter 5). It assumes that register 1 contains the address it contained when the program received control from the operating system. If no data was specified, the code generated returns a zero in register 15. If data was specified, the generated code moves the data into a field labeled by the user via the positional parameter &PARM (which the macro defines as part of its expansion), appends at least one blank after the data, and returns the length of the specified PARM data in register 15. The macro allows the user to specify a label for the code that is generated. Coding Example 3.3.3 contains the macro definition of GETPARM.

Coding Example 3.3.3

The following coding example contains the macro definition for GETPARM.

```
         MACRO
&LABEL   GETPARM &PARM
&LABEL   B    *+106            BRANCH AROUND PARM HOLD AREA
&PARM    DC   102CL1' '        DEFINE MAX LEN OF JCL PARM + 2 FOR
*                              ALIGNMENT
         L    1,0(0,1)         LOAD JCL PARM ADR INTO REG 1
         LH   15,0(0,1)        LOAD LEN OF JCL PARM INTO REG 15
         LTR  15,15            WAS JCL PARM SPECIFIED?
         BZ   *+24             IF NO, BRANCH OUT OF MACRO
         BCTR 15,0             IF YES, DECR REG 15 FOR EX INSTR
         EX   15,*+8           MOVE JCL PARM INTO PARM HOLD AREA
         B    *+10             BRANCH AROUND MVC INSTR
         MVC  &PARM,2(1)       SUBJECT INSTR FOR EX INSTR
         LA   15,1(0,15)       INCR REG 15 BACK TO PARM LENGTH
         MEND
```

The code generated by GETPARM contains some relative addressing. In Chapter 1, we mentioned that relative addressing should be avoided in most coding situations. However, it is tolerable in a macro expansion for small displacements in code that will probably never change, such as this code. Using relative addressing eliminates the need to use Conditional Assembler to generate unique labels. However, when many labels are required due to the size and complexity of the code generated or when relative addressing is required to branch around many instructions, then unique labels should be generated. Generating code with fixed labels should be avoided because it prevents the user from using the macro more than once, if applicable, in the same program because of duplicate label names. The fixed label names may also conflict with the other labels used in the program. Section 3.5.1 discusses techniques for generating unique labels.

Notice that the field genarated by GETPARM to hold the JCL PARM is allocated to be 102 bytes by using the duplication factor of the DC instruction. If the field was allocated with the operand coded as CL102' ', then the EX instruction would not function properly. (Why not?) Hint: the EX instruction would function properly either way if the subject instruction was coded as MVC &PARM(0),2(1).

Also notice that the generated instructions that use registers do not specify the registers as EQU names. This is because the macro definition does not know whether the user defined an EQU table for the registers and, if defined, what the EQU names are. One way to enable the macro definiton to generate registers with EQU names is to provide the user with a keyword parameter for specifying the prefix of the EQU names. Using this technique, the macro definition would have to assume that the EQU names end with the actual number of the register. The default of the prefix of the EQU names would be defined as null (by specifying no value after the equal sign in the prototype statement). If the user does not use this facility to provide the prefix for the EQU names, then the macro would generate the register numbers as is.

The macro definition, PUTTBL, is an example of a macro that allows the user the flexibility of altering the fields of the generated code. The macro is used to add entries into a table. Each entry has a key or id field that is defined to start at the first byte of each entry. The length of the key is specified by the user via one of the symbolic parameters. All new entries are placed into the table at the end. If an entry, with the same key, is already in the table, then it is replaced by the new entry. All vacant slots in the table contain binary zeros and the physical end of the table or table segment (for an expandable table) contains binary ones in the last slot. The code returns a zero in register 15 when a new entry is inserted at the end of the table, a four in register 15 when an existing entry is replaced, and an eight in register 15 when the vacant slots are exhausted. All the symbolic parameters of PUTTBL are positional. &TABLE requires a label that points to the beginning of the table. &ENTRY requires a label that points to a field that contains the entry to be inserted into the table. &ENTLEN requires a self-defining term that indicates the length of each entry (fixed length entries are assumed). &KEYLEN requires a self-defining term that indicates the length of the key field of each entry. Coding Example 3.3.4 contains the macro definition of PUTTBL.

Coding Example 3.3.4

The following coding example contains the macro definition for PUTTBL.

```
          MACRO
&LABEL    PUTTBL &TABLE,&ENTRY,&ENTLEN,&KEYLEN
&LABEL    LA     14,&TABLE              LOAD ADR OF BG OF TBL INTO REG 14
$SCANTBL  CLI    0(14),X'00'            CHK FOR VACANT SPOT IN TBL
          BE     $INSTBL                IF YES, BRANCH TO INSERT RTN
          CLC    0(&KEYLEN,14),&ENTRY   CHK FOR DUPL ENTRY
          BE     $UPDTBL                IF YES, BRANCH TO UPDATE RTN
          CLI    0(14),X'FF'            CHK FOR END OF TBL
          BE     $TBLEND                IF YES, BRANCH TO TBLEND RTN
          LA     14,&ENTLEN.(0,14)      INCR TO NEXT TABLE SLOT
          B      $SCANTBL               BRANCH BACK TO BG OF LOOP
$INSTBL   MVC    0(&ENTLEN,14),&ENTRY   MOVE NEW ENTRY INTO TBL
          LA     15,0                   NEW ENTRY, SET RC = 0
          B      $PTBLEND               BRANCH OUT OF MACRO
$UPDTBL   MVC    0(&ENTLEN,14),&ENTRY   REPLACE DUPL ENTRY
          LA     15,4                   REPLACE ENTRY, SET RC = 4
          B      $PTBLEND               BRANCH OUT OF MACRO
$TBLEND   LA     15,8                   END OF TBL, SET RC = 8
$PTBLEND  DS     0H
          MEND
```

The macro definition PUTTBL provides the user with the flexibility of altering the entry length and the key length so that this macro may be used to build tables with a variety of specifications. The code generated contains fixed labels. This is to eliminate the need to use Conditional Assembler to generate unique labels. To minimize the chances of those labels conflicting with labels defined in open code, each generated label is prefixed with a dollar sign.

Despite the flexibility that this macro provides, it does have some shortcomings. Besides generating fixed labels, it does not enable the user to specify the parameters via a register specification. The programmer must specify a label to indicate the starting address of the table and of the new entry, and must also specify a self-defining term to indicate the length of the entry and of the key. Also, the macro definition does not validate the input parameters.

The macro definition, as it stands now, is fine if the user does not have a requirement to use a register specification for any of the parameters and if the macro is not required to be invoked more than once in the same program.

In Section 3.5 below, this macro is recoded using Conditional Assembler to provide the user with the flexibility to optionally specify the parameters via a register specification and to generate unique labels in order to eliminate the need for relative addressing and/or fixed labels. In addition, Conditional Assembler is used to perform certain verifications, such as verifying that the specified label does not exceed eight characters and that self-defining terms, when specified for &ENTLEN and &KEYLEN, are specified correctly.

3.4 CONDITIONAL ASSEMBLER LANGUAGE

This section discusses the elements, functions, and coding of Conditional Assembler language and how to use it to provide additional facilities and flexibility in macro definitions and in open code.

3.4.1 What is Conditional Assembler Language?

Conditional Assembler language is a sublanguage that operates within Assembler language at pre-assembly time. Pre-assembly time refers to that time in an assembly before any Assembler instructions or machine instructions are assembled. It is the time when variable symbols are processed and replaced by their values, the model statements that are to be part of the functioning program are generated from macro definitions and/or selected from open code, and the model statements that are generated and/or selected are altered (if applicable) via variable symbols to their final state.

ELEMENTS OF CONDITIONAL ASSEMBLER LANGUAGE

The elements of Conditional Assembler include the following:

- SET symbols, which are used to define and manipulate arithmetic, character string and binary bit values. SET symbols were discussed in Section 3.2.3.
- Compare and branch instructions, which are used to cause branching to statements at pre-assembly time, either unconditionally or conditionally based upon the results of an arithmetic, character, or logical relation condition test. The Conditional Assembler compare and branch instructions are discussed in Section 3.4.2.
- Sequence symbols, which function as labels for branching to statements at pre-assembly time. Sequence symbols are discussed in Section 3.4.2.
- Data attributes, which represent different characteristics of data. Data attributes are discussed in Section 3.4.3.

FUNCTIONS OF CONDITIONAL ASSEMBLER LANGUAGE

Conditional Assembler may be coded in macro definitions or in open code. The Assembler normally processes all Assembler statements present in a program and processes them sequentially. However, when Conditional Assembler is coded, it controls which Assembler statements will be processed by the Assembler and in which sequence.

This is accomplished by the actual logic of the Conditional Assembler and by the variable symbols set by the programmer and/or by the system (Assembler), which the Conditional Assembler examines. The Assembler statements (model statements) that are in the path of the Conditional Assembler execution are generated from macro definitions and selected from open code to become part of the active or functioning program; that is, the part of the program that gets assembled. In addition, the Assembler statements that get generated/selected are altered when the variable symbols, that they contain, if any, are substituted with their actual values.

USES OF CONDITIONAL ASSEMBLER LANGUAGE

Conditional Assembler is used in macro definitions to enable the macro to provide various sophisticated functions and processing techniques. This enables a macro definition to be flexable and versatile. Section 3.5 discusses the use of Conditional Assembler in macro definitions in detail and provides numerous coding examples. Additional coding examples are presented in Section 3.6.

In open code, Conditional Assembler can be used to select specific portions of the program code to be assembled. This could be accomplished by defining and setting various SET symbols, which the Conditional Assembler examines. This may be particularly useful if the program contains all the code required to generate different versions of the same program. The different versions could be required for the following reasons:

- To support different releases or versions of the same operating system, such as MVS/370, MVS/XA, and MVS/ESA. The different code can suppress or include code for the new facilities offered based upon which version of the operating system the program will execute.
- To select the proper code to execute under different operating systems, such as OS/MVS and DOS/VSE.
- To customize the program to include or exclude specific functions or options and/or set different defaults based upon certain criteria.

3.4.2 Compare and Branch Instructions

The Conditional Assembler language provides two instructions, AIF and AGO, that can be used to alter the sequence in which the statements of an Assembler language program are processed during an assembly. The labels that the compare and branch instructions branch to are called sequence symbols. In addition, Conditional Assembler provides two additional instructions, ANOP and ACTR, that are used to assist and control, respectively, the AIF and AGO instructions.

SEQUENCE SYMBOLS

Sequence symbols are, in effect, labels that are used during pre-assembly time to indicate the statements that are the objects of the Conditional Assembler branches.

The rules for defining sequence symbol names are the following:

- The first character must be a period (.) followed by one to seven characters.
- The second character must be an alpha character (A–Z) or a national character (@, #, $).
- The third through eigth characters may be alphameric characters (A–Z, 0–9) or national characters.

The scope of sequence symbols is local. That means that the same sequence symbols may be used in different macro definitions or in open code without conflicting with or relating to each other.

THE AIF INSTRUCTION

The AIF instruction provides the capability of branching based upon the result of a condition test. The following is the format of the AIF instruction:

Name	Operation	Operand
Sequence symbol or blank	AIF	(logical expression).sequence symbol

The operand of an AIF instruction is a logical expression (discussed in Section 3.2.3) enclosed within parentheses and immediately followed by a sequence symbol.

If the logical expression is true, then a branch is taken and control is passed to the statement that has the same sequence symbol as the one that appears after the logical expression in the operand of the AIF instruction; otherwise, execution continues with the next sequential statement. The statement that is identified by the sequence symbol must appear within the same local scope as the AIF instruction. This means that the object statement must appear in the same macro definition as the AIF instruction or it must appear in open code if the AIF instruction is located in open code. The statement that is identified by the sequence symbol may appear before or after the AIF instruction.

The AIF instruction is used to control which model statements are selected to be part of the active source program, to control which Conditional Assembler statements are to execute, to control loops, and to provide error checking. Consider the following example:

```
&CODE     SETC   'X2'
          ...
          AIF    ('&CODE' EQ 'X1').GENX1
          AIF    ('&CODE' EQ 'X2').GENX2
          AIF    ('&CODE' EQ 'X3').GENX3
          ...
.GENX2    MVC    STATUS,INFOX2
```

In the above example, the first AIF instruction does not branch because the value in &CODE is not X1, the second AIF instruction causes a branch to the statement that has the sequence symbol .GENX2 because the value of &CODE is X2 and the MVC instruction is selected to be part of the active source program, and the third AIF statement does not execute.

THE AGO INSTRUCTION

The AGO instruction provides the capability of unconditional branching. The following is the format of the AGO instruction:

Name	Operation	Operand
Sequence symbol or blank	AGO	Sequence symbol

The AGO instruction is used to exit from either a loop or a series of statements to other statements. Consider the following example:

```
.CHKOPT    AIF    ('&OPT' EQ 'A').OPTA
           AIF    ('&OPT' EQ 'B').OPTB
           AIF    ('&OPT' EQ 'C').OPTC
           AGO    .INVOPT
```

In the above example, the AGO instruction is used to exit the Conditional Assembler routine labeled by the sequence symbol .CHKOPT by passing control to the statement that has the sequence symbol .INVOPT in its name field.

THE ANOP INSTRUCTION

The ANOP instruction performs no operation. It is used to provide a sequence symbol for an instruction that is required to be branched to from an AIF or AGO instruction when the instruction already contains another symbol in its name field. The following is the format of the ANOP instruction:

Name	Operation	Operand
Sequence symbol or blank	ANOP	None

The ANOP is placed immediately before the instruction that is to receive control. Consider the following example:

```
          AIF    ('&FUNC' EQ '1').SETF1
          AIF    ('&FUNC' EQ '2').SETF2
          AIF    ('&FUNC' EQ '3').SETF3
          ...
.SETF1    ANOP
&FUNCIND SETA    1
```

In the above example, the particular SETA instruction shown will execute if &FUNC contains the character **1**. The SETA instruction has the name of an arithmetic SET symbol in its name field; therefore, it cannot also contain a sequence symbol in its name field. This problem is resolved by placing an ANOP instruction, containing the required sequence symbol in its name field, immediately before the SETA instruction.

THE ACTR INSTRUCTION

The Assembler maintains a Conditional Assembler loop counter for each individual macro definition and for open code. The ACTR instruction provides the capability of setting values for those loop counters. The following is the format of the ACTR instruction:

Name	Operation	Operand
Sequence symbol or blank	ACTR	Any valid arithmetic symbol(SETA) expression

The operand of the ACTR instruction indicates the limit of the total number of branches allowed by AIF and AGO instructions in a particular macro definition or in open code. Each time the Assembler processes an AIF instruction, which results in a branch, or an AGO instruction, the loop counter for that part of the program is decremented by one. When the total number of Conditional Assembler branches taken is equal to the number assigned by the ACTR instruction to the loop counter for that part of the program, the Assembler exits from the macro definition or stops processing statements in open code.

When the limit is reached in a macro definition, the Assembler exits the macro and no statements are generated. When the limit is reached in open code, the Assembler will process the remainder of the statements in the source as comments.

The scope of the Conditional Assembler loop counters is local. This means that each loop counter is separate from the others. If a macro definition calls an inner macro, the loop counter associated with the inner macro is decremented for each branch taken in the inner macro and has no effect on the loop counter of the calling macro. The scope of the ACTR instruction is also local; therefore, it may set only the value of the loop counter that is within the same scope.

The value of the loop counter may be reassigned throughout a macro definition and in open code by specifying additional ACTR instructions.

The Assembler sets its own internal loop counter for each macro definition and for open code. The Assembler assigns a default value of 4096 to each loop counter that is not assigned a value by an ACTR instruction.

The ACTR instruction is used to prevent excessive branching at pre-assembly time due to an unforeseen situation or to prevent a logic error in Conditional Assembler from causing the Assembler to abnormally terminate (ABEND). An endless loop in Conditional Assembler could exhaust the amount of DASD work space allocated to the Assembler (SB37 or SD37 ABEND) or could exceed the amount of CPU time allocated to the Assembler (S322 ABEND).

3.4.3 Data Attributes

Data attributes represent different characteristics of data. The data that is defined in a source program, such as machine instructions, macro instructions, constants, storage areas, and so on, can be described in terms of one or more of the data attributes supported by the Assembler. The data attributes are Type (T'), Length (L'), Count (K'), Number (N'), Integer (I'), and Scaling (S'). The integer and scaling attributes will not be discussed.

The format of data attribute notation is the one letter indicator of the desired attribute, followed by an apostrophe, followed by an ordinary or variable symbol. The following are some examples of data attribute notation:

```
T'CHARSTNG
N'&SYSLIST(&POS)
K'&LABEL
```

The actual attribute is a single character or a number, depending upon the particular attribute reference. The following sections indicate the actual values that the Assembler substitutes for the various data attributes.

Data attribute notation may be used only in the operands of SETA (only length, count, number, integer, and scaling), SETC (only type), and AIF instructions, except for the length attribute, which may also be used in the operands of machine and Assembler instructions. Data attribute notation may be used in macro definitions and in open code. When used in a macro definition, it may reference the symbolic parameters of the operand to determine the characteristics of the data that is being passed into the macro definition.

Using data attributes provides a very powerful facility for controlling the logic of Conditional Assembler (which determines which model statements get generated) altering the generated model statements, and performing data validation to determine if the specified data is in the proper format before it is processed. The following sections describe the various data attributes and indicate some of their main uses.

TYPE ATTRIBUTE

The type attribute distinguishes one form of data from another. Examples of such forms are: character data, hexadecimal data, binary data, machine instructions, and so on. The type attribute may also be used to determine if a value for a positional parameter of a macro call statement was specified or omitted. The type attribute may be used in macro definitions or in open code and may reference ordinary symbols, symbolic parameters, or SET symbols.

The values that are substituted for the result of the type attribute request are contained in Table 3.4.1.

Table 3.4.1

This table contains the characters used to represent the various type attributes and the meaning of those characters.

Type Attribute	Data Description
For symbols that are defined as labels for DC/DS instructions, and that may be used as values for the symbolic parameters in the operand of a macro call statement:	
A	A-type address constant, implicit length, aligned, or a CXD instruction

(Table 3.4.1, continued)

Type Attribute	Data Description
B	Binary constant
C	Character constant
D	Long floating-point constant, implicit length, aligned
E	Short floating-point constant, implicit length, aligned
F	Fullword fixed-point constant, implicit length, aligned
G	Fixed-point constant, explicit length
H	Halfword fixed-point constant, implicit length, aligned
I	Machine instruction
J	CSECT instruction
K	Floating-point constant, explicit length
L	Extended floating-point constant, implicit length, aligned
M	Macro instruction
O	SETC symbol that contains a null value
P	Packed decimal constant
Q	Q-type address constant, implicit length, aligned
R	A-, Q-, S-, V-, or Y-type address constant, explicit length
S	S-type address constant, implicit length, aligned
U	Undefined, none of the other type attributes apply
V	V-type address constant, implicit length, aligned
W	CCW instruction
X	Hexadecimal constant
Y	Y-type address constant, implicit length, aligned
Z	Zoned decimal constant
For symbols that are defined as operands of EXTRN or WXTRN:	
T	External symbol defined by EXTRN instruction
$	External symbol defined by WXTRN instruction
For values that are specified for the symbolic parameters in the operand of a macro call statement:	
N	Self-defining term or a SETA or SETB symbol
O	Omitted (for positional parameters only)

The following Assembler statements and SETC instructions illustrate how the type attribute values are set:

```
MOVE      MVC    AREA1,AREA2
GETREC    GET    DCBNAME,IOAREA
NUMB      DC     X'1A'
TBLADR    DC     A(TABLE)
LENGTH    DC     AL2(200)
RATE      DC     P'25'
REGSAVE   DS     F
&C1       SETC   T'MOVE                   Value of &C1 = I
&C2       SETC   T'GETREC                 Value of &C2 = M
```

```
&C3          SETC     T'NUMB                    Value of &C3 = X
&C4          SETC     T'TBLADR                  Value of &C4 = A
&C5          SETC     T'LENGTH                  Value of &C5 = R
&C6          SETC     T'RATE                    Value of &C6 = P
&C7          SETC     T'REGSAVE                 Value of &C7 = F
```

The following partial macro definition illustrates how the type attribute might be used to validate data. The requirements of the macro are that the value specified for &TABLE may be only an ADCON or a label of a DS instruction and that the value specified for &LEN must be a self-defining term that does not exceed 4095:

```
             MACRO                              HEADER
             MAC14    &TABLE,&LEN               PROTOTYPE STATEMENT
             ...
             AIF      (T'&TABLE EQ 'A').ADCON   CHECK IF ADCON SPECIFIED
             LA       R14,&TABLE                LOAD TBL ADR INTO REG 14
             AGO      .GENCODE                  GENERATE REST OF CODE
.ADCON       L        R14,&TABLE                LOAD TBL ADR INTO REG 14
.GENCODE     ANOP
             ...
             AIF      (T'&LEN EQ 'O').NOLEN     CHECK IF LEN SPECIFIED
             AIF      (T'&LEN NE 'N').INVLEN    CHECK IF SELF-DEF TERM
             AIF      (&LEN GT 4095).INVLEN     CHECK MAX LENGTH
             LA       R15,&LEN                  LOAD TBL LEN INTO REG 15
             ...
             MEND                               TRAILER
```

The macro definition, MAC14, checks if the value specified for &TABLE is an ADCON and checks if the value specified for &LEN is present and is a self-defining term. If the value for &TABLE is an ADCON, then a load (L) instruction is generated to load the address into register 14. If the value for &TABLE is not an ADCON (DS label assumed), then a load address (LA) instruction is generated to load the address into register 14. If the value of &LEN is omitted, then control is passed to the instructions that start at the sequence symbol .NOLEN. The instructions there may set a default value for &LEN or issue an error message (via the MNOTE instruction, discussed in Section 3.5.2) and terminate the macro expansion. If a value of &LEN is specified, then the macro definition verifies that it is a self-defining term that is also less than 4096.

LENGTH ATTRIBUTE

The value of the length attribute is the number of bytes occupied by the data represented by the symbol that the length attribute references. The length attribute may be used in macro definitions and in open code and may reference an ordinary symbol at assembly time, or an ordinary or variable symbol at pre-assembly time. If the length attribute references a variable symbol, then that variable symbol must ultimatley represent the name field of an Assembler statement in open code.

The following Conditional Assembler statements illustrate how the length attribute values are set:

```
             MAC16    DATA2                     MACRO CALL STATEMENT
             MAC16    &P1                       PROTOTYPE STATEMENT
             LCLA     &LEN1,&LEN2
             ...
&LEN1        SETA     L'DATA1                   Value of &LEN1 = 5
&LEN2        SETA     L'&P1                     Value of &LEN2 = 10
             ...
             MEND
```

```
         ...
DATA1    DS       CL5
DATA2    DS       CL10
```

The length attribute may be used to determine the number of bytes contained in an area defined by a DC/DS statement whose label is specified as input to a macro instruction.

COUNT ATTRIBUTE

The count attribute may reference only symbolic parameters, SET symbols, and the system variable symbols and may be used in both macro definitions and open code. The count attribute notation may be used only in arithmetic expressions.

The value of the count attribute is equal to the number of characters contained in the value of the variable symbol being referenced. The value of the count attribute is zero if it references an omitted symbolic parameter or a SETC symbol that contains no characters.

The following Conditional Assembler statements illustrate how the count attribute values are set:

```
&C1      SETC     'ABCDEF'
&A1      SETA     K'&C1                Value of &A1 = 6
&A2      SETA     0025
&A3      SETA     K'&A2                Value of &A3 = 2
&A4      SETA     K'&SYSNDX            Value of &A4 = 4
```

The count attribute may be used to verify that the length of a name or a character string does not exceed a certain number of characters. This is illustrated by the following coding example:

```
         AIF      (K'&LABEL GT 8).BADLAB
```

The difference between the length attribute and the count attribute is that the length attribute refers to the data length of an actual Assembler statement, such as a DC, DS, machine instruction, and so on, while the count attribute refers to the length of a string of data specified as input to a macro instruction or defined within the body of the macro definition.

NUMBER ATTRIBUTE

The number attribute may be used only in macro definitions and applies to the operands of macro call statements. The value of the number attribute is the number of positional parameters specified in a macro call statement or the number of sublist entries in a particular positional parameter. The number attribute notation may be used only in arithmetic expressions.

The number attribute of the system variable &SYSLIST indicates the total number of positional parameters specified and the number attribute of &SYSLIST(n) indicates the number of sublist entries specified in the n'th positional parameter.

The following macro call statement and SETA instructions illustrate how the number attribute values are set:

```
         MAC15    (A,B,C),P22,(,XYZ),(99,,B50),KW1=(XY,Z),KW2=25
&A1      SETA     N'&SYSLIST           Value of &A1 = 4
&A2      SETA     N'&SYSLIST(1)        Value of &A2 = 3
&A3      SETA     N'&SYSLIST(2)        Value of &A3 = 1
&A4      SETA     N'&SYSLIST(3)        Value of &A4 = 2
&A5      SETA     N'&SYSLIST(4)        Value of &A5 = 3
```

The number attribute may be used when processing a variable number of positional parameters or a variable number of sublist entries by providing the total number of parameters specified that could be used to determine the end of the list. Scanning the parameter-list for a type attribute of O (omitted) will not suffice to determine the end of the parameter-list because the list could contain embedded omitted parameters.

3.4.4 Substring Notation

Substring notation provides the capability of referencing one or more characters within a character string. The referenced characters may be selected to form other character strings, concatenated with other character strings, used for comparisons, or used for substitution. Substring notation may be used with character strings or with any variable symbols.

Substring notation is indicated by specifying two arithmetic values, separated by a comma and enclosed within parentheses immediately following a character string or variable symbol. The character strings or variable symbols, which are used with substring notation, must be enclosed within apostrophes. Substring notation may be used in the operands of SETC and AIF instructions. The following indicates the syntax of substring notation:

```
'ccc'(b,n)
```

where: ccc is a character string or variable symbol (maximum length is 255)

b is a valid SETA value that indicates the position, starting with one, of the first character of the string that is to be referenced; b must be in the range from 1 to 255; zero or negative numbers are not allowed. The specified value of b must not exceed the length of the character string.

n is a valid SETA value that indicates the total number of characters, starting with the character specified by b, which are to be referenced; n should be in the range from 1 to 255; if 0 is specified, then the resultant character string is the null character; negative numbers are not allowed. If the specified value of n (with a valid value of b) results in a reference that exceeds the character string, then only the characters up to the end of the string will be extracted.

The following examples illustrate the coding of substring notation:

```
&C1      SETC      'ABCD'(2,3)               Value of &C1 = BCD
&A1      SETA      1234
&C2      SETC      '&A1'(1,2)                Value of &C2 = 12
&C3      SETC      '&C1'.'&C2'(2,1)          Value of &C3 = BCD2

For System Variable &SYSNDX = 0015:
&SUFX    SETC      'SYSNDX'(2,3)             Value of &SUFX = 015

For Symbolic Parameter &P1 = (10):
         AIF       ('&P1'(1,1) EQ '(').REG   Value of '&P1'(1,1) = (
```

3.5 CODING COMPLEX MACRO DEFINITIONS

This section will discuss the coding of macro definitions using Conditional Assembler. The use of Conditional Assembler in the body of a macro definition provides the macro with the ability to perform various sophisticated functions such as:

- Validate input parameters;
- Select which model statements will be generated based upon input parameters and/or system parameters;
- Define unique labels;
- Manipulate character strings; and
- Process a variable number of positional parameters.

Before attempting to write a complex macro definition using Conditional Assembler language, it is a good idea to first write and test the code that is to be generated. After the code is debugged and functioning properly, then the macro definition can be written. This sequence of events enables the macro developer to know the objective (what code to generate) of the macro definition before its development is started. It is easier to know the appearance of the code that is to be generated in advance than it is to develop and test the generated code while the macro definition and Conditional Assembler are also being developed and tested.

The macro definitions ADD and PUTTBL, presented in previous sections, will be enhanced in this section to incorporate Conditional Assembler to provide additional and important functions.

3.5.1 Guidelines for Generating Labels

In Section 3.3, we discussed the writing of simple macro definitions. Those macros contained no Conditional Assembler; therefore, among other shortcomings, any labels generated by those macros were fixed.

In this section, we will discuss the generation of unique labels. Unique labels are labels generated by macro definitions that are different with each invocation of the same or different macros and do not conflict with the labels in open code.

To assist in generating unique labels, the system variable &SYSNDX is used. &SYSNDX was discussed in Section 3.2.2. Different labels could be guaranteed among multiple invocations of the same macro or among different macros by generating labels with the current value of &SYSNDX appended to a fixed base. For example, let us say that a particular macro definition uses the base LAB1 for one of its labels. If the macro is called twice in the same program (and is the fifth and eight macro call of the program), then the label would be coded and generated as follows:

```
LAB1&SYSNDX = LAB10005 (first call)
LAB1&SYSNDX = LAB10008 (second call)
```

This technique is adequate, but it does not guarantee that the generated labels will not conflict with the labels in open code. Actually, there is no way of guaranteeing this; however, the chances of it occurring could be mimimized. One way would be to define the fixed base portion of the label with a national character (@, #, $) as the first character.

The convention used in this book for generating unique labels in macro definitions is as follows:

- Define a 4-character fixed base:
  - First character is a dollar sign.
  - Next three characters are an abbreviation of the macro name.
- Append the last three bytes of &SYSNDX to the fixed base. This becomes the variable base of the label. Each label of the same invocation of the macro will have the first seven characters in common. Labels of different invocations of the same macro will have the first four characters in common.
- To define different labels in the same macro invocation, append an additional unique character to the variable base, starting with A, B, and so on. This convention will provide 39 (A–Z, 0–9, @, #, and $) usable labels for the code generated by the macro definition.

  For the macro PUTTBL, the 4-character fix base could be $PTB. The following shows the code required to generate the 7-character variable base.

```
         LCLC   &LAB
&LAB     SETC   '$'.'PTB'.'&SYSNDX'(2,3)
```

The following shows how to generate different labels in the same macro definition. The current value of &SYSNDX is assumed to be five:

```
&LAB.A = $PTB005A
&LAB.B = $PTB005B
```

```
&LAB.C = $PTB005C
etc.
```

This convention will guarantee unique labels for the first 999 macro calls. If more than 999 macro calls are made (which is highly unlikely) in the same program, then there is a remote possibility of duplicate labels occurring.

3.5.2 Generating Messages from a Macro Definition

While the Conditional Assembler is executing to validate input parameters and to determine which model statements are to be generated, it may be desirable to generate information, warning, and/or error messages to the programmer. This could be accomplished with the MNOTE instruction. The MNOTE instruction may be used in macro definitions and in open code. The format of the MNOTE instruction is as follows:

Name	Operation	Operand
A sequence symbol or blank	MNOTE	One of following: n,'message' ,'message' *,'message' 'message'

The operand of the MNOTE instruction may be specified in one or four formats. When the message is preceded by n or by a comma, then it implies a warning or error message and is printed with the other diagnostic message produced by the Assembler. The n is used to specifiy a severity code. The range of the severity code may be from 0 to 255. It may be specified as any arithmetic expression that is valid in the operand of the SETA instruction. If the severity code is omitted, as indicated by a comma, then the defaut is one. The highest severity code issued by MNOTE instructions or by the Assembler is used as the return code, which may be checked with the JCL COND parameter.

When the MNOTE message is preceded by an asterisk or by nothing, then the message is generated as a comment.

The message defined in the MNOTE instruction is generated only when the MNOTE instruction is in the path of the Conditional Assembler execution or if the macro definition contains no Conditional Assembler.

3.5.3 Examples of Complex Macro Definitions

This section will enhance two previously defined macro instructions to illustrate the additional functions that can be provided with the use of Conditional Assembler and will present another macro definition to illustrate other Conditional Assembler facilities.

ENHANCEMENT OF THE ADD MACRO DEFINITION

The ADD macro definition will be enhanced to provide the following additional functions:

- Verify that the specified label for the macro instruction does not exceed eight characters. If the specified label is longer than eight characters, then only the first eight chacarters are used for the label.
- Verify that the two positional parameters are specified.
- If specified, verify that the values are self-defining terms.
- If self-defining terms, verify that their values do not exceed 4095.
- Provide internal comments to describe function.

In addition, the use of the internal macro comment statement is illustrated. Coding Example 3.5.1 contains the enhanced macro definition of ADD.

Coding Example 3.5.1

This coding example contains the enhanced macro definition for ADD.

```
         MACRO                         HEADER STATEMENT
&LABEL   ADD      &NUMB1,&NUMB2        PROTOTYPE STATEMENT
         LCLC     &LAB                 DECLARE SETC SYMBOL FOR EDITED LABEL
         LCLC     &ERRSW               DECLARE SETC SYMBOL FOR PARM VALIDATION
&ERRSW   SETC     '0'                  INIT ERRSW TO INDICATE NO ERRORS
&LAB     SETC     '&LABEL'
         AIF      (K'&LAB LE 8).LABOK       CHECK LABEL LENGTH
&LAB     SETC     '&LABEL'(1,8)        SELECT FIRST 8 CHARACTERS
         MNOTE    *,'LABEL EXCEEDS 8 CHARACTERS---LEFT MOST 8 USED'
.LABOK   ANOP
.*
.*    THE FOLLOWING AIF INSTRUCTIONS VALIDATE THE VALUE SPECIFIED FOR
.*    THE SYMBOLIC PARAMETER &NUMB1
.*
         AIF      (T'&NUMB1 EQ 'O').NON1
         AIF      (T'&NUMB1 NE 'N').INVN1
         AIF      (&NUMB1 GT 4095).BIGN1
.*
.*    THE FOLLOWING AIF INSTRUCTIONS VALIDATE THE VALUE SPECIFIED FOR
.*    THE SYMBOLIC PARAMETER &NUMB2
.*
.V2      AIF      (T'&NUMB2 EQ 'O').NON2
         AIF      (T'&NUMB2 NE 'N').INVN2
         AIF      (&NUMB2 GT 4095).BIGN2
         AIF      ('ERRSW' EQ '0').GENCODE
         MEXIT
.GENCODE ANOP
.*
.*    THE FOLLOWING MODEL STATEMENTS ARE GENERATED IF THE VALUES FOR
.*    &NUMB1 AND &NUMB2 ARE SPECIFIED CORRECTLY
.*
&LAB     LA       R14,&NUMB1
         LA       R15,&NUMB2
         AR       R14,R15
         MEXIT
.*
.*    MNOTES FOR THE VALIDATION OF &NUMB1 AND &NUMB2
.*
.NON1    MNOTE    8,'FIRST NUMBER OMITTED---MACRO NOT GENERATED'
&ERRSW   SETC     '1'                  TURN ON ERRSW TO INDICATE PARM ERROR
         AGO      .V2
.INVN1   MNOTE    8,'FIRST NUMBER IS INVALID---MACRO NOT GENERATED'
&ERRSW   SETC     '1'                  TURN ON ERRSW TO INDICATE PARM ERROR
         AGO      .V2
.BIGN1   MNOTE    8,'FIRST NUMBER EXCEEDS 4095---MACRO NOT GENERATED'
&ERRSW   SETC     '1'                  TURN ON ERRSW TO INDICATE PARM ERROR
         AGO      .V2
.NON2    MNOTE    8,'SECOND NUMBER OMITTED---MACRO NOT GENERATED'
         MEXIT
.INVN2   MNOTE    8,'SECOND NUMBER IS INVALID---MACRO NOT GENERATED'
         MEXIT
.BIGN2   MNOTE    8,'SECOND NUMBER EXCEEDS 4095---MACRO NOT GENERATED'
.*
         MEND                    TRAILER STATEMENT
```

ENHANCEMENT OF THE PUTTBL MACRO DEFINITION

The PUTTBL macro definition will be enhanced to provide the following additional functions:

- Provide the facilitity to specify the address for the symbolic parameters &TABLE and &ENTRY as a register as well as a label. When a register is specified, it must be enclosed in parentheses.
- Generate unique labels.
- Verify that the specified values for the symbolic parameters &ENTLEN and &KEYLEN are self-defining terms that do not exceed 255.
- Verify that the value specified for &KEYLEN is equal to or less than the value specified for &ENTLEN.

Coding Example 3.5.2 contains the enhanced macro definition of PUTTBL. As an exercise, the reader may attempt to code the additional enhancements:

- Validate the length of the label specified for the macro instruction.
- Provide the facility to specify the value of &ENTLEN and &KEYLEN in a register as well as a self-defining term.
- Allow the user to specify a 1-byte physical end-of-table indicator. Default to X'FF' if not specified.

Coding Example 3.5.2

This coding example contains the enhanced macro definition for PUTTBL.

```
         MACRO
&LABEL   PUTTBL &TABLE,&ENTRY,&ENTLEN,&KEYLEN
         LCLC   &LBL
&LBL     SETC   '$'.'PTB'.'&SYSNDX'(2,3) DEFINE LABEL BASE
.*
.*   VERIFY THAT BOTH &ENTLEN AND &KEYLEN ARE SELF-DEFINING TERMS
.*
         AIF    (T'&ENTLEN EQ 'N' AND T'&KEYLEN EQ 'N').VRFY255
         MNOTE  4,'SPECIFIED ENTRY-LENGTH OR SPECIFIED KEY-LENGTH NOT VA-
                LID--MACRO NOT GENERATED'
         MEXIT
.*
.*   VERIFY THAT BOTH &ENTLEN AND &KEYLEN ARE LESS THAN 256
.*
.VRFY255 AIF    (&ENTLEN LE 255 AND &KEYLEN LE 255).CHKREL
         MNOTE  4,'SPECIFIED ENTRY-LENGTH OR SPECIFIED KEY-LENGTH EXCEED-
                 255--MACRO NOT GENERATED'
         MEXIT
.*
.*   VERIFY THAT &ENTLEN IS GREATER THAN OR EQUAL TO &KEYLEN
.*
.CHKREL  AIF    (&ENTLEN GE &KEYLEN).CHKREGT
         MNOTE  4,'SPECIFIED KEY-LENGTH IS GREATER THAN SPECIFIED ENTRY-
                LENGTH--MACRO NOT GENERATED'
         MEXIT
.*
.*   CHECK IF &TABLE IS SPECIFIED AS A REGISTER
.*
.CHKREGT AIF  ('&TABLE'(1,1) EQ '(').REGTBL
         LA     14,&TABLE                 LD ADR OF BG OF TBL INTO REG 14
         AGO    .B1
.REGTBL  LR     14,&TABLE(1)              LD ADR OF BG OF TBL INTO REG 14
.B1      ANOP
&LBL.A   CLI    0(14),X'00'               CHK FOR VACANT SPOT IN TBL
```

```
         BE    &LBL.B                   IF YES, BRANCH TO INSERT RTN
.*
.*   CHECK IF &ENTRY IS SPECIFIED AS A REGISTER
.*
.CHKREGE AIF   ('&ENTRY'(1,1) EQ '(').REGENT1
         CLC   0(&KEYLEN,14),&ENTRY     CHK FOR DUPL ENTRY
         AGO   .B2
.REGENT1 CLC   0(&KEYLEN,14),0&ENTRY(1) CHK FOR DUPL ENTRY
.B2      BE    &LBL.C                   IF YES, BRANCH TO UPDATE RTN
         CLI   0(14),X'FF'              CHK FOR END OF TBL
         BE    &LBL.D                   IF YES, BRANCH TO TBLEND RTN
         LA    14,&ENTLEN.(0,14)        INCR TO NEXT TABLE SLOT
         B     &LBL.A                   BRANCH BACK TO BG OF LOOP
         AIF   ('&ENTRY'(1,1) EQ '(').REGENT2
&LBL.B   MVC   0(&ENTLEN,14),&ENTRY     MOVE NEW ENTRY INTO TBL
         AGO   .B3
.REGENT2 ANOP
&LBL.B   MVC   0(&ENTLEN,14),0&ENTRY(1) MOVE NEW ENTRY INTO TBL
.B3      LA    15,0                     NEW ENTRY, SET RC = 0
         B     &LBL.E                   BRANCH OUT OF MACRO
         AIF   ('&ENTRY'(1,1) EQ '(').REGENT3
&LBL.C   MVC   0(&ENTLEN,14),&ENTRY     REPLACE DUPL ENTRY
         AGO   .B4
.REGENT3 ANOP
&LBL.C   MVC   0(&ENTLEN,14),0&ENTRY(1) REPLACE DUPL ENTRY
.B4      LA    15,4                     REPLACE ENTRY, SET RC = 4
         B     &LBL.E                   BRANCH OUT OF MACRO
&LBL.D   LA    15,8                     END OF TBL, SET RC = 8
&LBL.E   DS    0H
         MEND
```

NOTES:

- The parentheses are removed from the specified registers by the use of sublist notation. This is illustrated in the model statements referenced by the sequence symbols: .REGTBL, .REGENT1, .REGENT2, and .REGENT3.

THE BLDTBL MACRO INSTRUCTION

To illustrate some more uses of Conditional Assembler in macro development, the macro definition of the BLDTBL macro instruction, mentioned in Section 3.1.3, is coded in Coding Example 3.5.3.

The BLDTBL macro instruction has the following specifications:

- Accepts a label and only positional parameters.
- Each positional parameter is an entry in a table.
- Each positional parameter contains two sub-values (sublist of two):
  - The first sub-value contains a 4-byte key.
  - The second sub-value contains a 1- to 8-byte information character string that equates to the key.
- Each table entry generated is 16 bytes. The information value is padded with low order blanks, if necessary. Each entry is generated with the following fields:
  - 4-byte key;
  - 4-byte field containing the month and day of date of assembly; and
  - 8-byte field of information character string.
- A 16-byte entry of binary ones is generated at the end of the table.
- An invalid entry (positional parameter) is ignored and an appropriate MNOTE is generated. One or more of the following invalidates an entry:

- The key value is not four bytes in length.
- The information value exceeds eight bytes.
- If either the key, information, or both values are omitted.

■ The table is not generated if the day of the month is the 1st, 2nd or 3rd day or past the 25th day.

Coding Example 3.5.3 contains the macro definition of BLDTBL.

Coding Example 3.5.3

This coding example contains the macro definition for BLDTBL.

```
                  MACRO
&LABEL            BLDTBL
                  LCLA     &POS,&TOTPOS
                  LCLB     &OKBIT
                  LCLC     &LAB,&MM,&DD,&DATE
&POS              SETA     1                  INITIALIZE RUNNING POS PARM COUNT
&TOTPOS           SET      N'&SYSLIST         TOTAL POS PARMS SPECIFIED
                  AIF      (&TOTPOS EQ 0).NOPARMS     CHECK IF ANY POS PARMS SPEC
&MM               SETC     '&SYSDATE'(1,2)            EXTRACT MONTH
&DD               SETC     '&SYSDATE'(4,2)            EXTRACT DAY
                  AIF      ('&DD' LT '04' OR '&DD' GT '25').INVDATE  CHECK VALID
DATE
&DATE             SETC     '&MM'.'&DD'
&LAB              SETC     '&LABEL'
                  AIF      (K'&LAB LE 8).LABOK        CHECK LABEL LENGTH
&LAB              SETC     '&LABEL'(1,8)              SELECT FIRST 8 CHARACTERS
.LABOK            ANOP
&LAB              DS       0H
.LOOP             ANOP
.*
.*   SET UP VALIDATION LOGIC FOR POS PARM IN SETB INSTRUCTION
.*
&OKBIT            SETB     ((K'&SYSLIST(&POS,1) EQ 4)   AND             -
                           (K'&SYSLIST(&POS,2) LE 8)    AND             -
                           (T'&SYSLIST(&POS,1) NE 'O') AND              -
                           (T'&SYSLIST(&POS,2) NE 'O'))
                  AIF      (&OKBIT EQ 0).INVPARM     CHK IF POS PARM OK
.*
.*   DEFINE TABLE ENTRY
.*
                  DC       C'&SYSLIST(&POS,1)',C'&DATE',CL8'&SYSLIST(&POS,2)'
.INCRPOS          ANOP
&POS              SETA     &POS+1                     INCR POS PARM COUNT
                  AIF      (&POS GT &TOTPOS).TBLEND   CHECK FOR POS PARM END
                  AGO      .LOOP
.TBLEND           DC       16XL1'FF'                  INDICATE TABLE END
                  MEXIT
.*
.*   MNOTES FOR ERROR CONDITIONS
.*
.NOPARMS          MNOTE    8,'NO TABLE ENTRIES SPECIFIED--MACRO NOT GENERATED'
                  MEXIT
.INVDATE          MNOTE    4,'MACRO NOT GENERATED BECAUSE OF INVALID DATE'
                  MEXIT
.INVPARM          MNOTE    4,'POSITIONAL PARAMETER NUMBER &POS: &SYSLIST(&POS) -
                           IS INVALID--MACRO NOT GENERATED'
                  AGO      .INCRPOS
                  MEND
```

3.6 SOME USEFUL MACRO DEFINITIONS

This section will present the macro definitions of two useful macro instructions: INITL and RCNTL. These two macro instructions will be used throughout the book in various programming examples. The INITL macro instruction is used to initialize an Assembler language program and the RCNTL macro instruction is used to return control to the calling program or to the operating system. Besides the usefulness of these macros, examination of the coding techniques may be helpful.

The macro definition for the INITL macro instruction is presented in Coding Example 3.6.1 and the macro definition for the RCNTL macro instruction is presented in Coding Example 3.6.2.

3.6.1 The INITL Macro Instruction

The INITL macro instruction has the following specifications:

- Accepts from 1 to 15 base registers as positional parameters. Register 0 is rejected, if specified.
- Register 13 may be used as a base register if it is specified as the first positional parameter.
- If register 13 is specified, then the user has the option of specifying the name of the savearea via the SA= keyword parameter.
- Reentrant code is generated if register 13 is not used as a base register.
- An optional equate table may be generated by specifying the EQU= keyword parameter. The value of EQU= is a 1- to 6-character prefix that is appended to the register number (1–15).

Coding Example 3.6.1

This coding example contains the macro definition for INITL.

```
         MACRO
&LABEL   INITL  &EQU=,&ID=,&SA=
         LCLA   &POS,&TOTOPD,&DISP,&STOPSW,&REG13SW
         LCLC   &SVAR,&LBL,&PRFX
         LCLC   &REGS,&REG1,&REG2
         AIF    (T'&LABEL NE 'O').B1
         MNOTE  *,'NO LABEL SPECIFIED'
         AGO    .CHKEQU
.B1      AIF    (K'&LABEL LE 8).LABOK
         MNOTE  'LABEL EXCEEDS 8 CHARACTERS---LEFT MOST 8 USED'
.LABOK   ANOP
&LBL     SETC   '&LABEL'(1,8)
.CHKEQU  AIF    (T'&EQU EQ 'O').B8
         AIF    (K'&EQU LE 6).EQUOK
         MNOTE  'EQU PREFIX EXCEEDS 6 CHARACTERS---LEFT MOST 6 USED'
.EQUOK   ANOP
&PRFX    SETC   '&EQU'(1,6)
.B8      ANOP
&SVAR    SETC   'SVAR'.'&SYSNDX'
&TOTOPD  SETA   N'&SYSLIST
         AIF    (&TOTOPD EQ 0).NOREG
         AIF    (&TOTOPD LE 15).PROCEED
         MNOTE  0,'MORE THAN 15 REGISTERS HAVE BEEN SPECIFIED---SURPLUS -
                ONES HAVE BEEN IGNORED'
&TOTOPD  SETA   15
.PROCEED ANOP
```

```
         AIF    (T'&EQU NE '0').EQUTBL
.B2      ANOP
         AIF    (T'&ID NE '0').SETID
.B3      ANOP
.ULOOP   ANOP
&POS     SETA   &POS+1
         AIF    (&POS GT &TOTOPD).USING
         AIF    ('&SYSLIST(&POS)' EQ '13').REG13
         AIF    ('&SYSLIST(&POS)' EQ '0').INVREG
.B4      ANOP
&REGS    SETC   '&REGS'.','.'&PRFX'.'&SYSLIST(&POS)'
         AGO    .ULOOP
.USING   ANOP
         AIF    (&REG13SW EQ 1).USING13
&LBL     STM    &PRFX.14,&PRFX.12,12(&PRFX.13)
         BALR   &PRFX.&SYSLIST(1),0
         USING  *&REGS
.B5      ANOP
&POS     SETA   1
         AIF    (&TOTOPD EQ 1).REST
.NXLOAD  ANOP
&POS     SETA   &POS+1
         AIF    (&POS GT &TOTOPD).REST
&REG1    SETC   '&SYSLIST(&POS-1)'
&REG2    SETC   '&SYSLIST(&POS)'
         LA     &PRFX.&REG2,2048
         LA     &PRFX.&REG2,2048(&PRFX.&REG1,&PRFX.&REG2)
         AGO    .NXLOAD
.REG13   AIF    (&POS GT 1).INVREG
&REG13SW SETA   1
         AGO    .B4
.USING13 ANOP
         AIF    (T'&SA EQ '0').B6
&SVAR    SETC   '&SA'(1,8)
.B6      ANOP
&LBL     STM    &PRFX.14,&PRFX.12,12(&PRFX.13)
         LR     &PRFX.2,&PRFX.13
         BALR   &PRFX.12,0
         BAL    &PRFX.13,76(0,&PRFX.12)
&SVAR    DC     18F'0'
         USING  &SVAR&REGS
         AGO    .B5
.REST    AIF    (&REG13SW EQ 1).B7
         GETMAIN R,LV=72,SP=1
         ST     &PRFX.13,4(0,&PRFX.1)
         ST     &PRFX.1,8(0,&PRFX.13)
         LR     &PRFX.13,&PRFX.1
         L      &PRFX.1,4(0,&PRFX.13)
         L      &PRFX.1,24(0,&PRFX.1)
         MEXIT
.B7      ST     &PRFX.2,4(0,&PRFX.13)
         ST     &PRFX.13,8(0,&PRFX.2)
         MEXIT
.EQUTBL  ANOP
&PRFX.0  EQU    0
&PRFX.1  EQU    1
&PRFX.2  EQU    2
&PRFX.3  EQU    3
&PRFX.4  EQU    4
&PRFX.5  EQU    5
&PRFX.6  EQU    6
&PRFX.7  EQU    7
&PRFX.8  EQU    8
&PRFX.9  EQU    9
```

```
&PRFX.10 EQU    10
&PRFX.11 EQU    11
&PRFX.12 EQU    12
&PRFX.13 EQU    13
&PRFX.14 EQU    14
&PRFX.15 EQU    15
         AIF    (&REG13SW EQ 1).B5
         AGO    .B2
.SETID   B      12(0,&PRFX.15)
         AIF    ('&ID'(1,1) EQ '*').CSECTNM
         DC     CL8'&ID'
         AGO    .B3
.CSECTNM DC     CL8'&SYSECT'
         AGO    .B3
.NOREG   MNOTE  12,'NO REGISTERS SPECIFIED---MACRO NOT GENERATED'
         MEXIT
.INVREG  MNOTE  12,'INVALID REGISTER SPECIFIED---MACRO GENERATION TERMIN-
                ATED'
         MEND
```

3.6.2 The RCNTL Macro Instruction

The RCNTL macro instruction has the following specifications:

- Obtains the address of the savearea of the calling program from the savearea pointed to by register 13.
- Restores the registers from the savearea of the calling program.
- A return code may be optionally specified via the RC= keyword parameter. A decimal number from 0 to 4095 may be specified, or (15) may be specified, which indicates that the return code is in register 15.

Coding Example 3.6.2

This coding example contains the macro definition for RCNTL.

```
         MACRO
&LABEL   RCNTL  &RC=,&SA=
         LCLC   &SVAR
         AIF    (K'&LABEL LE 8).LABOK
         MNOTE  0,'LABEL CONTAINS MORE THAN 8 CHARACTERS---MACRO NOT GEN-
                ERATED'
         MEXIT
.LABOK   ANOP
         AIF    (T'&SA EQ 'O').NOSA
         AIF    ('&SA'(1,1) EQ '(').SAREG
&SVAR    SETC   '&SA'(1,8)
&LABEL   LA     13,&SVAR+4
         AGO    .CHKRC
.SAREG   ANOP
&LABEL   L      13,4(0,&SA(1))
         AGO    .CHKRC
.NOSA    ANOP
&LABEL   L      13,4(0,13)
.CHKRC   AIF    (T'&RC EQ 'O').NORC
         AIF    ('&RC'(1,1) EQ '(').RCREG
         AIF    (T'&RC NE 'N').RCINVAL
         AIF    (&RC GT 4095).RCINVAL
         LA     15,&RC
         AGO    .RCOK
```

```
.RCREG   AIF    (&RC(1) EQ 15).RCOK
         MNOTE  0,'INVALID REGISTER SPECIFIED FOR RETURN CODE--RC IGNOR-
                ED'
         AGO    .NORC
.RCINVAL MNOTE  0,'RETURN CODE SPECIFIED IS INVALID--RC IGNORED'
         AGO    .NORC
.RCOK    L      14,12(0,13)
         LM     0,12,20(13)
         BR     14
         MEXIT
.NORC    LM     14,12,12(13)
         BR     14
         MEND
```

BIBLIOGRAPHY FOR CHAPTER 3

The following IBM manuals contain reference material for the topics discussed in this chapter.

ID	TITLE
GC33-4010	*OS/VS—DOS/VSE VM/370—Assembler Language*
GC33-4021	*OS/VS—VM/370 Assembler Programmer's Guide*
SC26-4036	*Assembler H Version 2 Application Programming: Guide*
GC26-4037	*Assembler H Version 2 Application Programming: Language Reference*

4

Supervisor Services and Macro Instructions

This chapter discusses the functions, interface requirements and use of the more frequently used supervisor services. The macro instructions presented in this chapter do not require an authorized caller in order to be used. Since the macro instructions presented in this chapter are commonly used and many programmers are familiar with them, the format of these macro instructions is presented informally and all the possible operand parameters of each macro instruction are not necessarily discussed. Only the more important or frequently used parameters are discussed.

The presentation of the selected macro instructions will include a detailed explanation of the facilities provided by the macro instructions, typical uses of the facilities, and some coding examples to illustrate how to code the macro instructions, as well as other pertinent parts of the programs that use those macro instructions.

The programmer should consult the Bibliography at the end of this chapter for the names and ID numbers of the appropriate IBM manuals for a full description of all the operand parameters and syntax for the macro instructions discussed in this chapter.

4.1 WHAT ARE SUPERVISOR SERVICES?

Supervisor services are various facilities provided by the operating system to Assembler language programs via macro instructions. The proper use of these facilities will enable application and system programs to do the following:

- Execute more efficiently;
- Provide special services to its users;
- Fullfill special execution requirements; and
- Provide flexibility in design and maintenance.

4.2 STANDARD, LIST, AND EXECUTE FORMS OF MACRO INSTRUCTIONS

Besides the standard form, most IBM-supplied macro instructions are also provided with the list and execute forms. The standard form of the macro is the form that is ordinarily specified and results in the invoking of the function of the macro instruction. The standard form expands into a parameter-list and executable code. The list form of a macro instruction expands into only a parameter-list, and the execute form expands into executable code that refers to the parameter-list generated by the list form of the macro instruction. The execute form could also specify parameters that override the ones specified in the list form.

The list and execute forms of a macro instruction work together and are functionally equivalent to the standard form of the macro instruction. The list and execute forms of a macro instruction may be used to write reentrant programs (discussed in Chapter 5). They may also be used if the function of the macro instruction is used many times in a program, with slight changes to the operands. In this case, instead of coding the standard form of the macro instruction each time and generating a parameter-list and executable code, the list form could be specified once with the operands that are normally used. The execute form could then be specified in the appropriate places in the program and refer to the parameter-list generated by the list form of the macro instruction and provide any required parameter changes.

The list form of the macro is indicated by specifying the keyword parameter value of MF=L in the operand. The execute form of the macro instruction is indicated by specifying the keyword parameter value of MF=(E,list-addr) in the operand, where list-addr is the address of the expansion of the list form of the macro instruction. The address may be specified as either the name associated with the expansion of the macro instruction or a register, enclosed in parentheses, containing the address of the expansion. In most macro instructions, all or most of the parameters valid in the standard form of the macro instruction are valid in the list and execute forms. Some macro instructions use the keyword parameter SF= instead MF= in the list and execute forms.

4.3 THE EXTRACT MACRO INSTRUCTION

The EXTRACT macro instruction is used to obtain information from specified fields of the TCB and associated control blocks. The TCB may be for the task that issues the EXTRACT macro instruction, or the TCB may be for one of the substasks (if any) of the task that issues the macro instruction. The information is returned into an answer area provided by the programmer. The EXTRACT macro instruction may be used only by programs that reside in 24-bit addressable virtual storage.

The first two positional parameters of the EXTRACT macro instruction specify the address of the answer area and the TCB address, respectively. The address may be specified as a label (A-type address) or as a register, enclosed in parentheses, containing the address. The answer area must be on a fullword boundary and contain one fullword for each request. If the information is for the issuing task, then the TCB address may be omitted or specified as 'S'.

The requested information is specified via the FIELDS keyword parameter with information ids. The information ids, described below, may be specified in any combination and in any sequence. The information ids must be separated by commas and enclosed in parentheses, if more than one is specified. The requested information is placed in the provided answer area in the same relative sequence as specified by the FIELDS parameter. The following are the meanings of the information ids:

`ALL`	Requests the following information in the following sequence: GRS, FRS, reserved, AETX, PRI, CMC, TIOT. If ALL is specified, seven fullwords are required in the answer area.
`GRS`	The address of the savearea used by the operating system to save the general registers 0-15 when the task is not active.
`FRS`	The address of the savearea used by the operating system to save the floating point registers 0, 2, 4, and 6 when the task is not active.

AETX	The address of the end-of-task exit routine specified in the ETXR parameter of the ATTACH macro instruction used to create the task.
PRI	The limit and dispatching priorities of the task. The two high- order bytes are zero. The third byte is the current limit priority, and the fourth byte is the current dispatching priority.
CMC	The task completion code. If the task has not completed, the field is zero.
TIOT	The address of the task input/output table.
ASID	The address space identifer, which is extracted from the ASCB.
COMM	The address of the Command Scheduler communications list.
PSB	The address of the TSO protected storage control block, which is extracted from the JSCB.
TJID	The address space identifer for a TSO address space and zero for a non-TSO address space.
TSO	The address of a byte. The high order bit has a value of 1 if the task is contained in a TSO address space, and contains a value of 0 if the task is contained in a non-TSO address space.

Coding Example 4.3.1

This coding example shows how to obtain the address space ID, priorities, and completion code of the subtask whose TCB address is stored in the fullword labeled STCB1ADR.

```
         EXTRACT TCBINFO,STCB1ADR,FIELDS=(ASID,PRI,CMC)
         ...
STCB1ADR DS   F
TCBINFO  DS   0F
TCBASID  DS   F
TCBPRIO  DS   F
TCBCMCD  DS   F
```

Coding Example 4.3.2

This coding example shows how to obtain the jobname of the task that issued the EXTRACT macro.

```
         EXTRACT TIOTADR,'S',FIELDS=TIOT
         L       R10,TIOTADR
         MVC     JOBNAME,0(R10)
         ...
TIOTADR  DS      F
JOBNAME  DS      CL8
```

NOTES:

- The first eight bytes of the TIOT contains the jobname.

4.4 PROGRAM MANAGEMENT

The information in this section is pertinent to the sections below that discuss the LOAD, LINK, XCTL, and ATTACH macro instructions, and therefore, should be read before those sections.

A program can be designed in one of three structures: simple, planned overlay and dynamic.

A simple structure program is composed of a single load module that does not call any other load modules during execution; however, the load module may contain multiple CSECTs (which may have been object modules or load modules) that communicate via the CALL macro instruction. The entire simple structure load module (with all its CSECTs) is created as a single load module at linkedit time, and the entire load module is loaded into virtual storage when invoked (via JCL or by another load module).

A planned overlay structure program is composed of a root segment and overlay segments. When invoked, only the root segment is loaded into virtual storage and remains there until termination. The overlay segments (which are other CSECTs), which are invoked via the CALL macro instruction from the root segment, are loaded into virtual storage as required and use the same virtual storage area, which means that they overlay each other as required. The entire planned overlay structure is defined at linkedit time and is created as a single load module.

A dynamic structure program is composed of a single load module that dynamically invokes other load modules during execution to satisfy the function of the program. The other load modules are loaded into virtual storage only as required and are self-contained (since they are separate load modules).

This rest of this section will discuss dynamic structure programs. These programs are implemented with the use of the LINK, LOAD, DELETE, XCTL and ATTACH macro instructions. The terms program and load module will be used interchangeably in the rest of this section and in the sections that follow that deal with the macro instructions mentioned above.

In order to be managable, load modules (or programs) may have the attributes of serially-reusable, reentrant, and refreshable (which is similar to the reentrant attribute and is used for recovery). These attributes are set at linkedit time and determine if the load module can be executed by only one task at a time or executed concurrently by multiple tasks and if reloading into virtual storage is required between executions. If a load module does not have any of those attributes, then it is considered to be nonreusable.

A nonreusable load module modifies itself; therefore, only one task at a time may execute it and it may be executed only once per load. A serially-reusable load module also modifies itself; but, it either resets itself before termination or initializes itself at the beginning of execution. Therefore, like a nonreusable load module, only one task at a time may execute a serially-reusable load module, but, unlike a nonreusable load module, a serially-reusable load module may be executed more than once per load. A reentrant (and refreshable) load module does not modify itself. Therefore, it may be executed concurrently by multiple tasks and may also be executed more than once per load. It should be noted that the only requirement for a program to be reentrant is that multiple tasks may execute it concurrently with a single load; therefore, a reentrant program may modify itself under certain conditions. The code that is modified must be serially-reusable and executed by only one task at a time. The single threading must be enforced by the reentrant program by the use of ENQ/DEQ or similar mechanism.

When load modules are loaded into virtual storage, they may be loaded into either the Link Pack Area or the Job Pack Area (JPA). The link pack area, which may be fixed (FLPA) or pageable (PLPA and MLPA) is a global area that is accessible by the entire system. The load modules in this area must be reentrant and are mainly system modules that are required by many address spaces. User programs will be usually loaded into the JPA (but some select ones may reside in the link pack area). Each address space has its own JPA, which is accessible only to that address space (not considering the use of Cross Memory Services). The rest of this section will discuss only the JPA (unless it explicitly mentions otherwise).

In order to efficiently use the virtual storage allocated to the JPA, the operating system maintains two responsibility counts for each load module that is loaded into that area. One responsibility count is used for loads in response to the LOAD macro instruction, and the other responsibility count is used for loads in response to the LINK, XCTL, and ATTACH macro instructions. The counts are maintained in the following ways:

- The first responsibility count mentioned is incremented by one for load modules when they are loaded via the LOAD macro instruction.

  For load modules that were loaded via LOAD, that count is decremented:

  - By one, when those load modules are released via the DELETE macro instruction; and
  - By the number of outstanding LOAD requests made by a specific task or subtask for those load modules when that task or subtask terminates.

- The second responsibility count mentioned is incremented by one for load modules that receive control via the the LINK, XCTL, or ATTACH macro instructions or via JCL.That count is decremented by one for those load modules:

  - Which received control via LINK, when they return control to the caller;
  - When they issue the XCTL macro instruction; and
  - Which are specified by the ATTACH macro instruction, when the subtask terminates.

The total responsibility or use count is maintained in a field of the Contents Directory Entry (CDE) for the load module. When the count reaches zero, the virtual storage occupied by that load module is released (only for JPA).

When a load module is invoked, the operating system searches for it in a number of locations in a specific sequence. The sequence of the search is as follows:

- Job Pack Area;
- Libraries defined by DCB/TASKLIB parameter;
- Libraries defined by JOBLIB/STEPLIB JCL DD statement (if DCB/TASKLIB not defined);
- Link Pack Area (MLPA, FLPA, PLPA); and
- Libraries defined by the system link list

The job pack area and link pack area were discussed above.

An optional DCB parameter may be specified for the LOAD, LINK, XCTL, and ATTACH macro instructions. The DCB parameter requires the address of an opened DCB that is associated with a JCL DD statement that points to a load library(s). This address is placed into the TCBJLB field of the TCB for the life of the macro instruction execution and indicates the library(s) that is to be searched to locate the load module that is named in the macro instruction. That library(s) is used only for the macro instructions that explicitly specify the DCB parameter. The DCB specification, in effect, replaces the JOBLIB/STEPLIB specification for those macro instructions. If the load module is not located in the load library(s) indicated by the DCB parameter, then the JOBLIB/STEPLIB load library(s) will not be searched.

Besides a DCB parameter, an optional TASKLIB parameter may also be specified for the ATTACH macro instruction. The TASKLIB parameter also requires the address of an opened DCB that is associated with a JCL DD statement that points to a load library(s). This address is placed into the TCBJLB field of the TCB of the created subtask and indicates the load library(s) that is to be searched to locate load modules requested by the subtask. The TASKLIB specification, in effect, replaces the JOBLIB/STEPLIB specification for the subtask. If the load module is not located in the load library(s) indicated by the TASKLIB parameter, then the JOBLIB/STEPLIB load library(s) is not searched. The subtask could override the TASKLIB library(s) by specifying the DCB parameter with any of the load module invoking macro instructions that were mentioned above.

The JOBLIB and STEPLIB JCL DD statements are specified in the JCL jobstream and point to load library(s). The JOBLIB load library(s) is used for all steps of the job that do not specify a STEPLIB. The STEPLIB load library(s) is used only for the steps that specify a STEPLIB DD statement. If the load module does not reside in the STEPLIB load library(s), then the JOBLIB load library(s) will not be searched.

The system link list refers to the system load library—SYS1.LINKLIB—and all the load libraries that are concatenated to it via the LNKLSTxx member of SYS1.PARMLIB.

When a job step is initiated, the JPA of the address space contains no load modules. Therefore, even though it is first in the search sequence, the JOBLIB/STEPLIB load library(s) (assuming DCB/TASKLIB were not specified) is, in effect, actually searched first and gives the programmer the most flexibility in determining which libraries are to be used to locate the desired versions of the load modules (for testing, etc.). If DCB/TASKLIB load libraries are hard-coded in the load module, the programmer still retains flexibility by specifying the desired load library(s) in the JCL for the ddname(s) associated with DCB/TASKLIB. Besides, for selecting the proper versions of the load modules, the purpose of overriding the default search sequence is to enable the operating system to search more efficiently (fewer directory searches) for the desired load modules.

After the job step starts to execute, especialy if subtasking is being used, the JPA will start to become populated with load modules (based upon requests and responsibility counts). When requests are made for load modules, the operating system will search the JPA to determine if a usable copy exists. If one does exist, then the operating system will use that copy of the load module to satisfy the request and save the time required to reload that load module from the library into the JPA. The operating system determines if an existing copy is usable by examining its attributes and current status (executing or not). Load modules that are reentrant (or refreshable) are always usable. A serially-reusable load module is usable only if it is not currently being executed. A task is put into a wait state if it requests the use of a serially-reusable load module that is currently being executed by another task. It should be emphasized that the reusability integrity of a load module is protected by the operating system only if the operating system is used to pass control to the load module. This is accomplished by use of the LINK, XCTL, and ATTACH macro instructions. If a load module is loaded into virtual storage via the LOAD macro instruction and then receives control via a branch instruction or the CALL macro instruction, then it is the programmer's responsibility to maintain the reusability integrity of the load module.

The section "Writing Reusable Programs" in Chapter 5 contains more information concerning the topics presented in this section.

4.5 THE LOAD AND DELETE MACRO INSTRUCTIONS

The section "Program Management," above, should be read first because it contains prerequisite information to this section.

The LOAD macro instruction is used to bring a load module into virtual storage. The programmer specifies an entry point name that must be a member name or an alias name in the directory of a partitioned dataset (library), or must have been previously specified by an IDENTIFY macro instruction. The corresponding load module is loaded into virtual storage if a usable copy is not available. However, control is not passed to the load module; instead, the virtual storage address of the specified entry point is returned in register 0, and the authorization code and load module length are returned in the high order byte of register 1 and the low order three bytes of register 1, respectively.

The DELETE macro instruction is used to release the virtual storage occupied by the load module loaded by a previous LOAD macro instruction. In order for the DELETE macro instruction to be effective, it must specify the same entry point name as that specified in the LOAD macro instruction, which brought the load module into virtual storage, and be issued by the same task that issued the LOAD macro instruction.

The LOAD macro instruction can be used to provide better program management performance by causing the operating system to bring load modules into virtual storage more efficiently. The LOAD macro instruction should be used only for load modules that have the reentrant or serially-reusable attributes (and must be used for load modules that have the only-loadable (OL) attribute). There is no performance advantage by LOADing nonreusable load modules because they are required to be reloaded each time that they are executed. If a load module is required to be executed many times during the life of a task or by multiple tasks of the same job step, then the load module can be either called (via the LINK, XCTL, or ATTACH macro instructions) each time it is required or it can be LOADed once before it is required and then called each time that it is required. If the load module is called (without an initial LOAD), then each time it returns control (when called by LINK or ATTACH) or relinquishes control (via XCTL), then its responsibility count becomes zero (if and when there are no other tasks executing that load module or waiting to execute it) and it is removed from virtual storage (from JPA only); therefore, it must be reloaded each time it is required. If the same load module is LOADed first, and is then called when required, it will remain in virtual storage because its responsibility count will always be at least one (because of the outstanding LOAD).

The LOAD macro instruction can also provide a performance advantage for infrequently used, but access time-sensitive load modules. If a special load module and/or a special task that executes that load module requires quick access time, then the use of the LOAD macro instruction can eliminate the overhead of reloading that load module into virtual storage each it is called. When the load module is no longer required, then the DELETE macro instruction can be used to free the virtual storage.

When a load module is LOADed, it should receive control via the LINK, XCTL, or ATTACH macro instructions in order for the operating system to protect the reusability integrity of the load module. If the programmer elects to pass control to the LOADed program via a branch instruction in a multi-tasking address space, then it is the programmer's responsibility to insure the load module's reusability integrity. If reentrant programs are involved, then there are no integrity exposures. If serially-reusable programs are involved, then the ENQ/DEQ mechanism must be used to provide the required serialization. If nonreusable programs are involved, they should never receive control via a branch instruction (this is true for both a single or a multi-tasking environment) because, since those programs modify themselves, unpredictable results will occur after the first execution if they are not reloaded. If the programmer does not know the program's attributes or know if multi-tasking is occurring, then the LINK, XCTL, or ATTACH macro instructions should be used to pass control.

The name of the load module, which LOAD brings into virtual storage, may be specified in one of three ways. One way to specify the name of the load module is to hard-code it with the EP parameter as follows:

```
          LOAD EP=PROG01
```

Instead of hard-coding the name of the load module in the macro instruction operand, the name of the load module may be specified in an 8-byte area and its address specified by the EPLOC parameter as follows:

```
          MVC   PGMNAME,=CL8'PROG01'
          ...
          LOAD  EPLOC=PGMNAME
          ...
PGMNAME   DS    CL8
```

The area that contains the load module name must be padded with low order blanks if the the name is less than eight characters. This method should be used if the required load module name varies based upon execution requirements or if many load modules are to be loaded during the course of the execution.

The desired load module may also be specified by using the DE parameter to point to the PDS (library) directory entry of the load module. The directory entry is obtained by use of the BLDL macro instruction (discussed in Chapter 8). This method will provide a performance advantage if more than one load module is required to be loaded because BLDL reads the directory once and loads the directory entries of all the desired load modules into the area provided. The LOAD macro instruction must perform a directory search if the load module name is specified via the EP or the EPLOC parameters. If the desired load module directory entry is specified via the DE parameter, then the LOAD macro instruction saves the processing time required to perform the directory search. No performance advantage is gained if only one load module is to be loaded because either method (EP/EPLOC or BLDL/DE) would require one directory search. Coding Example 4.5.1 shows the required code to use the DE parameter to request the LOADing of a load module.

Coding Example 4.5.1

This coding example illustrates the code required to load three load modules using the DE parameter and the BLDL macro instruction. The zero in the first positional parameter of the BLDL macro instruction indicates that the current load library group (via JOBLIB, STEPLIB, etc.) for the jobstep is to be used.

```
                BAL   R6,DOBLDL      BUILD BLDL-LIST FOR REQR PRGMS
                BAL   R6,LOADPGMS    LOAD REQUIRED PRGMS
                ...
DOBLDL          BLDL  0,BLDLIST      SEARCH CURRENT LOAD LIBS
                BR    R6             RETURN TO CALLING RTN
                ...
LOADPGMS        LOAD  DE=P1ENTRY
                ST    R0,P1EPADR     SAVE EPA OF PRGM01
                LOAD  DE=P2ENTRY
                ST    R0,P2EPADR     SAVE EPA OF PRGM02
                LOAD  DE=P3ENTRY
                ST    R0,P3EPADR     SAVE EPA OF PRGM03
                BR    R6             RETURN TO CALLING RTN
                ...
BLDLIST         DC    H'3'           SPECIFY 3 DIR ENTRIES REQUESTED
                DC    H'60'          ONLY 1ST 60 BYTES OF EACH ENTRY REQR
P1ENTRY         DC    CL8'PRGM01'
                DS    CL52
P2ENTRY         DC    CL8'PRGM02'
                DS    CL52
P3ENTRY         DC    CL8'PRGM03'
                DS    CL52
                ...
P1EPADR         DS    F
P2EPADR         DS    F
P3EPADR         DS    F
```

The LOAD macro instruction may specify the load library(s) where the operating system should search for the specified load module. This is accomplished with the DCB parameter. Coding Example 4.5.2 shows the required code to use this facility.

The LOAD macro instruction provides the facility to limit the search for load modules to only the JPA and the first group (via concatenation) of libraries specified in the search sequence. This is accomplished by specifying the LSEARCH=YES parameter. If the DCB parameter is also specified, then the search will be limited to the JPA and the load library(s) pointed to by the DCB parameter. If the JOBLIB/STEPLIB JCL DD statement is specified and the DCB parameter is not specified with LSEARCH=YES, then the search for the load module will be limited to the JPA and the library(s) pointed to by JOBLIB/STEPLIB. This facility will prevent the LOAD macro instruction from searching the system areas (MLPA, FLPA, and PLPA) and the system load libraries (LNKLSTxx) to locate a load module. If the requested load module is not located in the JPA or the specified user load libraries, then LSEARCH=YES will cause an S806 ABEND even if the load module resides in the LPA or in the link list libraries. This facility will provide a performance advantage and integrity. If a user load module is not located in the user load libraries, then this facility will prevent the operating system from performing additional directory searches looking for a load module in libraries where the load module should not exist. If, however, a new version of a load module that normally resides in the system area is being tested or if a user load module has the same name as a system load module (which should be avoided), then this facility will prevent the operating system from LOADing the wrong load module if the user load module was inadvertently not placed into the proper user load library.

If the LOAD request results in an ABEND condition, the ABEND could be suppressed with the use of the ERRET parameter. The ERRET parameter specifies the address of a user-provided routine that is to receive control when an ABEND condition occurs. This routine could analyze the ABEND code and determine if a recovery is possible. When the routine receives control, register 1 contains the ABEND code and register 15 contains the reason code. Coding Example 4.5.3 shows the required code to use this facility.

Coding Example 4.5.2

This coding example illustrates the code required to direct the LOAD macro instruction to search the load library(s) pointed to by the DCB parameter. In this example, the LOAD macro instruction is directed to search the load libraries USER.LOADLIB1 and USER.LOADLIB2 for the program PROG02.

```
          BAL    R6,OPENLIB
          BAL    R6,LOADPGM
          ...
OPENLIB   OPEN   PRIVLIB
          ...                              CHECK FOR GOOD OPEN
          BR     R6
          ...
LOADPGM   LOAD   EP=PROG02,DCB=PRIVLIB
          ST     R0,EPAP2                  SAVE ENTRY POINT OF PROG02
          BR     R6
          ...
EPAP2     DS     F
PRIVLIB   DCB    DSORG=PO,MACRF=R,DDNAME=PRIVLIB
```

JCL DD Statement:

```
//PRIVLIB DD DSN=USER.LOADLIB1,DISP=SHR
//        DD DSN=USER.LOADLIB2,DISP=SHR
```

Coding Example 4.5.3

This coding example illustrates how to suppress an ABEND if the LOAD macro instruction is unable to complete successfully. The example shows how to attempt a recovery from a S106-C (insuffcent storage for load module) ABEND.

```
LOAD03    LA     R7,CHKERR3       LOAD ADR OF RECVRY CHK RTN
          LOAD   EP=PROG03,ERRET=LOADERR3
```

```
         BR       R6              RETURN TO CALLING RTN
CHKERR3  C        R15,BIN4        CHK IF RECOVERY POSSIBLE
         BE       LOAD03          IF YES, TRY LOAD AGAIN
         ABEND    ...             IF NO, ABEND
         ...
LOADERR3 C        R1,ERR106       CHK FOR S106 ABEND
         BE       CHKER106        IF S106, CHK REASON CODE
         C        R1,ERR806       CHK FOR S806 ABEND
         BE       NOPROG          IF YES, IND PGM NOT FOUND
         LA       R15,8           INDICATE NON-RECVRY ERROR
         BR       R7              RETURN TO LOAD RTN
CHKER106 C        R15,BIN12       CHK REASON CODE FOR NO VIR STOR
         BE       NOVSTOR         IF YES, ATTEMPT RECVRY
         LA       R15,8           INDICATE NON-RECRY ERROR
         BR       R7              RETURN TO LOAD RTN
NOVSTOR  CLI      RCVRYSW,C'1'    CHK IF RECRY ALREADY ATTEMPTED
         BE       NOVSRCRY        IF YES, NON-RECVRY ERROR
         DELETE   ...             DELETE NOT NEEDED PRGMS
         FREEMAIN ...             FREE NOT NEEDED VIRT STORAGE
         MVI      RCVRYSW,C'1'    INDICATE RECVRY ATTEMPTED
         LA       R15,4           INDICATE TRY LOAD AGAIN
         BR       R7              RETURN TO LOAD RTN
NOVSRCRY WTO      '*** INSUFFICIENT VIRTUAL STORAGE FOR PROG03 ***'
         LA       R15,8           IND NON-RECRY ERROR
         BR       R7              RETURN TO LOAD RTN
NOPROG   WTO      '*** PROGRAM PROG03 NOT FOUND ***'
         LA       R15,8           IND NON-RECRY ERROR
         BR       R7              RETURN TO LOAD RTN
         ...
RCVRYSW  DC       C'0'
BIN4     DC       F'4'
BIN12    DC       F'12'
ERR106   DC       X'00000106'
ERR806   DC       X'00000806'
```

NOTES:

- A recovery suggestion for a S806 ABEND would be for the program to request the dataset name of the library that contains the load module via the WTOR macro instruction. The dataset could then be dynamically allocated (discussed in Chapter 7) and the LOAD retried with the DCB parameter specified pointing to the ddname assigned by dynamic allocation.

The DELETE macro instruction may specify the name of the load module that is to be released using one of the three parameters: EP, EPLOC, or DE. The parameters have the same meaning as in the LOAD macro instruction. The following shows how to release the load module PROG01 by hard-coding its name:

```
         DELETE EP=PROG01
```

4.6 THE LINK MACRO INSTRUCTION

The section "Program Management," above, should be read first because it contains prerequisite information to this section.

The LINK macro instruction is used to pass control to (call) a load module. The programmer specifies an entry point name, which must be a member name or an alias name in the directory of a partitioned dataset (library), or must have been previously specified by an IDENTIFY macro instruction.

The corresponding load module is loaded into virtual storage if a usable copy is not available and receives control. The execution is synchronous, which means that the calling program waits for the called program to complete execution before the calling program can execute again.

When the called program completes execution, control is returned to the calling program at the instruction following the LINK macro instruction. The calling program can communicate with the called program by passing a parameter-list to it. The parameter-list can be used to pass and/or receive information.

The calling and called programs use standard MVS linkage conventions, or else unpredictable results could occur. The called program returns control to the calling program by branching to the address that was in register 14 when control was received. Register 14 is set by the operating system and is not the address of the instruction following the Link macro instruction. Instead, it points to a location in the MVS Nucleus that contains an SVC 3 instruction, which passes control back to the next highest request block (the calling program).

The name of the load module that receives control via LINK may be specified by using one of the three parameters: EP, EPLOC, or DE. The parameters have the same meaning as in the LOAD macro instruction. The following shows how to LINK to the load module PROG01 by hard-coding its name:

```
LINK EP=PROG01
```

Like the LOAD macro instruction, the LINK macro instruction also supports the facilities provided by the DCB, LSEARCH, and ERRET parameters. The explanations and examples for the LOAD macro instruction, above, are also applicable for the LINK macro instruction.

The LINK macro instruction can pass a parameter-list to the called load module with the use of the PARAM parameter. The calling load module specifies a list of the addresses of the virtual storage areas that contain information for the called load module and/or are to receive information from the called load module. The addresses may be specified as the names of the areas or as registers, enclosed in parantheses, containing the addresses of the areas. The LINK macro instruction generates a list of full words containing the addresses specified in the PARAM parameter in the same sequence and sets register 1 to point to the beginning of the list. Coding Example 4.6.1 shows how to code the PARAM parameter and how the called program processes the parameter-list.

Coding Example 4.6.1

This coding example illustrates how to call a program and pass it a parameter list. In this example, the calling program calls PROG02 and passes it the addresses of the virtual storage areas CODE1, CODE2, and RESPONSE. CODE1 and CODE2 contain information for PROG02, and RESPONSE is to receive information from PROG02.

Calling Program

```
         LA      R10,CODE2
         LINK    EP=PROG02,PARAM=(CODE1,(R10),RESPONSE)
         LTR     R15,R15           TEST RC FROM CALLED PROGRAM
         BZ      LISTRESP
         ...
LISTRESP MVC     #INF001,RESPONSE
         ...
CODE1    DC      C'123'
CODE2    DC      C'XYZ'
RESPONSE DS      CL10
LINE     DS      0CL133
         ...
#INF001  DS      CL10
```

Called Program

```
PROGO2    CSECT
          INITL     3,EQU=R
          L         R10,0(0,R1)        LOAD ADDR OF 1ST PARM (CODE1)
          L         R11,4(0,R1)        LOAD ADDR OF 2ND PARM (CODE2)
          L         R12,8(0,R1)        LOAD ADDR OF 3RD PARM (RESPONSE)
          ...
          MVC       0(L'INFORM01,R12),INFORM01  PUT REPLY INTO 3RD PARM AREA
          ...
          RCNTL     RC=0
          ...
INFORM01  DC        CL10'...'          INFORMATION FOR CODE: 123/XYZ
          ...
          END
```

If the LINK macro instruction passes a variable number of parameters, then the paramater VL=1 should be coded with the PARAM parameter. This causes the LINK macro instruction to set the high order bit of the last fullword to 1 to indicate the end of the parameter-list. The following shows how to code the LINK macro instruction when it passes a variable number of parameters.

```
LINK EP=PROGO3,PARAM=(P1,P2,P3),VL=1
```

In the above example, three parameters are being passed and the VL=1 enables the called program to determine how many parameters have been passed. Coding Example 4.6.2 shows the code that can be used to enable the called program to determine the end of the parameter-list.

Coding Example 4.6.2

This coding example illustrates how a called program could check for the last fullword address when a variable length parmameter-list is passed.

```
GETNXADR  TM        0(R1),X'80'        CHK FOR HI ORDER BIT ON
          BO        PARMEND            IF ON, END OF PARMLIST
          L         R10,0(0,R1)        LOAD PARM ADR IN REG 10
          LA        R1,4(0,R1)         INCR TO NEXT FWD ADR
          LA        R15,0              IND THAT PARM ADR IS NOT LAST ONE
          BR        R6                 RETURN TO CALLING RTN
PARMEND   L         R10,0(0,R1)        LOAD LAST PARM ADR INTO REG 10
          LA        R15,4              IND THAT THIS IS LAST ADR
          BR        R6                 RETURN TO CALLING RTN
```

If a variable number of parameters are being passed to the called program, then some convention should be set up to indicate when no parameters are being passed. If the PARAM parameter is not specified, the LINK macro instruction does not modify register 1. Therefore, one possible convention could be to set register 1 to zeros before issuing the LINK macro instruction if no parameter-list is being passed to the called program.

4.7 THE XCTL MACRO INSTRUCTION

The section "Program Management," above, should be read first because it contains prerequisite information to this section.

The XCTL macro instruction is used to transfer control to (call) a load module. The programmer specifies an entry point name that must be a member name or an alias name in the directory of a partitioned dataset (library), or must have been previously specified by an IDENTIFY macro instruction

The corresponding load module is loaded into virtual storage, and receives control if a usable copy is not available. However, unlike the LINK macro instruction, control is not returned to the calling program. The calling program is logically removed from the calling chain, and its responsibility count is decremented by one. Instead, control is returned to the load module that passed control (via non-XCTL) to the load module that issued the XCTL macro instruction.

The name of the load module that receives control via XCTL may be specified by using one of the three parameters: EP, EPLOC, or DE. The parameters have the same meaning as in the LOAD macro instruction. The following shows how to XCTL to the load module PROG03:

```
         XCTL EP=PROG03
```

Like the LOAD macro instruction, the XCTL macro instruction also supports the facilities provided by the DCB and LSEARCH parameters (XCTL does not support the ERRET parameter). The explanations and examples for the LOAD macro instruction, above, are also applicable for the XCTL macro instruction.

There are certain considerations for the program that issuses the XCTL macro instruction. Since the program that issues XCTL is no longer in the calling chain and may be removed from virtual storage (if its responsibility becomes zero), it must restore the environment that existed when it received control and it cannot pass any parameters to the the XCTLed program that may cause a reference to the called program. To satisfy these requirements, the calling program must do the following:

- Restore registers 2 through 14 to the contents that existed when it received control. Registers 0, 1, and 15 would not normally be required to be restored. This will provide the called program with the address of the savearea and register content of the previous program (the program that called the calling program). This will assure that the XCTLed program will return control properly.
- If a parameter-list is to be passed to the XCTLed program, then the calling program must assure that the storage area(s), which contains the parameter-list and/or is referenced by the addresses in the parameter-list, are not contained in the calling program. This is necessary because if the responsibility count of the calling program becomes zero due to the XCTL macro instruction, then the calling program is removed from virtual storage and any storage areas, that were contained in it are no longer available. If a parameter-list is to be passed, then one method that can be used is to place the parameter-list and its referenced virtual storage into storage obtained via the GETMAIN macro instruction.

One more consideration must be mentioned. When the registers are restored to that of the previous program, the program that issues XCTL will no longer have addressability because its base register(s) would have been overlayed. The program that issues XCTL has two options for restoring registers. One is to restore the registers immediately before issuing XCTL. If the registers are restored in this manner, then the EP parameter of XCTL cannot be used to provide the name of the called program because that form of the XCTL macro instruction generates code that requires addressability. However, the EPLOC and DE parameters have no such restriction. The other method of restoring registers is to let the XCTL macro instruction do it. This can be done by specifying the register range, enclosed in parentheses, as the first positional parameter of XCTL. The registers will be restored from the savearea that is currently pointed to by register 13. Therefore, register 13 must be restored to the address of the previous programs savearea by the calling program before it issues the XCTL macro instruction. The following example shows how to direct XCTL to restore all the registers except 13, which was already restored by the calling program:

```
         L        R13,4(0,R13)
         XCTL     (R14,R12),EP=PROG04
```

The PARAM parameter is supported in only the execute form of the XCTL macro instruction. If a parameter-list is required to be sent to the calling program and if the normal form of the macro is used, then the programmer must setup the parameter-list and load its address into register 1. In this case, the programmer must not direct XCTL to restore register 1 since this would overlay the address of the parameter-list. Coding Example 4.7.1 shows the code required to pass a parameter-list to the XCTLed program.

Coding Example 4.7.1

This coding example illustrates how to set up the registers before issuing the XCTL macro instruction when a parameter-list is being passed to the called program.

```
         BAL      R6,GETMAIN
         B        DOXCTL
         ...
GETMAIN  GETMAIN  EC,LV=x,A=PARMADR
         ...
         BR       R6
         ...
DOXCTL   L        R13,4(0,R13)       RESTORE ADR OF PREV PROG SA
         L        R14,12(0,R13)      RESTORE RET ADR OF PREV PROG
         L        R1,PARMADR         LOAD PARMLIST ADR
         XCTL     (R2,R12),EP=PROG04
         ...
PARMADR  DS       F
```

The XCTL macro instruction can be used in a situation when a program can be repackaged into smaller programs whose functions are required only once during an execution. An example of such a situation would be to divide a large program into four smaller programs (or design it that way initially) whose functions are initization, data input and editing, validation, and processing the data. In this structure, the first program performs various initialization functions and XCTLs to the next program. The next program reads data from a dataset, edits it, reformats it, and stages it into either another dataset or into virtual storage and then XCTLs to the next program. The third program validates the edited data and then XCTLs to the final program, which does the actual processing of the data. This structure would eliminate the need to have a control program or router that LINKs to other programs as required. The main function of XCTL is to enable the task to save virtual storage and to use real storage frames more efficiently.

4.8 THE ATTACH, DETACH AND CHAP MACRO INSTRUCTIONS

The section "Program Management," above, should be read first because it contains prerequisite information to this section.

When a job is initiated, the operating system creates a task. This task is called the Job Step Task. The ATTACH macro instruction may then be used to cause the operating system to create new tasks to execute in the same address space as that of the task issuing the macro instruction. The programmer specifies an entry point name, which must be a member name or an alias name in the directory of a partitioned dataset (library), or must have been previously specified by an IDENTIFY macro instruction. The corresponding load module is loaded into virtual storage if a usable copy is not available and receives control when the subtask is dispatched.

The ATTACH macro instruction may override the normal search sequence used by the operating system to locate the specified load module. This is accomplished by use of the optional DCB and TASKLIB parameters. The DCB and TASKLIB parameters require the address of an opened DCB that is associated with a JCL DD statement that points to a load library(s). The DCB parameter overrides the JOBLIB/STEPLIB load library(s) for the life of the ATTACH macro instruction for locating the load module that is specified to execute as the first load module of the subtask. The TASKLIB parameter permanently overrides the JOBLIB/STEPLIB load library(s) for the subtask.

To illustrate the use of the DCB and TASKLIB parameters, consider Coding Example 4.8.1. Based upon that example, if the specified load modules are not located in the JPA, then the next place where the operating system looks for these load modules is indicated below:

```
Program PROGS1 of first ATTACH of parent task:
USER.LOADLIB

Program PROGS2 of second ATTACH of parent task:
PRIV.LOADLIB

Program PROGS1A of LOAD of first subtask:
USER.LOADLIB

Program PROGS2A of first LOAD of second subtask:
SUBT.LOADLIB, if not found, then SUBT.LOADLIB2

Program PROGS2B of second LOAD of second subtask:
PRIV.LOADLIB2
```

Coding Example 4.8.1

This coding example illustrates how the DCB and TASKLIB parameters are used. It shows the ATTACH macro instructions issued by a parent task, the LOAD macro instructions issued by the subtasks created, and selected JCL DD statements specified for the job step.

Parent Task

```
ATTACH EP=PROGS1
ATTACH EP=PROGS2,DCB=PRIVLIB,TASKLIB=ST2LIB
```

Subtask-1

```
LOAD EP=PROGS1A
```

Subtask-2

```
LOAD EP=PROGS2A
LOAD EP=PROGS2B,DCB=PRIVLIB2
```

Selected JCL DD statements for job step

```
//STEPLIB  DD DSN=USER.LOADLIB,DISP=SHR
//PRIVLIB  DD DSN=PRIV.LOADLIB,DISP=SHR
//PRIVLIB2 DD DSN=PRIV.LOADLIB2,DISP=SHR
//ST2LIB   DD DSN=SUBT.LOADLIB,DISP=SHR
//         DD DSN=SUBT.LOADLIB2,DISP=SHR
```

When the ATTACH processing is complete, control is returned to the issuing program at the instruction following the ATTACH macro instruction, and the address of the TCB for the new task is returned in register 1. The new task is called a subtask of the originating task. The originating task, which may also be called the parent task (or mother task), is the task that issued the ATTACH macro instruction. A task could be both a parent task and a subtask. (See Figure 4.8.1.) The significance of distinguishing whether a task is functioning as a parent task or a subtask is for when the task issues certain macro instructions such as ATTACH, DETACH, CHAP, ABEND, and so on.

The execution of all parent tasks and all of their subtasks is asynchronous which means that the tasks execute concurrently.

The subtask assumes the same limit and dispatching priorities of the originating task unless they are changed in the ATTACH macro instruction.

Since each task in an address space would normally be performing a portion of the entire job step work requirement, ATTACH processing provides a mechanism to permit communications between the parent tasks and their subtasks. The parent task may communicate with its subtasks by passing a parameter-list to them for sending and/or receiving information, and also by providing an ECB or an exit routine address to determine when the subtask completes (normally or abnormally).

If an ECB is provided, the operating system posts it when the subtask completes execution. The completion code is placed in the last three bytes of the ECB.

If an exit routine address is provided, it receives control, asynchronously to the parent task, when the subtask completes execution. The completion code may be obtained from the TCBCMPC field of the TCB of the subtask. The exit routine must be resident in virtual storage when it is required to receive control. It may be a CSECT of the program executing for the parent task (therefore, already in virtual storage) or it may be a separate program. If it is a separate program, then it may be loaded into virtual storage via the LOAD macro instruction. The exit routine assumes the same dispatching priority of the task that issued the ATTACH macro instruction and competes with other tasks in the address space for CPU time. The exit routine must establish addressability and save and restore the registers.

When the exit routine receives control, the contents of the registers are as follows:

`Register 0`	Information used by operating system.
`Register 1`	Address of TCB of subtask whose termination is driving the exit.
`Register 13`	Address of savearea provided by operating system
`Register 14`	Return address (to operating system).
`Register 15`	Address of exit routine entry point.

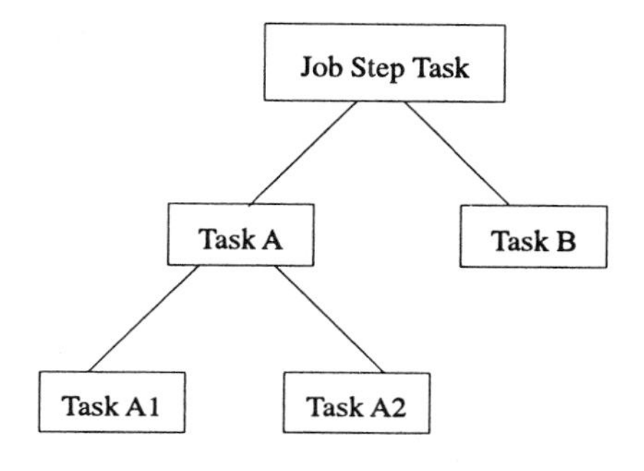

Figure 4.8.1. This figure indicates the task levels in a job step.Task A and Task B are subtasks of the Job Step Task, but Task A is also the parent task of Tasks A1 and A2.

The contents of registers 2 through 12 do not contain any significant information for the exit, but should be saved and restored.

The exit routine is a good place to issue the DETACH macro instruction. If any information from the TCB of the subtask is required, such as the completion code, then that information should be extracted before the DETACH macro instruction is issued. Since the exit routine must provide its own addressability and since there is no facility provided for the parent task to pass a parameter-list to the exit routine, then there appears to be no direct way for the parent task to communicate with the exit routine. The section of this chapter that discusses the STIMER macro instruction shows a coding technique that allows the main program and the exit routine to reference the same storage areas using the same labels.

When should an ECB be used and when should an exit routine be provided to determine when a subtask completes execution? This depends on the structure, design, and execution requirements of the parent task. However, there are a few informal guidelines. A different ECB must be used for each subtask in order to know which subtask has completed execution, but only one exit routine is required to determine which subtask has completed, since register 1 contains the TCB address of the subtask that completed when the exit received control. If a parent task has many subtasks and if the parent task performs work independent of the subtasks and requires only to periodically check for the completion of the subtasks to process the results, then an exit routine would be more practical. By providing an exit routine, the parent task would not require the code and the processing time to periodically check numerous ECBs for completion. Instead, it could use that processing time to perform useful work and be informed automatically by the operating system of subtask completion by the exit routine receiving control. If a parent task has very few subtasks, the ECB method may be more practical since it is easier to test an ECB for completion than it is to write and interface to (if necessary) an exit routine. However, if the parent task functions like a router or scheduler and depends upon the completion of subtasks in order to have work to process, then the ECB method would be better. In this case, the parent task would issue the WAIT macro instruction for an ECB list with an event number of one. The parent task will receive control only when one or more subtasks have completed and can scan the ECBs to determine which subtasks have completed and execute accordingly.

The parent task can direct its subtasks to terminate processing using the following technique. The parent task passes the address of a parameter field to the subtasks at ATTACH time. When required, the parent task could then post the parameter field to indicate that the subtasks are to terminate. For this technique to function, the subtasks would be required to periodically check the parameter field to determine if the parent task requested termination. This technique could be expanded to direct only a portion of the subtasks to terminate. This can be accomplished in one of two ways. The actual code, that is posted in the parameter field could indicate which subtasks are to terminate and when (immediately or after certain processing is complete). The other way would be to group the subtasks by function, if possible, and each group could receive a separate parameter field to check. In this case, the parent task need only select the proper parameter field(s) to post. This will direct all the subtasks in that group(s) to terminate.

Coding Example 4.8.2

The following coding example illustrates how the parent task could direct a subtask to terminate its processing. In this example, the parent task passes the address of the parameter field EXECIND to the subtask. When the parent task requires that the subtask terminate, the parent task will execute the STOPSUB subroutine. When the subtask initially receives control, it saves the address of the parameter field EXECIND in INDADR. As the subtask executes, it will periodically execute the CHKIND subroutine to determine if the parent task is requesting subtask termination.

Parent Task

```
         ATTACH   EP=PROGSUB1,PARAM=EXECIND
         ...
STOPSUB  MVI      EXECIND,C'S'      DIRECT SUBTASK TO STOP
         BR       R7                RETURN TO CALLING RTN
         ...
EXECIND  DC       C'E'              INIT INDICATOR, "E" FOR EXECUTE
```

Subtask

```
CHKIND   L        R10,INDADR        LOAD ADR OF EXECIND PARM FIELD
         CLI      0(R10),'S'        CHK IF PARENT IS REQ TERMINATION
         BE       STASKEND          IF YES, TERMINATE
         BR       R7                IF NO, RETURN TO CALLING RTN
         ...
INDADR   DS       F
```

When a subtask completes execution, the parent task must issue a DETACH macro instruction to remove the subtask's TCB from the system if the parent task provided an ECB or an exit routine address for that subtask. The DETACH macro instruction, if required, must be issued before the parent task terminates. If the parent task requires information from the terminating subtask's TCB, such as the completion code, then that information must be extracted before the DETACH macro instruction is issued. The subtask's TCB is removed automatically by the operating system if the parent task did not provide an ECB or an exit routine address.

Coding Example 4.8.3

This coding example illustrates how to create a subtask, pass it the addresses of parameter fields, and check for subtask completion via an ECB. In this example, the addresses of the parameter fields REQCODE and REQINFO are passed to the program INQUIRY. REQCODE contains a code used to request certain information from a database, table, and so on, and REQINFO is the receiving field for the information obtained. The parent task checks the ECB, specified in the ATTACH macro instruction, to determine when the subtask completes. The ECB may be required to be checked during two different processing conditions of the parent task. One possible condition is when the parent task is busy performing other processing and it periodically checks if the subtask is complete. The other condition is when the parent task has completed all its work and it waiting for the subtask to complete. Depending on how the parent task is designed, either one or both conditions may be required.

```
ATTACHS1 XC       ECBS1,ECBS1       CLEAR ECB FOR ATTACH
         ATTACH   EP=INQUIRY,PARAM=(REQCODE,REQINFO),ECB=ECBS1
         ST       R1,TCBADRS1       SAVE TCB ADR OF SUBTASK
         BR       R7                RETURN TO CALLING RTN
         ...
CHKECBS1 TM       ECBS1,X'40'       CHECK IF POST BIT ON
         BO       S1END             IF YES, DETACH SUBTASK
         LA       R15,4             INDICATE SUBTASK NOT COMPLETE
         BR       R7                RETURN TO CALLING RTN
S1END    DETACH   TCBADRS1          REMOVE SUBTASK'S TCB
         LA       R15,0             INDICATE SUBTASK COMPLETE
         BR       R7                RETURN TO CALLING RTN
```

```
              ...
MAINEND       WAIT    1,ECB=ECBS1        PARENT TASK INACTIVE/END,
*                                        WAIT FOR SUBTASK END
              DETACH TCBADRS1            REMOVE SUBTASK'S TCB
              BR      R7                 RETURN TO CALLING RTN
              ...
ECBS1         DS      F
TCBADRS1      DS      F
REQCODE       DS      CL4
REQINFO       DS      CL20
```

The CHAP macro instruction is used to change the dispatching priority of the issuing task or any of its subtasks.

There are two categories of execution priorities: limit priority and dispatching priority. Dispatching priority is further subdivided into two types: address space dispatching priority and task dispatching priority. Address spaces compete with each other for CPU time based upon their dispatching priorities. When a particular address space is active, the tasks (parent tasks and subtasks) within that address space then compete with each other for CPU time based upon their relative dispatching priorities.

The dispatching priority of an address space is set by the operating system based upon parameters received from the user or data center. The user may set the dispatching priority directly via the PRTY or DPRTY JCL parameters or indirectly via the PERFORM parameter or may not specify any of these parameters and take the defaults. The data center also has the option to restrict or ignore those parameters via an SMF or a JES2/JES3 exit or via the SRM (System Resource Manager).

There is no limit priority associated with address spaces, and their dispatching priorities are adjusted up or down by the operating system in order to maintain an efficient workload balance on the system. Tasks have limit priorities and dispatching priorities. The limit priority of the job step task is set equal to the initial dispatching priority. Tasks may then CHAP their own dispatching priorities up or down but not above their own limit priorities. Parent tasks may CHAP their subtasks dispatching priorities up or down. If a parent task CHAPs the dispatching priority of its subtask above the subtask's limit priority, then the limit priority is adjusted up to equal the new dispatching priority; however, a parent task may not raise the limit priority of its subtask above its own limit priority.

In order to effectively use the CHAP facility for a performance advantage, tasks that are I/O-bound should be set to a higher dispatching priority than tasks that are CPU-bound. If a task has periods when it is I/O-bound and periods when it is CPU-bound, then the CHAP macro instruction should be used to raise the dispatching priority when the task is I/O-bound and lower the dispatching priority when the task is CPU-bound. The determination of I/O bound versus CPU-bound is relative among the tasks within a particular address space.

Performance based upon an efficient mix of I/O-bound and CPU-bound tasks is not the only consideration for dynamically changing dispatching priorities. Certain tasks that are considered to be important may also need to execute at higher dispatching priorities regardless of the amount of I/O that they perform. Such tasks may include tasks that control terminals that require quick response time or monitors that may be in a wait state most of the time.

Consider the following scenario. Let us say that the parent task reads records from a slow source such as a terminal and/or teleprocessing line. It extracts somes fields from each record, does some processing, and writes new shorter, modified records to a DASD queue. The subtask periodically reads a batch of ten records from the DASD queue, performs complex mathematical calculations and logical manipulations on the fields of the records, and then writes a one line result for each record onto a printer. The process described so far indicates that the parent task is I/O-bound and the subtask is CPU-bound.

Let us say that the parent task is initialized with a dispatching priority (DP) of 120 and a limit priority (LP) of 120. The parent task ATTACHes the subtask with a DP of 100 and an LP of 100. At this point in the processing, the parent task is executing with a DP of 120 and the subtask is executing with a DP of 100. Since the parent task is I/O-bound relative to the subtask, this is an efficient arrangement. The ATTACH macro instruction would be coded as follows:

```
ATTACH EP=PROGST01,DPMOD=-20,LPMOD=20
```

The DP of the subtask (the DPMOD parameter) is specified as a signed number that is algebraically added to the current DP of the originating task. The LP (the LPMOD parameter) of the subtask is specified as an unsigned number that is subtracted from the limit priority of the originating task.

Now, let us say that between 1:00 P.M. and 2:00 P.M. every afternoon the results from the subtask must be calculated and printed very quickly. This implies that during this period the subtask must execute with a DP higher than its parent task. But, with the current arrangement, this is not possible since the LP priority of the subtask is less than the DP of the parent task. To remedy this situation, the parent task should initially execute with a DP priority higher than the subtask, but provide the subtask with an LP that is higher than the DP of the parent task so that the subtask could raise its DP higher than the DP of the parent task when the situation warrents it. One way of accomplishing this is for the parent task to ATTACH the subtask with a DP of 100 and an LP of 110. Then the parent task CHAPs its DP down to 105. With this arrangement, the parent task executes with a DP of 105 and the subtask executes with a DP of 100, which satisfies the requirement that the parent task executes with a higher DP. But, with this arrangement, the subtask, with an LP of 110, now has the ability to raise its DP above the DP of the parent task when required. The ATTACH and CHAP macro instructions would be coded as follows:

```
          ATTACH   EP=PROGST01,DPMOD=-20,LPMOD=10
          ST       R1,TCBADRS1
          CHAP     -15
          ...
TCBADRS1  DS       F
```

During the required time interval, the DP of the subtask could be raised by either the parent task or the subtask. If the parent task raises the DP of the subtask, then it must specify the TCB address in the second positional parameter of the CHAP macro instruction. If the parent task raises the DP of the subtask to 110, then the CHAP macro instruction would be coded as follows:

```
CHAP     +10,TCBADRS1
```

If the subtask raises its own DP, then the specification of the TCB address is not required since the default is the TCB address of the issuing task. The CHAP macro instruction would be coded as follows if issued by the subtask:

```
CHAP     +10
```

The parent task will now be executing at a DP of 105 and the subtask will be executing at a DP of 110, which satisfies the relative importance of the two tasks between the time interval of 1:00 P.M. to 2:00 P.M.

If the parent task abnormally terminates or issues the ABEND macro instruction, then all its subtasks are also abnormally terminated. If a subtask is abnormally terminated or issues the ABEND macro instrucion (without the STEP parameter), then only the subtask abnormally terminates.

If a subtask abnormally terminates, the parent task can intercept it by coding the ESTAI parameter of the ATTACH macro intruction. This parameter sets up an ESTAE environment (the ESTAE macro instruction is discussed in Chapter 6).

4.9 THE WAIT AND POST MACRO INSTRUCTIONS

The WAIT macro instruction is used to inform the operating system that the task issuing the macro instruction cannot continue to execute until one or more events, each represented by a different event control block (ECB), have completed.

The POST macro instruction is used to indicate that the event, represented by the specified ECB, has completed, and then optionally provide a completion code.

An ECB is a fullword aligned on a fullword boundary. The first two bits of the ECB must be set to 0 before the WAIT macro instruction is issued for that ECB. When the WAIT macro instruction is issued, the high order bit of the ECB is set to 1 to indicate that it is in a wait state. The POST macro instruction causes bit-0 (wait bit) to be set to 0 and bit-1 (post bit) to be set to 1. The WAIT processing is satisfied when the value of the high order two bits of the specified ECB is 01. When all the specified waiting events have completed, control is returned to the waiting program at the instruction following the WAIT macro instruction.

The first positional parameter of the WAIT macro instruction specifies the number of events that must occur to satisfy the wait. If the number specified is one (or omitted, which defaults to one), then the ECB address is specified via the ECB keyword parameter. If the number of events specified is greater than one (maximum 255), then the ECBLIST keyword parameter must be used to specify the address of a list of ECB addresses. The number of ECB addresses in the list must be equal to or greater than the number of events specified. The end of the list is indicated by setting the high order bit of the last ECB address to one. The number of events may be specified as a symbol or decimal number, or as a register, enclosed in parentheses, containing the event number. The address for the ECB and ECBLIST parameters may be specified as a label (A-type address) or as a register enclosed in parentheses. Coding Example 4.9.1 shows how to code the WAIT macro instruction to wait for single and multiple events. When control is returned from a multiple event wait, the program can determine which events have completed by scanning the ECBs of the list. The ECBs that contain B'01xxxxxx' in the first byte have been posted. More ECBs may have been posted than the number specified in the WAIT macro instruction since that number specifies only the minimum amount of ECBs that must be posted to satisfy the wait.

The first positional parameter of the POST macro instruction is the address of the ECB that is to be posted. It may be specified as a label or as a register enclosed in parentheses. In most cases, a register is specified because the ECB is not located in the routine that issues the POST macro instruction. The second positional parameter is the optional completion code that is to be sent to the task that is waiting for the ECB to be posted. It may be specified as a symbol or decimal number, or as a register, enclosed in parentheses, containing the completion code. The default is zero.

Coding Example 4.9.1

This coding example shows how to code the WAIT macro instruction to wait for the completion of both one event and multiple events. The multiple events example specifies a list of five ECBs for the WAIT macro instruction, and requests that control be returned to the issuing task when at least three of those ECBs have been posted.

Wait for one event

```
         WAIT      ECB=ECB01
         ...
ECB01    DC        F'0'
```

Wait for multiple events

```
          WAIT      3,ECBLIST=ECBLIST1
          ...
ECBLIST1  DC        A(ECB01)
          DC        A(ECB02)
          DC        A(ECB03)
          DC        A(ECB04)
          DC        X'80'
          DC        AL3(ECB05)
*
ECB01     DC        F'0'
ECB02     DC        F'0'
ECB03     DC        F'0'
ECB04     DC        F'0'
ECB05     DC        F'0'
```

The WAIT macro instruction may be specified after other macro instructions that require an ECB to be posted to indicate that the service requested has been completed. Those macro instructions return control to the issuing program before the event is complete. Such macro instructions include basic access I/O macro instructions such as READ and WRITE, whose specified ECBs are posted after the I/O is complete. Also included are the EXCP macro instruction (discussed in Chapter 11) and the WTOR macro instructions (discussed in this chapter). For these macro instructions (and others), the operating system issues the POST macro instruction.

If the program can do other processing while waiting for the event(s) to be completed, then the issuing of the WAIT macro instruction can be deferred. But, when the WAIT macro instruction is issued, the task will stay in a wait state until the specified number of events have been completed. In some situations, the issuing of the WAIT macro instruction may not be desired at all because the design of the program or the timing of the event completion may be such that that the resulting wait state would be impractical and/or inefficient. In those cases, a test under mask (TM) instruction could be executed periodically to test the ECB for completion. Coding Example 4.9.2 shows the required code. Other examples of such processing are described in the sections of this chapter that deal with the ATTACH and the WTOR macro instructions.

Coding Example 4.9.2

This coding example illustrates how to periodically test an ECB for completion using the TM instruction.

```
TESTECB    TM     ECB01,X'40'     TEST IF ECB HAS BEEN POSTED
           BO     POSTED          YES, ECB POSTED
           BR     R6              NO, CONTIN PROC, CHK AGAIN LATER
```

In most cases, when a program issues a WAIT macro instruction, the ECB is for some operating system-provided service; therefore, the operating system issues the POST macro instruction. However, a programmer may design his/her programs to use the WAIT/POST facility to signal the completion of an event. In this case, the user program issues the

POST macro instruction. The following shows how to code the POST macro instruction to post one of the ECBs from Coding Example 4.9.1, and specify a completion code of 4. The address of the ECB to be posted is in register 10:

```
POST (R10),4
```

Obviously, the POST macro instruction must be issued from a task other than the one that issued the WAIT macro instruction. WAIT/POST communication may occur between tasks within the same address space or between tasks across address spaces.

Under certain conditions, an ECB may be posted without issuing a POST macro instruction (which expands into an SVC instruction), thereby obtaining a performance advantage. This may be done only if the WAIT macro instruction has not yet been issued for the ECB that is to be posted. This can be determined by testing the high order bit of the ECB with the TM instruction. If this bit is 0, then the WAIT macro instruction has not been issued. Posting the ECB requires that bit-0 be set to 0 and bit-1 be set to 1, plus setting bits 2 through 31 with a completion code, if required. There are a number of instructions available that will perform that task (MVC, ST, XC, etc.), but there is a special consideration when posting an ECB in this fashion. If the WAIT macro instruction is issued for that ECB bewteen the execution of the TM instruction and the setting of the bits, then this method will not work because the WAIT macro instruction would have been issued before the bits were set. To handle this situation, a compare and swap (CS) instruction should be used instead. When a CS instruction is executed, the hardware performs a serialization function before the operand is fetched and again after the operation is complete. If the CS instruction determines that the bit configuration of the ECB has changed since the execution of the TM instruction, then the ECB is not changed and a condition code of one (mask 4) is set in the PSW. If the WAIT macro instruction has been issued, then the POST macro instruction must be issued to post the ECB. Coding Example 4.9.3 shows the required code.

Coding Example 4.9.3

This coding example illustrates how to post an ECB without issuing the POST macro instruction. In this example, the routine that issues the POST macro instruction receives the address of the ECB that is to be posted and stores it into ECBADR until required. A completion code of decimal 255 is required to be sent to the task that is waiting for the ECB to be posted. The contents of NEWECB contains the information that is to be placed into the ECB when posted.

```
POSTECB  L     R12,ECBADR          LOAD ECB ADR
         L     R10,0(0,R12)        LOAD CONTENTS OF ECB
         L     R11,NEWECB          LOAD CONTENTS OF NEW ECB
         TM    0(R12),X'80'        CHECK IF WAIT ISSUED
         BO    DOPOST              IF YES, ISSUE POST MACRO
         CS    R10,R11,0(R12)      IF NO, TRY QUICK POST
         BC    4,DOPOST            IF UNSUCCESSFUL, ISSUE POST MACRO
         BR    R6                  IF OK, RETURN TO CALLING RTN
DOPOST   POST  (R12),255
         BR    R6                  RETURN TO CALLING RTN
ECBADR   DS    F
NEWECB   DC    X'400000FF'         ECB WITH POST BIT ON AND CC=255
```

4.10 THE ENQ AND DEQ MACRO INSTRUCTIONS

The ENQ macro instruction is used to cause the operating system to assign control of one or more serially resuable resources to the task that issued the macro instruction. The user may request shared control or exclusive control. If any of the requested resources are not available, the task may optionally go into a wait state until all the requested resources become available.

The user identifies the resources for which control is requested by specifying a qname (queue) and an rname (resource) together with a scope value that indicates if the qname/rname combination should be considered a global resource or a local resource.

The operating system does not actually control access to the specified resource. Instead, it maintains a global queue and a local queue of user-assigned qnames/rnames (a QCB is dynamically created for each combination). Each requester (TCB address) for a specific qname/rname and scope combination is queued to the appropiate QCB (via QEL and QXB control blocks). The Operating System will assure that the execution of the tasks, ENQing on specific qname/rname and scope combinations, will be concurrent or serialized relative to each other, according to the specified requests of the ENQ macro instruction.

The ENQ/DEQ mechanism will function properly only if all the tasks that require serialization of specific resources adhere to the same rules and conventions. It is the user's responsibility to define those rules and conventions and then enforce them. The following considerations are necessary:

- Qnames and rnames must be defined and equated to the specific serially reusable resources that are required to be serialized among tasks within the same address space (local scope) or among tasks within all address spaces of a single CPU or multiple CPUs (global scope).
- A single qname/rname may be equated to a single resource or a group of resources that are required to be serialized together.
- All tasks that require serialization of the resources must use the ENQ/DEQ macro instructions with the appropriate qnames/rnames and scope to allow the operating system to control access to the resources.
- Since the other tasks (and possibly MVS) may be waiting to use the ENQed resource, the DEQ should be done immediately after control of the resource is no longer required.
- Since the operating system knows only about the qnames/rnames and scope and not about the actual resource, if a task attempts to access one of the resources without using the ENQ macro instruction with the appropiate request, then the operating system will allow access (permit the task to execute) even though another task may have "exclusive" control of the resource.

The same qname/rname with different scope values are considered to be different resources. The operating system will allow a group of tasks that are requesting shared ENQs for the same qname/rname and the same scope value to execute concurrently. A group of tasks that are requesting exclusive ENQs or a combination of exclusive and shared ENQs for the same qname/rname and same scope value will be prevented from executing concurrently.

The resource could be anything that the user needs to serialize. It could be a program, a dataset, a group of instructions, an area of virtual storage, and so forth.

The DEQ macro instruction is used to cause the operating system to relinquish control of one or more serially reusable resources (actually, to remove the appropiate QEL/QXB control blocks from the QCB chain). Control of the resources must have been previously obtained by the same task via the ENQ macro instruction.

Based upon the request sequence and type of ENQ requests presented in Table 4.10.1, the operating system will assign control of the resource (actually, permit the requesting tasks to execute) in the following manner.

Table 4.10.1

This table is a logical representation of a sequence of ENQ requests for a qname/rname that have the same scope value. The table shows the ID of the requesting task and the type of control required.

Task A	—	SHARED
Task B	—	SHARED
Task C	—	SHARED
Task D	—	EXCLUSIVE
Task E	—	EXCLUSIVE
Task F	—	SHARED
Task G	—	SHARED
Task H	—	EXCLUSIVE

Tasks A, B, and C will be permitted to execute concurrently. Tasks D, E, F, G, and H will wait. Tasks F and G, even though they requested SHARED control of the resource, will wait because of the intervening EXCLUSIVE request of Tasks D and E. When Tasks A, B, and C all relinquish control of the resource via DEQ macro instructions, then Task D will be permitted to execute alone because it requested EXCLUSIVE control of the resource. When Task D relinquishes control of the resource, then Task E will be permitted to execute alone because it requested EXCLUSIVE control of the resource. When Task E relinquishes control of the resource, then Tasks F and G are permitted to execute concurrently because they requested SHARED control of the resource and there was no intervening EXCLUSIVE request for the resource, but Task H still waits because it requested EXCLUSIVE control of the resource. When Tasks F and G both relinquish control of the resource, then Task H is permitted to execute.

The operand of the ENQ/DEQ instruction contains one sublist positional parameter and one keyword parameter. In the following sequence, the positional parameter specifies the qname address, rname address, control type indicator (only for ENQ; E for exclusive, S for shared), rname length (optional, if omitted the assembled length of rname is used), and scope (STEP, SYSTEM, or SYSTEMS). The keyword RET is optional and indicates if the request is conditional or unconditional and if the resource is available (ENQ only). Multiple resouces may be specified on a single ENQ/DEQ macro instruction by coding the set of positional sub-parameters for each resource in a string separated by commas and enclosed in parentheses. However, the RET parameter pertains to all the specified resources.

The qname and rname address may be specified as a label or as a register, enclosed in parentheses, containing the address of the virtual storage location that contains the name. The length of the qname must be 8 characters and the length of the rname may be from 1 to 255 characters.

A scope of STEP indicates a local resource and means that serialization is only for the address space (among parent tasks and subtasks). A scope of SYSTEM indicates a global resource, which includes all address spaces controlled by a single operating system. A scope of SYSTEMS indicates a global resource, which includes all address spaces controlled by multiple operating systems. A specification of SYSTEMS requires that the IBM program product Global Resource Serialization (GRS) or similar product be installed to handle the serialization across operating systems.

The values and their meaning for the RET parameter for the ENQ macro instruction are the following:

`CHNG`	Change the control type of the specified resource from shared to exclusive.
`HAVE`	Assign control of the resource only if a request has not been made previously by the same task. This is a conditional request.

TEST	Test the availability of the resource, but do not assign control of it.
USE	Assign control of the resource only if it is immediately available. This is a conditional request.
NONE	The default. Requests unconditional control of the specified resource. If it is not available, the task is put into a wait state until the resource becomes available. No return code is provided if RET=NONE is specified or defaulted.

The values and their meaning for the RET parameter for the DEQ macro instruction are the following:

HAVE	Release the specified resources only if they are assigned to the requesting task.
NONE	The default. Requests unconditional release of the specified resources. The requesting task is ABENDed if control of any of the specified resources was not assigned to it. No return code is provided if RET=NONE is specified or defaulted.

When the ENQ and the DEQ macro instructions return control to the issuing program, a return code is provided for each resource request only if the RET parameter was specified. If RET was not specified, then when (or if) control is returned to the issuing program, it may assume that the ENQ/DEQ was successful. If the return code is 0 for all the requests, then register 15 contains 0. If any of the return codes are not 0, then register 15 contains the address of a virtual storage area that contains the list of return codes. Part of the ENQ/DEQ expansion is a parameter-list that describes the specified resources. A 12-byte entry is built in the parameter-list for each specified resource in the sequence specified. The return code is placed in the third byte of each entry. If register 15 does not contain 0, then it points to the first 12-byte entry of the parameter-list. Table 4.10.2 contains a list of the return codes and their meanings.

Table 4.10.2

This table contains the return codes issued by the ENQ and DEQ macro instructions if the RET parameter was specified.

The following return codes are issued by the ENQ macro instruction:

Return Code (Hex)	Meaning
00	CHNG: The control type of the specified resource has been changed to exclusive. HAVE: Control of the specified resource has been assigned to the requesting task. TEST: The specified resource is immediately available. USE: Control of the specified resource has been assigned to the requesting task.
04	CHNG: The status of the specified resource cannot be changed to exclusive. HAVE: The specified resource is not immediately available. TEST: The specified resource is not immediately available.

(Table 4.10.2, continued)

Return Code (Hex)	Meaning
08	CHNG: The requesting task does not have control over the specified resource, and the specified resource is available. USE: The specified resource is not immediately available HAVE: The requesting task has made a previous request for control of the specified resource and has control of it. TEST: Same as HAVE. USE: Same as HAVE.
14	CHNG: Not applicable. HAVE: The requesting task has made a previous request for control of the specified resource, and the task does not have control of the resource. TEST: Same as HAVE. USE: Same as HAVE.
18	CHNG: Not applicable. HAVE: The limit for the number of concurrent resource requests has been reached. TEST: Not applicable. USE: Same as HAVE.

The following return codes are issued by the DEQ macro instruction:

Return Code (Hex)	Meaning
00	The resource has been released.
04	Control of the resource has been requested by the task, but the task has not been assigned control and remains in the wait state. This return code would normally not occur unless DEQ is issued in an exit routine that received control due to an interruption.
08	The requesting task does not have control of the specified resource.

Coding Example 4.10.1

This coding example illustrates how to code the ENQ macro instruction. In this example, The program requests conditional exclusive global control of the resource represented by the queue name EMPINFO and resource name DEPT850. If the resource is available, then an update is performed. If the resource is not available, then other processing is done and the update is tried again later.

```
         BAL   R6,UPDATE        UPDATE EMPLY INFO FILE
         ...
UPDATE   BAL   R7,DOENQ         DO ENQ BEFORE UPDATE
         LTR   R15,R15          CHK IF IN CONTROL OF RESOURCE
```

```
         BZ     DOUPDT            IF YES, DO UPDATE
         MVI    NOUPDTSW,C'1'     IF NO, INDICATE IT
         BR     R6                RET TO CALLING RTN, TRY UPDATE LATER
DOUPDT   MVI    NOUPDTSW,C'0'     INDICATE UPDATE WILL BE DONE
         ...                      DO UPDATE
         BAL    R7,DODEQ          DO DEQ AFTER UPDATE
         BR     R6                RETURN TO CALLING RTN
         ...
DOENQ    ENQ    (QNAME,RNAME,E,,SYSTEMS),RET=USE
         BR     R7                RETURN TO CALLING RTN
         ...
DODEQ    DEQ    (QNAME,RNAME,,SYSTEMS),RET=HAVE
         BR     R7                RETURN TO CALLING RTN
         ...
NOUPDTSW DC     C'0'
QNAME    DC     CL8'EMPINFO'
RNAME    DC     C'DEPT850'
```

Coding Example 4.10.2

This coding example illustrates how to code the ENQ macro instruction. In this example, the issuing task tests the availability of two resources. If resource-1 is under the shared control or under no control of the other tasks in the same address space as the issuing task and if resource-2 is under no control of any of the other tasks of the same address space, then ENQ issues a return code of 0.

```
         ENQ    (QNAME1,RNAME1,S,,STEP,QNAME2,RNAME2,E,,STEP),RET=TEST
         LTR    R15,R15           TEST IF ALL SPEC RSRCS ARE AVAIL
         BZ     RSRCAVAL          YES, ALL SPEC RSRCS ARE AVAIL
         ...
```

4.11 THE WTO MACRO INSTRUCTION

The WTO macro instruction causes a message to be written to one or more operator/system consoles and/or hardopy joblog. The programmer specifies the actual message that is to be written and optionally specifies route and descriptor codes for the message via the ROUTCDE and DESC parameters, respectively.

The operating system supports multiple consoles (MCS). The normal convention is to place the consoles at strategic locations throughout the data center and programming areas. The systems programmer assigns default route codes via SYSGEN (via CONSOLxx member of SYS1.PARMLIB with MVS/XA version 2.2 and MVS/ESA) for the various consoles, consistent with their locations. The operator could change those route codes via the MVS VARY command.

The system compares the route codes specified on the WTO macro instruction to the route codes assigned to the various consoles. If the ROUTCDE parameter is not specified, then the default is all route codes. A console will receive the message only if at least one of its assigned route codes matches at least one of the specified route codes on the WTO macro instruction. Table 4.11.1 contains the list of the route codes with their meanings and intended locations.

The objective of MCS is to send only those messages that are pertinent to the specific locations where the consoles reside. An example would be to locate a console in the tape drive pool area. This console would be assigned route code 3 (see Table 4.11.1), which will cause only tape mount messages to be sent there. The operator assigned to that area would have no need to see the other messages since his/her function is only to mount tapes.

Table 4.11.1

This table lists the WTO/WTOR route codes with their meanings.

1—Master Console, Action	9—System Security
2—Master Console, Information	10—System Error/ Maintenance
3—Tape Drive Pool	11—Programmer Information
4—DASD Pool	12—Emulators
5—Tape Library	13—Reserved for Data Center use
6—DASD Library	14—Reserved for Data Center use
7—Printer Pool	15—Reserved for Data Center use
8—Teleprocessing Control	16—Reserved for future IBM use

As can be seen from Table 4.11.1, most of the route codes are used by MVS. The route codes that would normally be used by programmers are 2 and 11. Route code 2 would be used if the programmer needed to send a message to the master console operator. If the message was only for the programmer's use, then route code 11 should be used. This would cause the message to be displayed only on the programmer's job listing (if route code 11 was not assigned to any consoles). If messages are required to be sent to a location not covered by Table 4.11.1, such as the Help Desk or the Production Control area, then route codes 13, 14, or 15 could be assigned by the Data Center for that purpose.

There are also 16 descriptor codes. They are normally used by MVS and have little use for programmers. However, the DESC parameter could be used to highlight an important message. If the IBM color defaults are being used, then descriptor codes 1 and 11 will be displayed in red and descriptor code 2 will be displayed in white. Descriptor codes 1 and 2 are for authorized programs only and will be changed to descriptor code 7 if an unauthorized program specified them, but descriptor 11 could be used by an unauthorized program. Messages with descriptor 11 will not roll off the console screen automatically; they must be explicitly deleted by the operator. In view of the characteristics of specifying DESC=11 for a message, prudence and consideration should be exercised when planning to use it.

The following coding example shows how to use the WTO macro instruction to display an important message to the master console operator:

```
         WTO   '*** JOB PRODXYZ ABENDING, NOTIFY PRODUCTION CONTROL -
               IMMEDIATELY ***',ROUTCDE=2,DESC=11
```

The WTO macro instruction has no facility for changing sections of the message dynamically (the list and execute forms of WTO can be used to change the entire message). This facility would be useful for displaying messages that contain a fixed section and a variable section. With this facility, the variable section may be changed from execution to execution and/or multiple times during one execution of the program.

This facility could be provided by coding the actual WTO expansion and assigning labels for the sections of the message that are required to be changed. Then, via the MVC instruction, those areas could be dynamically changed, as required, by referencing the corresponding labels. After the appropriate changes are made, then the message could be displayed by using the execute form of the WTO macro instruction and pointing it to the programmer-supplied WTO expansion.

Coding Example 4.11.1

This coding example illustrates how to dynamically change sections of a WTO message before displaying it. In this example, the WTO message is modified to display a user-provided volser, as well as the corresponding unit address where the volume is mounted.

```
          BAL    R6,GETVSER              OBTAIN VOLSER FROM USER
          BAL    R6,SCANUCBS             SCAN UCB TABLE FOR VOLSER
          BAL    R6,GETUADR              GET CORRESPONDING UNIT ADR
          BAL    R6,DPLYINFO             MODIFY AND DSPLY WTO MSG
          ...
DPLYINFO  MVC    W1VOLSER,VOLSER         MOVE VOLSER INTO WTO MSG
          MVC    W1UNADR,UNITADR         MOVE UNIT ADR INTO WTO MSG
          LA     R1,WTOLST1              SET R1 TO POINT TO WTO LIST
          WTO    MF=(E,(R1))             ISSUE EXEC FORM OF WTO
          BR     R6                      RETURN TO CALLING RTN
          ...
          CNOP   0,4
WTOLST1   DC     AL2(WTOLST1X-WTOLST1)
          DC     H'0'
          DC     C'VOLSER '
W1VOLSER  DS     CL6
          DC     C' IS MOUNTED ON '
W1UNADR   DS     CL3
WTOLST1X  EQU    *
```

NOTES:

- The UCB table can be scanned (in MVS/XA and MVS/ESA) with the IBM-provided program IOSVSUCB. The entry point is contained in the field CVTUCBSC of the CVT.

If DESC and ROUTCDE values are not specified, then the default values are used. The default values for DESC and ROUTCDE are DESC=7 and all route codes, respectively. The default value for DESC may be acceptable in most situations, but a specification of all route codes may not be desired.

If the default values of DESC and/or ROUTCDE are required to be changed, then the WTO-list needs to be modified. The second halfword is changed to X'8000' to indicate that the DESC and ROUTECDE values are specified, respectively, as 2-byte fields, after the message. The WTO-list count field contained in the first two bytes of the list does not include the lengths of the DESC and ROUTCDE fields. The bit numbers that are turned on indicate the DESC/ROUTCDE values. For example, if bit-1 and bit-2 (note: in this case, the bits are numbered from 1 to 16, left to right) are set to 1 for the ROUTCDE field, then that indicates ROUTCDE = (1,2). Coding example 4.11.2 illustrates the required code for the modified WTO-list.

Coding Example 4.11.2

This coding example illustrates the required WTO-list to include DESC and ROUTCDE values.

```
          CNOP   0,4
WTO1LST   DC     AL2(WTO1LSTX-WTO1LST)
          DC     X'8000'            INDICATE DESC/ROUTCDE INCLUDED
          DC     C'***ACTUAL MESSAGE***'
WTO1LSTX  EQU    *
```

```
         DC    X'0000'                 DESC DEFAULT
         DC    X'0020'                 ROUTCDE=11
```

4.12 THE WTOR MACRO INSTRUCTION

The WTOR macro instruction causes a message that requires a reply, to be written to one or more operator/system consoles. The programmer specifies four positional parameters to contain, in the following sequence, the actual message that is to be written, the address of the reply area that the system is to use to store the reply, the length of the reply, and the address of the ECB that is to be posted when the reply is issued. The optional ROUTCDE follows the positional parameters.

The route codes are used in the same way as indicated in the discussion of the WTO macro instruction above. The WTOR macro instruction assigns a descriptor code of 7 and ignores any specified ones.

When the program issues the WTOR macro instruction to obtain information from the operator, it may optionally go into a wait state until a reply is issued by issuing a WAIT macro instruction for the specified ECB or it may periodically check the ECB for completion via the TM machine instruction while it performs other processing. The program could also be coded to contain additional sophisticated logic to go into a wait state for a predetermined amount of time and then check the ECB for completion. If a reply has not been received yet, the program could then issue a warning or reminder message to the operator via the WTO macro instruction and then go into a wait state again for a predetermined amount of time. The end of this section contains coding examples showing all three methods.

The ECB must be set to binary zeros before it is used or reused for a WTOR macro instruction (or any other macro instruction that uses an ECB). This is because the value of the first two bits are changed when the ECB is posted. If the WAIT macro instruction is used with an ECB that already has been posted, then the WAIT will indicate that the event has completed, which in this case means that the operator replied to the WTOR and the WAIT will pass control to the following instruction. This instruction will probably check the reply. Since the reply was not issued yet, the reply area will probably be initialized to contain what appears to be an invalid reply (or contain the previous reply, which may have been invalid). The code of the routine will probably issue a WTO macro instruction indicating that the reply was invalid and then reissue the WTOR macro instruction. Since the CPU and the display console function much faster than the operator can type, a WTO/WTOR loop will occur, flooding the operator/system console display unit until the operator is finally able to respond with the correct reply. This is why it is important to clear the ECB each time before it is used.

The WTOR macro instruction could also be used to enable the operator to communicate with a program and, when required, to dynamically pass parameters, commands, and so on. This can be done by issuing a WTOR macro instruction at the beginning of the execution of the program and allow it to be outstanding until the operator has a requirement, if ever, to communicate with the program. In the meantime, the program executes and periodically checks the ECB to determine if the operator has communicated with the program. However, a better technique would be via the MVS MODIFY and STOP commands as described in Chapter 5. This technique does not require that a WTOR macro instruction be outstanding for the life of the program, but does require that the program be initiated via the MVS START command and requires additional coding to set up the environment to accept those commands; however, this is the better, more professional way of satisfying such a requirement.

If the information-requesting message requires multiple lines, then only the last line should be written with the WTOR macro instruction. The preceding lines of the message should be written with the WTO macro instruction.

Coding Example 4.12.1

This coding example illustrates how to issue a WTOR macro instruction to request information required before the program can continue to execute and how to wait for the reply via the WAIT macro instruction.

```
WTORO1    XC      ECB01,ECB01          CLEAR ECB BEFORE WTOR
          MVC     REPLY01,BLANKS       INIT REPLY AREA TO BLANKS
          WTO     '*** REPLY "F1" FOR FUNCTION-1 PROCESSING;'
          WTO     '*** REPLY "F2" FOR FUNCTION-2 PROCESSING; OR'
          WTOR    '*** REPLY "T" TO TERMINATE PROGRAM',REPLY01,2,ECB01
          WAIT    1,ECB=ECB01          WAIT FOR REPLY
          CLC     REPLY01,=C'F1'       CHK REPLY FOR FUNC-1 PROC
          BE      SETF1                IF YES, IND IT
          CLC     REPLY01,=C'F2'       CHK REPLY FOR FUNC-2 PROC
          BE      SETF2                IF YES, IND IT
          CLC     REPLY01,=C'T         ' CHK REPLY FOR TERMINATION
          BE      SETEND               IF YES, IND IT
          WTO     '*** INVALID REPLY ***'
          B       WTORO1               REISSUE WTOR
SETF1     DS      0H
          ...
          BR      R6                   RETURN TO CALLING RTN
*
SETF2     DS      0H
          ...
          BR      R6                   RETURN TO CALLING RTN
*
SETEND    DS      0H
          ...
          BR      R6                   RETURN TO CALLING RTN
*
ECB01     DS      F
REPLY01   DS      CL2
BLANKS    DC      CL2' '
```

Coding Example 4.12.2

This coding example shows how to issue a WTOR macro instruction that requests information that is either optional or not immediately required, and how to check for the reply periodically via the TM machine instruction while execution continues.

```
          BAL     R6,WTORO2            ISSUE OUTSTANDING WTOR
CONTIN    BAL     R6,PROCESS           PROCESS A UNIT OR WORK
          BAL     R6,TESTWRO2          CHECK IF WTOR HAS REPLY
          B       CONTIN               CONTINUE PROCESSING
*
WTORO2    XC      ECB02,ECB02          CLEAR ECB FOR WTOR
          L       R10,=A(L'REPLY02)    LOAD REPLY LEN IN R10 FOR WTOR
          WTOR    '*** REPLY "S" FOR ORDERLY SHUTDOWN ***',REPLY02,(R10), -
                  ECB02
          BR      R6                   RETURN TO CALLING RTN
*
PROCESS   CLI     SDSW,C'1'            CHECK IF SHUTDOWN REQUESTED
          BE      SHUTDOWN             IF YES, GO TO SHUTDOWN RTN
```

```
         ...                          IF NO, PERFORM NORMAL PROCESSING
         BR     R6                    RETURN TO CALLING RTN
*
SHUTDOWN DS     0H
         ...                            PERFORM SHUTDOWN PROCESSING
*
TESTWR02 TM     ECB02,X'40'           CHECK IF WTOR ECB POSTED
         BO     CHKREPLY              IF YES, CHECK REPLY
         BR     R6                    IF NO, RETURN TO CALLING RTN
CHKREPLY CLI    REPLY02,C'S'          CHK IF SHUTDOWN REQ
         BE     SETSD                 IF YES, IND IT
         CLI    REPLY02,X'A2'         CHECK FOR LOWER CASE "S'
         BE     SETSD                 IF YES, IND IT
         WTO    '*** INVALID REPLY ***'
         ST     R6,SAVR6              SAVE RETURN ADDRESS
         BAL    R6,WTOR02             REISSUE WTOR
         L      R6,SAVR6              RESTORE RETURN ADDRESS
         BR     R6                    RETURN TO CALLING RTN
SETSD    MVI    SDSW,C'1'             INDICATE SHUTDOWN REQUESTED
         BR     R6                    RETURN TO CALLING RTN
*
ECB02    DS     F
SAVR6    DS     F
REPLY02  DS     CL1
SDSW     DC     C'0'
```

Coding Example 4.12.3

This coding example shows how to issue a WTOR macro instruction that requests information that is required before an important program can continue to execute, as well as how to remind the operator, via a WTO macro instruction, that the reply has not yet been issued after a predetermined amount of time has elapsed.

```
WTOR03   XC     ECB03,ECB03         CLEAR ECB FOR WTOR
         WTO    '*** ERRORS DETECTED IN PARAMETERS FOR JOB jjjjjjjj ***'
         WTO    '*** SHOULD PROCESSING CONTINUE WITH DEFAULTS ... ***'
         WTOR   '*** REPLY "Y" FOR YES, OR "T" TO TERMINATE JOB ***', -
                REPLY03,1,ECB03
SETWAIT  STIMER WAIT,DINTVL=WR3WTTME
         TM     ECB03,X'40'         CHECK IF ECB POSTED
         BO     CHKREPLY            IF YES, CHECK REPLY
         WTO    '*** OPERATOR, PLEASE REPLY TO OUTSTANDING MESSAGE FOR J-
                OB: xxxxxxxx ***',DESC=11
         B      SETWAIT             REISSUE WAIT
CHKREPLY CLI    REPLY03,C'Y'        CHK IF DEFAULT REQ
         BE     SETDFLT             IF YES, IND IT
         CLI    REPLY03,C'T'        CHK IF TERMINATION REQ
         BE     SETTERM             IF YES, IND IT
         WTO    '*** INVALID REPLY ***'
         B      WTOR03              REISSUE WTOR
SETDFLT  MVI    DFLTSW,C'1'         IND DEFAULT USAGE
         BR     R6                  RETURN TO CALLING RTN
SETTERM  MVI    TERMSW,C'1'         IND TERMINATION
         BR     R6                  RTCT
         ...
ECB03    DS     F
REPLY03  DS     CL1
DFLTSW   DC     C'0'
TERMSW   DC     C'0'
         DS     0D
WR3WTTME DC     C'00001500'         15 SECONDS WAIT TIME
```

NOTES:

- The jobname (xxxxxxxx) may be hardcoded if it is never expected to change. It may also be obtained via the EXTRACT macro instruction (from the TIOT), which is the better method. The jobname can then be inserted into the WTO message, using the technique described in the section of this chapter that discusses the WTO macro instruction.
- The programmer also has the option of deleting the outstanding WTOR message, using the DOM macro instruction and reissuing the WTOR after displaying the reminder message. However, this method is impractical because it causes the operating system to provide a different reply id number for the message, causing confusion and additional work if the operator was in the process of replying to the message.

4.13 THE GETMAIN AND FREEMAIN MACRO INSTRUCTIONS

The GETMAIN macro instruction is used to request the operating system to allocate one or more areas of virtual storage to the task that issued the macro instruction. The storage is allocated from the specified subpool and is aligned on a fullword or page boundary. If the subpool is located within the tasks address space, then it is cleared to binary zeros for the initial allocation. Any subsequent allocation via GETMAIN of the same virtual storage area (after an intervening FREEMAIN of that storage area) will not be cleared. If the allocated storage is located in the common area (this technique is discussed in Chapter 13), then the area is always cleared to binary zeros.

The FREEMAIN macro instruction is used to request the operating system to release one or more areas of virtual storage or an entire subpool that were allocated by a previous GETMAIN macro instruction issued from the same task.

The GETMAIN macro instruction provides a number of ways of requesting virtual storage, and each way may be requested as conditional (C) or unconditional (U). The various ways are are as follows:

`Element` EC or EU requests a single area of virtual storage. The length is specified by the LV parameter, and the address of the allocated virtual storage is returned at the address specified by the A parameter.

`List` LC or LU requests one or more areas of virtual storage. The length of each request is contained in one of the entries of a list of fullwords pointed to by the LA parameter. The address of each allocated virtual storage area is returned in the same relative entry of another list of fullwords pointed to by the A parameter. The end of the list, pointed to by the LA parameter, is indicated by setting the high order bit of the last address to one.

`Variable` VC or VU requests a single area of virtual storage whose length is between two values. The two values are contained in consecutive fullwords pointed to by the LA parameter. The operating system will attempt to allocate the largest area of contiguous virtual storage within the range of the values specified. The address and the actual length of the allocated virtual storage is returned in the two consecutive fullwords, respectively, pointed to by the A parameter.

`Register` — RC, RU, or R (unconditional) requests a single area of virtual storage. The length is specified by the LV parameter, and the address of the allocated virtual storage is returned in register 1. This version of the GETMAIN macro instruction may be used to obtain virtual storage for a reentrant program. (Reentrant programs are discussed in Chapter 5.)

`Variable Register` — VRC or VRU requests a single area of virtual storage, whose length is between two values, similar to the VC/VU specification. The maximum and minimum lengths are specified by the LV parameter as consecutive lengths, respectively, separated by a comma and enclosed within parentheses. The address of the allocated storage is returned in register 1, and the actual length allocated is returned in register 0. This version of the GETMAIN macro instruction may be used to obtain virtual storage for a reentrant program.

The length value of the LV parameter may be specified as either an EQU symbol or a decimal number, or as a register, enclosed within parentheses, containing the length. The address specified by the A and LA parameters may be specified as the name (A-type address) associated with the area or as a register, enclosed in parentheses, containing the address.

The subpool number, from which the virtual storage is to be allocated, may be specified with the SP parameter as an EQU symbol, or a decimal number, or as a register, enclosed within parentheses, containing the subpool number. Subpool numbers of 0 to 127 may be specified by non-authorized programs. If the subpool number is not specified, then the default is zero.

The programmer may also specify that the allocated virtual storage be aligned on a doubleword or a page boundary via the BNDRY=DBLWD (default) and BNDRY=PAGE parameters, respectively.

Upon return from GETMAIN and FREEMAIN, if a conditional request was made, then register 15 is set to 0 if the request was succsessful and to 4 if the request was not successful. If the request was unconditional, then a system ABEND occurs if the request was unsuccessful.

Coding Example 4.13.1

This coding example illustrates how to conditionally request 2000 bytes of virtual storage from subpool 0.

```
         GETMAIN  EC,LV=2000,A=VSADR
         LTR      R15,R15          CHK IF GM ALLO OK
         BNZ      GMERR
         L        R10,VSAD         LOAD VS ADR INTO REG 10 (TO USE IT)
         BR       R6               RETURN TO CALLING RTN
         ...
VSADR    DS       F
```

Coding Example 4.13.2

This coding example illustrates how to unconditionally request three areas of virtual storage of lengths of 1,000, 5,000, and 2,000 bytes from subpool 10, with one GETMAIN macro instruction.

```
            GETMAIN   LU,LA=GMLENS,A=GMADRS,SP=10
            ...
GMLENS      DS        0F
GMLEN1      DC        A(1000)
GMLEN2      DC        A(5000)
GMLEN3      DC        X'80'
            DC        AL3(2000)
*
GMADRS      DS        0F
GMADR1      DS        F
GMADR2      DS        F
GMADR3      DS        F
```

Coding Example 4.13.3

This coding example illustrates how to conditionally request a virtual storage area with a length of at least 4,096 bytes, but no more than 16,384 bytes.

```
GETVS       GETMAIN   VC,LA=GMREQLEN,A=GMRESP
            LTR       R15,R15      CHECK IF VS OBTAINED
            BZR       R6           IF YES, RET TO CALLING RTN
            B         NOVS         IF NO, VS NOT AVAILABLE
            ...
GMREQLEN    DS        0F
GMMIN       DC        A(4096)      MINIMUM STOR REQUESTED
GMMAX       DC        A(16384)     MAXIMUM STOR REQUESTED
*
GMRESP      DS        0F
GMVADR      DS        F            RETURNED ADR OF ALLO STOR
GMVLEN      DS        F            RETURNED LEN OF ALLO STOR
```

Coding Example 4.13.4

This coding example illustrates how to conditionally request 4,096 bytes of virtual storage from subpool 25 for a workarea for a reentrant program.

```
            LA        R10,25       LOAD SP NUMBER INTO R10
            GETMAIN   RC,LV=4096,SP=(R10)
            LTR       R15,R15      CHECK IF VS OBTAINED
            ...
```

Coding Example 4.13.5

This coding example illustrates how to conditionally release the virtual storage obtained in Coding Example 4.13.1

```
            FREEMAIN  EC,LV=2000,A=VSADR
            LTR       R15,R15      CHECK IF VS RELEASED
              ...
```

Coding Example 4.13.6

This coding example illustrates how to unconditionally release the second virtual storage area obtained in Coding Example 4.13.2

```
            L         R10,GMLEN2
            LA        R11,GMADR2
            FREEMAIN  EU,LV=(R10),A=(R11),SP=10
```

Coding Example 4.13.7

This coding example illustrates how to conditionally release the last area of virtual storage obtained in Coding Example 4.13.2 and the virtual storage area obtained in Coding Example 4.13.3.

```
         MVC      FMLEN1,GMLEN3     MOVE LEN OF 1ST VS AREA
         NI       FMLEN1,X'7F'      TURN OFF HI ORDER BIT
         MVC      FMADR1,GMADR3     MOVE ADR OF 1ST VS AREA
         MVC      FMLEN2,GMVLEN     MOVE LEN OF 2ND VS AREA
         OI       FMLEN2,X'80'      TURN ON HI ORDER BIT
         MVC      FMADR2,GMVADR     MOVE ADR OF 2ND VS AREA
         FREEMAIN LC,LA=FMLENS,A=FMADRS
         LTR      R15,R15           CHECK FOR GOOD FREEMAIN
         ...
FMLENS   DS       0F
FMLEN1   DS       F                 LEN OF STOR AREA-1
FMLEN2   DS       F                 LEN OF STOR AREA-2
*
FMADRS   DS       0F
FMADR1   DS       F                 ADR OF STOR AREA-1
FMADR2   DS       F                 ADR OF STOR AREA-2
```

Coding Example 4.13.8

This coding example illustrates how to conditionally release all of the virtual storage allocated from subpool 25 by a previous GETMAIN macro instruction.

```
         FREEMAIN RC,SP=25
         LTR      R15,R15
         ...
```

4.14 THE STIMER MACRO INSTRUCTION

The STIMER macro instruction is used to set a program (24-hour) timer. The timer may be set to a specific time of day interval or to a specific time quantity that starts to elapse after the macro instruction completes exucution.

The time interval may be measured in real time (specified by REAL or WAIT) or task time (specified by TASK). Real time means that the timer runs continuously whether the task is active or not. Task time means that the timer runs only when the task is active. If real time is specified, then the task has the option of either being active or being put into a wait.

An optional exit routine address may be specified (only for REAL or TASK) to receive control, asynchronously, when the timer interval is satisfied. If an exit routine address is not specified, then no indication is provided that the timer interval was satisfied. If the task elects to be in an STIMER wait state while the timer is running, then the instruction following the STIMER macro instuction will receive control when the timer interval is satisfied.

The time interval may be specified in a number of different formats. If time of day is specified, then local (TOD) or Greenwich mean time (GMT) may be specified. If a time quantity is specified, then it may be specified in binary (BINTVL), decimal (DINTVL), microseconds (MICVL), or CPU timer units (TUINTVL).

For the TOD, GMT, and DINTVL parameters, the value is the address of a doubleword on a doubleword boundary that contains the time in zoned decimal digits in the following format.

HHMMSSth, where:
HH is hours (24-hour clock)
MM is minutes
SS is seconds
th is tenths and hundredths of a second

For the BINTVL and TUINTVL parameters, the value is the address of a fullword on a fullword boundary that contains an unsigned 32-bit binary number. For BINTVL, the low order bit has a value of 0.01 seconds. For TUINTVL, the low order bit has a value of one timer unit (approximately 26.04166 microseconds).

The value of the MICVL parameter is the address of a doubleword on a doubleword boundary that contains an unsigned 64-bit binary number. Only bits 0 through 51 are significant, and the value of bit 51 is one microsecond.

Coding Example 4.14.1

This coding example illustrates how to code the STIMER macro instruction to put the issuing task into a wait state for 7 minutes and 30 seconds. When the wait interval is complete, the issuing program receives control at the instruction following the STIMER marco instruction.

```
         STIMER   WAIT,DECINTVL=WAITTIME
         ...
         ...      *** CODE TO RECEIVE CONTROL AFTER STIMER WAIT ***
         ...
         DS       0D
WAITTIME DC       C'00073000'    7 MINS, 30 SECS
```

For the REAL and TASK timer options, an exit routine may be provided by specifying its address as the second positional operand. If an exit routine address is provided, it receives control asynchronously to the issuing task when the specified time interval expires. The exit routine must establish addressability and save and restore the registers.

When the exit routine receives control, the contents of the registers are as follows:

Register 0	Information used by operating system.
Register 1	Information used by operating system.
Register 13	Address of savearea provided by operating system.
Register 14	Return address (to operating system).
Register 15	Address of exit routine entry point.

The contents of registers 2 through 12 do not contain any significant information for the exit, but should be saved and restored.

Since the exit routine must provide its own addressability and since the operating system provides no facility for passing any parameters to the exit routine, then there appears to be no direct way for the main program (the one that issued the STIMER macro instruction) to communicate with the exit routine, if required. If the exit routine is coded in the same CSECT as the main program, the exit routine still cannot reference the areas in the program using the same labels since the addressability will be different. This is easily explained. The storage areas of the main program are addressed by the base registers established by the program plus the displacement of the storage area into the program from the appropriate base register. When the exit routine receives control, the contents of those base registers have been destroyed. Some programmers elect to use register 15 to establish addressability since it containes the entry point of the exit routine. This is fine if the exit is a self-contained CSECT (or load module) has no requirements to communicate with the main program, does no I/O, and does not use most other MVS services.

The main program and exit routine could communicate via a shared DASD dataset or via a virtual storage area located in the CSA, but this may be impractical. There is, however, a technical trick that could be used to enable the main program and the exit routine to reference the same storage areas with the same labels if the exit routine is coded in the same CSECT as the main program.

The following describes this technique:

- Place the code for the exit routine after the code that initializes the main program.
- Supply a label for the first instruction that is addressed by the first base register. This would usually be the instruction that follows the BALR instruction.
- Code an EQU instruction with the operand defined as the difference between the addresses of the exit routine and the first instruction that is addressed by the first base register. The difference must be less than 4096. To ensure this, the exit routine is placed after the program initialization.
- At the beginning of the exit routine, restore the values of the base registers, as set by the main program, by using the address contained in register 15 and the EQU value.

Coding Example 4.14.2 illustrates this technique.

Coding Example 4.14.2

This coding example illustrates how to provide addressability for the STIMER exit routine such that it could reference the storage areas defined in the main program, using the same labels.

```
MAINPGM  CSECT
R0       EQU    0
         ...
R15      EQU    15
         STM    R14,R12,12(R13)   SAVE REGS INTO CALLERS SA
         BALR   R3,0              LOAD 1ST BASE REGISTER
         USING  *,R3,R4           ASSIGN R3 AND R4 AS BASE REGS
BASEBG   LA     R4,4095           LOAD 2ND
         LA     R4,1(R3,R4)       BASE REGISTER
         ...
         ...    *** CODE FOR SA LINKAGE ***
         ...
         B      MAINCODE          BRANCH TO MAIN PROGRAM
*
XOFFSET  EQU    EXITRTN-BASEBG    OFFSET BETW 1ST BASE REG ADR AND EXIT
*
EXITRTN  STM    R14,R12,12(R13)   SAVE REGS IN SYS PROV SA
         LR     R3,R15            LD MAIN PGM BASE REG WITH EXIT EPA
         LA     R15,XOFFSET       LD OFFSET OF EXIT FROM MAIN PGM BASE
         SR     R3,R15            LD 1ST BASE REG TO ADR SET BY MAIN PGM
         LA     R4,4095           LOAD 2ND BASE REG TO ADR SET
         LA     R4,1(R3,R4)       BY THE MAIN PGM
         LR     R12,R13           SAVE ADR OF SYS PROV SA
         LA     R13,EXITSA        LOAD ADR OF EXIT SA
         ST     R12,4(0,R13)      SAVE SYS PROV SA ADR IN OWN SA
         ST     R13,8(0,R12)      SAVE OWN SA ADR IN SYS PROV SA
         ...
         ...    *** CODE FOR EXIT ROUTINE ***
         ...
         MVI    EXITSW,C'1'       SET SW TO IND TIME INTV EXPIRED
```

```
         ...
         ...
         L       R13,4(0,R13)       RESTORE SYS PROV SA ADR
         LM      R14,R12,12(R13)    RESTORE REGISTERS
         BR      R14                RETURN TO MVS
EXITSA   DS      18F
*
MAINCODE ...     *** CODE FOR MAIN PROGRAM ***
         ...
         STIMER  TASK,EXITRTN,DINTVL=TIME01
         ...
         ...     *** CODE FOR MAIN PROGRAM ***
         ...
         CLI     EXITSW,C'1'        CHK IF TIME INTV EXPIRED
         BE      TIMEEND
         ...
*
TIME01   DC      C'00100000'        TASK TIME INTERVAL - 10 MINUTES
EXITSW   DC      C'0'               SW FOR TIME INTV EXPIRATION
*
         END
```

NOTES:

- The code in the exit routine and the code in the main program could reference the same storage areas using the same labels. This will enable the exit routine to set an indicator that the main program could test.

4.15 THE TTIMER MACRO INSTRUCTION

The TTIMER macro instruction is used to test the time interval previously set by an STIMER macro instruction issued by the same task.

If the time interval has not been set or has already expired, then binary zeros are returned.

If the time interval has not expired, then the amount of time remaining in the time interval is returned. The time remaining is returned in the specified units. The programmer may specify CPU timer units (TU) or microseconds (MIC). TU and MIC have the same meaning as in the STIMER macro instruction. If TU is specified, then the remaining time is returned in register 0. If MIC is specified, then the remaining time is returned in the specified doubleword, which is aligned on a doubleword. The units are specified as the second positional parameter. The doubleword for MIC is specified as the third positional parameter.

If the time interval returned is required to be in hours, minutes, and seconds, then the MIC option should be specified. The high order four bytes of the doubleword returned by TTIMER contains the number of whole seconds in binary and the low order four bytes contains the fractional part of a second in binary. The conversion into seconds (dropping the fraction) requires that the binary value contained in the high order four bytes be multiplied by 1024^2 and that number be divided by 1,000,000. Coding Example 4.15.1 shows the required code for the conversion.

The TTIMER macro instruction may also be used to cancel any remaining time interval if CANCEL is specified as the first positional parameter. When CANCEL is specified, the time that was remaining is still returned as defined by the units (TU or MIC) specified. The CANCEL option has no effect if WAIT was specified on the STIMER macro instruction.

Coding Example 4.15.1

This coding example illustrates how to convert the time remaining in MIC units, returned from the TTIMER macro instruction, into seconds. The answer will be contained in register 9 as a binary number. The number could be converted into packed decimal format via the CVD instruction. Converting the seconds into hours, minutes, and seconds and putting it into the same format as the DINTVL specification of the STIMER macro instruction is left as an exercise for the reader.

```
          STIMER TASK,EXITRTN,DINTVL=TIMEINTV
          ...
          TTIMER ,MIC,TIMELEFT
          LA     R8,0           CLEAR R8 FOR MR INSTR
          L      R9,TIMELEFT    EXTRACT HI-ORDER 4 BYTES
          L      R10,ONEMEG     LD R10 WITH 1024 X 1024 FOR DR INSTR
          MR     R8,R10         HI-ORDER 4 BYTES VALUE X 1024 X 1024
          L      R10,ONEMIL     LD R10 WITH 1 MILLION FOR DR INSTR
          DR     R8,R10         DIV BY 1 MILLION TO GET SECONDS
          CVD    R9,PKSECS      CONV BIN SECS INTO PACK SECS
          ...
TIMELEFT  DS     D
ONEMEG    DC     X'00100000'    1024 X 1024
ONEMIL    DC     A(1000000)     1,000,000
PKSECS    DS     D
```

Coding Example 4.15.2

This coding example illustrates how to use the STIMER and TTIMER macro instructions to accomplish the following requirement.

Data is being received from a group of terminals. The data is validated, edited, and written to a DASD dataset for processing. A job must be submitted by 6 P.M. to process that data. If all the data is received before 6 P.M., then the job may be submitted then. The routine DATAEND receives control when all the data is received and processed. If data is still being received at 6 P.M., then the file must be closed, additional data written to another file to be processed tomorrow, and the job submitted.

```
          STIMER REAL,EXITRTN,TOD=JOBTIME
          ...
NEXTDATA  BAL    R6,GETDATA     RECEIVE DATA
          BAL    R6,VALIDATE    VALIDATE DATA
          BAL    R6,EDIT        EDIT DATA
          BAL    R6,PUTFILE     WRITE RECS TO ACTIVE FILE
          BAL    R6,CHKTIME     CHECK IF TIME TO SUBMIT JOB
          B      NEXTDATA       PROCESS NEXT GROUP OF DATA
*
DATAEND   TTIMER CANCEL         ALL DATA PROC, CANCEL TIME EXIT
          BAL    R7,CLOSE       CLOSE FILES
          BAL    R7,SUBMIT      SUBMIT JOB
          ...
CHKTIME   CLI    TIMESW,C'1'    CHK IF TIME EXIT ENTERED
          BNER   R6             IF NO, CONTIN PROC
          BAL    R7,FLIPFILE    IF YES, FLIP FLOP OUTPUT FILES
          BAL    R7,SUBMIT      SUBMIT JOB
          ...
*
EXITRTN   ...                   INITIALIZE AS C.E. 4.14.2
          MVI    TIMESW,C'1'    INDICATE THAT TIME EXIT ENTERED
          ...
          BR     R14            RETURN TO MVS
          ...
```

```
TIMESW      DC      C'0'
JOBTIME     DC      C'18000000'        TOD - 6:00 PM
```

Coding Example 4.15.3

This coding example illustrates how to use the STIMER and TTIMER macro instructions to accomplish the following requirement.

Three actions must be performed at certain time intervals while a program is executing. The actions must be performed 10 minutes, 45 minutes, and 1 hour after a certain event completes. The STIMER macro instruction is issued after the event occurs.

```
         BAL     R6,SETTIMER        SET PROGRAM TIMER
CONTIN   BAL     R6,PROCESS         PERFORM SOME PROCESSING
         BAL     R6,CHKTIME         CHK IF A TIME INTV HAS ELAPSED
         B       CONTIN             PERFORM SOME MORE PROCESSING
         ...
SETTIMER STIMER  REAL,DINTVL=TIMEINTV      *** NOTICE, NO EXIT ADR ***
         LA      R10,TIMETBL        LOAD BG ADR OF TIME TBL
         ST      R10,TMTBLPTR       STORE ADR OF 1ST ENTRY
         BR      R6                 RETURN TO CALLING RTN
*
PROCESS  ...
         BR      R6                 RETURN TO CALLING RTN
*
CHKTIME  CLI     TMENDSW,C'1'       CHK IF ALL TIME INTV PROCESSED
         BER     R6                 IF YES, RET TO CALLING RTN
         TTIMER  ,MIC,TIMELEFT      IF NO, GET TIME LEFT
         BAL     R7,CVTOSECS        CONVERT MICROSECS INTO PACKED SECS
         L       R10,TMTBLPTR       LOAD CURRENT TIME TBL ENTRY ADR
         CP      SECSLEFT,0(8,R10)  CHK IF CURRENT TIME INTV ELAPSED
         BNH     DOACTION           IF YES, PERFORM ACTION
         BR      R6                 IF NO, RET TO CALLING RTN
DOACTION BAL     R7,PERFORM         PERFORM TIME DEPENDENT ACTION
         CP      0(8,R10),PACKZERO  CHK IF LAST TIME INTERVAL
         BE      ALLDONE            IF YES, INDICATE IT
         LA      R10,8(0,R10)       IF NO, INCR TO NXT TIME TBL ENT ADR
         ST      R10,TMTBLPTR       STORE NEW TIME TBL ENTRY ADR
         BR      R6                 RETURN TO CALLING RTN
ALLDONE  MVI     TMENDSW,C'1'       INDICATE ALL TIME INTV PROCESSED
         BR      R6                 RETURN TO CALLING RTN
*
CVTOSECS ...     ***                SEE C.E. 4.15.1 ***
         BR      R7                 RETURN TO CALLING RTN
*
PERFORM  ...                        ACTION FOR EACH INTERVAL
         BR      R7                 RETURN TO CALLING RTN
         ...
*
TMENDSW  DC      C'0'
TIMEINTV DC      C'01000000'        1 HOUR TIME INTERVAL FOR STIMER
TIMETBL  DC      PL8'3000'          10 MINUTES ELAPSED (3000 SECS LEFT)
         DC      PL8'900'           45 MINUTES ELAPSED (900 SECS LEFT)
         DC      PL8'0'             1 HOUR ELAPSED (0 SECS LEFT)
TMTBLPTR DS      F
TIMELEFT DS      D
SECSLEFT DS      D                  PACKED SECONDS FROM CVTOSECS RTN
PACKZERO DC      P'0'
```

NOTES:

- This processing could also be accomplished by issuing three STIMER macro instructions with time intervals of 10 minutes, 35 minutes, and 15 minutes, respectively. But, that would require the coding of an exit routine (the system overhead involved in scheduling the asynchronous exit three times) and be less accurate because the time lag (due to issuing the STIMER macro instruction two additional times and due to the system processing other tasks and the relative dispatching priority of the issuing task) is cumulative.

4.16 THE TIME MACRO INSTRUCTION

The TIME macro instruction is used to request the operating system to return the time of day (local or Greenwich mean time) and date. The accuracy of the time returned is dependant upon the accuracy of the time entered by the system operator and on the response time of the system.

The time of day, based on a 24-hour clock, is returned in either register 0 or in an 8-byte storage area in different formats, depending on the specified parameters.

The format of the time may be requested by specifying one of the following codes as the first positional parameter.

`DEC` The time of day is returned in register 0 in the following format. HHMMSSth, where
HH is hours (24-hour clock);
MM is minutes;
SS is seconds; and
th is tenths and hundredths of a second.

`BIN` The time of day is returned in register 0 as an unsigned 32-bit binary number. The low order bit is equivalent to 0.01 seconds.

`TU` The time of day is returned in register 0 as an unsigned 32-bit binary number. The low order bit is equivalent to one timer unit (approximately 26.04166 microseconds).

`MIC` The time of day is returned in microseconds from midnight in the supplied 8-byte area where bit 51 is equivalent to one microsecond. The address of the area is specified as the second positional parameter. The address may be specified as a label (A-type address) or as a register, enclosed within parentheses, and must be specified as a 24-bit address.

The time may be requested to be local time by specifying ZONE=LT or may be requested to be Greenwich mean time by specifying ZONE=GMT. The GMT will not be accurate unless the PARMTZ member (MVS/370 and MVS/XA prior to version 2.2) or the CLOCKxx member (MVS/XA version 2.2 or later and MVS/ESA) of SYS1.PARMLIB is defined properly.

The date is returned in register 1 as packed decimal digits in the following format.

00YYDDDF, where:
00 is as is;
YY is the last two digits of the year;
DDD is the day of the year starting with 001; and
F is as is, and is the sign of the packed decimal number.

Coding Example 4.16.1

This coding example illustrates how to code the TIME macro instruction to request that the time of day be returned in register 0, in the format HHMMSSth, and that the date be returned in register 1, in the format 00YYDDDF.

```
         TIME    DEC
```

4.17 THE SNAP MACRO INSTRUCTION

The SNAP macro instruction is used to obtain a dump of all or selected portions of virtual storage assigned to and/or selected control blocks created for the current job step, and then permits the requesting task to continue executing.

The user may select specific areas of virtual storage to be dumped by specifying one or more pairs of beginning and ending addresses of the desired storage via the STORAGE parameter or LIST parameter. The addresses may point to areas within the program that issued the SNAP macro instruction, to other areas within the address space that are assigned to the job step, or to areas within the common system areas that are accessible to the job step.

The STORAGE parameter specifies the beginning and ending addresses as a series of labels and/or registers. The entire series of addresses is separated by commas and enclosed within parentheses. The LIST parameter specifies the address of a list as a label or register. The list is composed of consecutive fullwords containing the begining and ending addresses. The end of the list is indicated by setting the high order bit of the last address to one.

Besides specific addresses of virtual storage areas, other information such as control blocks (ASCBs, TCBs, RBs, etc.), system areas (Nucleus, SQA, etc.), and program information (PSW, registers, etc.) may be dumped. This is requested by specifying various codes associated with those areas via the SDATA (system related information) and PDATA (program related information) parameters.

Some of the SDATA information codes and their meanings are the following:

ALL	All the following codes.
NUC	The nucleus, except the system trace table.
SQA	The system queue area.
LSQA	The local system queue area.
SWA	The schedule work area.
CB	The control blocks for the task.
Q	The ENQ and GRS control blocks.
TRT	The system trace table.
DM	The data management control blocks.
IO	The I/O control blocks.

Some of the PDATA information codes and their meanings are the following:

ALL	All of the following codes.
PSW	The PSW when the SNAP macro instruction was issued.
REGS	The contents of the registers when the SNAP macro instruction was issued.
SA	The savearea linkage information.
JPA	The contents of the job pack area for the address space.
LPA	The load modules from the link pack area that are currently being referenced.
ALLPA	Both the JPA and LPA.
SPLS	The active virtual storage subpools for the task.

The programmer also has the option of requesting that the SNAP dumps be printed with some sort of descriptive header. This can be accomplished with the ID and/or STRHDR parameters. This option is particularly useful if multiple SNAP dumps are requested for various parts and/or execution conditions of the program.

The ID parameter specifies a number to be printed as part of the header of the requested dump. The ID may be specified as a symbol, decimal number, or register. The range of the number must be 0 through 255.

The STRHDR parameter may be used to specify a header of up to 100 characters for each requested dump. The specified heading information consists of a 1-byte header length followed by the actual header.

When STRHDR is used with the STORAGE parameter, STRHDR indicates the address, as a label or register, of one header for each address pair specified by STORAGE. The desired headers are specified in the same sequence as the corresponding address pairs to which the headers refer. If more than one header is requested, then their addresses must be separated by commas and enclosed in parentheses. If a header is not desired for a particular storage area, then a comma must be used to indicate the header's absence. Coding Example 4.17.1 shows how to code the STORAGE and STRHDR parameters.

When STRHDR is used with the LIST parameter, STRHDR indicates the address, as a label or register, of a list of header addresses. The header addresses are specified in the same sequence as the corresponding address pairs to which the headers refer. The end of the list is indicated by setting the high order bit of the last address to one. Coding Example 4.17.2 shows how to code the LIST and STDHDR parameters.

Before the SNAP macro instruction is issued, a dataset must be defined in the jobstream to contain the dump, and an opened DCB, pointing to that dataset, must be provided. The dataset may be a SYSOUT dataset or may be a sequential DASD or magnetic tape dataset. If the SNAP macro instruction is issued and the DCB is not opened, then the SNAP request will be ignored. The address of the opened DCB is specified to the SNAP macro instruction via the DCB parameter as a label or register. The specified parameters of the DCB macro instruction must contain the following:

```
DSORG=PS,MACRF=W,RECFM=VBA,BLKSIZE=,LRECL=125,DDNAME=
```

The BLKSIZE may be either 882 or 1632 and the DDNAME may be any name except SYSABEND, SYSMDUMP, SYSUDUMP or any other ddname used by the operating system (JOBLIB, JOBCAT, etc.).

Coding Example 4.17.1

This coding example illustrates how to code the SNAP macro instruction to do the following:

- Use the STORAGE parameter to dump the storage addresses between the labels BG1 and END1, BG2 and END2, and between the addresses contained in registers 10 and 11;
- Provide the id number 10;
- Provide the header HDR1 for the address range BG1/END1, no header for the address range BG2/END2, and the header HDR2 for the address range contained in registers 10 and 11; and
- Dump the PSW, registers, task control blocks, and all the virtual storage subpools of the address space.

```
         OPEN    (SNAPDCB,(OUTPUT))
         ...
         SNAP    DCB=SNAPDCB,STORAGE=(BG1,END1,BG2,END2,(R10),(R11)),  -
                 ID=10,STRHDR=(HDR1,,HDR2),SDATA=(CB),                 -
                 PDATA=(PSW,REGS,SPLS)
         ...
BG1      EQU     *
```

```
         ...     SECTION OF PROGRAM TO BE DUMPED
END1     EQU     *
         ...
BG2      EQU     *
         ...     SECTION OF PROGRAM TO BE DUMPED
END2     EQU     *
         ...
HDR1     DC      AL1(L'HDR1TXT)
HDR1TXT  DC      C'*** STORAGE AREA-1 ***'
HDR2     DC      AL1(L'HDR2TXT)
HDR2TXT  DC      C'*** STORAGE AREA-2 ***'
         ...
SNAPDCB  DCB     DSORG=PS,MACRF=W,RECFM=VBA,BLKSIZE=1632,LRECL=125,      -
                 DDNAME=SNAPDUMP
```

Coding Example 4.17.2

This coding example illustrates how to code the SNAP macro instruction to do the following:

- Use the LIST parameter to dump the storage addresses between the labels BG3 and END3, BG4 and END4, and between the addresses contained in registers 10 and 11.
- Provide the header HDR3 for the address range BG3/END3, header HDR4 for the address range BG4/END4, and header HDR5 for the address range contained in registers 10 and 11; and
- Dump the PSW, registers, task control blocks, data management control blocks, and all the modules from the job pack area.

```
           OPEN      (SNAPDCB,(OUTPUT))
           ...
           ST        R10,BGADR5
           ST        R11,ENDADR5
           OI        ENDADR5,X'80'       SET END OF ADDRESS INDICATOR
           SNAP      DCB=SNAPDCB,LIST=DUMPLST1,STRHDR=HDRLST1,           -
                     PDATA=(PSW,REGS,JPA),SDATA=(CB,DM)
           ...
BG3        EQU       *
           ...       SECTION OF PROGRAM TO BE DUMPED
END3       EQU       *
           ...
BG4        EQU       *
           ...       SECTION OF PROGRAM TO BE DUMPED
END4       EQU       *
           ...
DUMPLST1   DC        A(BG3)
           DC        A(END3)
           DC        A(BG4)
           DC        A(END4)
BGADR5     DS        F
ENDADR5    DS        F
*
HDRLST1    DC        A(HDR3)
           DC        A(HDR4)
           DC        X'80',AL3(HDR5)
*
HDR3       DC        AL1(L'HDR3TXT)
HDR3TXT    DC        C'*** STORAGE AREA-3 ***'
HDR4       DC        AL1(L'HDR4TXT)
HDR4TXT    DC        C'*** STORAGE AREA-4 ***'
HDR5       DC        AL1(L'HDR5TXT)
HDR5TXT    DC        C'*** STORAGE AREA-5 ***'
           ...
```

```
SNAPDCB      DCB        DSORG=PS,MACRF=W,RECFM=VBA,BLKSIZE=1632,LRECL=125, -
                        DDNAME=SNAPDUMP
```

Since the SNAP macro instruction is very useful for debugging, it would be useful to develop a macro definition to facilitate the coding of the SNAP macro instruction. Coding Example 4.17.3 shows the macro definition for such a macro instruction, called SNAPA, together with its specifications. The reader is encouraged to enhance the macro defintion if additional features are desired.

Coding Example 4.17.3

This coding example illustrates the code required for the SNAPA macro definition. This macro instruction has the following features:

- Generates and opens the appropriate DCB required for the SNAP macro instruction the first time that the SNAPA macro instruction is issued.
- Facilitates the coding of the STORAGE parameter. This is accomplished by the user specifying two optional positional parameters, which contain the begining and ending addresses, respectively. The addresses may be specified as a label or as a register. Only one set of addresses are supported.
- Facilitates the coding of PDATA and SDATA. This is accomplished by providing one keyword parameter, DATA, which is used to specify a set of codes that generate the more frequently used sets of PDATA and SDATA codes. If the DATA parameter is omitted, then only the registers are dumped. The following lists the values coded for DATA and the corresponding PDATA and SDATA codes generated:

```
CBP          DATA=(PSW,SA,REGS), SDATA=(CB,Q)
JLPA         PDATA=(ALLPA,REGS)
SPLS         PDATA=(SPLS,REGS)
ALL          PDATA=(PSW,ALLPA,SA,SPLS,REGS), SDATA=(CB,Q)
```

- Does not support the STRHDR parameter, but generates a unique ID number for each SNAP dump requested.
- Saves and restores all register that it uses, which are 0, 1, 14, and 15.
- The user may specify SNAP=NO in the operand of the SNAPA macro instruction to generate only the DCB and the OPEN. If multiple SNAP macro instructions are requested and if the sequence of execution is not known, then specifying SNAP=NO at the beginning of the program will guarantee that the DCB is opened before the first SNAP executes.

The following is the macro definition of SNAPA:

```
         MACRO
&LABEL   SNAPA    &BGADR,&ENDADR,&DATA=0,&SNAP=0
         GBLA     &SNAPA
         GBLC     &SNAPA1
         LCLA     &SUB,&OPT,&JLPA,&CB,&SPLS,&NOADRSW
         LCLC     &LBL
&SNAPA   SETA     &SNAPA+1
&LBL     SETC     '$'.'SNP'.'&SYSNDX'(2,3)
         AIF      (&SNAPA GT 1).B7
&SNAPA1  SETC     '&LBL'
.B7      ANOP
&LABEL   STM      14,1,&SNAPA1
         AIF      (&SNAPA GT 1).B1
         B        &LBL.A
```

```
SNAPDCB    DCB      DSORG=PS,RECFM=VBA,MACRF=W,BLKSIZE=882,LRECL=125,
                    DDNAME=SNAPDUMP
&SNAPA1    DS       4F
&LBL.A     EQU      *
           OPEN     (SNAPDCB,(OUTPUT))
.B1        AIF      ('&SNAP' EQ 'NO').ENDX
           AIF      (T'&BGADR EQ 'O').NOADR
           AIF      (T'&ENDADR EQ 'O').NOADR
           AIF      ('&BGADR'(1,1) EQ '(').BGREG
           LA       14,&BGADR
.B6        AIF      ('&ENDADR'(1,1) EQ '(').ENDREG
           LA       15,&ENDADR
           AGO      .B2
.NOADR     ANOP
&NOADRSW   SETA     1
.B2        ANOP
           AIF      ('&DATA' EQ 'O').SNAPO
&SUB       SETA     N'&DATA+1
.B3        ANOP
&SUB       SETA     &SUB-1
           AIF      (&SUB EQ 0).NOMORE
           AIF      ('&DATA(&SUB)' EQ 'ALL').SNAP1
           AIF      ('&DATA(&SUB)' EQ 'JLPA').JLPA
           AIF      ('&DATA(&SUB)' EQ 'CB').CB
           AIF      ('&DATA(&SUB)' EQ 'SPLS').SPLS
           MNOTE    'INVALID CODE SPECIFIED---CODE IGNORED'
           AGO      .B3
.JLPA      ANOP
&JLPA      SETA     1
           AGO      .B3
.CB        ANOP
&CB        SETA     1
           AGO      .B3
.SPLS      ANOP
&SPLS      SETA     1
           AGO      .B3
.BGREG     AIF      ('&BGADR' EQ '(14)').B6
           LR       14,&BGADR(1)
           AGO      .B6
.ENDREG    AIF      ('&ENDADR' EQ '(15)').B2
           LR       15,&ENDADR(1)
           AGO      .B2
.NOMORE    ANOP
           AIF      (&JLPA EQ 1).MKJPA
.B4        AIF      (&CB EQ 1).MKCB
.B5        AIF      (&SPLS EQ 1).MKSPLS
           AGO      .CHKOPT
.MKJPA     ANOP
&OPT       SETA     &OPT+100
           AGO      .B4
.MKCB      ANOP
&OPT       SETA     &OPT+10
           AGO      .B5
.MKSPLS    ANOP
&OPT       SETA     &OPT+1
.CHKOPT    AIF      (&OPT EQ 111).SNAP1
           AIF      (&OPT EQ 110).SNAP2
           AIF      (&OPT EQ 101).SNAP3
           AIF      (&OPT EQ 100).SNAP4
           AIF      (&OPT EQ 11).SNAP5
           AIF      (&OPT EQ 10).SNAP6
           AIF      (&OPT EQ 1).SNAP7
.SNAPO     ANOP
           AIF      (&NOADRSW EQ 1).SNAPOA
```

```
         SNAP  DCB=SNAPDCB,STORAGE=((14),(15)),PDATA=REGS,ID=&SNAPA
         AGO   .END
.SNAP0A  ANOP
         SNAP  DCB=SNAPDCB,PDATA=REGS,ID=&SNAPA
         AGO   .END
.SNAP1   ANOP
         AIF   (&NOADRSW EQ 1).SNAP1A
         SNAP  DCB=SNAPDCB,STORAGE=((14),(15)),SDATA=(CB,Q),          -
               PDATA=(REGS,ALLPA,PSW,SA,SPLS),ID=&SNAPA
         AGO   .END
.SNAP1A  ANOP
         SNAP  DCB=SNAPDCB,SDATA=(CB,Q),                              -
               PDATA=(REGS,ALLPA,PSW,SA,SPLS),ID=&SNAPA
         AGO   .END
.SNAP2   ANOP
         AIF   (&NOADRSW EQ 1).SNAP2A
         SNAP  DCB=SNAPDCB,STORAGE=((14),(15)),SDATA=(CB,Q),          -
               PDATA=(REGS,ALLPA,PSW,SA),ID=&SNAPA
         AGO   .END
.SNAP2A  ANOP
         SNAP  DCB=SNAPDCB,SDATA=(CB,Q),                              -
               PDATA=(REGS,ALLPA,PSW,SA),ID=&SNAPA
         AGO   .END
.SNAP3   ANOP
         AIF   (&NOADRSW EQ 1).SNAP3A
         SNAP  DCB=SNAPDCB,STORAGE=((14),(15)),                       -
               PDATA=(REGS,ALLPA,SPLS),ID=&SNAPA
         AGO   .END
.SNAP3A  ANOP
         SNAP  DCB=SNAPDCB,PDATA=(REGS,ALLPA,SPLS),ID=&SNAPA
         AGO   .END
.SNAP4   ANOP
         AIF   (&NOADRSW EQ 1).SNAP4A
         SNAP  DCB=SNAPDCB,STORAGE=((14),(15)),PDATA=(REGS,ALLPA),    -
               ID=&SNAPA
         AGO   .END
.SNAP4A  ANOP
         SNAP  DCB=SNAPDCB,PDATA=(REGS,ALLPA),ID=&SNAPA
         AGO   .END
.SNAP5   ANOP
         AIF   (&NOADRSW EQ 1).SNAP5A
         SNAP  DCB=SNAPDCB,STORAGE=((14),(15)),SDATA=(CB,Q),          -
               PDATA=(REGS,PSW,SA,SPLS),ID=&SNAPA
         AGO   .END
.SNAP5A  ANOP
         SNAP  DCB=SNAPDCB,SDATA=(CB,Q),                              -
               PDATA=(REGS,PSW,SA,SPLS),ID=&SNAPA
         AGO   .END
.SNAP6   ANOP
         AIF   (&NOADRSW EQ 1).SNAP6A
         SNAP  DCB=SNAPDCB,STORAGE=((14),(15)),SDATA=(CB,Q),          -
               PDATA=(REGS,PSW,SA),ID=&SNAPA
         AGO   .END
.SNAP6A  ANOP
         SNAP  DCB=SNAPDCB,SDATA=(CB,Q),                              -
               PDATA=(REGS,PSW,SA),ID=&SNAPA
         AGO   .END
.SNAP7   ANOP
         AIF   (&NOADRSW EQ 1).SNAP7A
         SNAP  DCB=SNAPDCB,STORAGE=((14),(15)),PDATA=(REGS,SPLS),
               ID=&SNAPA
         AGO   .END
.SNAP7A  ANOP
         SNAP  DCB=SNAPDCB,PDATA=(REGS,SPLS),ID=&SNAPA
```

```
.END      ANOP
*
          MNOTE    *,'ID # FOR THIS SNAP IS &SNAPA'
*
.ENDX     LM       14,1,&SNAPA1
          MEND
```

4.18 THE ABEND MACRO INSTRUCTION

The ABEND macro instruction is used to terminate a task abnormally. The programmer must specify a completion code, specified as the first positional parameter, associated with the abnormal termination. The programmer can optionally request a full dump or a tailored dump of virtual storage areas and control blocks pertaining to the tasks being abnormally terminated and may also optionally request job step termination.

If the job step task (the first one created in the address space) issues the ABEND macro instruction or if any of the subtasks issue the ABEND macro instruction and requests job step termination (via the STEP parameter), then all the tasks of the address space are terminated.

If the issuing of the ABEND macro instruction does not result in job step termination, then the following processing occurs:

- The task that issues the ABEND macro instruction is abnormally terminated and all of its subtasks, if any, are also terminated, but the parent task and the other subtasks, if any, are not terminated.
- The end of task exit routine of the parent task is given control, but the end of task exit routine of the subtasks is not given control.
- The specified completion code is placed in the TCBCMPC field of the TCB of the task that issued the ABEND macro instruction.

The ABEND macro instruction contains four positional parameters. The positional parameters specify, in sequence, the completion code, DUMP to indicate that a storage dump is requested, STEP to indicate that the entire jobstep is to be abnormally terminated, and USER (default) or SYSTEM to indicate that the specified completion code should be treated as a user or as a system code, respectively.

The completion code must be in the range 0–4095 and may be specified as a decimal number, a hexadecimal number, a symbol, or a register (enclosed within parentheses) containing the completion code.

Besides specifying DUMP as the second positional parameter, a SYSABEND, SYSUDUMP, or SYSMDUMP JCL DD statement is also required in the JCL stream in order for a dump to be produced. The dumps produced when SYSUDUMP and SYSABEND are specified are formatted so that they can be printed directly. The dump produced when SYSMDUMP is specified is unformatted, machine-readable, and used with IPCS. A SYSUDUMP dump contains only address space related information and in most cases is sufficient for problem determination and resolution. A SYSABEND dump includes all the information that is contained in a SYSUDUMP dump plus system related information. The contents of the dumps can be changed by operator command (CHNGDUMP and SLIP) or by system parameters (IEADMPxx and IEADMRxx).

The programmer may specify a reason code via the REASON keyword parameter (this parameter is valid only in MVS/XA and MVS/ESA). The reason code may be specified as a 31-bit decimal number, 32-bit hexadecimal number, a symbol or a register (enclosed within parentheses) containing the reason code. The reason code is used to supplement the completion code. Recovery Termination Management propagates the reason code to each subsequent ESTAE recovery exit routine via the SDWA and also places it in the TCB of the issuing task.

The programmer may customize the requested storage dump by specifying the address of a parameter-list of dump options via the DUMPOPT keyword parameter. The parameter-list may be produced by the list form of the SNAP macro instruction. The TCB, DCB, ID and STRHDR options may not be specified in the SNAP macro instruction which is used to produce the list. The TCB of the issuing task is used and MVS provides its own DCB.

Coding Example 4.18.1

This coding example illustrates how to code the ABEND macro instruction to abnormally terminate a program with a User ABEND code of 900 and request a storage dump.

```
         ABEND     900,DUMP
```

NOTES:

- The dump will be produced only if a SYSABEND, SYSUDUMP, or a SYSMDUMP JCL DD statement is provided in the JCL stream, and the contents of the dump will depend upon which one of those JCL DD statements is provided.

Coding Example 4.18.2

This coding example illustrates how to code the ABEND macro instruction to abnormally terminate the entire jobstep without a storage dump and with the User ABEND code contained in register 10.

```
         ABEND   (R10),,STEP
```

Coding Example 4.18.3

This coding example illustrates how to code the ABEND macro instruction to abnormally terminate a program with a system completion code of S213 and produce a customized dump as specified by the parameter-list DMOPT01.

```
         ABEND     X'213',DUMP,,SYSTEM,DUMPOPT=DMOPT01
         ...
DMOPT01  SNAP      PDATA=(PSW,REGS),SDATA=(CB,DM,SWA),MF=L
```

BIBLIOGRAPHY FOR CHAPTER 4

The following IBM manuals contain reference material for the topics discussed in this chapter.

ID	Title
GC28-1114	*OS/VS2 MVS Supervisor Services and Macro Instructions*
GC28-1154	*MVS/XA Supervisor Services and Macro Instructions*
GC28-1821	*MVS/ESA Application Development Guide*
GC28-1822	*MVS/ESA Application Development Macro Reference*

5

Advanced Assembler Language Techniques

This chapter discusses the coding of various useful techniques that may be accomplished in Assembler language. Some of the techniques discussed also involve the use of MVS facilities. Whenever a coding technique involves the use of an MVS facility, the facility is first discussed and then the implementation of it is demonstrated with the appropriate Assembler language coding.

5.1 USING GENERAL PURPOSE REGISTER 13 AS A BASE REGISTER

Linkage convention between programs requires that a linkage/register savearea be defined in a program and that register 13 point to that savearea during the execution of the program. Actually, register 13 must point to the savearea only when another program is called (some Data Management macro instructions also call programs); however, it is normal procedure to have register 13 point to the savearea at all times during the execution of the program.

If register 13 could be used as a base register, then the programmer will have an extra register available for a base register or for another purpose. This could be very useful for certain programs.

In order to use register 13 as a base register, register 13 must simultaneously point to the savearea and to the beginning of a 4K area within the program. The coding is easier if register 13 is used to point the first 4K of required addressability.

Coding Example 5.1.1

This coding example illustrates how to initialize an Assembler language program and how to use registers 13, 3, and 4, respectively, as base registers.

```
PROGRAM   CSECT
R0        EQU       0                   DEFINE SYMBOLS
          ...                           FOR
R15       EQU       15                  REGISTERS
          STM       R14,R12,12(R13)     SAVE REGS 14 THRU 12 INTO CALLERS SA
          LR        R2,R13              SAVE CALLERS SA ADR IN REG 2
          BALR      R12,0               LOAD REG 12 WITH NEXT INSTR ADDR
          BAL       R13,76(0,R12)       LOAD REG 13 WITH ADR OF OWN SA ADDR
```

```
*                                          AND 1ST 4K OF PROGRAM ADDRESSABILITY,
*                                          THEN BRANCH AROUND OWN SA
SAVEAREA  DS      18F                      DEFINE OWN 72-BYTE SAVEAREA
          USING   SAVEAREA,R13,R3,R4       TELL ASMBLR, REGS 13, 3, & 4 WILL BE
*                                          BASE REGS AND RELATIVE ADR OF THEM
          LA      R3,4095                  LOAD REG 3 WITH 4K-1 FOR NEXT INSTR
          LA      R3,1(R13,R3)             LOAD REG 3 WITH ADR 4K PAST REG 13
          LA      R4,4095                  LOAD REG 4 WITH 4K-1 FOR NEXT INSTR
          LA      R4,1(R3,R4)              LOAD REG 4 WITH ADR 4K PAST REG 3
          ST      R2,4(0,R13)              SAVE CALLERS SA ADR INTO OWN SA+4
          ST      R13,8(0,R2)              SAVE OWN SA ADR INTO CALLERS SA+8
*
*         ...                              MAINSTREAM OF PROGRAM STARTS HERE
```

5.2 ACCESSING THE DATA FROM THE PARM PARAMETER OF THE JCL EXEC STATEMENT

Up to 100 bytes of data can be passed from the JCL to an executing program. This data can be used to provide various control or other information to the program and influence how it executes under certain conditions. Passing information this way in lieu of a dataset such as SYSIN has the advantage of not requiring the program to contain the necessary control blocks and code to read and store the information and eliminates the need to place the data into a dataset. Like a dataset, the data specified via JCL can be changed from execution to execution. However, since only 100 bytes can be passed to the program via JCL, this method is not applicable if a large quantity of data or control information is required.

The format of the PARM parameter of the JCL EXEC statement is as follows:

```
//STEP    EXEC    PGM=ppp,PARM=ddd
```

where:

- ppp is the name of the program that is to be invoked.
- ddd is the data that is to be passed to the program. It may contain up to 100 bytes of data. If the data contains special characters (other than the period), then the entire string must be enclosed within apostrophes. The framing apostrophes are not passed to the program as data.

When a program is invoked, the operating system loads register 1 with the address of a halfword that contains the length, in binary, of the data string specified by the PARM parameter of the JCL EXEC statement. The high order bit of the address is set to one to indicate that it is the only address being passed to the program. The actual data immediately follows the halfword. If the PARM parameter is not specified, then the halfword contains zeros.

Coding Example 5.2.1

This coding example illustrates how to load the length of the data, specified via the PARM parameter, into register 15 and how to load the address of the actual data into register 1.

```
L       R1,0(0,R1)        LOAD JCL PARM LEN/DATA ADR INTO REG 1
LH      R15,0(0,R1)       LOAD LEN OF JCL PARM INTO REG 15
LA      R1,2(0,R1)        LOAD ADR OF JCL PARM INTO REG 1
```

Whether the PARM parameter was specified can be determined by testing register 15 for zeros as follows:

```
LTR    R15,R15          TEST REG 15 FOR ZERO
BZ     NOPARM           IF ZERO, NO PARM SPECIFIED
```

If PARM was specified, then register 1 can be used as a base register to access the data.

The macro instruction GETPARM, defined in Chapter 3 (Section 3.3.2), generates code that accesses the PARM data.

If a program calls another program that accepts the JCL PARM parameter value, then the calling program must set up the same environment that is set up by the operating system. Register 1 must point to a PARM value in the same format or indicate that no PARM value is being passed. The following examples illustrate the code required to call a program that expects a PARM value. The programs in the examples below are called via the LINK macro instruction (discussed in Chapter 4).

Coding Example 5.2.2

This coding example illustrates how to call the Assembler and pass it parameters.

```
         LINK     EP=IEV90,PARAM=APARMLST,VL=1
         ...
APARMLST DC       H'APARMEND-APARMVAL'
APARMVAL DC       C'XREF,NOLOAD'
APARMEND EQU      *
```

The VL=1 parameter is specified to cause the LINK macro instruction to turn on the high order bit of the address of the parameter. Some programs, such as the Assembler and Linkage Editor, have code to process multiple parameter addresses (the second parameter address of the Assembler and Linkage Editor points to an optional ddname list used to change the ddnames) when they are being called. If the high order bit is not on and only one address is being passed, then those programs will expect that another parameter address follows and will attempt to process it. Since a valid address does not follow, the called program may ABEND with an S0C4.

Coding Example 5.2.3

This coding example illustrates how the IBM utility program IEBCOPY is called with an indication that no PARM value is being passed.

```
         LINK     EP=IEBCOPY,PARAM=DUMYPARM,VL=1
         ...
DUMYPARM DC       H'0'
```

5.3 USING DSECTS

A DSECT (Dummy Section) is located in a program's source code and is used to map (provide names for the fields of) virtual storage that is not located in the program, such as the storage obtained via a GETMAIN macro instruction or received from a locate-mode GET macro instruction. The DSECT itself occupies no virtual storage since it is used only as an overlay for existing virtual storage.

A DSECT starts with the DSECT Assembler instruction and terminates with another DSECT statement, a CSECT statement, or an END statement. The name of a DSECT is defined in the name field of the DSECT statement. The field names of the DSECT follow the

DSECT statement. The DSECT may contain DS, DC, and EQU statements. A DC statement may be used to define the length of a field, but the actual constant is not preserved.

As many DSECTs as required may be defined in a program. A DSECT may be hard-coded in the program, be invoked via the CALL macro instruction, or be invoked from a macro instruction expansion.

Coding Example 5.3.1

This coding example illustrates a sample DSECT. This DSECT could be used to map an I/O record read, using a locate-mode GET macro instruction. The column to the left of the DSECT shows the displacements (in hexadecimal) into the DSECT.

```
0000    EMPLYREC    DSECT
0000    EMPNAME     DS     CL20    EMPLOYEE NAME
0014    EMPADDR     DS     0CL22   HOME ADDRESS
0014    EMPSTRET    DS     CL15    STREET
0023    EMPSTATE    DS     CL2     STATE
0025    EMPCITY     DS     CL15    CITY
0034    EMPZIP      DS     CL5     ZIP CODE
0039    EMPSSNO     DS     CL9     SOCIAL SECURITY NUMBER
0042    EMPSDATE    DS     CL6     WORK START DATE
0048    EMPRDATE    DS     CL6     REVIEW DATE
004E    EMPBFLGS    DS     CL1     BENEFIT FLAGS
        EMPBBLIN    EQU    X'80'   BIT FOR BASIC LIFE INSURANCE
        EMPBELIN    EQU    X'40'   BIT FOR EXTENDED LIFE INSURANCE
        EMPBBHIN    EQU    X'20'   BIT FOR BASIC HEALTH INSURANCE
        EMPBMSUR    EQU    X'10'   BIT FOR MAJOR SURGERY
        EMPBDENT    EQU    X'08'   BIT FOR DENTAL PLAN
004F    EMPDEPT     DS     CL10    DEPARTMENT
0059    EMPSALRY    DS     CL9     SALARY
```

For convenience, DSECTs should be located at the end of the program, just before the END statement. If DSECTs are located in the middle of a program, then they are required to be delimited by a CSECT statement. If the code that follows that DSECT statement is part of the CSECT that preceded the DSECT, then both CSECT statments must contain the same name, or addressability errors will occur. This additional work and potential problem is avoided by placing the DSECTs at the end of the program.

Coding Example 5.3.2

This coding example illustrates the required CSECT statements when a DSECT is defined in the middle of a program.

```
MAINPGM   CSECT
          ...
          Machine instructions, macros, and Assembler instructions.
          ...
DSECT01   DSECT
D1FLD01   DS      CL10
D1FLD02   DS      CL10
D1FLD03   DS      CL10
*
MAINPGM   CSECT                              CONTINUATION OF CSECT
          ...
          Machine instructions, macros, and Assembler instructions.
          ...
          END
```

Setting up and using a DSECT instructure requires that a task be performed at Assembler time and again at execution time. In order to use a DSECT to map a particular area of virtual storage, the following must be done:

- Define the DSECT in the source of the program in which it will be used.
- Indicate to the Assembler:
  - That it is to provide addressability for the fields of the DSECT by generating the proper code wherever those fields are referenced; and
  - Which register should be use for the addressability.

  The above is done via the USING statement.
- At execution time, load the DSECT register with the address of the virtual storage area that is to be mapped by the DSECT before those fields are referenced.

Coding Example 5.3.3

This coding example illustrates how to set up the DSECT, defined in Coding Example 5.3.1, so that the Assembler generates the proper code and the program executes properly.

```
          USING  EMPLYREC,R10        TELL ASM TO USE REG 10 FOR DSECT
          ...
          L      R10,EMRECADR        LOAD ADR OF I/O AREA INTO DSECT REG
          MVC    #NAME,EMPNAME       REFERENCE A FIELD MAPPED BY DSECT
          MVC    #SALARY,EMPSALRY    REFERENCE A FIELD MAPPED BY DSECT
          ...
EMRECADR  DS     F                   ADDRESS OF I/O AREA
```

A separate register need not be devoted to each DSECT. If only a few DSECTs are used and the registers are available, then each DSECT may have its own register. However, this is not good practice because this is a waste (except for the special cases discussed below) of registers that may be required at a later time if the program is modified. If a program uses many DSECTs and/or many registers, then unique registers for DSECTs are also not possible. Addressability can be accomplished by the use of only one register for all DSECTs (if they are not being used at the same time). To do this, specify the USING statement just before the routine that requires addressability. Specify the DROP statement after the routine. The DROP statement instructs the Assembler to release the register (generate no more code using that register as a base register) so that it can be used in another USING statement to provide addressability for another DSECT (or the same one). Remember, the USING and DROP statements are not executable. They are simply instructions to the Assembler to insure that the proper code is generated in the proper place in the program; therefore, their physical location in the program is significant. They must be specified physically before and after the routine, respectively, that requires the use of the DSECT, regardless of how and when the routine receives control.

A valid reason for using unique registers for DSECTs are the following:

- If the fields of the DSECT will be referenced throughout most of the program. In this case, the DSECT register contains the address of the virtual storage area that is being mapped for most of the life of the program.
- If fields of multiple DSECTs are referenced in the same instruction or in the same routine. In this case, unique registers must be used.

If unique registers are being used, then the USING statement(s) should be located at the beginning of the program for documentation reasons. If unique registers are not being used, then the USING statements must be placed before the routine that references the fields of the DSECT, and for documentation reasons, those USING statements should be placed immediately before the routines so that they are easy to notice. If DROP statements are required, then they should be placed immediately after the routine that is using the DSECT, again for documentation reasons.

Coding Example 5.3.4

This coding example illustrates how to use multiple DSECTs with the same register.

```
         USING  DSECT01,R10       DEFINE REG FOR DSECT01 DSECT
RTN001   L      R10,AREA1ADR      LOAD ADR OF AREA MAPPED BY DSECT
         ...                      REF FIELDS DEFINED IN DSECT01 DSECT
         BR     R6                RETURN TO CALLING RTN
         DROP   R10               RELEASE DSECT REG
         ...
         USING  DSECT02,R10       DEFINE REG FOR DSECT02 DSECT
RTN02    L      R10,AREA2ADR      LOAD ADR OF AREA MAPPED BY DSECT
         ...                      REF FIELDS DEFINED IN DSECT02 DSECT
         BR     R6                RETURN TO CALLING RTN
         DROP   R10               RELEASE DSECT REG
         ...
AREA1ADR DS     F                 ADDRESS OF AREA MAPPED BY DSECT01
AREA2ADR DS     F                 ADDRESS OF AREA MAPPED BY DSECT02
```

How does a DSECT work? Technically, a DSECT works very simply. For ease of reference, good documentation, and good program practice, the programmer references an area of virtual storage by using the names of the fields as defined by the DSECT instead of using relative addressing (e.g., AREA+10(5)). The Assembler uses the displacement associated with that field name (see Coding Examples 5.3.1 and 5.3.3) and, in effect, adds it to the register defined (via the USING statement) for use with that DSECT. The Assembler accomplishes this by generating the address of the field, using the specified register as the base of the address and the displacement into the DSECT for the field name as the displacement of the address. For example, the address of the field name EMPSSNO is generated by using register 10 (X'A') as the base and 57 (X'039') as the displacement. The programmers responsibility, besides coding the USING statement in the proper place in the program, is to load the specified DSECT register with the address of the virtual storage area that coincides with the beginning of the fields (defined in the DSECT) before those fields are referenced.

The fields mapped by a DSECT may also be accessed without setting up addressability with the USING statement. This can be accomplished by using the explicit form of an instruction. A register is loaded with the beginning address of the area, and the displacement of the individual fields within that area are determined by subtracting the label associated with the beginning of the DSECT from the label associated with the individual fields. Coding Example 5.3.5 illustrates this technique.

Coding Example 5.3.5

This coding example illustrates how to access a field of an area using a DSECT and the explicit form of the MVC instruction. In this example, the contents of the field EMPSALRY from the I/O area pointed to by register 10 is moved into the area #SALARY. The DSECT defined in Coding Example 5.3.1 is used in this example.

```
          LA     R10,IOAREA
          MVC    #SALARY,EMPSALRY-EMPLYREC(R10)
          ...
EMPLYREC  DSECT
          ...
```

5.4 CONVERTING FROM HEXADECIMAL INTO CHARACTER

Since all data is stored in hexadecimal (actually binary), let's define what is meant by converting from hexadecimal into character.

Converting from hexadecimal into character means that the converted data will be translated such that, when displayed on a CRT or printer, it will appear as the actual hexadecimal data that is stored in virtual storage or auxiliary storage. For example, the hexadecimal representation of the character A (X'C1') will be translated to X'C3F1', which will appear as C1 instead of A when displayed. This technique could be used to display data as it actually appears in virtual storage or on an auxiliary storage medium such as DASD or magnetic tape, or it could be used to display hexadecimal return codes or ABEND codes.

Therefore, hexadecimal character conversion requires that each byte of hexadecimal data be translated into two bytes in character format that, when displayed, appear as the actual hexadecimal data. This requires that the first hexadecimal digit or zone (high order four bits) part of the hexadecimal data byte be translated into a byte in character format and that the second hexadecimal digit or numeric (low order four bits) part of the hexadecimal data byte be translated into another byte in character format. Isolating the zone and the numeric parts of the hexadecimal data byte can be done with the MVZ and MVN instructions, respectively. Moving the four bits of the zone and the four 4 bits of the numeric parts of the hexadecimal data byte into separate bytes satisfies the reqirement of translating one byte into two bytes. By setting the other 4 bits of each of the two bytes not affected by the MVZ and MVN instructions to a known value such as binary zeros provides two bytes suitable as argument bytes for the TR instruction. Coding Example 5.4.1 illustrates how to isolate the two hexadecimal digits of the hexadecimal data byte and place them into separate bytes.

Coding Example 5.4.1

This coding example illustrates how to extract the two hexademical digits, which represent the character A, and place each of them into a separate byte.

```
          MVZ    BYTE1,CHARA
          MVN    BYTE2,CHARA
          ...
CHARA     DC     X'C1'

Before execution:
BYTE1     DC     X'00'
BYTE2     DC     X'00'

After execution:
BYTE1     DC     X'C0'
BYTE2     DC     X'01'
```

The translation table would need to be set up such that the two bytes containing the extracted hexadecimal digits would translate to the character that would display as the hexadecimal digit. For example, the hexadecimal digit F could appear, depending if it were in the zone part or numeric part of the character, as either X'F0' or X'0F' after it was extracted from the hexadecimal byte. Therefore, the translation table would be required to translate both X'F0' and X'0F' into X'C6'. Coding Example 5.4.2 shows the required translation table and Coding Example 5.4.3 shows the actual code required to use that translation table to convert a string of hexadecimal data into the equivalent string of character data.

Coding Example 5.4.2

This coding example illustrates how to set up the TR table required to translate the bytes containing the extracted hexadecimal digits into the proper characters.

```
HEXTBL   DC    X'F0F1F2F3F4F5F6F7F8F9C1C2C3C4C5C6'    00-0F
         DC    X'F1',X15'00'                          10-1F
         DC    X'F2',X15'00'                          20-2F
         DC    X'F3',X15'00'                          30-3F
         DC    X'F4',X15'00'                          40-4F
         DC    X'F5',X15'00'                          50-5F
         DC    X'F6',X15'00'                          60-6F
         DC    X'F7',X15'00'                          70-7F
         DC    X'F8',X15'00'                          80-8F
         DC    X'F9',X15'00'                          90-9F
         DC    X'C1',X15'00'                          A0-AF
         DC    X'C2',X15'00'                          B0-BF
         DC    X'C3',X15'00'                          C0-CF
         DC    X'C4',X15'00'                          D0-DF
         DC    X'C5',X15'00'                          E0-EF
         DC    X'C6',X15'00'                          F0-FF
```

Coding Example 5.4.3

This coding example illustrates how to code the routine to convert hexcadecimal into character. After the routine TRNSLTXC executes, CHARLIST will contain X'C3F1C3F2C3F3C6F1C6F2C6F3F0F4C1C6'. This will display as C1C2C3F1F2F304AF, which is the character equivalent of the specified hexadecimal data.

```
TRNSLTXC  L     R0,HEXLEN          LOAD LENGTH OF HEX STRING TO TRANS
          LA    R14,HEXLIST        LOAD ADR OF HEX STRING TO TRANS
          LA    R15,CHARLIST       LOAD ADR OF RECV AREA FOR TRANS
NEXTCHAR  MVZ   BYTE1,0(R14)       ISOLATE HIGH ORDER HEX DIGIT
          MVN   BYTE2,0(R14)       ISOLATE LOW ORDER HEX DIGIT
          TR    BYTE1,HEXTBL       TRANS HI ORDER HEX DIGIT INTO CHAR
          TR    BYTE2,HEXTBL       TRANS LO ORDER HEX DIGIT INTO CHAR
          MVC   0(1,R15),BYTE1     MOVE 1ST TRANS HEX CHAR INTO RECV AREA
          MVC   1(1,R15),BYTE2     MOVE 2ND TRANS HEX CHAR INTO RECV AREA
          LA    R14,1(0,R14)       INCR TO NEXT HEX BYTE
          LA    R15,2(0,R15)       INCR TO NEXT RECV AREA SLOT
          BCT   R0,NEXTCHAR        TRANS NEXT HEX BYTE
          BR    R6                 ALL HEX BYTES TRANS, RET TO CALLING RTN
          ...
HEXLIST   DC    C'ABC123',X'04AF'  HEX BYTES TO CONVERT INTO CHAR
HEXLEN    DC    A(*-HEXLIST)       LENGTH OF HEX STRING TO TRANS
CHARLIST  DS    CL(L'HEXLIST*2)    RECV AREA FOR TRANS
BYTE1     DC    X'00'
BYTE2     DC    X'00'
```

5.5 VALIDATING NUMERIC DATA

A main reason why a functioning program ABENDs due to a user error is faulty input data. This faulty data is usually a bad numeric field and causes a SOC7 ABEND. A good Assembler language program should always validate any numeric fields to verify that they are in the proper format (zoned decimal or packed decimal) before processing them.

There are a few ways of verifying that a zoned decimal data field contains valid data. One simple way is to increment through the length of the entire field and verify that each byte contains a value within the range of X'F0' to X'F9'. Coding Example 5.5.1 shows the code to accomplish this.

Coding Example 5.5.1

This coding example illustrates how to verify that a data field contains zoned decimal data by using the CLI instruction.

```
         LA    R0,ZDNOLEN        LD LENGTH OF FIELD TO VALIDATE
         LA    R10,ZDNUMB        LD ADR OF FIELD TO VALIDATE
         BAL   R7,VALDTZD        VALIDATE FIELD FOR ZONED DEC DATA
         LTR   R15,R15           CHK IF FIELD CONTAIN VALID DATA
         BZ    DATAOK            IF 0, FIELD CONTAINS VALID ZD NUMB
         B     DATAINV           IF NOT, FIELD CONTAINS INV ZD NUMB
*
*
************************************************************************
*   THIS SUBROUTINE CHECKS IF A FIELD OF DATA CONTAINS ZONED DECIMAL
*   NUMBERS. THIS SUBROUTINE PERFORMS THE VALIDATION BY VERIFYING THAT
*   EACH BYTE OF THE FIELD IS IN THE RANGE X'F0' TO X'F9'. A RC IS SET
*   IN REGISTER 15 FOR THE CALLING ROUTINE; X'00' INDICATES VALID DATA,
*   X'04' INDICATES INVALID DATA.
************************************************************************
*
VALDTZD  DS    0H
NEXTDIG  CLI   0(R10),X'F0'      COMPARE A BYTE OF FIELD TO ZD ZERO
         BL    BADZDD            IF LESS THAN ZD 0, BAD ZD DATA
         CLI   0(R10),X'F9'      COMPARE A BYTE OF FIELD TO ZD NINE
         BH    BADZDD            IF GREATER THAN ZD 9, BAD ZD DATA
         LA    R10,1(0,R10)      INCR TO NEXT BYTE OF FIELD
         BCT   R0,NEXTDIG        IF MORE BYTES, COMPARE NEXT ONE
         LA    R15,0             IF NO MORE BYTES, DATA OK—IND IT
         BR    R7                RETURN TO CALLING RTN
BADZDD   LA    R15,4             INDICATE BAD ZD DATA
         BR    R7                RETURN TO CALLING RTN
*                                VALIDATED FOR ZONED DECIMAL DATA
ZDNOLEN  EQU   L'ZDNUMB          CONTAINS THE LENGTH OF ZDNUMB
ZDNUMB   DC    ...               THE FIELD THAT IS TO BE VALIDATED
*                                FOR ZONED DECIMAL DATA
```

Zoned decimal data may also be verified by using the translate and test (TRT) instruction. This would require that a TRT table be set up. In the table, the valid bit combinations are required to be equated to X'00' and the invalid combinations are required to be equated to a non-zero entry. Coding Example 5.5.2 shows the required code to verify that a data field contains zoned decimal data, using the TRT instructions.

Coding Example 5.5.2

This coding example illustrates how to verify that a data field contains zoned decimal data by using the TRT instruction.

```
VALDTZD    TRT     ZDNUMB,TABLE       COMPARE ALL BYTES OF FIELD
           BC      8,DATAOK           IF CC=0, ALL BYTES CONTAIN ZD
           LA      R15,4              IF NOT, BAD DATA—IND IT
           BR      R7                 RETURN TO CALLING RTN
DATAOK     LA      R15,0              IND GOOD ZD DATA
           BR      R7                 RETURN TO CALLING RTN
*
ZDNUMB     DC      ...                THE FIELD THAT IS TO BE VALIDATED
*                                     FOR ZONED DECIMAL DATA
TABLE      DC      256XL1'01'
           ORG     TABLE+C'0'
           DC      10XL1'00'
           ORG     TABLE+256
```

NOTES:

- The length attribute of the field ZDNUMB must indicate the correct number of bytes in the field or the TRT instruction will not function properly, in which case an alternate means would be required to provide the data length to the TRT instruction.

Since this verification facility is required frequently, it would be useful to develop a macro definition to generate the required code. Coding Example 5.5.3 shows such a macro definition together with the instructions for its use.

Coding Example 5.5.3

This coding example illustrates the code required for the VALNUMB macro definition, which will verify that a data field contains zoned decimal data. This macro instruction accepts two positional parameters. The first positional parameter specifies the address of the data field and the second positional parameter specifies the length of the data field. Either parameter may be specified as a register enclosed in parentheses. If the first parameter is specified as a label, then the second parameter is optional. If omitted, the assembled length of the field is used; if specified, it must be specified as a self-defining term. If the first parameter specifies the address in a register, then the second parameter is required. In this case, the second parameter may be specified as a self-defining term or as a register that contains the length. When the macro instruction returns control, register 15 contains either X'00' (if the data field contains zoned decimal data) or X'04' if the data field contains invalid data).

```
           MACRO
&LABEL     VALNUMB  &ADR,&LEN
           LCLC     &LBL
&LBL       SETC     '$'.'VAL'.'&SYSNDX'(2,3)
           AIF      (T'&ADR EQ 'O').NOADR
           AIF      ('&ADR'(1,1) EQ '(').REGA
           AIF      (T'&LEN EQ 'O').ADRONLY
           AIF      (T'&LEN NE 'N').INVLEN
&LABEL     TRT      &ADR.(&LEN),&LBL.A
           AGO      .BC
.ADRONLY   ANOP
&LABEL     TRT      &ADR,&LBL.A
.BC        BC       8,&LBL.B
           B        &LBL.C
           AGO      .REST
.REGA      AIF      (T'&LEN EQ 'O').NOLEN
```

```
         AIF   ('&LEN'(1,1) EQ '(').REGAL
&LABEL   TRT   0(&LEN,&ADR(1)),&LBL.A
         BC    8,&LBL.B
         B     &LBL.C
         AGO   .REST
.REGAL   ANOP
&LABEL   BCTR  &LEN(1),0
         EX    &LEN(1),&LBL.E
         LA    &LEN(1),1(0,&LEN(1))
         BC    8,&LBL.B
         B     &LBL.C
&LBL.E   TRT   0(0,&ADR(1)),&LBL.A
.REST    ANOP
&LBL.A   DC    256XL1'01'
         ORG   &LBL.A+C'0'
         DC    10XL1'00'
         ORG   &LBL.A+256
&LBL.B   LA    R15,0
         B     &LBL.D
&LBL.C   LA    R15,4
         B     &LBL.D
&LBL.D   DS    0H
         MEXIT
.NOADR   MNOTE 4,'DATA FIELD ADDRESS NOT SPECIFIED---MACRO NOT GENERATED'
         MEXIT
.NOLEN   MNOTE 4,'LENGTH NOT SPECIFIED---MACRO NOT GENERATED'
         MEXIT
.INVLEN  MNOTE 4,'INVALID LENGTH SPECIFIED---MACRO NOT GENERATED'
         MEXIT
         MEND
```

Verifying packed decimal data is a little more involved than verifying zoned decimal data. Each byte (except the last) is required to have a value in the range of X'00' to X'09' or X'10 to X'19' or ... or X'90' to X'99'. The last byte, which contains the sign, is required to have the zoned part (bits 0–3) contain a value in the range of X'0' to X'9' and the numeric part (bits 4–7) to contain a value of X'C' or X'D' or X'F'. It would be easier to perform the validation using the TRT instruction than to use a series of numerious CLI and branch instructions. The TRT instruction would require two tables. One table for all the bytes of the data field except the last one and the second table for the last byte. Coding Example 5.5.4 shows the required tables.

TABLE2 would be simpler to code if the zone and numeric parts of the last byte were reversed. To use the table in that form would require the use of the UNPK instruction. The last byte could be UNPKed into itself, and then, after the validation, the UNPK instruction could be used again to restore the last byte. Coding Example 5.5.5 shows the modified TABLE2. Coding Example 5.5.6 shows the required code to verify that a data field contains packed data.

Coding Example 5.5.4

This coding example illustrates the TRT tables required to verify that a data field contains packed decimal data. TABLE1 is for all the bytes of the field except the last one, and TABLE2 is for the last byte.

```
TABLE1   DC    256XL1'01'
         ORG   TABLE1+X'00'
         DC    XL10'00'
         ORG   TABLE1+X'10'
         DC    XL10'00'
         ORG   TABLE1+X'20'
         DC    XL10'00'
```

```
                 ...      .
                 ORG      TABLE1+X'90'
                 DC       XL10'00'
                 ORG      TABLE1+256
*
TABLE2           DC       256XL1'01'
                 ORG      TABLE2+X'0C'
                 DC       X'00'
                 ORG      TABLE2+X'1C'
                 DC       X'00'
                 ...
                 ORG      TABLE2+X'9C'
                 DC       X'00'
                 ORG      TABLE2+X'0D'
                 DC       X'00'
                 ORG      TABLE2+X'1D'
                 DC       X'00'
                 ...
                 ORG      TABLE2+X'9D'
                 DC       X'00'
                 ORG      TABLE2+X'0F'
                 DC       X'00'
                 ORG      TABLE2+X'1F'
                 DC       X'00'
                 ...
                 ORG      TABLE2+X'9F'
                 DC       X'00'
                 ORG      TABLE2+256
```

Coding Example 5.5.5

This coding example illustrates the simpler TABLE2 for the TRT instruction if the zone and numeric parts of the last byte of the packed decimal data field were reversed.

```
TABLE2           DC       256XL1'01'
                 ORG      TABLE2+X'C0'
                 DC       XL10'00'
                 ORG      TABLE2+X'D0'
                 DC       XL10'00'
                 ORG      TABLE2+X'F0'
                 DC       XL10'00'
                 ORG      TABLE2+256
```

Coding Example 5.5.6

This coding example illustrates how to verify that a data field contains packed decimal data by using the TRT instruction and TABLE1 from Coding Example 5.5.4 and TABLE2 from Coding Example 5.5.5.

```
                 LA       R0,PDNOLEN         LD LENGTH OF FIELD TO VALIDATE
                 LA       R10,PDNUMB         LD ADR OF FIELD TO VALIDATE
                 BAL      R7,VALDTPD         VALIDATE FIELD FOR PACKED DEC DATA
                 LTR      R15,R15            CHK IF FIELD CONTAINS VALID DATA
                 BZ       DATAOK             IF 0, FIELD CONTAINS VALID PD NUMB
                 B        DATAINV            IF NOT, FIELD CONTAINS INV PD NUMB
*
*
*********************************************************************
*    THIS SUBROUTINE CHECKS IF A FIELD OF DATA CONTAINS PACKED DECIMAL
*    NUMBERS. THIS SUBROUTINE PERFORMES THE VALIDATION BY USING TWO
*    TRANSLATION TABLES. ONE TABLE TO VALIDATE ALL THE BYTES EXCEPT THE
*    LAST ONE AND THE OTHER TABLE TO VALIDATE THE LAST BYTE (THE ONE
```

```
*   THAT CONTAINS THE SIGN). A RC IS SET IN REGISTER 15 FOR THE CALLING
*   ROUTINE; X'00' INDICATES VALID DATA, X'04' INDICATES INVALID DATA.
**********************************************************************
*
VALDTPD    C      R0,BINONE            CHK IF FIELD CONTAINS ONLY 1 BYTE
           BE     CHKSIGN              IF YES, DO ONLY LAST BYTE TEST
           C      R0,BIN16             CHK IF LEN OF FIELD EXCEEDS 16 BYTES
           BH     PDATAINV             IF YES, PD FIELD TOO LONG
           LR     R14,R0               LD FD LEN INTO R14 FOR S + EX INSTR
           LR     R15,R10              LD ADR OF BG OF FD INTO R15 (SAVE R10)
           S      R14,BINTWO           DECR LEN BY 2, 1 FOR SIGN, 1 FOR EX
           EX     R14,TRT1             CHK IF ALL BYTES (EXCEPT SIGN) VALID
           BC     8,CHKSIGN            IF ALL BYTES OK, CHK SIGN BYTE
           LA     R15,4                IF NOT, IND IT
           BR     R7                   RETURN TO CALLING RTN
TRT1       TRT    0(0,R10),TABLE1      TRT INSTR FOR EX
CHKSIGN    LR     R14,R0               LD FD LEN IN R14 FOR LA INSTR
           LA     R15,0(R14,R10)       LD ADR OF BYTE PAST FIELD
           BCTR   R15,0                SET ADR TO POINT TO SIGN (LAST) BYTE
           UNPK   0(1,R15),0(1,R15)    REVERSE SIGN AND DIGIT FOR TABLE2
           TRT    0(1,R15),TABLE2      CHK IF LAST BYTE VALID
           UNPK   0(1,R15),0(1,R15)    RESTORE LAST BYTE
           BC     8,PDATAOK            CHK IF LAST BYTE OK
PDATAINV   LA     R15,4                IF NOT, IND IT
           BR     R7                   RETURN TO CALLING RTN
PDATAOK    LA     R15,0                DATA OK, IND IT
           BR     R7                   RETURN TO CALLING RTN
*
BINONE     DC     F'1'
BINTWO     DC     F'2'
BIN16      DC     F'16'
PDNOLEN    EQU    L'PDNUMB             CONTAINS THE LEN OF PDNUMB (IN BYTES)
PDNUMB     DC     ...                  THE FIELD THAT IS TO BE VALIDATED
*                                      FOR PACKED DECIMAL DATA
```

NOTES:

- Since the UNPK instruction does not cause a condition code to be set, it may be placed after the TRT instruction before the condition code is tested.

As an exercise, it is recommended that the reader try to enhance the VALNUMB macro definition, described above, to provide packed decimal data support. A third positional parameter could be defined to indicate the data format. Let Z (the default) indicate zoned decimal and P indicate packed decimal.

5.6 EXTERNAL SUBROUTINES

External subroutines are located in different CSECTs of the same load module. Each external subroutine may be coded as a separate program or as a separate CSECT within a multi-CSECT program. Then all the CSECTs are combined together via the Linkage Editor to form one multi-CSECT load module. Any CSECT of the load module may call any other external subroutine (CSECT) via the CALL macro instruction and may, optionally, pass parameters to it.

Besides the CALL macro instruction, the Assembler provides the ENTRY and the EXTRN Assembler instructions and VCONs to set up an external subroutine environment. An ENTRY statement is used to specify symbols that are defined in the same CSECT as the ENTRY statement but are referenced by other CSECTs. An EXTRN statement is used to specify symbols that are defined in other CSECTs but are referenced by the CSECT in which the EXTRN statement appears.

When a program is assembled, the Assembler creates an external symbol dictionary (ESD) as part of the object module and, optionally, a relocation dictionary (RLD). The name of each CSECT is automatically placed into the ESD. In addition, each name that is specified in the operands of ENTRY and of EXTRN statements are also placed into the ESD. Each name specified as the object of a VCON are placed into the ESD and the RLD. Symbols specified by the EXTRN statement may be referenced by ADCONs without causing an assembly error due to an undefined symbol because the EXTRN statement indicates to the Assembler that those symbols are defined in other CSECTs. The Assembler generates an RLD entry for the name specified as the object of an ADCON. A combination of an EXTRN statement and an ADCON for the same symbol is equivalent to a VCON.

A symbol must be defined in the ESD if it is to be referenced by another CSECT. Such a symbol may be the name of a CSECT that is called by another CSECT or may be the name associated with a storage area that is referenced by another CSECT (this does not pertain to parameters that are passed via the CALL macro instruction). The ESD entries are used by the Linkage Editor to provide a relative address into the load module where that symbol is located.

A symbol must be defined in the RLD if it is used to reference an area located in another CSECT. Such a symbol may be the name of another CSECT that is called or the name of a storage area that is located in another CSECT. As part of its expansion, the CALL macro instruction generates a VCON, which causes the Assembler to generate an RLD entry for the CSECT name that is being called.

When the Linkage Editor creates a load module from multiple CSECTs, it matches any RLD entries with the corresponding ESD entries and resolves the addresses (displacements into the load module).

Coding Example 5.6.1

This coding example illustrates the required JCL to assemble two separate programs, how to combine them into a single multi-CSECT load module, and how to execute it. The program (CSECT) named MAIN calls the program (CSECT) named SUBRTN. When SUBRTN completes execution, it returns control to MAIN.

```
//jobname        JOB        -
//STEP1          EXEC       ASMHC
//A.SYSPUNCH     DD         DSN=USER.OBJLIB(SUBRTN),DISP=SHR
//A.SYSIN        DD  *
*
SUBRTN           CSECT
                 INITL      3,EQU=R
                 ...
                 RCNTL      RC=0
                 END
//*
//STEP2          EXEC       ASMHCLG
//A.SYSIN        DD         *
*
MAIN             CSECT
                 INITL      3,EQU=R
                 ...
                 CALL       SUBRTN
                 ...
                 RCNTL      RC=0
                 END
//*
//L.OBJLIB       DD         DSN=USER.OBJLIB,DISP=SHR
//L.SYSIN        DD         *
  INCLUDE OBJLIB(SUBRTN)
//
```

NOTES:

- An ESD entry is created for name MAIN in the object module for program MAIN and an ESD entry is created for the name SUBRTN in the object module for program SUBRTN because they are CSECT names. This enables the Linkage Editor to record relative addresses into the load module for the starting locations for those names.
- An RLD entry is created for SUBRTN in the object module for the program MAIN due to the VCON generated by the CALL macro instruction.
- The Linkage Editor provides the VCON for SUBRTN (RLD entry) in the load module for the CSECT MAIN, with the relative address of SUBRTN (from the ESD entry).

Coding Example 5.6.2

This coding example expands the functions of Coding Example 5.6.1 and illustrates how MAIN passes two parameters to SUBRTN and how SUBRTN references a storage area (other than those parameters) defined in MAIN.

```
SUBRTN     CSECT
           EXTRN   TABLE              INDICATE TABLE IS IN ANOTHER CSECT
           INITL   3,EQU=R
           L       R10,0(0,R1)        LD ADR OF 1ST PARM (P1)
           L       R11,4(0,R2)        LD ADR OF 2ND PARM (P2)
           L       R12,TBLADR         LD ADR OF TABLE
           ...
           RCNTL   RC=0
TBLADR     DC      A(TABLE)           ADR OF TABLE (RESOLVED BY L.E.)
           END
*
MAIN       CSECT
           ENTRY   TABLE              INDICATE THAT TABLE IS LOCATED IN
*                                     THIS CSECT AND MAY BE REF BY
*                                      ANOTHER CSECT
           INITL   3,EQU=R
           ...
           CALL    SUBRTN,PARM=(P1,P2) CALL SUBRTN AND PASS IT THE ADRS OF
*                                     THE PARAMETERS P1 AND P2
           ...
           RCNTL   RC=0
P1         DC      C'PARM-1'
P2         DC      C'PARM-2'
*
TABLE      DC      C'ENTRY-1'
           DC      C'ENTRY-2'
           DC      C'ENTRY-3'
           ...
           DC      C'ENTRY-N'
           DC      X'FF'
           END
```

NOTES:

- For SUBRTN, the EXTRN statement could be omitted and TBLADR could be defined as a VCON instead, DC V(TABLE).
- In addition to the ESD and RLD entries mentioned in Coding Example 5.6.1, an ESD entry is created for TABLE in the object module for the program MAIN due to the ENTRY statement specified and an RLD entry is created for TABLE in the object module for the program SUBRTN due to the ADCON statement specified (or VCON, if specified instead).

External subroutines could be used to isolate program functions at the CSECT level. When a program is structured this way, a function could be modified by reassembling only the CSECT affected, and then relinkediting the load module with the modified CSECT. There is no need to reassemble all the program source. An external subroutine structure could also be used if a program has become so large that there are not enough registers available to be used as base registers and a single load module is still desired.

5.7 WRITING REUSABLE PROGRAMS

A reusable program is a program that may be reused without an intervening load into virtual storage. Reusable programs have one or more of the linkedit attributes of serially-reusable (PARM=REUS), reentrant (PARM=RENT), or refreshable (PARM=REFR). The section "Program Management" in Chapter 4 discusses how the operating system maintains the integrity of reusable programs.

A serially-reusable program is one that may be loaded into virtual storage once and used (executed) by multiple tasks one at a time. To accomplish this, the code in the program must either initialize itself at the beginning of program execution or reset itself at the end of program execution. This means that all switches, counters, control blocks, and so on, must be set as if the program was just loaded into virtual storage and being executed for the first time.

A reentrant program is usually coded as a read-only program and may be executed concurrently by two or more tasks. Read-only means that the program may not modify any instructions (except with the EX instruction), write into any areas defined with DC or DS instructions, or issue any macro instructions whose expansions are modified. The read-only requirement is necessary to accommodate the execution of multiple tasks concurrently. When multiple tasks are executing the same physical program, different tasks (depending upon start time, dispatching priority, and swap recommendations) will be executing different sections of the program and passing each other in the program as execution progresses. Therefore, for each task to execute properly, the reentrant program must be the same (contain the same instructions and constants) to each task and not contain the results of the previous task's execution.

A reentrant program does not have to be read-only throughout its code. The only requirement that a reentrant program must have is that it can support the execution of multiple tasks concurrently with the same load of the program. If a reentrant program elects to modify itself (this is strongly discouraged), then the section of the code that modifies itself must be serially-reusable. This means that this section of the code must initialize itself before it is excecuted or reset itself after it is executed. Also, it is the responsibility of the reentrant program to assure that only one task at a time executes that section of the code. This can be enforced by framing the code with the ENQ and DEQ macro instructions, respectively. This kind of reentrant program is sometimes called a quasi-reentrant program.

A reentrant program is loaded into the Job Pack Area (JPA) of the address space where it is executing or may be preloaded into the Link Pack Area (LPA). When loaded into the JPA, the program resides in either subpool 251 in the PSW protection key of the job step task (field TCBPKF of TCB), or in subpool 252 in PSW protection key zero if it is loaded from an authorized library. When loaded into the LPA, the program may reside in the Modified LPA (MLPA), Fixed LPA (FLPA), or Pageable LPA (PLPA).

If a reentrant program is designed to modify itself, then the serially-reusable section of code can modify itself while executing in either the same protection key as the job step task, in key zero, or not at all, depending on where the program resides. If the program resides in subpool 251, then the TCB key suffices; key zero is required if the program resides in subpool 252. If the program resides in the MPLA or the FPLA, then key zero is required if page protection is not turned on (via the NOPROT specification of the IEALPAxx and

IEAFIXxx members, respectively, of SYS1.PARMLIB). If page protection is turned on, then the program cannot modify itself even if it is executing in key zero. If the program resides in the PLPA, then it is treated automatically as a refreshable program and must not modify itself. If a reentrant program attempts to modify itself while resident in subpool 252 without executing in key zero, while resident in the MLPA or the FLPA with page protection on, or while resident in the PLPA, then it will ABEND with an S0C4. As you can see, attempting to execute a reentrant program that modifies itself (using the proper technique or not) could become quite involved and unpredictable. This is a good reason to write reentrant programs that do not contain any serially- reusable sections of code.

A refreshable program is a program that must be strictly reentrant. This means that the entire program must be read-only. Unlike a reentrant program, a refreshable program must not contain any sections that are serially-reusable. A refreshable program may be used in a certain way during system recovery. A program with the refreshable attribute indicates that the operating system, in order to recover from a recoverable software/hardware error, may reload the program while it is being executed without affecting the remainder of the execution. If the program had a serially-reusable section of code (like a reentrant program may have), then successful execution cannot be guaranteed after reload because if the serially-reusable section of the code were being executed when recovery was attempted, then the reload would lose the changes made to the program.

The remainder of this section will discuss reentrant programs that are read-only (contain no serially-reusable sections of code). Therefore, the rest of this section will also apply to refreshable programs.

A reentrant program may, however, modify the contents of general registers since their contents are saved and restored by MVS between the dispatching of tasks. If a reentrant program requires virtual storage areas to modify for use as a linkage and register savearea, I/O area, counters, switches, and so on, then that virtual storage area must be obtained via a GETMAIN macro instruction. This will not cause a conflict between tasks because each task allocates its own unique GETMAINed area. However, an R-type GETMAIN is required so that the address of the requested virtual storage is returned in a register (register 1). Also, a register must be assigned, for the life of the program, to contain the address of the GETMAINed area since that address cannot be stored in a virtual storage area. However, if multiple GETMAINed areas are obtained, then the address of only one GETMAINed area is required to be saved in a register, and fields in that GETMAINed area could be used to save the addresses of the other GETMAINed areas. DSECTs should be used to map the fields of the GETMAINed areas.

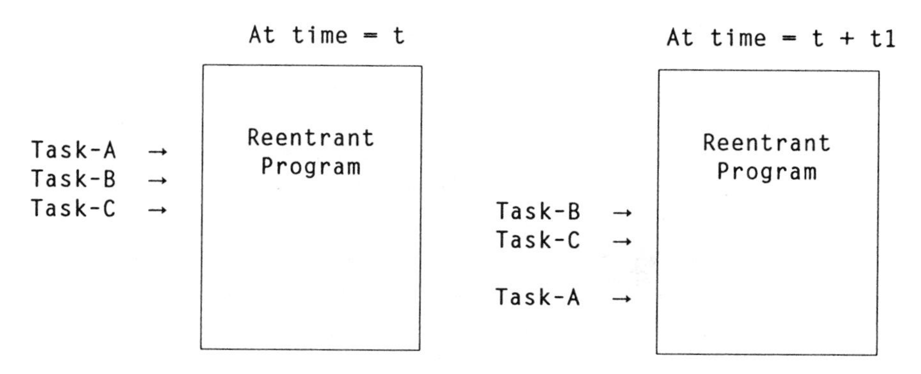

Figure 5.7.1. This figure illustrates how the execution of three tasks might progress while executing the same reentrant (or refreshable) program.

If the facilities provided by various IBM macro instructions are required by a reentrant program, then the list and execute forms of these macro instructions must be used. The list form of the macro instruction is coded in the program; the expansion is copied into a GETMAINed area; and the execute form of the macro instruction refers to the list in the GETMAINed area. If a macro instruction generates a control block, that is modified during the execution of the program, such as the DCB macro instruction, then that macro instruction is coded in the program, the expansion is copied into a GETMAINed area, and any references to the expansion are done by specifying the address (which points to the GETMAINed area) in a register. If a macro instruction does not have a list and an execute form, such as the GET and the PUT macro instructions, then the address of the parameters must be specified as registers that point to a GETMAINed area.

The advantages of using reentrant programs over nonreusable programs and serially-reusable programs are the following:

- Virtual storage can be saved since only one copy of the program is required. A reentrant program may be loaded into the Link Pack Area if the program is required to be shared across address spaces and may be loaded into the Job Pack Area if the program is required to be shared only among tasks in the same address space.
- There is also a performance advantage since:
  - Unlike a nonreusable program, the program is not required to be loaded into virtual storage each time that it is required to be used.
  - Unlike a serially-reusable program, tasks do not have to wait to execute the program if another task is currently executing the program.

Coding Example 5.7.1

This coding example illustrates how to code a reentrant program to perform I/O. In this example, the program reads file-1, selects certain fields from each record, and uses these fields to create the records of file-2. The records are read, using the locate-mode of the GET macro instruction, which eliminates the requirement to allocate the input I/O area from a GETMAINed area. This program also qualifies as a refreshable program.

```
         TITLE 'REENTRANT I/O PROGRAM EXAMPLE'
*
*
**********************************************************************
*
*        EXAMPLE OF REENTRANT I/O PROGRAM
*
*        FILE-1 IS READ, AND SELECTED FIELDS FROM EACH RECORD
*        ARE USED TO CREATE THE RECORDS OF FILE-2.
*
*        ALSO, A RECORD COUNTER IS MAINTAINED IN THE PROGRAM AND
*        ITS CONTENTS ARE USED AS ONE OF THE FIELDS OF THE RECORDS
*        OF FILE-2.
*
*        REGISTER 9 IS USED TO HOLD THE ADDRESS OF THE FIRST
*        GETMAINED AREA DURING THE ENTIRE EXECUTION OF THE PROGRAM.
*
**********************************************************************
*
*
RENTIO   CSECT
*
*
**********************************************************************
*        INITIALIZATION
```

```
**********************************************************************
*
          INITL   3,EQU=R             INITIALIZE PROGRAM
          USING   WORKAREA,R9         DEFINE REG FOR WA DSECT
          USING   RECORD1,R11         DEFINE REG FOR REC1 DSECT
          USING   RECORD2,R12         DEFINE REG FOR REC2 DSECT
*
*
**********************************************************************
*       MAINSTREAM OF PROGRAM
**********************************************************************
*
          BAL     R6,GETMAIN1         GET STOR FOR WORKAREA
          BAL     R6,GETMAIN2         GET STOR FOR MACRO EXPNS, I/O AREAS
          BAL     R6,BLDCNTLS         MOVE MACRO EXPNS INTO GM AREA
          BAL     R6,OPENFLS          OPEN FILES
NEXTREC   BAL     R6,GETREC           READ A RECORD
          BAL     R6,BLDREC           BUILD OUTPUT RECORD
          BAL     R6,PUTREC           WRITE A RECORD
          B       NEXTREC             PROCESS NEXT RECORD
RECEND    BAL     R6,CLOSEFLS         CLOSE FILES
          B       RETURN              RETURN TO MVS OR TO CALLING PROG
*
*
**********************************************************************
*       THIS ROUTINE OBTAINS STORAGE FOR THE PROGRAM WORKAREA AND SAVES
*       THAT ADDRESS IN REGISTER 9.
**********************************************************************
*
GETMAIN1  GETMAIN RU,LV=WKARLEN
          LR      R9,R1               SET ADRBLTY FOR WA DSECT
          BR      R6                  RETURN TO CALLING RTN
*
*
**********************************************************************
*       THIS ROUTINE OBTAINS STORAGE FOR THE I/O MACRO EXPANSIONS AND
*       THE I/O AREAS AND SAVES THE ADDRESSES OF THOSE STORAGE AREAS
*       IN FIELDS OF THE PREVIOUS GETMAINED AREA.
**********************************************************************
*
GETMAIN2  GETMAIN RU,LV=OPENLEN
          ST      R1,OPENADR
          GETMAIN RU,LV=CLOSELEN
          ST      R1,CLOSEADR
          GETMAIN RU,LV=DCB1LEN
          ST      R1,DCB1ADR
          GETMAIN RU,LV=DCB2LEN
          ST      R1,DCB2ADR
          GETMAIN RU,LV=REC2LEN
          ST      R1,REC2ADR
          BR      R6                  RETURN TO CALLING RTN
*
*
**********************************************************************
*       THIS ROUTINE COPIES THE I/O MACRO EXPANSIONS INTO THE
*       GETMAINED STORAGE AREAS.
**********************************************************************
*
BLDCNTLS  L       R10,OPENADR
          MVC     0(OPENLEN,R10),OPEN
          L       R10,CLOSEADR
          MVC     0(CLOSELEN,R10),CLOSE
          L       R10,DCB1ADR
          MVC     0(DCB1LEN,R10),DCB1
```

```
          L       R10,DCB2ADR
          MVC     0(DCB2LEN,R10),DCB2
          BR      R6                  RETURN TO CALLING RTN
*
*
*********************************************************************
*      THIS ROUTINE OPENS THE DCBS FROM THE GETMAINED AREAS
*      AND ZEROS THE RECORD COUNTER FOR FILE-2
*********************************************************************
*
OPENFLS   L       R1,OPENADR          LOAD ADR OF OPEN LIST FROM GM AREA
          L       R10,DCB1ADR         LOAD ADR OF DCB1 FROM GM AREA
          L       R11,DCB2ADR         LOAD ADR OF DCB2 FROM GM AREA
          OPEN    ((R10),,(R11)),MF=(E,(R1))    DO REENTRANT OPEN
          ZAP     REC2CTR,ZERO        CLEAR RECORD COUNTER
          BR      R6                  RETURN TO CALLING RTN
*
*
*********************************************************************
*      THIS ROUTINE READS A RECORD FORM FILE-1.
*********************************************************************
*
GETREC    L       R10,DCB1ADR         LOAD ADR OF DCB1 FROM GM AREA
          GET     (R10)               DO REENTRANT GET
          LR      R11,R1              SET ADRBLTY FOR REC1 DSECT
          BR      R6                  RETURN TO CALLING RTN
*
*
*********************************************************************
*      THIS ROUTINE CREATES THE RECORDS FOR FILE-2.
*********************************************************************
*
BLDREC    L       R12,REC2ADR         SET ADRBLTY FOR REC2 DSECT
          AP      REC2CTR,ONE         INCR RECORD COUNTER
          MVC     ORECNUM,REC2CTR
          MVC     OFIELD1,IFIELD2
          MVC     OFIELD2,IFIELD4
          BR      R6                  RETURN TO CALLING RTN
*
*
*********************************************************************
*      THIS SUBROUTINE WRITES THE RECORDS INTO FILE-2.
*********************************************************************
*
PUTREC    L       R10,DCB2ADR         LOAD ADR OF DCB2 FROM GM AREA
          L       R12,REC2ADR         LD ADR OF REC2 I/O AREA FROM GM AREA
          PUT     (R10),(R12)         DO REENTRANT PUT
          BR      R6                  RETURN TO CALLING RTN
*
*
*********************************************************************
*      THIS ROUTINE CLOSES THE DCBS FROM THE GETMAINED AREAS
*********************************************************************
*
CLOSEFLS  L       R1,CLOSEADR         LOAD ADR OF CLOSE LIST FROM GM AREA
          L       R10,DCB1ADR         LOAD ADR OF DCB1 FROM GM AREA
          L       R11,DCB2ADR         LOAD ADR OF DCB2 FROM GM AREA
          CLOSE   ((R10),,(R11)),MF=(E,(R1))    DO REENTRANT CLOSE
          BR      R6                  RETURN TO CALLING RTN
*
*
*********************************************************************
*      THIS ROUTINE RESTORES THE REGISTERS AND RETURNS CONTROL.
*********************************************************************
```

```
*
RETURN     RCNTL   RC=0               RETURN TO MVS OR CALLING PROG
*
*******************************************************************
*      CONSTANTS USED BY PROGRAM
*******************************************************************
*
ZERO       DC      P'0'
ONE        DC      P'1'
*
*
*******************************************************************
*      LIST FORM OF I/O MACRO INSTRUCTIONS
*******************************************************************
*
OPEN       OPEN    (DCB1,(INPUT),DCB2,(OUTPUT)),MF=L
OPENLEN    EQU     (*-OPEN)
*
CLOSE      CLOSE   (DCB1,,DCB2),MF=L
CLOSELEN   EQU     (*-CLOSE)
*
*
*******************************************************************
*      DCB MACRO INSTRUCTIONS
*******************************************************************
*
FILE1DCB   DCB     DSORG=PS,MACRF=GL,RECFM=FB,LRECL=80,EODAD=RECEND,    -
                   DDNAME=INDATADD
DCB1LEN    EQU     (*-FILE1DCB)
*
FILE2DCB   DCB     DSORG=PS,MACRF=PM,RECFM=FB,LRECL=50,DDNAME=OUTDATDD -
DCB2LEN    EQU     (*-FILE2DCB)
*
*
*******************************************************************
*      DSECTS USED BY PROGRAM
*******************************************************************
*
WORKAREA   DSECT
OPENADR    DS      F                  ADDR OF OPEN LIST IN GM AREA
CLOSEADR   DS      F                  ADDR OF CLOSE LIST IN GM AREA
DCB1ADR    DS      F                  ADDR OF DCB1 IN GM AREA
DCB2ADR    DS      F                  ADDR OF DCB2 IN GM AREA
REC2ADR    DS      F                  ADDR OF OUT REC I/O AREA IN GM AREA
REC2CTR    DS      PL5                ADDR OF RECORD COUNTER
WKARLEN    EQU     (*-WORKAREA)       LEN OF WORK AREA
*
RECORD1    DSECT
IFIELD1    DS      CL15
IFIELD2    DS      CL20
IFIELD3    DS      CL10
IFIELD4    DS      CL25
IFIELD5    DS      CL10
*
RECORD2    DSECT
ORECNUM    DS      CL5
OFIELD1    DS      CL20
OFIELD2    DS      CL25
REC2LEN    EQU     (*-RECORD2)        LEN OF OUTPUT RECORD
*
*
*******************************************************************
*      END OF PROGRAM
*******************************************************************
```

```
*
         END
*
```

The Assembler can be used to verify that the code is reentrant if PARM=RENT is specified when the Assembler is invoked. This will cause the Assembler to verify that the receiving operands of all machine instructions that modify virtual storage (MVC, L, ST, etc.) are defined explicitly (base register and displacement) or reference the names of virtual storage areas that are contained in DSECTs. However, the Assembler will not verify that the registers used to provide addressability for the DSECTs are loaded with a proper address, and it will not verify that the proper forms (list and execute) of the macro instructions are used.

After the program is assembled, it must be linkedited with PARM=RENT for the resulting load module to receive the reentrant attribute. The Linkage Editor does not verify that the code of the program is reentrant. If multiple programs are being linkedited together to create one load module, then the Linkage Editor will check the reentrant attribute of each program. If any program is not marked reentrant, then the Linkage Editor will mark the resultant load module as not reentrant.

5.8 BUILDING AN EXPANDABLE VARIABLE LENGTH TABLE

When a program processes data, there are times when it is convenient, efficient or even necessary to store the data into a table in virtual storage and process it there. Such tables are defined and processed in a number of different ways. One way is to simply allocate a large fixed amount of storage either with a DS instruction in the actual program or with a GETMAIN macro instruction. However, this method has a serious shortcoming if more data is processed than the fixed length table can accommodate. For this occurrence, the method would have two options. One option would be to stop processing the data and issue an error or warning message to the user. However, a message to the user, who has a requirement to process all the data, does not get the job done. The other option would be to modify the program to create a larger fixed length table. This action is only a temporary solution until the amount of data processed again exceeds the capacity of the table. It also delays the user from processing the required amount of data until the program is modified.

A much better solution is to write the code that will create a table that expands dynamically, according to the amount of data that is required to be processed for any given execution of the program. This method always accommodates the amount of data that is processed, provided that enough virtual storage is available. In the unlikely event that the available virtual storage cannot accommodate the amount of data processed, the program need not be modified since the amount of virtual storage available is controlled by the JCL and the architecture of the operating system.

The storage is allocated for such a table by performing successive GETMAINs, as required, and linking the areas together to join them logically. The initial or base allocation for the table should be large enough to accommodate all or most of the data for a typical run (if it is possible to estimate). This will save the overhead of excessive GETMAINs. The initial allocation should also be accomplished with a GETMAIN as opposed to a DS instruction because a large storage allocation in the program will use a large portion of the available addressability range of the base registers. Conditional GETMAINs should be used to prevent the program from ABENDing if the available amount of virtual storage is exhausted and also to enable the program to issue a meaningful message for such an occurrence. Also, conventions for linkage between the GETMAINed areas and end-of-data indication need to be established.

One convention that is used is to set the first word of the last slot of each GETMAINed area (that is followed by another GETMAINed area) to binary ones and the second word to the address of the next GETMAINed area, and to set the first word of the slot (after the last data entry) to binary zeros. Therefore, if the first word of a slot does not contain binary ones or binary zeros, then it contains a data entry.

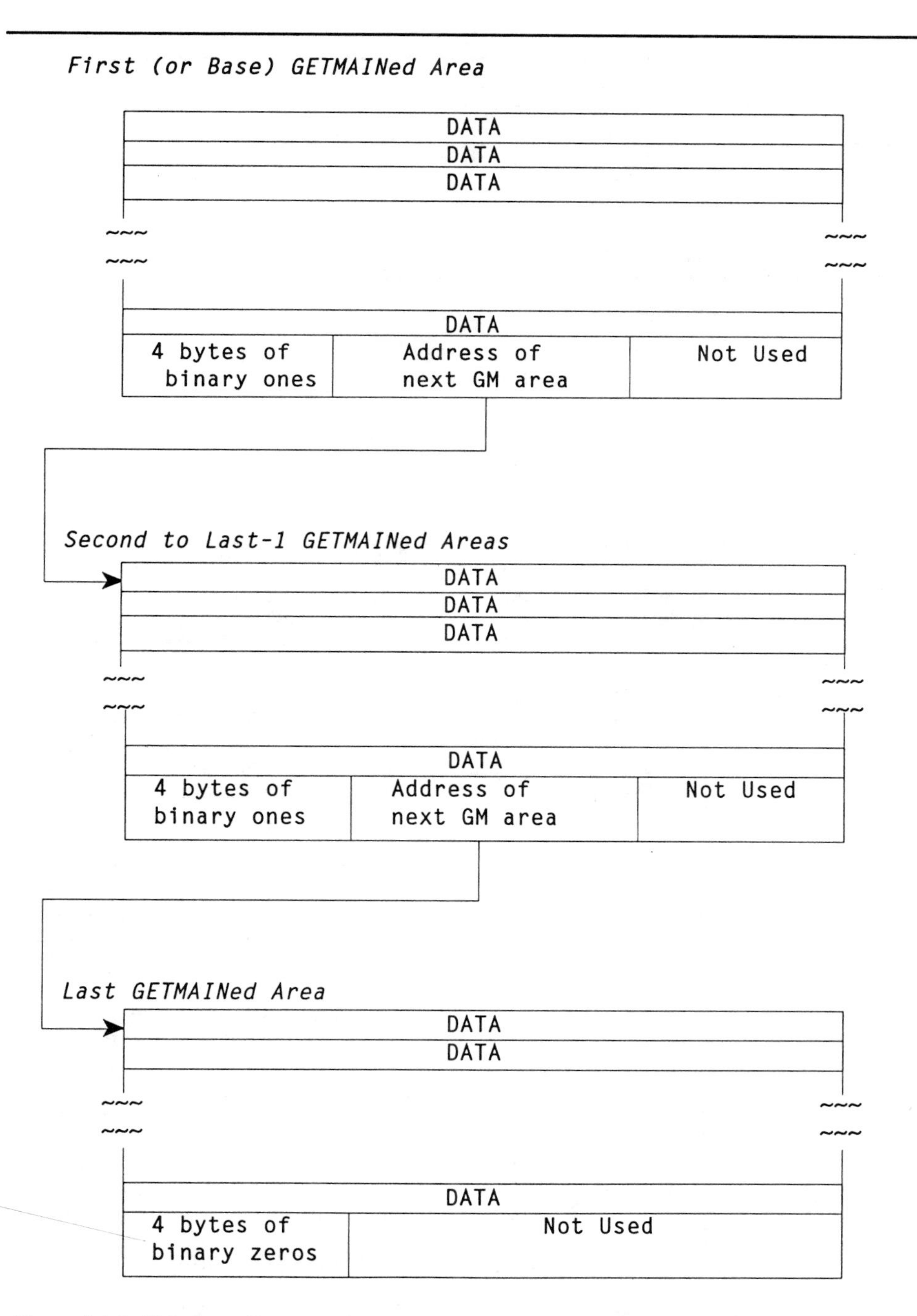

Figure 5.8.1. This figure illustrates the contents of each GETMAINed area of an expandable table.

Coding Example 5.8.1

This coding example illustrates the code to create an expandable table. Fixed length data entries are assumed (variable length entries are discussed below). Let us also assume that the entry size is 100 bytes, the base allocation will be large enough to hold 500 entries, and each extension will be large enough to hold 75 additional entries.

```
EXPDTBL   CSECT
*
*
***************************************************************************
*      INITIALIZATION
***************************************************************************
*
          INITL     3,EQU=R                   INITIALIZE PROGRAM
*
*
***************************************************************************
*      MAINSTREAM OF PROGRAM
***************************************************************************
*
          ...
          BAL       R6,ALLOBASE               ALLOCATE TABLE BASE
NEXTDATA  BAL       R6,GETDATA                GET A DATA RECORD
          BAL       R6,BLDTBL                 PUT RECORD INTO TABLE
          B         NEXTDATA                  GET NEXT DATA RECORD
DATAEND   BAL       R6,SETBLEND               SET END OF DATA INDICATOR
          ...
*
*
***************************************************************************
*      THIS ROUTINE ALLOCATES THE VIRTUAL STORAGE FOR THE TABLE BASE. THE
*      ADDRESS OF THE FIRST TABLE SLOT IS STORED IN SLOTPTR AND THE TOTAL
*      NUMBER OF SLOTS IN THE BASE AREA IS STORED IN SLOTCT.
***************************************************************************
*
ALLOBASE  GETMAIN   EC,LV=GM1LEN,SP=10,A=GM1ADDR
          MVC       SLOTPTR,GM1ADDR           STORE FIRST AVAIL SLOT ADDR
          LA        R10,BASECT+1              LOAD NUMBER OF SLOTS IN GM1 AREA
          ST        R10,SLOTCT                STORE NUMBER OF SLOTS
          BR        R6                        RETURN TO CALLING RTN
*
*
***************************************************************************
*      THIS ROUTINE GETS THE DATA FOR THE EXPANDABLE TABLE FROM SOME
*      EXTERNAL SOURCE AND PLACES THE DATA ENTRY INTO THE AREA DATA.
***************************************************************************
*
GETDATA   DS        0H
          ...                                 GET DATA FROM EXTERNAL SOURCE
          BR        R6                        RETURN TO CALLING RTN
*
*
***************************************************************************
*      THIS ROUTINE BUILDS THE EXPANDABLE TABLE BY INSERTING THE DATA,
*      WHICH IS PASSED TO IT IN THE AREA DATA, INTO THE TABLE SLOTS. THE
*      ADDRESS OF THE NEXT SLOT IS STORED IN SLOTPTR AND THE NUMBER OF
*      SLOTS LEFT IN THE TABLE SEGMENT IS STORED IN SLOTCT. THIS ROUTINE
*      DOES THE FOLLOWING:
*             * INSERTS THE DATA ENTRY INTO THE TABLE SLOT POINTED TO BY
*               SLOTPTR;
*             * UPDATES SLOTPTR TO POINT TO THE NEXT TABLE SLOT;
*             * UPDATES SLOTCT BY DECREMENTING THE COUNT BY ONE;
```

```
*           * BRANCHES AND LINKS TO THE ALLOXTEN ROUTINE TO ALLOCATE VIRTUAL
*             STORAGE FOR ANOTHER TABLE SEGMENT WHEN THE CURRENT SEGMENT IS
*             EXHAUSTED.
*       THE INITIAL VALUES OF SLOTPTR AND SLOTCT ARE SET EACH TIME THAT
*       VIRTUAL STORAGE IS ALLOCATED FOR A NEW TABLE SEGMENT BY THE ROUTINE
*       THAT DOES THE ALLOCATION.
***************************************************************************
*
BLDTBL    L       R10,SLOTCT                LOAD NUMBER OF AVAIL SLOTS
          BCTR    R10,0                     DECR AVAIL SLOT COUNT
          LTR     R10,R10                   CHECK IF LAST SLOT
          BZ      LASTSLOT                  IF YES, BRANCH
          L       R11,SLOTPTR               LOAD ADR OF NEXT AVAIL SLOT
          MVC     0(ENTRYLEN,R11),DATA      MOVE DATA INTO TABLE
          LA      R11,ENTRYLEN(0,R11)       INCR TO NEXT SLOT ADDR
          ST      R11,SLOTPTR               STORE ADR OF NEXT AVAIL SLOT
          BR      R6                        RETURN TO CALLING RTN
LASTSLOT  MVC     SLOTXPTR,SLOTPTR          STORE ADR OF LAST SLOT
          BAL     R7,ALLOXTEN               OBTAIN NEXT GM AREA
          L       R11,SLOTXPTR              LOAD ADR OF LAST SLOT OF PREV GM
          MVC     0(4,R11),BINONES          SET LINK WORD IN PREV GM AREA
          MVC     4(4,R11),GMXADDR          STORE ADR OF NEXT GM INTO PREV GM
          B       BLDTBL                    PUT CURRENT DATA ENTRY INTO TBL
*
*
***************************************************************************
*       THIS SUBROUTINE ALLOCATES VIRTUAL STORAGE FOR A TABLE EXTENSION. IT
*       RECEIVES CONTROL EACH TIME THAT THE CURRENT TABLE SEGMENT IS
*       EXHAUSTED AND INITIALIZES THE SLOTPTR AND SLOTCT AREAS EACH TIME
*       THAT ADDITIONAL VIRTUAL STORAGE IS ALLOCATED.
***************************************************************************
*
ALLOXTEN  GETMAIN EC,LV=GMXLEN,SP=10,A=GMXADDR
          MVC     SLOTPTR,GMXADDR           STORE FIRST AVAIL SLOT ADDR
          LA      R10,EXTENCT+1             LOAD NUMBER OF SLOTS IN GMX AREA
          ST      R10,SLOTCT                STORE NUMBER OF SLOTS
          BR      R7                        RETURN TO CALLING RTN
*
*
**************************************************************************
*       THIS ROUTINE RECEIVES CONTROL WHEN ALL THE DATA IS INSERTED INTO THE
*       TABLE AND PUTS AN END-OF-TABLE INDICATOR AFTER THE LAST DATA ENTRY.
***************************************************************************
*
SETBLEND  L       R11,SLOTPTR               LOAD ADR OF NEXT AVAIL SLOT
          MVC     0(4,R11),BINZEROS         SET END-OF-DATA INDICATOR
          BR      R6                        RETURN TO CALLING RTN
*
*
***************************************************************************
*       DC/DS/EQU STATEMENTS
***************************************************************************
*
ENTRYLEN  EQU     100                       LENGTH OF DATA ENTRY
BASECT    EQU     500                       CAPACITY OF TABLE BASE
EXTENCT   EQU     75                        CAPACITY OF EACH TABLE EXTENSION
GM1LEN    EQU     (BASECT+1)*ENTRYLEN       LENGTH OF BASE GETMAIN
GMXLEN    EQU     (EXTENCT+1)*ENTRYLEN      LENGTH OF EACH ADDITIONAL GETMAIN
BINZEROS  DC      4XL1'00'                  END-OF-DATA INDICATOR
BINONES   DC      4XL1'FF'                  LINK INDICATOR
GM1ADDR   DS      F                         ADR OF BG OF TABLE
GMXADDR   DS      F                         ADR OF EACH TABLE EXTENSION
SLOTPTR   DS      F                         RUNNING ADR OF NEXT AVAIL SLOT
SLOTXPTR  DS      F                         ADR OF LAST SLOT OF EACH GM AREA
```

```
SLOTCT      DS      F                     RUNNING COUNT OF SLOTS AVAIL
DATA        DS      CL100                 DATA ENTRY
                    ...
*
*
************************************************************************
*       END OF PROGRAM
************************************************************************
*
            END
```

NOTES:

- Notice the easy-to-understand, modular program structure and the use of EQUs to facilitate any future length changes.
- Subpool 10 is used to isolate the table in its own storage subpool. This will facilitate locating it in a storage dump to verify that it is being built properly.
- As an excercise, the reader might try to write a routine to sequentially read all the entries of the table created by this coding example.

Variable length entries can be supported by appending an entry-length-field to the beginning of each entry. A 4-byte entry-length-field is convenient and efficient since its contents are loaded into a register during processing. The contents of the entry-length-field may contain the length of only the entry (exclusive of the entry-length-field) or may contain the length of the entry-length-field plus the entry. The entry-length-fields used in this section will include both. The length of the entry should be supplied by the calling routine.

An expandable table with variable length entries requires considerations for determining the following:

- Number of entries that can be accommodated in each table segment;
- Location of the next available entry slot when the table is being created;
- Location of the next entry when the table is read;
- End-of-segment.

The number of entries that can be accommodated in a table segment can only be estimated based upon average entry length. The length of the GETMAIN for the table base allocation and for each successive GETMAIN for the table extensions can be based upon the average length of the entries or can be a fixed length.

The location of the next available slot after an entry is inserted into the table can be determined by adding the address of the current slot to the length of the entry (including the entry-length-field). Coding Example 5.8.2 shows the code for the subroutine that moves the new entry into the next available slot of the table and then calculates the next available slot address.

Coding Example 5.8.2

This coding example illustrates how to build an expandable table containing variable-length entries. When BLDTBLV receives control, SLOTPTR contains the address of the next available slot of the table, DATA contains the new entry, and register 10 contains the length of the new entry.

```
BLDTBLV   L       R11,SLOTPTR       LOAD ADR OF NEXT AVAIL SLOT
          BCTR    R10,0             DECR ENTRY LEN FOR EX INTR
          EX      R10,MOVEDATA      MOVE NEW ENTRY INTO TABLE
          LA      R10,5(0,R10)      RESTR ENTRY LEN, ADD LEN OF LEN-FIELD
          ST      R10,0(0,R11)      APPEND ENTRY LENGTH TO BG OF ENTRY
          LA      R11,0(R10,R11)    GET ADR OF NEXT AVAIL SLOT
          ST      R11,SLOTPTR       SAVE ADR OF NEXT AVAIL SLOT
```

```
         BR      R7                 RETURN TO CALLING RTN
MOVEDATA MVC     4(0,R11),DATA      MVC INSTR FOR EX INSTR
```

NOTES:

- This subroutine should include code to check when the virtual storage of the table segment has been exhausted.

When the table is read sequentially, the address of the next entry is calculated simply by adding the length of the current entry to the address of the current entry. Coding Example 5.8.3 illustrates the required code.

Coding Example 5.8.3

This coding example illustrates how to read the variable length entries of the expandable table sequentially.

```
GETENTRY L       R1,SLOTPTR         LD ADR OF CURRENT ENTRY
         CLC     0(4,R1),BINZEROS CHK IF CURRENT ENTRY IS TBL-END-IND
         BE      TBLEND             IF YES, END-OF-TABLE
         L       R14,0(0,R1)        LD LEN OF CURRENT ENTRY
         LA      R11,0(R14,R1)      CALC ADR OF NEXT ENTRY
         S       R14,BIN4           SUBT LEN OF ENTRY-LEN-FIELD
         LA      R1,4(0,R1)         INCR PAST ENTRY-LEN-FIELD
         CLC     0(4,R11),BINONES CHK IF NEXT ENTRY IS LINK ENTRY
         BE      GETNXSEG           IF YES, GET ADR OF NEXT TBL SEG
         ST      R11,SLOTPTR        IF NO, SAVE ADR OF NEXT ENTRY
         LA      R15,0              IND REG 1 CONTAINS CUR ENTRY ADR
         BR      R7                 RETURN TO CALLING RTN
GETNXSEG L       R11,4(0,R11)       LD ADR OF NEXT TBL SEG
         ST      R11,SLOTPTR        SAVE ADR OF NEXT ENTRY
         LA      R15,0              IND REG 1 CONTAINS CUR ENTRY ADR
         BR      R7                 RETURN TO CALLING RTN
TBLEND   LA      R15,4              IND END-OF-TABLE
         BR      R7                 RETURN TO CALLING RTN
         ...
BIN4     DC      F'4'
```

NOTES:

- When GETENTRY returns control, register 1 points to the data section of the entry (4 bytes past the beginning of the stored entry, skipping the entry-length-field), and register 14 contains the length of the entry (not counting the length of the entry-length-field).

The end-of-segment cannot be determined by counting the number of entries that are inserted as was the case in Coding Example 5.8.1, with fixed length entries. The length of the entries (including the appended entry-length-field) that are inserted into the table segment must be accumulated. The counter must start with eight to allow for the link fields (four bytes for the indicator and four bytes for the address of the next GETMAINed area) located at the end of the segment. The end of the table segment occurs when the length of a new entry causes the accumulated length to exceed the length of the segment. This is when the next segment is allocated, and that entry becomes the first entry in the next segment.

As an exercise, the reader might try to modify Coding Example 5.8.1 to support variable length records and then write a routine to sequentially read the variable length entries of the table.

5.9 MULTI-LEVEL TABLES

Before discussing multi-level tables, let us first review single-level tables. A single-level table (or just table) equates one key or id field with a specific piece of information. The following is a typical table:

```
TABLE      EQU    *
           DC     X'0001',CL24'INFORMATION FOR CODE 0001'
ENTRYLEN   EQU    *-TABLE
           DC     X'0002',CL24'INFORMATION FOR CODE 0002'
           DC     X'0003',CL24'INFORMATION FOR CODE 0003'
           ...
           DC     X'nnnn',CL24'INFORMATION FOR CODE nnnn'
ENTRIES    EQU    (*-TABLE)/ENTRYLEN
```

The first 2 bytes of each entry is the key field, and the remaining 24 bytes contain the information associated with that key. The processing would consist of scanning the key fields of each entry for a specific code. When the code is located, the remainder of the entry contains the information that satisfies the search.

A multi-level table contains multiple entries or subentries for each key field. The subentries for each key field contain key fields that may also point to multiple entries. The initial key field search leads to other key field searches until a unique entry is located. Since entries point to multiple entries, each of those entries could conveniently be stored in another table. Therefore, the structure of a multi-level table is such that each entry in the first table points to another table. The entries in the next table may also point to other tables until the last set of tables that contain the actual information that is the object of the search are defined.

As an example of the use of a multi-level table, let us consider the following situation. A manufacturer produces a particular product (let us say stock number 0123) in three different sizes: small, medium, and large. Each size is produced in two quality categories: standard and deluxe. All combinations of the product sell in three different geographical locations: East, Central, and West. The selling price of the product varies according to size, quality, and selling location. The selling prices for the various combinations are tabulated in Table 5.9.1.

Table 5.9.1

This table contains the selling prices of product 0123 for all possible combinations and locations.

Combination		Location/Price		
Size	Quality	East	Central	West
S	Standard	10.00	7.10	9.90
	Deluxe	14.95	12.00	14.00
M	Standard	15.00	11.50	13.05
	Deluxe	21.80	17.25	20.50
L	Standard	19.90	14.90	17.05
	Deluxe	30.00	23.00	27.00

The initial task for implementing a multi-level table is to design the table in virtual storage. The DC instructions required to represent the the multi-level table described in Table 5.9.1 are coded in Coding Example 5.9.1.

Coding Example 5.9.1

This coding example illustrates how to code the DC instructions required to represent the multi-level table described in Table 5.9.1.

```
*
************************************************************************
* MULTI-LEVEL TABLE FOR PRODUCT NUMBER 0123
************************************************************************
*
*
*     TABLE OF PRODUCT SIZES
*
P0123TBL        EQU       *
                DC        C'S',CL3' ',A(P0123SQ)        SMALL
                DC        C'M',CL3' ',A(P0123MQ)        MEDIUM
                DC        C'L',CL3' ',A(P0123LQ)        LARGE
                DC        X'FF'
*
*
*     TABLE OF QUALITY FOR SMALL SIZE
*
P0123SQ         EQU       *
                DC        C'S',CL3' ',A(P0123SSL)       SMALL STANDARD
                DC        C'D',CL3' ',A(P0123SDL)       SMALL DELUXE
                DC        X'FF'
*
*
*     TABLE OF LOCATION/PRICE FOR STANDARD SMALL SIZE
*
P0123SSL        EQU       *
                DC        C'E',PL3'1000'                SMALL STANDARD EAST
                DC        C'C',PL3'0710'                SMALL STANDARD CENTRAL
                DC        C'W',PL3'0990'                SMALL STANDARD WEST
                DC        X'FF'
*
*
*     TABLE OF LOCATION/PRICE FOR DELUXE SMALL SIZE
*
P0123SDL        EQU       *
                DC        C'E',PL3'1495'                SMALL DELUXE EAST
                DC        C'C',PL3'1200'                SMALL DELUXE CENTRAL
                DC        C'W',PL3'1400'                SMALL DELUXE WEST
                DC        X'FF'
*
*
*     TABLE OF QUALITY FOR MEDIUM SIZE
*
P0123MQ         EQU       *
                DC        C'S',CL3' ',A(P0123MSL)       MEDIUM STANDARD
                DC        C'D',CL3' ',A(P0123MDL)       MEDIUM DELUXE
                DC        X'FF'
*
*
*     TABLE OF LOCATION/PRICE FOR STANDARD MEDIUM SIZE
*
P0123MSL        EQU       *
                DC        C'E',PL3'1500'                MEDIUM STANDARD EAST
```

```
                DC        C'C',PL3'1150'              MEDIUM STANDARD CENTRAL
                DC        C'W',PL3'1305'              MEDIUM STANDARD WEST
                DC        X'FF'
*
*
*     TABLE OF LOCATION/PRICE FOR DELUXE MEDIUM SIZE
*
P0123MDL        EQU       *
                DC        C'E',PL3'2180'              MEDIUM DELUXE EAST
                DC        C'C',PL3'1725'              MEDIUM DELUXE CENTRAL
                DC        C'W',PL3'2050'              MEDIUM DELUXE WEST
                DC        X'FF'
*
*
*     TABLE OF QUALITY FOR LARGE SIZE
*
P0123LQ         EQU       *
                DC        C'S',CL3' ',A(P0123LSL)     LARGE STANDARD
                DC        C'D',CL3' ',A(P0123LDL)     LARGE DELUXE
                DC        X'FF'
*
*
*     TABLE OF LOCATION/PRICE FOR STANDARD LARGE SIZE
*
P0123LSL        EQU       *
                DC        C'E',PL3'1990'              LARGE STANDARD EAST
                DC        C'C',PL3'1490'              LARGE STANDARD CENTRAL
                DC        C'W',PL3'1705'              LARGE STANDARD WEST
                DC        X'FF'
*
*
*     TABLE OF LOCATION/PRICE FOR DELUXE LARGE SIZE
*
P0123LDL        EQU       *
                DC        C'E',PL3'3000'              LARGE DELUXE EAST
                DC        C'C',PL3'2300'              LARGE DELUXE CENTRAL
                DC        C'W',PL3'2700'              LARGE DELUXE WEST
                DC        X'FF'
*
*
***********************************************************************
*     DSECTS FOR MULTI-LEVEL TABLE
***********************************************************************
*
DSIZETBL        DSECT
$SIZE           DS        CL1                         SIZE CODE
                DS        CL3                         *** FOR ALIGNMENT ***
$QTBLADR        DS        CL4                         POINTER TO CORRESPONDING
*                                                      QUALITY TABLE
$SENTLEN        EQU       *-DSIZETBL                  ENTRY LENGTH
*
DQUALTBL        DSECT
$QUAL           DS        CL1                         QUALITY CODE
                DS        CL3                         *** FOR ALIGNMENT ***
$LTBLADR        DS        CL4                         POINTER TO CORRESPONDING
*                                                      LOCATION TABLE
$QENTLEN        EQU       *-DQUALTBL                  ENTRY LENGTH
*
DLOCTBL         DSECT
$LOC            DS        CL1                         LOCATION CODE
$PRICE          DS        PL3                         PRICE
$LENTLEN        EQU       *-DLOCTBL                   ENTRY LENGTH
```

The information described in Table 5.9.1 could also be represented in a single-level table, but this is not advisable because the resulting table would be unwieldy, difficult to maintain, and less efficient to process. Each entry would be required to contain every possibility for the initial key (size). Each entry would be excessively long, contain many subfields, be difficult to follow (because the information from three tables are merged into one table), and be very sensitive to field length changes.

Another way to design the single-level table would be to simpilfy the entries by merging all the keys (size, quality, location) together to form one super key. Using that design would require additional code to merge the three discreet keys (size, quality, location) into one key before the table is searched. Using the super key method would simplify the search process, but would create many more entries and would require a serial search, thereby, requiring more time to search the table.

The price table is logically three tables: size, quality, and location/price. By structuring it as a multi-level table, each logical table is also set up as a physical table. This provides easier maintenance because, since each separate group of information (size, quality, etc.) is stored in a separate table instead of merged with others, it is easier to follow, and each separate group of information (table) can be changed independently of the others. Also, searching a multi-level table is more efficient because the search is serial within category (size, quality, location and price) instead of completely serial as in a single-level table.

Coding Example 5.9.2

This coding example illustrates the code required to search the multi-level table described in Table 5.9.1. The multi-level table and DSECTs used by this program are defined in Coding Example 5.9.1. The routine GETPRICE is the generalized routine that searches a multi-level table in the format described above. When GETPRICE receives control, it expects the address of the appropriate table to be loaded into register 10 by the caller. The routine GETP0123 loads the address of the multi-table for product number 0123 and then calls GETPRICE to obtain the price. The fields ARGSIZE, ARGQUAL, and ARGLOC, which contain the size, quality, and selling location, respectively, of the product are assumed to be set elsewhere in the program. When control is returned from GETPRICE, if the requested price was found, then register 15 contains a return code of X'00', and the price of the product is located in the area PRICE in packed decimal.

```
***********************************************************************
*    THIS ROUTINE OBTAINS THE PRICE FOR PRODUCT NUMBER 0123.
***********************************************************************
*
GETP0123  LA    R10,P0123TBL           LD ADR OF ML-TBL FOR PROD-0123
          BAL   R8,GETPRICE            GET PRICE OF PROD-0123
          BR    R7                     RETURN TO CALLING RTN
*
*
***********************************************************************
*    THIS SUBROUTINE OBTAINS THE PRICE OF THE PRODUCT SPECIFIED BY THE
*    CALLING ROUTINE. WHEN THIS SUBROUTINE RECEIVES CONTROL, IT EXPECTS
*    THE ADDRESS OF THE MULTI-LEVEL PRICE TABLE FOR THE PRODUCT WHOSE
*    PRICE IS DESIRED, TO BE LOADED INTO REGISTER 10.
***********************************************************************
*
          USING DSIZETBL,R10           DEF REG FOR SIZE-TABLE DSECT
GETPRICE  DS    0H
NEXTSIZE  CLI   $SIZE,TBLENDID         CHECK FOR END OF TABLE
          BE    INVSIZE                IF TBL END, INV SIZE SPEC
          CLC   $SIZE,ARGSIZE          SEARCH FOR REQUIRED SIZE
          BE    SETQTBL                IF FOUND, LOAD QUAL TABLE
```

```
         LA    R10,$SENTLEN(0,R10)     INCR TO NEXT SIZE ENTRY
         B     NEXTSIZE                SEARCH NEXT SIZE ENTRY
INVSIZE  LA    R15,4                   INDICATE INVALID SIZE
         BR    R8                      RETURN TO CALLING RTN
*
SETQTBL  L     R10,$QTBLADR            LOAD ADR OF CORRES QUAL TBL
         DROP  R10                     MAKE R10 AVAILABLE FOR DSECT
         USING DQUALTBL,R10            DEF REG FOR QUAL-TABLE DSECT
NEXTQUAL CLI   $QUAL,TBLENDID          CHECK FOR END OF TABLE
         BE    INVQUAL                 IF TBL END, INV QUAL SPEC
         CLC   $QUAL,ARGQUAL           SEARCH FOR REQUIRED QUAL
         BE    SETLTBL                 IF FOUND, LOAD LOC TABLE
         LA    R10,$QENTLEN(0,R10)     INCR TO NEXT QUAL ENTRY
         B     NEXTQUAL                SEARCH NEXT QUAL ENTRY
INVQUAL  LA    R15,8                   INDICATE INVALID QUAL
         BR    R8                      RETURN TO CALLING RTN
*
SETLTBL  L     R10,$LTBLADR            LOAD ADR OF CORRES LOC TBL
         DROP  R10                     MAKE R10 AVAIL FOR DSECT
         USING DLOCTBL,R10             DEF REG FOR LOC-TBL DSECT
NEXTLOC  CLC   $LOC,ARGLOC             SEARCH FOR REQUIRED LOC
         BE    SETPRICE                IF FOUND, GET PRICE
         CLI   $LOC,$TBLENDID          CHECK FOR END OF TABLE
         BE    INVLOC                  IF TBL END, INV LOC SPEC
         LA    R10,$LENTLEN(0,R10)     INCR TO NEXT LOC ENTRY
         B     NEXTLOC                 SEARCH NEXT LOC ENTRY
INVLOC   LA    R15,12                  INDICATE INVALID LOC
         BR    R8                      RETURN TO CALLING RTN
*
SETPRICE ZAP   PRICE,$PRICE            LOAD PRICE FOR CALLER
         LA    R15,0                   INDICATE PRICE SEARCH OK
         BR    R8                      RETURN TO CALLING RTN
*
*
**********************************************************************
*    DC/DS/EQU STATEMENTS
**********************************************************************
*
TBLENDID EQU   X'FF'
ARGSIZE  DS    CL1
ARGQUAL  DS    CL1
ARGLOC   DS    CL1
PRICE    DS    PL3
```

5.10 LINKED LISTS

A linked-list is a group of entries that are sequenced logically (but not necessarily physically) by some key field within the entries. The entries may be located one behind the other in contiguious virtual storage in the physical sequence in which they are added to the linked-list, or they may be scattered in virtual storage in no particular physical sequence.

Each time a new entry is inserted, the program code used to build the linked-list reorders the list logically to assure that the new entry is in the proper logical location relative to the other entries in the linked-list. To accomplished this, each entry is appended with a link field as it is inserted into the linked-list. The link field points to the next sequential entry in the linked-list. Therefore, to insert a new entry into the linked-list in sequence requires only that the link field of the entry, which is logically sequenced immediately before, be adjusted. In addition, the structure of a linked-list requires two pointers. One pointer points to the logical begining of the linked-list (the entry with the lowest or highest key, depending on sequencing criterion) and the other pointer points to the next available slot of the linked-list.

The routine that creates the linked-list requires logic to handle the following three conditions:

- Condition-1. The insertion of a new entry somewhere in the middle of the linked-list. That is, the new entry will not be the new first or new last entry of the linked-list.
- Condition-2. The insertion of a new entry that will become the new last entry of the linked-list.
- Condition-3. The insertion of a new entry that will become the new first entry of the linked-list.

When the linked-list creation routine is being developed, it is easier to code it to handle condition-1 first. After that code has been successfully developed and tested, the code for condition-2 and then the code for condition-3 can be developed and incorporated into the routine. Coding Example 5.10.1 illustrates the code required for condition-1. Coding Examples 5.10.2 and 5.10.3 illustrate the additional code required to implement condition-2 and condition-3, respectively.

The virtual storage for a linked-list may be obtained in the same manner as it is for an expandable table (discussed in this chapter). A GETMAIN macro instruction is issued for a block of virtual storage large enough to accomodate a certain predefined number of entries (including the appended link field). The entries are physically placed one behind the other until the block of virtual storage is exhausted. Additional virtual storage is obtained via GETMAINs, as required, to accommodate other entries.

Coding Example 5.10.1

This coding example illustrates how to code the portion of the linked-list creation routine to handle condition-1, which is illustrated in Figures 5.10.1 and 5.10.2. When the PUTENTRY routine receives control, it expects the new entry to be in the area labeled NEWENTRY.

```
                USING     ENTRYMAP,R11         DEFINE REG FOR DSECT
*
PUTENTRY        L         R10,LLENTONE         LOAD ADR OF FIRST LOG ENTRY OF LL
                L         R12,LLENTNXT         LOAD ADR OF NEXT AVAIL SLOT OF LL
                LA        R11,NEWENTRY         LOAD ADR OF NEW ENTRY
NXTENTRY        CLC       4(ENTKYLEN,R10),ENTRYKEY     COMPARE KEY OF A LL ENTRY
*                                                      TO KEY OF NEW ENTRY
                BH        INSERT               IF HIGH, INSERT NEW ENTRY
                BE        DUPENTRY             IF EQUAL, ENTRY ALREADY EXISTS
                ST        R10,PRVENTRY         STORE ADR OF CURRENT ENTRY
                L         R10,0(0,R10)         LOAD ADR OF NEXT ENTRY IN SEQ
                B         NXTENTRY             COMPARE NEXT ENTRY KEY TO NEW KEY
*
INSERT          L         R10,PRVENTRY         LOAD ADR OF ENTRY BEFORE NEW ENTRY
                MVC       0(4,R12),0(R10)      MOVE NEXT ENTRY PTR TO NEW ENTRY
*                                              LINK FIELD
                MVC       4(ENTRYLEN,R12),ENTRY        MOVE NEW ENTRY INTO NEXT
*                                                      SLOT+4 (PASSED LINK FIELD)
                ST        R12,0(0,R10)         MOVE ADR OF NEW ENTRY INTO LINK
*                                              FIELD OF PREV ENTRY
                LA        R12,LLENTLEN(0,R12)  CALC ADR OF NEW NEXT AVAIL SLOT
                ST        R12,LLENTNXT         SAVE ADR OF NEXT AVAIL SLOT
                BR        R6                   RETURN TO CALLING RTN
*
```

```
LLENTONE: X'00010000' (Pointer to logical beginning
                       of list)
LLENTNXT: X'00010028' (Pointer to the next available
                       slot of list)
NEWENTRY: DDDDDD
```

Entry Address	Link Field Pointer	Actual Entry
X'10000'	X'10000A'	BBBBBB
X'1000A'	X'10001E'	CCCCCC
X'10014'	4XL1'FF'	GGGGGG
X'1001E'	X'10014'	FFFFFF

Figure 5.10.1. This figure illustrates a linked-list that has already been created. The list currently contains four entries. For illustration purposes, the length of the entries will be small, and each byte will have the same character. Each entry has a length of six bytes, and the first two bytes of each entry is the key. A 4-byte link field is appended to the beginning of each entry before it is inserted into the list. Notice that the link field of each entry points to the next sequential entry. The link field of the last entry of the list contains binary ones to indicate the end-of-LL. NEWENTRY contains the next entry that is to be inserted into the list. This figure illustrates condition-1, when a new entry is inserted into list, but does not become the new logical first or new logical last entry of the list.

```
LLENTONE: X'00010000'
LLENTNXT: X'00010032' *** Changed ***
NEWENTRY: DDDDDD
```

Entry Address	Link Field Pointer	Actual Entry	
X'10000'	X'1000A'	BBBBBB	
X'1000A'	X'10028'	CCCCCC	*** Link Field Changed ***
X'10014'	4XL1'FF'	GGGGGG	
X'1001E'	X'10014'	FFFFFF	
X'10028'	X'1001E'	DDDDDD	*** New Entry ***
X'10032'			

Figure 5.10.2. This figure illustrates the linked-list after NEWENTRY from Figure 5.10.1 has been inserted. Notice that the link field of entry CCCCCC has been changed to point to the new entry DDDDDD, the old link field of entry CCCCCC (X'1001E') was placed into the link field of the new entry DDDDDD, and the next slot pointer (LLENTNXT) has been changed from X'00010028' to X'00010032'.

Coding Example 5.10.1 (Cont.)

```
LLENTONE        DS       F
LLENTNXT        DS       F
PRVENTRY        DS       F
NEWENTRY        DS       CL6
*
ENTRYMAP        DSECT
ENTRY           EQU      *
ENTKEY          DS       CL2
ENTKYLEN        EQU      *-ENTKEY
ENTFLD01        DS       CL4
ENTRYLEN        EQU      *-ENTRYMAP
LLENTLEN        EQU      ENTRYLEN+4
```

Now, let us consider condition-2, when the new entry becomes the new last entry of the linked-list. We now need to add code to the routine in Coding Example 5.10.1 to check for the logical end of the linked-list and to add the new entry to the logical end of the list. Figure 5.10.3 illustrates the linked-list after a new last entry is added and Coding Example 5.10.2 illustrates the required new code to incorporate into the linked-list building routine illustrated in Coding Example 5.10.1.

Coding Example 5.10.2

This coding example illustrates the new code that has been incorporated into the code in Coding Example 5.10.1 to support condition-2. The new instructions are denoted with (2) preceding the comment.

```
LLENTONE: X'00010000'
LLENTNXT: X'0001003C' *** Changed ***
NEWENTRY: MMMMMM
```

Entry Address	Link Field Pointer	Actual Entry	
X'10000'	X'1000A'	BBBBBB	
X'1000A'	X'10028'	CCCCCC	
X'10014'	X'10032'	GGGGGG	*** Link Field Changed ***
X'1001E'	X'10014'	FFFFFF	
X'10028'	X'1001E'	DDDDDD	
X'10032'	4XL1'FF'	MMMMMM	*** New Entry ***
X'1003C'			

Figure 5.10.3. This figure illustrates the linked-list from Figure 5.10.2, after the new entry, contained in NEWENTRY, has been inserted into it. This figure illustrates condition-2, when the new entry becomes the new logical last entry of the linked-list.

```
         USING    ENTRYMAP,R11           DEFINE REG FOR DESCT
*
PUTENTRY L        R10,LLENTONE           LOAD ADR OF FIRST LOG ENTRY OF LL
         L        R12,LLENTNXT           LOAD ADR OF NEXT AVAIL SLOT OF LL
         LA       R11,NEWENTRY           LOAD ADR OF NEW ENTRY
NXTENTRY CLC      0(4,R10),BINONES       (2) CHECK FOR LOG END OF LL
         BE       INSERTX                (2) IF END, INSERT NEW ENTRY AT
                                             END
         CLC      4(ENTKYLEN,R10),ENTRYKEY COMPARE KEY OF A LL ENTRY
*                                        TO KEY OF NEW ENTRY
         BH       INSERT                 IF HIGH, INSERT NEW ENTRY
         BE       DUPENTRY               IF EQUAL, ENTRY ALREADY
*                                        EXISTS
         ST       R10,PRVENTRY           STORE ADR OF CURRENT
*                                        ENTRY
         L        R10,0(0,R10)           LOAD ADR OF NEXT ENTRY IN SEQ
         B        NXTENTRY               COMPARE NEXT ENTRY KEY TO NEW KEY
*
INSERT   L        R10,PRVENTRY           LOAD ADR OF ENTRY BEFORE NEW ENTRY
         MVC      0(4,R12),0(R10)        MOVE NEXT ENTRY PTR TO NEW ENTRY
*                                        LINK FIELD
         MVC      4(ENTRYLEN,R12),ENTRY  MOVE NEW ENTRY INTO NEXT
*                                        SLOT+4 (PASSED LINK FIELD)
         ST       R12,0(0,R10)           MOVE ADR OF NEW ENTRY INTO LINK FIELD
*                                        OF PREV ENTRY
         LA       R12,LLENTLEN(0,R12)    CALC ADR OF NEW NEXT AVAIL SLOT
         ST       R12,LLENTNXT           SAVE ADR OF NEXT AVAIL SLOT
         BR       R6                     RETURN TO CALLING RTN
*
INSERTX  MVC      4(ENTRYLEN,R12),ENTRY  (2) MOVE NEW ENTRY INTO NEXT
*                                        SLOT+4 (PASSED LINK FIELD)
         ST       R12,0(0,R10)           (2) MOVE ADR OF NEW ENTRY INTO LINK
*                                        FIELD OF CURRENT LAST ENTRY
         MVC      0(4,R12),BINONES       (2) MOVE END-OF-LL INDICATOR INTO
*                                        LINK FIELD OF NEW LAST ENTRY
         LA       R12,LLENTLEN(0,R12)    (2) CALC ADR OF NEXT AVAIL
*                                        SLOT OF LL
         ST       R12,LLENTNXT           (2) SAVE ADR OF NEXT AVAIL SLOT
         BR       R6                     (2) RETURN TO CALLING RTN
*
BINONES  DC       4XL1'FF'
LLENTONE DS       F
LLENTNXT DS       F
PRVENTRY DS       F
NEWENTRY DS       CL6
*
ENTRYMAP DSECT
ENTRY    EQU      *
ENTKEY   DS       CL2
ENTKYLEN EQU      *-ENTKEY
ENTFLD01 DS       CL4
ENTRYLEN EQU      *-ENTRYMAP
LLENTLEN EQU      ENTRYLEN+4
```

Now, let us consider condition-3, when the new entry becomes the new first entry (or logical beginning) of the linked-list. We now need to add code to the routine in Coding Example 5.10.2 to add the new entry to the logical beginning of the list. Figure 5.10.4 illustrates the listed-list after a new first entry is added and Coding Example 5.10.3 illustrates the required new code to incorporate into the linked-list building routine illustrated in Coding Example 5.10.2.

```
LLENTONE: X'0001003C' *** Changed ***
LLENTNXT: X'00010046' *** Changed ***
NEWENTRY: AAAAAA
```

Entry Address	Link Field Pointer	Actual Entry	
X'10000'	X'1000A'	BBBBBB	
X'1000A'	X'10028'	CCCCCC	
X'10014'	X'10032'	GGGGGG	
X'1001E'	X'10014'	FFFFFF	
X'10028'	X'1001E'	DDDDDD	
X'10032'	4XL1'FF'	MMMMMM	
X'1003C'	X'10000'	AAAAAA	*** New Entry ***
X'10046'			

Figure 5.10.4. This figure illustrates the linked-list from Figure 5.10.3, after the new entry, contained in NEWENTRY, has been inserted into it. This figure illustrates condition-3, when the new entry becomes the new logically first entry of the linked-list.

Coding Example 5.10.3

This coding example illustrates the new code that has been incorporated into the code in Coding Example 5.10.2 to support condition-3. The new instructions are denoted with (3) preceding the comment.

```
             USING    ENTRYMAP,R11               DEFINE REG FOR DESCT
*
PUTENTRY     MVI      IN1SW,C'1'                 (3) INIT NEW FIRST ENTRY SWITCH
             L        R10,LLENTONE               LOAD ADR OF FIRST LOG ENTRY OF LL
             L        R12,LLENTNXT               LOAD ADR OF NEXT AVAIL SLOT OF LL
             LA       R11,NEWENTRY               LOAD ADR OF NEW ENTRY
NXTENTRY     CLC      0(4,R10),BINONES           (2) CHECK FOR LOG END OF LL
             BE       INSERTX                    (2) IF END, INSERT NEW ENTRY
*                                                    AT END
             CLC      4(ENTKYLEN,R10),ENTRYKEY   COMPARE KEY OF A LL ENTRY
*                                                TO KEY OF NEW ENTRY
             BH       INSERT                     IF HIGH, INSERT NEW ENTRY
             BE       DUPENTRY                   IF EQUAL, ENTRY ALREADY EXISTS
             MVI      IN1SW,C'0'                 (3) TURN OFF NEW FIRST ENTRY SW
             ST       R10,PRVENTRY               STORE ADR OF CURRENT ENTRY
             L        R10,0(0,R10)               LOAD ADR OF NEXT ENTRY IN SEQ
             B        NXTENTRY                   COMPARE NEXT ENTRY KEY TO NEW KEY
*
INSERT       CLI      IN1SW,C'1'                 (3) CHECK IF NEW FIRST ENTRY
*                                                    SW SET
             BE       INSERT1                    (3) IF YES, INSERT NEW FIRST ENTRY
```

```
         L        R10,PRVENTRY            LOAD ADR OF ENTRY BEFORE NEW ENTRY
         MVC      0(4,R12),0(R10)         MOVE NEXT ENTRY PTR TO NEW ENTRY
*                                         LINK FIELD
         MVC      4(ENTRYLEN,R12),ENTRY   MOVE NEW ENTRY INTO NEXT
*                                         SLOT+4 (PASSED LINK FIELD)
         ST       R12,0(0,R10)            MOVE ADR OF NEW ENTRY INTO LINK
*                                         FIELD OF PREV ENTRY
         LA       R12,LLENTLEN(0,R12)     CALC ADR OF NEW NEXT AVAIL SLOT
         ST       R12,LLENTNXT            SAVE ADR OF NEXT AVAIL SLOT
         BR       R6                      RETURN TO CALLING RTN
*
INSERT1  MVC      4(4,R12),0(R11)         (3) MOVE NEW ENTRY INTO NEXT
*                                         SLOT+4 (PASSED LINK FIELD)
         ST       R10,0(0,R12)            (3) MOVE ADR OF OLD FIRST ENTRY INTO
*                                         LINK FIELD OF NEW FIRST ENTRY
         ST       R12,LLENTONE            (3) SAVE ADR OF NEW FIRST ENTRY
         LA       R12,LLENTLEN(0,R12)     (3) CALC ADR OF NEXT AVAIL SLOT
         ST       R12,LLENTNXT            (3) SAVE ADR OF NEXT AVAIL SLOT
         BR       R6                      (3) RETURN TO CALLING RTN
*
INSERTX  MVC      4(ENTRYLEN,R12),ENTRY   (2) MOVE NEW ENTRY INTO NEXT
*                                         SLOT+4 (PASSED LINK FIELD)
         ST       R12,0(0,R10)            (2) MOVE ADR OF NEW ENTRY INTO LINK
*                                         FIELD OF CURRENT LAST ENTRY
         MVC      0(4,R12),BINONES        (2) MOVE END-OF-LL INDICATOR INTO
*                                         LINK FIELD OF NEW LAST ENTRY
         LA       R12,LLENTLEN(0,R12)     (2) CALC ADR OF NEXT AVAIL
*                                         SLOT OF LL
         ST       R12,LLENTNXT            (2) SAVE ADR OF NEXT AVAIL SLOT
         BR       R6                      (2) RETURN TO CALLING RTN
*
IN1SW    DS       CL1
BINONES  DC       4XL1'FF'
LLENTONE DS       F
LLENTNXT DS       F
PRVENTRY DS       F
NEWENTRY DS       CL6
*
ENTRYMAP DSECT
ENTRY    EQU      *
ENTKEY   DS       CL2
ENTKYLEN EQU      *-ENTKEY
ENTFLD01 DS       CL4
ENTRYLEN EQU      *-ENTRYMAP
LLENTLEN EQU      ENTRYLEN+4
```

Coding example 5.10.3 shows the complete routine that is required to build the linked-list and satisfy all three conditions. The routine does not contain the code required to allocate virtual storage. This code would normally be in another routine and should be modeled after the routine used for building an expandable table (discussed in this chapter). Two routines are still required to maintain the linked-list—one to read it and the other one to delete entries from it. Coding Example 5.10.4 illustrates the code required the print all the entries of the listed-list. This routine could also be used during testing to determine if the linked-list building routine is functioning properly.

Entries could be deleted from the linked-list either physically or logically. When done physically, the link field of the entry, which is logically immediately before the entry that is to be deleted, is replaced by the link field of the deleted entry. This method is illustrated in Figure 5.10.5. When done logically, a deletion flag is inserted in the entries that are to be deleted. One convention that could be used is to insert a byte of binary ones in the first byte of the entry (first byte after the link field). If this method is used, then the routine that reads the linked-list would be required to check that byte and ignore the entry if the byte is set. This method is illustrated in Figure 5.10.6.

Both methods of deleting entries from the linked-list have advantages and disadvantages. Deleting physically would have the advantage of keeping the size of the logical linked-list to a minimum and would require less time to read the entire list and scan it for new insertions, since the logical linked-list would contain no deleted entries. However, additional code would be required to implement this method and slighty more processing time would be required to adjust the pointers each time an entry had to be deleted. The physical size of the listed-list, however, will not decrease because the deleted entries remain in virtual storage. Deleting logically would require less code to implement and slightly less time to execute when deleting entries, but the logical linked-list would continually expand and require additional time to read because it would contain the active entries and the deleted entries. Fewer deleted entries would be carried in the logical linked-list, using the logical deletion method, if the building routine reused the deleted entries, but this would require additional code in the building routine and additional processing time to search for deleted entries instead of simply adding the new entries at the physical end of the linked-list. The search for deleted entries could be made more efficient if the deletion routine maintained a count of deleted entries and/or pointers to them, but this also would require additional code and additional processing time for the deletion routine. If the deleted entries are reused, then the logical deletion method would use less virtual storage than the physical deletion method for the linked-list because the virtual storage used by the deleted entries would be reclaimed. There is no way of reclaiming the virtual storage used by the deleted entries with the physical deletion method because there are no pointers to them.

```
LLENTONE: X'0001003C'
LLENTNXT: X'00010046'
DELKEY:   DD
```

Entry Address	Link Field Pointer	Actual Entry	
X'10000'	X'1000A'	BBBBBB	
X'1000A'	X'1001E'	CCCCCC	*** Link Field Changed ***
X'10014'	X'10032'	GGGGGG	
X'1001E'	X'10014'	FFFFFF	
X'10028'	X'1001E'	DDDDDD	*** Deleted ***
X'10032'	4XL1'FF'	MMMMMM	
X'1003C'	X'10000'	AAAAAA	
X'10046'			

Figure 5.10.5. This figure illustrates the linked-list from Figure 5.10.4, after the entry, whose key is contained in DELKEY, has been physically deleted from the list.

```
LLENTONE: X'0001003C'
LLENTNXT: X'00010046'
DELKEY: DD
```

Entry Address	Link Field Pointer	Actual Entry	
X'10000'	X'1000A'	BBBBBB	
X'1000A'	X'10028'	CCCCCC	*** Link Field Changed ***
X'10014'	X'10032'	GGGGGG	
X'1001E'	X'10014'	FFFFFF	
X'10028'	X'1001E'	X'FF' DDDDD	*** Deleted ***
X'10032'	4XL1'FF'	MMMMMM	
X'1003C'	X'10000'	AAAAAA	
X'10046'			

Figure 5.10.6. This figure illustrates the linked-list from Figure 5.10.4, after the entry, whose key is contained in DELKEY, has been logically deleted from the list.

The actual method selected would depend on the activity (frequency of insertions and deletions) of the linked-list, performance requirements, and amount of virtual storage available.

Coding Example 5.10.4

This coding example illustrates how to read and print all the entires of the previously created linked-list.

```
DSPLYLL   L      R10,LLENTONE                LOAD BG ADR OF LL
NXTLLENT  MVC    ENTRY(ENTRYLEN),4(R10)      MOVE ENTRY (WITHOUT LINK FIELD)
          BAL    R7,PRINT                    PRINT ENTRY
          C      R10,BINONES                 CHECK FOR END OF LL
          BER    R6                          IF END, RETURN TO CALLING RTN
          L      R10,0(0,R10)                IF NOT, LOAD ADR OF NEXT SEQ
*                                            ENTRY
          B      NXTLLENT                    GET NEXT ENTRY
*
PRINT     PUT    REPORT,LINE                 PRINT AN ENTRY OF LL
          BR     R7                          RETURN TO CALLING RTN
*
          DS     0F
BINONES   DC     4XL1'FF'                    END-OF-LL INDICATOR
LINE      DS     0CL133
          DC     C' '
ENTRY     DC     CL132' '
*
REPORT    DCB    DSORG=PS,MACRF=PM,BLKSIZE=3990,LRECL=133,RECFM=FBA,  -
                 DDNAME=REPORT
```

When virtual storage is allocated for the linked-list, it and the linked-list pointers LLENTONE and LLENTNXT must be initialized to indicate that the linked-list is empty. The LLENTONE and LLENTNXT must point to the beginning of the linked-list, and the link field of the first (dummy) entry in the linked-list must contain binary ones.

Coding Example 5.10.5

This coding example illustrates how to obtain virtual storage to accommodate 100 entries for the previously discussed linked-list as well as how to initialize it.

```
INITLL     GETMAIN    EC,LV=1000,A=LLADR
           LTR        R15,R15                   CHECK IF GM OK
           BNZ        NOSTOR                    IF NO, ...
           MVC        LLENTONE,LLADR            INIT PTR TO BG OF LL
           MVC        LLENTNXT,LLADR            INIT PTR TO NEXT SLOT OF LL
           L          R10,LLADR                 LOAD ADR OF BG OF LL
           MVC        0(4,R10),BINONES          PUT END-OF-LL IND IN 1ST ENTRY
           BR         R6                        RETURN TO CALLING RTN
*
LLADR      DS         F
```

Linked-lists may be used as queues when the individual entries must be maintained in some predetermined sequence other than the order of insertion, such as priority value, ID number, alphabetical, and so forth. The TCB queue of an address space in MVS and the active DCA queue in CICS are examples of linked-lists.

The linked-lists that have been discussed have entries that contain forward pointers to the next sequential entry. A linked-list may also be built with forward and backward pointers, in which case a second link field would be appended to each entry. This is done if there is a requirement that the entries be read backward. If backward reading is required, then a pointer to the logical last entry should also be maintained.

5.11 BRANCH TABLES

Branch tables are used to pass control to a specific routine based upon an index value received from another routine or called program. Structurally, a branch table is an ordered sequential list of unconditional branch instructions. The following is an example of a branch table.

```
BRNCHTBL  B    RTN01
          B    RTN02
          B    RTN03
          ...
          B    RTNnn
```

Branch tables are a convenient and efficient way of passing control to a specific routine based upon a predetermined decision. The program performing the branch into the branch table requires no desision-making code, since that was already done by the called program.

Control is passed to the appropriate B instruction, within the branch table, with the following instruction:

```
B   n(r)
```

where: n is the name associated with the beginning of the branch table,
r is a general register (usually 15) that contains the index value received from another routine or a called program.

The index value is added to the address of the name (beginning of branch table) to form the address of the branch instruction that receives control.

Since a branch table is built with 4-byte branch instructions, the index value must be a multiple of four. When control is returned from an IBM-supplied program, register 15 contains a return code that is appropriate to be used as an index into a branch table (this is why the return codes are in increments of four).

Before control is passed into a branch table, the index value should be validated to assure that it is a multiple of four and that it will not cause a branch beyond the branch table.

Coding Example 5.11.1

This coding example illustrates how to validate the index value used for a branch table. The index value is assumed to be in register 15.

```
VALDTINX  STC    R15,LOWBYTE           EXTRACT LOW ORDER BYTE OF INX VALUE
          TM     LOWBYTE,X'03'         IS INX MULT OF 4 (LOW 2 BITS 0)?
          BZ     CHKINXSZ              IF YES, CHECK INX SIZE
          B      INDXBAD1              IF NO, ERROR
CHKINXSZ  C      R15,MAXINX            CHK IF INX NOT LARGER THAN BR-TBL
          BNH    INDEXOK               IF INX WITHIN BR-TBL, OK
          B      INDXBAD2              IF NO, ERROR
INDEXOK   BR     R7                    INDEX OK, RETURN TO CALLING RTN
INDXBAD1  WTO    '*** INDEX VALUE NOT MULTIPLE OF FOUR ***'
          ABEND  901
INDXBAD2  WTO    '*** INDEX VALUE TOO LARGE ***',ROUTECDE=11
          ABEND  902
          ...
LOWBYTE   DS     CL1
```

Coding Example 5.11.2

This coding example illustrates how to pass control into a branch table using the index value returned by a called program.

```
          LINK   EP=PROGM01
          BAL    R7,VALDTINX           SEE C.E. 5.11.1
          B      BRNCHTBL(R15)         BRANCH INTO BRANCH-TABLE
          ...
BRNCHTBL  B      RQUESTOK
          B      WARNING
          B      ERROR01
          B      ERROR02
BRTBLEND  EQU    *
MAXINX    DC     A(BRTBLEND-BRNCHTBL-4)  MAX ALLOW INX (DSPLM INTO TBL)
```

If required, the branch table may contain BR instructions if the register is preloaded with the appropriate branch address and if two slack bytes are specified after the instruction to maintain alignment with the other B instructions. Branch tables may be used with subroutines that are required to pass control back to the caller. Coding Example 5.11.3 illustrates this.

Coding Example 5.11.3

This coding example illustrates how to structure a subroutine and the branch table, such that control could be returned to the calling routine via a link register. The parameters required by the program INQUIRE are set by the routine that calls GETINFO.

```
          BAL       R7,GETINFO
          ...
GETINFO   LINK      EP=INQUIRE,PARAM=(KEY1,KEY2,RECORD)
          BAL       R8,VALDTINX                SEE C.E. 5.11.1
          B         BRNCHTBL(R15)              BRANCH INTO BRANCH-TABLE
          ...
BRNCHTBL  BR        R7                         REQ INFO RETURNED,
*                                              RETURN TO CALLING RTN
          DS        H                          FOR ALIGNMENT
          B         GETDATA1                   GET ADDITIONAL DATA-1
          B         GETDATA2                   GET ADDITIONAL DATA-2
          B         NOINFO                     NO INFO AVAIL
MAXINX    DC        A(*-BRNCHTBL-4)            MAX INDEX ALLOWED
*
GETDATA1  ...                                  OBTAIN COMMON DATA-1
          BR        R7                         RETURN TO CALLING RTN
*
GETDATA2  ...                                  OBTAIN COMMON DATA-2
          BR        R7                         RETURN TO CALLING RTN
*
NOINFO    ...                                  PERFORM NO-INFO-AVAIL PROCESSING
          BR        R7                         RETURN TO CALLING RTN
```

The structure of a branch table does not lend itself to structured programming as discussed in Chapters 1 and 2. Also, if there is a wild branch in one of the subroutines that receives control via the branch table, then there is not link register available to indicate which subroutine has the bad code. This could be remedied by making some modifications in the standard branch table. Those modifications are illustrated in Coding Example 5.11.4.

In that coding example, each of the subroutines that receives control via the branch table returns control to the routine that called them. In addition, if there is a wild branch in any of these subroutines, then link register 8 indicates which subroutine had control when the wild branch occurred. Note, link register 8 is not used for linkage, but only as a passive trace register as discussed in the section "Suggestions for Debugging Difficult Problems" in Chapter 2.

Coding Example 5.11.4

This coding example illustrates how to modify the standard branch table to enable it to be used in a structured program.

```
          BAL       R7,GETINFO
          ...
GETINFO   LINK      EP=PROGINQ
          BAL       R8,VALTINX                 SEE C.E. 5.11.1
          LA        R9,GETINFOX                LD RET ADR FOR SUBRTN
          B         BRNCHTBL(R15)              BRANCH TO APPROPRIATE SUBRTN
GETINFOX  BR        R7                         RETURN TO CALLING RTN
          ...
BRNCHTBL  BAL       R8,RTN1
          BAL       R8,RTN2
          BAL       R8,RTN3
MAXINX    DC        A(*-BRNCHTBL-4)
```

```
*
RTN1         ...
             BR        R9                           RETURN TO CALLING RTN
*
RTN2         ...
             BR        R9                           RETURN TO CALLING RTN
*
RTN3         ...
             BR        R9                           RETURN TO CALLING RTN
```

5.12 COMMUNICATING WITH A PROBLEM PROGRAM VIA SYSTEM COMMANDS

The MVS system operator can communicate with an executing problem program if it was invoked via the START command. This communication can be accomplished with the MVS MODIFY and/or STOP commands. Communication can also be accomplished via the WTOR macro, but that technique was discussed in Chapter 4.

A problem program must contain certain code in order to be aware that the MODIFY and STOP commands are being issued and, of course, contain additional code to respond to those commands.

The Command Schedule Communications ECB, associated with a particular started task, is posted whenever the operator issuses a MODIFY or STOP command for that task. In order to gain access to this ECB, the program issues the EXTRACT macro instruction requesting the Command Schedule Communications list (CSCL) as follows:

```
         EXTRACT   answer-area,FIELDS=COMM
```

The answer-area is defined as a full word and will contain the address of the CSCL upon return from EXTRACT. The contents and format of the CSCL is illustrated in Figure 5.12.1.

The token field is for an internal START command only and is discussed in Section 5.13 below.

The Command Input Buffer (CIB) contains information associated with the START, STOP, and MODIFY commands. If the task was invoked from the console via the START command, the CSCL will point to the START CIB. If the task was invoked as a batch job via a reader (JES2 internal reader, etc.), the CIB address will contain binary zeros. Note that a task is considered a started task (STC) only if the operand of the START command contains the actual PROC that invokes the task. A task is not considered a started task if it is invoked when the START command invokes a task that reads a JCL library and passes the JCL (that also contains a JOB statement) to the JES2/JES3 internal reader. The contents and format of the CIB are illustrated in Figure 5.12.2.

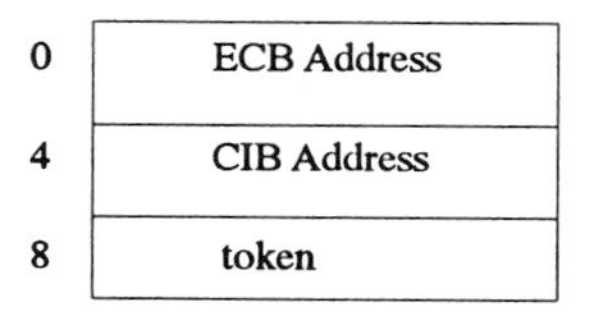

Figure 5.12.1. This figure illustrates the contents and format of the CSCL.

Offset				
0	Address of next CIB			
4	Verb Code	CIB Length	Reserved	
8	Reserved		Address Space ID	
12	Console ID	Reserved	Length of Data Field	
16	Variable Length Data Specified on the Command			

Figure 5.12.2. This figure illustrates the contents and format of the CIB.

After the information contained in the CIB has been referenced, the CIB should be freed. This is accomplished with the QEDIT macro instruction as follows:

```
QEDIT   ORIGIN=address-of-CIB-pointer,BLOCK=address-of-CIB
```

The parameter ORIGIN contains the address of the beginning of the CIB chain. This is the address of the second word (not the address contained in the second word) of the CSCL when the EXTRACT macro instruction returns control. The parameter BLOCK contains the address of the actual CIB, in the chain, to be freed.

After the START CIB is freed, the CIB counter should then be set to allow CIBs to be chained and MODIFY commands to be accepted for the started task. This is also accomplished by the QEDIT macro instruction and is coded as follows:

```
QEDIT   ORIGIN=address-of-CIB-pointer,CIBCTR=n
```

The value of n may be any interger from 0 to 255 and indicates the maximum number of MODIFY and STOP commands that may be issued before any of their CIBs are freed. If n is set to zero, then no MODIFY commands will be accepted for the started task; however, one CIB will always be available for a STOP command. If the START CIB is not freed and CIBCTR is set to a value of less than two, then MODIFY commands will not be accepted, but a STOP command will be accepted and the information for that STOP command will be contained in the second CIB in the chain (even though chaining was not requested).

If n is set to a value greater than one, then one or more MODIFY commands (up the the value of CIBCTR) may be specified by the operator, and the CIBs representing those MODIFY commands are chained together. In most cases, chained MODIFY commands are probably not required and CIBCTR=1 would suffice. If outstanding MODIFY commands are allowed (n set to a value greater than 1), then the program would require additional code to scan the CIB chain and process all the MODIFY commands represented by those CIBs.

If a MODIFY command is issued and one of the following conditions exist:

- The MODIFY command exceeds the size of the specified CIB chain;
- The CIBCTR is set to zero;
- The START CIB is not deleted and CIBCTR is set to one; or
- The program, which is invoked by the START command, contains no code to recognize MODIFY commands;

then MVS will issue the following message:

```
IEE342I   MODIFY REJECTED - TASK BUSY
```

MODIFY commands will be accepted again when one or more of the CIBs have been freed (when CIBCTR is set to a value greater than zero). When a CIB is processed, it should be freed with the QEDIT macro instruction (as mentioned above). The Command Schedule Communications ECB is cleared when there is at least one CIB slot available on the CIB chain.

The program should periodically test the ECB to determine if a MODIFY or STOP command was issued. This testing should not be done with the WAIT macro instruction because this will put the program into a wait state until a command is issued, and prevent the program from doing any useful work. The testing can be done with a TM instruction. This will enable the program to perform various processing until a MODIFY or STOP command is issued, and then perform the appropriate processing based upon the command.

Coding Example 5.12.1

This coding example illustrates the code required by a program, initiated by the START command, to recognize and process the MODIFY and STOP commands.

```
STCDEMO   CSECT
*
*
*************************************************************************
*     INITIALIZATION
*************************************************************************
*
          INITL     3,EQU=R                    INITIALIZE PROGRAM
          USING     CSCL,R10                   DEFINE ADRBLTY REG FOR CSCL DSECT
          USING     CIB,R11                    DEFINE ADRBLTY REG FOR CIB DSECT
*
*
*************************************************************************
*     MAINSTREAM OF PROGRAM
*************************************************************************
*
          BAL       R6,EXTRACT                 GET ADR OF CMD SCHED COMM LIST
          BAL       R6,CHKSTC                  CHECK IF STARTED TASK
          BAL       R6,SETCIBCT                SET CIB CHAIN COUNT
LOOP      BAL       R6,PROCESS                 PERFORM FUNCTION OF PROGRAM
          BAL       R6,CHKECB                  CHECK IF MODIFY/STOP CMD ENTERED
          B         LOOP                       CONTINUE PROCESSING
POSTED    BAL       R6,CHKCMD                  CHECK IF MODIFY OR STOP CMD
          B         LOOP                       CONTINUE PROCESSING
STOPPROG  B         RETURN                     RETURN TO MVS
*
*
*************************************************************************
*     THIS ROUTINE OBTAINS THE ADDRESS OF THE COMMAND SCHEDULE
*     COMMUNICATIONS LIST (CSCL). THE CSCL CONTAINS THE ADDRESS OF THE
*     COMMAND SCHEDULE COMMUNICATIONS ECB AND THE ADDRESS OF THE COMMAND
*     INPUT BUFFER (CIB), WHICH ARE REQUIRED BY THE PROGRAM TO PROCESS
*     ANY MODIFY AND STOP COMMANDS ISSUED BY THE OPERATOR.
*************************************************************************
*
EXTRACT   EXTRACT   CSCLADDR,FIELDS=COMM
          BR        R6                         RETURN TO CALLING RTN
*
*
*************************************************************************
*     THIS ROUTINE VERIFIES THAT THE PROGRAM WAS INVOKED AS A STARTED TASK
*     AND RELEASES THE ALLOCATED STORAGE FOR THE CIB, WHICH CONTAINS THE
*     START COMMAND.
```

```
***********************************************************************
*
CHKSTC    L        R10,CSCLADDR              LOAD ADR OF CSCL, SET ADRBLTY FOR DSECT
          CLC      COMCIBPT,BINZEROS         CHECK IF CIB PRESENT
          BE       NOSTC                     IF NO, NOT STARTED TASK
          WTO      '*** STC TASK ***'        *** FOR TESING ONLY ***
          BAL      R7,DELTCIB                DELETE START-CIB
          BR       R6                        RETURN TO CALLING RTN
NOSTC     WTO      '*** BATCH TASK---PROGRAM TERMINATED ***'
          B        RETURN                    RETURN TO MVS
*
*
***********************************************************************
*    THIS SUBROUTINE RELEASES THE STORAGE ALLOCATED FOR THE SPECIFIED CIB.
***********************************************************************
*
DELTCIB   L        R10,CSCLADDR              LOAD ADR OF CSCL, SET ADRBLTY FOR DSECT
          LA       R11,COMCIBPT              LOAD ADR OF PTR TO CIB CHAIN
          L        R12,0(0,R11)              LOAD ADR OF CIB TO BE FREED
          QEDIT    ORIGIN=(R11),BLOCK=(R12) FREE PROCESSED CIB
          BR       R7                        RETURN TO CALLING RTN
*
*
***********************************************************************
*    THIS ROUTINE SETS THE LIMIT FOR THE NUMBER OF MODIFY COMMANDS THAT
*    MAY BE SPECIFIED BY THE OPERATOR BEFORE THE CIB'S CONTAINING THOSE
*    COMMANDS MUST BE RELEASED.
***********************************************************************
*
SETCIBCT  L        R10,CSCLADDR              LOAD ADR OF CSCL, SET ADRBLTY FOR DSECT
          LA       R11,COMCIBPT              LOAD ADR OF PTR TO CIB CHAIN
          QEDIT    ORIGIN=(R11),CIBCTR=1     SET CIB CHAIN COUNT
          BR       R6                        RETURN TO CALLING RTN
*
*
***********************************************************************
*    THIS ROUTINE PERFORMS THE ACTUAL PROCESSING OF THE PROGRAM.
***********************************************************************
*
PROCESS   DS       0H
          ...                                PERFORM A UNIT OF PROCESSING
          BR       R6                        RETURN TO CALLING RTN
*
*
***********************************************************************
*    THIS ROUTINE RECEIVES CONTROL PERIODICALLY TO CHECK IF THE ECB OF
*    THE COMMAND SCHEDULER HAS BEEN POSTED, WHICH INDICATES THAT A MODIFY
*    OR A STOP COMMAND WAS SPECIFIED BY THE OPERATOR.
***********************************************************************
*
CHKECB    L        R10,CSCLADDR              LOAD ADR OF CSCL, SET ADRBLTY FOR DSECT
          L        R11,COMECBPT              LOAD ADR OF CMD SCHED COMM ECB
          TM       0(R11),X'40'              TEST IF ECB POSTED
          BO       POSTED                    IF YES, CHK COMMAND
          BR       R6                        RETURN TO CALLING RTN
*
*
***********************************************************************
*    THIS ROUTINE RECEIVES CONTROL WHEN THE COMMAND SCHEDULER ECB IS
*    POSTED. THIS ROUTINE PROCESSES THE CIB (COMMAND ISSUED BY OPERATOR)
*    POINTED TO BY THE CSCL.
***********************************************************************
*
CHKCMD    L        R10,CSCLADDR              LOAD ADR OF CSCL, SET ADRBLTY FOR DSECT
```

```
         L       R11,COMCIBPT               LOAD ADR OF CIB, SET ADRBLTY FOR DSECT
         CLI     CIBVERB,CIBMODFY           CHECK IF MODIFY CMD
         BE      MODIFY                     IF YES, PROCESS MDFY CMD
         CLI     CIBVERB,CIBSTOP            CHECK IF STOP CMD
         BE      STOP                       IF YES, PROCESS STOP CMD
         WTO     '*** NOT MODIFY/STOP COMMAND ***'
         ABEND   901
MODIFY   WTO     '*** MODIFY COMMAND ACCEPTED ***'
         BAL     R7,PROCMDFY                PERFORM MODIFY PROCESSING
         BAL     R7,DELTCIB                 DELETE MODIFY-CIB
         BR      R6                         CONTINUE PROCESSING
STOP     WTO     '*** STOP COMMAND ISSUED---PROGRAM TERMINATED ***'
         BAL     R7,PROCSTOP                PERFORM STOP PROCESSING
         B       STOPPROG                   RETURN TO MVS
*
*
***********************************************************************
*   THIS SUBROUTINE PROCESSES ANY MODIFY COMMANDS ISSUED BY THE OPERATOR.
***********************************************************************
*
PROCMDFY LH      R15,CIBDATLN               LOAD LENGTH OF MODIFY-DATA
         BCTR    R15,0                      DECR DATA LENGTH FOR EX INSTR
         LA      R12,CIBDATA                LOAD ADR OF MODIFY-DATA
         EX      R15,MVCBDATA               COPY MODIFY-DATA INTO USER AREA
         ...                                PERFORM MDFY PROCESSING
         XC      MDFYDATA,MDFYDATA          CLEAR MODIFY-DATA USER AREA
         BR      R7                         RETURN TO CALLING RTN
MVCBDATA MVC     MDFYDATA(0),0(R12)         MVC INSTR FOR EX INSTR
*
*
***********************************************************************
*   THIS SUBROUTINE PROCESSES THE STOP COMMAND ISSUED BY THE OPERATOR.
***********************************************************************
*
PROCSTOP DS      0H
         ...                                PERFORM STOP PROCESSING
         BR      R7                         RETURN TO CALLING RTN
*
*
***********************************************************************
*   THIS ROUTINE RESTORES THE REGISTERS AND RETURNS CONTROL.
***********************************************************************
*
RETURN   RCNTL   RC=0                       RETURN TO MVS
*
*
***********************************************************************
*   DC/DS STATEMENTS
***********************************************************************
*
BINZEROS DC      XL4'00'
CSCLADDR DS      F
MDFYDATA DC      XL100'00'
*
*
***********************************************************************
*   THE DSECTS
***********************************************************************
*
         PRINT   NOGEN
CSCL     DSECT
         IEZCOM                             GENERATES CSCL DSECT
*
CIB      DSECT
```

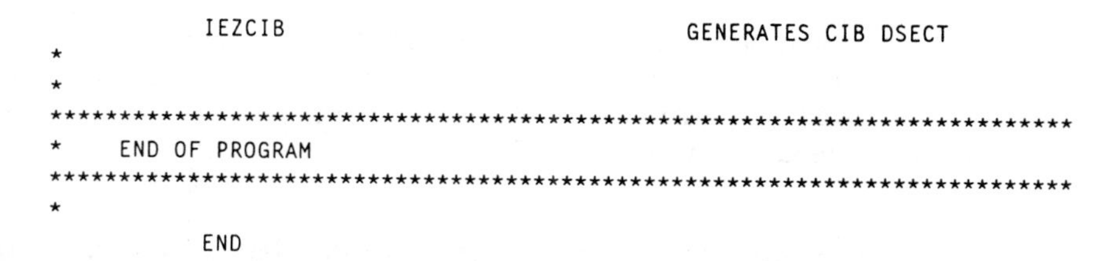
```
         IEZCIB                                     GENERATES CIB DSECT
*
*
***********************************************************************
*    END OF PROGRAM
***********************************************************************
*
         END
```

NOTES:

- If the name of the PROC, which was invoked to start the problem program, is required to be known, then the EXTRACT macro instruction may be used to request the address of the TIOT. For a started task, the name of the PROC is contained in the TIOT field TIOCNJOB and also in the TIOT field TIOCSTEP.

Coding Example 5.12.2

This coding example illustrates how to obtain the name of the PROC that was invoked by the START command.

```
          USING     TIOT1,R10
          ...
          EXTRACT   TIOTADR,FIELDS=(TIOT)
          L         R10,TIOTADR
          ...
          MVC       PROCNAME,TIOCNJOB
```
or
```
          MVC       PROCNAME,TIOCSTEP
          ...
TIOTADR   DS        F
PROCNAME  DS        CL8
          ...
          DSECT
          IEFTIOT1
```

5.13 ISSUING COMMANDS AND SUBMITTING JOBS FROM A PROBLEM PROGRAM

There are two ways to issue JES2 and MVS commands and submit jobs from a problem program. One way is through the JES2 internal reader and the other way is by issuing SVC 34 via the MGCR macro instruction. Both methods have advantages and disadvantages.

The program is not required to be authorized to submit commands or jobs through the JES2 internal reader; however, the internal reader must be defined via JES2 parameters, to authorize all commands. Also, the operator could change the authorization via a JES2 command to suppress the issuing of MVS commands and certain JES2 commands. Therefore, the program does not have complete control of the effect of issuing commands this way, but may submit jobs with no restriction.

Issuing commands via SVC 34 cannot be suppressed by any system parameters or by the opereator; therefore, the program has complete control of the effect of issuing commands this way. However, the program must execute in supervisor state and PSW key 0-7 in order to use the MGCR macro instruction.

Submitting commands in this matter is very sensitive. Caution and planning are required. As mentioned above, the execution of certain JES2 commands submitted via the internal reader may be suppressed via a JES2 initialization parameter (INTRDR AUTH=x) or via a JES2 operator command ($T RDI,A=x). The use of the MGCR macro instruction can be controlled by restricting the use of authorized libraries by protecting them with the IBM program product RACF or a similar product.

5.13.1 Issuing Commands and Submitting Jobs Via JES2 Internal Reader

The JES2 internal reader is defined in the JCL jobstream by the following JCL DD statement:

```
//ddname   DD   SYSOUT=(x,INTRDR)
```

The internal reader is treated as an output sequential dataset with LRECL=80 and RECFM=FB. JES2 supplies a default BLKSIZE if the programmer does not specify one. The dataset is opened and card-image records containing the commands/JCL statements are written to the dataset.

For JES2 commands, the card-image record must contain a /* in the first two positions, immediately followed by the actual command.

For MVS commands, the card-image record must contain a /* in the first two positions, immediately followed by the JES2 command $VS,'mvs-command'. The MVS command, which is to be issued, is specified within the apostrophes.

Jobs may be submitted via the JES2 internal reader by defining a complete JCL jobstream (starting with a JCL JOB statement) and writing the JCL statements to the internal reader.

JES2 responds to the submitted commands and/or JCL statements when the internal reader is closed. If commands and/or JCL statements are sent to the internal reader intermittently while other processing is being performed, then it would be impractical or inefficient to close the internal reader each time. In this case, the JES2 command /*EOF can follow the last command or JCL statement and have the same effect as the CLOSE macro instruction, causing JES2 to process the submitted commands/JCL statements as they are written to the internal reader.

A sequential access method is required for writing to the internal reader. The QSAM, BSAM, or VSAM access methods may be used. For submitting commands, all those access methods provide the same service; but for submitting jobs, the VSAM access method will also return the JES2 assigned job number to the program. The job number is returned in the 8-byte RPLRBAR field of the RPL. The information returned is in the format: JOBnnnnn, where nnnnn is the JES2 assigned job number.

Coding Example 5.13.1

This coding example illustrates how to issue MVS commands and JES2 commands via the JES2 internal reader. In this example, a JES2 $DA command, an MVS D A command and an MVS START command are issued via the JES2 internal reader.

```
         CSECT
*
*
***************************************************************************
*    INITIALIZATION
***************************************************************************
*
         INITL     3,EQU=R                    INITIALIZE PROGRAM
*
*
```

```
***********************************************************************
*    MAINSTREAM OF PROGRAM
***********************************************************************
*
         BAL       R6,OPEN                       OPEN JES2 INTERNAL READER
         BAL       R6,ISSUCMDS                   ISSUE COMMANDS
         BAL       R6,CLOSE                      CLOSE INTERNAL READER
         B         RETURN                        RETURN TO MVS OR CALLING PROG
*
*
***********************************************************************
*    THIS ROUTINE OPENS THE JES2 INTERNAL READER.
***********************************************************************
*
OPEN     OPEN (JES2IRDR,(OUTPUT))                OPEN IRDR
         ...                                     CHK FOR GOOD OPEN
         BR        R6                            RETURN TO CALLING RTN
*
*
***********************************************************************
*    THIS ROUTINE ISSUES ALL THE SPECIFIED COMMANDS IN THE COMMAND
*    TABLE. IN ORDER TO ACCOMPLISH THIS TASK, THIS ROUTINE CALLS THE
*    SUBROUTINES WITH THE FOLLOWING FUNCTIONS:
*          * EXTRACT A COMMAND FROM THE COMMAND TABLE;
*          * WRITE THE COMMAND TO THE JES2 INTERNAL READER.
***********************************************************************
*
ISSUCMDS LA        R10,COMMTBL                   LD ADR OF BG OF CMD TBL
NEXTCOMM BAL       R7,GETCOMM                    GET A COMMAND FROM TBL
         CLI       0(R10),X'00'                  CHK FOR END-OF-TABLE
         BER       R6                            IF END, RET TO CALLING RTN
         BAL       R7,PUTCOMM                    IF NOT END, ISSUE COMMAND
         B         NEXTCOMM                      GET NEXT CMD FROM TBL
*
*
***********************************************************************
*    THIS SUBROUTINE EXTRACTS THE CURRENT COMMAND ENTRY FROM THE COMMAND
*    TABLE AND MOVES THE COMMAND INTO THE I/O AREA USED BY THE JES2
*    INTERNAL READER AND THEN INCREMENTS THE POINTER TO THE NEXT COMMAND
*    ENTRY. THE CURRENT COMMAND ENTRY IS POINTED TO BY REGISTER 10.
***********************************************************************
*
GETCOMM  MVC       COMMAND,0(R10)                MOVE CMD FROM TBL TO INTRDR BUF
         LA        R10,80(0,R10)                 INCR TO NEXT CMD
         BR        R7                            RETURN TO CALLING RTN
*
*
***********************************************************************
*    THIS SUBROUTINE WRITES THE COMMAND TO THE JES2 INTERNAL READER.
***********************************************************************
*
PUTCOMM  PUT       JES2IRDR,COMMAND              WRITE CMD TO INTRDR
         BR        R7                            RETURN TO CALLING RTN
*
*
***********************************************************************
*    THIS ROUTINE CLOSES THE JES2 INTERNAL READER.
***********************************************************************
*
CLOSE    CLOSE     JES2IRDR                      CLOSE IRDR
         BR        R6                            RETURN TO CALLING RTN
*
*
***********************************************************************
```

```
*     THIS ROUTINE RESTORES THE REGISTERS AND RETURNS CONTROL.
***********************************************************************
*
RETURN    RCNTL     RC=0                    RETURN TO MVS OR CALLING PROG
*
*
***********************************************************************
*     THE COMMAND TABLE
***********************************************************************
*
COMMTBL   DS        0H
          DC        CL80'/*$DA'             JES2 $DA COMMAND
          DC        CL80'/*$VS,'D A,L'      MVS D A COMMAND
          DC        CL80'/*$VS,'S xxxx'     MVS START COMMAND
          DC        CL80'/*EOF'             REQD ONLY IF INTRDR IS NOT CLOSED
          DC        X'00'                   END-OF-TBL INDICATOR
*
*
***********************************************************************
*     THE I/O AREA AND QSAM DCB FOR THE JES2 INTERNAL READER
***********************************************************************
*
COMMAND   DS        CL80
JES2IRDR  DCB       DSORG=PS,MACRF=PM,RECFM=FB,LRECL=80,DDNAME=JESIRDR
*
*
***********************************************************************
*     END OF PROGRAM
***********************************************************************
*
          END
```

Coding Example 5.13.2

This coding example illustrates how to submit a job through the JES2 internal reader using VSAM and how to obtain the JES2 assigned job number.

```
PUTIRDRV  CSECT
*
*
***********************************************************************
*     INITIALIZATION
***********************************************************************
*
          INITL     3,EQU=R                 INITIALIZE PROGRAM
          USING     IFGRPL,R10              DEFINE REG FOR RPL DSECT
*
*
***********************************************************************
*     MAINSTREAM OF PROGRAM
***********************************************************************
*
          BAL       R6,OPENRDR              OPEN INTERNAL RDR
          BAL       R6,SENDJCL              WRITE JCL TO INTRDR
          BAL       R6,GETJOBNO             GET JOB NUMB OF SUBM JOB
          BAL       R6,CLOSERDR             CLOSE INTERNAL RDR
          B         RETURN                  RETURN TO MVS OR CALLING PROG
*
*
***********************************************************************
*     THIS ROUTINE OPENS THE JES2 INTERNAL READER.
***********************************************************************
```

```
*
OPENRDR   OPEN    (IRDRACB,(OUTPUT))
          ...                          CHECK FOR GOOD OPEN
          BR      R6                   RETURN TO CALLING RTN
*
*
***********************************************************************
*    THIS ROUTINE SUBMITS THE JOB BY WRITING ALL THE JCL STATEMENTS
*    TO THE INTERNAL READER.
***********************************************************************
*
SENDJCL   LA      R10,JCL              LOAD ADR OF BG OF JCL STREAM
NEXTJCL   CLI     0(R10),X'00'         CHK FOR END-OF-JCL
          BER     R6                   IF END, RET TO CALLING RTN
          MVC     JCLSTMT,0(R10)       MOVE JCL STMT INTO VSAM WKAR
          LA      R10,80(0,R10)        INCR TO NEXT JCL STMT
          PUT     RPL=IRDRRPL          WRITE JCL STMT TO INTRDR
          B       NEXTJCL              GET NEXT JCL STMT
*
*
***********************************************************************
*    THIS ROUTINE OBTAINS THE JOB NUMBER OF THE SUBMITTED JOB.
***********************************************************************
*
GETJOBNO  ENDREQ  RPL=IRDRRPL          INDICATE END-OF-JCL
          LA      R10,IRDRRPL          SET ADRBLTY FOR RPL DSECT
          MVC     JOBID,RPLRBAR        GET JOB NUMBER FROM RPL
          BR      R6                   RETURN TO CALLING RTN
*
*
***********************************************************************
*    THIS ROUTINE CLOSES THE JES2 INTERNAL READER.
***********************************************************************
*
CLOSERDR  CLOSE   IRDRACB
          BR      R6                   RETURN TO CALLING RTN
*
*
***********************************************************************
*    THIS ROUTINE RESTORES THE REGISTERS AND RETURNS CONTROL.
***********************************************************************
*
RETURN    RCNTL   RC=0                 RETURN TO MVS OR CALLING PROG
*
*
***********************************************************************
*    THE JCL STATEMENTS TO BE SUBMITTED
***********************************************************************
*
JCL       DC      CL80'//DEMOJOB JOB ACCTNO,NAME,CLASS=A'
          DC      CL80'//STEP EXEC PGM=IEFBR14'
          DC      CL80'//'
          DC      X'00'                END-OF-JCL INDICATOR
*
*
***********************************************************************
*    THE DC/DS STATEMENTS
***********************************************************************
*
JOBID     DS      CL8
JCLSTMT   DS      CL80
*
*
***********************************************************************
```

```
*     THE VSAM ACB AND RPL
***********************************************************************
*
IRDRACB    ACB      AM=VSAM,MACRF=(ADR,SEQ,OUT),DDNAME=INTRDR
IRDRRPL    RPL      AM=VSAM,ACB=IRDRACB,OPTCD=(ADR,SEQ,SYN,NUP,MVE),  -
                    AREA=JCLSTMT,AREALEN=80,RECLEN=80
*
*
***********************************************************************
*     THE DSECTS
***********************************************************************
*
           PRINT    NOGEN
           IFGRPL                          GENERATES THE RPL DSECT
*
*
***********************************************************************
*     END OF PROGRAM
***********************************************************************
*
           END
```

NOTES:

- The ENDREQ macro instruction has the same effect as the JES2 /*EOF command.

5.13.2 Issuing Commands Via the MGCR Macro Instruction

The format of the MGCR macro instruction is as follows:

```
[name]    MGCR command-buffer-address
```

`command-buffer-address`

Specifies the address of a command buffer. The address may be specified as a label (A-type address) or as a register, enclosed within parentheses. The format of the command buffer is as follows. The number in parentheses indicates the length of the field in bytes:

`Flags-1 (1)`	Bit 0 is set to 1 to indicate that Flags-2 contains meaningful information. Bits 1–7 must be set to zero.
`Length (1)`	The length of the command buffer up to but not including the token field.
`Flags-2 (2)`	X'8000' indicates that token is present. X'0000' indicates that token is not present.
`Text (maximum 126)`	The actual text of the command, just as it would be entered on the system console.
`Token (4)`	Optional field that may contain any desired information. When specified, only the low order 31-bits are used and the operating system turns on the high order bit. This field is meaningful only for MVS START commands; and the contents is passed to the program which is invoked via the START command.

Commands can be changed dynamically by providing a label for the command text field and modifying it before issuing the MGCR macro instruction. Trailing blanks and/or comments may be specified in the command text.

For a START command (referred to as an internal START command when issued via the MGCR macro instruction), if data is to be passed to the invoked program and if the data can be specified in only 31 bits, then the data can be specified, as is, in the token field. However, if more data is required to be sent to the program invoked by the START command, then the token field should contain an address that points to a parameter-list. The parameter-list should be contained in the CSA since the START command causes a different address space to be created. Also, if the CSA storage, containing the parameter-list, is allocated below the 16 Mb line, then a program executing in either 24-bit or 31-bit addressing mode could access the data. If a 24-bit address is used, then it is the programmer's responsibility to insure that the high order seven bits of the address contains zeros. Coding Example 5.13.6 shows the required code to access the token field from the program invoked by the START command.

Jobs can be submitted via the MGCR macro instruction by defining an internal START command, which invokes a PROC, which in turn invokes a program to read a JCL jobstream from a sequential dataset or from a member of a partitioned dataset and writes the JCL statements to the JES2 internal reader. If jobs are to be submitted only, then using the JES2 internal directly would be a better choice.

Coding Example 5.13.3

This coding example illustrates how to code the MGCR macro instruction and command buffer to issue an MVS command. In this example, an MVS Display Active command is issued.

```
          MGCR     CMDBUFF              INVOKE SVC 34, ISSUE COMMAND
          ...
CMDBUFF   DC       X'80'                IND FLAG-2 CONTAINS MEANINGFUL INFO
          DC       AL1(CMDBUFFX-CMDBUFF)      LENGTH OF COMMAND BUFFER
          DC       X'0000'              INDICATES TOKEN FIELD NOT PRESENT
          DC       C'D A,L'             COMMAND
CMDBUFFX  EQU      *
```

Coding Example 5.13.4

This coding example illustrates how to code the MGCR macro instruction and command buffers to issue JES2 commands. In this example, the job classes processed by Initiator 5 are changed to A, B and X, and Initiator 10 is stopped.

```
          MVC      COMMAND,J2COMM01       PUT JES2 CMD-1 INTO COMMAND BUFFER
          BAL      R7,ISSUECMD            ISSUE JES2 COMMAND VIA SVC 34
          MVC      COMMAND,J2COMM02       PUT JES2 CMD-2 INTO COMMAND BUFFER
          BAL      R7,ISSUECMD            ISSUE JES2 COMMAND VIA SVC 34
          ...
ISSUECMD  MGCR     CMDBUFF                INVOKE SVC 34, ISSUE COMMAND
          BR       R7                     RETURN TO CALLING RTN
          ...
CMDBUFF   DC       X'80'                  IND FLAG-2 CONTAINS MEANINGFUL INFO
          DC       AL1(CMDBUFFX-CMDBUFF)  LENGTH OF COMMAND BUFFER
          DC       X'0000'                INDICATES TOKEN FIELD NOT PRESENT
COMMAND   DS       CL10                   COMMAND AREA
CMDBUFFX  EQU      *
          ...
J2COMM01  DC       CL10'$TI5,ABX'         JES2 COMMAND-1
J2COMM02  DC       CL10'$PI10'            JES2 COMMAND-2
```

Coding Example 5.13.5

This coding example illustrates how to code the MGCR macro instruction and command buffer to issue an MVS START command. In this example, the START command invokes the procname PROC01 and passes the program, which is invoked by PROC01, the parameter S01 in the low order three bytes of the token field.

```
         MGCR      CMDBUFF                 INVOKE SVC 34, ISSUE COMMAND
         ...
CMDBUFF  DC        X'80'                   IND FLAG-2 CONTAINS MEANINGFUL INFO
         DC        AL1(CMDBUFFX-CMDBUFF)   LENGTH OF COMMAND BUFFER (NOT
*                                          INCLUDING TOKEN FIELD)
         DC        X'8000'                 INDICATES TOKEN FIELD IS PRESENT
         DC        C'S PROC01'             COMMAND
CMDBUFFX EQU       *
STARTID  DC        X'00',C'S01'            TOKEN FIELD
```

Coding Example 5.13.6

This coding example illustrates a practical use of issuing an internal START command with a parameter-list address specified as the token field. In this example, a user-specified WTO/WTOR exit is written. This exit is defined via the Message Processing Facility (MPF). (This facility is available in MVS/XA and MVS/ESA.) The purpose of the exit routine is to notify the operator via WTO and WTOR macro instructions whenever a production job abnormally terminates and to request that the operator create a trouble report (TR) for the job. To confirm that the operator notices the ABEND message and issues a TR, the WTO/WTOR indicates the jobname and the stepname of the job that abnormally terminated and requests that the operator replies "A" to acknowledge the ABEND and the request for the TR.

To accomplish this, the following requirements and considerations are necessary:

- Indicate to MPF to pass control to the exit routine whenever the IEF450I (Job ABEND) system message is encountered. This is accomplished by specifying the following entry in the active MPFLSTxx member of SYS1.PARMLIB.

```
IEF450I,SUP(NO),USEREXIT(ABNDNOTE)
where: ABNDNOTE is the user-assigned name of the exit.
```

- Since it is necessary to wait for the operator's reply, the WTOR macro instruction cannot be issued in the WTO/WTOR exit routine since the exit routine is not allowed to perform any wait processing.
- The solution to the above problem is to have the exit routine process the IEF450I message and extract the jobname and the stepname. CSA storage is allocated below the 16 Mb line and is used to store the jobname and the stepname and for the MGCR buffer in order to maintain reentrancy in the WTO/WTOR exit. Finally, the exit routine issues the MGCR macro instruction to START a program that issues the WTOR macro instruction and waits for the operator's reply. The address of the allocated CSA storage is passed to the invoked program via the token field.
- The name of the WTO/WTOR exit routine is ABNDNOTE, and it must be reentrant and execute in 31-bit addressing mode. The name of the PROC, which is invoked by the internal START command issued by ABNDNOTE, is OPERALRT. The name of the program invoked by the PROC is also named OPERALRT.
- The program OPERALRT issues the EXTRACT macro instruction to obtain the address of the Command Schedule Communications list (CSCL), which contains the address of the token field. The EXTRACT macro instruction requires that its parameter-list be located below the 16 Mb line.
- Production jobs have the charcater "P" in the first position of the jobname. The exit routine invokes OPERALRT via the internal START command only if a production job ABENDs.
- OPERALRT does the FREEMAIN for the CSA storage obtained by ABNDNOTE.
- When the exit routine receives control, register 1 contains a pointer to the communications task exit parameter-list (CTXT). Field CTXTTXPJ of the CTXT contains the

address of the CTXTATTR. Field CTXTTMSG of the CTXTATTR contains the actual message starting with the first character of the message ID.

The code for ABNDNOTE

```
ABNDNOTE  CSECT
ABNDNOTE  AMODE 31                               SPEC ADR MODE IS 31 BITS
ABNDNOTE  RMODE ANY                              SPEC RES MODE IS ANYWHERE
*
*
***********************************************************************
* INITIALIZATION
***********************************************************************
*
          INITL    3,EQU=R                       INITIALIZE PROGRAM
          USING    CTXT,R10                      DEFINE REG FOR CTXT DSECT
          USING    CTXTATTR,R11                  DEFINE REG FOR CTXTATTR DSECT
          USING    CSAWORK,R12                   DEFINE REG FOR CSAWORK DSECT
*
*
***********************************************************************
* MAINSTREAM OF PROGRAM
***********************************************************************
*
          BAL      R6,GETMSG                     GET ADR OF MSG IEF450I
          BAL      R6,CKJOBPFX                   CHK IF PROD JOB
          BAL      R6,GETCSA                     ALLO CSA FOR PARM-LIST ADR
          BAL      R6,BLDPARM                    BUILD PARM-LIST IN CSA
          BAL      R6,DOSTART                    ISSUE START CMD VIA SVC 34
          B        RETURN                        RETURN TO MVS
*
*
***********************************************************************
* THIS ROUTINE OBTAINS THE ADDRESS OF THE BEGINNING OF MESSAGE IEF450I.
***********************************************************************
*
GETMSG    L        R10,0(0,R1)                   SET ADRBLTY FOR CTXT DSECT
          L        R11,CTXTTXPJ                  SET ADRBLTY FOR CTXTATTR DSECT
          LA       R11,CTXTTMSG                  LD ADR OF BG OF MESSAGE IEF450I
          BR       R6                            RETURN TO CALLING RTN
*
*
***********************************************************************
* THIS ROUTINE CHECKS THE FIRST CHARACTER OF THE JOBNAME LOCATED IN
* MESSAGE IEF450I FOR THE PRODUCTION PREFIX ("P" IN FIRST POSITION).
* IF THE JOB IS NOT A PRODUCTION JOB, NO OTHER PROCESSING IS PERFORMED.
***********************************************************************
*
CKJOBPFX  CLI      8(R11),C'P'                   CHK 1ST CHAR OF JOBNM FOR PROD JOB
          BER      R6                            IF PROD JOB, RET TO CALLING RTN
          B        RETURN                        IF NOT PROD JOB, RETURN TO MVS
*
*
***********************************************************************
* THIS ROUTINE ALLOCATES VIRTUAL STORAGE FROM THE CSA, WHICH IS USED TO
* STORE THE PARAMETERS PASSED TO THE PROGRAM INITIATED VIA THE INTERNAL
* START COMMAND.
***********************************************************************
*
GETCSA    GETMAIN  RC,LV=CSAGMLEN,SP=241,LOC=BELOW
          LTR      R15,R15                       CHK IF CSA ALLOC OK
          BNZ      RETURN                        IF CSA UNAVAIL, RETURN TO MVS
          LR       R12,R1                        SET ADRBLTY FOR CSAWORK DSECT
```

```
         ST    R1,CSATOKEN           STORE ALLO CSA ADR IN TOKEN FIELD
         MVC   CSAJOBNM,BLANKS       BLANK OUT CSA JOBNAME FIELD
         MVC   CSASTEPN,BLANKS       BLANK OUT CSA STEPNAME FIELD
         BR    R6                    RETURN TO CALLING RTN
*
*
***********************************************************************
* THIS ROUTINE OBTAINS THE JOBNAME AND THE STEPNAME OF THE ABENDING
* PRODUCTION JOB FROM MESSAGE IEF450I AND INSERTS THEM INTO THE
* PARAMETER-LIST.
***********************************************************************
*
BLDPARM  LA    R0,8                  SET MAX JOBNAME COUNT
         LA    R11,8(0,R11)          LD ADR OF BG OF JOBNM IN MSG IEF450I
         LA    R10,CSAJOBNM          LD ADR OF JOBNAME PARM IN CSA
NEXTJPOS CLI   0(R11),C' '           CHK FOR END OF JOBNAME
         BE    GETSTEP               AT END, START TO EXTR STEPNAME
         MVC   0(1,R10),0(R11)       MOVE A CHAR OF JOBNM TO PARM IN CSA
         LA    R11,1(0,R11)          INCR JOBNAME IN MSG IEF450I
         LA    R10,1(0,R10)          INCR JOBNAME PARM IN CSA
         BCT   R0,NEXTJPOS           MOVE NEXT JOBNAME CHAR
GETSTEP  LA    R0,8                  AT JOBNAME END, SET MAX STEPNAME
*                                    COUNT
         LA    R11,1(0,R11)          INCR PAST BLANK BETW JBNM AND STEPNM
         LA    R10,CSASTEPN          LD ADR OF STEPNAME PARM IN CSA
NEXTSPOS CLI   0(R11),C' '           CHK FOR END OF STEPNAME
         BER   R6                    AT END, RETURN TO CALLING RTN
         MVC   0(1,R10),0(R11)       MOVE A CHAR OF STEPNM TO PARM IN CSA
         LA    R11,1(0,R11)          INCR STEPNAME IN MSG IEF450I
         LA    R10,1(0,R10)          INCR STEPNAME PARM IN CSA
         BCT   R0,NEXTSPOS           MOVE NEXT STEPNAME CHAR
         BR    R6                    AT STEPNAME END, RET TO CALLING RTN
*
*
***********************************************************************
* THIS ROUTINE ISSUES THE INTERNAL START COMMAND VIA THE MGCR MACRO
* (SVC 34).
***********************************************************************
*
DOSTART  MVC   CSABUF34,MGCRBUFF      MOVE MSGBUF INTO CSA
         LA    R0,0                  ZERO REG 0 FOR SVC 34
         LA    R10,CSABUF34          LD ADR OF MSGBUF IN CSA
         MGCR  (R10)                 ISSUE SVC 34
         BR    R6                    RETURN TO CALLING RTN
*
*
***********************************************************************
* THIS ROUTINE RESTORES THE REGISTERS AND RETURNS CONTROL.
***********************************************************************
*
RETURN   RCNTL RC=0                  RETURN TO MVS
*
*
***********************************************************************
* CONSTANTS
***********************************************************************
*
BLANKS   DC    CL8' '
*
*
***********************************************************************
* PARAMETER-LIST FOR SVC 34
***********************************************************************
*
```

```
MGCRBUFF   DC        X'80'
           DC        AL1(BUFFLEN)
           DC        X'8000'                   INDICATE TOKEN PRESENT
           DC        C'S OPERALRT'
MGCRBUFX   EQU       *
BUFFLEN    EQU       (MGCRBUFX-MGCRBUFF)
*
*
************************************************************************
* THE DSECTS
************************************************************************
*
           PRINT     NOGEN
           IEZVX100                            GENERATES CTXT, CTXTATTR DSECTS
*
CSAWORK    DSECT
CSAJOBNM   DS        CL8
CSASTEPN   DS        CL8
CSABUF34   DS        CL(BUFFLEN)
CSATOKEN   DS        CL4
CSAGMLEN   ORG       *-CSAWORK
*
*
************************************************************************
* END OF PROGRAM
************************************************************************
*
           END
```

The code for OPERALRT

```
OPERALRT   CSECT
*
*
************************************************************************
* INITIALIZATION
************************************************************************
*
           INITL     3,EQU=R                   INITIALIZE PROGRAM
           USING     CSCL,R10                  DEFINE REG FOR CSCL DSECT
           USING     CSAPARM,R11               DEFINE REG FOR CSAPARM DSECT
*
*
************************************************************************
* MAINSTREAM OF PROGRAM
************************************************************************
*
           BAL       R6,EXTRACT                GET ADR OF C.S.C.L.
           BAL       R6,GETPARM                GET CSA ADR FROM TOKEN FIELD
           BAL       R6,DOWTOR                 NOTIFY OPER OF ABEND VIA WTOR
           BAL       R6,RELCSA                 RELEASE CSA ALLO BY WTO/WTOR EXIT
           B         RETURN                    RETURN TO MVS
*
*
************************************************************************
* THIS ROUTINE OBTAINS THE ADDRESS OF THE COMMAND SCHEDULER
* COMMUNICATIONS LIST (CSCL), WHICH CONTAINS THE TOKEN (PARAMETER-LIST
* ADDRESS) PASSED BY THE INTERNAL START COMMAND ISSUED BY THE WTO/WTOR
* EXIT.
************************************************************************
*
EXTRACT    EXTRACT   CSCLADDR,FIELDS=(COMM)
           BR        R6                        RETURN TO CALLING RTN
*
```

```
*
************************************************************************
* THIS ROUTINE OBTAINS THE TOKEN CONTAINED IN THE CSCL. THE TOKEN
* CONTAINS THE ADDRESS OF THE VIRTUAL STORAGE ALLOCATED FROM THE CSA,
* WHICH CONTAINS THE PARAMETER-LIST PASSED BY THE WTO/WTOR EXIT.
************************************************************************
*
GETPARM   L        R10,CSCLADDR          SET ADRBLTY FOR CSCL DSECT
          TM       COMTOKEN,COMTOKHR     CHK IF TOKEN PRESENT
          BNO      NOTOKEN               IF NO, ERROR
          MVC      CSAADR,COMTOKEN       MOVE ADR OF ALLO CSA (CSAPARM)
          BR       R6                    RETURN TO CALLING RTN
NOTOKEN   WTO      '*** NO PARM SPECIFIED---PROGRAM TERMINATED ***'
          WTO      '*** NOTIFY SYSTEMS PROGRAMMING DEPARTMENT ***'
          ABEND    901
*
*
************************************************************************
* THIS ROUTINE INSERTS THE JOBNAME AND THE STEPNAME OF THE PRODUCTION
* JOB THAT ABENDED INTO THE WTO-LIST. IT THEN ISSUES THE WTO/WTOR
* MACRO TO INFORM THE OPERATOR THAT A PRODUCTION JOB HAS ABENDED AND
* WAITS FOR A REPLY FROM THE OPERATOR, WHICH INDICATES THAT THE
* OPERATOR SAW THE MASSEAGE AND IS PREPARING A TROUBLE REPORT.
************************************************************************
*
DOWTOR    L        R11,CSAADR            SET ADRBLTY FOR CSAPARM DSECT
          MVC      WTO1JBNM,CSAJOBNM     MOVE JOBNAME INTO WTO-LIST
          MVC      WTO1STEP,CSASTEPN     MOVE STEPNAME INTO WTO-LIST
WTOR      LA       R1,WTOLST1            LOAD ADR OF WTO-LIST
          WTO      MF=(E,(R1))           ISSUE EXEC-FORM OF WTO
          XC       ECB,ECB               CLEAR ECB FOR WTOR
          WTOR     '*** REPLY "A" TO ACKNOWLEDGE AND ISSUE TR ***',  -
                   REPLY,1,ECB
          WAIT     1,ECB=ECB             WAIT FOR REPLY
          CLI      REPLY,C'A'            CHK FOR PROPER REPLY
          BER      R6                    IF REPLY OK, RET TO CALLING RTN
          WTO      '*** INVALID REPLY ***'
          B        WTOR                  REISSUE WTOR
*
*
************************************************************************
* THIS ROUTINE RELEASES THE CSA STORAGE ALLOCATED BY THE WTO/WTOR EXIT.
************************************************************************
*
RELCSA    LA       R11,CSAADR            LOAD ADR OF CSAPARM ADR
          FREEMAIN EC,LV=100,SP=241,A(R11)
          BR       R6                    RETURN TO CALLING RTN
*
*
************************************************************************
* THIS ROUTINE RESTORES THE REGISTERS AND RETURNS CONTROL.
************************************************************************
*
RETURN    RCNTL    RC=0                  RETURN TO MVS
*
*
************************************************************************
* DC/DS STATEMENTS
************************************************************************
*
CSCLADDR  DS       F
CSAADR    DS       F
ECB       DS       F
REPLY     DS       CL1
```

```
*
*
***************************************************************************
* THE WTO-LIST USED FOR INSERTING THE JOBNAME AND THE STEPNAME OF THE
* ABENDING JOB.
***************************************************************************
*
          DS        0F
WTOLST1   DC        AL2(WTOLST1X-WTOLST1)
          DC        X'8000'
          DC        C'*** OPERATIONS: JOB '
WTO1JBNM  DS        CL8
          DC        C' HAS ABENDED AT STEP '
WTO1STEP  DS        CL8
          DC        C' ***'
WTOLST1X  EQU       *
          DC        X'4000'                 DESC=2
          DC        X'4000'                 ROUT=2
*
*
***************************************************************************
* THE DSECTS
***************************************************************************
*
          PRINT     NOGEN
CSCL      DSECT
          IEZCOM                            GENERATES CSCL DSECT
*
CSAPARM   DSECT
CSAJOBNM  DS        CL8
CSASTEPN  DS        CL8
*
*
***************************************************************************
* END OF PROGRAM
***************************************************************************
*
          END
```

5.14 OBTAINING THE ADDRESSES OF THE TCB AND THE ASCB

There may be times when a program requires to known the addresses of its Task Control Block (TCB) and its Address Space Control Block (ASCB). There are at least three ways of obtaining this information.

The simplest way is to have an SVC routine available that returns those addresses to the calling program. When an SVC routine receives control, the operating system provides it with the addresses of the calling program's TCB and ASCB. The code for such an SVC routine is presented in Chapter 12.

The most direct and efficient way is to extract the information from the Prefixed Save Area (PSA). The PSA can be located by running a number of pointers. The CVT has a pointer (the CVTPCCAT field) to the Physical Configuration Communication Area Vector Table (PCCAVT). The PCCAVT contains up to 16 fullwords that contain the addresses of the PCCAs for each of the CPUs of a multiprocessing (MP) system. The PCCA contains a pointer (the PCCAPSAV or the PCCAPSAR field) to the PSA. The PSATOLD field contains the address of the currently dispatched TCB (the one for the program that is currently examining the PSA), and the PSAAOLD field contains the address of the currently dispatched ASCB (the one that contains the TCB pointed to by PSATOLD). The problem with this method is determining on which CPU the program is executing. However, there is a simple solution. The PSA is used to map low storage (PSWs, etc.) and starts at location 0 for the CPU of a uniprocessor system or for each CPU of a multiprocessor system. Therefore, the PSA can be located by setting the DSECT register to 0 and extracting the information from the appropriate fields of the PSA DSECT.

Coding Example 5.14.1

This coding example illustrates how to obtain the addresses of the currently dispatched TCB and ASCB from the PSA.

```
         USING    PSA,R10               DEFINE REG FOR PSA DSECT
         ...
         LA       .R10,0                LOAD ADR OF PSA
         MVC      TCBADR,PSATOLD        EXTRACT TCB ADR
         MVC      ASCBADR,PSAAOLD       EXTRACT ASCB ADR
         ...
TCBADR   DS       F
ASCBADR  DS       F
         ...
         IHAPSA                         GENERATES PSA DSECT
```

If an SVC routine is not available and if the programmer does not know how to access the PSA, then the TCB and ASCB addresses can be obtained by the use of the ATTACH, EXTRACT, and LOCASCB macro instructions. The ATTACH macro instruction is used to ATTACH a dummy subtask (IEFBR14 is a good choice for the program). The address of the TCB of the subtask is returned in register 1. The TCBOTC field of the subtask's TCB has the address of the TCB of the attaching task. The EXTRACT macro instruction can be used to request the Address Space ID (ASID) of the issuing task. The LOCASCB macro instruction can be used to obtain the address of the ASCB for the specified ASID.

Coding Example 5.14.2

This coding example illustrates how to obtain the addresses of the TCB and the ASCB and the ASID of a program using nonrestricted macro instructions.

```
GETINFO  ATTACH   EP=IEFBR14
         MVC      TCBADR,TCBOTC-TCB(R1)   STORE TCB ADR
         EXTRACT  ASID,FIELDS=(ASID)      GET ASID
         L        R10,ASID
         LOCASCB  ASID=(R10)
         ST       R1,ASCDADR              STORE ASCB ADR
         BR       R7                      RETURN TO CALLING RTN
         ...
TCBADR   DS       F
ASID     DS       F
ASCBADR  DS       F
         ...
         IKJTCB                           GENERATES THE TCB DSECT
         ...
```

BIBLIOGRAPHY FOR CHAPTER 5

The following IBM manuals contain reference material for the topics discussed in this chapter.

ID	TITLE
GC28-1114	*OS/VS2 MVS Supervisor Services and Macro Instructions*
GC28-1046	*OS/VS2 SPL: Supervisor*
GC26-3838	*OS/VS VSAM Programmer's Guide*
GC28-1147	*MVS/XA SPL: User Exits*
GC28-1150	*MVS/XA SPL: System Macros and Facilities Volume 1*
GC28-1151	*MVS/XA SPL: System Macros and Facilities Volume 2*
GC28-1154	*MVS/XA Supervisor Services and Macro Instructions*
GC26-4016	*MVS/XA VSAM Reference*
GC28-1821	*MVS/ESA Application Development Guide*
GC28-1822	*MVS/ESA Application Development Macro Reference*
GC28-1836	*MVS/ESA SPL: User Exits*
GC28-1852	*MVS/ESA SPL: Application Development Guide*
GC28-1857	*MVS/ESA SPL: Application Development Macro Reference*
SC26-4517	*MVS/ESA VSAM Administration: Macro Instruction Reference*

6 Programming ABEND Recovery

MVS provides recovery facilities for programs that abnormally terminate. Program exception ABENDs (S0C1 to S0CF) may be intercepted by using the SPIE/ESPIE macro instruction and other system ABENDs (including the program exceptions intercepted by SPIE/ESPIE) may be intercepted by using the ESTAE macro instruction or the SETFRR macro instruction. The ESTAE macro instruction is used for programs that execute in task mode (enabled, unlocked, and under control of a TCB), and the SETFRR macro instruction is used for programs that execute in system mode (disabled or locked or in SRB mode). This chapter discusses the recovery facilities provided by the SPIE\ESPIE and the ESTAE macro instructions.

6.1 RECOVERING FROM PROGRAM INTERRUPTION ABENDS

A program interruption occurs when a program attempts to perform an invalid function, such as executing an invalid machine instruction, processing data that is in an invalid format, accessing real or virtual storage that is not owned by the task under which the program executes, and so on. The CPU indicates this group of errors by causing a program interruption and posting the appropriate interruption code in the Old Program PSW (BC mode) and in low storage (EC mode). The interruption codes are X'01' to X'0F', X'10' to X'13', X'40', and X'80'. MVS converts the interruption codes X'01' to X'0F' into the program exception ABEND codes S0C1 to S0CF, respectively. By means of the SPM (Set Program Mask) machine instruction, the programmer has the facility of disabling certain program interruption types (X'08', X'0A', X'0D', and X'0E').

During normal processing, the Recovery/Termination Management (RTM) component of MVS abnormally terminates the program, which causes a program interruption. However, the programmer has the option of writing a recovery exit routine, which will handle the program interruption instead of RTM. This is accomplished by using the SPIE/ESPIE macro instruction (or the ESTAE macro instruction which is discussed in section 6.2).

The SPIE/ESPIE macro instruction enables the programmer to specify a recovery exit routine, which receives control when one of the specified program interruption types occurs. If the SPIE/ESPIE macro instruction specifies a program interruption type that has been disabled (via the SPM machine instruction), then MVS enables that program interruption type when the macro instruction is executed.

When the recovery exit routine receives control, the content of the registers are as follows:

Register 0	Used by operating system.
Register 1	Points to the PIE control block if the recovery environment was established by the SPIE macro instruction or points to the EPIE control block if the recovery environment was established by the ESPIE macro instruction.
Registers 2	12 Same as when the program interruption occurred.
Register 13	Address of the savearea of the main program. The area must not be used by the exit routine.
Register 14	Return address (to operating system).
Register 15	Address of exit routine.

Only one SPIE/ESPIE recovery environment may be active at a time for a task. When a new recovery environment is established, it replaces the previous one. The recovery environment established by SPIE/ESPIE exists for the life of the task, but may be changed in one of the following ways:

- A new recovery environment is established.
- The program that created the SPIE/ESPIE recovery environment terminates. This processing is different between version 1 (MVS/370) of the operating system and version 2 and later (MVS/XA and MVS/ESA) of the operating system. In MVS/370, if the program that established the SPIE recovery environment terminates or transfers control (via XCTL), then the SPIE recovery environment stays in effect if the task continues to execute. In MVS/XA and MVS/ESA, the SPIE/ESPIE recovery environment is cancelled when the program that established the SPIE/ESPIE recovery environment terminates, even if the task continues to execute.
- The recovery environment is cancelled by specifying a blank operand or a zero exit routine address in the SPIE macro instruction, or by specifying a token containing zero in the ESPIE macro instruction, with the RESET option. If the SPIE/ESPIE recovery environment is to be cancelled, then it should be cancelled in the main program. If the recovery environment is cancelled in the exit routine, then the main program will not receive control when the exit routine returns control.

Processing is easier if the recovery exit routine is located in the program that issues the SPIE/ESPIE macro instruction. Since the contents of registers 2-12 remain intact when the exit routine receives control, setting up addressability is not required. Therefore, the exit routine and the rest of the program can communicate by simply referencing the same storage areas, using the same labels. However, the exit routine should not pass control back to the main program by branching to a label in the main program because then that routine would be considered to be part of the exit routine. Since program interruptions that occur in the exit routine are not intercepted, then any routine that receives control directly via a branch will not be protected by the SPIE/ESPIE recovery environment. The exit routine must return control by branching to the address that was in register 14 when control was received. When control is returned via a branch to register 14, the main program receives control at the instruction following the one that caused the program interruption. If control is required to be passed to another instruction, then the address of that instruction must be placed into the PIE/EPIE control block (replacing the PSW interruption address), and then control should be returned via a branch to register 14.

The recovery exit routine could also change the contents of the registers that the main program receives when control is returned. If the recovery environment was defined by SPIE, then registers 14–2 can be changed by changing the corresponding fields in the PIE since the operating system restores those registers from the PIE before returning control to the main program. The other registers, 3–13, can be changed by simply changing them directly before returning control. If the recovery environment was defined by the ESPIE macro instruction, then registers 0–15 can be changed by changing the corresponding fields in the EPIE since the operating system restores all registers from the EPIE before returning control. Care should be taken so as not to change the contents of the base registers or the savearea register.

6.1.1 Difference Between the SPIE and the ESPIE Macro Instructions

The SPIE macro instruction can be used only by programs that execute in 24-bit addressing mode and may be used in MVS/370, MVS/XA, and MVS/ESA operating systems. The ESPIE macro instruction may be used by programs which execute in either 24-bit or 31-bit addressing mode. It performs the same functions as the SPIE macro instruction plus some additional ones, but the macro instruction format is different. For ESPIE, the exit routine receives control in the addressing mode that was in effect when the ESPIE macro instruction was issued. The ESPIE macro instruction may be used only in MVS/XA and MVS/ESA operating systems.

The expansion of each standard or list form of the SPIE macro instruction contains a parameter-list called a Program Interruption Control Area (PICA). The PICA contains the specified interruption codes and the address of the exit routine that is to receive control when one of the interruption types occurs. The contents and format of the PICA is presented in Figure 6.1.1. IBM provides the macro instruction IHAPICA to generate the DSECT for mapping the PICA.

Also, during the first time in a task that an SPIE macro instruction is executed (or after its effect has been cancelled), MVS creates a control block called the Program Interruption Element (PIE) in virtual storage. The current PICA and the PIE together are referred to as the SPIE recovery environment.

The PIE is used for communications between the SPIE service routine and the user recovery exit routine. The contents and format of the PIE is presented in Figure 6.1.2. IBM provides the macro instruction IHAPIE to generate the the DSECT for mapping the PIE.

Offset		
0	PICAPRMK	PICEXITA
4	PICITMK1	PICITMK2
6	PICITMK3	PICITMK4

Figure 6.1.1. This figure illustrates the contents and format of the PICA. The field names used are the names contained in the IBM provided DSECT.

Offset		Field
0		PIEPICAA
4	PIEPSW	
12	PIEGR14	
16	PIEGR15	
20	PIEGR0	
24	PIEGR1	
28	PIEGR2	

Figure 6.1.2. This figure illustrates the contents and format of the PIE. The field names used are the names contained in the IBM-provided DSECT.

The following descibes the contents of the fields of the PICA. The number in parentheses, following the field name, is the length of the field.

`PICAPRMK (1)`

The first four bits are zero, and the second four bits contain the required mask to enable any specified interruption type codes that can be disabled.

`PICEXITA (3)`

The address of the recovery exit routine.

`PICITMK1 (2)`

Mask-1 indicates which program interruption types were specified. This field indicates interruption type codes 1–7.

`PICITMK2 (2)`

Mask-2 indicates which program interruption types were specified. This field indicates interruption type codes 8–15. When fields PICITMK1 and PICITMK2 are used together, bit 1 corresponds to interruption type code 1, bit 2 corresponds to interruption type code 2, and so on.

`PICITMK3 (2)`

N/A

`PICITMK4 (2)`

Not used.

The following describes the contents of the fields of the PIE.

`PIEPICAA (3)`

The address of the current PICA. The label PIEPICA is also provided in the DSECT to refer to the entire word.

`PIEPSW (8)`

The contents of the old program interruption PSW (in BC mode) at interruption time. Offset three for a length of one contains the interruption code and offset five for a length of three contains the address of the next instruction that will receive control when the exit routine returns control.

`PIEGR14 (4)`

The contents of register 14 at the time of the interruption.

PIEGR15 (4)

The contents of register 15 at the time of the interruption.

PIEGR0 (4)

The contents of register 0 at the time of the interruption.

PIEGR1 (4)

The contents of register 1 at the time of the interruption.

PIEGR2 (4)

The contents of register 2 at the time of the interruption.

The format of the SPIE macro instruction is as follows:

```
[name]     SPIE exit-address,(interruption-codes)
```

---

exit-address

Specifies the address of the routine to receive control when a program interruption of the type specified occurs. The address may be specified as a label (A-type address) or as a register, enclosed within parentheses. A zero address or omitted operand cancels the SPIE recovery environment.

interruption-codes

Specifies the codes for the interruption types that are to cause the exit routine to receive control. The following codes, with their meaning, are the ones that may be specified:

Code	Interruption Type	Code	Interruption Type
1	Operation	9	Fixed-point divide
2	Privileged operation	10	Decimal overflow
3	Execute	11	Decimal divide
4	Protection	12	Exponent overflow
5	Addressing	13	Exponent underflow
6	Specification	14	Significance
7	Data	15	Floating-point divide
8	Fixed-point overflow		

The codes may be specified in any sequence, separated by commas and enclosed within parentheses. Consecutive code numbers may be indicated by specifying the first code and the last code, separated by a comma and enclosed within parentheses. Valid combinations include the following:

((1,15))—Indicates all codes.

(1,3,8)—Indicates codes 1, 3, and 8.

((1,5),9,(12,14))—Indicates codes 1, 2, 3, 4, 5, 9, 12, 13, and 14.

During the first time in a task that an ESPIE macro instruction is executed (or after its effect has been cancelled), MVS creates a control block called the Extented Program Interruption Element (EPIE) in virtual storage. The EPIE is used for communications between the ESPIE service routine and the user recovery exit routine. The contents and format of the EPIE is presented in Figure 6.1.3. IBM provides the macro instruction IHAEPIE to generate the DSECT for mapping the EPIE.

The following describes the contents of the fields of the EPIE. The number in parentheses, following the field name, is the length of the field.

0	EPIEEPIE
4	EPIEPARM
8	EPIEGPR
72	EPIEPSW
80	EPIEINT
84	N/A
88	Reserved

Figure 6.1.3. This figure illustrates the contents and format of the EPIE. The names used are the names contained in the IBM-provided DSECT.

`EPIEEPIE (4)`
The charcaters EPIE for control block identification.

`EPIEPARM (4)`
The address of the user-supplied parameter-list. Contains zero if no parameter-list is passed.

`EPIEGRP (64)`
The contents of the registers at the time of the program interruption. The registers are stored in the sequence 0–15.

`EPIEPSW (8)`
The contents of the old program interruption PSW (in EC mode) at interruption time. Offset four for a length of four contains the address of the next instruction that will receive control when the exist routine returns control.

`EPIEINT (4)`
The 2-byte ILC (instruction length code) followed by the 2-byte interruption code at the time of the program interruption.

The ESPIE macro instruction provides three options: SET, RESET, and TEST. The SPIE macro instruction provides functions equivalent to SET, RESET, and TEST. In addition, the ESPIE macro instruction also enables the programmer to pass a parameter-list to the exit routine.

The format of the ESPIE macro instruction is as follows:

For SET option:

```
[name] ESPIE SET,exit-address,(interruption-codes)[,PARAM=list-address]
```

`SET`
Indicates that an ESPIE recovery environment is to be established.

`exit-address`
Specifies the address of the routine to receive control when a program interruption of the type specified occurs. The address may be specified as a label (A-type address) or as a register, enclosed within parentheses.

`interruption-codes`

Specifies the codes for the interruption types that are to cause the exit routine to receive control. The codes are the same as described in the SPIE macro instruction description and are specified using the same syntax.

`PARAM=list-address (Default: none)`

Specifies the address of a user-defined parameter-list that is to be passed to the recovery exit routine. The address must be aligned on a fullword boundary and may be specified as a label (A-type address) or as a register, enclosed in parentheses. The parameter-list consists of consecutive fullword addresses that point to the virtual storage areas that are to be passed to the exit routine.

For RESET option:

```
[name] ESPIE RESET,token-address
```

`RESET`

Indicates that the current ESPIE recovery environment is to be cancelled and a previous ESPIE recovery environment is to be restored.

`token-address`

Specifies the address of a fullword that contains a token representing the ESPIE recovery environment that is to be restored. This is the same token that is returned in register 1 when the ESPIE macro instruction is issued with the SET option.

For TEST option:

```
[name] ESPIE TEST,parameter-list-address
```

`TEST`

Indicates a request for information concerning the active SPIE/ESPIE recovery environment. The information is returned in the parameter-list specified.

`parameter-list-address`

Specifies the address of a four-word parameter-list aligned on a fullword boundary. If there is an active ESPIE recovery environment, then the parameter-list contains the following when control is returned:

Word	Contents
0	Address of the recovery exit routine. The address is a 31-bit address with the high order bit set to 0. If the exit routine is executing in 24-bit mode, then the high order seven bits of the address are 0.
1	Address of the parameter-list. (Same address convention as Word-0).
2	Mask of specified program interruption type codes. Only the first two bytes are used. Bit 1 corresponds to interruption type code 1, bit 2 corresponds to interruption type code 2, and so on.
3	Zero.

When control is returned from ESPIE TEST, register 15 contains one of the following return codes:

Return Code (Hex)	Meaning
00	An ESPIE recovery environment is active, and the contents of the four words of the parameter-list are as described above.
04	A SPIE recovery environment is active, and word-0 of the parameter-list contains the address of the current PICA.
08	A SPIE/ESPIE recovery environment is not active.

6.1.2 Using the SPIE Macro Instruction

When the SPIE macro instruction is issued, the address of the previous PICA (or zero if this is the first time the macro instruction executes) is returned in register 1. This information is useful if one program of a task creates an SPIE recovery environment and then calls another program (or subroutine) of the same task that has its own SPIE recovery environment requirements. The called program would issue the SPIE macro instruction with its own requirements, replacing the specifications of the previous SPIE (from the calling program). Upon completion, the called program (or subroutine) would restore the SPIE recovery environment to that of the calling program and then return control. The execute form of the SPIE macro instruction, pointing to the previous PICA, is used to restore the SPIE recovery environment.

Coding Example 6.1.1

This coding example illustrates how to use the SPIE macro instruction to intercept certain program interruption types. In this example, the main program reads and processes records from a master file. The processing requirements are to skip processing of all records that contain invalid data. The SPIE macro instruction is used to intercept all decimal data (packed) calculation related interruption types. If such an ABEND is intercepted, the assumption is made that the record currently being processed contains bad data. When the exit recovery routine receives control, it produces a hexadecimal dump of the entire record that has the bad data and then causes control to be passed to the NEXTREC routine in the main program.

```
SPIE01    CSECT
*
*
***********************************************************************
* INITIALIZATION
***********************************************************************
*
          INITL     3,EQU=R                    INITIALIZE PROGRAM
          USING     PIE,R11                    DEFINE REG FOR PIE DSECT
*
*
***********************************************************************
* MAINSTREAM OF PROGRAM
***********************************************************************
*
```

```
          ...
          BAL       R6,SETSPIE                ESTAB SPIE ENVIR
NEXTREC   BAL       R6,READMSTR               READ A REC FROM MASTR FILE
          BAL       R6,PROCESS                PROCESS RECORD
          B         NEXTREC                   READ NEXT REC
          ...
*
*
***************************************************************************
* THIS ROUTINE ESTABLISHES THE SPIE RECOVERY ENVIRONMENT. IT SPECIFIES
* THAT THE FOLLOWING INTERRUPTION TYPES ARE TO BE INTERCEPTED:
*          * DATA EXCEPTION (7);
*          * DECIMAL OVERFLOW (10);
*          * DECIMAL DIVIDE (11).
* WHEN ONE OF THE SPECIFIED INTERRUPTION TYPES IS ENCOUNTERED, CONTROL
* IS PASSED TO THE RECOVERY ROUTINE DATACHK, WHICH PROCESSES THE ABEND.
***************************************************************************
*
SETSPIE   SPIE      DATACHK,(7,10,11)
          BR        R6                        RETURN TO CALLING RTN
*
*
***************************************************************************
* THIS ROUTINE RECEIVES CONTROL VIA THE SPIE SERVICE ROUTINE WHEN THE
* PROGRAM ENCOUNTERS A SOC7, SOCA OR SOCB ABEND. WHEN THE ABEND
* PROCESSING IS COMPLETE, DATACHK RETURNS CONTROL TO THE NEXTREC
* ROUTINE OF THE MAIN PROGRAM.
***************************************************************************
*
DATACHK   ST        R14,SAVR14                SAVE RETURN ADR TO SPIE
          LR        R11,R1                    SET ADRBLTY FOR PIE DSECT
          CLI       PIEPSW+3,X'07'            CHK IF 07 INTERRUPTION TYPE
          BE        INCROC7                   IF YES, INCR OC7 ERROR CTR
          B         INCROCAB                  IF NO, INCR OCA/OCB ERROR CTR
INCROC7   AP        ERR1CTR,ONE               INCR OC7 ERROR CTR
          B         DODUMP                    DUMP RECORD
INCROCAB  AP        ERR2CTR,ONE               INCR OCA/OCB ERROR CTR
DODUMP    BAL       R7,DUMP                   PRODUCE HEX DUMP OF RECORD
          L         R10,=A(NEXTREC)           LOAD RETRY ADR TO MAIN PROG
          ST        R10,PIEPSW+4              PUT RETRY ADR INTO PIE
          L         R14,SAVR14                RESTORE REG 14
          BR        R14                       PASS CNTRL TO NEXTREC RTN VIA SPIE
*
*
***************************************************************************
* THE SUBROUTINE PRODUCES A HEX DUMP OF EACH RECORD THAT CONTAINS BAD
* DATA.
***************************************************************************
*
DUMP      ...                                 DO REQUIRED DUMP
          BR        R7                        RETURN TO CALLING RTN
          ...
*
*
***************************************************************************
* DC/DS STATEMENTS
***************************************************************************
*
SAVR14    DS        F
ONE       DC        P'1'
ERR1CTR   DC        PL3'0'                    ERROR CTR FOR SOC7 ABENDS
ERR2CTR   DC        PL3'0'                    ERROR CTR FOR SOCA/SOCB ABENDS
          ...
*
```

```
*
***************************************************************************
* THE DSECTS
***************************************************************************
*
          IHAPIE                              GENERATES PIE DSECT
*
*
***************************************************************************
* END OF PROGRAM
***************************************************************************
*
          END
```

Coding Example 6.1.2

This coding example illustrates how to establish an SPIE recovery environment and how to save and restore the previous SPIE recovery environment. In this example, PROG01 established an SPIE environment to intercept operation exceptions, protection exceptions, and data exceptions. PROG1 LINKs to PROG02, which establishes its own SPIE recovery environment to intercept decimal divide exceptions. When PROG02 terminates, it restores the SPIE recovery environment of PROG01 before returning control.

Calling Program:

```
PROG01    CSECT
          ...
          SPIE      EXIT01,(1,4,7)
          ...
          LINK      EP=PROG02
          ...
          END
```

Called Program:

```
PROG02    CSECT
          ...
SETSPIE   SPIE      EXIT02,(11)
          ST        R1,PICAADR                SAVE PREV PICA ADR
          BR        R6                        RETURN TO CALLING RTN
          ...
RETURN    L         R10,PICADDR               LOAD PREV PICA ADR
          SPIE      MF=(E,(R10))              RESTORE SPIE ENVIR OF CALLING PROG
          L         R13,4(0,R13)              RESTORE ADR OF PREV SA
          LM        R14,R12,12(R13)           RESTORE REGS OF CALLING PROG
          BR        R14                       RETURN TO CALLING PROG
          ...
PICAADR   DS        F
          ...
          END
```

6.1.3 Using the ESPIE Macro Instruction

When the ESPIE macro instruction with the SET option is issued, a token, representing the previous ESPIE recovery environment, is returned in register 1. If there was no previous recovery environment established, then the token contains zero. This information is useful if one program of a task creates an ESPIE recovery environment and then calls another program (or subroutine) of the same task that has its own ESPIE recovery environment requirements. The called program would issue the ESPIE macro instruction with its own requirements, replacing the specifications of the previous ESPIE (from the calling program). Upon completion, the called program (or subroutine) would restore the ESPIE recovery environment to that of the calling program and then return control. The ESPIE recovery environment is restored by using the ESPIE macro instruction with the RESET option and specifying the token returned from the ESPIE macro instruction which was used to establish the current recovery environment.

Coding Example 6.1.3

This coding example illustrates how to use the ESPIE macro instruction to perform the same function as the SPIE macro instruction in Coding Example 6.1.1. The only difference is that this example uses the PARAM parameter (SPIE does not provide a PARAM parameter) to pass the retry address to the exit routine.

```
ESPIE01   CSECT
*
*
***********************************************************************
* INITIALIZATION
***********************************************************************
*
          INITL    3,EQU=R                     INITIALIZE PROGRAM
          USING    EPIE,R11                    DEFINE REG FOR EPIE DSECT
*
*
***********************************************************************
* MAINSTREAM OF PROGRAM
***********************************************************************
*
          ...
          BAL      R6,SETESPIE                 ESTAB ESPIE ENVIR
NEXTREC   BAL      R6,READMSTR                 READ A REC FROM MASTR FILE
          BAL      R6,PROCESS                  PROCESS RECORD
          B        NEXTREC                     READ NEXT RECORD
          ...
*
*
***********************************************************************
* THIS ROUTINE ESTABLISHES THE ESPIE RECOVERY ENVIRONMENT. IT SPECIFIES
* THAT THE FOLLOWING INTERRUPTION TYPES ARE TO BE INTERCEPTED:
*          * DATA EXCEPTION (7);
*          * DECIMAL OVERFLOW (10);
*          * DECIMAL DIVIDE (11).
* WHEN ONE OF THE SPECIFIED INTERRUPTION TYPES IS ENCOUNTERED, CONTROL
* IS PASSED TO THE RECOVERY ROUTINE DATACHK, WHICH PROCESSES THE ABEND.
* THE RETRY ADDRESS IS PASSED TO DATACHK VIA THE PARAM PARAMETER.
***********************************************************************
*
SETESPIE  ESPIE    SET,DATACHK,(7,10,11),PARAM=RETRYADR
          BR       R6                          RETURN TO CALLING RTN
*
*
***********************************************************************
* THIS ROUTINE RECEIVES CONTROL VIA THE ESPIE SERVICE ROUTINE WHEN THE
* PROGRAM ENCOUNTERS A SOC7, SOCA, OR SOCB ABEND. WHEN THE ABEND
* PROCESSING IS COMPLETE, DATACHK RETURNS CONTROL TO THE MAIN PROGRAM
* AT THE ADDRESS SPECIFIED VIA THE PARAM PARAMETER PASSED BY ESPIE.
***********************************************************************
*
```

```
DATACHK  ST    R14,SAVR14           SAVE RETURN ADR TO ESPIE
         LR    R11,R1               SET ADRBLTY FOR EPIE DSECT
         L     R10,EPIEPARM         LOAD ADR OF PARM-LIST
         L     R10,0(0,R10)         LOAD RETRY ADR TO MAIN PROG
         CLI   EPIEINT+3,X'07'      CHK IF 07 INTERRUPTION TYPE
         BE    INCROC7              IF YES, INCR OC7 ERROR CTR
         AP    ERR2CTR,ONE          IF NO, INCR OCA/OCB ERROR CTR
         B     DODUMP               BYPASS THE INCR OF OC7 ERR CTR
INCROC7  AP    ERR1CTR,ONE          INCR OC7 ERROR CTR
DODUMP   BAL   R7,DUMP              PRODUCE HEX DUMP OF REC
         ST    R10,EPIEPSW+4        PUT RETRY RTN ADR INTO EPIE
         L     R14,SAVR14           RESTORE REG 14
         BR    R14                  PASS CONTROL TO NEXTREC RTN VIA ESPIE
*
*
***********************************************************************
* THE SUBROUTINE PRODUCES A HEX DUMP OF EACH RECORD THAT CONTAINS BAD
* DATA.
***********************************************************************
*
DUMP     ...                        DO REQUIRED DUMP
         BR    R7                   RETURN TO CALLING RTN
*
*
***********************************************************************
* DC/DS STATEMENTS
***********************************************************************
*
         ...
ONE      DC    P'1'
ERR1CTR  DC    PL3'0'               ERROR CTR FOR SOC7 ABENDS
ERR2CTR  DC    PL3'0'               ERROR CTR FOR SOCA/SOCB ABENDS
RETRYADR DC    A(NEXTREC)
         ...
*
*
***********************************************************************
* THE DSECTS
***********************************************************************
*
IHAEPIE                             GENERATES EPIE DSECT
*
*
***********************************************************************
* END OF PROGRAM
***********************************************************************
*
         END
```

Coding Example 6.1.4

This coding example illustrates how to use the ESPIE macro instruction to perform the same function as the SPIE macro instruction in Coding Example 6.1.2.

Calling Program:

```
PROG01   CSECT
         ...
         ESPIE    SET,EXIT01,(1,4,7)
         ...
         LINK     EP=PROG02
         ...
         END
```

Called Program:

```
PROG02    CSECT
          ...
SETESPIE  ESPIE    SET,EXIT02,(11)
          ST       R1,TOKEN              SAVE TOKEN OF PREV ESPIE ENVIR
          BR       R6                    RETURN TO CALLING RTN
          ...
RETURN    ESPIE    RESET,TOKEN           RESTORE ESPIE ENVIR OF CALLING PROG
          L        R13,4(0,R13)          RESTORE ADR OF PREV SA
          LM       R14,R12,12(R13)       RESTORE REGS OF CALLING PROG
          BR       R14                   RETURN TO MVS OR CALLING PROG
          ...
TOKEN     DS       F
          ...
          END
```

6.1.4 Mixing the SPIE and the ESPIE Macro Instructions

The use of the SPIE and the ESPIE macro instructions could be intermixed in the same task to establish and restore recovery environments. However, this should not be done on purpose. Any new programs that are developed or existing ones that require program interruption recovery should use the ESPIE macro instruction. However, if an existing program, that uses SPIE is called by another program that uses ESPIE, or vice versa, then the previous recovery environment could still be saved and restored. This is true because the contents retured in register 1, after issuing SPIE/ESPIE, is compatible to the other macro instruction for restoring the environment. Therefore, the code for PROG02 in Coding Example 6.1.3 and in Coding Example 6.1.4 will function correctly, as is, regardless if the previous recovery environment was established by SPIE or by ESPIE.

6.2 RECOVERING FROM SYSTEM AND USER ABENDS

In the previous section, we saw that ABENDs due to program exceptions (S0C1-S0CF) could be intercepted by use of the SPIE/ESPIE macro instruction. This section discusses intercepting the ABENDs that are not intercepted by SPIE/ESPIE for programs that execute in task mode. This will be accomplished by using of the ESTAE macro instruction. The ESTAE macro instruction can also intercept the program exception ABENDs.

6.2.1 Brief Overview of RTM

When a task terminates, normally or abnormally, the Recovery Termination Management (RTM) component of MVS receives control. During abnormal termination, RTM will either route control to a programmer-provided recovery exit routine or, if one has not been provided, abnormally terminate the task.

A task may have more than one ESTAE recovery exit routine outstanding at a time. The same program may issue multiple ESTAEs or more typically Program-A calls Program-B which calls Program-C, etc. and each program defines its own ESTAE recovery environoment. In this scenario, the ESTAE environment established by Program-A protects itself and optionally protects Program-B and Program-C; and the ESTAE environment established by Program-B protects itself and optionally protects Program-C. The ESTAE recovery environment established by a program protects the called program if the called program does not establish its own recovery environment or requests that the termination (ABEND) continues when exiting its recovery exit routine.

When the ESTAE macro instruction is issued to define a recovery exit routine, RTM creates a STAE control block (SCB). The SCB contains such information as the ESTAE exit routine address, parameter-list address, etc. The addresses of the SCBs are chained on a LIFO stack which is pointed to by the TCBSTABB field of the TCB.

When RTM receives control (due to an ABEND), it attempts to obtain virtual storage for a work area which RTM initializes to contain information about the ABEND, before passing control to the ESTAE recovery exit routine. The work area is called a System Diagnostic Work Area (SDWA) and is the control block used for communications between RTM and the ESTAE recovery exit routine. When the exit routine receives control, the contents of the registers will vary depending on whether or not RTM was successful in obtaining storage for the SDWA. Also, the way the exit routine returns control will vary based upon the existence of a SDWA. When the exit routine receives control the code in register 0 will contain X'0C' if RTM was unable to obtain storage for the SDWA. This almost never happens, but the exit routine must be coded for such an occurrence. IBM provides the macro instruction IEHSDWA to generate the DSECT for mapping the SDWA. Some of the fields of the SDWA, which are relevant to ESTAE recovery exits, are described in Table 6.2.1.

When the ESTAE recovery exit routine completes processing, it returns control to RTM with an indication of retry or terminate. If retry is selected, then RTM passes control to the retry address specified by the recovery exit routine. If termination is selected, then RTM passes control to the next ESTAE recovery exit routine defined on the stack. This is known as percolation. If there are no other exit routines on the stack, then RTM abnormally terminates the task.

Table 6.2.1

The following contains a description of the fields of the SDWA, which may be of relevance to ESTAE exits. The names of the fields are the names used in the IBM provided DSECT.

SDWAPARM (4 bytes)	The address of the parameter-list specified in the ESTAE macro instruction. Set to zero if no parameter-list.
SDWACMPC (3 bytes)	The ABEND code. The high order 12 bits contain the system ABEND code and the low order 12 bits contain the user ABEND code.
SDWAEC1 (8 bytes)	The EC PSW of the program which ABENDed at the time of the ABEND.
SDWAGRSV (64 bytes)	The contents of registers 0-15, respectively, of the program which ABENDed at the time of the ABEND.
SDWAEC2 (8 bytes)	The EC PSW of the program, that issued the ESTAE macro instruction at the time of the ABEND.
SDWASRSV (64 bytes)	The contents of registers 0–15, respectively, of the program that issued the ESTAE macro instruction at the time of the ABEND.
SDWAERRA (1 byte)	Contains flags that indicate the type of error. For example, machine check, program check.
SDWAERRB (1 byte)	Contains flags that indicate the status of the system at the time of the ABEND. For example, task mode, SRB mode.
SDWAERRC (1 byte)	Contains flags that indicate previous RTM processing. For example, if this exit routine received control as a result of percolation.
SDWAERRD (1 byte)	Contains flags that indicate additional information. For example, whether retry is allowed for this ABEND.
SDWASPID (1 byte)	The virtual storage subpool number of the SDWA.
SDWALNTH (3 bytes)	The length, in bytes, of the SDWA.

NOTES:

- The contents of the fields SDWAEC1 and SDWAGRSV are the same as the contents of the fields SDWAEC2 and SDWASRSV when the program that issued the ESTAE macro instruction ABENDs. They are different when the program that issued ESTAE calls (via LINK) another program that has the ABEND. In this case, the information in SDWAEC1 and SDWAGRSV is for the program that was called and ABENDed, and the information in SDWAEC2 and SDWASRSV is for the program that issued ESTAE at the time the LINK macro instruction was issued.

6.2.2 The ESTAE Macro Instruction

The ESTAE macro instruction (extended STAE) is used to define a recovery exit routine address and ABEND processing-related options to RTM. The exit routine will receive control during an ABEND. The ESTAE macro instruction extends the recovery capabilities of the STAE macro instruction and changes the defaults for some of its parameters to the most commonly used options. The increased capability over STAE enables the ESTAE exit routine to perform "clean-up" processing during certain ABENDS for which the STAE exit routine does not receive control, such as an S222 (Job Cancel by Operator) ABEND.

The format of the ESTAE macro instruction is as follows:

```
[name]      ESTAE {exit-routine-address|0}
            [,CT|OV]
            [,PARAM=parameter-list-address]
            [,XCTL={YES|NO}]
            [,PURGE={NONE|QUIESCE|HALT}]
            [,ASYNCH={YES|NO}]
            [,TERM={YES|NO}]
```

`exit-routine-address|0`

Specifies the address of the recovery exit routine. The address may be specified as a label (A-type address) or as a register, enclosed in parentheses, containing the address. If 0 is specified, the most recent exit address (SCB entry on the stack) is cancelled.

`CT`
`OV (Default: CT)`

CT indicates that a new exit address is to be defined (new SCB put onto the stack). OV indicates that the most recent SCB on the stack is to be overlayed with the new information specified.

`PARAM=parameter-list-address (Default: none)`

Specifies the address of a user-defined parameter-list that is to be passed to the recovery exit routine. The address must be aligned on a fullword boundary and may be specified as a label (A-type address) or as a register, enclosed in parentheses. The parameter-list consists of consecutive fullword addresses that point to the virtual storage areas that are to be passed to the exit routine.

`XCTL=YES`
`XCTL=NO (Default: NO)`

Specifies whether the ESTAE request is the be cancelled (XCTL=NO) or is not to be cancelled (XCTL=YES) if the program that issued ESTAE subsequently issues an XCTL macro instruction.

PURGE=NONE
PURGE=QUIESCE
PURGE=HALT (Default: NONE)

Specifies the action that is to be taken for outstanding I/O processing when the ABEND occurs.

NONE	indicates that I/O processing continues normally when the ESTAE exit routine receives control.
QUIESCE	indicates that all outstanding requests for I/O operations that are in progress are allowed to complete, and all I/O operations that are queued are saved when the ESTAE exit routine receives control. The saved I/O operations are restorable and may be resumed with the RESTORE macro instruction.
HALT	indicates that all outstanding requests for I/O operations will be stopped and not saved; therefore, these I/O operations are not restorable.

ASYNCH=YES
ASYNCH=NO (Default: YES)

Specifies whether asynchronous exit processing will be allowed (ASYNCH=YES) or prohibited (ASYNCH=NO) while the ESTAE exit routine has control. ASYNCH=YES must be specified if I/O is allowed to continue (PURGE=NONE or PURGE=QUIESCE) or if the exit routine requests any supervisor services that require asynchronous processing to complete.

TERM=YES
TERM=NO (Default: NO)

Specifies if the exit routine will be allowed to receive control (TERM=YES) or not allowed to receive control (TERM=NO) during the following situations:

- Job cancel by operator (S122 or S222);
- Forced logoff (S122 or S222);
- Job or job step timer expiring (S322);
- Exceeding the wait time limit for a job step (S522);
- ABENDING the parent task when the ESTAE macro instruction was issued by a subtask; and
- ABENDING the job step task when a subtask issued the ABEND macro instruction with the STEP option.

When the exit routine is entered due to one of the above reasons, only "clean-up" processing is allowed. A retry is not permitted. This is indicated by RTM setting the SDWACLUP bit in the SDWAERRD field.

Coding Example 6.2.1

The following coding example illustrates how to code the ESTAE macro instruction to specify a new recovery exit routine address defined by the label EXITRTN and to pass the addresses of RETRYRTN and STATUS to the exit routine.

```
          ESTAE     EXITRTN,CT,PARAM=PARMLIST
          ...
EXITRTN   DS        OH
          ...
RETRYRTN  DS        OH
          ...
STATUS    DC        X'00'
          ...
PARMLIST  DC        A(RETRYRTN)
          DC        A(STATUS)
```

6.2.3 The SETRP Macro Instruction

If RTM provided an SDWA, then the recovery exit routine may use the SETRP macro instruction to set the appropiate fields of the SDWA to indicate to RTM which actions are to be taken when control is returned. It is easier to use the SETRP macro instruction to perform that task than it is for the exit routine to explicitly modify the appropriate SDWA fields.

The format of the SETRP macro instruction is as follows:

```
[name]     SETRP     [WKAREA=(reg)]
                     [,REGS={(reg1)|(reg1,reg2)}]
                     [,DUMP={IGNORE|YES|NO}]
                     [,DUMPOPT=parm-list-addr]
                     [,RC={0|4|16}]
                     [,RETADDR=addr]
                     [,RETREGS={YES|YES,RUB|NO}]
                     [,FRESDWA={YES|NO}]
                     [,REASON=code]
                     [,COMPCOD={comp-code|(comp-code,USER)|(comp-code,SYSTEM)}]
```

`WKAREA=(reg) (Default: (1))`

Specifies a register that contains the address of the SDWA. This is the address that was received from RTM. The register must be specified as a decimal number enclosed within parentheses.

`REGS=(reg1)`
`REGS=(reg1,reg2) (Default: none)`

Specifies the register or range of registers to be restored and causes control to be returned to MVS via a branch on register 14. The registers are restored from the savearea pointed to by register 13. If REGS is not specified, then the programmer is responsible for returning control.

`DUMP=IGNORE`
`DUMP=YES`
`DUMP=NO (Default: IGNORE)`

IGNORE	The previously specified dump request is honored.
YES	A dump will be produced if the appropriate JCL DD statement is specified.
NO	A dump request, if any, is suppressed.

`DUMPOPT=parm-list-addr (Default: none)`

Specifies the address of a parameter-list of dump options. The format of the parameter-list is the same as that of the SNAP macro instruction and may be created with the list form of that macro instruction. The TCB, DCB, and STRHDR options are ignored if specified. The operating system uses the TCB of the task that ABENDed and uses its own DCB with one of the standard ddnames for dumps.

`RC=0`
`RC=4`
`RC=16 (Default: 0)`

Indicates what action RTM is to take when control is returned.

0	Indicates that abnormal termination is to continue. Previously defined recovery routines, if any, receive control.
4	Indicates that control is to be passed to the specified retry address.

`16`	Suppresses further STAI/ESTAI processing (used only with recovery environment established with ATTACH macro instruction).

`RETADDR=addr`

Specifies the address of the retry routine that is to receive control. May be specified as a label or a register, enclosed within parentheses. This parameter must be specified only when RC=4 is specified.

`RETREGS=YES`
`RETREGS=YES,RUB`
`RETREGS=NO (Default: NO)`

Specifies the contents of the registers when the retry routine receives control.

`YES`	Registers 0–15 are restored from the contents of SDWASRSV.
`YES,RUB`	Only the registers specified in the programmer supplied RUB (register update block) are updated. The RUB has a maximum length of 66 bytes. The first 2 bytes indicate which registers are to be updated. Bit 0 on indicates register 0, bit 1 on indicates register 1, and so on. The next 4 to 64 bytes contain the contents of the registers indicated, in the sequence 0–15.
`NO`	Only registers 14–2 are restored.

`FRESDWA=YES`
`FRESDWA=NO (Default: NO)`

Specifies that the virtual storage occupied by the SDWA is to be freed (FRESDWA=YES) or not freed (FRESDWA=NO). If the retry routine requires examining the SDWA, then NO should be specified and the retry routine should release the storage occupied by the SDWA.

`REASON=code (Default: none)`

Specifies a reason code, which is used to supplement the completion code. RTM propagates the reason code to each subsequent ESTAE recovery exit routines via the SDWA. The reason code may be specified as a 31-bit decimal number, 32-bit hexadecimal number, symbol, or a register, enclosed within parentheses, containing the reason code.

`COMPCOD=comp-code`
`COMPCOD=(comp-code,USER)`
`COMPCOD=(comp-code,SYSTEM) (Default: none)`

Specifies a completion code that is to be passed to subsequent ESTAE exit routines. The completion code may be specified as a symbol, decimal number, or a register, enclosed in parentheses, containing the completion code. The range of the completion code may be from 0–4095. USER indicates that the completion code is stored in the low order 12 bits of the field SDWACMPC, and SYSTEM indicates that the completion code is stored in the high order 12 bits of the field SDWACMPC. If the completion code is specified without USER or SYSTEM, then the default is USER.

6.2.4 Writing an ESTAE Recovery Exit Routine

The purpose of an ESTAE recovery exit routine is to obtain the ABEND code and analyze the reason and/or implications of it, perform any required clean-up processing, and determine if abnormal termination is to continue or if a retry is possible.

The ABEND code can be determined and analyzed by examining the following SDWA fields: SDWACMPC, SDWAEC1, SDWAGRSV, SDWAEC2, SDWASRSV, and SDWAERRx. If an SDWA has not been provided, then only the ABEND code is available (in register 1).

The action to be performed may be based solely on the ABEND code, or it may be based upon additional information as well. Such information may be the section of the program or the processing stage of the program that was executing at the time of the ABEND. This information may possibly be determined by the values in the registers. A better technique would be for the program to set certain bits in a status field, as the program executes, and pass that status field to the exit routine as a parameter. The program maintaining a status field and passing it to the exit routine will enable the exit routine to know what processing was being performed, and so on, at the time of the ABEND. This will assist the exit routine in determining the required clean-up processing and the appropriate recovery action.

Clean-up processing may involve one or more of the following:

- Releasing GETMAINed storage that is not automatically released at step termination, such as storage areas allocated from the SQA and the CSA. If a security table, accouting table, or other table is being created in such an area and the ABEND caused it to be unusable, then this storage should be released. In this case, the address of the virtual storage should be passed to the exit routine as a parameter.
- Restoring dynamic hooks to original code. This refers to programs that make dynamic coding changes to resident system code located in the SVC table, the Nucleus, and so on. These programs reset the code when they terminate. If the program ABENDs, the code must still be reset or the systems integrity will be compromised.
- Closing output datasets, and perhaps writing a control record before the close.
- Flushing buffers. This refers to programs that process and store large amounts of data in virtual storage and periodically write the data into a dataset. After an ABEND, the processed data residing in virtual storage should be saved by writing them to the dataset. To accomplish this, the address of the buffer pool is passed as a parameter to the exit routine. The buffer pool would be designed to indicate which buffers contain active data that have not been written to the dataset yet.

Recovery action involves determining if a program can continue to execute and still perform useful processing after an ABEND. Some reasons why a program ABENDs are because it received and attempted to process faulty data or the program was unable to obtain a desired or required resource, such as a dataset, additional DASD space, a load module, and so on.

The ESTAE recovery exit routine receives control unlocked and enabled in TCB mode and in the same addressing-mode as the program that issued the ESTAE macro instruction. Since the exit routine executes under the control of a TCB, it may issue macro instructions that expand into an SVC instruction.

When the recovery exit routine receives control, before it performs any processing, it must determine if RTM provided an SDWA. This is necessary because of the following reasons:

- The content of the registers, at entry to the exit routine, varies according to the existence of an SDWA.
- The way the exit routine returns control will vary based upon the existence of an SDWA.
- The SETRP macro instruction may not be used if RTM did not provide an SDWA.
- The diagnostic logic of the exit routine will vary based upon the existence of an SDWA.

When the recovery exit routine receives control and an SDWA is provided, the contents of the registers are as follows:

`Register 0`	One of the following codes:
`X'00'`	Active I/O has been quiesced and is restorable.
`X'04'`	Active I/O has been halted and is not restorable.
`X'08'`	No I/O was active when the ABEND occurred.

X'16'	I/O is continuing normally.
Register 1	Address of the SWDA.
Register 13	Address of savearea provided by operating system.
Register 14	Return address (to operating system).
Register 15	Address of exit routine entry point.

The contents of registers 2-12 do not contain any significant information for the exit routine.

When the recovery exit routine receives control and an SDWA is not provided, the contents of the registers are as follows:

Register 0	X'0C', which indicates that no SDWA is provided.
Register 1	ABEND code.
Register 2	Address of the parameter-list specified in the ESTAE macro instruction or X'00' if no parameter-list was specified.
Register 14	Return address (to operating system).
Register 15	Address of exit routine entry point.

The contents of registers 3-13 do not contain any significant information for the exit routine.

Coding Example 6.2.2

This coding example illsutrates how to code an ESTAE recovery exit routine, which will perform "clean-up" processing after an ABEND and then let the ABEND continue for the program with the following processing specifications and "clean-up" requirements:

- The program performs the following two tasks:
  - Creates a security table in the Commom Service Area (CSA); and
  - Copies and updates data from one DASD dataset to another DASD dataset.

The following describes the processing sequence of the program and the "clean-up" requirements for each processing stage:

- Allocate virtual storage from the CSA.
- Create a security table in the allocated CSA storage.

  Clean-up requirement:

  - If the program ABENDs while the table is in the process of being created, then the table is considered unusable and the CSA storage must be released.
  - If the program ABENDs after the table creation is complete, then the table is to be kept and no "clean-up" is required.

- Virtual storage is obtained via GETMAIN large enough for a buffer pool to accomodate RECGROUP (equal to 10 in this example) records and for the creation of a control record that will be written to the output dataset after the last updated record is written. The storage is obtained from the address space of the executing program.
- A predetermined amount (RECGROUP) of records are read from the input dataset and loaded into the buffer pool.
- All the records in the buffer pool are validated and updated, and the the control record is updated. Then, all the processed records from the buffer pool are written into the output dataset. Then, the next group of records are read into the buffer pool and processed, etc.

until all the records have been processed and written into the output dataset. Finally, the control record is written into the output dataset.

Clean-up requirement:

- If the program ABENDs after all the records in the buffer pool and the control record have been successfully updated, then all the records are to be written from the buffer pool to the output dataset. The control record is then to be written to the output dataset and the output dataset closed.
- If the program ABENDs while the records in the buffer pool are in the process of being updated, then only the control record is to be written to the output dataset and the output dataset closed.

■ If the program ABENDs while the output dataset is not opened, then no clean-up is required for the dataset.

This coding example contains the code for the main program and the ESTAE recovery exit routine. Only the pertinent code is shown.

```
ESTAE01   CSECT
*
*
*************************************************************************
* INITIALIZATION
*************************************************************************
*
          INITL     3,EQU=R                     INITIALIZE PROGRAM
*
*
*************************************************************************
* MAINSTREAM OF PROGRAM
*************************************************************************
*
          BAL       R6,SETESTAE                 SETUP ESTAE ENVIRONMENT
          BAL       R6,ALLOCSA                  ALLOCATE STORAGE FROM CSA
          BAL       R6,BLDTBL                   BUILD SECURITY TABLE
          BAL       R6,ALLOBUFF                 ALLO STOR FOR BUFF POOL & CNTL REC
          BAL       R6,OPEN                     OPEN DATASETS
NXGROUP   BAL       R6,GETRECS                  READ A GROUP OF RECS INTO BUF POOL
          BAL       R6,PROCESS                  PROCESS RECORDS IN BUFFER POOL
          BAL       R6,PUTRECS                  WRITE BUFFER POOL RECS INTO DATASET
          B         NXGROUP                     READ NEXT GROUP OF RECORDS
DATAEND   BAL       R6,PUTCNTL                  WRITE CONTROL RECORD
          BAL       R6,CLOSE                    CLOSE DATASETS
          B         RETURN                      RETURN TO MVS OR CALLING PROGRAM
*
*
*************************************************************************
* THIS ROUTINE ESTABLISHES THE ESTAE RECOVERY ENVIRONMENT. WHEN A
* SYSTEM OR A USER ABEND IS ENCOUNTERED, THE RECOVERY EXIT ROUTINE
* RECVEXIT RECEIVES CONTROL AND THE ADDRESSES OF THE PARAMETERS POINTED
* TO BY PARMLIST ARE PASSED TO THE RECOVERY EXIT ROUTINE.
*************************************************************************
*
SETESTAE  ESTAE     RECVEXIT,CT,TERM=YES,PARAM=PARMLIST
          BR        R6                          RETURN TO CALLING RTN
*
*
*************************************************************************
* THIS ROUTINE ALLOCATES VIRTUAL STORAGE FROM THE CSA FOR THE
* SECURITY TABLE. WHEN THE CSA STORAGE IS SUCCESSFULLY ALLOCATED, AN
* INDICATOR BIT IS SET IN THE STATUS BYTE.
```

```
*************************************************************************
*
ALLOCSA    L         R10,CSALEN                LOAD LEN OF REQD CSA STOR
           GETMAIN   EC,LV=(R10),SP=241,A=CSAADR
           OI        STATUS,INDCSA             INDICATE CSA ALLOCATED
           BR        R6                        RETURN TO CALLING RTN
*
*
*************************************************************************
* THIS ROUTINE CREATES THE SECURITY TABLE IN THE CSA. WHEN THE CREATION
* OF THE TABLE IS SUCCESSFULLY COMPLETED, AN INDICATOR BIT IS SET IN
* THE STATUS BYTE.
*************************************************************************
*
BLDTBL     ...
           OI        STATUS,INDTBLOK           INDICATE TABLE CREATED OK
           BR        R6                        RETURN TO CALLING RTN
*
*
*************************************************************************
* THIS ROUTINE ALLOCATES VIRTUAL STORAGE FOR THE BUFFER POOL AND THE
* CONTROL RECORD. THE LENGTH OF THE GETMAIN IS GOVERNED BY THE EQU
* SYMBOL GMLEN WHICH IS CALCULATED (BY THE ASSEMBLER) BY MULTIPLYING
* THE DESIRED NUMBER OF RECORDS (RECGROUP) IN THE BUFFER POOL BY THE
* RECORD LENGTH PLUS THE LENGTH OF THE CONTROL RECORD.
*************************************************************************
*          .
ALLOBUFF   GETMAIN   RC,LV=GMLEN               ALLOC STOR FOR BUFF POOL + CNTL REC
           ...       CHK                       IF GM OK
           ST        R1,BUFFADR                SAVE ADR OF BG OF BUFF POOL
           LA        R1,BUFFLEN(0,R1)          INCR PASS BUFF POOL TO CNTL REC
           ST        R1,CNTLADR                SAVE ADR OF CNTL REC
           BR        R6                        RETURN TO CALLING RTN
*
*
*************************************************************************
* THIS ROUTINE OPENS ALL THE DCBS. AN INDICATOR BIT IS SET IN THE
* STATUS BYTE WHEN THE OUTPUT DCB IS SUCCESSFULLY OPENED.
*************************************************************************
*
OPEN       OPEN      (DCB1,,DCB2,(OUTPUT))
           ...       CHECK                     IF OPEN OK
           OI        STATUS,INDDCB2            INDICATE THAT OUTPUT DCB OPENED
           BR        R6                        RETURN TO CALLING RTN
*
*
*************************************************************************
* THIS ROUTINE READS RECGROUP NUMBER OF RECORDS FROM THE INPUT DATASET
* AND CALLS THE SUBROUTINE PUTBUFF AFTER EACH READ TO MOVE THE RECORD
* INTO THE BUFFER POOL.
*************************************************************************
*
GETRECS    LA        R10,RECGROUP              SET NUMB OF RECS IN BUFF POOL
NEXTREC    GET       .DCB1                     READ A LOGICAL REC
           LR        R2,R1                     SAVE ADR OF LOGICAL RECORD
           BAL       R7,PUTBUFF                MOVE REC INTO A BUFF OF THE POOL
           BCT       R10,NEXTREC               IF BUFF POOL NOT FILLED, READ REC
           BR        R6                        IF FILLED, RETURN TO CALLING RTN
*
*
*************************************************************************
* THIS ROUTINE PROCESSES THE RECORDS IN THE BUFFER POOL. IN ORDER TO
* PERFORM THAT TASK, THIS ROUTINE BRANCHES AND LINKS TO THE SUBROUTINES
* THAT HAVE THE FOLLOWING FUNCTIONS:
```

```
*           * VALIDATE EACH RECORD IN THE BUFFER POOL;
*           * UPDATE THE RECORDS IN THE BUFFER POOL;
*           * UPDATE THE CONTROL RECORD WHEN ALL THE RECORDS IN THE BUFFER
*             POOL ARE PROCESSED.
* WHEN PROCESSING IS SUCCESSFULLY COMPLETED, THEN TWO INDICATOR BITS
* ARE SET IN THE STATUS BYTE. ONE BIT TO INDICATE THAT THE RECORDS WERE
* UPDATED AND THE OTHER BIT TO INDICATE THAT THE CONTROL RECORD WAS
* UPDATED.
***********************************************************************
*
PROCESS    BAL       R7,VALIDATE              VALIDATE RECS IN BUFF POOL
           BAL       R7,UPDRECS               UPDATE RECS IN BUFF POOL
           BAL       R7,UPDCNTL               UPDATE CNTL REC IN VIR STOR
           OI        STATUS,INDBUF            IND THAT ALL BUFF RECS UPDATED
           OI        STATUS,INDCNTL           IND THAT CNTL REC UPDATED
           BR        R6                       RETURN TO CALLING RTN
*
*
***********************************************************************
* THIS ROUTINE WRITES THE UPDATED RECORDS FROM THE BUFFER POOL INTO
* THE OUTPUT DATASET. WHEN ALL THE RECORDS FROM THE BUFFER POOL HAVE
* BEEN SUCCESSFULLY WRITTEN, THEN THE INDICATOR BIT IS RESET IN THE
* STATUS BYTE.
***********************************************************************
*
PUTRECS    ...                                WRITE UPDATED RECORDS INTO DATASET
           NI        STATUS,INDXBUFF          IND THAT RECS IN BUFF POOL WRITTEN
           BR        R6                       RETURN TO CALLING RTN
*
*
***********************************************************************
* THIS ROUTINE WRITES THE CONTROL RECORD INTO THE OUTPUT DATASET WHEN
* ALL THE INPUT RECORDS ARE PROCESSED.
***********************************************************************
*
PUTCNTL    L         R10,CNTLADR              LOAD ADR OF CNTL REC
           PUT       DCB2,(R10)               WRITE CNTL REC
           OI        STATUS,INDXCNTL          IND THAT CNTL REC WRITTEN
           BR        R6                       RETURN TO CALLING RTN
*
*
***********************************************************************
* THIS ROUTINE CLOSES ALL THE DCBS. THE INDICATOR BIT IS RESET IN THE
* STATUS BYTE WHEN THE OUTPUT DCB IS SUCCESSFULLY CLOSED.
***********************************************************************
*
CLOSE      CLOSE     (DCB1,,DCB2)
           NI        STATUS,INDXDCB2          INDICATE THAT OUTPUT DCB CLOSED
           BR        R6                       RETURN TO CALLING RTN
*
*
***********************************************************************
* THIS ROUTINE RESTORES THE REGISTERS AND RETURNS CONTROL.
***********************************************************************
*
RETURN     RCNTL     RC=0                     RETURN TO MVS OR CALLING PROG
*
*
***********************************************************************
* THIS IS THE PARMLIST THAT IS PASSED BY THE ESTAE SERVICE ROUTINE TO
* THE RECOVERY EXIT ROUTINE.
***********************************************************************
*
PARMLIST   DC        A(STATUS)                ADR OF STATUS BYTE
```

```
         DC        A(CSAADR)                  ADR OF FWD CONTAINING CSA STOR ADR
         DC        A(CSALEN)                  ADR OF FWD CONTAINING CSA STOR LEN
         DC        A(DCB2)                    ADR OF OUTPUT DCB ADR
BUFFADR  DS        F                          ADR OF BG OF BUFFER POOL
CNTLADR  DS        F                          ADR OF CONTROL RECORD
*
*** END OF PARMLIST ***
*
CSAADR   DS        F                          ADR OF ALLO CSA STOR
CSALEN   DC        A(4096)                    LENGTH OF ALLO CSA STOR
*
*
***********************************************************************
* EQU'S FOR STATUS INDICATOR BIT SETTINGS.
***********************************************************************
*
STATUS   DC        X'00'                      STATUS BYTE CONTAINING INDICATORS
INDCSA   EQU       X'80'                      CSA ALLOCATED
INDTBLOK EQU       X'40'                      TABLE SUCCESSFULLY CREATED
INDDCB2  EQU       X'20'                      OUTPUT DCB OPENED
INDXDCB2 EQU       X'DF'                      OUTPUT DCB CLOSED
INDBUFF  EQU       X'10'                      BUFFER POOL CONTAINS RECS TO WRITE
INDXBUFF EQU       X'EF'                      RECS IN BUFFER POOL WRITTEN
INDCNTL  EQU       X'01'                      CONTROL RECORD NOT WRITTEN YET
INDXCNTL EQU       X'FE'                      CONTROL RECORD WRITTEN
*
*
***********************************************************************
* EQU'S USED TO CALCULATE GETMAIN LENGTH FOR BUFFER POOL AND CONTROL
* RECORD.
***********************************************************************
*
LRECL    EQU       80                         LENGTH OF DATA RECS AND CNTL REC
RECGROUP EQU       10                         DESIRED NUMBER OF RECS IN BUFF POOL
BUFFLEN  EQU       LRECL*RECGROUP             LENGTH OF BUFF REQD FOR DATA RECS
GMLEN    EQU       BUFFLEN+LRECL              GM LEN = BUFFLEN + CNTLREC LEN
*
*
***********************************************************************
* THE DCBS
***********************************************************************
*
DCB1     DCB       ...
DCB2     DCB       ...
*
*
*
*
***********************************************************************
* THE FOLLOWING CSECT IS THE ESTAE RECOVERY EXIT REFERENCED IN THE
* ESTAE MACRO IN THE MAIN PROGRAM.
***********************************************************************
*
RECVEXIT CSECT
*
*
***********************************************************************
* INITIALIZATION
***********************************************************************
*
         USING     *,R3                       DEFINE BASE REG
         USING     SDWA,R12                   DEFINE REG FOR SDWA DSECT
         LR        R3,R15                     SET ADRBLTY FOR REVC EXIT RTN
         ST        R14,SAVR14                 SAVE RETURN ADR TO RTM
```

```
*
*
***********************************************************************
* THE FOLLOWING CODE DETERMINES IF A SDWA HAS BEEN PROVIDED.
***********************************************************************
*
         C     R0,BIN12                CHK IF SDWA CREATED
         BE    NOSDWA                  PROCESS WITHOUT SDWA
         B     YESSDWA                 PROCESS USING SDWA
*
*
***********************************************************************
* THIS ROUTINE RECEIVES CONTROL IF A SDWA WAS NOT PROVIDED. THIS
* ROUTINE LOADS THE PARAMETER-LIST ADDRESS INTO THE REGISTER EXPECTED
* BY THE RECOVERY ROUTINE; BRANCHES AND LINKS TO THE RECOVERY ROUTINE;
* INDICATES THAT A SDWA WAS NOT PROVIDED; AND PASSES CONTROL TO THE
* RECOVERY-EXIT RETURN ROUTINE.
***********************************************************************
*
NOSDWA   LR    R10,R2                  LOAD ADR OF PARM-LIST
         BAL   R6,RECVYRTN             DO RECOVERY
         LA    R15,0                   IND NO SDWA
         B     EXITRET                 EXIT RECOVERY-EXIT
*
*
***********************************************************************
* THIS ROUTINE RECEIVES CONTROL IF A SDWA WAS PROVIDED. THIS ROUTINE
* SAVES THE ADDRESS OF THE SDWA; LOADS THE PARAMETER-LIST ADDRESS INTO
* THE REGISTER EXPECTED BY THE RECOVERY ROUTINE; BRANCHES AND LINKS TO
* THE RECOVERY ROUTINE; INDICATES THAT A SDWA WAS PROVIDED; AND PASSES
* CONTROL TO THE RECOVERY-EXIT RETURN ROUTINE.
***********************************************************************
*
YESSDWA  LR    R12,R1                  SET ADRBLTY FOR SDWA DSECT
         L     R10,SDWAPARM            LOAD ADR OF PARM-LIST
         BAL   R6,RECVYRTN             DO RECOVERY
         LA    R15,4                   IND SDWA PROVIDED
         B     EXITRET                 EXIT RECOVERY-EXIT
*
*
***********************************************************************
* THE MAINSTREAM OF THE RECOVERY EXIT ROUTINE
***********************************************************************
*
RECVYRTN BAL   R7,GETPARMS             GET PARM ADRS
         BAL   R7,FREEMAIN             CHK IF CSA FREEMAIN REQUIRED
         BAL   R7,PUTRECSX             CHK IF BUFF WRITE REQUIRED
         BAL   R7,PUTCNTLX             CHK IF CNTL-REC WRITE REQUIRED
         BAL   R7,CLOSEX               CHK IF CLOSE REQUIRED
         BR    R6                      RETURN TO CALLING RTN
*
*
***********************************************************************
* THIS ROUTINE OBTAINS THE ADDRESSES OF THE PARAMETERS SPECIFIED BY
* THE ESTAE MACRO AND PASSED TO THE RECOVERY ROUTINE BY RTM.
***********************************************************************
*
GETPARMS L     R11,0(0,R10)            LD ADR OF PARM STATUS
         ST    R11,STATADRX            STORE ADR OF STATUS
         L     R11,4(0,R10)            LD ADR OF PARM CSAADR
         ST    R11,GMADRX              STORE ADR OF ADR OF CSA STOR
         L     R11,8(0,R10)            LD ADR OF PARM CSALEN
         ST    R11,GMLENX              STORE ADR OF CSALEN
         L     R11,12(0,R10)           LD ADR OF PARM DCB2
```

```
          ST        R11,DCB2ADRX               STORE ADR OF DCB2
          L         R11,16(0,R10)              LD ADR OF PARM BUFFADR
          ST        R11,BUFFADRX               STORE ADR OF BG OF BUFF POOL
          L         R11,20(0,R10)              LD ADR OF PARM CNTLADR
          ST        R11,CNTLADRX               STORE ADR OF CNTL REC
          BR        R7                         RETURN TO CALLING RTN
*
*
************************************************************************
* THIS ROUTINE CHECKS THE STATUS BYTE TO DETERMINE IF THE ALLOCATED
* CSA STORAGE IS TO BE RELEASED. THIS DECISION IS MADE BY VERIFYING IF
* THE SECURITY TABLE WAS CREATED OK. IF THE TABLE WAS SUCCESSFULLY
* CREATED, THEN THE CSA STORAGE REMAINS ALLOCATED.
************************************************************************
*
FREEMAIN  L         R11,STATADRX               LOAD ADR OF STATUS FIELD
          TM        0(R11),INDCSA              WAS CSA ALLO
          BZR       R7                         IF NO, RETURN TO CALLING RTN
          TM        0(R11),INDTBLOK            IF YES, CHK IF TBL CREATED OK
          BOR       R7                         IF YES, RETURN TO CALLING RTN
          L         R10,GMLENX                 IF NO, RELEASE IT -LOAD CSA LEN
          LA        R11,GMADRX                 LOAD ADR OF FWD WHICH HAS CSA ADR
          FREEMAIN  EU,LV=(R10),SP=241,A=(R11)
          BR        R7                         RETURN TO CALLING RTN
*
*
************************************************************************
* THIS ROUTINE CHECKS THE STATUS BYTE TO DETERMINE IF THE BUFFER POOL
* CONTAINS RECORDS THAT ARE TO BE WRITTEN INTO THE OUTPUT DATASET.
************************************************************************
*
PUTRECSX  L         R11,STATADRX               LOAD ADR OF STATUS FIELD
          TM        0(R11),INDBUFF             CHK IF BUFF HAS RECS TO WRITE
          BZR       R7                         IF NO, RETURN TO CALLING RTN
          ...                                  IF YES, WRITE THEM
          BR        R7                         RETURN TO CALLING RTN
*
*
************************************************************************
* THIS ROUTINE CHECKS THE STATUS BYTE TO DETERMINE IF THE CONTROL
* RECORD, WHICH IS IN VIRTUAL SRORAGE, IS TO BE WRITTEN INTO THE
* OUTPUT DATASET.
************************************************************************
*
PUTCNTLX  L         R11,STATADRX               LOAD ADR OF STATUS FIELD
          TM        0(R11),INDCNTL             CHK IF CNTL REC HAS TO BE WRITTEN
          BZR       R7                         IF NO, RETURN TO CALLING RTN
          L         R11,DCB2ADRX               IF YES, LOAD DCB2 ADR
          L         R12,CNTLADRX               LOAD CNTL REC ADR
          PUT       (R11),(R12)                WRITE CNTL REC
          BR        R7                         RETURN TO CALLING RTN
*
*
************************************************************************
* THIS ROUTINE CHECKS THE STATUS BYTE TO DETERMINE IF THE OUTPUT DCB
* IS REQUIRED TO BE CLOSED.
************************************************************************
*
CLOSEX    L         R11,STATADRX               LOAD ADR OF STATUS FIELD
          TM        0(R11),INDDCB2             CHK IF DCB2 OPENED
          BZR       R7                         IF NO, RETURN TO CALLING RTN
          L         R11,DCB2ADRX               IF YES, LOAD DCB2 ADR
          CLOSE     (R11)                      CLOSE DCB2
          BR        R7                         RETURN TO CALLING RTN
```

```
*
*
***********************************************************************
* THIS ROUTINE RECEIVES CONTROL WHEN THE RECOVERY EXIT ROUTINE IS TO
* RETURN CONTROL TO RTM. THIS ROUTINE CHECKS WHETHER A SDWA WAS
* PROVIDED AND CAUSES CONTROL TO BE RETURNED ACCORDINGLY.
***********************************************************************
*
EXITRET   LTR      R15,R15                  CHK IF SDWA PROVIDED
          BZ       RETXSDWA                 IF NO, RETURN WITHOUT SDWA
          B        RETSDWA                  IF YES, RETURN WITH SDWA
*
*
***********************************************************************
* THIS ROUTINE RETURNS CONTROL WHEN A SDWA WAS NOT PROVIDED.
***********************************************************************
*
RETXSDWA  LA       R15,0                    INDICATE CONTINUE WITH ABEND
          L        R14,SAVR14               RESTORE RETURN ADR
          BR       R14                      RETURN TO RTM
*
*
***********************************************************************
* THIS ROUTINE RETURNS CONTROL WHEN A SDWA WAS PROVIDED.
***********************************************************************
*
RETSDWA   SETRP    WKAREA=(R12),RC=0,DUMP=NO RC=0 - CONTIN WITH ABEND
          L        R14,SAVR14               RESTORE RETURN ADR
          BR       R14                      RETURN TO RTM
*
*
***********************************************************************
* THE FULLWORDS USED TO STORE THE PARAMETER ADDRESSES RECEIVED FROM
* THE ESTAE SERVICE ROUTINE; AND THE FULLWORD TO SAVE THE RETURN
* ADDRESS TO RTM.
***********************************************************************
*
STATADRX  DS       F                        ADR OF THE STATUS BYTE
GMADRX    DS       F                        ADR OF THE ADR OF THE ALLO CSA STOR
GMLENX    DS       F                        ADR OF THE LENGTH OF THE ALLO CSA
*                                           STOR
DCB2ADRX  DS       F                        ADR OF THE OUTPUT DCB
BUFFADRX  DS       F                        ADR OF THE BG OF THE BUFFER POOL
CNTLADRX  DS       F                        ADR OF THE CONTROL RECORD
*
SAVR14    DS       F                        RETURN ADR TO RTM
*
*
***********************************************************************
* CONSTANTS USED BY EXIT ROUTINE
***********************************************************************
*
BIN12     DC       F'12'
*
*
***********************************************************************
* THE DSECTS
***********************************************************************
*
          PRINT    NOGEN
          IHASDWA                           GENERATES SDWA DSECT
*
*
***********************************************************************
```

```
* END OF PROGRAM
*************************************************************************************
*
          END
```

NOTES:

- Notice that in the PROCESS routine, the indicator (INDBUF) for the records-updates-complete situation is set after both the records and control record are updated. This is necessary because if the program ABENDs while the control record is being updated, then the updated records in the buffer pool must not be written to the dataset because the control record will not indicate the proper status/count, and so on, of the updated records.
- The PUTBUFF and PUTRECS/PUTRECSX routines should contain code to indicate and process, respectively, an incomplete buffer pool.

Coding Example 6.2.3

This coding example illustrates how to code a generic ESTAE recovery exit routine. A list of ABEND codes with their corresponding retry addresses are passed to the exit routine as parameters by a program. The exit routine compares the current ABEND code with the ones in the list. If the ABEND code is found in the list, then the exit routine causes control to be passed to the corresponding retry address. If the ABEND code is not found in the list, then the exit routine directs RTM to allow the ABEND to continue.

In this example, the program attempts to process all the datasets whose names are in a list. The datasets are assumed to reside on the DASD volume pointed to by the FILESDD JCL DD statement. The datasets are opened one at a time and read and/or updated. The program requires that the exit routine intercepts all S213 ABENDs (dataset not found on specified DASD volume) and passes control back to the program at the specified retry address. Also, while updating/expanding the dataset, if DASD space is exhausted, then those ABENDs (SB37, SD37, and SE37) are to be intercepted by the exit routine and control passed back to the program at the specified retry address. The program will then terminate processing of that dataset, close it, and issue an error message. Then the program will attempt to process the next dataset in the list until all datasets in the list have been processed. The datasets in the list are allocated via the modified JFCB technique (discussed in Chapter 7).

```
ESTAE02   CSECT
*
*
*************************************************************************
* INITIALIZATION
*************************************************************************
*
          INITL    3,EQU=R                  INITIALIZE PROGRAM
          USING    INFMJFCB,R10             DEFINE REG FOR JFCB DSECT
*
*
*************************************************************************
* MAINSTREAM OF PROGRAM
*************************************************************************
*
          BAL      R6,SETESTAE              SETUP ESTAE ENVIRONMENT
          BAL      R6,RDJFCB                READ JFCB INTO PROG AREA
NEXTDSNM  BAL      R6,SETDSNM               PUT REQD DATASET NAME INTO JFCB
          BAL      R6,OPENJ                 OPEN USING MODIFIED JFCB
          BAL      R6,PROCESS               PROCESS DATASET
DATAEND   BAL      R6,CLOSE                 ALL RECS READ, CLOSE DCB
```

```
         B       NEXTDSNM                  ALLO NEXT DATASET
DATAERR1 BAL     R6,CLOSE                  S213 ABEND, CLOSE DCB
         BAL     R6,DOERMSG1               DSPLY ERR MSG FOR S213
         B       NEXTDSNM                  ALLO NEXT DATASET
DATAERR2 BAL     R6,CLOSE                  SX37 ABEND, CLOSE DCB
         BAL     R6,DOERMSG2               DSPLY ERR MSG FOR SX37
         B       NEXTDSNM                  ALLO NEXT DATASET
DSNMEND  B       RETURN                    RETURN TO MVS OR CALLING PROG
*
*
***********************************************************************
* THIS ROUTINE ESTABLISHES THE ESTAE RECOVERY ENVIRONMENT. WHEN A
* SYSTEM OR A USER ABEND IS ENCOUNTERED, THE RECOVERY EXIT ROUTINE
* RECVEXIT RECEIVES CONTROL AND THE ADDRESSES OF THE PARAMETERS POINTED
* TO BY PARMLIST ARE PASSED TO THE RECOVERY EXIT ROUTINE.
***********************************************************************
*
SETESTAE ESTAE   RECVEXIT,CT,PARAM=PARMLIST
         BR      R6                        RETURN TO CALLING RTN
*
*
***********************************************************************
* THIS ROUTINE READS THE JFCB INTO THE AREA DEFINED IN THE PROGRAM AND
* INITIALIZES THE DATASET NAME TABLE POINTER TO POINT TO THE FIRST
* ENTRY.
***********************************************************************
*
RDJFCB   RDJFCB  DCB01
         ...     CHK                       IF DD STMT IN JCL
         LA      R10,DSNMTBL               LD ADR OF 1ST DSNM ENTRY OF TBL
         ST      R10,DSNMPTR               STORE ADR OF NEXT ENTRY TO BE PROC
         BR      R6                        RETURN TO CALLING RTN
*
*
***********************************************************************
* THIS ROUTINE PUTS THE DATASET NAME OF THE CURRENT ENTRY OF THE
* DATASET NAME TABLE INTO THE JFCB AND INCREMENTS TO THE NEXT ENTRY.
***********************************************************************
*
SETDSNM  L       R10,DSNMPTR               LD ADR OF DATASET ENTRY TO BE PROC
         CLI     0(R10),X'00'              CHK FOR END-OF-TBL
         BE      DSNMEND                   IF YES, TERMINATE PROG
         MVC     JFCBDSNM,0(R10)           IF NO, PUT DSNM INTO JFCB
         LA      R10,ENTLEN(0,R10)         INCR TO NEXT DSNM ENTRY
         ST      R10,DSNMPTR               STORE ADR OF NEXT ENTRY TO BE PROC
         BR      R6                        RETURN TO CALLING RTN
*
*
***********************************************************************
* THIS ROUTINE OPENS THE DCB AND ALLOCATES THE DATASET NAMED IN THE
* JFCB.
***********************************************************************
*
OPENJ    OPEN    DCB01,TYPE=J              OPEN USING MDFY JFCB
         ...                               CHK FOR GOOD OPEN
         BR      R6                        RETURN TO CALLING RTN
*
*
***********************************************************************
* THIS ROUTINE PROCESSES THE DATASET.
***********************************************************************
*
PROCESS  ...                               PROCESS DATASET
         BR      R6                        RETURN TO CALLING RTN
```

```
*
*
***********************************************************************
* THIS ROUTINE CLOSES THE DCB.
***********************************************************************
*
CLOSE    CLOSE    DCB01                    CLOSE DCB OF CUR DATASET
         BR       R6                       RETURN TO CALLING RTN
*
*
***********************************************************************
* THIS ROUTINE DISPLAYS A MESSAGE ON THE HARDCOPY JOBLOG TO INDICATE
* THAT A S213 ABEND WAS INTERCEPTED FOR THE SPECIFIED DATASET NAME.
***********************************************************************
*
DOERMSG1 ...
         BR       R6
*
***********************************************************************
* THIS ROUTINE DISPLAYS A MESSAGE ON THE HARDCOPY JOBLOG TO INDICATE
* THAT A SX37 ABEND WAS INTERCEPTED FOR THE SPECIFIED DATASET NAME.
***********************************************************************
*
DOERMSG2 ...
         BR       R6
*
*
***********************************************************************
* THIS ROUTINE RESTORES THE REGISTERS AND RETURNS CONTROL.
***********************************************************************
*
RETURN   RCNTL    RC=0                     RETURN TO MVS OR CALLING PROG
*
*
***********************************************************************
* THE DATASET NAME TABLE. THIS TABLE CONTAINS THE NAMES OF ALL THE
* DATASETS THAT ARE TO BE ALLOCATED AND PROCESSED.
***********************************************************************
*
ENTLEN   EQU      44
DSNMTBL  DC       CL44'USER.FILE1'
         DC       CL44'USER.FILE2'
         DC       CL44'USER.FILE3'
         DC       CL44'USER.FILE4'
         DC       CL44'USER.FILE5'
         DC       X'00'                    END-OF-TBL INDICATOR
DSNMPTR  DS       F                        POINTER TO CURRENT ENTRY
*
*
***********************************************************************
* THIS IS THE PARMLIST THAT IS PASSED BY THE ESTAE SERVICE ROUTINE TO
* THE RECOVERY EXIT ROUTINE.
***********************************************************************
*
PARMLIST DC       A(ABCODTBL)
         DC       A(RETRYTBL)
*
*
***********************************************************************
* THE ABEND-CODE TABLE. THIS TABLE CONTAINS THE LIST OF ALL THE ABEND
* CODES FOR WHICH A RETRY IS TO BE PERFORMED. THE RETRY ADDRESS IS
* SPECIFIED IN THE CORRESPONDING ENTRY OF THE RETRY-ADDRESS TABLE.
***********************************************************************
*
```

```
ABCODTBL  DC        X'21300000'              ABEND CODE-1 TO INTERCEPT
          DC        X'B3700000'              ABEND CODE-2 TO INTERCEPT
          DC        X'D3700000'              ABEND CODE-3 TO INTERCEPT
          DC        X'E3700000'              ABEND CODE-4 TO INTERCEPT
          DC        XL4'00'                  END OF ABEND-CODE TABLE
*
*
***********************************************************************
* THE RETRY-ADDRESS TABLE. THIS TABLE CONTAINS THE LIST OF ALL THE
* RETRY ADDRESSES THAT CORRESPOND TO THE ENTRIES IN THE SAME RELATIVE
* LOCATION OF THE ABEND-CODE TABLE.
***********************************************************************
*
RETRYTBL  DC        A(DATAERR1)              RETRY ADR FOR ABEND CODE-1
          DC        A(DATAERR2)              RETRY ADR FOR ABEND CODE-2
          DC        A(DATAERR2)              RETRY ADR FOR ABEND CODE-3
          DC        A(DATAERR2)              RETRY ADR FOR ABEND CODE-4
          DC        XL4'00'                  END OF RETRY-ADR TABLE
*
*
***********************************************************************
* THE JFCB LIST AND THE DCB
***********************************************************************
*
          CNOP      0,4
JFCBPTR   DC        X'87'
          DC        AL3(JFCB)
JFCB      DS        44F
*
DCB01     DCB       DSORG=PS,MACRF=GL,EXLST=JFCBPTR,EODAD=DATAEND,    -
                    DDNAME=FILESDD
*
*
*
*
***********************************************************************
* THE FOLLOWING CSECT IS THE ESTAE RECOVERY EXIT REFERENCED IN THE
* ESTAE MACRO IN THE MAIN PROGRAM.
***********************************************************************
*
RECVEXIT  CSECT
*
*
***********************************************************************
* INITIALIZATION
***********************************************************************
*
          USING     *,R3                     DEFINE BASE REG
          USING     SDWA,R12                 DEFINE REG FOR SDWA DSECT
          LR        R3,R15                   SET ADRBLTY FOR RECV EXIT RTN
          ST        R14,SAVR14               SAVE RETURN ADR TO RTM
*
*
***********************************************************************
* THE FOLLOWING CODE DETERMINES IF A SDWA HAS BEEN PROVIDED.
***********************************************************************
*
          C         R0,BIN12                 CHK IF SDWA CREATED
          BE        NOSDWA                   PROCESS WITHOUT SDWA
          B         YESSDWA                  PROCESS USING SDWA
*
*
***********************************************************************
* THIS ROUTINE RECEIVES CONTROL IF A SDWA WAS NOT PROVIDED. THIS
```

```
* ROUTINE LOADS THE PARAMETER-LIST ADDRESS INTO THE REGISTER EXPECTED
* BY THE RECOVERY ROUTINE; BRANCHES AND LINKS TO THE RECOVERY ROUTINE;
* INDICATES THAT A SDWA WAS NOT PROVIDED; AND PASSES CONTROL TO THE
* RECOVERY-EXIT RETURN ROUTINE.
***********************************************************************
*
NOSDWA   LR    R10,R2                   LD ADR OF PARM-LIST
         ST    R1,ABCODE                STORE ABEND CODE
         BAL   R6,RECVYRTN              DO RECOVERY
         LA    R10,0                    IND NO SDWA
         B     EXITRET                  EXIT RECOVERY-EXIT
*
*
***********************************************************************
* THIS ROUTINE RECEIVES CONTROL IF A SDWA WAS PROVIDED. THIS ROUTINE
* SAVES THE ADDRESS OF THE SDWA; LOADS THE PARAMETER-LIST ADDRESS INTO
* THE REGISTER EXPECTED BY THE RECOVERY ROUTINE; BRANCHES AND LINKS TO
* THE RECOVERY ROUTINE; INDICATES THAT A SDWA WAS PROVIDED; AND PASSES
* CONTROL TO THE RECOVERY-EXIT RETURN ROUTINE.
***********************************************************************
*
YESSDWA  LR    R12,R1                   SET ADRBLTY FOR SDWA DSECT
         L     R10,SDWAPARM             LOAD ADR OF PARM-LIST
         XC    ABCODE,ABCODE            CLEAR ABEND CODE HOLD AREA
         MVC   ABCODE(3),SDWACMPC       STORE ABEND CODE
         BAL   R6,RECVYRTN              DO RECOVERY
         LA    R10,4                    IND SDWA PROVIDED
         B     EXITRET                  EXIT RECOVERY-EXIT
*
*
***********************************************************************
* THE MAINSTREAM OF THE RECOVERY EXIT ROUTINE
***********************************************************************
*
RECVYRTN BAL   R7,GETPARMS              GET PARM ADRS
         BAL   R7,CHKABCOD              CHK ABEND CODE, DO ABEND OR RETRY
         BR    R6                       RETURN TO CALLING RTN
*
*
***********************************************************************
* THIS ROUTINE OBTAINS THE ADDRESSES OF THE PARAMETERS SPECIFIED BY
* THE ESTAE MACRO AND PASSED TO THE RECOVERY ROUTINE BY RTM.
***********************************************************************
*
GETPARMS L     R11,0(0,R10)             LD ADR OF PARM ABEND-CODE-TBL
         ST    R11,ABTBLADR             SAVE ADR OF ABEND-CODE-TBL
         L     R11,4(0,R10)             LD ADR OF PARM RCVRY-ADR-TBL
         ST    R11,RETBLADR             SAVE ADR OF RCVRY-ADR-TBL
         BR    R7                       RETURN TO CALLING RTN
*
*
***********************************************************************
* THIS ROUTINE CHECKS THE ABEND CODE TO DETERMINE IF IT IS ONE OF THE
* ONES FOR WHICH A RETRY IS REQUIRED. IF THE ABEND CODE IS FOUND IN
* THE ABEND-CODE TABLE, THEN THE RETRY ADDRESS IN THE SAME RELATIVE
* LOCATION IN THE RETRY-ADDRESS TABLE IS USED AS THE RETRY ADDRESS, AND
* REGISTER 15 IS SET WITH A RETURN CODE OF X'04' TO INDICATE RETRY. IF
* THE ABEND CODE IS NOT FOUND IN THE ABEND-CODE TABLE, THEN THE ABEND
* IS TO CONTINUE AND REGISTER 15 IS SET WITH A RETURN CODE OF X'00' TO
* INDICATE ABEND.
***********************************************************************
*
CHKABCOD L     R10,ABTBLADR             LD ADR OF ABEND-CODE-TBL
         L     R11,RETBLADR             LD ADR OF RCVRY-ADR-TBL
```

```
NXABCODE  CLI       0(R10),X'00'                CHK FOR END-OF-TBL
          BE        ABEND                       IF END, DO ABEND
          CLC       ABCODE,0(R10)               CHK IF ABEND CODE IN TBL
          BE        RETRY                       IF YES, DO RETRY
          LA        R10,4(0,R10)                INCR TO NEXT ABEND CODE IN TBL
          LA        R11,4(0,R11)                INCR TO NEXT RCVRY ADR IN TBL
          B         NXABCODE                    COMP ABEND CODE TO NEXT TBL ENTRY
ABEND     LA        R15,0                       IND ABEND REQUIRED
          BR        R7                          RETURN TO CALLING RTN
RETRY     MVC       RETRYADR,0(R11)             EXTRACT CORRESPONDING RETRY ADR
          LA        R15,4                       IND RETRY REQUIRED
          BR        R7                          RETURN TO CALLING RTN
*
*
***********************************************************************
* THIS ROUTINE RECEIVES CONTROL WHEN THE RECOVERY EXIT ROUTINE IS TO
* RETURN CONTROL TO RTM. THIS ROUTINE CHECKS WHETHER OR NOT A SDWA WAS
* PROVIDED AND CAUSES CONTROL TO BE RETURNED ACCORDINGLY.
***********************************************************************
*
EXITRET   LTR       R10,R10                     CHK IF SDWA PROVIDED
          BZ        RETSDWAX                    RETURN WITHOUT SDWA
          B         RETSDWA                     RETURN USING SDWA
*
*
***********************************************************************
* THIS ROUTINE RETURNS CONTROL WHEN A SDWA WAS NOT PROVIDED. IF
* REGISTER 15 CONTAINS A RETURN CODE OF X'00', THEN THE ABEND IS TO
* CONTINUE. IF REGISTER 15 CONTAINS A RETURN CODE OF X'04', THEN THE
* RETRY ADDRESS, WHICH WAS SELECTED FROM THE CHKABCOD ROUTINE, IS USED
* TO RETURN CONTROL TO THE MAIN PROGRAM.
***********************************************************************
*
RETSDWAX  LTR       R15,R15                     CHK IF ABEND OR RETRY REQUIRED
          BZ        DOABENDX                    IF RC=0, DO ABEND
          L         R0,RETRYADR                 LD RETRY ADR
          L         R14,SAVR14                  RESTORE RETURN ADR
          BR        R14                         RETURN TO RTM
DOABENDX  L         R14,SAVR14                  RESTORE RETURN ADR
          BR        R14                         RETURN TO RTM
*
*
***********************************************************************
* THIS ROUTINE RETURNS CONTROL WHEN A SDWA WAS PROVIDED. IF
* REGISTER 15 CONTAINS A RETURN CODE OF X'00', THEN THE ABEND IS TO
* CONTINUE. IF REGISTER 15 CONTAINS A RETURN CODE OF X'04', THEN THE
* RETRY ADDRESS, WHICH WAS SELECTED FROM THE CHKABCOD ROUTINE, IS USED
* TO RETURN CONTROL TO THE MAIN PROGRAM.
***********************************************************************
*
RETSDWA   LTR       R15,R15                     CHK IF ABEND OR RETRY REQUIRED
          BZ        DOABEND                     IF RC=0, DO ABEND
          L         R10,RETRYADR                LD RETRY ADR
          SETRP     WKAREA=(R12),RC=4,RETADDR=(R10),RETREGS=YES,FRESDWA=YES
*                                               RC=4 - PROVIDE RETRY ADDRESS
          L         R14,SAVR14                  RESTORE RETURN ADR
          BR        R14                         RETURN TO RTM
DOABEND   SETRP     WKAREA=(R12),RC=0           RC=0 - CONTIN WITH ABEND
          LR        R14,SAVR14                  RESTORE RETURN ADR
          BR        R14                         RETURN TO RTM
*
*
***********************************************************************
* DC/DS STATEMENTS USED BY EXIT ROUTINE
```

```
*************************************************************************
*
SAVR14     DS       F
BIN12      DC       F'12'
ABCODE     DS       F
ABTBLADR   DS       F
RETBLADR   DS       F
RETRYADR   DS       F
*
*
*************************************************************************
* THE DSECTS
*************************************************************************
*
           PRINT    NOGEN
           DSECT
           IEFJFCBN                            GENERATES JFCB DSECT
*
           IHASDWA                             GENERATES SDWA DSECT
*
*
*************************************************************************
* END OF PROGRAM
*************************************************************************
*
           END
```

BIBLIOGRAPHY FOR CHAPTER 6

The following IBM manuals contain reference material for the topics discussed in this chapter.

ID	TITLE
GC28-1114	*OS/VS2 MVS Supervisor Services and Macro Instructions*
GC28-1154	*MVS/XA Supervisor Services and Macro Instructions*
GC28-1821	*MVS/ESA Application Development Guide*
GC28-1822	*MVS/ESA Application Development Macro Reference*

7

Programming Dataset Allocation

In MVS, datasets may be allocated via Job Control Language (JCL) or programmatically. MVS provides the programmer two methods for allocating datasets via a program. One is by modifying the Job File Control Block (JFCB) before OPEN processing, and the other is via Dynamic Allocation (SVC 99).

The Job Management component of MVS creates the JFCB and stores it in the Scheduler Work Area (SWA). The JFCB contains the contents of the JCL DD statement and other information. A JCL DD statement must be provided in the jobstream for the JFCB to be created and then modified by the program. Datasets are allocated by changing the dataset name field (and volser field, if required) in the JFCB before issuing the OPEN macro instruction. However, only datasets that reside on the same unit type (3375, 3380, 3400, etc.) that was specified in the JCL DD statement can be allocated since the unit is allocated by the Initiator and cannot be changed by modifying the JFCB.

Dynamic Allocation does not require a JCL DD statement and is more flexible than the JFCB modification method, but its use also requires more programming effort.

With the MVT operating system (predecessor to MVS), SVC 32 was provided and could dynamically allocate a dataset if it were passed a JFCB address (via register 0) and a UCB address (via register 1). This method is still supported but is documented only in the DADSM Logic manual, is cummbersome to use, and requires that the user be authorized. Since SVC 99 has effectively replaced SVC 32 and since SVC 99 is a standard, well-documented interface, the SVC 32 method will not be discussed any further.

7.1 MODIFYING THE JOB FILE CONTROL BLOCK

In order to function, the OPEN processing requires certain information that is provided in the JCL DD statement (and other sources). The information specified in the JCL is made available to OPEN via the JFCB. The JFCB is built by the Interpreter and stored in the SWA. A program may access the JFCB by using the RDJFCB macro instruction. By examining the JFCB, the program can determine what parameters were specified on the JCL DD statement for the specified dataset. These parameters may be changed by modifying the appropriate fields of the JFCB. If the modifications are done before the dataset is

OPENed, the effect is as if these modifications were actually coded on the JCL DD statement. However, information specified in the UNIT parameter cannot be changed because the unit is allocated by the Initiator. Also, unit information is stored in the Task I/O Table (TIOT), not the JFCB.

The dataset name and other dataset-related parameters can be changed because the Initiator does not actually locate the dataset; it allocates the unit and volume based upon either the information specified in the JCL or stored in the catalog. The Initiator enqueues on the dataset name (based upon the DISP parameter), but OPEN processing actually locates the dataset by searching the specified volume. If the volume is to be changed, then the JCL should specify DEFER in the UNIT parameter to prevent two mount messages (one by the Initiator and one by OPEN) for datasets residing on magnetic tape volumes or removable DASD volumes.

7.1.1 Typical Reasons for Modifying the JFCB

Some of the reasons for modifying the JFCB within a program would include the following:

- Reading all the datasets on a multi-file magnetic tape volume. This could be accomplished by changing the dataset name and sequence number and OPENing each dataset until they are all accessed. If the dataset names are unknown, then LABEL=(1,BLP) can be specified in the JCL and RECFM=U specified in the DCB macro instruction. BLP means Bypass Label Processing. It directs MVS to treat all records (labels, if any and data) on the volume as data. A specification of NL in the LABEL parameter cannot be used because NL specifically indicates that the volume must be unlabeled. If labels are found, the volume will not be processed. The number that precedes BLP in the LABEL parameter indicates the file number. If the volume contains standard labels, then a specification of (1,BLP) will cause the tape volume to be positioned at the standard label (VOL1/HDR1/HDR2).

  If BLP is specified, then only the dataset sequence number need be changed. Coding Example 7.1.1 shows the code required to read all the data for each file of a multi-file magnetic tape volume with the use of only one JCL DD statement.
- Changing the dataset name. This enables a program to reference different datasets on the same volume, using only one JCL DD statement. This facility would be useful if a program is required to reference a large number of datasets whose names may not be known until execution. The dataset names may come from control statements, be created dynamically based upon input data, or be obtained by reading the VTOC. In this case, specifying a separate JCL DD statement for each dataset would be impractical, if not impossible.

  Note: if a DASD dataset name is changed, then the program must issue the ENQ/DEQ macro instructions using the same qname and rname as the operating system to insure dataset integrity. Coding Example 7.1.2 shows the proper names to use.
- Changing the dataset name and volser. This enables a program to reference different datasets, located on different volumes, using only one JCL DD statement. The reasons for doing this would be the same as those specified above. In order to accomplish this, the allocated unit must support removeable volumes. Such units include magnetic tape drives and 3330 DASDs.
- Accessing more than one member of a PDS, using QSAM or BSAM. Chapter 8 discusses this technique.
- Examining the DCB attributes specified on a JCL DD statement. For a new dataset, the program can provide the DCB attributes if they are omitted, thereby providing the user with the flexibility of providing DCB attributes in the JCL for a new dataset and

preventing an ABEND if they are not specified. Coding Example 7.1.3 shows the code to accomplish this.

- OPENing the VTOC. Coding Example 7.1.4 shows the code to accomplish this.
- Adding secondary allocation to a DASD dataset allocated with only primary allocation.

7.1.2 The RDJFCB Macro Instruction

The RDJFCB macro instruction will cause the JFCB for the ddname of each DCB address specified to be copied from the SWA into the area provided by the program.

The operand of the RDJFCB macro instruction has the same content and syntax as the OPEN macro instruction.

Upon completion, the RDJFCB macro instruction will post the following return codes in register 15.

Return Code (Hex)	Meaning
00	Successful completion.
04	One or more of the ddname(s) of the specified DCB(s) is not in the JCL stream or is specified as blanks.

7.1.3 Setting Up for RDJFCB

Before the RDJFCB macro instruction can be executed, certain control information must be defined. The DCB macro instruction must specify an exit list (via the EXLST parameter) to indicate the address of the user-provided JFCB area. This is coded as follows.

```
MSTRFILE DCB ....,EXLST=JFCBPTR1,DDNAME=MSTRFILE
```

The symbol JFCBPTR1 points to an exit-list that must be aligned on a fullword boundary. Each entry in the list is four bytes long. Data management provides many exits (DCB Open, End-of-Volume, etc.); therefore, the high order byte of each exit list entry must indicate the exit type. An X'07' indicates a JFCB exit. The next three bytes contain the address of the user-provided JFCB area. The size of the JFCB is 176 bytes. Since an exit list may contain many entries, the high order bit of the first byte of the last entry should be set to one to indiacte the end of the list.

The following coding example illustrates how to code the JFCB exit entry when it is the only entry in the exit-list.

```
                0F
JFCBPTR1    DC      X'87'
            DC      AL3(JFCB1)
JFCB1       DS      CL176
```

When the RDJFCB macro instruction is executed with the DCB name MSTRFILE specified, the corresponding JFCB will be copied into the area labeled JFCB1.

7.1.4 Required JCL DD Statement for RDJFCB

There are two ways to code the JCL DD statement for use by the RDJFCB macro instruction. One way is to code it in the normal way, specifying all required parameters. The other way is to just allocate the unit and volume by coding the JCL DD statement in the following way.

```
//DD1 DD UNIT=SYSDA,VOL=SER=123456,DISP=SHR
```

In the above example, the Initiator will allocate the DASD that has the volume with the serial number 123456 mounted. Since no dataset name is specified, a temporary dataset name is generated. The generated temporary dataset name does not exist on the volume, but a JCL error or allocation error does not occur because the initiator makes no attempt to locate the dataset (this is done by OPEN). The DISP refers to the dataset, not the volume. When the JFCB is modified to contain the desired dataset name, the specified DISP will be used by OPEN (since it is now in the JFCB), unless that information is also changed.

7.1.5 The OPEN and CLOSE Macro Instructions

OPEN processing will normally use the JFCB that is in the SWA for each DCB address specified. When a modified JFCB is provided by the program, it is indicated to OPEN via the TYPE=J parameter of the macro instruction.

The format of the OPEN macro instruction used with the RDJFCB macro instruction is as follows:

```
[name] OPEN (dcb-address,[(options)],...),TYPE=J
```

`dcb-address`

The address of the DCB containing the EXLST parameter that contains a pointer to the programmer-supplied JFCB. The address may be specified as the name of the DCB macro instruction or specified in a register.

`options`

The same ones which may be specified in the normal OPEN macro instruction.

`TYPE=J`

Indicates to OPEN processing that, for each DCB address specified, it is to use the modified JFCB provided by the programmer.

The CLOSE macro instruction that is used for the TYPE=J OPEN is the same as normally used.

7.1.6 JFCB Modification Coding Examples

This section contains coding examples that show how to modify the JFCB for various useful applications.

Coding Example 7.1.1

This coding example illustrates how to read all the datasets on a magnetic tape volume with the use of only one JCL DD statement. In this coding example, the following coding technique is used:

- The JCL DD statement, which points to the magnetic tape volume, is required to contain only the UNIT, VOL=SER, DISP and LABEL parameters.
- DISP=(OLD,PASS) or VOL=(RETAIN,...) should be coded on the JCL DD statement to prevent the magnetic tape volume from unloading for each CLOSE.
- LABEL=(1,BLP) must be specified. BLP cannot be forced by modifying the JFCB unless the program is authorized. The program verifies that BLP was specified by examining the JFCBLTYP field.
- The file sequence number field (JFCBFLSQ) of the JFCB is set to one for the first OPENJ and incremented by one for each successive OPENJ.
- The DCB macro instruction specifies MACRF=GL, BLKSIZE=32760 and RECFM=U. After each read (via the GET macro instruction), the length of the record read will be posted in the DCBLRECL field of the DCB.
- There are two consecutive tape marks after the last dataset on the volume. An immediate end-of-data condition (first GET/READ after OPEN) can be interpreted as end-of-volume (assuming that all datasets contain data) when using QSAM or BSAM to read the magnetic tape volume. (The presence of two consecutive tape marks can be determined directly by using EXCP).

```
READTAPE  CSECT
*
*
***************************************************************************
* INITIALIZATION
***************************************************************************
*
          INITL     3,EQU=R                  INITIALIZE PROGRAM
          USING     INFMJFCB,R10             DEFINE REG FOR JFCB DSECT
*
*
***************************************************************************
* MAINSTREAM OF PROGRAM
***************************************************************************
*
          BAL       R6,OPENPRT               OPEN SYSPRINT
          BAL       R6,RDJFCB                READ JFCB INTO PROG AREA
NEXTFILE  BAL       R6,MDFYJFCB              MODIFY JFCB-INCR FILE SEQ NUM
          BAL       R6,OPENTAP               OPEN NEXT TAPE DATASET
NEXTREC   BAL       R6,READREC               READ A REC FROM TAPE DATASET
          BAL       R6,PRINT                 PRINT A REC FROM TAPE DATASET
          B         NEXTREC                  READ NEXT REC FROM TAPE DATASET
ENDFILE   BAL       R6,CKENDVOL              CHECK IF END OF TAPE VOL
          BAL       R6,CLOSETAP              CLOSE TAPE DATASET
          B         NEXTFILE                 PROCESS NEXT TAPE DATASET
ENDVOL    BAL       R6,CLOSE                 LAST TAPE DATASET, CLOSE ALL DCBS
          B         RETURN                   RETURN TO MVS OR CALLING PROG
*
*
***************************************************************************
* THIS ROUTINE OPENS THE SYSPRINT DCB.
***************************************************************************
*
OPENPRT   OPEN      (SYSPRINT,(OUTPUT))
          ...                                CHECK FOR GOOD OPEN
          BR        R6                       RETURN TO CALLING RTN
```

```
*
*
************************************************************************
* THIS ROUTINE READS THE JFCB AND COPIES IT FROM THE SWA INTO THE
* PROGRAMMER-SUPPLIED AREA.
************************************************************************
*
RDJFCB   LA       R10,JFCB               SETUP ADRBLTY FOR JFCB DSECT
         RDJFCB   SYSUT1
         LTR      R15,R15                CHK IF DD STMT IN JCL
         BNZ      NODD                   IF RC NOT 0, DD MISSING
         TM       JFCBLTYP,JFCBLP        CHK IF BLP SPECIFIED
         BNO      NOBLP                  IF NOT 1, NO BLP
         BR       R6                     RETURN TO CALLING RTN
NODD     WTO      '*** SYSUT1 JCL DD STATEMENT MISSING ***',ROUTCDE=11
         ABEND    901
NOBLP    WTO      '*** LABEL=(1,BLP) NOT SPECIFIED FOR SYSUT1 ***',  -
                  ROUTCDE=11
         ABEND    902
*
*
************************************************************************
* THIS ROUTINE MODIFIES THE JFCB. EACH TIME THIS ROUTINE RECEIVES
* CONTROL, IT INCREMENTS THE FILE-SEQUENCE-NUMBER BY ONE AND INSERTS
* THE NEW VALUE INTO THE JFCB.
************************************************************************
*
MDFYJFCB LA       R10,JFCB               SET ADRBLTY FOR JFCB DSECT
         L        R11,FILENUM            LOAD PREV FILE SEQ NUM
         LA       R11,1(0,R11)           INCR FILE SEQ NUM
         ST       R11,FILENUM            STORE NEW FILE SEQ NUM
         MVC      JFCBFLSQ,FILENUM+2     PUT NEW FILE SEQ NUM INTO JFCB
         BR       R6                     RETURN TO CALLING RTN
*
*
************************************************************************
* THIS ROUTINE OPENS THE TAPE DATASET DCB AND USES THE MODIFIED JFCB
* SUPPLIED BY THE PROGRAMMER TO POSITION THE TAPE VOLUME TO THE NEXT
* DATASET.
************************************************************************
*
OPENTAP  OPEN     SYSUT1,TYPE=J          OPEN, USE JFCB IN PROG
         TM       DCBOFLGS,DCBOFOPN      CHK IF OPEN OK
         BNO      OPENBAD                IF NOT 1, OPEN UNSUCCESSFUL
         MVI      NORECSW,C'1'           INIT NO-REC-SW TO DETM END-OF-VOL
         BR       R6                     RETURN TO CALLING RTN
OPENBAD  WTO      '*** OPEN ERROR FOR FILEDD ***',ROUTCDE=11
         ABEND    903
*
*
************************************************************************
* THIS ROUTINE READS A RECORD FROM THE CURRENT TAPE DATASET.
************************************************************************
*
READREC  GET      SYSUT1                 GET A RECORD FROM TAPE DS
         MVI      NORECSW,C'0'           IND THAT DS CONTAINS A RECORD
         BR       R6                     RETURN TO CALLING RTN
*
*
************************************************************************
* THIS ROUTINE PRINTS THE RECORD READ FROM THE TAPE DATASET.
************************************************************************
*
PRINT    ...                             PRINT RECS FROM TAPE DATASETS
```

```
         BR        R6                      RETURN TO CALLING RTN
*
*
***********************************************************************
* THIS ROUTINE CHECKS IF ALL THE DATASETS ON THE TAPE VOLUME HAVE
* BEEN PROCESSED.
***********************************************************************
*
CKENDVOL CLI       NORECSW,C'1'            CHK IF IMED END-OF-FILE FROM LAST GET
         BE        ENDVOL                  IF YES, ALL DATASETS READ
         CLI       NORECSW,X'00'           CHK IF VOL HAS ANY DATA
         BE        NODATA                  IF X'00', NO DATA ON TAPE
         BR        R6                      RETURN TO CALLING RTN
NODATA   WTO       '*** TAPE VOLUME CONTAINS NO DATA ***',ROUTCDE=11
*
*
***********************************************************************
* THIS ROUTINE CLOSES THE DCB FOR THE CURRENT TAPE DATASET.
***********************************************************************
*
CLOSETAP CLOSE     SYSUT1                  CLOSE TAPE DCB
         BR        R6                      RETURN TO CALLING RTN
*
*
***********************************************************************
* THIS ROUTINE CLOSES ALL THE DCBS.
***********************************************************************
*
CLOSE    CLOSE     (SYSUT1,,SYSPRINT)      CLOSE ALL DCBS
         BR        R6                      RETURN TO CALLING RTN
*
*
***********************************************************************
* THIS ROUTINE RESTORES THE REGISTERS AND RETURNS CONTROL.
***********************************************************************
*
RETURN   RCNTL     RC=0                    RETURN TO MVS OR CALLING PROG
*
*
***********************************************************************
* DC/DS STATEMENTS
***********************************************************************
*
FILENUM  DC        F'0'
NORECSW  DC        X'00'
*
*
***********************************************************************
* THE JFCB-LIST AND THE DCBS
***********************************************************************
*
JFCB     DS        44F
JFCBPTR  DC        X'87'
         DC        AL3(JFCB)
*
SYSUT1   DCB       DSORG=PS,MACRF=GL,RECFM=U,BLKSIZE=32760,
                   EXLST=JFCBPTR,EODAD=ENDFILE,DDNAME=SYSUT1
SYSPRINT DCB       ...
*
*
***********************************************************************
* THE DSECTS
***********************************************************************
*
```

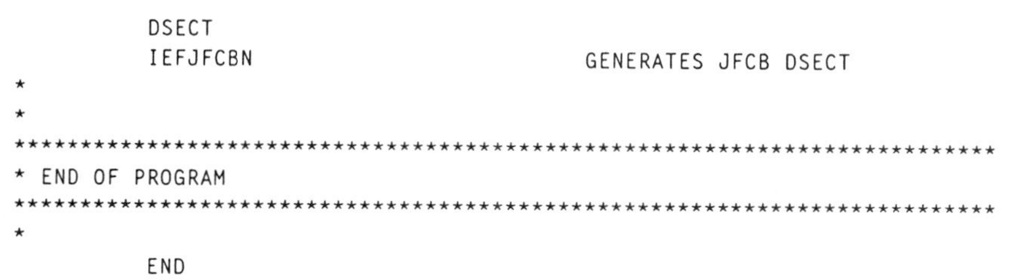

```
         DSECT
         IEFJFCBN                      GENERATES JFCB DSECT
*
*
**************************************************************************
* END OF PROGRAM
**************************************************************************
*
         END
```

NOTES:

- If the magnetic tape volume is read using BSAM (MACRF=R specified in DCB and READ macro instruction), then a GETMAIN of 32760 bytes is required to obtain the buffer used with the READ macro instruction.
- Chapter 11 discusses the structure of magnetic tape volumes and the use of EXCP to read from and write to a magnetic tape volume.
- The writing of the PRINT routine is left as an exercise for the reader. This routine can perform various processing based upon the contents of the magnetic tape volume and the objectives of the program. The following contains some suggestions and considerations:
  - Each record read from the magnetic tape volume can be printed as is. This would include labels (if any) and data.
  - It can be determined whether the magnetic tape volume contains standard labels by checking the first four bytes of each record for the character strings: VOL1 (first file only, and should be the first record on the magnetic tape volume, if present), HDR1, HDR2, EOF1, EOF2, EOV1, and EOV2. As another check, these label records are 80 bytes in length. This is indicated in the DCBLRECL field of the DCB after the record is read. The dataset name is contained in the HDR1 (and EOF1/EOV1) label, and the DCB attributes are contained in the HDR2 (and EOF2/EOV2) label record. The dataset name can be printed before the records that it contains, and the DCB attributes can be used to deblock the records read.
  - If the magnetic tape volume contains no labels (indicated by the first record not containing the character string VOL1 in the first four positions), then the records of each unlabeled file can be preceded with its file sequence number.

Coding Example 7.1.2

This coding example illustrates how to allocate various DASD datasets, which are located on the same DASD volume, by changing the dataset name in the JFCB.

```
READDISK   CSECT
*
*
**************************************************************************
* INITIALIZATION
**************************************************************************
*
           INITL     3,EQU=R                 INITIALIZE PROGRAM
           USING     INFMJFCB,R10            DEFINE REG FOR JFCB DSECT
           USING     IHADCB,R11              DEFINE REG FOR DCB DSECT
           USING     DSTBLMAP,R12            DEFINE REG FOR USER DSN-TBL DSECT
*
*
**************************************************************************
* MAINSTREAM OF PROGRAM
**************************************************************************
*
           BAL       R6,RDJFCB               READ JFCB INTO PROG AREA
NEXTFILE   BAL       R6,MDFYJFCB             MODIFY JFCB WITH NEXT DATASET NAME
```

```
             BAL      R6,ENQ                   ENQ ON DATASET NAME
             BAL      R6,OPEN                  OPEN NEXT DATASET
             BAL      R6,PROCESS               PROCESS DATASET
DATAEND      BAL      R6,CLOSE                 CLOSE DATASET
             BAL      R6,DEQ                   DEQ ON DATASET NAME
             B        NEXTFILE                 ALLOCATE NEXT DATASET
VOLEND       B        RETURN                   ALL DATASETS ON VOL PROC, RETURN
*
*
**********************************************************************
* THIS ROUTINE READS THE JFCB AND COPIES IT FROM THE SWA INTO THE
* PROGRAMMER-SUPPLIED AREA.
**********************************************************************
*
RDJFCB       RDJFCB   FILEDCB
             LTR      R15,R15                  CHK IF DD STMT IN JCL
             BNZ      NODD                     IF RC NOT 0, DD STMT MISSING
             BR       R6                       RETURN TO CALLING RTN
NODD         WTO      '*** FILEDD NOT SPECIFIED IN JCL ***',ROUTCDE=11
             ABEND    901
*
*
**********************************************************************
* THIS ROUTINE MODIFIES THE JFCB. THE CURRENT DASD DATASET NAME FROM
* THE TABLE IS PUT INTO THE DATASET-NAME FIELD OF THE JFCB.
**********************************************************************
*
MDFYJFCB     LA       R10,JFCB                 SET ADRBLTY FOR JFCB DSECT
             L        R12,DSTBLPTR             LD CUR DSN ENTRY ADR, SET DSECT ADRBLTY
             CLI      DSNAME,X'00'             CHK FOR LAST DSN ENTRY
             BE       VOLEND                   IF YES, ALL DSNMS PROCESSED
             MVC      JFCBDSNM,DSNAME          PUT CUR DSN INTO JFCB
             LA       R14,TBLENLEN(0,R12)      INCR TO NEXT DSN ENTRY
             ST       R14,DSTBLPTR             SAVE ADR OF NEXT DSN ENTRY
             BR       R6                       RETURN TO CALLING RTN
*
*
**********************************************************************
* THIS ROUTINE ENQ'S THE DATASET THAT WILL BE ALLOCATED VIA OPEN.
**********************************************************************
*
ENQ          MVC      RNAME,DSNAME             MOVE DSNAME FOR ENQ
             L        R2,DSNMLEN               LOAD LEN OF RNAME
             ENQ      (QNAME,RNAME,S,(R2),SYSTEMS)
             BR       R6                       RETURN TO CALLING RTN
*
*
**********************************************************************
* THIS ROUTINE OPENS THE DCB AND ALLOCATES THE DSNAME SPECIFIED IN
* THE PROGRAMMER-SUPPLIED JFCB.
**********************************************************************
*
OPEN         LA       R11,FILEDCB              SET ADRBLTY FOR DCB DSECT
             OPEN     FILEDCB,TYPE=J           OPEN, USE JFCB IN PROG
             ...                               CHK FOR GOOD OPEN
             BR       R6                       IF YES, RET TO CALLING RTN
*
*
**********************************************************************
* THIS ROUTINE READS A RECORD FROM THE DATASET AND PROCESSES IT.
**********************************************************************
*
PROCESS      GET      FILEDCB                  READ A RECORD FROM DATASET
             ...                               PROCESS A RECORD
```

```
         BR        R6                       RETURN TO CALLING RTN
*
*
***********************************************************************
* THIS ROUTINE CLOSES THE DCB.
***********************************************************************
*
CLOSE    CLOSE     FILEDCB                  CLOSE DATASET
         BR        R6                       RETURN TO CALLING RTN
*
*
***********************************************************************
* THIS ROUTINE DEQ'S THE DATASET.
***********************************************************************
*
DEQ      L         R2,DSNMLEN
         DEQ       (QNAME,RNAME,(R2),SYSTEMS)
         BR        R6
*
*
***********************************************************************
* THIS ROUTINE RESTORES THE REGISTERS AND RETURNS CONTROL.
***********************************************************************
*
RETURN   RCNTL     RC=0                     RETURN TO MVS OR CALLING PROG
*
*
***********************************************************************
* DC/DS STATEMENTS FOR DASD DATASET NAME TABLE
***********************************************************************
*
DSTBLPTR DC        A(DSNTBL)
*
DSNTBL   DS        0F
TBLENTBG EQU       *
         DC        A(L'DS01)
DS01     DC        C'USER.FILE01'
         DC        CL(45-L'DS01)' '
TBLENTX  EQU       *
         DC        A(L'DS02)
DS02     DC        C'USER.FILE02'
         DC        CL(45-L'DS02)' '
         DC        A(L'DS03)
DS03     DC        C'USER.FILE03'
         DC        CL(45-L'DS03)' '
         DC        F'0'                     INDICATE END-OF-DSN TABLE
TBLENLEN EQU       TBLENTX-TBLENTBG         TBL ENTRY LENGTH
*
*
***********************************************************************
* DC/DS STATEMENTS FOR ENQ/DEQ MACROS
***********************************************************************
*
QNAME    DC        CL8'SYSDSN'
RNAME    DS        CL44
*
*
***********************************************************************
* THE JFCB-LIST AND THE DCB
***********************************************************************
*
JFCB     DS        44F
JFCBPTR  DC        X'87'
         DC        AL3(JFCB)
```

```
*
FILEDCB    DCB     DSORG=PS,MACRF=GL,EXLST=JFCBPTR,EODAD=DATAEND, -
                   DDNAME=FILEDD
*
*
***************************************************************************
* THE DSECTS
***************************************************************************
*
           DSECT
           IEFJFCBN                         GENERATES JFCB DSECT
*
DSTBLMAP   DSECT
DSNMLEN    DS      CL4
DSNAME     DS      CL44
           DS      CL1                      REQD TO PREVENT ASM ERROR
*
*
***************************************************************************
* END OF PROGRAM
***************************************************************************
*
*
           END
```

NOTES:

- Since the dataset name was changed in the JFCB, an ENQ macro instruction must be issued to maintain dataset integrity. The major name (qname) must be SYS-DSNbb (two low-order blanks are added since the qname must be eight characters) and the minor (rname) must be the dataset name. The length of the rname must be the actual length of the dataset name, not 44 (unless that is the actual length). Also, the DEQ macro instruction should be issued as soon as possible to make the dataset available to other users. In order to issue the ENQ/DEQ macro instruction with the system qname of SYSDSNbb, the program must be authorized.
- In this example, the dataset names are hard-coded in a table located in the program. This is for illustration purposes and not necessarily a good technique. A better technique would be to code the dataset names on control statements that are read and processed by the program, or for the program to read the VTOC and select dataset names that meet certain criteria.

Coding Example 7.1.3

This coding example illustrates how to check the DCB BLKSIZE parameter, which is specified on the JCL DD statement. In this example, if the BLKSIZE parameter is not specified for a new dataset, then the program provides a default BLKSIZE to prevent an S013 ABEND. If the BLKSIZE is specified, then the program verifies that the BLKSIZE is a multiple of the LRECL, which is specified by the program via the DCB macro instruction. If the BLKSIZE is not a multiple of the LRECL, then the program replaces it with the default BLKSIZE. If the specified BLKSIZE is a multiple of the LRECL, then the program verifies that is it at least a minimum size, otherwise it is replaced by the minimum BLKSIZE (hardcoded in program).

```
CHKBLKSZ   CSECT
*
*
***************************************************************************
* INITIALIZATION
***************************************************************************
```

```
*
            INITL     3,EQU=R                  INITIALIZE PROGRAM
            USING     INFMJFCB,R10             DEFINE REG FOR JFCB DSECT
            USING     IHADCB,R11               DEFINE REG FOR DCB DESCT
*
*
***********************************************************************
* MAINSTREAM OF PROGRAM
***********************************************************************
*
            BAL       R6,RDJFCB                READ JFCB INTO PROG AREA
            BAL       R6,VALBLKSZ              VALIDATE BLKSZ SPEC ON JCL STMT
            BAL       R6,MDFYJFCB              SET DEFAULT BLKSZ
            BAL       R6,OPEN                  OPEN DCB, CHK IF JFCB MDFY REQR
            BAL       R6,PROCESS               PROCESS DATASET
            B         RETURN                   RETURN TO MVS OR CALLING PROG
*
*
***********************************************************************
* THIS ROUTINE READS THE JFCB AND COPIES IT FROM THE SWA INTO THE
* PROGRAMMER-SUPPLIED AREA.
***********************************************************************
*
RDJFCB      RDJFCB    FILEDCB
            LTR       R15,R15                  CHK IF DD STMT IN JCL
            BNZ       NODD                     IF RC NOT 0, DD STMT MISSING
            BR        R6                       RETURN TO CALLING RTN
NODD        WTO       '*** FILEDD NOT SPECIFIED IN JCL ***',ROUTCDE=11
            ABEND     901
*
*
***********************************************************************
* THIS ROUTINE EXAMINES THE BLKSIZE SPECIFIED IN THE REFERENCED JCL
* STATEMENT ONLY FOR DISP=NEW DATASETS. IF ONE OF THE FOLLOWING
* CONDITIONS IS TRUE:
*       * THE BLKSIZE IS OMITTED;
*       * THE BLKSIZE IS NOT A MULTIPLE OF THE LRECL SPECIFIED IN THE
*         DCB MACRO;
*       * THE BLKSIZE IS LESS A PREDEFINED MINIMUM;
* THEN REGISTER 15 IS SET WITH A NON-ZERO RC TO INDICATE THAT THE
* SPECIFIED BLKSIZE IS TO BE REPLACED WITH THE DEFAULT BLKSIZE.
***********************************************************************
*
VALBLKSZ    LA        R10,JFCB                 SET ADRBLTY FOR JFCB DSECT
            LA        R11,FILEDCB              SET ADRBLTY FOR DCB DSECT
            TM        JFCBIND2,JFCNEW          CHK IF DISP=NEW ON JCL STMT
            BO        NEWDS                    IF YES, CHK BLKSZ
            LA        R15,0                    IF NO, INDICATE BLKSZ OK
            BR        R6                       RETURN TO CALLING RTN
NEWDS       CLC       JFCBLKSI,BINZEROS        CHK IF BLKSZ IN JCL
            BNE       CHKBSZ1                  IF YES, CHK IT
            LA        R15,4                    IF NO, IND BLKSZ MOD REQR
            BR        R6                       RETURN TO CALLING RTN
CHKBSZ1     LH        R15,JFCBLKSI             LOAD R15 WITH BLKSZ FROM JCL
            LA        R14,0                    SET R14 TO ZERO FOR DR INSTR
            LH        R12,DCBLRECL             LOAD R12 WITH LRECL FROM PROG
            DR        R14,R12                  DIVIDE LRECL INTO BLKSZ
            LTR       R14,R14                  CHK IF BLKSZ MULT OF LRECL (REMDR=0)
            BZ        CHKBSZ2                  IF YES, CHK MIN BLKSZ
            LA        R15,4                    IF NO, IND BLKSZ MOD REQR
            BR        R6                       RETURN TO CALLING RTN
CHKBSZ2     CLC       JFCBLKSI,MINBLKSZ        COMP JCL BLKSZ TO MIN BLKSZ
            BNL       BLKSZOK                  OK, IF JCL BLKSZ EQ OR GT MIN BLKSZ
            LA        R15,4                    IF LT MIN, IND BLKSZ MOD REQR
```

```
         BR    R6                       RETURN TO CALLING RTN
BLKSZOK  LA    R15,0                    IND BLKSZ OK
         BR    R6                       RETURN TO CALLING RTN
*
*
***********************************************************************
* THIS ROUTINE MODIFIES THE JFCB IF REQUIRED (RC IN REGISTER 15 IS
* NON-ZERO). IF REQUIRED, THE DEFAULT BLKSIZE IS PUT INTO THE JFCB
* AND OVERRIDES THE ONE SPECIFIED IN THE JCL (IF ANY).
***********************************************************************
*
MDFYJFCB LTR   R15,R15                  CHK IF BLKSZ MOD REQUIRED
         BZR   R6                       IF NO, RET TO CALLING RTN
         MVC   JFCBLKSI,DFLTBSZ         IF YES, USE DEFAULT BLKSZ
         BR    R6                       RETURN TO CALLING RTN
*
*
***********************************************************************
* THIS ROUTINE OPENS THE DCB. IF THE RC IN REGISTER 15 IS NON-ZERO,
* THEN THE PROGRAMMER-SUPPLIED JFCB IS USED WITH THE NEW BLKSIZE.
***********************************************************************
*
OPEN     LTR   R15,R15                  CHK IF BLKSZ MOD REQUIRED
         BNZ   OPENJ                    IF YES, USE MOD JFCB FOR OPEN
         OPEN  (FILEDCB,(OUTPUT))
         B     CHKOPEN
OPENJ    OPEN  (FILEDCB,(OUTPUT)),TYPE=J
         B     CHKOPEN
CHKOPEN  TM    DCBOFLGS,DCBOFOPN        CHK FOR GOOD OPEN
         BNO   OPENBAD                  IF NOT 1, OPEN UNSUCCESSFUL
         BR    R6                       RETURN TO CALLING RTN
OPENBAD  WTO   '*** OPEN ERROR FOR FILEDD ***',ROUTCDE=11
         ABEND 902
*
*
***********************************************************************
* THIS ROUTINE DOES THE ACTUAL PROCESSING.
***********************************************************************
*
PROCESS  ...
         BR    R6                       RETURN TO CALLING RTN
*
*
***********************************************************************
* THIS ROUTINE RESTORES THE REGISTERS AND RETURNS CONTROL.
***********************************************************************
*
RETURN   RCNTL RC=0                     RETURN TO MVS OR CALLING PROG
*
*
***********************************************************************
* CONSTANTS
***********************************************************************
*
BINZEROS DC    H'0'
MINBLKSZ DC    H'4080'                  MINIMUM BLKSIZE
DFLTBSZ  DC    H'4080'                  DEFAULT BLKSIZE
*
*
***********************************************************************
* THE JFCB-LIST AND THE DCB
***********************************************************************
*
JFCB     DS    44F
```

```
JFCBPTR      DC        X'87'
             DC        AL3(JFCB)
*
FILEDCB      DCB       DSORG=PS,MACRF=PM,EXLST=JFCBPTR,DDNAME=FILEDD, -
                       LRECL=80,RECFM=FB
*
*
***********************************************************************
* THE DSECTS
***********************************************************************
*
             DSECT
             IEFJFCBN                         GENERATES JFCB DSECT
*
             DCBD      DSORG=PS               GENERATES PS-DCB DSECT
*
*
***********************************************************************
* END OF PROGRAM
***********************************************************************
*
             END
```

Coding Example 7.1.4

This coding example illustrates how to OPEN the VTOC and read the DSCBs. The "dataset name" of the VTOC is 44 consecutive X'04's. This character string is inserted into the dataset-name field of the JFCB before issuing the OPEN macro instruction. In this example, BSAM is used to read each DSCB of the VTOC. Only the format-1 DSCBs (the ones that contain the dataset name) are processed. The total length of a DSCB is 140 bytes. The first set of 44 bytes is the key area of the record (contains the dataset name for a format-1 DSCB), and the last set of 96 bytes is the data area of the record. In this example, QSAM cannot be used to read the VTOC because it reads only the 96-byte data area, but the entire record (key area plus data area) is required.

```
READVTOC     CSECT
*
*
***********************************************************************
* INITIALIZATION
***********************************************************************
*
             INITL     3,EQU=R                INITIALIZE PROGRAM
             USING     INFMJFCB,R10           DEFINE REG FOR JFCB DSECT
             USING     IECSDSF1,R11           DEFINE REG FOR DSCB-1 DSECT
*
*
***********************************************************************
* MAINSTREAM OF PROGRAM
***********************************************************************
*
             BAL       R6,RDJFCB              READ JFCB INTO PROG AREA
             BAL       R6,MDFYJFCB            MODIFY JFCB WITH VTOC NAME
             BAL       R6,OPEN                OPEN VTOC
NEXTDSCB     BAL       R6,READVTOC            READ A DSCB
             BAL       R6,PROCESS             PROCESS FORMAT-1 DSCBS
             B         NEXTDSCB               READ NEXT DSCB
DSCBEND      BAL       R6,CLOSE               CLOSE VTOC
             B         RETURN                 RETURN TO MVS OR CALLING PROG
*
*
```

```
************************************************************************
* THIS ROUTINE READS THE JFCB AND COPIES IT FROM THE SWA INTO THE
* PROGRAMMER-SUPPLIED AREA.
************************************************************************
*
RDJFCB    RDJFCB   VTOCDCB
          LTR      R15,R15                CHK IF DD STMT IN JCL
          BNZ      NODD                   IF RC NOT 0, DD STMT MISSING
          BR       R6                     RETURN TO CALLING RTN
NODD      WTO      '*** VTOCDD NOT SPECIFIED IN JCL ***',ROUTCDE=11
          ABEND    901
*
*
************************************************************************
* THIS ROUTINE MODIFIES THE JFCB. THE DATASET NAME OF THE VTOC IS PUT
* INTO THE DATASET-NAME FIELD OF THE JFCB.
************************************************************************
*
MDFYJFCB  LA       R10,JFCB               SET ADRBLTY FOR JFCB DSECT
          MVC      JFCBDSNM,VTOCNAME      PUT VTOC LABEL INTO JFCB DSNAME
*                                         FIELD
          BR       R6                     RETURN TO CALLING RTN
*
*
************************************************************************
* THIS ROUTINE OPENS THE VTOC BY USING THE MODIFIED JFCB SUPPLIED
* BY THE PROGRAMMER.
************************************************************************
*
OPEN      OPEN     VTOCDCB,TYPE=J
          ...                             CHECK FOR GOOD OPEN
          BR       R6                     RETURN TO CALLING RTN
*
*
************************************************************************
* THIS ROUTINE READS DSCBS FROM THE VTOC AND CHECKS THEIR TYPE. ONLY
* FORMAT-1 DSCBS ARE RETURNED TO THE CALLING ROUTINE.
************************************************************************
*
READVTOC  LA       R11,DSCB               SET ADRBLTY FOR DSCB-1 DSECT
          READ     VTOCDECB,SF,VTOCDCB,(R11)   READ A DSCB
          CHECK    VTOCDECB               CHECK FOR GOOD READ
          CLI      DS1FMTID,C'1'          CHECK IF FORMAT-1 DSCB
          BNE      READVTOC               IF NO, READ ANOTHER DSCB
          BR       R6                     IF YES, RET TO CALLING RTN
*
*
************************************************************************
* THIS ROUTINE PROCESSES THE FORMAT-1 DSCBS.
************************************************************************
*
PROCESS   DS       0H
          ...                             PROCESS FORMAT-1 DSCB
          BR       R6                     RETURN TO CALLING RTN
*
*
************************************************************************
* THIS ROUTINE CLOSES THE VTOC DCB.
************************************************************************
*
CLOSE     CLOSE    VTOCDCB
          BR       R6                     RETURN TO CALLING RTN
*
*
```

```
***********************************************************************
* THIS ROUTINE RESTORES THE REGISTERS AND RETURNS CONTROL.
***********************************************************************
*
RETURN     RCNTL     RC=0                      RETURN TO MVS OR CALLING PROG
*
*
***********************************************************************
* DC/DS STATEMENTS
***********************************************************************
*
VTOCNAME   DC        44XL1'04'                 THE LABEL OF THE VTOC
DSCB       DS        CL140
*
*
***********************************************************************
* THE JFCB-LIST AND THE DCB
***********************************************************************
*
JFCB       DS        44F
JFCBPTR    DC        X'87'
           DC        AL3(JFCB)
*
VTOCDCB    DCB       DSORG=PS,MACRF=R,EXLST=JFCBPTR,EODAD=DSCBEND,  -
                     KEYLEN=44,BLKSIZE=96,LRECL=96,RECFM=F,DDNAME=VTOCDD
*
*
***********************************************************************
* THE DSECTS
***********************************************************************
*
           DSECT
           IEFJFCBN                  GENERATES DSECT FOR JFCB
*
           DSECT
           IECSDSL1  1               GENERATES DSECT FOR FORMAT-1 DSCB
*
*
***********************************************************************
* END OF PROGRAM
***********************************************************************
*
           END
```

NOTES:

- A Volume Table of Contents (VTOC) is located on each DASD volume. The VTOC is a dataset that describes the contents of the DASD volume. The VTOC contains records called DataSet Control Blocks (DSCBs). There are seven DSCB types or formats, format-0 through format-6. The format-1 DSCB contains the dataset name and various information about the dataset, such as DCB attributes, beginning and ending DASD locations (CCHHR) of the first three extents on the volume, and so forth. All DSCB records are 140 bytes in length. The first 44 bytes is the key area and the remaining 96 bytes is the data area. The 44-byte key area of a format-1 DSCB contains the dataset name. The sequence of the dataset names in the VTOC is in the sequence in which the dataset is allocated except when a dataset is deleted (format-1 DSCB becomes a format-0 DSCB), in which case that DSCB is reused. When a DASD volume is initialized, a VTOC Index may optionally be requested. One of the functions of the VTOC Index is to provide the means to perform a quicker search for a specific format-1 DSCB. The VTOC may also be read serially until the required DSCB is located. IBM provides various macro instructions to read and update the

VTOC, such as the DADSM/CAMLST series of macro instructions and the CVAF series of macro instructions.
- This example shows how to read the DSCBs of the VTOC serially without using any of the IBM-provided VTOC access macro instructions.

7.2 DYNAMIC ALLOCATION (SVC 99)

Allocating datasets using dynamic allocation is more flexible than the JFCB modification method, but also requires more coding. Unlike the JFCB modification method, dynamic allocation requires no JCL DD statements, allocates units as well as datasets, and can perform additional functions. However, dynamic allocation is not intended to be a replacement for processing the JFCB since this technique offers functions that dynamic allocation cannot perform, such as examining specified JCL DD statements and changing them as required.

The term dynamic allocation is actually the name used for SVC 99. However, SVC 99 has additional functions. The following are the functions that are provided by SVC 99:

- Dynamic allocation;
- Dynamic unallocation;
- Dynamic concatenation;
- Dynamic deconcatenation; and
- Dynamic information retrieval.

Performing dynamic allocation via SVC 99 is the most widely used function and the most involved to code. SVC 99 may be used in a time-sharing environment and in a batch environment. The use of SVC 99 in time-sharing and batch environments are the same, but some additional facilities are available that enable the use of SVC 99 to be more efficient in a time-sharing environment.

ADVANTAGES AND DISADVANTAGES OF USING SVC 99

Since dynamic allocation (SVC 99) allocates and deallocates dynamically, it may be used to enable programs to use resources more efficiently, which may increase availability and throughput.

One type of job that will benefit from the use of SVC 99 is one that executes programs that require temporary use of resources for which there is heavy contention (high activity datasets, DASD work space, tape drives, etc.). SVC 99 provides the facility for a program to allocate these resources for only the duration in which they are actually required (instead of the entire life of the jobstep as with JCL allocation) and then to release (unallocate) them in order to make them available for other jobs while the original job continues to execute.

Another type of job that will benefit from the use of SVC 99 is one that executes programs whose resource requirements are large and may vary from execution to execution. The typical method of running this type of job would be to allocate all possible required resources via JCL. This may require numerous tape drives, hugh amounts of DASD work space, exclusive use of datasets, and so forth. Some or most of these resources may never be used during the job, but would be allocated and, therefore, unavailable for use by other jobs. The resources required for a particular run for this type of job are known when the program starts to execute and examines its input data, parameters, and so on. Therefore, the data center's resources would be used more efficiently if the program used

SVC 99 to allocate only the resources that it determines are required for each particular run and let the unrequired resources be available for use by other jobs.

The use of the JCL DD parameter FREE=CLOSE may be used to unallocate a dataset that was allocated via JCL when it is no longer required by the program, but using this method requires additional planning and consideration. Using this method requires that the CLOSE macro instruction be placed in the proper location in the program to cause the dataset to be unallocated when it is no longer required. After the dataset is CLOSEd, it cannot be OPENed and reused again unless it is dynamically allocated (and available). Also, if the dataset is not required for a particular run, then the dataset is required to be OPENed and CLOSEd to unallocate it. In this case, the unrequired dataset would be allocated between the time of step initiation and CLOSE. Using SVC 99, unrequired datasets are not allocated at all.

Allocating and unallocating via SVC 99 is not always an advantage. If a required resource is known before execution and is used for the entire (or most of the) life of the program execution, then little or nothing is gained by dynamic allocation/unallocation. In this case, the disadvantages would be the additional time and effort required to develop the code for the SVC 99 requests as well as the lack of JCL DD statements in the JCL stream necessitating additional documentaion and/or the need to examine the program source to determine what datasets are being used.

SVC 99 ATTRIBUTES

SVC 99 provides some attributes (control features), most of which are applicable in a time-sharing environment, but may be used in a batch environment. The attributes are the following:

`In-Use Attribute` — The in-use attribute is automatically turned on when a dataset is allocated dynamically or via JCL. In a time-sharing environment (TSO/ISPF/PDF, etc.), the Terminal Monitor Propram (TMP) turns off the in-use attribute of all datasets that were dynamically allocated by a command processor (Edit, etc.), when that command processor terminates. Turning off the in-use attribute does not unallocate the dataset. When the same or another command processor receives control from the TMP and requests dymanic allocation of a dataset that is allocated with the in-use attribute off, the in-use attribute is turned on (by SVC 99) and the dataset is made available without the overhead of another allocation. Allocated datasets with the in-use attribute off (the longest) will be unallocated automatically by SVC 99 to satisfy other allocation requests when the *control limit* is exceeded. The control limit is a mechanism used to control the amount of dynamic allocations that may be active at any one time during a jobstep or a TSO logon session. The control limit is specified by the user and is the sum of the number specified by the JCL EXEC DYNAMNBR parameter and the number of step JCL DD statements. The maximum value is 1635.

`Permanently Allocated Attribute` — This attribute is automatically assigned to a dataset when it is allocated via JCL and optionally assigned (by user) via dynamic allocation. This attribute prevents SVC 99 from automatically unallocating a dataset that has the in-use attribute off in order the satisfy the control limit when allocating another dataset.

`Permanently Concatenated Attribute` — This attribute is automatically assigned to a concatenation dataset group when allocated via JCL and optionally assigned (by user) via dynamic concatenation. A concatenated dataset group with this attribute cannot be dynamically deconcatenated into its individual datasets. This is particularly useful if one concatenated group is concatenated with other datasets to form a new (and larger) non-permanently concatenated group. If the smaller concatenation group is to remain concatenated when the new concatenation group is dynamically deconcatenated, then the smaller concatenation group is concatenated with the permanently concatenated attribute. To unallocate all the datasets of a permanently concatenated group requires the specification of the ddname (instead of dataset names) with the unallocation request.

REQUESTING SERVICES FROM SVC 99

The functions of SVC 99 are requested by passing it a parameter-list containing a Request Block pointer, a Request Block, a Text Unit Pointer list, and one or more Text Units. Figure 7.2.1 shows the structure of the SVC 99 parameter-list.

The Request Block contains various information that controls the SVC 99 request. It contains information such as the type of request (allocation, unallocation, etc.), pointer to the Text Units, various flag bits that control how requests are satisfied, and areas for feedback information from SVC 99.

The Text Unit Pointer list points to all the Text Units required for a particular SVC 99 request. The list is composed of consecutive fullwords, each of which points to a different Text Unit.

The Text Units are variable length areas with multiple fields that define a discreet piece of information (such as an individual JCL parameter) required by SVC 99 to satisfy the request. For example, for a dynamic allocation request, many Text Units would be defined. Each one would define a different JCL parameter (such as dataset name, disposition, etc.) and its corresponding value. Collectively, the Text Units define all the required JCL parameters to allocate a dataset.

IBM provides a number of macro instructions to assist in the use of SVC 99. The DYNALLOC macro instruction invokes SVC 99. The macro instruction requires no operands. The parameter-list must be built and register 1 must be loaded with the address of the Request Block Pointer before DYNALLOC is issued. The macro instruction IEFZB4D0 generates DSECTS for mapping the Request Block Pointer, Request Block, Text Unit Pointer list, and the Text Units, as well as EQU symbols for the parameters specified for the Request Block. The macro instruction IEFZB4D2 generates EQU symbols for the various Text Unit keys (DSN, DISP, etc.) for each Request Block verb code (allocation, etc.).

SVC 99 PARAMETER-LIST

The structure of the SVC 99 parameter-list is illustrated in Figure 7.2.1.

The following is a description of the fields in the SVC 99 parameter-list. The names in parentheses, that follow the field names, are the field names defined in the DSECTs generated by the IEFZB4D0 macro instruction. The number following the comma after the DSECT field name is the length of the field:

`Register 1` — Register 1 must be loaded with the address of the Request Block pointer before SVC 99 receives control.

`Request Block Pointer (DSECT Name is S99RBPTR,4)` — This is a fullword that contains the address of the Request Block. The high order bit must be set to one.

Request Block (DSECT Name is S99RB,20)	The format and contents of the Request Block is as follows:
Length (S99RBLN,1)	The length of the Request Block. The length is 20 (X'14') bytes for all requests.
Verb (S99VERB,1)	The verb code that indicates the type of request. The verb codes are as follows:
X'01'	Dataset Allocation (S99VRBAL)
X'02'	Unallocation (S99VRBUN)

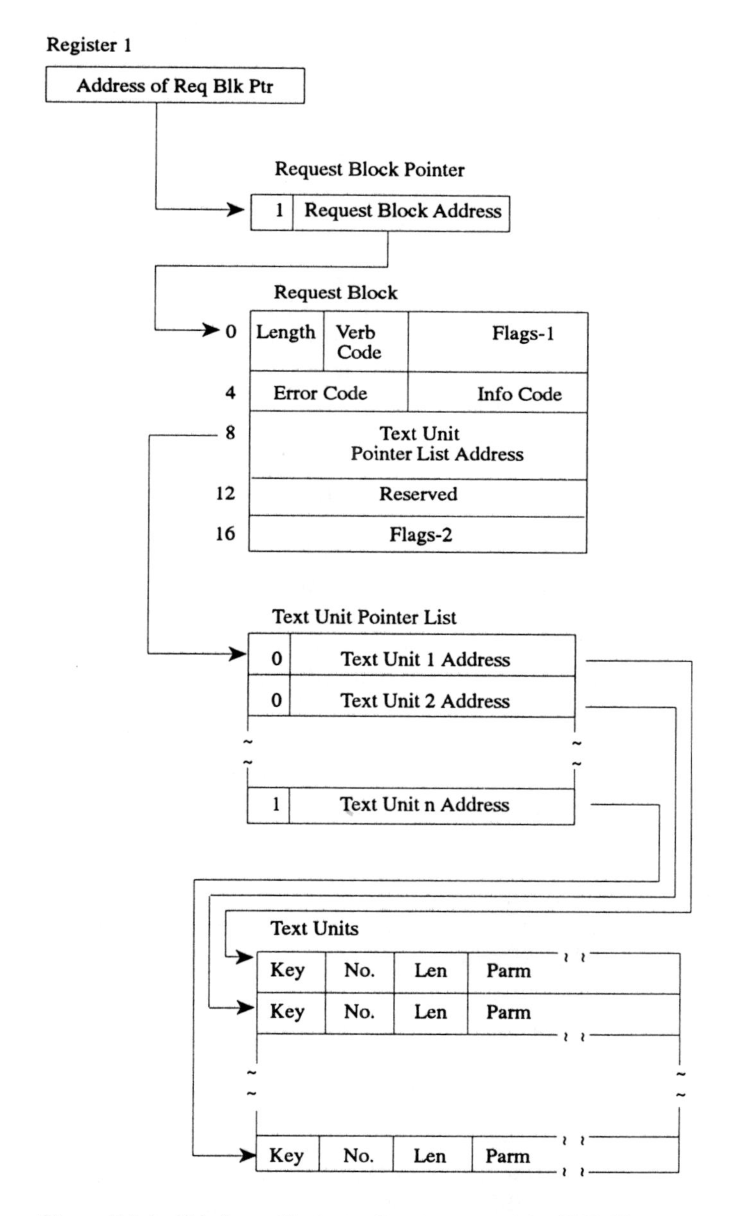

Figure 7.2.1. This figure illustrates the structure of the SVC 99 parameter-list.

X'03'	Concatenation (S99VRBCC)
X'04'	Deconcatenation (S99VRBDC)
X'05'	Remove In-Use Attribute (S99VRBRI)
X'06'	Ddname Allocation (S99VRBDN)
X'07'	Information Retrieval (S99VRBIN)
Flags-1 (S99FLAG1,2)	Used to indicate how dataset allocation is satisfied.
Error Code (S99ERROR,2)	Area in which SVC 99 returns an error reason code if the request was unsuccessful.
Information Code (S99INFO,2)	Area in which SVC 99 returns an information reason code to provide futher information about an error.
Text Unit Pointer List Address (S99TXTPP,4)	The address of the Text Unit Pointer list.
Flags-2 (S99FLGS2,4)	Used to request authorized functions.
Text Unit Pointer List (DSECT name is S99TUPL)	This is a list of fullwords. Each fullword contains the address of a Text Unit. The name in the DSECT used for a Text Unit Pointer is S99TUPTR. The end of the list is indicated by the high order bit of the last address being set to one.
Text Units (DSECT Name is S99TUNIT, Variable)	Each Text Unit has the fields key, number, length, and parameter. The contents of the fields depends on the key specified, and the selection of the key depends upon the verb code indicated in the Request Block.
Key (S99TUKEY,2)	Indicates the kind of information that is contained in the parameter field of the Text Unit, such as ddname, dataset name, volser, and so on. A list of text unit keys are generated by the IEFZB4D2 macro instruction and is also contained in the appropriate IBM manual as described in the Bibliography at the end of this Chapter.
Number (S99TUNUM,2)	Indicates the number of length/parameter entries that are contained in the Text Unit. This field normally contains one, but some keys (such as DASD space units, etc.) require no parameter and, therefore, length/parameter number of zero. Some keys (such as volser) may require multiple parameters (more than one serial number), in which case this field may indicate a value of two or more.
Length (S99TULNG,2)	Indicates the length of the parameter that follows.
Parameter (S99TUPAR,var)	Contains the actual parameter in the Text Unit

GENERAL PROCEDURE FOR USING SVC 99

In order to request the services of SVC 99, the following procedure should be followed:

- Determine all the parameters that are required for the request and then define a Text Unit for each parameter. The Text Unit keys should be specified by using the EQU symbols generated by the IEFZB4D2 macro instruction.
- Create the Text Unit Pointer list. This is a series of consecutive fullwords. Each contains the address of one of the Text Units. The Text Unit addresses may be specified in any

sequence. The high order bit of the last fullword address must be set to one to indicate the end of the list.

- Construct the SVC 99 Request Block or modify an existing one. Specify the following required fields:

  - The verb code of the request type (allocation, unallocation, etc.). The verb code should be specified by using the EQU symbols generated by the IEFZB4D0 macro instruction.
  - The length of the Request Block (S99RBEND-S99RB).
  - The address of the beginning of the Text Unit Pointer List.
  - Set the Flags-1 and Flags-2 fields as required. Usually these fields are set to zeros.

- Define a fullword for the Request Block Pointer and load into it the address of the beginning of the Request Block. The high order bit is required to be turned on to indicate that the Request Block address is the only address being specified.
- Load the address of the Request Block Pointer into register 1.
- Issue the DYNALLOC macro instruction.
- Check the return code posted in register 15, and the error/information reason codes posted in the Request Block, if applicable.

7.2.1 Dynamic Allocation

A dataset may be dynamically allocated by the dataset name method (verb code X'01') or by the ddname method (verb code X'06'). The first time that a dataset is allocated, it must be allocated by the dataset name method. The ddnames JOBLIB, STEPLIB, JOBCAT, and STEPCAT may not be used for a dynamic allocation request.

DYNAMIC ALLOCATION VIA DATASET NAME

In order to allocate a dataset using SVC 99, the general procedure, as outlined above, should be followed. In addition, the specific requirements for dynamic allocation are as follows:

- Determine all the JCL parameters that are required for the allocation. Then, define a Text Unit for each parameter. For a new DASD dataset, unlike JCL, SVC 99 provides a default for the SPACE parameter if it is not specified. The default is SPACE=(1000,(10, 50),RLSE). Also, unlike JCL, the ddname is not required. If the ddname is specified, it must be different from other ddnames currently allocated either via JCL or via SVC 99. If the ddname is not specified, then SVC 99 generates a ddname prefixed by SYS and followed by a 5-digit number. If the generated ddname is required, it may be obtained by using the information retrieval facility of SVC 99.
- Some parameters could be hard-coded in the program and others may need to be determined after the program starts to execute. A good example is dataset name. If only the same dataset is required to be dyamically allocated, then its name may be hard-coded in the program. However, if the dataset name(s) is not known and may vary from execution to execution, then the dataset name would need to be dynamically built based upon control statements, processing requirements, and so forth. In this case, to facilitate that processing, a label should be associated with the dataset length field and dataset name field of the appropriate Text Unit. Labels should also be associated with other Text Unit fields that are to receive values dynamically.
- Specify a verb code of X'01' (S99VRBAL) in the Request Block.
- Set the Flags-1 and Flags-2 fields as required. Usually, these fields are set to zeros.

Coding Example 7.2.1

Consider the following JCL DD statement.

```
//DD1 DD DSN=USER.NEWDATA,DISP=(NEW,CATLG),UNIT=SYSDA,VOL=SER=123456,
//       DCB=(BLKSIZE=4080,LRECL=80,RECFM=FB),SPACE=(CYL,(10,1),,RLSE)
```

This coding example illustrates how to allocate the same dataset using the dynamic allocation function of SVC 99.

```
SVC99ALO  CSECT
*
*
***********************************************************************
* INITIALIZATION
***********************************************************************
*
          INITL    3,EQU=R                 INITIALIZE PROGRAM
          USING    S99RBP,R10              DEFINE REG FOR REQ BLK PTR DSECT
          USING    S99RB,R11               DEFINE REG FOR REQ BLOCK DSECT
*
*
***********************************************************************
* MAINSTREAM OF PROGRAM
***********************************************************************
*
          BAL      R6,SETRB001             SETUP RB FOR ALLOC
          BAL      R6,SETRBPTR             SETUP RB PTR
          BAL      R6,DOSVC99              ISSUE SVC 99
          B        RETURN                  RETURN TO MVS OR CALLING PROG
*
*
***********************************************************************
* THIS ROUTINE SETS UP THE SVC99 REQUEST BLOCK.
***********************************************************************
*
SETRB001  LA       R11,REQBLK              SET ADRBLTY FOR RB DSECT
          XC       REQBLK,REQBLK           CLEAR RB
          MVI      S99RBLN,REQBLKLN        SET RB LEN
          MVI      S99VERB,S99VRBAL        SET ALLOCATION VERB
          LA       R10,TUPTR001            LD ADR OF BG OF TEXT-UNIT-PTR LIST
          ST       R10,S99TXTPP            STORE THAT ADR INTO RB
          BR       R6                      RETURN TO CALLING RTN
*
*
***********************************************************************
* THIS ROUTINE SETS UP THE SVC99 REQUEST-BLOCK-POINTER.
***********************************************************************
*
SETRBPTR  LA       R10,RBPTR               SET ADRBLTY FOR RBPTR DSECT
          LA       R11,REQBLK              LD ADR OF RB
          ST       R11,S99RBPTR            STORE RB ADR INTO RB PTR
          OI       S99RBPTR,S99RBPND       TURN ON HIGH ORDER BIT
          BR       R6                      RETURN TO CALLING RTN
*
*
***********************************************************************
* THIS ROUTINE ISSUES SVC 99 VIA THE DYNALLOC MACRO.
***********************************************************************
*
DOSVC99   LA       R1,RBPTR                LD ADR OF RB PTR INTO R1 FOR SVC 99
          DYNALLOC                         ISSUE SVC 99
```

```
             LTR       R15,R15                 CHK RC
             BNZ       CHKERR                  IF NOT ZERO, CHK ERROR/INFO FIELDS
             BR        R6                      IF OK, RETURN TO CALLING RTN
CHKERR       ...
*
*
*************************************************************************
* THIS ROUTINE RESTORES THE REGISTERS AND RETURNS
*************************************************************************
*
RETURN       RCNTL     RC=0                    RETURN TO MVS OR CALLING PROG
*
*
*************************************************************************
* SVC99 REQ-BLOCK-POINTER AND REQUEST BLOCK
*************************************************************************
*
RBPTR        DS        F
REQBLK       DS        CL(S99RBEND-S99RB)
REQBLKLN     EQU       L'REQBLK
*
*
*************************************************************************
* TEXT-UNITS-POINTERS LIST
*************************************************************************
*
TUPTR001     DS        0F
             DC        A(TUDDNA1)              ADR OF TU FOR DDNAME
             DC        A(TUDSNA1)              ADR OF TU FOR DSNAME
             DC        A(TUDSSA1)              ADR OF TU FOR DS STATUS
             DC        A(TUDNDA1)              ADR OF TU FOR DS NORM TERM DISP
             DC        A(TUUNTA1)              ADR OF TU FOR UNIT
             DC        A(TUVOLA1)              ADR OF TU FOR VOLSER
             DC        A(TUBLKA1)              ADR OF TU FOR DCB BLKSZ
             DC        A(TULRLA1)              ADR OF TU FOR DCB LRECL
             DC        A(TURFMA1)              ADR OF TU FOR DCB RECFM
             DC        A(TUCYLA1)              ADR OF TU FOR SPACE IN CYL
             DC        A(TUPRMA1)              ADR OF TU FOR PRIM SPACE
             DC        A(TUSECA1)              ADR OF TU FOR SEC SPACE
             DC        X'80'                   INDICATES LAST TU ADDRESS
             DC        AL3(TURLSA1)            ADR OF TU FOR SPACE RLSE
*
*
*************************************************************************
* TEXT UNITS
*************************************************************************
*
TUDDNA1      DC        AL2(DALDDNAM)           TU KEY FOR DDNAME
             DC        AL2(1)                  NUMBER OF ENTRIES
             DC        AL2(8)                  LENGTH OF DDNAME
             DC        CL8'DD1'                DDNAME
*
TUDSNA1      DC        AL2(DALDSNAM),AL2(1),AL2(44),CL44'USER.NEWDATA'
TUDSSA1      DC        AL2(DALSTATS),AL2(1),AL2(1),X'04'
TUDNDA1      DC        AL2(DALNDISP),AL2(1),AL2(1),X'02'
TUUNTA1      DC        AL2(DALUNIT),AL2(1),AL2(5),C'SYSDA'
TUVOLA1      DC        AL2(DALVLSER),AL2(1),AL2(6),C'123456'
TUBLKA1      DC        AL2(DALBLKSZ),AL2(1),AL2(2),AL(4080)
TULRLA1      DC        AL2(DALLRECL),AL2(1),AL2(2),AL2(80)
TURFMA1      DC        AL2(DALRECFM),AL2(1),AL2(1),X'90'
TUCYLA1      DC        AL2(DALCYL),AL2(0)
TUPRMA1      DC        AL2(DALPRIME),AL2(1),AL2(3),AL3(10)
TUSECA1      DC        AL2(DALSECND),AL2(1),AL2(3),AL3(1)
TURLSA1      DC        AL2(DASPFRM),AL2(0)
```

```
*
*
***********************************************************************
* THE DSECTS
***********************************************************************
*
         IEFZB4D0          GENS DSECT FOR REQ BLOCK, TEXT UNIT, ETC.
         IEFZB4D2          GENS TABLE OF EQUATES FOR TU KEYS
*
*
***********************************************************************
* END OF PROGRAM
***********************************************************************
*
         END
```

NOTES:

- The lengths of the ddname and the dsname values in the Text Unit may be specified as 8 and 44, respectively, or as the actual length. If the maximum length is specified, then the ddname and the dsname must be padded with low order blanks. If these names are built dynamically, then the area that is to contain them should be defined as maximum length to accommodate any required value.

DYNAMIC ALLOCATION VIA DDNAME

Allocating a dataset via ddname is normally used in a time-sharing environment. This method allocates a dataset that was previously allocated and has been marked not-in-use (in-use attribute bit off). A ddname allocation sets the in-use attribute bit on. The only required Text Unit is one that contains the ddname.

Coding Example 7.2.2

This coding example illustrates how to allocate the not-in-use dataset that was previously allocated with the ddname DD1.

```
***********************************************************************
* THIS ROUTINE SETS UP THE SVC99 REQUEST BLOCK.
***********************************************************************
*
SETRB002 ...
         MVI   S99VERB,S99VRBDN        SET DDNAME ALLO VERB
         LA    R10,TUPTR002            LD ADR OF BG OF TEXT-UNIT-PTR LIST
         ST    R10,S99TXTPP            STORE THAT ADR INTO RB
         BR    R6                      RETURN TO CALLING RTN
*
*
***********************************************************************
* TEXT-UNITS-POINTERS LIST
***********************************************************************
*
TUPTR002 DS    0F
         DC    X'80'                   INDICATES LAST TU ADDRESS
         DC    AL3(TUDDNA2)            ADR OF TU FOR DDNAME FOR RE-ALLO
*
*
***********************************************************************
* TEXT UNIT
***********************************************************************
*
```

```
TUDDNA2     DC      AL2(DDNDDNAM)           TU KEY FOR DDNAME ALLO
            DC      AL2(1)                  NUMBER OF ENTRIES
            DC      AL2(3)                  LENGTH OF DDNAME
            DC      C'DD1'                  DDNAME
```

7.2.2 Dynamic Unallocation

A dataset may be dynamically unallocated by specifying either the dataset name or the ddname that was specified (or assigned by the system) when the dataset was allocated. The dataset may have been allocated via JCL or dynamically. Also, the dataset must be CLOSEd or the unallocation request will fail.

In order to unallocate a dataset using SVC 99, the general procedure, as outlined above, should be followed. In addition, the specific requirements for dynamic unallocation are as follows:

- Define a Text Unit containing either the dataset name of the dataset that is to be unallocated or the ddname associated with that dataset.
- Specify a verb code of X'02' (S99VRBUN) in the Request Block.

Coding Example 7.2.3

This coding example illustrates how to dynamically unallocate a dataset that was previously dynamically allocated with the ddname SYS00009.

```
***************************************************************************
* THIS ROUTINE SETS UP THE SVC99 REQUEST BLOCK.
***************************************************************************
*
SETRB003    ...
            MVI     S99VERB,S99VRBUN        SET UNALLOCATION VERB
            LA      R10,TUPTR003            LD ADR OF BG OF TEXT-UNIT-PRT LIST
            ST      R10,S99TXTPP            STORE THAT ADR INTO RB
            BR      R6                      RETURN TO CALLING RTN
*
*
***************************************************************************
* TEXT-UNITS-POINTERS LIST
***************************************************************************
*
TUPTR003    DS      OF
            DC      X'80'                   INDICATES LAST TU ADDRESS
            DC      AL3(TUDDNU1)            ADR OF TU FOR UNALLO DDNAME
*
*
***************************************************************************
* TEXT UNIT
***************************************************************************
*
TUDDNU1     DC      AL2(DUNDDNAM)           TU KEY FOR DDNAME UNALLO
            DC      AL2(1)                  NUMBER OF ENTRIES
            DC      AL2(8)                  LENGTH OF DDNAME
            DC      C'SYS00009'             DDNAME
```

REMOVING THE IN-USE ATTRIBUTE

Instead of unallocating a dataset, the in-use attribute could be turned off. This would normally be done in a time-sharing environment in anticipation of a reallocation of the same dataset. There are two ways of turning off the in-use attribute bit.

One way is to remove the in-use attribute for individual datasets by specifying the DUNREMOV key in the Text Unit. This key has a length/parameter number of zero. Specifying this key with the ddname or dataset name Text Unit will cause the in-use attribute to be removed, but the dataset remains allocated.

Another way to remove the in-use attribute is by task. This method will remove the in-use attribute of all datasets associated with only the current task or with only the current task's subtasks. Using this method requires that the request be made via the verb code X'05' (S99VRBRI) in the Request Block. The Text Unit key DRITCBAD indicates that the in-use attribute should be removed for all datasets associated only with the current task, and the Text Unit key DRICURNT indicates that the in-use attribute should be removed from all datasets associated only with the subtasks of the current task. In both cases, the length field of the Text Unit is four, and the parameter field contains the TCB address of the current task.

7.2.3 Dynamic Concatenation

Datasets may be dynamically concatenated (logically connected) by specifying the ddnames associated with the datasets that are to be concatenated. The datasets must already be allocated either via JCL or dynamically and must all be CLOSEd, or the dynamic concatenation request will fail. One Text Unit is specified for all the ddnames. The number field of the Text Unit contains the number (must be at least two) of ddnames and each length/parameter field that follows contains a length and ddname. The datasets are concatenated in the same sequence as specified. The first ddname specified is the name associated with the concatenated group, and the other ddnames are no longer associated with any datasets. If any of the specified ddnames point to a concatenated group, then all those datasets become part of the new concatenated group.

In order to concatenate a group of datasets using SVC 99, the general procedure, as outlined above, should be followed. In addition, the specific requirements for dynamic concatenation are as follows:

- Determine all the datasets and their associated ddnames that are to be concatenated, the ddname of the concatenated group, the required sequence of the concatenation, and if the concatenation group is to have the permanently concatenated attribute.
- Define one Text Unit containing the ddnames, in the proper sequence, for all the datasets that are to be concatenated.
- Specify a verb code of X'03' (S99VRBCC) in the Request Block.

Coding Example 7.2.4

This coding example illustrates how to dynamically concatenate the datasets with the ddnames PRIVLIB, SYS00010, and TESTLIB (in that sequence). In the example, the ddname associated with the concatenated group is PRIVLIB, and the concatenated group is assigned the permanently concatenated attribute.

```
**************************************************************************
* THIS ROUTINE SETS UP THE SVC99 REQUEST BLOCK.
**************************************************************************
*
SETRB004    ...
            MVI      S99VERB,S99VRBCC        SET CONCATENATION VERB
```

```
         LA      R10,TUPTR004          LD BG ADR OF TEXT-UNIT-PTR LIST
         ST      R10,S99TXTPP          STORE THAT ADR INTO RB
         BR      R6                    RETURN TO CALLING RTN
*
*
***********************************************************************
* TEXT-UNITS-POINTERS LIST
***********************************************************************
*
TUPTR004 DS      0F
         DC      A(TUPCA)              ADR OF TU FOR PERM CONCAT ATTR
         DC      X'80'                 INDICATES LAST TU ADDRESS
         DC      AL3(TUDDNSC1)         ADR OF TU FOR CONCAT DDNAME LIST
*
*
***********************************************************************
* TEXT UNITS
***********************************************************************
*
TUPCA    DC      AL2(DCCPERMC)         TU KEY FOR PARM CONCAT ATTR
         DC      AL2(0)                NO LEN/PARM VALUE REQUIRED
*
TUDDNSC1 DC      AL2(DCCDDNAM)         TU KEY FOR DDNAME CONCAT
         DC      AL2(3)                NUMBER OF DDNAMES
         DC      AL2(7)                LENGTH OF 1ST DDNAME
         DC      C'PRIVLIB'            DDNAME-1, NAME ASSO WITH CONCAT GROUP
         DC      AL2(8)                LENGTH OF 2ND DDNAME
         DC      C'SYS00010'           DDNAME-2
         DC      AL2(7)                LENGTH OF 3RD DDNAME
         DC      C'TESTLIB'            DDNAME-3
```

7.2.4 Dynamic Deconcatenation

A previously dynamically concatenated dataset group may be deconcatenated by specifying the ddname associated with the group. The concatenated dataset group must be CLOSEd or the dynamic deconcatenation request will fail. After deconcatenation, the ddnames that were associated with the datasets before they were concatenated are restored unless this would result in duplicate ddnames, in which case the dynamic deconcatenation request would fail. This situation could be caused if one or more of the ddnames associated with the datasets of the concatenation group were used for a dynamic allocation request after the dynamic concatenation.

In order to deconcatenate the datasets of a concatenated group using SVC 99, the general procedure, as outlined above, should be followed. In addition, the specific requirements for dynamic deconcatenation are as follows:

- Determine ddname of the concatenated group that is to be deconcatenated.
- Define a Text Unit containing a ddname.
- Specify a verb code of X'04' (S99VRBDC) in the Request Block.

Coding Example 7.2.5

This coding example illustrates how to dynamically deconcatenate the datasets that are in the concatenated group with the ddname TESTLIB.

```
***********************************************************************
* THIS ROUTINE SETS UP THE SVC99 REQUEST BLOCK.
***********************************************************************
```

```
*
SETRB005    ...
            MVI       S99VERB,S99VRBDC          SET DECONCATENATION VERB
            LA        R10,TUPTR005              LD BG ADR OF TEXT-UNIT-PTR LIST
            ST        R10,S99TXTPP              STORE THAT ADR INTO RB
            BR        R6                        RETURN TO CALLING RTN
*
*
***********************************************************************
* TEXT-UNITS-POINTERS LIST
***********************************************************************
*
TUPTR005    DS        0F
            DC        X'80'                     INDICATES LAST TU ADDRESS
            DC        AL3(TUDDND1)              ADR OF TU FOR DECONCAT DDNAME
*
*
***********************************************************************
* TEXT UNIT
***********************************************************************
*
TUDDND1     DC        AL2(DDCDDNAM)             TU KEY FOR DDNAME DECAT
            DC        AL2(1)                    NUMBER OF ENTRIES
            DC        AL2(7)                    LENGTH OF DDNAME
            DC        C'TESTLIB'                DDNAME ASSO WITH CONCAT GROUP
```

7.2.5 Dynamic Information Retrieval

Dynamic information retrieval provides the facility to obtain information about the current allocation environment. The user may identify the dataset for which information is required by dataset name, ddname, or relative request number (first, second, etc., allocation request). Information may be retrieved for datasets allocated via JCL or dynamically. When a relative request number is used, the datasets requested via JCL will have lower numbers (since they were allocated first) than the datasets allocated dynamically.

The requested information is returned in the parameter field of the appropriate Text Unit and, therefore, the length of that field must be large enough to contain the largest expected value for the request. The length field of the Text Unit is posted with the actual length of the returned value.

Coding Example 7.2.6

This coding example illustrates how to dynamically retrieve the system-generated ddname of the dataset USER.WORK01. The returned ddname is placed in the paramater field (I1DDNAME) of the Text Unit with the key DINRTDDN.

```
***********************************************************************
* THIS ROUTINE SETS UP THE SVC99 REQUEST BLOCK.
***********************************************************************
*
SETRB006    ...
            MVI       S99VERB,S99VRBIN          SET DYNM INFOR RETRV VERB
            LA        R10,TUPTR006              LD BG ADR OF TEXT-UNIT-PTR LIST
            ST        R10,S99TXTPP              STORE THAT ADR INTO RB
            BR        R6                        RETURN TO CALLING RTN
*
*
***********************************************************************
* TEXT-UNITS-POINTERS LIST
***********************************************************************
```

```
*
TUPTR006    DS       0F
            DC       A(TUDSNI1)           ADR OF TU FOR SPECIFIED DSNAME
            DC       X'80'                INDICATES LAST TU ADDRESS
            DC       AL3(TURDDNI1)        ADR OF TU FOR RETURNED DDNAME
*
*
************************************************************************
* TEXT UNITS
************************************************************************
*
TUDSNI1     DC       AL2(DINDSNAM)        TU KEY FOR SPECIFIED DSNAME
            DC       AL2(1)               NUMBER OF ENTRIES
            DC       AL2(44)              LENGTH OF DSNAME
I1DSNAME    DC       CL44'USER.WORK01'    SPECIFIED DSNAME
*
TURDDNI1    DC       AL2(DINRTDDN)        TU KEY FOR RETURNED DDNAME
            DC       AL2(1)               NUMBER OF ENTRIES
            DS       CL2                  RETURNED LENGTH OF DDNAME
I1DDNAME    DS       CL8                  RETURNED DDNAME
```

Coding Example 7.2.7

This coding example illustrates how to dynamically retrieve the dataset name and associated ddname of each allocation request for the current job step. In this example, the relative request number is incremented from one to the last request. The last request is determined by specifying a Text Unit with the DINRTLST key. The parameter field of this Text Unit is posted with X'80' if the specified relative number was the last request; otherwise, an X'00' is returned. The datasets allocated via JCL will be returned first (since they were allocated first), followed by the datasets that were allocated dynamically.

```
SVC99INR    CSECT
*
*
************************************************************************
* INITIALIZATION
************************************************************************
*
            INITL    3,EQU=R              INITIALIZE PROGRAM
            USING    S99RBP,R10           DEFINE REG FOR REG BLK PTR DSECT
            USING    S99RB,R11            DEFINE REG FOR REQ BLOCK DSECT
*
*
************************************************************************
* MAINSTREAM OF PROGRAM
************************************************************************
*
            BAL      R6,SETRB007          SETUP RB FOR DYNM INFO RETV
            BAL      R6,SETRBPTR          SETUP RB PTR
NEXTINFO    BAL      R6,SETRELNO          INCR REL NO AND STORE INTO TU
            BAL      R6,DOSVC99           ISSUE SVC 99
            BAL      R6,RETVINFO          OBTAIN DDN/DSN INFO
            BAL      R6,PROCESS           PROCESS DDN/DSN INFO
            B        NEXTINFO             GET NEXT DDN/DSN INFO
INFOEND     B        RETURN               RETURN TO MVS OR CALLING PROG
*
*
************************************************************************
* THIS ROUTINE SETS UP THE SVC99 REQUEST BLOCK.
************************************************************************
*
SETRB007    LA       R11,REQBLK           SET ADRBLTY FOR RB DSECT
```

```
            XC       REQBLK,REQBLK          CLEAR RB
            MVI      S99RBLN,REQBLKLN       SET RB LEN
            MVI      S99VERB,S99VRBIN       SET DYNM INFO RETV VERB
            LA       R10,TUPTR007           LD ADR OF BG OF TEXT-UNIT-PTR LIST
            ST       R10,S99TXTPP           STORE THAT ADR INTO RB
            BR       R6                     RETURN TO CALLING RTN
*
*
***********************************************************************
* THIS ROUTINE SETS UP THE SVC99 REQUEST-BLOCK-POINTER.
***********************************************************************
*
SETRBPTR    LA       R10,RBPTR              SET ADRBLTY FOR RBPTR DSECT
            LA       R11,REQBLK             LD ADR OF RB
            ST       R11,S99RBPTR           STORE RB ADR INTO RB PTR
            OI       S99RBPTR,S99RBPND      TURN HIGH ORDER BIT
            BR       R6                     RETURN TO CALLING RTN
*
*
***********************************************************************
* THIS ROUTINE INCREMENTS THE RELATIVE NUMBER OF THE ALLOCATION AND
* STORES THE NEW RELATIVE NUMBER INTO THE RELATIVE-NUMBER TEXT UNIT
***********************************************************************
*
SETRELNO    L        R12,RELNO              LD LAST REL NUMB
            LA       R12,1(0,R12)           INCR REL NUMB
            ST       R12,RELNO              SAVE CUR REL NUMB
            ST       R12,I2RELNO            STORE CUR REL NUMB INTO TU
            BR       R6                     RETURN TO CALLING RTN
*
*
***********************************************************************
* THIS ROUTINE ISSUES SVC 99 VIA THE DYNALLOC MACRO.
***********************************************************************
*
DOSVC99     LA       R1,RBPTR               LD ADR OF RB PTR INTO R1 FOR SVC 99
            DYNALLOC                        ISSUE SVC 99
            LTR      R15,R15                CHK RC
            BNZ      CHKERR                 IF NOT ZERO, CHK ERROR/INFO FIELDS
            BR       R6                     IF OK, RETURN TO CALLING RTN
CHKERR      ...
*
*
***********************************************************************
* THIS ROUTINE EXTRACTS THE DDNAME AND DATASET NAME OF THE ALLOCATION
* ASSOCIATED WITH THE SPECIFIED RELATIVE NUMBER.
***********************************************************************
*
RETVINFO    MVC      DDNAME,DDNAME-1        CLEAR AREA FOR DDNAME
            MVC      DSNAME,DSNAME-1        CLEAR AREA FOR DSNAME
            LH       R12,I2DDNLEN           LD LEN OF RETURNED DDN
            BCTR     R12,0                  DECR LEN FOR EX INSTR
            EX       R12,MOVEDDN            GET DDNAME
            LH       R12,I2DSNLEN           LD LEN OF RETURNED DSN
            BCTR     R12,0                  DECR LEN FOR EX INSTR
            EX       R12,MOVEDSN            GET DSNAME
            CLI      I2LESW,X'80'           CHK IND FOR LAST DD STMT
            BE       INFOEND                IF YES, GO TO END-DD-STMT RTN
            BR       R6                     IF NO, RETURN TO CALLING RTN
MOVEDDN     MVC      DDNAME(0),I2DDNAME     MVC INTR FOR EX
MOVEDSN     MVC      DSNAME(0),I2DSNAME     MVC INTR FOR EX
*
*
***********************************************************************
```

```
* THE ROUTINE PROCESSES THE DDN/DSN INFORMATION.
************************************************************************
*
PROCESS   ...                             PROCESS INFORMATION
          BR        R6                    RETURN TO CALLING RTN
*
*
************************************************************************
* THIS ROUTINE RESTORES THE REGISTERS AND RETURNS.
************************************************************************
*
RETURN    RCNTL     RC=0                  RETURN TO MVS OR CALLING PROG
*
*
************************************************************************
* SVC99 REQ-BLOCK-POINTER AND REQUEST BLOCK
************************************************************************
*
RBPTR     DS        F                     PTR TO SVC 99 REQ BLOCK
REQBLK    DS        CL(S99RBEND-S99RB)    STORAGE FOR REQ BLOCK
REQBLKLN  EQU       L'REQBLK              LENGTH OF REQ BLOCK
*
*
************************************************************************
* TEXT-UNITS-POINTERS LIST
************************************************************************
*
TUPTR007  DS        0F
          DC        A(TURLNOI2)           ADR OF TU FOR REL NUMB
          DC        A(TURDDNI2)           ADR OF TU FOR RET-DDN
          DC        A(TURDSNI2)           ADR OF TU FOR RET-DSN
          DC        X'80'                 INDICATES LAST TU ADDRESS
          DC        AL3(TULESWI2)         ADR OF TU FOR LAST-DD-STMT IND
*
*
************************************************************************
* TEXT UNITS
************************************************************************
*
TURLNOI2  DC        AL2(DINRELNO),AL2(1),AL2(2)
I2RELNO   DS        CL2                   RELATIVE NUMBER OF ALLOCATION
*
TURDDNI2  DC        AL2(DINRTDDN),AL2(1)
I2DDNLEN  DS        CL2                   RETURNED LENGTH OF DDNAME
I2DDNAME  DS        CL8                   RETURNED DDNAME
*
TURDSNI2  DC        AL2(DINRTDSN),AL2(1).
I2DSNLEN  DS        CL2                   RETURNED LENGTH OF DSNAME
I2DSNAME  DS        CL44                  RETURNED DSNAME
*
TULESWI2  DC        AL2(DINRTLST),AL2(1),AL2(1)
I2LESW    DS        CL1                   LAST DD-STMT INDICATOR
*
*
************************************************************************
* DC/DS STATEMENTS
************************************************************************
*
RELNO     DC        F'0'                  REL NUM FOR DYNAM INFO RETRV
          DC        C' '                  USED TO BLANK DDNAME
DDNAME    DS        CL8                   AREA TO SAVE DDN FROM INFO RETV
          DC        C' '                  USED TO BLANK DSNAME
DSNAME    DS        CL44                  AREA TO SAVE DSN FROM INFO RETV
*
```

```
*
***************************************************************************
* THE DSECTS
***************************************************************************
*
         IEFZB4D0                        GENS DSECT FOR REQ BLOCK, TEXT
UNIT, ETC.
         IEFZB4D2                        GENS TABLE OF EQUATES FOR TU KEYS
*
*
***************************************************************************
* END OF PROGRAM
***************************************************************************
*
END
```

7.2.6 SVC 99 Feedback

When SVC 99 returns control to the issuing program, it posts a return code in register 15 and may, depending on the return code, provide additional information in the S99ERROR (error reason code) and may, depending on the error reason code, provide additional information in the S99INFO (information reason code) fields of the SVC 99 Request Block.

The return codes that can appear in register 15 are the following:

Return Code (Hex)	Meaning
00	Successful completion.
04	Error resulting from current environment such as the unavailability of a resource. An error reason code is also posted.
08	The installation validation routine denied this request.
0C	Invalid parameter-list. An error reason code is also posted.

See the Bibliography at the end of this chapter for the names and ID numbers of the IBM manuals that contain the list of the error and information codes that may appear in the S99ERROR and S99INFO fields.

BIBLIOGRAPHY FOR CHAPTER 7

The following IBM manuals contain reference material for the topics discussed in this chapter.

ID	TITLE
GC26-3830	*OS/VS2 SPL: Data Management*
GC28-1303	*OS/VS2 SPL: Job Management*
GC26-4010	*MVS/XA SPL: Data Management*
GC28-1150	*MVS/XA SPL: System Macros and Facilities Volume 1*
GC28-1852	*MVS/ESA SPL: Application Development Guide*
SC26-4515	*MVS/ESA SPL: System–Data Administration*

8

Processing a Partitioned Dataset

Partitioned datasets (PDS), which are also called libraries, are used by MVS to contain various system data such as load modules, parameters, JCL procedures, and so forth. They also have user applications and may contain such data as program source code, control statements, job streams, and so forth.

This chapter discusses the structure of a partitioned dataset and the ways of processing one without the use of the various utility programs that are available. The discussion includes the IBM-supplied access methods and macro instructions, other IBM facilities and various programming techniques for processing the PDS directory and individual members.

8.1 WHAT IS A PARTITIONED DATASET?

A partitioned dataset is composed of one or more members and a directory. Each member has a unique name and contains one or more records organized sequentially. Each member is a single entity within the dataset and each member contains an end-of-data indicator after its last record. The directory of the PDS is physically located at the beginning of the dataset and the individual members follow. The directory contains an entry for each member of the PDS. An entry contains the member name, its location within the PDS, and other information. Entries are arranged and maintained in the directory by member name in System/370 collating sequence. Members may be read, created, updated, deleted, or renamed. A member has a primary name and optionally additional alias names. A partitioned dataset can reside only on a single volume direct access storage device (DASD).

When a new member is added to the PDS, the actual data of the member is written behind the physically last member of the dataset, but the new member's directory entry is placed in the proper location (in collating sequence by member name) in the directory. Therefore, the directory is reorganized each time a new member name is added to (or deleted from) the PDS directory.

When an existing member is updated (not in-place), the new version of the member is written behind the physically last member in the PDS (just as if it were a new member), but the member's entry in the directory remains in the same place (since it already was in the proper place). The location field in the entry is changed to reflect the location of the new version of the member. The old version of the member remains physically in the dataset, but is no longer accessible (unless it has an alias name that was not updated) because the updated directory entry points only to the latest version of the member.

During a delete or rename operation, only the PDS directory is processed. When a member is deleted, its entry is removed from the PDS directory. For a member rename, only the name field of the directory entry is changed. Then the entry with the new name is repositioned into the proper place in the directory, but actual data records of the member remain in the same place in the dataset.

Alias names are assigned to existing members by adding new entries to the directory. Each alias entry contains an alias name, an indicator that it is an alias name, and a pointer (same pointer value as primary name entry) to the actual member.

Since the space occupied by the old versions of updated members and by deleted members is not relinquished during update and delete operations, the PDS will eventually become full. The unused space will be interspersed throughout the member data portion of the PDS. MVS indicates that a PDS is full (cannot accommodate any more new or updated members) with an ABEND code of SD37-04 or SE37-04 when an attempt is made to write additional records into the PDS. To reclaim this unused space, the PDS must be reorganized (compressed). During a compress operation, each member is rewritten in the same sequence as it appears in the directory, and the location field of each member's directory entry is changed (if necessary) to reflect the new location of the member. After the compress is completed, all the unused space is located at the physical end of the PDS, where it is usable and the members are in the same sequence as they appear in the directory. If a compress operation is attempted and is not required (all unused space is located after the last member of the dataset), then the members are not rewritten. Besides a compress in-place, a compress could also be performed by copying the PDS to a newly allocated (with the same size and DCB attributes, unless changes are required) and empty PDS. In this case, the new PDS is automatically compressed. This method followed by a delete of the old PDS and a rename of the new PDS to the name of the original PDS is the preferred way of compressing a PDS because there is no danger of damaging the original PDS due to a job cancel or system failure condition.

A PDS directory can also become full. MVS indicates this condition with an ABEND code of SB14-0C or a return code of 12 from the STOW macro instruction. Since the PDS directory is reorganized (when required) whenever it is updated, there is no such operation as a compress to reclaim unused directory space. When the PDS directory becomes full, there are one of two actions that may be performed to provide directory space for new members. One is to delete members that are no longer required causing additional directory space to become available. The other is to reallocate the PDS with a larger directory. This can be accomplished by allocating a new PDS with a larger directory, copying the old PDS into the new PDS, deleting the old PDS, and renaming the new PDS to the name of the old PDS.

8.2 THE STRUCTURE OF THE PDS DIRECTORY

The PDS directory is located at the beginning of the dataset and is composed of 256-byte unblocked records. The end of the directory has an end-of-file indicator (zero count record, see Chapter 11 for a discussion of DASD track and record format). The number of 256-byte records (the term block is used for PDS directory records) is specified by the user when the dataset is allocated. Each directory block contains one or more directory entries. The length of each directory entry is a mimimum of 12 bytes and a maximum of 74 bytes. Therefore, each directory block may contain a variable number of directory entires. Figure 8.2.1 shows the format of a directory entry.

`Member Name (8 bytes)`

The name of the member that this entry describes. The field may also contain an alias name for the member.

Member Name	TTR	C	Optional User-Data

Figure 8.2.1. This figure shows the format of a directory entry of a PDS directory.

`TTR (3 bytes)`

The relative location, within the PDS, of the beginning of the member. This field contains the number of tracks from the beginning of the PDS and the record number on the first track where the actual member begins. For multiple extent datasets, this field treats the dataset as one contiguous dataset.

`C (1 byte)`

Contains the following control information:

`Bit 0`

When set to 0, it indicates that this entry contains the primary name of the member. When set to 1, it indicates that this entry contains an alias name.

`Bits 1-2`

Number of user-data TTRNs (not discussed).

`Bits 3-7`

Binary value indicating the number of halfwords of user-data. This value must also include the space used by the TTRNs (if any) as indicated above.

`User-Data (2-62 bytes)`

This field is optional. If specified, it may contain any user information in any format. If TTRNs are used, they must be placed first in the user-data field.

Each directory block has an external key area associated with it, which is used to provide efficient directory searches. The length of this key area is 8 bytes and it contains the last member name in that directory block. The length of the data area of each PDS directory block is 256 bytes. The first 2 bytes contain a count field containing the number of bytes used (including the 2-byte count field) in that directory block. The remaining 254 bytes contain as many complete member entries as can fit.

Directory blocks are used sequentially until they are exhausted. The external key of the last directory block used contains binary ones and the member name field in the last entry also contains binary ones. All the directory blocks that follow that one are unused, and their external keys contain binary zeros.

8.3 READING THE ENTIRE PDS DIRECTORY

At times, all the members of a PDS are required to be processed. Such processing may include listing all the members, scanning all the members to locate a specific character string, searching for members whose names have a certain prefix (or some other criteria), updating

Count	Key	Data					
	Name of last entry in block	Dir bytes used	Member Entry 1 1	Member Entry 2 2	......	Member Entry n	Unused

Figure 8.2.2. This figure shows the complete (CKD) format of a directory block.

all members, and so on. In those situations, it would be cumbersome and impractical for the user to specify the names of all the members as input to the program. Therefore, the program would need to read the PDS directory to obtain the entire list of member names in order to process each one. IBM software does not provide such a facility. The BLDL macro instruction is provided, but it does not read the entire directory. It returns the directory information only for specific members when their names are provided by the program.

The PDS directory can be read with QSAM, BSAM, or EXCP. Using QSAM is easier to code than BSAM, but since the directory is not blocked, using BSAM is less involved than it would normally be. Using BSAM would enable the program to read the external key area associated with each directory block while QSAM would not. However, this information is not necessary if the entire directory is to be read. Reading the directory using EXCP will not be discussed.

This section will provide coding examples to illustrate how to read the entire PDS directory and determine if the member name is a primary name or an alias name. Coding examples will include both QSAM and BSAM.

8.3.1 Reading the PDS Directory Using QSAM

Coding Example 8.3.1

This coding example illustrates how to read a PDS directory using QSAM. In this example, each time that the routine GETENTRY is called, it returns the member name (either primary or alias name), the TTRC fields and any user-data in the virtual storage areas MEMBNAME, TTRC, and USERDATA, respectively. If no user-data is present, USERDATA is set to binary zeros.

```
 ...
            BAL       R6,OPENDIR                OPEN PDS DIRECTORY
NXTENTRY    BAL       R6,GETDRBLK               READ WHOLE PDS DIR BLOCK
            BAL       R6,GETENTRY               GET INDIV PDS DIR ENTRY
            ...                                 PROCESS
            B         NXTENTRY                  GET NEXT PDS DIR ENTRY
DIREND      BAL       R6,CLOSEDIR               DIR END, CLOSE PDS DIR
            ...
*
*
***************************************************************************
* THIS ROUTINE OPENS THE DCB FOR THE PDS DIRECTORY.
***************************************************************************
*
OPENDIR     OPEN      PODIRDCB                  OPEN PDS DIR
            ...                                 CHK FOR GOOD OPEN
            BR        R6                        RETURN TO CALLING RTN
*
*
***************************************************************************
* THIS ROUTINE USES QSAM TO READ AN ENTIRE PDS DIRECTORY BLOCK. WHEN
* THIS ROUTINE RETURNS CONTROL TO THE CALLING ROUTINE REGISTERS 14, 15,
* 0, AND 1 ARE SAVED IN THE AREA SAVEREGS, AND REGISTERS 1, 14, AND 15
* CONTAIN THE FOLLOWING CONTROL INFORMATION:
*      * REGISTER 1  -  ADDRESS OF THE FIRST ENTRY OF THE PDS DIRECTORY
*        BLOCK;
*      * REGISTER 14  -  NUMBER OF USED BYTES IN THE DIRECTORY BLOCK;
*      * REGISTER 15  -  NUMBER OF BYTES OF DIRECTORY BLOCK PROCESSED,
*                        INITIALLY SET TO 2 FOR DIR BLK COUNT FIELD.
***************************************************************************
*
GETDRBLK    CLI       GETDBSW,C'0'              CHK IF GET REQUIRED
            BER       R6                        IF NO, RET TO CALLING RTN
```

```
         GET      PODIRDCB,DIRBLOCK       GET A DIR BLOCK
         MVI      GETDBSW,C'0'            INDICATE GET DONE
         LA       R15,2                   START RUNNING DIR BLK COUNT,
*                                         2 BYTES FOR DIR COUNT FIELD
         LH       R14,DIRBLOCK            LOAD REG14 WITH DIR BLK COUNT
         LA       R1,DIRBLOCK+2           LOAD REG1 WITH FIRST ENTRY ADR
         STM      R14,R1,SAVEREGS         SAVE REGS FOR GETENTRY RTN
         BR       R6                      RETURN TO CALLING RTN
*
*
***********************************************************************
* THIS ROUTINE GETS THE NEXT PDS DIRECTORY ENTRY. WHEN THIS ROUTINE
* RECEIVES CONTROL REGISTERS 14 THROUGH 1 ARE SAVED IN THE AREA
* SAVEREGS. THE REGISTERS IN SAVEREGS CONTAIN THE FOLLOWING CONTROL
* INFORMATION:
*    * REGISTER 14 -  NUMBER OF USED BYTES IN THE DIRECTORY BLOCK;
*    * REGISTER 15 -  NUMBER OF BYTES OF DIRECTORY BLOCK PROCESSED
*                         SO FAR;
*    * REGISTER 1  -  ADDRESS OF THE PREVIOUS ENTRY OF THE PDS
*                         DIRECTORY BLOCK.
* WHEN THIS ROUTINE RETURNS CONTROL TO THE CALLING ROUTINE, THE
* FOLLOWING AREAS CONTAIN THE FOLLOWING INFORMATION:
*    MEMBNAME  -  THE MEMBER NAME OR ALIAS;
*    TTRC      -  THE TTRC FIELD OF THE PDS DIR ENTRY;
*    USER-DATA -  ANY USERDATA CONTAINED IN THE PDS DIR ENTRY OR
*                   BINARY ZEROS IF THERE IS NO USERDATA.
* IN ADDITION, THE CONTROL INFORMATION IN REGISTERS 1 AND 15 IS
* UPDATED, AND REGISTERS 14 THROUGH 1 ARE SAVED IN THE AREA SAVEREGS.
***********************************************************************
*
GETENTRY LM       R14,R1,SAVEREGS         RESTORE REGS
         CLC      0(8,R1),BINONES         CHK FOR LOGICAL END OF DIR
         BE       DIREND                  IF YES, END OF DIR
         MVC      MEMBNAME,0(R1)          MOVE MEMBER NAME
         MVC      TTRC,8(R1)              MOVE TTRC
         XC       USERDATA,USERDATA       CLEAR USER-DATA AREA FOR EX INSTR
         MVC      UDATALEN+3(1),TTRC+3    MOVE ENTRY CONTROL FIELD
         NI       UDATALEN+3(1),X'1F'     ZERO HIGH ORDER 3 BITS TO
*                                         ISOLATE USER-DATA LENGTH
         L        R2,UDATALEN             LOAD REG2 WITH USER-DATA LENGTH
*                                         IN HALFWORDS
         SLL      R2,1                    CONVERT HALFWORDS TO BYTES
         BAL      R7,GETUDATA             GET USER-DATA
         LA       R2,12(0,R2)             LOAD REG2 WITH ENTRY LENGTH,
*                                         (MINIMUM 12 + USER-DATA)
         AR       R15,R2                  ADD ENTRY LEN TO RUNNING DIR BLK CT
         CR       R15,R14                 COMPARE RUNNING DIR BLK COUNT TO
*                                         DIR BLK COUNT
         BNL      DRBLKEND                IF NOT LOW, ENTIRE DIR BLK PROCESSED
         B        SETNXENT                IF MORE DIR, INCR REG1 TO NEXT ENTRY
DRBLKEND MVI      GETDBSW,C'1'            IND THAT GET NEXT DIR BLK REQUIRED
         BR       R6                      RETURN TO CALLING RTN
SETNXENT LA       R1,0(R2,R1)             INCR REG1 TO NEXT DIR ENTRY ADR
         STM      R14,R1,SAVEREGS         SAVE REGS FOR NEXT GETENTRY EXEC
         BR       R6                      RETURN TO CALLING RTN
*
*
***********************************************************************
* THIS SUBROUTINE GETS THE USER-DATA OF THE PDS DIRECTORY. WHEN THIS
* SUBROUTINE RECEIVES CONTROL, REGISTER 2 CONTAINS THE LENGTH OF THE
* USER-DATA IN BYTES AND REGISTER 1 CONTAINS THE ADDRESS OF THE
* BEGINNING OF THE PDS DIRECTORY ENTRY. WHEN THIS SUBROUTINE RETURNS
* CONTROL TO THE CALLING ROUTINE, THE AREA USER-DATA CONTAINS THE
* USER-DATA OF THE PDS DIRECTORY ENTRY OR BINARY ZEROS IF THE ENTRY
```

```
* CONTAINS NO USER-DATA.
***************************************************************************
*
GETUDATA    LTR     R2,R2                   CHK IF USER-DATA PRESENT
            BZR     R7                      IF NO, BACK TO CALLER
            BCTR    R2,0                    DECR REG2 LEN FOR EX INSTR
            EX      R2,MOVUDATA             MOVE USER-DATA
            LA      R2,1(0,R2)              RESTORE REG2 LEN
            BR      R7                      RETURN TO CALLING RTN
MOVUDATA    MVC     USERDATA(0),12(R1)      MOVE ONLY SPECIFIED USER-DATA
*
*
***************************************************************************
* THIS ROUTINE CLOSES THE DCB FOR THE PDS DIRECTORY.
***************************************************************************
*
CLOSEDIR    CLOSE   PODIRDCB                CLOSE PDS DIR
            BR      R6                      RETURN TO CALLING RTN
*
*
***************************************************************************
* DC/DS STATEMENTS
***************************************************************************
*
GETDBSW     DC      C'1'
BINONES     DC      8XL1'FF'
DIRBLOCK    DS      CL256
MEMBNAME    DS      CL8
TTRC        DS      CL4
USERDATA    DS      CL62
UDATALEN    DC      F'0'
SAVEREGS    DS      4F
*
*
***************************************************************************
* THE DCB FOR THE PDS DIRECTORY
***************************************************************************
*
PODIRDCB    DCB     DSORG=PS,MACRF=GM,BLKSIZE=256,LRECL=256,RECFM=F,   -
                    EODAD=DIREND,DDNAME=LIBDD
            ...
```

8.3.2 Reading the PDS Directory Using BSAM

Coding Example 8.3.2

This coding example illustrates how to read a PDS directory using BSAM. In this example, each time that the routine GETDRBLK is called, it returns the external key of the directory block in the virtual storage area DIRKEY, and each time that the routine GETENTRY is called, it returns the member name (either primary or alias name), the TTRC fields, and any user-data in the virtual storage areas MEMBNAME, TTRC, and USERDATA, respectively. If no user-data is present, USERDATA is set to binary zeros.

If a specific entry is required, then the search performance could be improved by using the information in DIRKEY. Since the key area of each directory block contains the last member name in that directory, if the argument member name is higher than the member name in the key area, then the scan of that directory block could be skipped. The argument member name could be compared to the key area of each directory block until the argument member name is low or equal to the member name in the key area and then the scan of that directory block is performed.

```
          ...
          BAL      R6,OPENDIR              OPEN PDS DIRECTORY
NXTENTRY  BAL      R6,GETDRBLK             READ A DIRECTORY BLOCK
          BAL      R6,GETENTRY             EXTRACT AN ENTRY FROM DIR BLOCK
          ...
          B        NXTENTRY                OBTAIN NEXT DIR ENTRY
DIREND    BAL      R6,CLOSEDIR             CLOSE PDS DIR DCB
          ...
*
OPENDIR   OPEN     PODIRDCB                OPEN PDS DIR DCB
          ...                              CHK FOR GOOD OPEN
          BR       R6                      RETURN TO CALLING RTN
*
GETDRBLK  CLI      GETDBSW,C'0'            CHK IF GET REQUIRED
          BER      R6                      IF NO, RET TO CALLING RTN
          READ     DIRDECB,SF,PODIRDCB,DIRBLOCK
          CHECK    DIRDECB
          MVI      GETDBSW,C'0'            INDICATE GET DONE
          LA       R15,2                   START RUNNING DIR BLK COUNT
          LH       R14,DIRDATA             LOAD REG14 WITH DIR BLK COUNT
          LA       R1,DIRDATA+2            LOAD REG1 WITH FIRST ENTRY ADR
          STM      R14,R1,SAVEREGS         SAVE REGS FOR GETENTRY RTN
          BR       R6                      RETURN TO CALLING RTN
*
GETENTRY  LM       R14,R1,SAVEREGS         RESTORE REGS
          CLC      0(8,R1),BINONES         CHK FOR LOGICAL END OF DIR
          BE       DIREND                  IF YES, END OF DIR
          MVC      MEMBNAME,0(R1)          MOVE MEMBER NAME
          MVC      TTRC,8(R1)              MOVE TTRC FIELDS
          XC       USERDATA,USERDATA       CLEAR USER-DATA REC AREA
          MVC      UDATALEN+3(1),TTRC+3    MOVE ENTRY CONTROL FIELD
          NI       UDATALEN+3(1),X'1F'     ZERO HIGH ORDER 3 BITS TO
*                                          ISOLATE USER-DATA LENGTH
          L        R2,UDATALEN             LOAD REG2 WITH USER-DATA LENGTH
*                                          IN HALFWORDS
          SLL      R2,1                    CONVERT HALFWORDS TO BYTES
          BAL      R7,GETUDATA             GET USER-DATA
          LA       R2,12(0,R2)             LOAD REG2 WITH ENTRY LENGTH
          AR       R15,R2                  ADD ENTRY LENGTH TO RUNNING DIR BLK
*                                          COUNT
          CR       R15,R14                 COMPARE RUNNING DIR BLK COUNT TO
*                                          DIR BLK COUNT
          BNL      DRBLKEND                IF NOT LOW, ENTIRE DIR BLK PROCESSED
          B        SETNXENT                IF MORE DIR, INCR REG1 TO NEXT ENTRY
DRBLKEND  MVI      GETDBSW,C'1'            INDICATE THAT GET NEXT DIR BLK REQRD
          BR       R6                      RETURN TO CALLING RTN
SETNXENT  LA       R1,0(R2,R1)             INCR REG1 TO NEXT DIR ENTRY
          STM      R14,R1,SAVEREGS         SAVE REGS FOR NEXT GETENTRY EXEC
          BR       R6                      RETURN TO CALLING RTN
*
GETUDATA  LTR      R2,R2                   CHK IF USER-DATA PRESENT
          BZR      R7                      IF NO, BACK TO CALLER
          BCTR     R2,0                    DECR REG2 LEN FOR EX INSTR
          EX       R2,MOVUDATA             MOVE USER-DATA
          LA       R2,1(0,R2)              RESTORE REG2 LEN
          BR       R7                      RETURN TO CALLING RTN
MOVUDATA  MVC      USERDATA(0),12(R1)      MVC FOR EX INSTR
*
CLOSEDIR  CLOSE    PODIRDCB                CLOSE PDS DIRECTORY DCB
          BR       R6                      RETURN TO CALLING RTN
*
GETDBSW   DC       C'1'
BINONES   DC       8XL1'FF'
DIRBLOCK  DS       0CL264
```

```
DIRKEY      DS     CL8
DIRDATA     DS     CL256
MEMBNAME    DS     CL8
TTRC        DS     CL4
USER-DATA   DS     CL62
UDATALEN    DC     F'0'
SAVEREGS    DS     4F
*
PODIRDCB    DCB    DSORG=PS,MACRF=R,KEYLEN=8,BLKSIZE=256,LRECL=256,  -
                   RECFM=F,EODAD=DIREND,DDNAME=LIBDD
                   ...
```

NOTES:

- The code for reading the PDS directory is the same for QSAM and BSAM except for the following:
  - The DCB macro instruction specifies different parameters.
  - The GET macro instruction is used for QSAM, and the READ and the CHECK macro instructions are used for BSAM.
  - The I/O buffer for BSAM is eight bytes longer because each BSAM READ returns the 8-byte external key of the PDS directory (at the beginning of the buffer) and a QSAM GET does not.
- The routine header comments are omitted since they are identical to the QSAM example above, except for the header comment for the routine GETDRBLK, which requires that the word QSAM be changed to BSAM.

8.3.3 A Macro Instruction Definition to Read the PDS Directory

The following macro definition reads the entire PDS directory. The macro name is READDIR and requires only one positional parameter. The parameter specifies the ddname of the JCL DD statement that points to a partitioned dataset. The macro uses QSAM to read the directory, defines the DCB required for the directory read, and OPENs the directory DCB. Each time the macro instruction is passed control, it will:

- Return the name of the next member (in collating sequence) from the directory into the area labeled $MEMBER (defined in the macro expansion);
- Return the corresponding TTRC field in the area labeled $TTRC (defined in the macro expansion);
- Return the beginning address (starting with the name field) of the corresponding directory entry in register 1; and
- Post a return code in register 15.

The following are the return codes issued by READDIR when it returns control:

Return Code (Hex)	Meaning
00	$MEMBER contains a primary member name.
04	$MEMBER contains an alias member name.
08	End-of-directory, $MEMBER contains binary zeros.
0C	JCL DD statement not in jobstream.

Coding Example 8.3.3

This coding example contains the macro definition for READDIR.

```
            MACRO
&LABEL      READDIR   &DDNAME
            GBLA      &RDIRSW         USED TO PREVENT DUPL GEN  OF $-AREAS
            LCLC      &LBL            USED TO GEN UNIQUE LABELS
&LBL        SETC      '$'.'RDR'.'&SYSNDX'(2,3)  SET LABEL PREFIX
&LABEL      LM        14,1,&LBL.A     RESTORE REG 14, 15, 0, 1 FROM PREV
*                                     EXEC OF READDIR MACRO
            ST        2,&LBL.B        SAVE REG 2
            B         &LBL.O          BRANCH AROUND CONSTANTS
&LBL.A      DS        4F              SAVE AREA FOR REGS 14, 15, 0, 1
&LBL.B      DS        F               SAVE AREA FOR REG 2
&LBL.C      DC        F'0'            AREA TO EXPAND DIR ENTRY SIZE FIELD
*                                     TO FULLWORD
            AIF       (&RDIRSW EQ 1).BYPASS   CHECK IF $-AREAS WERE DEFINED
$MEMBER     DS        CL8             MEMBER NAME
$TTRC       DS        CL4             TTRC FIELD
&RDIRSW     SETA      1               INDICATE THAT $MEMBER AND $TTRC
*                                     ARE DEFINED
.BYPASS     ANOP
*           DCB       BLKSIZE=256,LRECL=256,RECFM=F,DDNAME=&DDNAME,
*                     MACRF=GM,DSORG=PS,EODAD=&LBL.J
&LBL.D      DCB       BLKSIZE=256,LRECL=256,RECFM=F,DDNAME=&DDNAME, -
                      MACRF=GM,DSORG=PS,EODAD=&LBL.J
&LBL.E      DC        C'0'            OPEN SWITCH
&LBL.H      DS        CL256           DIRECTORY AREA
&LBL.N      DC        8XL1'FF'        END OF DIR INDICATOR
&LBL.O      CLI       &LBL.E,C'1'     CHK IF DIR OPENED
            BE        &LBL.F          IF YES, BRANCH AROUND OPEN AND
*                                     FIRST GET
*           OPEN      &LBL.D          OPEN DIR DCB
            OPEN      &LBL.D
            TM        &LBL.D+48,X'10' CHECK IF PDS JCL DD STMT SPECIFIED
            BNO       &LBL.P          IF NOT, INDICATE IT
            MVI       &LBL.E,C'1'     SET OPEN SWITCH
*                    GET        &LBL.D,&LBL.H  GET DIR BLOCK
&LBL.G      GET       &LBL.D,&LBL.H
            LA        15,2            START RUNNING DIR BLOCK COUNT
            LA        1,2(0,1)        INCR REG1 PAST DIR COUNT FIELD
            LH        14,&LBL.H       LOAD REG14 WITH DIR BLOCK COUNT
            B         &LBL.I          GET MEMBER NAME
&LBL.F      MVC       &LBL.C+3(1),11(1) EXPAND ENTRY SIZE FIELD TO FULLWORD
            NI        &LBL.C+3,X'1F' ZERO HIGH ORDER 3 BITS TO ISOLATE
*                                     USER-DATA LENGTH
            L         2,&LBL.C        LOAD ENTRY USER-DATA LEN (HALFWORDS)
*                                     INTO REG2
            LA        2,12(2,2)       LOAD ENTRY LENGTH (BYTES) INTO REG2
            AR        15,2            ADD CURRENT ENTRY LEN TO RUNNING DIR
*                                     BLOCK COUNT
            CR        15,14           COMPARE RUNNING DIR BLOCK COUNT TO
*                                     DIR BLOCK COUNT
            BNL       &LBL.G          IF NOT LOW, ENTIRE DIR BLK PROCESSED
            LA        1,0(2,1)        INCR REG1 TO NEXT ENTRY
&LBL.I      CLC       0(8,1),&LBL.N   COMPARE FOR LOGICAL END OF DIR
            BE        &LBL.J          IF EQUAL, DIR END
            MVC       $MEMBER,0(1)    MOVE MEMBER NAME
            MVC       $TTRC,8(1)      MOVE TTRC FIELD
            TM        11(1),X'80'     CHK IF MEMBER NAME IS AN ALIAS
            BO        &LBL.K          IF BIT ON, ALIAS
            B         &LBL.L          NORMAL END
&LBL.P      LA        R15,12          INDICATE PDS JCL DD STMT MISSING
```

```
         B       &LBL.M         BRANCH OUT OF MACRO
&LBL.J   MVI     &LBL.E,C'O'    ZERO OPEN SWITCH
*        CLOSE   &LBL.D         CLOSE DIR DCB
         CLOSE   &LBL.D
         XC      $MEMBER,$MEMBER CLEAR MEMBER NAME AT END OF DIR
         LA      15,8           INDICATE END OF DIR
         B       &LBL.M         BRANCH OUT OF MACRO
&LBL.K   STM     14,1,&LBL.A    SAVE REG 14, 15, 1
         LA      15,4           INDICATE ALIAS
         B       &LBL.M         BRANCH OUT OF MACRO
&LBL.L   STM     14,1,&LBL.A    SAVE REG 14, 15, 1
         LA      15,0           NORMAL END
         B       &LBL.M         BRANCH OUT OF MACRO
&LBL.M   L       2,&LBL.B       RESTORE REG2
         MEND
```

8.4 READING INDIVIDUAL MEMBERS OF A PDS

Individual members may be read from a PDS using a sequential access method (QSAM or BSAM) or BPAM. Using QSAM is easier to use than BSAM; therefore, only QSAM will be discussed for processing a PDS, using a sequential access method. If only one member is to be read each time the program executes, then QSAM would be the preferred way because it is easier to code than BPAM. When using QSAM (and BSAM), the same set of code is used to read a member of a PDS or a sequential dataset. If multiple members are to be read, then BPAM is the preferred way because it is more efficient. Multiple members can be read using QSAM (and BSAM) if the JFCB is modified to contain each member name that is to be read. This is very inefficient because it requires that the QSAM DCB be OPENed and CLOSEd for each member read in this fashion. Using BPAM is more involved than using QSAM because more macro instructions, additional code and deblocking is required because the basic access methods (BSAM, BPAM, BDAM and formerly BISAM) read only whole blocks. Therefore, selecting QSAM or BPAM to read multiple members of the same PDS is a trade-off between ease of programming (QSAM) and program performance (BPAM).

The section discusses the programming methods required to read members of a PDS, using QSAM and BPAM.

8.4.1 Reading Members with QSAM

When members of a PDS are read using QSAM, the names of the members may be specified in two ways. If only one member is to be read, then its name may be specified in the JCL. If multiple members are to be read, then the modified JFCB method (discussed in Chapter 7) must be used.

SPECIFYING MEMBER NAMES IN JCL

The member name is specified in the JCL by qualifying the DSNAME parameter of the JCL DD statement with the member name, as follows:

```
//PDSDD DD DSN=USER.SRCLIB(PRGM01),DISP=SHR
```

When the dataset USER.SRCLIB is OPENed, the PDS directory is automatically searched for the member name PRGM01, and its location is placed into the DCB. Then, when the GET macro instruction is issued, the logical records of the member PRGM01 are read sequentially (one for each execution of GET) just like a sequential dataset was being read. The end-of-member condition causes the end-of-data routine (specified via the

EODAD parameter of DCB macro instruction) to receive control. The logic of the program is the same as if it were reading a sequential dataset.

SPECIFYING MEMBER NAMES IN MODIFIED JFCB

Multiple members of the same PDS may be read using QSAM only if the desired member names are specified via a modified JFCB. The name of each member that is to be read must be specified in the JFCB after the previous member has been read. Since the OPEN routine does the actual locating of the member, the DCB of the dataset is required to be OPENed for each member that is to be read. Using this method, the JCL DD statement points to the PDS without any member name specified.

Coding Example 8.4.1

This coding example illustrates how to read multiple members of a PDS, using QSAM. The members that are to be read may be specified as input to the program or by reading the directory. In this example, the READDIR macro instruction is used to read the entire directory.

```
READPDSQ    CSECT
*
*
***************************************************************************
* INITIALIZATION
***************************************************************************
*
            INITL       3,EQU=R               INITIALIZE PROGRAM
            USING       IHADCB,R10            DEFINE REG FOR DCB DSECT
            USING       INFMJFCB,R11          DEFINE REG FOR JFCB DSECT
*
*
***************************************************************************
* MAINSTREAM OF PROGRAM
***************************************************************************
*
            BAL         R6,RDJFCB             READ JFCB INTO PROG AREA
NEXTMEMB    BAL         R6,GETNAME            GET NEXT MEMBER NAME FROM PDS DIR
            BAL         R6,SETNAME            PUT MEMBER NAME INTO JFCB
            BAL         R6,OPEN               OPEN PDS, POS TO MEMBER
NEXTREC     BAL         R6,READ               READ A RECORD OF MEMBER
            BAL         R6,PROCMEMB           PROCESS RECORD
            B           NEXTREC               GET NEXT MEMBER RECORD
MEMBEND     BAL         R6,CLOSE              ALL MEMB RECS READ, CLOSE PDS
            B           NEXTMEMB              GET NEXT MEMBER NAME
MEMBENDX    BAL         R6,CLOSE              ALL MEMBERS READ, CLOSE PDS
            B           RETURN                RETURN TO MVS OR CALLING PROGRAM
*
*
***************************************************************************
* THIS ROUTINE READS THE JFCB AND COPIES IT FROM THE SWA INTO THE
* PROGRAMMER-SUPPLIED AREA.
***************************************************************************
*
RDJFCB      RDJFCB      PDSQDCB
            LTR         R15,R15               CHK IF DD STMT IN JCL
            BNZ         NODDSTMT              DD STMT MISSING
            BR          R6                    RETURN TO CALLING RTN
NODDSTMT    WTO         '*** DDNAME "PDSDD" IS NOT IN JOBSTREAM ***',ROUTCDE=11
            ABEND       901
*
*
***************************************************************************
```

```
* THIS ROUTINE USES THE READDIR MACRO TO OBTAIN THE MEMBER NAME IN THE
* NEXT PDS DIRECTORY ENTRY. ALIAS NAMES ARE IGNORED.
***********************************************************************
*
GETNAME    READDIR    PDSDD
           LTR        R15,R15              CHECK IF PRIMARY NAME
           BZR        R6                   IF YES, RET TO CALLING RET
           C          R15,BIN4             CHECK IF ALIAS
           BE         GETNAME              IF YES, IGNORE GET NEXT NAME
           B          MEMBENDX             END OF DIR, BRANCH TO END-OF-MEMB RTN
*
*
***********************************************************************
* THIS ROUTINE MODIFIES THE JFCB. THE NAME OF THE NEXT PDS MEMBER TO
* BE READ IS INSERTED INTO THE PDS-MEMBER-NAME FIELD OF THE JFCB.
***********************************************************************
*
SETNAME    LA         R11,JFCB             SET ADRBLTY FOR PDS DCB DSECT
           MVC        JFCBELNM,$MEMBER     MOVE CURRENT MEMB NAME INTO JFCB
           OI         JFCBIND1,JFCPDS      IND THAT MEMB NAME SPEC IN JFCB
           BR         R6                   RETURN TO CALLING RTN
*
*
***********************************************************************
* THIS ROUTINE OPENS THE PDS DCB, USING THE INFORMATION IN THE MODIFIED
* JFCB. THE OPEN WILL CAUSE THE NEXT GET TO READ THE FIRST LOGICAL
* RECORD OF THE MEMBER WHOSE NAME IS SPECIFIED IN THE JFCB.
***********************************************************************
*
OPEN       OPEN       PDSQDCB,TYPE=J       TELL OPEN TO USE MODIFIED JFCB
           ...                             CHK FOR GOOD OPEN
           BR         R6                   RETURN TO CALLING RTN
*
*
***********************************************************************
* THIS ROUTINE USES QSAM TO READ A LOGICAL RECORD OF THE MEMBER.
***********************************************************************
*
READ       GET        PDSQDCB              GET A MEMBER RECORD
           LR         R2,R1                SAVE ADR OF RECORD IN REG 2
           BR         R6                   RETURN TO CALLING RTN
*
*
***********************************************************************
* THIS ROUTINE PROCESSES EACH LOGICAL RECORD OF THE MEMBER.
***********************************************************************
*
PROCMEMB   ...                             PROC RECORDS OF MEMBER
           BR         R6                   RETURN TO CALLING RTN
*
*
***********************************************************************
* THIS ROUTINE CLOSES PDS DCB.
***********************************************************************
*
CLOSE      CLOSE      PDSQDCB              CLOSE PDS
           BR         R6                   RETURN TO CALLING RTN
*
*
***********************************************************************
* THIS ROUTINE RESTORES THE REGISTERS AND RETURNS CONTROL.
***********************************************************************
*
RETURN     RCNTL      RC=0                 RETURN TO MVS OR CALLING PROG
```

```
*
*
*************************************************************************
* DC/DS STATEMENTS
*************************************************************************
*
BIN4         DC          F'4'
*
*
*************************************************************************
* THE JFCB-LIST AND THE DCB FOR THE PDS
*************************************************************************
*
JFCB         DS          44F
JFCBPTR      DC          X'87'
             DC          AL3(JFCB)
*
PDSQDCB      DCB         DSORG=PS,MACRF=GL,EODAD=MEMBEND,EXLST=JFCBPTR, -
.                        DDNAME=PDSDD
*
*
*************************************************************************
* THE DSECTS
*************************************************************************
*
             PRINT       NOGEN
             DCBD        DSORG=PS              GENERATES PS-DCB DSECT
*
             DSECT
             IEFJFCBN                          GENERATES JFCB DSECT
*
*
*************************************************************************
* END OF PROGRAM
*************************************************************************
*
             END
```

NOTES:

- The DCB for the PDS is defined as a sequential dataset since it is being processed via QSAM.

8.4.2 Reading Members Using BPAM

Unlike QSAM, reading multiple members of the same PDS with BPAM does not require that the dataset be OPENed and CLOSEd for each member. Individual members may be read by specifying the FIND macro instruction. The FIND macro instruction causes the location of the beginning of the specified member to be placed into the DCB. Then, when the READ macro instruction is issued, the physical blocks of the member are read (one for each execution of READ). The member may be specified by name or location in the FIND macro instruction. It is easier to specify the member name, but more efficient to specify the member location. The member location can be obtained with the use of the BLDL macro instruction. If many members are to be read, then the additional coding required to use the BLDL macro instruction to obtain the location of the member for the FIND macro instruction is justified because it would cause the program to execute more efficiently. The location of multiple members may be obtained with one execution of the BLDL macro instruction. This results in one directory read. If the member name is specified in the FIND macro instruction, then the directory must be read (by FIND) for each member in order to obtain its location. If the BLDL macro instruction is used to locate only one member, then no performance advantage is gained.

When records are read using a basic access method (such as BPAM or BSAM), only whole blocks are read. If the blocks are defined as fixed length and contain more than one logical record, then the programmer must supply the appropriate code to do the deblocking. Coding Example 8.4.2 shows a subroutine that does deblocking. However, there is one more consideration when reading whole blocks and deblocking. There may be short blocks imbedded in the data, and although this is unlikely, the last block will usually be a short block (since it is unlikely that the total number of logical records in the dataset are an exact multiple of the blocking factor). If a short block is not processed properly, then the logical record slots in the block I/O area located after the short block will contain residual data from the previous read.

For variable length records, the length is contained in the block descriptor word located at the beginning of each block; therefore, no additional processing is required to determine the length for variable length records. For fixed length records, there are two ways to determine the length of a short block, if one is received.

One method is to subtract the residual byte count from the number of bytes requested (specified block size). If the residual byte count is zero, then a short block was not returned. The residual byte count is stored in the Channel Status Word (CSW). The contents of the last seven bytes of the CSW is located in field IOBCSW of the IOB. The IOB is pointed to by field DECIOBPT of the DECB. The DECB is generated in the expansion of the READ macro instruction, and the label that is specified as the first positional parameter of the READ macro instruction is assigned to the beginning of the DECB. The specified block size is located in field DCBBLKSI of the DCB. If the block size is specified in the READ macro instruction (which overrides the DCB value), then the number of bytes requested is located in field DECLNGTH of the DECB. The residual byte count is contained in the last two bytes of the CSW (IOBCSW+5(2)). This method will not work with track overflow records or if chained scheduling is being used. In these cases, another method would be required.

The other method to determine the length of a short block is to initialize the entire buffer (I/O area) or just the first byte of each logical record slot with binary zeros (or some other character that does not appear in the data) before each READ is performed. After the block is read, check the first byte of each logical record slot (during the deblocking operation) for the initialization character. If the initialization character is found, then the rest of the buffer can be discarded.

The first method requires more code to implement but is more reliable and perhaps even more efficient, especially if the second method initializes the entire buffer. The second method is easier to code, but not as reliable as the first method since it is possible that the initialization character may appear in the data, in which case, valid logical records would be discarded.

LOCATING MEMBERS WITHOUT USING THE BLDL MACRO INSTRUCTION

Members of a PDS may be found without using BLDL by specifying the member name in the FIND macro instruction.

Coding Example 8.4.2

This coding example illustrates how to read multiple members of a PDS, using BPAM, and how to specify the member's name via the FIND macro instruction. In this example, the program reads a sequential dataset containing a list of member names that are to be read. The members of the PDS contain fixed-length blocked records, which are read and deblocked.

```
READPDSB    CSECT
*
```

```
*
*************************************************************************
* INITIALIZATION
*************************************************************************
*
            INITL       3,EQU=R             INITIALIZE PROGRAM
            USING       IHADCB,R10          DEFINE REG FOR DCB DSECT
            USING       LRECMAP,R11         DEFINE REG FOR LREC DSECT
*
*
*************************************************************************
* MAINSTREAM OF PROGRAM
*************************************************************************
*
            BAL         R6,OPEN             OPEN DATASETS
            BAL         R6,GETMAIN          ALLO STOR FOR PDS BLOCK I/O AREA
            BAL         R6,GETLRINF         CALC NUMB OF LRECS PER BLOCK
NEXTMEMB    BAL         R6,LOCMEMB          LOCATE SPEC MEMBER IN PDS
NEXTLREC    BAL         R6,GETLREC          GET A LOGICAL RECORD OF MEMBER
            BAL         R6,PROCMEMB         PROCESS LOGICAL RECORD
            B           NEXTLREC            GET NEXT LOGICAL RECORD OF MEMBER
MEMBEND     B           NEXTMEMB            END-OF-MEMB, GET NEXT MEMBER
MEMBENDX    BAL         R6,CLOSE            ALL MEMBERS READ, CLOSE DATASETS
            B           RETURN              RETURN TO MVS OR CALLING PROG
*
*
*************************************************************************
* THIS ROUTINE OPENS ALL THE DCBS.
*************************************************************************
*
OPEN        OPEN        (SYSIN,,PDSBDCB)
            ...         CHECK FOR GOOD OPEN
            BR          R6                  RETURN TO CALLING RTN
*
*
*************************************************************************
* THIS ROUTINE OBTAINS THE BLKSIZE FROM THE PDS DCB AND ALLOCATES
* VIRTUAL STORAGE FOR THE PDS BLOCK I/O AREA.
*************************************************************************
*
GETMAIN     LA          R10,PDSBDCB         SET ADRBLTY FOR PDS DCB DSECT
            LH          R11,DCBBLKSI        LD PDS BLOCK SIZE
            GETMAIN     EC,LV=(R11),A=BLKADR
            ...                             CHECK IF GM OK
            BR          R6                  RETURN TO CALLING RTN
*
*
*************************************************************************
* THIS ROUTINE CALCULATES THE NUMBER OF LOGICAL RECORDS IN A FULL
* PHYSICAL BLOCK. THIS INFORMATION IS USED BY THE DEBLOCKING ROUTINE.
*************************************************************************
*
GETLRINF    LA          R10,PDSBDCB         SET ADRBLTY FOR PDS DCB DSECT
            LH          R12,DCBLRECL        LOAD PDS LRECL
            ST          R12,LRECLEN         SAVE PDS LRECL
            LA          R14,0               CLEAR REG 14 FOR DR INSTR
            LH          R15,DCBBLKSI        LOAD PDS BLKSZ
            DR          R14,R12             DIVIDE BLKSZ BY LRECL
            ST          R15,LRECMAX         SAVE NUMB OF LRECS PER BLOCK
            BR          R6                  RETURN TO CALLING RTN
*
*
*************************************************************************
* THIS ROUTINE LOCATES THE NEXT MEMBER THAT IS TO BE PROCESSED. IN ORDER
```

```
* TO PERFORM THAT TASK, THIS ROUTINE BRANCHES AND LINKS TO THE
* SUBROUTINES THAT PERFORM THE FOLLOWING FUNCTIONS:
*       * READ THE NEXT MEMBER NAME FROM THE SYSIN DATASET;
*       * SET THE DASD LOCATION IN THE PDS DCB TO THE BEGINNING OF THE
*         MEMBER THAT IS TO BE PROCESSED.
***********************************************************************
*
LOCMEMB     BAL        R7,GETNAME          GET A SPECIFIED MEMBER NAME
            BAL        R7,FINDMEMB         SET MEMB PTR IN PDS DCB
            LTR        R15,R15             CHK IF MEMB FOUND
            BNZ        LOCMEMB             IF NO, TRY NEXT SPEC MEMB
            BR         R6                  IF YES, RET TO CALLING RET
*
*
***********************************************************************
* THIS SUBROUTINE READS THE NAME OF THE NEXT MEMBER, THAT IS TO BE
* PROCESSED FROM THE SYSIN DATASET.
***********************************************************************
*
GETNAME     GET        SYSIN,MEMBNAME      GET A SPEC MEMB NAME FROM SEQ DS
            BR         R7                  RETURN TO CALLING RTN
*
*
***********************************************************************
* THIS SUBROUTINE CAUSES THE LOCATION OF THE BEGINNING OF THE
* SPECIFIED MEMBER TO BE PLACED INTO THE PDS DCB.
***********************************************************************
*
FINDMEMB    FIND       PDSBDCB,MEMBNAME,D  FIND MEMB WITH NAME SPECIFIED
            LTR        R15,R15             CHK IF SPEC MEMB FOUND
            BNZ        NOMEMB              IF NO, IND MEMB NOT FOUND
            BR         R7                  IF YES, RET TO CALLING RET
NOMEMB      ...
            BR         R7                  RETURN TO CALLING RTN
*
*
***********************************************************************
* THIS ROUTINE READS THE NEXT LOGICAL RECORD OF THE MEMBER. IN ORDER TO
* PERFORM THAT TASK, THIS ROUTINE BRANCHES AND LINKS TO THE SUBROUTINES
* THAT PERFORM THE FOLLOWING FUNCTIONS:
*       * READ THE NEXT PHYSICAL BLOCK OF THE MEMBER;
*       * DEBLOCK THE PHYSICAL BLOCK INTO LOGICAL RECORDS.
***********************************************************************
*
GETLREC     BAL        R7,READBLOK         READ A MEMB BLOCK FROM PDS
            BAL        R7,DEBLOCK          GET A LREC FROM BLOCK
            BR         R6                  RETURN TO CALLING RTN
*
*
***********************************************************************
* THIS SUBROUTINE READS AN ENTIRE PHYSICAL BLOCK OF THE MEMBER AND SETS
* THE LOGICAL RECORD POINTER TO THE BEGINNING OF THE BLOCK AND SETS THE
* LOGICAL RECORD NUMBER COUNTER TO ONE.
***********************************************************************
*
READBLOK    CLI        READSW,C'1'         CHK IF NEXT BLOCK READ REQUIRED
            BNER       R7                  IF NOT, RET TO CALLING RET
            MVI        READSW,C'0'
            L          R11,BLKADR          LD ADR OF BLOCK I/O AREA
            ST         R11,LRECPTR         INIT LREC PTR TO BG OF BLOCK
            L          LRECCTR,ONE         INIT LREC CTR TO ONE
            READ       RDDECB,SF,PDSBDCB,(R11)
            CHECK      RDRECB              CHECK IF READ OK
            BR         R7                  RETURN TO CALLING RTN
```

```
*
*
***************************************************************************
* THIS SUBROUTINE DEBLOCKS A PHYSICAL BLOCK OF THE PDS INTO LOGICAL
* RECORDS. IT USES THE INFORMATION IN LRECPTR (POINTER TO NEXT LOGICAL
* RECORD) AND LRECCTR (NUMBER OF THE NEXT LOGICAL RECORD IN THE BLOCK).
* THIS ROUTINE DOES THE FOLLOWING:
*       * UPDATES THE VALUES IN LRECPTR AND LRECCTR;
*       * CHECKS FOR END-OF-BLOCK (BY COMPARING THE NUMBER OF THE LOGICAL
*         RECORD TO THE TOTAL LOGICAL RECORDS IN A BLOCK);
*       * LOADS REGISTER 2 WITH THE ADDRESS OF THE CURRENT LOGICAL RECORD.
* THE INITIAL VALUES OF LRECPTR AND LRECCTR ARE SET BY THE READBLOK
* ROUTINE.
***************************************************************************
*
DEBLOCK     L           R10,LRECCTR         LOAD CURR LREC CTR
            L           R11,LRECPTR         LOAD CURR LREC PTR
            LR          R2,R11              SAVE CURR LREC PTR IN REG 2
            C           R10,LRECMAX         CHECK IF LAST LREC OF BLOCK
            BE          LRECEND             IF YES, IND IT
            LA          R10,1(0,R10)        INCR LREC COUNT
            ST          R10,LRECCTR         SAVE LREC COUNT
            L           R12,LRECLEN         LOAD PDS LRECL
            LA          R11,0(R12,R11)      INCR TO NEXT LREC ADR
            ST          R11,LRECPTR         SAVE NEXT LREC ADR
            BR          R7                  RETURN TO CALLING RTN
LRECEND     MVI         READSW,C'1'         IND THAT NEXT BLOCK READ REQUIRED
            BR          R7                  RETURN TO CALLING RTN
*
*
***************************************************************************
* THIS ROUTINE PROCESSES EACH LOGICAL RECORD OF THE MEMBER.
***************************************************************************
*
PROCMEMB    LR          R11,R2              LD ADR OF LREC, SET DSECT ADRBLTY
            ...
            BR          R6                  RETURN TO CALLING RTN
*
*
***************************************************************************
* THIS ROUTINE CLOSES ALL THE DCBS.
***************************************************************************
*
CLOSE       CLOSE       (SYSIN,,PDSBDCB)    CLOSE ALL DCBS
            BR          R6                  RETURN TO CALLING RTN
*
*
***************************************************************************
* THIS ROUTINE RESTORES THE REGISTERS AND RETURNS CONTROL.
***************************************************************************
*
RETURN      RCNTL       RC=0                RETURN TO MVS OR CALLING PROG
*
*
***************************************************************************
* DC/DS STATEMENTS
***************************************************************************
*
READSW      DC          C'1'
ONE         DC          F'1'
BLKADR      DS          F
LRECLEN     DS          F
LRECPTR     DS          F
LRECCTR     DS          F
```

```
LRECMAX      DS          F
MEMBNAME     DS          D
*
*
***********************************************************************
* THE DCBS
***********************************************************************
*
SYSIN        DCB         DSORG=PS,MACRF=GM,EODAD=MEMBENDX,DDNAME=SYSIN
PDSBDCB      DCB         DSORG=PO,MACRF=R,EODAD=MEMBEND,DDNAME=PDSDD
*
*
***********************************************************************
* THE DSECTS
***********************************************************************
*
             PRINT       NOGEN
             DCBD        DSORG=PO             GENERATES PO-DCB DSECT
             PRINT       GEN
*
             DSECT
             LRECMAP
             ...                              FIELDS OF LOGICAL RECORD
*
*
***********************************************************************
* END OF PROGRAM
***********************************************************************
*
             END
```

NOTES:

- The DEBLOCK routine returns the address of each logical record in register 2.
- The DEBLOCK routine assumes fixed length records. As an exercise, the reader might try to enhance the routine to process both fixed and variable length records.
- The DEBLOCK routine does not check for short blocks. As an exercise, the reader might try to enhance the routine to check for short blocks, using one of the methods described above.
- The "D" in the third positional parameter of the FIND macro instruction indicates that a member name is specified. A "C" indicates that a member location (TTR) is specified.

LOCATING MEMBERS USING THE BLDL MACRO INSTRUCTION

The BLDL macro instruction is used to return directory information into a programmer's defined virtual storage area (called a BLDL-List). The BLDL-list consists of one or more entries. The programmer supplies the names of the members, whose directory information is desired, into the BLDL-list. One entry is defined for each member name. The BLDL macro instruction returns the directory information in the appropriate entries for the member names supplied. The member location TTRK, returned by the BLDL macro instruction, may then be used by the FIND macro instruction.

THE BLDL MACRO INSTRUCTION

The format of the BLDL macro instruction is as follows.

```
[name] BLDL dcb-addr,list-addr
```

`dcb-addr`
: Specifies the address of the DCB. It may be the name associated with the DCB macro instruction or the address of the DCB in a register, enclosed in parentheses. The DCB must specify BPAM (DSORG=PO and MACRF= R or W) and must be OPENed for output. A specification of 0 indicates that the active load library is to be searched for the specified member name (STEPLIB/JOBLIB then link-list)

`list-addr`
: Specifies the address of the BLDL-list. The address may be specified as the name associated with the list area or in a register, enclosed in parentheses. The format of the BLDL-list is illustrated in Figure 8.4.1.

`FFLL`
: The BLDL-list description. The FF is two bytes and contains the number of entries in the BLDL-list. The LL is two bytes and contains the maximum length of the directory entry that is to be placed into each BLDL-list entry. The value of LL must be a minimum of 12 and a maximum of 74. This field is set by the programmer.

`NAME`
: The name of the member whose directory entry is desired. The name may be the primary name or an alias of the member. This field is set by the programmer.

`TTR`
: The starting location of the member relative from the beginning of the PDS. The same field as in the directory.

`K`
: Indicates if the member is from a concatenated dataset. Set to X'00' if the member is from the first or only dataset, X'01' if the member is from the second dataset and so on.

`Z`
: Source of directory entry: X'00' for private library (pointed to by DCB), X'01' for link-list library, and X'02' for job/step library.

`C`
: The same field as in the directory.

`USER-DATA`
: The same field as in the directory.

```
FFLL    (4)
BLDL    Entry-1
        NAME         (8)
        TTR          (3)
        K            (1)
        Z            (1)
        C            (1)
        USER-DATA    (0 to 31 Halfwords)
BLDL    Entry-2
...
BLDL    Entry-n
```

Figure 8.4.1. This figure illustrates the format of the BLDL-list. The numbers in parentheses are the lengths (in bytes, unless otherwise indicated) of the fields.

The LL field of the BLDL-list description controls how much data is placed into each BLDL-list entry. If only the control information is required, then specify a length of 14. That will provide the TTR and C fields of the directory entry. If all the user-data for each member is also required, but the maximum length of the user-data is not known, then specify the maximum BLDL-list entry length of 74. If less than the maximum length is specified, then only the amount of user-data that will fit will be placed into each BLDL-list entry.

When the BLDL macro instruction returns control, register 15 is posted with one the following return code:

Return Code (Hex)	Meaning
00	Successful completion.
04	One of more of the entries in the list could not be filled. This could indicate that the specified name was not found in the library or that the list is invalid.
08	I/O error searching directory, insufficient virtual storage for BLDL to process, or invalid DEB.

Since the previous program (Coding Example 8.4.2) was structured properly, it may be easily modified to use the BLDL macro instruction to provide the FIND macro intruction with the location of the member that is to be read. Only the LOCMEMB routine and its called subroutines need to be modified. The modified LOCMEMB routine is illustrated in Coding Example 8.4.3.

Coding Example 8.4.3

The following code modification of LOCMEMB (from Coding Example 8.4.2) and its subroutines illustrates the use of the BLDL macro instruction to assist in the reading of members:

```
LOCMEMB   BAL    R7,GETNAME          GET A SPECIFIED MEMBER NAME
          BAL    R7,GETTTRK          GET TTRK OF MEMBER
          LTR    R15,R15             CHK IF TTRK OF MEMB FOUND
          BNZ    LOCMEMB             IF NO, TRY TO LOC NEXT MEMB
          BAL    R7,FINDMEMB         IF YES, SET MEMB PTR IN PDS DCB
          BR     R6                  RETURN TO CALLING RTN
*
GETNAME   GET    SYSIN,MEMBNAME      GET A SPEC MEMB NAME FROM SEQ DS
          BR     R7                  RETURN TO CALLING RTN
*
GETTTRK   MVC    BLDLNAME,MEMBNAME   MOVE MEMB NAME INTO BLDL-LIST
          BLDL   PDSBDCB,BLDLLST     READ DIR ENTRY FOR SPEC MEMB
          LTR    R15,R15             CHK IF DIR ENTRY FOUND
          BNZ    NOMEMB              IF NO, INDICATE IT
          BR     R7                  RETURN TO CALLING RTN
NOMEMB    ...
          BR     R7                  RETURN TO CALLING RTN
*
FINDMEMB  FIND   PDSBDCB,BLDLTTRK,C  FIND MEMB WITH TTRK SPECIFIED
          BR     R7                  RETURN TO CALLING RTN
*
BLDLLST   DS     0CL16
BLDLFFLL  DC     X'0001',X000C'      1 ENTRY, 12 BYTES
```

```
BLDLNAME    DS          CL8
BLDLTTRK    DS          CL4
*
MEMBTTRK    DS          CL4
```

NOTES:

- The BLDL macro instruction is used to obtain the location of only one member at a time. This is for illustration purposes only. As an exercise, the reader might try to modify the code to cause BLDL to obtain directory information for ten members at a time, and provide the required code to process only one of these directory entries (members) at a time.
- Only the first 12 bytes of each directory entry is requested via the BLDL macro instruction because that is all that is required to obtain the information for the FIND macro instruction.

8.5 WRITING NEW MEMBERS INTO A PDS

New members may be added into a PDS, using either QSAM (or BSAM) or BPAM. There are the same advantages and disadvantages in using QSAM and BPAM for write operations as there were in the read operations described above. Using QSAM is easier than using BPAM, but BPAM is more efficient if more than one member is to be processed in the same PDS.

8.5.1 Creating New Members Using QSAM

When new members are written into a PDS, using QSAM, the names of the members may be specified in one of two ways. If only one member is to be created, then its name may be specified in the JCL. If multiple members are to be created, then the modified JFCB method must be used. Like the read operation described above, the logic of the program is the same as if the write were to a sequential dataset.

When new members are added into the PDS, the JCL DD statement that points to the PDS may specify DISP=OLD (SHR, if the program is doing its own ENQing) or DISP=MOD. The CLOSE macro instruction causes the PDS directory to be updated. If the member name already exists in the PDS, then it is replaced by the new member if DISP=OLD (or SHR) is specified. If this is not desired, then DISP=MOD must be specified. This will cause the CLOSE to ABEND with SB14-04 if the member name already exists in the PDS directory. The ABEND may be suppressed with the use of the ESTAE macro instruction (discussed in Chapter 6).

Coding Example 8.5.1

This coding example illustrates how to add one new member into a PDS. In this example, the member name is specified via the JCL, SEQDD points to a sequential dataset that contains the records of the new member, and PDSDD points to the PDS that is to receive the new member.

```
WRTPDSQ     CSECT
*
*
*********************************************************************
* INITIALIZATION
*********************************************************************
*
            INITL     3,EQU=R                       INITIALIZE PROGRAM
```

```
*
*
*************************************************************************
* MAINSTREAM OF PROGRAM
************************************************************************* *
         BAL    R6,OPEN                 OPEN DATASETS
NEXTREC  BAL    R6,GETRECS              READ A RECORD OF THE MEMBER
         BAL    R6,PUTRECS              WRITE A RECORD OF THE MEMBER INTO PDS
         B      NEXTREC                 READ NEXT RECORD
RECEND   BAL    R6,CLOSE                CLOSE DATASETS AND UPDATE PDS DIR
         B      RETURN                  RETURN TO MVS OR CALLING PROG
*
*
*************************************************************************
* THIS ROUTINE OPENS ALL THE DCBS AND CAUSES THE FIRST PUT TO THE PDS
* TO START WRITING AFTER THE LAST MEMBER IN THE PDS.
*************************************************************************
*
OPEN     OPEN   (SEQIN,,PDSOUT,(OUTPUT))
         ...                            CHECK FOR GOOD OPEN
         BR     R6                      RETURN TO CALLING RTN
*
*
*************************************************************************
* THIS ROUTINE READS THE RECORDS THAT ARE TO BE PUT INTO THE PDS.
*************************************************************************
*
GETRECS  GET    SEQIN,RECORD            READ MEMB REC FROM SEQ DATASET
         BR     R6                      RETURN TO CALLED
*
*
*************************************************************************
* THIS ROUTINE WRITES THE RECORDS INTO THE PDS.
*************************************************************************
*
PUTRECS  PUT    PDSOUT,RECORD           WRITE MEMB REC INTO PDS
         BR     R6                      RETURN TO CALLING RTN
*
*
*************************************************************************
* THIS ROUTINE CLOSES ALL THE DCBS AND IMPLICITLY CAUSES THE STOW
* FUNCTION TO UPDATE THE DIRECTORY OF THE PDS.
*************************************************************************
*
CLOSE    CLOSE  (SEQIN,,PDSOUT)         CLOSE DATASETS AND UPDT DIR
         BR     R6                      RETURN TO CALLING RTN
*
*
*************************************************************************
* THIS ROUTINE RESTORES THE REGISTERS AND RETURNS CONTROL.
*************************************************************************
*
RETURN   RCNTL  ,RC=0                   RETURN TO MVS OR CALLING PROG
*
*
*************************************************************************
* DC/DS STATEMENTS
*************************************************************************
*
RECORD   DS     CL80
*
*
*************************************************************************
* THE DCBS
```

```
************************************************************************
*
SEQIN     DCB      DSORG=PS,MACRF=GM,EODAD=RECEND,DDNAME=SEQDD
PDSOUT    DCB      DSORG=PS,MACRF=PM,DDNAME=PDSDD
*
*
************************************************************************
* END OF PROGRAM
************************************************************************
*
          END
```

NOTES:

- When the PDS DCB is OPENed for OUTPUT and if a member name was specified via the JCL or modified JFCB, then the location of the next available area in the PDS is placed in the DCB. Then, when the PUT macro instruction is issued, the member records will be written, starting at that location.
- When the PDS is CLOSEd, the PDS directory is updated to reflect the new member.

If multiple members are to be written to the PDS, then the modified JFCB method is used. The coding technique is the same as shown in Coding Example 8.4.1 in Section 8.4 for reading multiple members, except that the PUT macro instruction (MACRF=PM is specified in DCB) is used for the PDS instead of the GET macro instruction and the PDS DCB is OPENed for output.

8.5.2 Creating New Members Using BPAM

When new members are written into a PDS using BPAM, the STOW macro instruction, with the add (A) option, must be executed after the last record of each member is written, to update the directory.

THE STOW MACRO INSTRUCTION

The STOW macro instruction causes BPAM to update the PDS directory by adding, changing, replacing, or deleting an entry in the directory.

The format of the STOW macro instruction is as follows.

```
[name] STOW dcb-addr,list-addr,directory-action
```

`dcb-addr`

Specifies the address of the DCB. It may be the name of the DCB macro instruction or the address of the DCB in a register, enclosed in parentheses. The DCB must specify BPAM (DSORG=PO and MACRF=R or MACRF=W) and must be OPENed for output.

`list-addr`

Specifies the address of the STOW-list that contains the information required for the directory action specified. The address may be specified as the name associated with the list area or in a register, enclosed in parentheses. The format of the STOW-list is illustrated in Figure 8.5.1.

`directory-action`

Specifies one of the following actions:

A	Indicates that an entry is to be added to the directory.

C	Indicates that the primary name or alias name of an existing entry is to be changed.
D	Indicates that an existing entry is to be deleted.
R	Indicates that an existing directory entry is to be replaced by a new directory entry.This action is used to rewrite (update) an existing member and/or change or add user-data. If the entry is not found, then a new entry is added.

For the A and R directory actions

```
NAME (8); TTR (3); C (1); USER-DATA (0 to 31 halfwords)
```

NAME
: The name of the member, whose entry is being added or replaced. The name may be the primary name or an alias of the member.

TTR
: The starting location of the member, relative from the beginning of the PDS. This field is supplied by BPAM when a new entry is added or an existing entry is replaced. If an alias name is being added for an existing entry, then this field is supplied by the programmer and may be obtained via the BLDL macro instruction.

C
: Indicates the following control information:

Bit 0: 0 for primary name, 1 for alias name.
Bits 1-2: Number of TTRN fields in the user-data.
Bits 3-7: Length of user-data in halfwords.

USER-DATA
: From 0 to 62 (in increments of halfwords) of user-data.

For the C directory action

```
OLD-NAME (8); NEW-NAME (8)
```

OLD-NAME
: The primary or alias name of the existing member.

NEW-NAME
: The member name to which the existing name is to be changed.

For the D directory action

```
NAME (8)
```

NAME
: The primary or alias name of the existing member whose entry is to be deleted.

Figure 8.5.1. This figure illustrates the format of the STOW-list. The numbers in parentheses are the lengths (in bytes, unless otherwise indicated) of the fields.

When the STOW macro instruction returns control, register 15 is posted with one the following return code:

Return Code (Hex)	Meaning
00	For all functions: Directory update successful.
04	A: The directory already contains the member name. No directory update performed. C: The directory already contains the new member name. No directory update performed. D: Not applicable. R: Not applicable.
08	A: Not applicable. C: The specified old member name not in directory. No directory update performed. D: The specified member name not in directory. No directory update performed. R: The specified member name not in directory. Member name added to directory.
0C	A: No more space in directory. No directory update performed. C: No more space in directory. No directory update performed. D: Not applicable. R: No more space in directory. No directory update performed.
10	For all functions: Permanent I/O error. No directory update performed.
14	For all functions: The specified DCB is either not OPENed or not OPENed for output. No directory update performed.
18	For all functions: Insufficient virtual storage available to perform specified function.

Coding Example 8.5.2

This coding example illustrates how to add new members into a PDS, using BPAM. In this example, SEQDD points to a sequential dataset that contains the records of each new member, stacked one behind the other. Each member is preceded by a control record that contains "$$" in the first two positions, followed by the member name. PDSDD points to the PDS that is to receive the new members. Since BPAM writes only physical blocks, the program must also block the records.

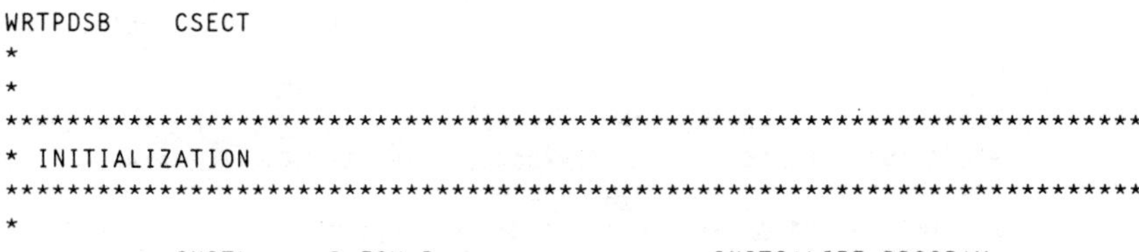

```
WRTPDSB    CSECT
*
*
***********************************************************************
* INITIALIZATION
***********************************************************************
*
           INITL     3,EQU=R                        INITIALIZE PROGRAM
```

```
          USING    IHADCB,R10                DEFINE REG FOR DCB DSECT
*
*
***************************************************************************
* MAINSTREAM OF PROGRAM
***************************************************************************
*
          BAL      R6,OPEN                   OPEN DATASETS
          BAL      R6,GETMAIN                ALLOC STOR FOR I/O BLOCK AREA
          BAL      R6,CALCRECS               FIND NUMB OF LRECS IN BLOCK
          BAL      R6,GETNAME1               GET AND SAVE FIRST MEMBER NAME
NEXTREC   BAL      R6,GETDATA                READ MEMB RECS, BLD BLOCK
          BAL      R6,WRTPDS                 WRITE WHOLE BLOCK INTO PDS
          B        NEXTREC                   GET NEXT MEMB REC
MEMBEND   BAL      R6,LASTBLK                MEMB-RECS-END, WRITE LAST INCOMP
*                                            BLOCK INTO PDS
          BAL      R6,STOW                   UPDATE PDS DIR
          B        NEXTREC                   GET NEXT MEMB RECORDS
DATAEND   BAL      R6,LASTBLK                END-OF-MEMBS, WRITE LAST INCOMP
*                                            BLOCK INTO PDS
          BAL      R6,STOW                   UPDATE PDS DIR FOR LAST MEMB
          BAL      R6,CLOSE                  CLOSE DATASETS
          B        RETURN                    RETURN TO MVS OR CALLING PROG
*
*
***************************************************************************
* THIS ROUTINE OPENS ALL THE DCBS.
***************************************************************************
*
OPEN      OPEN     (SEQDCB,,PDSDCB,(OUTPUT))
          ...                                CHECK FOR GOOD OPEN
          BR       R6                        RETURN TO CALLING RTN
*
*
***************************************************************************
* THIS ROUTINE OBTAINS THE BLKSIZE FROM THE PDS DCB AND ALLOCATES
* VIRTUAL STORAGE FOR THE PDS BLOCK I/O AREA.
***************************************************************************
*
GETMAIN   LA       R10,PDSDCB                SET ADRBLTY FOR PDS DCB DSECT
          LH       R11,DCBBLKSI              LD PDS BLKSZ FOR GETMAIN
          GETMAIN  EU,LV=(R11),A=BLKADR
          BR       R6                        RETURN TO CALLING RTN
*
*
***************************************************************************
* THIS ROUTINE CALCULATES THE NUMBER OF LOGICAL RECORDS IN A FULL
* PHYSICAL BLOCK. THIS INFORMATION IS USED BY THE BLOCKING ROUTINE.
***************************************************************************
*
CALCRECS  LA       R10,PDSDCB                SET ADRBLTY FOR PDS DCB DSECT
          LA       R14,0                     CLEAR REG 14 FOR DR INSTR
          LH       R15,DCBBLKSI              LD PDS BLKSZ
          LH       R12,DCBLRECL              LD PDS LRECL
          DR       R14,R12                   DIVIDE LRECL INTO BLKSZ
          ST       R15,BLKRECS               SAVE NUMB OF LRECS PER BLOCK
          BR       R6                        RETURN TO CALLING RTN
*
*
***************************************************************************
* THIS ROUTINE READS THE FIRST RECORD OF THE SEQUENTIAL DATASET AND
* VERIFIES THAT IT CONTAINS A MEMBER NAME.
***************************************************************************
*
```

```
GETNAME1  BAL     R7,GETSEQ               READ FIRST REC FROM SEQ DS
          CLC     0(2,R2),ID              CHK FOR MEMB NAME ID
          BNE     NONAME1                 IF NO, NO MEMB NAME
          MVC     SAVENAME,2(R2)          IF YES, SAVE MEMB NAME
          BR      R6                      RETURN TO CALLING RTN
NONAME1   WTO     '*** FIRST DATA RECORD DOES NOT CONTAIN MEMBER NAME ***'
          ABEND   901
*
*
*************************************************************************
* THIS SUBROUTINE READS A RECORD FROM THE SEQUENTIAL DATASET AND LOADS
* THE ADDRESS OF THAT RECORD INTO REGISTER 2.
*************************************************************************
*
GETSEQ    GET     SEQDCB                  GET A LREC OF MEMB FROM SEQ DS
          LR      R2,R1                   SAVE ADR OF LREC IN REG2
          BR      R7                      RETURN TO CALLING RTN
*
*
*************************************************************************
* THIS ROUTINE BUILDS A BLOCK OF DATA FOR THE PDS DATASET. IT
* CONTINUALLY BRANCHES AND LINKS TO THE GETSEQ SUBROUTINE TO READ A
* RECORD OF THE MEMBER FROM THE SEQUENTIAL DATASET UNTIL A WHOLE BLOCK
* IS BUILT.
*************************************************************************
*
GETDATA   LA      R10,PDSDCB              SET ADRBLTY FOR PDS DCB DSECT
          L       R11,BLKRECS             LD NUMB OF LRECS PER BLOCK
          L       R12,BLKADR              LD ADR OF I/O BLOCK AREA
          LA      R9,0                    CLEAR REG 9 FOR LREC CTR
NEXTGET   BAL     R7,GETSEQ               GET A LREC OF MEMB FROM SEQ DS
          CLC     0(2,R2),ID              CHK FOR MEMB NAME ID
          BE      SETNAME                 IF YES, BG OF NEW MEMB, DO STOW
          MVI     FULBLKSW,C'0'           IND BLOCK NOT WRITTEN YET
          LA      R9,1(0,R9)              INCR LREC CTR
          ST      R9,LRECCTR              SAVE LREC CTR
          MVC     0(80,R12),0(R2)         MOVE LREC INTO BLOCK AREA
          LA      R12,80(0,R12)           INCR TO NEXT LREC SLOT IN BLOCK
          BCT     R11,NEXTGET             CHK IF BLOCK FULL
          MVI     FULBLKSW,C'1'           IF FULL, IND IT
          BR      R6                      RETURN TO CALLING RTN
SETNAME   MVC     STOWNAME,SAVENAME       PUT CURR MEMB NAME INTO STOW-LIST
          MVC     SAVENAME,2(R1)          RESTORE NEXT MEMB NAME
          B       MEMBEND                 BRANCH TO MEMB-END RTN
*
*
*************************************************************************
* THIS ROUTINE WRITES A PHYSICAL BLOCK INTO THE PDS. THE SIZE OF THE
* BLOCK IS SPECIFIED IN THE PDS DCB.
*************************************************************************
*
WRTPDS    L       R12,BLKADR              LD ADR OF I/O BLOCK AREA
          WRITE   WDECB,SF,PDSDCB,(R12)
          CHECK   WDECB                   CHECK IF WRITE OK
          BR      R6                      RETURN TO CALLING RTN
*
*
*************************************************************************
* THIS ROUTINE RECEIVES CONTROL EACH TIME WHEN ALL THE RECORDS OF A
* MEMBER HAVE BEEN READ FROM THE SEQUENTIAL DATASET. THIS ROUTINE
* CHECKS IF THE LAST BLOCK IS INCOMPLETE AND IS REQUIRED TO BE WRITTEN
* INTO THE PDS. THE PDS DCB BLKSIZE IS SET TO THE SHORT BLKSIZE BEFORE
* THE WRITE AND THEN THE DCB BLKSIZE IS RESTORED TO THE NORMAL BLKSIZE.
*************************************************************************
```

```
*
LASTBLK  CLI    FULBLKSW,C'1'          CHK IF LAST BLOCK WRITTEN
         BER    R6                     IF YES, RETURN
         LA     R10,PDSDCB             IF NO, SET ADRBLTY FOR PDS DSECT
         LA     R14,0                  CLEAR REG 14 FOR MR INSTR
         LH     R15,DCBLRECL           LD PDS LRECL
         L      R12,LRECCTR            LD NUMB OF LRECS IN LAST BLOCK
         LTR    R12,R12                CHK IF NO LRECS IN LAST BLOCK
         BZ     NORECS                 IF NO LRECS, ERROR
         MR     R14,R12                CALC HOW MUCH OF BLOCK FULL
         MVC    SAVBLKSZ,DCBBLKSI      SAVE PDS NORMAL BLKSZ
         STH    R15,DCBBLKSI           PUT LEN OF LAST BLOCK INTO PDS DCB
         ST     R6,SAVREG6             SAVE REG 6 FOR BAL INSTR
         BAL    R6,WRTPDS              WRITE LAST BLOCK OF MEMB
         L      R6,SAVREGS             RESTORE REG 6 AFTER BAL DONE
         MVC    DCBBLKSI,SAVBLKSZ      RESTORE NORMAL PDS BLKSZ
         BR     R6                     RETURN TO CALLING RTN
NORECS   WTO    '*** NO DATA RECORDS IN SEQDD ***',ROUTCDE=11
         ABEND  902
*
*
**************************************************************************
* THIS ROUTINE ISSUES THE STOW MACRO TO UPDATE THE DIRECTORY OF
* THE PDS.
**************************************************************************
*
STOW     STOW   PDSDCB,STOWLST,A       UPDATE PDS DIR
         LTR    R15,R15                CHK RC
         BZR    R6                     IF OK, RET TO CALLING RET
         C      R15,BIN4               CHK IF DUP MEMB NAME
         BE     DUPNAME                IF YES, NO UPDT, DSPLY WARN MSG
         C      R15,BIN12              CHK FOR NO MORE DIR SPC
         BE     NODIRSPC               NO MORE ROOM IN DIR, DSPLY MSG
         ...                           CHECK OTHER RETURN CODES
DUPNAME  MVC    WTO1NAME,STOWNAME      PUT DUPL NAME INTO WTO MSG
         LA     R1,WTO1LST             LD LIST ADR FOR EXEC-FORM WTO
         WTO    MF=(E,(R1))            ISSUE EXEC-FORM OF WTO
         BR     R6                     RETURN TO CALLING RTN
NODIRSPC WTO    '*** NO MORE DIRECTORY SPACE FOR NEW MEMBER ***',  -
                ROUTCDE=11
         ABEND  903
*
*
**************************************************************************
* THIS ROUTINE CLOSES ALL THE DCBS.
**************************************************************************
*
CLOSE    CLOSE  (SEQDCB,,PDSDCB)       CLOSE ALL DCBS
         BR     R6                     RETURN TO CALLING RTN
*
*
**************************************************************************
* THIS ROUTINE RESTORES THE REGISTERS AND RETURNS CONTROL.
**************************************************************************
*
RETURN   RCNTL  RC=0
*
*
**************************************************************************
* DC/DS STATEMENTS
**************************************************************************
*
FULBLKSW DC     C'0'
ID       DC     C'$$'
```

```
BIN4      DC      F'4'
BIN12     DC      F'12'
BLKADR    DS      F
BLKRECS   DS      F
LRECCTR   DC      F'0'
SAVREG6   DS      F
SAVENAME  DS      CL8
SAVBLKSZ  DS      CL2
*
*
************************************************************************
* THE WTO-LIST
************************************************************************
*
          CNOP    0,4
WTO1LST   DC      AL2(WTO1LSTX-WTO1LST)
          DC      X'8000'                  INDICATE DESC/ROUTCDE INCLUDED
          DC      C'***SPECIFIED MEMBER NAME: '
WTO1NAME  DS      CL8
          DC      C' ALREADY EXISTS IN LIBRARY—MEMBER NOT ADDED ***'
WTO1LSTX  EQU     *
          DC      .X'0000'                 DESC DEFAULT
          DC      X'0020                   ROUTCDE=11
*
*
************************************************************************
* THE STOW-LIST
************************************************************************
*
STOWLST   DS      0CL12
STOWNAME  DS      CL8
STOWTTR   DS      CL3
STOWC     DC      X'00'
*
*
************************************************************************
* THE DCBS
************************************************************************
*
SEQDCB    DCB     DSORG=PS,MACRF=GL,LRECL=80,RECFM=FB,EODAD=DATAEND, -
                  DDNAME=SEQDD
PDSDCB    DCB     DSORG=PO,MACRF=W,LRECL=80,DDNAME=PDSDD
*
*
************************************************************************
* THE DSECTS
************************************************************************
*
          DSECT   -
          DCBD    DSORG=PO                 GENERATES PO-DCB DSECT
*
*
************************************************************************
* END OF PROGRAM
************************************************************************
*
          END
```

NOTES:

- The "A" option of the STOW macro instruction is used to add the new members to the directory. If duplicate members are to be replaced, then the "R" option could be specified instead.

- Since BPAM deals only with whole blocks, the LASTBLK routine is used to write the last short (incomplete) block, if required of the member.
- This program should verify that the block size of the PDS is a multiple of the logical record length of the input data. This is left as an exercise for the reader.

8.6 UPDATING EXISTING MEMBERS OF A PDS

Existing members of a PDS may be updated using either QSAM (or BSAM) or BPAM. There are the same advantages and disadvantages in using QSAM and BPAM for update operations as there are in the read operations described above. Although using QSAM is easier than using BPAM, BPAM is more efficient if more than one member is to be processed in the same PDS.

When an existing member is updated, it must be either rewritten or updated in-place. If records are added or deleted or record lengths are changed (in the case of variable length records), then the member must be rewritten. When a member is updated in-place, the same physical space is used; therefore, the TTRs are not changed and the STOW macro instruction (in the case of BPAM) is not required.

8.6.1 Alias Name Considerations when Updating Members of a PDS

There are no alias name considerations when members are updated in-place because the TTRs do not change. However, there are certain alias name considerations when members are rewritten.

If only the primary names are selected to be rewritten, then the alias names (if any) will point to the old version of the member instead of the updated version. If both the primary and alias names are selected for update, then this will result in a different physical member for each name instead of the same physical member for all the names.

There are two techniques that may be used to keep the alias names in sync with their primary names. Both methods involve using only the primary name for the update.

One technique is to perform all the updates and then execute a separate program that resets the alias names to the new TTR. This program requires, as input, a list of the alias names that are assigned to each primary name that was updated. Section 8.7 describes how to assign an alias name to an existing primary name.

Another technique is to have the update program, itself, reassign the alias names. This can be done only if the update program uses BPAM. The old and new TTRs of each member that is updated must be saved in a table. The old TTR is obtained with the BLDL macro instruction executing before the STOW macro instructon is executed for the update, and the new TTR is obtained with the BLDL macro instruction executing after the STOW macro instruction is executed. After all the updates are performed, the directory is scanned for only alias names. Any alias name whose TTR matches the old TTR is replaced (R) via the STOW macro instruction using the corresponding new TTR.

8.6.2 Updating (Rewriting) Existing Members Using QSAM

When existing members are rewritten into a PDS using QSAM, the names of the members may be specified in one of two ways. If only one member is to be rewritten, then its name may be specified in the JCL. If multiple members are to be rewritten, then the modified JFCB method must be used. Rewriting a member requires two DCBs—one for input and one for output. The two DCBs may point to the same JCL DD statement. When the dataset is CLOSEd, the old member is deleted and the new member is added (new TTR placed into existing directory entry).

Coding Example 8.6.1

This coding example illustrates how to rewrite multiple members, using QSAM and modifying the JFCB. In this example, the READDIR macro instruction is used to read all the member names. Alias names are ignored, and only primary names contain "PR" in the first two positions or a "W" in position 5 are selected for update.

```
PDSUPDTQ  CSECT
*
*
***************************************************************************
* INITIALIZATION
***************************************************************************
*
          INITL     3,EQU=R                       INITIALIZE PROGRAM
          USING     INFMJFCB,R10                  DEFINE REG 10 FOR JFCB DSECT
*
*
***************************************************************************
* MAINSTREAM OF PROGRAM
***************************************************************************
*
          BAL       R6,RDJFCB                     READ JFCB INTO PROG AREA
NEXTMEMB  BAL       R6,GETNAME                    GET NEXT QUAL MEMB NAME FROM DIR
          BAL       R6,SETMEMB                    PUT MEMB NAME INTO JFCB
          BAL       R6,OPEN                       OPEN PDS AND POS TO MEMB NAME
NEXTREC   BAL       R6,GETMEMB                    READ A LREC OF MEMB
          BAL       R6,UPDTMEMB                   UPDATE LREC
          BAL       R6,PUTMEMB                    REWRITE THE LREC
          B         NEXTREC                       GET NEXT LREC OF MEMB
MEMBEND   BAL       R6,CLOSE                      MEMB-END, CLOSE PDS AND UPDATE DIR
          B         NEXTMEMB                      GET NEXT QUAL MEMB
MEMBENDX  BAL       R6,CLOSE                      END-OF-MEMBS, CLOSE PDS AND UPT DIR
          B         RETURN                        RETURN TO MVS OR CALLING PROG
*
*
***************************************************************************
* THIS ROUTINE READS THE JFCBS AND COPIES THEM FROM THE SWA INTO THE
* PROGRAMMER-SUPPLIED AREA.
***************************************************************************
*
RDJFCB    RDJFCB    (PDSQDCBI,,PDSQDCBO,(OUTPUT))
          LTR       R15,R15                       CHK IF JCL DD STMT IN JOBSTREAM
          BNZ       NODDNM                        IF NO, ERROR
          BR        R6                            IF YES, RET TO CALLING RTN
NODDNM    WTO       '*** JCL DD STATEMENT(S) OMITTED ***',ROUTCDE=11
          ABEND     901
*
*
***************************************************************************
* THIS ROUTINE USES THE READDIR MACRO TO OBTAIN THE MEMBER NAME IN THE
* NEXT PDS DIRECTORY ENTRY. ALIAS NAMES ARE IGNORED.
***************************************************************************
*
GETNAME   READDIR   PDSDD                         GET NEXT DIR ENTRY
          LTR       R15,R15                       CHECK IF PRIM NAME
          BZ        CHKNAME                       IF YES, CHK IF QUAL NAME
          C         R15,BIN4                      CHECK IF ALIAS
          BE        GETNAME                       IF YES, IGNORE
          B         MEMBENDX                      END-OF-DIR, BRANCH TO E-OF-D RTN
CHKNAME   BAL       R7,TESTNAME                   CHECK IF MEMB NAME OK FOR UPDT
          LTR       R15,R15                       CHECK RC FOR MEMB NAME OK
```

```
          BNZ      GETNAME                    IF NO, GET NEXT DIR ENTRY
          BR       R6                         IF YES, RET TO CALLING RTN
*
*
***********************************************************************
* THIS SUBROUTINE EXAMINES THE NAMES OF THE MEMBERS TO DETERMINE IF
* THEY ARE TO BE UPDATED. IT SETS A RC OF X'00' IN REGISTER 15 IF THE
* MEMBER IS TO BE UPDATED AND SETS A RC OF X'04' IF THE MEMBER IS NOT
* TO BE UPDATED.
***********************************************************************
*
TESTNAME  CLC      $MEMBER(2),=C'PR'          CHECK IF MEMB NAME ACCEPTABLE
          BE       NAMEOK                     IF YES, IND IT
          CLC      $MEMBER+4,C'W'             CHECK IF MEMB NAME ACCEPTABLE
          BE       NAMEOK                     IF YES, IND IT
          LA       R15,4                      IND SKIP MEMB NAME
          BR       R7                         RETURN TO CALLING RTN
NAMEOK    LA       R15,0                      IND MEMB NAME OK
          BR       R7                         RETURN TO CALLING RTN
*
*
***********************************************************************
* THIS ROUTINE MODIFIES THE JFCBS. THE NAME OF THE NEXT PDS MEMBER TO
* BE UPDATED IS INSERTED INTO THE PDS-MEMBER-NAME FIELD OF THE JFCBS
* ASSOCIATED WITH THE INPUT AND THE OUTPUT DCBS.
***********************************************************************
*
SETMEMB   LA       R10,JFCBI                  SET ADRBLTY FOR PDS DCB DSECT
          MVC      JFCBELNM,$MEMBER           PUT MEMB NAME INTO INPUT JFCB
          OI       JFCBIND1,JFCPDS            IND MEMB NAME SUPPLIED
          LA       R10,JFCBO                  SET ADRBLTY FOR PDS DCB DSECT
          MVC      JFCBELNM,$MEMBER           PUT MEMB NAME INTO OUTPUT JFCB
          OI       JFCBIND1,JFCPDS            IND MEMB NAME SUPPLIED
          BR       R6                         RETURN TO CALLING RTN
*
*
***********************************************************************
* THIS ROUTINE OPENS THE PDS DCBS USING THE INFORMATION IN THE MODIFIED
* JFCBS. THE OPEN WILL CAUSE THE NEXT GET TO START READING FROM THE
* FIRST LOGICAL RECORD OF THE MEMBER WHOSE NAME IS SPECIFIED IN THE
* JFCB OF THE INPUT PDS AND WILL CAUSE THE NEXT PUT TO START WRITING
* AFTER THE LAST MEMBER WHOSE NAME IS SPECIFIED IN THE JFCB OF THE
* OUTPUT PDS.
***********************************************************************
*
OPEN      OPEN     (PDSQDCBI,,PDSQDCBO,(OUTPUT)),TYPE=J
          ...                                 CHECK FOR GOOD OPEN
          BR       R6                         RETURN TO CALLING RTN
*
*
***********************************************************************
* THIS ROUTINE READS A RECORD FROM THE MEMBER WHOSE NAME IS SPECIFIED
* IN THE JFCB.
***********************************************************************
*
GETMEMB   GET      PDSQDCBI,RECORD            GET A LREC OF MEMB
          BR       R6                         RETURN TO CALLING RTN
*
*
***********************************************************************
* THIS ROUTINE UPDATES THE RECORDS OF THE MEMBER BEING PROCESSED.
***********************************************************************
*
UPDTMEMB  ...                                 UPDATE RECORD
```

```
         BR       R6                         RETURN TO CALLING RTN
*
*
***************************************************************************
* THIS ROUTINE REWRITES THE RECORDS OF THE MEMBER WHOSE NAME IS
* SPECIFIED IN THE JFCB
***************************************************************************
*
PUTMEMB  PUT      PDSQDCBO,RECORD            REWRITE THE LREC
         BR       R6                         RETURN TO CALLING RTN
*
*
***************************************************************************
* THIS ROUTINE CLOSES ALL THE DCBS AND IMPLICITLY CAUSES THE STOW
* FUNCTION TO UPDATE THE DIRECTORY OF THE OUTPUT PDS.
***************************************************************************
*
CLOSE    CLOSE    (PDSQDCBI,,PDSQDCBO)       CLOSE ALL DCBS
         BR       R6                         RETURN TO CALLING RTN
*
*
***************************************************************************
* THIS ROUTINE RESTORES THE REGISTERS AND RETURNS CONTROL.
***************************************************************************
*
RETURN   RCNTL    RC=0                       RETURN TO MVS OR CALLING PROG
*
*
***************************************************************************
* DC/DS STATEMENTS
***************************************************************************
*
BIN4     DC       F'4'
RECORD   DS       CL80
*
*
***************************************************************************
* THE JFCB-LISTS AND THE DCBS
***************************************************************************
*
JFCBI    DS       44F
JFCBIPTR DC       X'87'
         DC       AL3(JFCBI)
JFCBO    DS       44F
JFCBOPTR DC       X'87'
         DC       AL3(JFCBO)
*
PDSDCB1I DCB      DSORG=PS,MACRF=GM,EODAD=MEMBEND,EXLST=JFCBIPTR,  -
                  DDNAME=PDSDD
PDSDCB1O DCB      DSORG=PS,MACRF=PM,EXLST=JFCBOPTR,DDNAME=PDSDD
*
*
***************************************************************************
* THE DSECTS
***************************************************************************
*
         PRINT    NOGEN
         DSECT
         IEFJFCBN                            GENERATES THE JFCB DSECT
*
*
***************************************************************************
* END OF PROGRAM
***************************************************************************
```

```
*
         END
```

NOTES:

- Since alias names are ignored, they will not point to the updated versions of the members.

8.6.3 Updating (Rewriting) Existing Members Using BPAM

Rewriting members in a PDS, using BPAM, requires two DCBs—one for input and one for output. The STOW macro instruction is required with the replace (R) option to be executed after each member is rewritten, to update the directory.

Coding Example 8.6.2

This coding example illustrates how to rewrite members of a PDS, using BPAM. In this example, the names of the members that are to be updated are specified via a sequential dataset, and the PDS contains unblocked fixed-length records of length 1000.

```
PDSUPDTB  CSECT
*
*
***********************************************************************
* INITIALIZATION
***********************************************************************
*
          INITL    3,EQU=R                     INITIALIZE PROGRAM
*
*
***********************************************************************
* MAINSTREAM OF PROGRAM
***********************************************************************
*
          BAL      R6,OPEN                     OPEN DATASETS
NEXTMEMB  BAL      R6,LOCMEMB                  LOC SPECIFIED MEMB IN PDS
NEXTREC   BAL      R6,READMEMB                 READ A REC OF MEMB
          BAL      R6,UPDTMEMB                 UPDATE REC
          BAL      R6,WRTMEMB                  REWRITE REC OF MEMB
          B        NEXTREC                     READ NEXT REC OF MEMB
MEMBEND   BAL      R6,STOW                     MEMB-END, UPDATE DIR
          B        NEXTMEMB                    GET NEXT MEMB
MEMBENDX  BAL      R6,CLOSE                    END-OF-MEMBS, CLOSE DATASETS
          B        RETURN                      RETURN TO MVS OR CALLING PROG
*
*
***********************************************************************
* THIS ROUTINE OPENS ALL THE DCBS.
***********************************************************************
*
OPEN      OPEN     (SYSIN,,PDSBDCBI,,PDSBDCBO,(OUTPUT))
          ...                                  CHECK FOR GOOD OPEN
          BR       R6                          RETURN TO CALLING RTN
*
*
***********************************************************************
* THIS ROUTINE LOCATES THE NEXT MEMBER THAT IS TO BE PROCESSED. IN
* ORDER TO PERFORM THAT TASK, THIS ROUTINE BRANCHES AND LINKS TO THE
* SUBROUTINES THAT PERFORM THE FOLLOWING FUNCTIONS:
*      * READ THE NEXT MEMBER NAME FROM THE SYSIN DATASET;
```

```
*      * SET THE DASD LOCATION IN THE PDS DCB TO THE BEGINNING OF THE
*        MEMBER THAT IS TO PROCESSED.
***********************************************************************
*
LOCMEMB   BAL      R7,GETNAME              GET A SPEC MEMB NAME FROM SEQ DS
          BAL      R7,FIND                 SET MEMB ADR IN PDS DCB
          LTR      R15,R15                 CHK IF SPEC MEMB IN PDS
          BNZ      LOCMEMB                 IF NO, GET NEXT SPEC MEMB
          BR       R6                      IF YES, RET TO CALLING RTN
*
*
***********************************************************************
* THIS SUBROUTINE READS THE NAME OF THE NEXT MEMBER THAT IS TO BE
* PROCESSED, FROM THE SYSIN DATASET.
***********************************************************************
*
GETNAME   GET      SYSIN,MEMBNAME          GET A SPEC MEMB NAME
          BR       R7                      RETURN TO CALLING RTN
*
*
***********************************************************************
* THIS SUBROUTINE CAUSES THE LOCATION OF THE BEGINNING OF THE
* SPECIFIED MEMBER TO BE PLACED INTO THE PDS DCB.
***********************************************************************
*
FIND      FIND     PDSBDCBI,MEMBNAME,D
          LTR      R15,R15                 CHK IF MEMB IN PDS
          BNZ      NOMEMB                  IF NO, PROC CONDITION
          BR       R7                      RETURN TO CALLING RTN
NOMEMB    ...                              ISSUE WARN MSG, ETC.
          BR       R7                      RETURN TO CALLING RTN
*
*
***********************************************************************
* THIS ROUTINE READS A RECORD OF THE SPECIFIED MEMBER FROM THE PDS.
***********************************************************************
*
READMEMB  READ     RDECB,SF,PDSBDCBI,BLOCK
          CHECK    RDECB                   CHECK IF READ OK
          BR       R6                      RETURN TO CALLING RTN
*
*
***********************************************************************
* THIS ROUTINE UPDATES THE RECORDS OF THE MEMBERS.
***********************************************************************
*
UPDTMEMB  ...                              UPDATE RECORD
          BR       R6                      RETURN TO CALLING RTN
*
*
***********************************************************************
* THIS ROUTINE REWRITES THE RECORDS OF THE MEMBERS TO THE PDS.
***********************************************************************
*
WRTMEMB   WRITE    WDECB,SF,PDSDCBO,BLOCK
          CHECK    WDECB                   CHECK IF WRITE OK
          BR       R6                      RETURN TO CALLING RTN
*
*
***********************************************************************
* THIS ROUTINE ISSUES THE STOW MACRO TO UPDATE THE TTR OF THE DIRECTORY
* ENTRY OF THE PDS TO POINT TO THE UPDATED MEMBER.
***********************************************************************
*
```

```
STOW      MVC      STOWNAME,MEMBNAME           PUT MEMB NAME INTO STOW-LIST
          STOW     PDSBDCBO,STOWLST,R          UPDATE DIR
          LTR      R15,R15                     CHK IF REPLACE OK
          BZR      R6                          IF YES, RET TO CALLING RTN
          C        R15,BIN12                   CHK FOR NO DIR SPC
          BE       NODIRSPC                    IF YES, DSPLY ERROR MSG
          ...                                  CHECK OTHER RETURN CODES
NODIRSPC  WTO      '*** NO MORE DIRECTORY SPACE FOR NEW MEMBER ***', -
                   ROUTCDE=11
          ABEND    901
*
*
************************************************************************
* THIS ROUTINE CLOSES ALL THE DCBS.
************************************************************************
*
CLOSE     CLOSE    (SYSIN,,PDSBDCBI,,PDSBDCBO)
          BR       R6
*
*
************************************************************************
* THIS ROUTINE RESTORES THE REGISTERS AND RETURNS CONTROL.
************************************************************************
*
RETURN    RCNTL    RC=0                        RETURN TO MVS OR CALLING PROG
*
*
************************************************************************
*         DC/DS STATEMENTS
************************************************************************
*
BIN12     DC       F'12'
BLOCK     DS       CL1000
MEMBNAME  DS       CL8
          DS       CL72
*
*
************************************************************************
* THE STOW-LIST
************************************************************************
*
STOWLST   DS       0CL12
STOWNAME  DS       CL8
STOWTTR   DS       CL3
STOWC     DC       X'00'
*
*
************************************************************************
* THE DCBS
************************************************************************
*
SYSIN     DCB      DSORG=PS,MACRF=GM,LRECL=80,RECFM=FB,EODAD=MEMBENDX, -
                   DDNAME=SYSIN
PDSBDCBI  DCB      DSORG=PO,MACRF=R,EODAD=MEMBEND,DDNAME=PDSDD
PDSBDCBO  DCB      DSORG=PO,MACRF=W,DDNAME=PDSDD
*
*
************************************************************************
* END OF PROGRAM
************************************************************************
*
          END
```

8.6.4 Updating In-Place Using QSAM

Updating a member in-place, using QSAM, requires that the DCB be OPENed for UPDAT and the use of the PUTX macro instruction. A record of the member must first be read using the GET macro instruction in locate mode. After the changes are made, the PUTX macro instruction is used to write the updated record back into its original place in the PDS. Unlike a rewrite operation, only one DCB macro instruction is required.

Coding Example 8.6.3

This coding example illustrates how to update one member in-place using QSAM. The member name is specified in the JCL.

```
PDSUPIPQ     CSECT
*
*
***************************************************************************
* INITIALIZATION
***************************************************************************
*
             INITL     3,EQU=R              INITIALIZE PROGRAM
*
*
***************************************************************************
* MAINSTREAM OF PROGRAM
***************************************************************************
*
             BAL       R6,OPEN              OPEN, POS TO JCL MEMB
NEXTREC      BAL       R6,GETREC            READ A REC OF MEMB
             BAL       R6,UPDTREC           UPDATE RECORD
             BAL       R6,PUTREC            PUT MEMB REC IN-PLACE
             B         NEXTREC              READ NEXT MEMB REC
ENDRECS      BAL       R6,CLOSE             CLOSE DATASET
             B         RETURN               RETURN TO MVS OR CALLING PROG
*
*
***************************************************************************
* THIS ROUTINE OPENS THE DCB OF THE PDS AND CAUSES THE NEXT GET TO
* START READING FROM THE BEGINNING OF THE MEMBER SPECIFIED IN THE JCL.
***************************************************************************
*
OPEN         OPEN      (PDSDCB,(UPDAT))
             ...                            CHECK IF GOOD OPEN
             BR        R6                   RETURN TO CALLING RTN
*
*
***************************************************************************
* THIS ROUTINE READS A RECORD OF THE MEMBER SPECIFIED IN THE JCL.
***************************************************************************
*
GETREC       GET       PDSDCB               GET LREC IN LOCATE-MODE
             LR        R2,R1                SAVE LREC ADR
             BR        R6                   RETURN TO CALLING RTN
*
*
***************************************************************************
* THIS ROUTINE UPDATES THE RECORDS OF THE MEMBER.
***************************************************************************
*
UPDTREC      ...                            UPDATE RECORD
             BR        R6                   RETURN TO CALLING RTN
```

```
*
*
***********************************************************************
* THIS ROUTINE UPDATES-IN-PLACE THE RECORDS OF THE MEMBER.
***********************************************************************
*
PUTREC       PUTX     PDSDCB              PUT RECORD IN-PLACE
             BR       R6                  RETURN TO CALLING RTN
*
*
***********************************************************************
* THIS ROUTINE CLOSES DCB OF THE PDS.
***********************************************************************
*
CLOSE        CLOSE    PDSDCB              CLOSE DATASET
             BR       R6                  RETURN TO CALLING RTN
*
*
***********************************************************************
* THIS ROUTINE RESTORES THE REGISTERS AND RETURNS CONTROL.
***********************************************************************
*
RETURN       RCNTL    RC=0                RETURN TO MVS OR CALLING PROG
*
*
***********************************************************************
* THE DCB
***********************************************************************
*
PDSDCB       DCB      DSORG=PS,MACRF=(GL,PM),EODAD=ENDRECS,DDNAME=PDSDD
*
*
***********************************************************************
* END OF PROGRAM
***********************************************************************
*
             END
```

NOTES:

- If multiple members are to be updated in-place using QSAM, then the modified JFCB method must be used. The code for obtaining each desired record is the same as presented in Coding Example 8.4.1. After the member is obtained, then the code for updating each member in-place is the same as presented in this coding example.

8.6.5 Updating In-Place Using BPAM

Updating a member in-place, using BPAM, requires that the DCB be OPENed for UPDAT and that the READ and WRITE macro instructions refer to the same DECB. A block must first be read using the READ macro instruction. After the changes are made, the WRITE macro instruction is used to write the updated block back into the PDS. In order to write the block back to its original place in the PDS, the READ and WRITE macro instructions must point to the same DECB. This is accomplished by defining the list form of the READ macro instruction and using that list for the execute forms of the READ and WRITE macro instructions. Since the TTRs do not change during an update in-place operation, the STOW macro instruction is not required. Unlike a rewrite operation, only one DCB macro instruction is required.

Coding Example 8.6.4

This coding example illustrates how to update multiple members in-place, using BPAM. In this example, the names of the members that are to be updated are specified via a sequential dataset, and the PDS contains unblocked fixed-length records.

```
PDSUPIPB    CSECT
*
*
***********************************************************************
* INITIALIZATION
***********************************************************************
*
            INITL    3,EQU=R              INITIALIZE PROGRAM
*
*
***********************************************************************
* MAINSTREAM OF PROGRAM
***********************************************************************
*
            BAL      R6,OPEN              OPEN DATASETS
NEXTMEMB    BAL      R6,LOCMEMB           LOC SPECIFIED MEMB IN PDS
NEXTREC     BAL      R6,READMEMB          READ A RECORD OF MEMB
            BAL      R6,UPDTMEMB          UPDATE RECORD
            BAL      R6,WRTMEMB           WRITE RECORD BACK TO PDS IN-PLACE
            B        NEXTREC              READ NEXT REC OF MEMB
MEMBEND     B        NEXTMEMB             MEMB-END, GET NEXT SPEC MEMB
MEMBENDX    BAL      R6,CLOSE             END-OF-MEMBS, CLOSE DATASETS
            B        RETURN               RETURN TO MVS OR CALLING PROG
*
*
***********************************************************************
* THIS ROUTINE OPENS ALL THE DCBS.
***********************************************************************
*
OPEN        OPEN     (SYSIN,,PDSBDCB,(UPDAT))
            ...                           CHECK FOR GOOD OPEN
            BR       R6                   RETURN TO CALLING RTN
*
*
***********************************************************************
* THIS ROUTINE LOCATES THE NEXT MEMBER THAT IS TO BE PROCESSED. IN
* ORDER TO PERFORM THAT TASK, THIS ROUTINE BRANCHES AND LINKS TO THE
* SUBROUTINES THAT PERFORM THE FOLLOWING FUNCTIONS:
*     * READ THE NEXT MEMBER NAME FROM THE SYSIN DATASET;
*     * SET THE DASD LOCATION IN THE PDS DCB TO THE BEGINNING OF THE
*       MEMBER THAT IS TO PROCESSED.
***********************************************************************
*
LOCMEMB     BAL      R7,GETNAME           GET A SPEC MEMB NAME FROM SEQ DS
            BAL      R7,FIND              SET MEMB ADR IN PDS DCB
            LTR      R15,R15              CHK IF SPEC MEMB IN PDS
            BNZ      LOCMEMB              IF NO, GET NEXT SPEC MEMB
            BR       R6                   IF YES, RET TO CALLING RTN
*
*
***********************************************************************
* THIS SUBROUTINE READS THE NAME OF THE NEXT MEMBER, THAT IS TO BE
* PROCESSED, FROM THE SYSIN DATASET.
***********************************************************************
*
GETNAME     ...                           SAME LOGIC AS IN C.E. 8.6.2
```

```
              BR        R7
*
*
******************************************************************************
* THIS SUBROUTINE CAUSES THE LOCATION OF THE BEGINNING OF THE
* SPECIFIED MEMBER TO BE PLACED INTO THE PDS DCB.
******************************************************************************
*
FIND          ...                          SAME LOGIC AS IN C.E. 8.6.2
              BR        R7
*
*
******************************************************************************
* THIS ROUTINE READS A RECORD OF THE SPECIFIED MEMBER OF THE PDS.
******************************************************************************
*
READMEMB      LA        R10,UDECB          LOAD ADR OF READ/WRITE LIST
              READ      (R10),SF,MF=E      READ REC USING SUPPLIED LIST
              CHECK     (R10)              CHECK IF READ OK
              BR        R6                 RETURN TO CALLING RTN
*
*
******************************************************************************
* THIS ROUTINE UPDATES THE RECORDS OF THE MEMBERS.
******************************************************************************
*
UPDTMEMB      ...                          UPDATE RECORD
              BR        R6                 RETURN TO CALLING RTN
*
*
******************************************************************************
* THIS ROUTINE UPDATES-IN-PLACE THE RECORDS OF THE MEMBERS OF THE PDS.
******************************************************************************
*
WRTMEMB       LA        R10,UDECB          LOAD ADR OF READ/WRITE LIST
              WRITE     (R10),SF,MF=E      WRITE IN-PLACE USING SUPPLIED LIST
              CHECK     (R10)              CHECK IF WRITE OK
              BR        R6                 RETURN TO CALLING RTN
*
*
******************************************************************************
* THIS ROUTINE CLOSES ALL THE DCBS.
******************************************************************************
*
CLOSE         CLOSE     (SYSIN,,PDSBDCB)   CLOSE ALL DCBS
              BR        R6                 RETURN TO CALLING RTN
*
*
******************************************************************************
* THIS ROUTINE RESTORES THE REGISTERS AND RETURNS CONTROL.
******************************************************************************
*
RETURN        RCNTL     RC=0               RETURN TO MVS OR CALLING PROG
*
*
******************************************************************************
* DC/DS STATEMENTS
******************************************************************************
*
BLOCK         DS        CL1000
*
*
******************************************************************************
* THE LIST-FORM OF THE READ MACRO
```

```
*************************************************************************
*
UPDTLST      READ     UDECB,SF,PDSBDCB,BLOCK,MF=L
*
*
*************************************************************************
* THE DCBS
*************************************************************************
*
SYSIN        DCB      DSORG=PS,MACRF=GL,LRECL=80,RECFM=FB,EODAD=MEMBENDX, -
                      DDNAME=SYSIN
PDSBDCB      DCB      DSORG=PO,MACRF=(R,W),EODAD=MEMBEND,DDNAME=PDSDD
*
*
*************************************************************************
* END OF PROGRAM
*************************************************************************
*
             END
```

8.7 OTHER PDS FACILITIES

Other PDS functions may be performed such as deleting a member name, changing (renaming) a member name, assigning an alias name to an existing member, and providing or changing user-data for a member. The delete, change, and alias functions require only a modification to the directory.

8.7.1 Deleting a Member Name

Deleting an existing member name from a PDS is accomplished by using the STOW macro instruction with the delete (D) option specified. The STOW macro instruction may be used only with BPAM. The member name may be the primary name of the member or may be an alias name.

When a member name is deleted, only the directory entry for that particular member name is removed from the directory. The member could still be accessed if the directory contains other references to the member. When all member names (primary and all aliases) are removed from the directory, then the member is no longer accessible, but the space occupied by the member is not released until the PDS is compressed.

Coding Example 8.7.1

This coding example illustrates how to code the STOW macro instruction to delete a member name.

```
          OPEN   (PDSBDCB,(OUTPUT))
          ...
          STOW   PDSBDCB,MEMBNAME,D     UPDATE DIRECTORY (DELETE MEMB)
          ...                           CHECK RETURN CODE
MEMBNAME  DS     CL8
PDSBDCB   DCB    DSORG=PO,...
```

NOTES:

- MEMBNAME must contain the member name that is to be deleted before the STOW macro instruction is issued.

8.7.2 Changing a Member Name

Changing an existing member name of a PDS to another name is accomplished by use of the STOW macro instruction, with the change (C) option specified. The STOW macro instruction may be used only with BPAM. The name that is changed may be the primary name of the member or may be an alias name.

Coding Example 8.7.2

This coding example illustrates how to code the STOW macro instruction to change a member name:

```
          OPEN     (PDSBDCB,(OUTPUT))
          ...
          MVC      STOWNAME,MEMBNAME     PUT EXISTING MEMB NAME INTO
*                                        STOW-LIST
          MVC      STOWNEWN,NEWNAME      PUT NEW MEMB NAME INTO STOW-LIST
          STOW     PDSBDCB,STOWLST,C     UPDATE DIRECTORY (RENAME MEMB)
          ...                            CHECK RETURN CODE
STOWLST   DS       0CL16
STOWNAME  DS       CL8
STOWNEWN  DS       CL8
*
MEMBNAME  DS       CL8
NEWNAME   DS       CL8
*
PDSBDCB   DCB      DSORG=PO,...
```

NOTES:

- MEMBNAME contains the name of the existing member that is to be renamed.
- NEWNAME contains the new name of the member.

8.7.3 Assigning an Alias Name to an Existing Member

One or more alias names may be specified for an existing member name of a PDS. This is accomplished by using the BLDL and STOW macro instructions. These macro instructions may be used only with BPAM.

Since an alias name is assigned for an existing member, the TTR of that member is required. The number of alias names that may be specified for the same member is limited only by the amount of directory space available. (There is a limit of 16 alias names for a load module member, but this limit is set by the Linkage Editor, not by BPAM.) The TTR may be obtained by use of the BLDL macro instruction. Either the primary name of the member or any of its alias names (the TTR is the same) may be specified in the BLDL macro instruction. The new alias name is assigned by specifying the following in the STOW-list for the STOW macro instruction using the add (A) option, the alias name, the TTR of the existing member that is to be assigned the alias name (obtained via the BLDL macro instruction), and the alias bit turned on in the C field.

Coding Example 8.7.3

The following coding example illustrates how to code the BLDL and STOW macro instructions to assign an alias name to an existing member.

```
          OPEN     (PDSBDCB,(OUTPUT))
          ...
          MVC      BLDLNAME,MEMBNAME     PUT EXISTING MEMB NAME INTO
*                                        BLDL-LIST
```

```
              BLDL      PDSBDCB,BLDLLST          OBTAIN TTRC OF MEMB
              ...
              MVC       STOWNAME,ALIASNAM        PUT ALIAS NAME INTO STOW-LIST
              MVC       STOWTTR,BLDLTTR          PUT LOC OF MEMB INTO STOW-LIST
              STOW      PDSBDCB,STOWLST,A        UPDATE DIRECTORY (ADD ALIAS)
              ...                                CHECK RETURN CODE
*
BLDLLST       DS        0CL16
BLDLFFLL      DC        X'0001',X'000C'          NUMB OF ENTRIES, MAX ENTRY LEN
BLDLNAME      DS        CL8
BLDLTTR       DS        CL3
BLDLK         DS        CL1
*
STOWLST       DS        0CL12
STOWNAME      DS        CL8
STOWTTR       DS        CL3                      HIGH ORDER BIT ON TO IND ALIAS
STOWC         DC        X'80'
*
MEMBNAME      DS        CL8
ALIASNAM      DS        CL8
*
PDSBDCB       DCB       DSORG=PO,...
```

NOTES:

- MEMBNAME contains the name of the existing member that is to be assigned an alias name.
- ALIASNAM contains the alias name.
- In the example, only the minimum directory entry length is used. If the directory entry contains user information that must be duplicated for the alias name, then the BLDL and STOW lists must be larger in order to accommodate the additional data. See Section 8.7.4 below.

8.7.4 Providing or Changing User-Data for a Member

User-data may optionally be specified for members. This data is stored in the member's directory entry. The user-data follows the TTR and C fields and may be up to 62 bytes. The five low order bits of the C field indicates the length of user-data in halfwords. User-data may be inserted into the directory entry during a STOW add (A) operation, or existing user-data may be changed during a STOW replace (R) operation. Existing user-data may be accessed by using the BLDL macro instruction. User-data may be inserted, changed, or referenced only with BPAM.

PROVIDING ORIGINAL USER-DATA

Coding Example 8.7.4

This coding example illustrates how to code the STOW macro instruction to provide user-data for a new member.

```
              OPEN      (PDSBDCB,(OUTPUT))
              ...                                      WRITE NEW MEMB RECORDS
              ...                                      INTO PDS
              MVC       STOWNAME,MEMBNAME              PUT NEW MEMBER NAME INTO
*                                                      STOW-LIST
              MVC       STOWUSER(L'USERDATA),USERDATA  MOVE USER-DATA INTO
                                                       STOW-LIST
              MVC       STOWC,USERLEN                  INDICATE USER-DATA LENGTH
```

```
              STOW     PDSBDCB,STOWLST,A            UPDATE DIRECTORY
              ...                                   CHECK RETURN CODE
STOWLST       DS       0CL74
STOWNAME      DS       CL8
STOWTTR       DS       CL3
STOWC         DS       CL1
STOWUSER      DS       CL62
*
MEMBNAME      DS       CL8
USERDATA      DC       CL40'...'                    USER-DATA FOR DIR ENTRY
USERLEN       DC       AL1(L'USERDATA/2)            LEN OF USER-DATA IN
*                                                   HALFWORDS
*
PSDBDCB       DCB      DSORG=PO,...
```

NOTES:

- MEMBNAME contains the name of the new member.
- USERDATA contains 40 bytes of user-data.
- USERLEN contains the binary value of 20 (the user-data length in halfwords).

CHANGING EXISTING USER-DATA

To change existing user-data requires that the member be rewritten. Section 8.6 above discussed how to do this. The directory entry for the existing member name is obtained by using the BLDL macro instruction. The directory entry contains the existing user-data. The user-data is changed by the program and the updated version is placed into the STOW-list. If the length of the user-data is not changed, then the C field may be copied from the BLDL-list to the STOW-list. If the length of the user-data is changed, then the program must insert the new length into the C field (but preserve the other bits) for the STOW-list.

Coding Example 8.7.5

This coding example illustrates how to code the BLDL and the STOW macro instructions to access existing user-data and to change it. In this example, the existing user-data contains the field names USERFLD1, USERFLD2, USERFLD3, and USERFLD4. USERFLD1 and USERFLD4 are changed and USERFLD5 is added.

```
              OPEN     (PDSBDCB,(OUTPUT))
              ...
              MVC      BLDLNAME,MEMBNAME        PUT EXISTING MEMB NAME INTO
*                                               BLDL-LIST
              BLDL     PDSBDCB,BLDLLST          OBTAIN USER-DATA OF MEMB
              ...
              MVC      USERDATA(USRLEN),BLDLUSER  EXTRACT CUR USER-DATA
              MVC      USERFLD1,UPDFLD1         UPDATE FLD-1 OF CUR USER-DATA
              MVC      USERFLD4,UPDFLD4         UPDATE FLD-4 OF CUR USER-DATA
              MVC      USERFLD5,NEWFLD5         INSERT FLD-5 INTO USER-DATA
              ...
              BAL      R6,REWRITE               REWRITE MEMBER
              ...
              MVC      STOWNAME,MEMBNAME        PUT MEMB NAME INTO STOW-LIST
              MVC      STOWC,BLDLC              PUT EXISTING C FIELD INTO STOW-
*                                               LIST
              NI       STOWC,X'E0'              ZERO OUT OLD LEN BITS
              O        STOWC,USRLENHW           INSERT NEW LEN BITS
              MVC      STOWUSER(L'USERDATA),USERDATA  MOVE NEW USER-DATA
              STOW     PDSBDCB,STOWLST,R        UPDATE DIRECTORY (REPLACE USER-
*                                               DATA)
              ...
```

```
BLDLLST    DS    0CL80
BLDLFFLL   DC    X'0001',X'004C'       NUMB ENTRIES, MAX ENTRY LEN
BLDLNAME   DS    CL8
BLDLTTR    DS    CL3
BLDLK      DS    CL1
BLDLZ      DS    CL1
BLDLC      DS    CL1
BLDLUSER   DS    CL62
*
STOWLST    DS    0CL74
STOWNAME   DS    CL8
STOWTTR    DS    CL3
STOWC      DS    CL1
STOWUSER   DS    CL62
*
MEMBNAME   DS    CL8
*
USERDATA   EQU   *
USERFLD1   DS    CL3                   EXISTING FIELD
USERFLD2   DS    CL4                   EXISTING FIELD
USERFLD3   DS    CL4                   EXISTING FIELD
USERFLD4   DS    CL5                   EXISTING FIELD
USERFLD5   DS    CL8                   NEW FIELD
USERFLDX   EQU   *
*
USRLEN     EQU   USERFLDX-USERDATA     LEN OF USER-DATA IN BYTES
USRLENHW   DC    AL1(USRLEN/2)         LEN OF USER-DATA IN HWDS
*
UPDFLD1    DC    CL3'...'
UPDFLD4    DC    CL5'...'
NEWFLD5    DC    CL8'...'
*
PSDBDCB    DCB   DSORG=PO,...
```

NOTES:

- The maximum length is specified for the user-data field of the BLDL and STOW lists to accommodate all situations.

BIBLIOGRAPHY FOR CHAPTER 8

The following IBM manuals contain reference material for the topics discussed in this chapter.

ID	TITLE
GC26-3873	*OS/VS2 MVS Data Management Macro Instructions*
GC26-3875	*OS/VS2 MVS Data Management Services Guide*
GC26-4013	*MVS/XA Data Management Services Guide*
GC26-4014	*MVS/XA Data Management Macro Instructions*
SC26-4505	*MVS/ESA Data Administration Guide*
SC26-4506	*MVS/ESA Data Administration: Macro Instruction Reference*

9

Programming Paging Efficiency

There are some programming techniques and MVS facilities that may be used in a program to benefit its paging performance. The programming techniques involve the placement of specific code and data relative to each other in the actual program. The MVS facilities involve the use of the PGFIX, PGFREE, PGRLSE, PGLOAD, and PGOUT macro instructions. The macro instructions PGFIX and PGFREE, which may be used only by authorized programs, are discussed in Chapter 10. The other macro instructions do not require an authorized caller and are discussed in this chapter.

9.1 BRIEF OVERVIEW OF MVS PAGING

Before we discuss the programming of paging efficiency, we should first have a general understanding of paging. This section discusses the basic paging structure and algorithms, as well as some of the terms used.

When a job step is initiated for execution, it is allocated an address space. The size of each address space is equal to the entire range of virtual storage. The maximum size of virtual storage is dependent upon the addressing scheme or addressing register of the CPU. In MVS/370 (non-XA version of MVS), the addressing scheme is based on 24 bits. In MVS/XA and MVS/ESA, which execute with the CPU in 370-XA mode and in ESA/370 mode, respectively, the addressing scheme is based on 31 bits. Therefore, the address range of vitrual storage is from 0 to 16M-1 (16,777,215) for MVS/370 and from 0 to 2G-1 (2,147,483,647) for MVS/XA and MVS/ESA. (Note: K is defined as 1024, M is defined as 1024^2 or 1,048,576, and G is defined as 1024^3 or 1,073,741,824.)

Virtual storage is divided into 4K byte blocks of storage called *pages*; real storage is divided into 4K byte blocks of storage called *frames*; and auxiliary storage (page datasets) is divided into 4K byte blocks of storage called *slots*. In order to provide storage protection between address spaces and for virtual storage management, virtual storage pages are grouped into segments. The size of a segment is 64K bytes for MVS/370 and 1M bytes for MVS/XA and MVS/ESA. Virtual storage protection is accomplished at the software level via the segment table. The hardware storage protection key cannot be used because all virtual storage (V=V) jobs execute in the same storage protection key (PSW storage key 8).

When a program is initially invoked, it is loaded into virtual storage. Virtual storage is allocated in whole segments, but only the pages required to contain the code and data are used. For example, if a 70K program is loaded into virtual storage of an MVS/370 system, two segments are allocated. All the pages from the first segment are used (64K), and only two pages from the second segment are used (for a total of 72K; only whole pages are used). The other pages of the second segment are allocated but are not used. As additional virtual storage is required (via GETMAINs, etc.), the allocated unused pages are used to satisfy the requests. During the lifetime of a program, the allocated and used pages of virtual storage, may reside in real storage frames or in auxiliary storage slots. The unallocated segments and the unused pages of the allocated segments do not exist anywhere (except for a representation of them in the segment tables and the page tables) since they contain no information.

In order for the program to execute its code or reference its data, the virtual storage page, which contains that information, must be located in real storage. As programs execute, their virtual storage pages are transferred between real storage and auxiliary storage, as required. This action is known as *paging*. A transfer from auxilary storage to real storage is called a *page-in* and a transfer from real storage to auxiliary storage is called a *page-out*.

There are various control blocks used by MVS to implement paging. The major ones are Segment Tables, Page Tables, External Page Tables, and the Page Frame Table. Each address space has its own Segment Table, Page Tables, and External Page Tables, but there is only one Page Frame Table for the entire system.

A Segment Table represents the entire range of virtual storage for each address space. It contains one entry for each segment. The segments are numbered from 0 to 255 (for MVS/370) and from 0 to 2047 (for MVS/XA and MVS/ESA). Each entry of the Segment Table contains the real address pointer to the Page Table for that particular segment.

There is one Page Table for each segment. A Page Table has one entry for each of the 16 pages (for MVS/370), or 256 pages (for MVS/XA and MVS/ESA) contained in a segment. If a virtual storage page is in a real storage frame, then its corresponding page table entry contains the real storage address of the frame that contains the page. If the page is not in real storage, then the page validity bit (commomly referred to as the invalid bit) of that entry is turned on, indicating that the page is on auxiliary storage.

There is an External Page Table associated with each Page Table. The External Page Table is located after its associated Page Table in real storage and contains a corresponding entry for each page in the Page Table. If the page validity bit is on for a particular page table entry, then the corresponding external page table entry (same relative entry location) contains the auxiliary storage DASD location of the slot that contains the page.

The Page Frame Table contains an entry for each real storage frame and keeps a record of the ownership and activity history of the pages in real storage. Each entry contains the address space ID of the owner of the page, segment and page number of the page, an indicator of whether the frame is available, unreferenced interval count (UIC) of the page, and the reference and change bits associated with the real storage that the page occupies. The UIC has a range from 0 to 255 and contains the number of seconds since the last time the page was referenced or changed. The reference and change bits are actually extentions of the storage protection key and are hardware controlled.

The addresses of virtual storage are consecutive and contiguous. However, when virtual storage pages reside in real storage, the corresponding addresses are not necessarily the same. Therefore, there must be some mechanism to translate the virtual address (the address that the program uses) into the corresponding real address (the address that the CPU uses). This is accomplished with a combination of hardware and software. The hardware mechanism is Dynamic Address Translation (DAT). The DAT is activated when the T-bit (bit 5) of the EC Mode PSW is turned on. (EC mode PSW is active when the C-bit (bit 12) is on.) DAT requires that the software (MVS) builds the segment and page tables. DAT also requires that the high order byte of control register 1 (not general purpose register 1; control register 1 is also known as the Segment Table Origin Register or STOR register) contains the size of the Segment Table and that the low order three bytes point to the real storage address of the Segment Table. It is the responsibility of MVS to assure that control register 1 points to the segment table of the address space that has control. Table 9.1 shows the structure of a virtual storage address for a 24-bit address and for a 31-bit address.

Table 9.1.1

The structure of a 24-bit virtual storage address is as follows:

Segment Address:	Bits 00 to 07 (8 bits)
Page address of that segment:	Bits 08 to 11 (4 bits)
Displacement into the page:	Bits 12 to 23 (12 bits)

The structure of a 31-bit virtual storage address is as follows:

Segment address:	Bits 00 to 10 (11 bits)
Page address of that segment:	Bits 11 to 18 (8 bits)
Displacement into the page:	Bits 19 to 30 (12 bits)

When a virtual storage address is required to be translated into a real storage address, the segment address part of the virtual storage address is used by DAT to locate the proper entry of the Segment Table. Then, the page address part of the virtual storage address is used by DAT to locate the proper entry of the Page Table for that segment. The page table entry contains the corresponding real storage address of the frame (if the page validity bit is off) that contains the virtual storage page. Finally, the displacement part of the virtual storage address is added to the real address of the frame to provide the corresponding real storage address of the virtual storage address. If the page validity bit of the page table entry is on, then the virtual storage page is not in real storage and DAT generates a *page fault* (a program interruption type X'11'). This causes MVS to handle the interruption and reference the corresponding entry in the External Page Table to obtain the DASD location of the virtual page and then perform a page-in operation.

As programs execute, the pages that contain the required information for program execution must be in real storage. When a required page is not in real storage, a page fault occurs and *demand paging* is required to load the page into real storage. Before MVS can do this, it must locate an available frame. It accomplishes this by examining the Page Frame Table. If there are no free frames, then MVS performs *page stealing*, which means that MVS takes a frame that is currently occupied by a page. The decision as to which frame to use is based upon the activity history of the pages that occupy the frames. The pages that have the highest UIC (indicating infrequent use) are candidates for page stealing. After MVS decides which page to steal, it checks the change bit of that page to determine if it has been changed since the last page-in. If the page has been changed, MVS saves its contents by performing a page-out operation. If the page has not been changed, then no page-out is performed. In either case, the page validity bit of the corresponding page table entry is turned on to indicate that the page is no longer in real storage. Then, the required page is paged-in, the page validity bit in its page table entry is turned off to indicate that the page is in real storage, and the Page Frame Table is updated to reflect the new owner of the frame.

9.2 EFFICIENT PROGRAM ORGANIZATION

A program could be organized such that, during execution, the paging rate could be minimized. This is accomplished by simply placing code that executes within close time intervals of each other next to each other in the program. Good candidates for this adjacent placement would be routines and their called subroutines. This would usually have the effect of packing code, that executes together into the same page. Extending this concept, the constants and workareas could be placed next to the code that references them. However, this placement would have the DC/DS instructions scattered all over the program. Also, more than one routine/subroutine may reference the same constants and workareas. It is probably better to place all the DC/DS instructions together for documentation reasons. Also, this placement would probably pack all the DC/DS instruction into the same page or two, which would also have the effect of decreasing the paging rate.

By using the structured and the top-down programming techniques, as described in Chapter 2, the code is automatically placed in the proper location of the program for efficient paging.

9.3 PAGING CONTROL MACRO INSTRUCTIONS

This section presents the format of the PGRLSE, PGLOAD, and PGOUT macro instructions and describes their functions. Also, coding examples are provided for each macro instruction. Addresses for parameters may be specified as a label (A-type address) or as a register containing the required address. When a register is specified, it must be enclosed within parentheses, and a register in the range 2–12 should be used.

The PGRLSE, PGLOAD, and PGOUT macro instructions may be used in the MVS/370, MVS/XA, and the MVS/ESA operating systems; however, those macro instructions operate only on pages located below the 16 Mb line. The PGSER macro instruction (discussed in Chapter 14) performs the PGRLSE, PGLOAD, and PGOUT functions for pages below or above the 16 Mb line and must be supplied with a 31-bit address.

9.3.1 The PGRLSE Macro Instruction

The PGRLSE macro instruction is used to release the real storage frames and the auxiliary storage slots, which contain the virtual storage pages that contain information that is no longer required. Only the real storage frames and auxiliary storage slots associated with virtual storage pages, which are completely within the address range specified, will be released. If the virtual storage addresses of the released pages are referenced again, they will contain binary zeros.

The format of the PGRLSE macro instruction is as follows.

```
[name] PGRLSE LA=start-addr,HA=end-addr
```

`LA=start-addr`

Specifies the starting address of the virtual storage area that is to be released.

`HA=end-addr`

Specifies the ending address + 1 of the virtual storage area that is to be released.

When the PGRLSE macro instruction returns control, register 15 is posted with one the following return codes:

Return Code (Hex)	Meaning
00	Successful completion.
04	Execution failed. The pages completely within the specified virtual storage area or a portion of those pages to be released are protected from the requesting program. Only the pages within the valid portion of the specified area preceding the protected area are released.

Coding Example 9.3.1

This coding example illustrates how to code the PGRLSE macro instruction. In this example, 4,096 bytes of virtual storage are obtained via the GETMAIN macro instruction, and then the virtual storage page, that contains that area is released. The allocation of the virtual storage area is requested to be on a page boundary.

```
         BAL     R6,GETMAIN1             GET A PAGE OF STORAGE
         ...
         BAL     R6,RLSEVS1              RELEASE THE PAGE OF STORAGE
         ...
GETMAIN1 GETMAIN EC,LV=4096,BNDRY=PAGE,A=PGADR
         ...
         BR      R6                      RETURN TO CALLING RTN
         ...
RLSEVS1  L       R10,PGADR               LOAD ADR OF VS AREA TO BE RELEASED
         LA      R11,4095(0,R10)         INCR TO LAST ADR OF THE VS AREA
         LA      R11,1(0,R11)            INCR TO 1 BYTE PAST VS AREA TO BE
REL
         PGRLSE  LA=(R10),HA=(R11)
         ...
         BR      R6                      RETURN TO CALLING RTN
         ...
PGADR    DS      F
```

NOTES:

- The address in register 11 points to one byte past the virtual storage area (page) that is to be released. This is required by the PGRLSE macro instruction. The virtual storage page will not be released if the HA address does not point to at least one byte past the end of the area.

9.3.2 The PGLOAD Macro Instruction

The PGLOAD macro instruction is used to cause the virtual storage pages that contain any portion of the address range specified to be loaded from auxiliary storage into real storage.

An ECB address should be specified. This will enable the program to know when all the requested virtual storage pages have been loaded. Specifying an ECB is important for the following reasons:

- It will assure that the program will reference the pages after they have been loaded, and therefore prevent a page fault from occurring.
- It will permit the program to do other useful work and periodically check the ECB for completion.

Before the page is loaded, the programmer has the option of discarding its contents. This means that the information stored in auxiliary storage is not required and the page-in is suppressed. However, the virtual storage page is indicated as being in a real storage frame (page validity bit off in corresponding page table entry), and therefore prevents a page fault from occurring when that virtual storage address is referenced.

If the virtual storage page is already in real storage when the PGLOAD macro instruction is issued, then no page-in operation is performed.

The format of the PGLOAD macro instruction is as follows.

```
[name] PGLOAD R,A=start-addr[,EA=end-addr][,ECB=ecb-addr]
              [,RELEASE={Y|N}]
```

R

Indicates that no parameter-list is being supplied. Always the case with this macro instruction.

A=start-addr

Specifies the starting address of the virtual storage area that is to be loaded into real storage.

EA=end-addr (Default: start-addr + 1)

Specifies the ending address of the virtual storage area that is to be loaded into real storage.

ECB=ecb-addr (Default: synchronous processing)

Specifies the address of the ECB that is to be posted when all the virtual storage pages are successfully loaded.

RELEASE=Y
RELEASE=N (Default: N)

Y	Specifies that the contents of the virtual pages, which are completely within the specified address range, are to be discarded.
N	Specifies that the contents of the virtual pages within the specified address range are to remain intact.

When the PGLOAD macro instruction returns control, register 15 is posted with one the following return codes:

Return Code (Hex)	Meaning
00	Successful completion; ECB posted complete.
08	Operation proceding; ECB will be posted complete when all page-ins are complete.

If an ECB is specified and checked, then there is no need to check the return code. If an ECB is not specified, then there is also no need to check the return code because PGLOAD will return control only if the operation is successful. If PGLOAD is unsuccessful, MVS will cause an ABEND.

Coding Example 9.3.2

This coding example illustrates how to code the PGLOAD macro instruction. In this example, the virtual storage page that contains the address specified will be loaded from auxiliary storage into real storage. When the load is succussfully completed, the ECB is posted.

```
         PGLOAD  R,A=(R10),ECB=PGECB
         WAIT    1,ECB=PGECB
```

Coding Example 9.3.3

This coding example illustrates how to code the PGLOAD macro instruction and then perform other processing until the PGLOAD operation is complete. In this example, real storage frames are assigned to the virtual storage pages that lie (whole or part) within the address range specified by registers 10 and 11, but no page-in will be performed. The CHKPGLD routine receives control periodically to check if the PGLOAD operation is complete.

```
LOADPGS   PGLOAD  R,A=(R10),EA=(R11),ECB=PGECB,RELEASE=Y
          BR      R6
          ...
CHKPGLD   TM      PGECB,X'40'           CHECK IF PGLOAD COMPLETE
          BO      CHKCC                 IF YES, CHK COMP CODE
          BAL     R7,DOWORK             IF NO, DO OTHER WORK
          B       CHKPGLD               CHECK AGAIN IF PGLOAD COMPLETE
CHKCC     CLC     PGECB+1(3),BINZEROS   CHECK COMP CODE
          BER     R6                    IF OK, RETURN TO CALLER
          ABEND   ...                   PGLOAD FAILED
          ...
PGECB     DC      F'0'
BINZEROS  DC      F'0'
```

9.3.3 The PGOUT Macro Instruction

The PGOUT macro instruction is used to cause the virtual storage pages that are completely within the address range specified to be paged-out.

The format of the PGOUT macro instruction is as follows.

```
[name] PGOUT R,A=start-addr[,EA=end-addr][,KEEPREL={Y|N}]
```

R

Indicates that no parameter-list is being supplied. Always the case with this macro instruction.

A=start-addr

Specifies the starting address of the virtual storage area that is to be paged-out.

EA=end-addr (Default: start-addr + 1)

Specifies the ending address + 1 of the virtual storage area that is to be paged-out.

```
KEEPREL=Y
KEEPREL=N (Default: N)
```

Y — Specifies that, after the page-out, the virtual storage pages also remain in real storage.

N — Specifies that, after the page-out, the real storage frames are released.

When the PGOUT macro instruction returns control, register 15 is posted with one the following return codes.

Return Code (Hex)	Meaning
00	Successful completion; paging I/O proceding asynchonously.
00	One or more pages specified to be paged out were not paged out. Either the pages were in the nucleus in unusable real frames, in SQA or LSQA, in a V=R area, were page fixed, or the system resources necessary to perform the page-out operations were momentary unavailable. Paging I/O is proceding normally for all other pages.

Coding Example 9.3.4

This coding example illustrates how to code the PGOUT macro instruction. In this example, the virtual storage pages that are completely within the address range specified by registers 10 and 11 will be paged-out, and the real storage frames that they occupied will be released.

```
         PGOUT R,A=(R10),EA=(R11)
```

9.4 USING THE PAGING CONTROL MACRO INSTRUCTIONS

This section will discuss some uses of the PGRLSE, PGLOAD, and PGOUT macro instructions. When properly used, these macro instructions could provide a paging performance advantage for both the issuing program and the operating system.

Since these macro instructions operate on complete pages, it would be efficient to allocate the virtuage storage that is to be manipulated with starting and ending address on page boundaries. If this is not done, then some of the performance advantage could be lost. One example would be using the PGLOAD and PGOUT macro instructions to control the timing of the page-in and page-out operations for certain virtual storage areas. If the entire virtual storage area does not encompass whole pages, then PGLOAD will still load the pages that contain any of the addresses within the specifed range, but PGOUT will not cause a page-out for a page unless the entire page is within the address range specified. Therefore, if the starting and ending addresses of the virtual storage area is not on page boundaries, then only some or none of the pages will be paged-out. Since PGRLSE has the same requirements as PGOUT for address boundaries, then the real storage frames and auxiliary storage slots will not be released for pages that lie partially outside of the address range specified.

9.4.1 Using the PGRLSE Macro Instruction

The PGRLSE macro instruction can be used to release the real storage frames and the auxiliary storage slots that contain information that is no longer required. The following example illustrates the use of the PGRLSE macro instruction. Let us say that an expandable table, like the one described in Chapter 5, is required to be created in virtual storage to store and process a large amount of data. After the data in this table is completely processed, then another expandable table is required to be created to store and process other data, and so on. There are a few ways to code the logic for this processing:

- A new series of GETMAIN macro instructions could be issued to obtain virtual storage for the new table. This method is inefficient for a few reasons. The data in the old table is no longer required, but since it remains in virtual storage, those virtual storage pages would still be subject to the normal paging processing. Since those virtual storage pages were being modified and referenced during processing, when the real storage frames (which are occupied by those virtual storage pages) are required to be used to contain other virtual storage pages, then those existing virtual storage pages, which were modified since the last page-in operation, will be paged-out and the data, which is no longer required, will be saved on auxiliary storage. This will increase the paging rate for both the system and the program and waste auxiliary storage. In addition, issuing a new series of GETMAIN macro instructions is inefficient for the following reasons. A GETMAIN macro instruction expansion contains an SVC instruction. The execution of an SVC instruction causes an SVC interruption. This causes the system to momentarily stop processing while the SVC First Level Interupt Handler processes the interruption and determines which SVC routine is to receive control. Then, the actual GETMAIN logic is executed. The additional system overhead due to the page-out operations for the un-required data of the previous table and due to the additional GETMAINs is unnecessary.
- The FREEMAIN macro instructions could be used to free all the virtual storage obtained for the current table since this data is no longer required and then issue a series of GETMAIN macro instructions to obtain storage for the new table. This method is a little better than the previous method. The FREEMAIN tells MVS that the data contained in the virtual storage area, which is being freed, is no longer required, and therefore does not need to be saved via a page-out operation. But the same additional system overhead is required for the issuing of a new series of GETMAINs, as mentioned in the previous method.
- Use the same GETMAINed virtual storage area for the next table, and physically erase all the existing data stored in that storage area by moving binary zeros into it. This method eliminates the system overhead required for a new series of GETMAINs for the new table but is inefficient because it causes excessive and unnecessary paging. Since the existing storage area is still being used, those virtual storage pages are subject to the normal paging process. Since binary zeros were moved into the entire area, this guarantees that every virtual page of that area was modified. Therefore, when the real storage frames, which are occupied by those virtual storage pages, are required to be used to contain other virtual storage pages, then those existing virtual storage pages will be paged-out, and the data that is no longer required from the previous table and/or the binary zeros will be saved on auxiliary storage. This will cause an unnecessary increase in the paging rate for both the system and the program and waste auxiliary storage.
- Use the PGRLSE macro instruction for the GETMAINed virtual storage areas that contain the current data. Then use the same GETMAINed storage areas for the next table, and logically delete the existing data either by setting a new end-of-data indicator or via pointers into the table. This method is the most efficient. PGRLSE indicates to MVS that all the data in the GETMAINed virtual storage area is no longer required, and therefore,

page-out operations are not necessary. This will eliminate unnecessary paging and, in addition, free all the real storage frames and auxiliary storage slots that contain those pages. Also, by using the same virtual storage area for the new table, the additional GETMAIN system overhead is eliminated. At this point, the virtual storage, obtained via the GETMAINs, is represented only by entries in the segment and page tables—no real storage or auxiliary storage is being used. As the next expandable table is created, only the required real storage frames and auxiliary storage slots will be used.

9.4.2 Using the PGLOAD Macro Instruction

The PGLOAD macro instruction can be used for anticipatory page-ins. If a section of a program is infrequently used and has not been referenced for awhile, then the pages that contain that information will probably be paged-out eventually. When that section of the program is to be referenced, paging overhead can be improved by the program issuing a PGLOAD for the virtual storage pages that contain that section of the program. Execution efficiency could be futher improved if the program could perform other useful work until the PGLOAD processing is complete. If the PGLOAD is not done prior to referencing that section of the program and if the virtual storage pages are not in real storage, then a page fault(s) occurs. A page fault causes a program interruption (interruption code X'0011'), which MVS must process. Either way (PGLOAD or page fault), the required virtual storage pages are paged-in. The PGLOAD is more efficient because it eliminates the additional system overhead required to process the page fault.

The PGLOAD should be done immediately before that section of the program is referenced because the virtual storage pages that are loaded into real storage frames via PGLOAD are also subject to the same paging processing as any other pages and could be paged-out if they are not referenced soon enough.

If the section of the program, that is to be referenced contains data that is no longer useful and is going to be overlayed, then page-in operations are not necessary. In this case, all that is required is for the virtual storage addresses to be assigned to real storage frames. To accomplish this, the PGLOAD macro instruction is coded with RELEASE=Y. This prevents unnecessary page-in operations and causes only the Page Table and the Page Frame Table to be updated.

9.4.3 Using the PGOUT Macro Instruction

The PGOUT macro instruction can be used to cause page-out operations of the virtual storage pages that contain sections of a program that are infrequently used. This action will free real storage frames, which will then be available when demain-paging is required. This will save MVS the overhead of performing page-stealing in order to free real storage frames to satisfy the demain-paging requirements. However, care should be exercised when using PGOUT. If it is misused, then excessive and needless paging may occur.

The following guidelines should be helpful in deciding when to use the PGOUT macro instruction:

- The PGOUT macro instruction should not be issued automatically after an infrequently used routine is executed or after infrequently used data is referenced. If the use of such routines or data is determined by certain data being processed or by user activity, then the timing of their use may be unpredictable. A routine may be executed infrequently during the life of a program, but those executions may be grouped together.
- If a routine or data is used only once or twice during the life of a program and if the reference to that routine or data is determined by various stages of the execution of the program as opposed to the type of input data received, then the use of PGOUT may be

efficient. Such routines or data may be the ones used for initialization/termination, and so on.

- The PGOUT macro instruction would also be efficiently used for routines or data that are used at certain times of day or at certain intervals. Such routines may be ones that are activated by the STIMER macro instruction (discussed in Chapter 5). In these situations, the PGOUT macro instruction could be used after the routine completes execution and/or the data is referenced. When the routine is activated, via STIMER, the PGLOAD macro instruction can then be used to load those pages into real storage frames before they are referenced again and prevent page faults.

BIBLIOGRAPHY FOR CHAPTER 9

The following IBM manuals contain reference material for the topics discussed in this chapter.

ID	TITLE
GC28-0984	*OS/VS2 MVS Overview*
GC28-1114	*OS/VS2 MVS Supervisor Services and Macro Instructions*
GC28-1348	*MVS/XA Overview*
GC28-1154	*MVS/XA Supervisor Services and Macro Instructions*
GC28-1821	*MVS/ESA Application Development Guide*
GC28-1822	*MVS/ESA Application Development Macro Reference*

10

Selected Advanced Supervisor Services Macros

This chapter discusses the facilities of some selected advanced supervisor services macro instructions. The discussions mention somes uses of these facilities and also provide coding examples. The user programs that issue the macro instructions presented in this chapter are required to be authorized. The requirements for authorizing a program are discussed in the first section of this chapter.

10.1 AUTHORIZING A USER PROGRAM

Performing certain functions or using certain MVS facilities requires that the requesting user program be authorized. A program could be authorized in one of three ways. It could be APF (Authorized Program Facility) authorized, be executing in supervisor state, or be executing in one of the PSW storage protection keys 0–7. Some facilities require that the requesting program be executing in both supervisor state and one of the PSW storage protection keys 0–7 (or only key 0).

APF AUTHORIZING A PROGRAM

There are two requirements to APF authorize a program that will be invoked via JCL. An APF authorized program must be linkedited with the authorization code set to one and reside in an authorized library. However, if a program is invoked by an authorized program, the called program need not have the authorization code set to one, but must still reside in an authorized library. The authorization code may be set with the Linkage Editor PARM parameter or with a Linkage Editor control statement.

Coding Example 10.1.1

This coding example illustrates how to set the authorization code for a user program. The IBM-supplied PROCs for assembling and linking a program (ASMFCL and ASMHCL) are used in the example.

```
//LKED          EXEC  ASMFCL,PARM.LKED='AC=1,...'
//LKED.SYSLMOD DD     DSN=USER.AUTHLIB(pgm-name),DISP=SHR
```

```
//
```

or

```
//L            EXEC  ASMHCL,PARM.L='...'
//L.SYSLMOD    DD    DSN=USER.AUTHLIB,DISP=SHR
//L.SYSIN      DD    *
  SETCODE AC(1)
  NAME pgm-name
//
```

The IBM-supplied authorized libraries are SYS1.LINKLIB, SYS1.SVCLIB, and SYS1.LPALIB (only during IPL). In addition, the user could authorize additional libraries by specifying the library names (dsname) and locations (volser) in the IEAAPFxx member of SYS1.PARMLIB.

User libraries could also be authorized if they are concatenated to SYS1.LINKLIB via the LNKLSTxx member of SYS1.PARMLIB and if LNKAUTH=APFTAB (MVS/XA and MVS/ESA only) is not specified in the member IEASYSxx. However, libraries that are authorized in this fashion will lose their authorization if they are pointed to by a JOBLIB/STEPLIB JCL DD statement.

SETTING SUPERVISOR STATE AND PSW STORAGE PROTECTION KEY ZERO

A program is automatically placed in supervisor state and protect key zero when it is invoked as an SVC routine or an SRB routine. (SVC routines are discussed in Chapter 12 and SRB routines are discussed in Chapter 15. In addition, a user program may place itself in supervisor state and/or PSW storage protection key zero by use of the MODESET macro instruction, discussed below.

SETTING PSW STORAGE PROTECTION KEYS 0–7

A program may be set to execute in one of the PSW storage protection keys 0–7 by placing an entry in the Program Properties Table (CSECT IEFSDPPT of load module IEFSD060, which resides in SYS1.LPALIB; or via the SCHEDxx member of SYS1.PARMLIB for MVS/XA version 2.2 or later and MVS/ESA). Each entry contains a program name, the PSW storage protection key that the program is to receive when it executes, and other program properties.

10.2 THE MODESET MACRO INSTRUCTION

The MODESET macro instruction is used to change the PSW mode (problem or supervisor) and the PSW protection key of the issuing program. The MODESET macro instruction has two forms. One form generates an SVC instruction and the other form generates inline code. Only the form that generates an SVC instruction will be discussed in this chapter. Only authorized programs may issue the MODESET macro instruction. The MODESET macro instruction may be used to enable an authorized program to execute in supervisor state and/or PSW protection key zero so that it can perform certain restricted actions, such as read from or write into the SQA, or issue certain restricted macro instructions, such as SETLOCK.

Coding Example 10.2.1

The following coding example illustrates how to use the MODESET macro instruction to change the PSW mode and the PSW protection key of the issuing program to supervisor state and key zero.

```
MODESET MODE=SUP,KEY=ZERO
```

The following coding example illustrates how to use the MODESET macro instruction to change the PSW mode and the PSW protection key of the issuing program to problem state and to the key number stored in the TCBPKF field of the TCB.

```
MODESET MODE=PROB,KEY=NZERO
```

The following coding example illustrates how to use the MODESET macro instruction to change the PSW mode of the issuing program to supervisor state. In this case, the PSW protection key remains the same as it was before the MODESET macro instruction was issued.

```
MODESET MODE=SUP
```

10.3 THE TESTAUTH MACRO INSTRUCTION

The TESTAUTH macro instruction is normally used by SVC routines. It permits the SVC routine to determine the authorization status of the calling program. Certain SVC routines have sensitive functions and therefore restrict their use only to authorized callers. A program is considered authorized if it is APF authorized, or executing in supervisor state, or executing in one of the PSW protection keys 0–7. TESTAUTH permits the SVC routines to test for all three types of authorization or any combinations of them. Depending upon the type of sensitive function that the SVC provides, it may require that the calling program be authorized by having any of the three types of authorization or it may require that the calling program be executing in both supervisor state and in PSW protection key 0–7.

The TESTAUTH macro instruction could be issued at the beginning of the SVC routine to restrict non-authorized programs from executing any portion of the SVC routine. Or, if the SVC routine provides multiple functions and if only some of those functions are sensitive, then the SVC routine could issue the TESTAUTH macro instruction only for the sensitive code and restrict non-authorized programs from invoking only those functions.

The format of the TESTAUTH macro instruction is as follows:

```
[name] TESTAUTH [FCTN=0|1]
                [,STATE=YES|NO]
                [,KEY=YES|NO]
                [,RBLEVEL=1|2]
```

FCTN

Specifies if the calling program should be checked for APF authorization; 0 indicates no and 1 indicates yes.

STATE

Specifies if the calling program should be checked for supervisor state.

KEY

Specifies if the calling program should be checked for PSW protection key of 0–7. If key zero is specifically required, then this can be determined by examining the first four bits of the TCBPKF field of the caller's TCB if this test is positive (RC=0). If the PSW protection key of the caller is zero, then all of those four bits are zero.

RBLEVEL (Default: 1)

Specifies the SVC type of the issuer of the TESTAUTH macro instruction; 1 indicates a type 2, 3, or 4 SVC, and 2 indicates a type 1 SVC.

If a specific authorization type check is not explicitly requested, then it is not performed. The specified authorization type checks is a logical OR test. If any of the specified checks are true, then the program calling the SVC routine is considered authorized. If the SVC routine requires that the calling program have more than one type of authorization, then a separate TESTAUTH macro instruction must be issued for each required authorization type.

When control is returned from TESTAUTH, register 15 is posted with a return code to indicate whether the caller of the SVC is authorized based upon the criteria specified in the TESTAUTH macro instruction. A return code of X'00' indicates authorized and a return code of X'04' indicates not authorized.

Coding Example 10.3.1

This coding example illustrates how to use the TESTAUTH macro instruction to check if the calling program is authorized in any of the three ways.

```
         TESTAUTH  FCTN=1,STATE=YES,KEY=YES
         LTR       R15,R15
         BZ        AUTH
         B         NOAUTH
```

Coding Example 10.3.2

The following coding example illustrates how to use the TESTAUTH macro instruction to check if the calling program is executing in supervisor state and in PSW protection key 0–7.

```
         TESTAUTH  STATE=YES
         LTR       R15,R15
         BZ        CHKKEY
         B         NOAUTH
CHKKEY   TESTAUTH  KEY=YES
         LTR       R15,R15
         BZ        AUTH
         B         NOAUTH
```

10.4 THE PGFIX AND PGFREE MACRO INSTRUCTION

The PGFIX and PGFREE macro instructions may be issued by only authorized programs. The PGFIX macro instruction causes virtual storage pages to be resident in real storage and ineligible for page-out operations (page-fixed) while the address space of the requesting TCB is swapped-in. When the address space is swapped-out, the fixed pages will be paged-out. A program can be made non-swappable by placing an entry in the Program Properties Table (discussed in Section 10.1 above) and turning on the appropriate bit. The virtual storage pages that are selected for the page-fixing reside below 16 Mb. The PGSER macro instruction (discussed in Chapter 14) performs the PGFIX and PGFREE functions for pages located below and above the 16 Mb line. Care should be taken when page-fixing because this decreases the supply of real frames available for paging for all address spaces.

The virtual storage pages that are fixed in real storage will become eligible for page-out operations when they are subsequently freed with the PGFREE macro instruction. The PGFREE macro instruction has no effect unless it is issued by the same task that issued the PGFIX macro instruction.

The reason why virtual storage pages are required to be page-fixed would be to eliminate the overhead involved to page-in the virtual storage areas when they are required by sensitive programs that require quick response time. The programmer is not required to page-fix virtual storage areas that contain I/O buffers because the operating system does the page-fix automatically in SQA and then moves the data from SQA to the user's buffers.

Pages that are frequently referenced do not necessarily need to be page-fixed to assure that they will remain in real storage because the operating system's paging algorithms will tend to keep frequency referenced pages in real storage. The PGFIX macro instruction should be used to cause the pages of sensitive program that are infrequently used or whose frequency of use varies during the execution of the program to stay paged-in.

The format of the PGFIX macro instruction is as follows.

```
[name] PGFIX {R|L},A=start-addr[,EA=end-addr][,ECB=ecb-addr]
             [,LONG={Y|N}],[,RELEASE={Y|N}]
```

R

Indicates that no parameter-list is being supplied with this request.

L

Indicates that a parameter-list is being supplied with this request. This option will not be discussed.

A=start-addr

Specifies the starting address of the virtual storage area that is to be fixed.

EA=end-addr (Default: start-addr + 1)

Specifies the ending address of the virtual storage area that is to be fixed.

ECB=ecb-addr (Default: synchronous processing)

Specifies the address of the ECB that is to be posted when all the virtual storage pages are fixed. If the ECB address is specified as 0 or is omitted, then control is returned when the fix request is completely satisfied.

LONG=Y
LONG=N (Default: Y)

Specifies the relative real time duration for the page fix. Y indicates long and N indicates short. The convention is that Y implies a second or more. The value Y should normally be specified (or defaulted). If N is specified, then the page is fixed in the V=R or non-preferred storage areas. If that page-fix actually has a long duration, then V=R functions and CONFIG STORAGE commands may be delayed.

RELEASE=Y
RELEASE=N (Default: N)

Y — Specifies that the contents of the virtual pages that are completely within the specified address range are to be discarded.

N — Specifies that the contents of the virtual pages within the specified address range are to remain intact.

The sections "The PGLOAD Macro Instruction" and "Using the PGLOAD Macro Instruction" in Chapter 9 discussed the meaning and use of the RELEASE parameter in more detail.

When the PGFIX macro instruction returns control, register 15 is posted with one of the following return codes:

Return Code (Hex)	Meaning
00	Successful completion; ECB posted complete.
08	Operation proceding; ECB will be posted complete when all specified pages are fixed in real storage.

If an ECB is specified and checked, then there is no need to check the return code. If an ECB is not specified, then there is also no need the check the return code because PGFIX will return control only if the operation is successful. If PGFIX is unsuccessful, MVS will cause an ABEND.

The format of the PGFREE macro instruction is as follows.

```
[name] PGFREE {R|L},A=start-addr[,EA=end-addr][,ECB=ecb-addr]
              [,RELEASE={Y|N}]
```

`R`

Indicates that no parameter-list is being supplied with this request.

`L`

Indicates that a parameter-list is being supplied with this request. This option will not be discussed.

`A=start-addr`

Specifies the starting address of the virtual storage area that is to be freed.

`EA=end-addr (Default: start-addr + 1)`

Specifies the ending address of the virtual storage area that is to be freed.

`ECB=ecb-addr (Default: none)`

Specifies the address of the ECB that was used in the previous PGFIX macro instruction. This parameter should be specified if there is any possibility that the ECB for the previously issued PGFIX was not posted complete. (One way in which this can happen is if the ECB was not tested for completion.)

`RELEASE=Y`
`RELEASE=N (Default: N)`

Y	Specifies that the contents of the virtual pages that are completely within the specified address range are to be discarded.
N	Specifies that the contents of the virtual pages within the specified address range are to remain intact.

The sections "The PGLOAD Macro Instruction" and "Using the PGLOAD Macro Instruction" in Chapter 9 discussed the meaning and use of the RELEASE parameter in more detail.

When the PGFREE macro instruction returns control, register 15 is posted with a return code of X'00' to indicate successful completion. If the operation is unsuccessful, then MVS will cause an ABEND.

Coding Example 10.4.1

This coding example illustrates how to code the PGFIX macro instruction. In this example, the virtual storage page that contains the address specified, will be page-fixed. Control is returned to the issuing program when the page-fix is complete.

```
         PGFIX R,A=(R10)
```

Coding Example 10.4.2

This coding example illustrates how to code the PGFIX macro instruction and then perform other processing until the PGFIX operation is complete. In this example, the virtual storage pages that lie (whole or part) within the address range specified by registers 10 and 11 are page-fixed. The CHKPGFX routine receives control periodically to check if the PGFIX operation is complete.

```
FIXPGS   PGFIX R,A=(R10),EA=(R11),ECB=PGFXECB
         BR    R6
         ...
CHKPGFX  TM    PGFXECB,X'40'        CHECK IF PGFIX COMPLETE
         BO    CHKCC                IF YES, CHK COMP CODE
         BAL   R7,DOWORK            IF NO, DO OTHER WORK
         B     CHKPGFX              CHECK AGAIN IF PGFIX COMPLETE
CHKCC    CLC   PGFXECB+1(3),BINZEROS    CHECK COMP CODE
         BER   R6                   IF OK, RETURN TO CALLER
         ABEND ...                  PGFIX FAILED
         ...
PGFXECB  DC    F'0'
BINZEROS DC    F'0'
```

Coding Example 10.4.3

This coding example illustrates how to code the PGFREE macro instruction to free the pages that were page-fixed in Coding Example 10.4.2. In this example, the virtual storage pages that lie (whole or part) within the address range specified by registers 10 and 11 are freed.

```
         PGFREE R,A=(R10),EA=(R11)
```

10.5 RESERVE MACRO INSTRUCTION

The program that issues the RESERVE macro instruction must be authorized only if the DASD unit that is to be RESERVEd is not allocated to the job step. The RESERVE macro instruction is used to lock out a specific DASD unit from other systems (CPUs with other operating systems) in a shared DASD environment. This is done at the hardware level through the DASD control unit. The RESERVE macro instruction also performs ENQ processing to cause other tasks that are executing in the same system to wait for access to the resource (provided that they issue an ENQ or RESERVE macro instruction with the same qname and rname). The qname and rname in the RESERVE macro instruction have the same meaning as in the ENQ macro instruction. The same qname/rname combination in the RESERVE macro instruction and in the ENQ macro instruction, with a scope of SYSTEMS, is considered to be the same resource.

If the RESERVE macro instruction is used only to serialize the use of a dataset or the VTOC area from other systems, then using RESERVE would be ineffficient because the use of an entire DASD unit (containing many datasets) is unavailable to other systems until the RESERVE is terminated (with a DEQ macro instruction). If the IBM program product Global Resource Serialization (GRS) or similar software is not available, then there is no alternative but to use RESERVE. If GRS or similar software is available, then ENQ with a scope of SYSTEMS should be used instead, since it will serialize only the specific resource across systems. If a program is currently using RESERVE and GRS was installed after the program was developed, then the RESERVE could be changed to an ENQ with a scope of SYSTEMS without changing the program. This could be accomplished by defining a RESERVE conversion resource name list (one of the name lists used by GRS) and specify the qnames and rnames used by the RESERVE macro instruction.

In order to use the RESERVE macro instruction, the UCB address of the DASD unit that is to be locked out from the other systems must be obtained and specified in the RESERVE macro instruction. One way that the unit address of the DASD could be specified is via a JCL DD statement with a specific ddname.

The format of the RESERVE macro instruction is as follows:

```
[name] RESERVE  (qname,rname,request-type,rname-length,scope),
                UCB=ucb-addr[,RET=cond-req][,ECB=ecb-addr]
```

All the parameters have the same meaning as the corresponding ones in the ENQ macro instruction except the following ones, which do not exist in the ENQ macro instruction. The ENQ macro instruction was discussed in Chapter 4.

`UCB=ucb-addr`

Specifies the address of a fullword that contains the address of the UCB for the device that is to be reserved. The UCB must be allocated by the job step before RESERVE is issued unless the issuer is authorized.

`ECB=ecb-addr (Default: synchronous processing)`

Specifies the address of an ECB and conditionally requests the specified resource(s). The ECB is posted complete when all the requested resource(s) are assigned to the issuing task. The ECB and the RET parameters may not be used together.

When the RESERVE macro instruction returns control, register 15 is posted with a return code of X'00' to indicate successful completion. If an ECB is specified, the return code should be checked first because the ECB is not posted if the return code is X'08' or greater, which indicates an error. A return code of X'04' indicates that its resource(s) is not immediately available.

Coding Example 10.5.1

This coding example illustrates how to code the RESERVE macro instruction. In this example, a cataloged dataset is specified on a JCL DD statement with the ddname LIBDD. The DASD unit, on which that dataset resides, is to be RESERVEd. The program receives control from RESERVE when the specified resource is available.

```
         USING JFCB,R10            DEFINE REG FOR JFCB DSECT
         ...
*
```

```
*
*************************************************************************
*    MAINSTREAM OF PROGRAM
*************************************************************************
*
          ...
          BAL    R6,RDJFCB          READ JFCB INTO PROG AREA
          BAL    R6,GETDSNM         GET SPECIFIED DATASET NAME
          BAL    R6,GETTIOT         GET TIOT ADR
          BAL    R6,GETUCB          GET UCB ADR FOR RESERVE
          BAL    R6,RESERVE         ISSUE RESERVE
          ...
*
*
*************************************************************************
*    THIS ROUTINE READS THE JFCB AND COPIES IT FROM THE SWA INTO THE
*    PROGRAMMER-SUPPLIED AREA.
*************************************************************************
*
RDJFCB    RDJFCB (DCB01,(OUTPUT))
          LTR    R15,R15            CHK IF DD STMT IN JCL
          BNZ    NODDNM1             IF NO, ERROR
          BR     R6                 IF YES, RET TO CALLING RTN
NODDNM1   WTO    '*** DDNAME "LIBDD" NOT SPECIFIED IN JCL ***',  -
                 ROUTCDE=11
          ABEND 901
*
*
*************************************************************************
*    THIS ROUTINE GETS THE SPECIFIED DATASET NAME FROM THE JFCB. THE
*    DATASET IS USED AS THE RNAME FOR THE RESERVE MACRO.
*************************************************************************
*
GETDSNM   LA     R10,JFCB           SET ADRBLTY FOR JFCB DSECT
          MVC    DSNAME,JFCBDSNM    EXTRACT SPEC DSNAME FROM JFCB
          BR     R6                 RETURN TO CALLIN RTN
*
*
*************************************************************************
*    THIS ROUTINE GETS THE TIOT ADDRESS, WHICH IS USED TO OBTAIN THE
*    UCB ADDRESS.
*************************************************************************
*
GETTIOT   EXTRACT TIOTADR,FIELDS=TIOT GET TIOT ADR
          BR   R6                      RETURN TO CALLING RTN
*
*
*************************************************************************
*    THIS ROUTINE GETS THE UCB ADDRESS BY SCANNING THE TIOT FOR THE
*    DDNAME LIBDD. THE TIOT ENTRY FOR THAT DDNAME CONTAINS THE REQUIRED
*    UCB ADDRESS.
*************************************************************************
*
GETUCB    L      R10,TIOTADR        LOAD ADR OF TIOT
          LA     R10,24(0,R10)      INCR PASS JOBNAME/STEPNAMES
*                                   TO FIRST TIOT DDNAME ENTRY
NEXTDDNM  CLC    0(4,R10),BINZEROS  CHECK FOR END OF TIOT
          BE     NODDNM             IF END, DDNAME NOT FOUND
          CLC    4(8,R10),DDNAME    CHK FOR DDNAME
          BE     MVUCBADR           IF FOUND, GET UCB ADDRESS
          IC     R11,0(0,R10)       STORE TIOT DDNAME ENTRY LEN
          LA     R10,0(R11,R10)     INCR TO NEXT TIOT DDNAME ENTRY
          B      NEXTDDNM           CHK NEXT DDN IN TIOT
MVUCBADR  MVC    UCBADR,16(R10)     GET UCB ADR FROM TIOT DDN ENTRY
```

```
         BR    R6                    RETURN TO CALLING RTN
NODDNM2  WTO   '*** DDNAME "LIBDD" NOT SPECIFIED IN JCL ***', -
               ROUTCDE=11
               ABEND 902
*
*
***********************************************************************
*    THIS ROUTINE ISSUES THE RESERVE MACRO FOR THE UCB ALLOCATED BY THE
*    JCL DD STATEMENT WITH THE DDNAME LIBDD AND USES THE SPECIFIED
*    DATASET NAME AS THE RNAME.
***********************************************************************
*
RESERVE  MVC   RNAME,DSNAME          USE DSNAME AS RNAME FOR RESERVE
         RESERVE (QNAME,RNAME,E,,SYSTEMS),UCB=UCBADR
         LTR   R15,R15               CHK IF RESERVE OK
         BNZ   RSRVBAD               IF RC NOT 0, ERROR
         BR    R6                    RETURN TO CALLING RTN
RSRVBAD  WTO   '*** RESERVE ERROR ***',ROUTCDE=11
         ABEND 903
*
*
***********************************************************************
*    DC/DS STATEMENTS
***********************************************************************
*
BINZEROS DC    F'0'
DSNAME   DS    CL44
DDNAME   DC    CL8'LIBDD'
TIOTADR  DS    F
UCBADR   DS    F
QNAME    DC    CL8'USER'
RNAME    DS    CL44
*
*
***********************************************************************
*    THE JFCB-LIST AND THE DCBS
***********************************************************************
*
JFCB     DS    44F
JFCBPTR  DC    X'87'
         DC    AL3(JFCB)
*
DCB01    DCB   DSORG=PS,MACRF=PM,EXLST=JFCBPTR,DDNAME=LIBDD
*
*
         ...
```

10.6 THE SETLOCK MACRO INSTRUCTION

MVS uses a locking mechanism to serialize the use of sensitive system reusable resources among processors in a multiprocessor (MP) system. An MP system is a system composed of multiple (from 2 to 16) CPUs (processors) that share the same real and virtual storage, and the same operating system. The term tightly-coupled CPUs is sometimes used to refer to an MP system, as opposed to the term loosely-coupled CPUs, which referes to multiple CPUs, each with its own unique operating system, sharing the same DASD pool. When MVS executes on a uniprocessor (one CPU) system, the same locking mechanism is also used.

In pre-MVS and non-multiprocessor (MP) systems, reusable resources were serialized by CPU disablement and/or by the ENQ/DEQ facility. However, in an MP system, a CPU executing disabled (disabled for I/O and external interruptions) does not prevent the programs executing in the other CPUs from accessing the same resources, and the ENQ/DEQ mechanism is designed to serialize at the task level, not the processor level.

Besides serializing reusable resources among processors, the locking mechanism also serializes reusable resources among programs executing within the same processor.

There are two categories of locks: global locks and local locks.

- Global locks protect serially resusable resources related to more than one address space, such as the UCB table or the control blocks used by GETMAIN for the allocation of virtual storage from the SQA or the CSA.
- Local locks protect serially resuable resources assigned to a particular address space, such as the control blocks used by GETMAIN for the allocation of virtual storage for user subpools within the address space.

There are two types of locks: spin locks and suspend locks. The type of lock determines what happens when a program executing on one processor in an MP system makes an unconditional request for a lock that is held by a program executing on another processor of an MP system.

- Spin locks prevent the requesting program from executing and prevents the processor on which the requesting program executes from doing any work.
- Suspend locks prevent the requesting program from executing but allows the processor to continue doing other work.

The valid combinations of lock category and lock type provides the following three groups of locks:

- Global spin locks;
- Local suspend locks; and
- Global suspend locks.

A global spin lock is used to provide serialization among processors for reusable resources that are addressable from any address space. While a program is executing under a global spin lock, the processor is disabled for I/O and external interruptions.

A local suspend lock is used to provide serialization among programs, that execute in the same or different processors for reusable resources within the same address space. There is one local suspend lock per address space and the lockword that represents it is located in the ASCB of the particular address space.

A global suspend lock is used to provide serialization among programs that execute in the same or different processors for reusable resources that are addressable from any address space. While a program is executing under a global suspend lock, the processor is enabled for I/O and external interruptions.

Each lock has its own unique lock-id (or name). Table 10.6.1 shows the names of the locks provided by MVS and a description of the resource that the lock serializes.

The locks are represented by a lockword. The global lockwords are located in common addressable storage (most are in the MVS Nucleus), and the lockwords for the local locks (CML and LOCAL) are located in each ASCB. The Prefixed Save Area (PSA) of each CPU points to the global lockwords. (Note: Each CPU has its own unique PSA.) A field in the PSA (PSACHLS) indicates which locks are held by the processor.

The lockwords for global spin locks and for local suspend locks contain the id (0-15) of the processor that currently holds the lock. The lockwords for global suspend locks contain the address of the ASCB.

There are two classes of locks: single locks and multiple locks.

- Single locks means that only one lock exists at a given level of the locking hierarchy. Table 10.6.2 indicates which locks are single class locks.
- Multiple locks means that more that one lock exists at a given level of the locking hierarchy. An example is the IOSUCB lock, which is used to serialize the use of the UCB table. There is a separate lockword for each UCB, which is located in the UCBLOCK field in the prefixed area of each UCB. Table 10.6.2 indicates which locks are multiple class locks.

The locks are arranged in a hierarchy to prevent a deadlock from occurring between processors. An example of how a deadlock can occur is as follows:

Program/processor A, holding the SRM lock, requests the VSMPAG lock.
Program/processor B, holding the VSMPAG lock, requests the SRM lock.

In the above scenario, processor A and processor B will continually wait for each to release the required lock. To eliminate the possibility of a deadlock, a program can request unconditionally only those locks that are higher in the hierarchy than any of the lock(s) currently held by the processor on which the program executes. Also, a processor is allowed to hold only one global lock at the same level in the hierarchy (except for the CML lock). For example, if a processor holds one of the IOSUCB locks (this is a multiple class lock), then it cannot hold another IOSUCB lock until the first one is released. Table 10.6.2 shows the hierarchy and the characteristics of the locks.

Table 10.6.1

This table contains the names of the locks provided by MVS, with a description of the resource serialized.

RSMGL (Real Storage Management Global lock)—Serializes RSM global resources.

VSMFIX (Virtual Storage Management Fixed Subpools lock)—Serializes the allocation of SQA and fixed CSA. (This lock exists only in MVS/XA and MVS/ESA.)

ASM (Auxiliary Storage Management lock)—Serializes ASM resources on an address space level.

ASMGL (Auxiliary Storage Management Global lock)—Serializes ASM resources on a global level.

RSMDS (Real Storage Management lock)—Used for various serializations required by RSM.

RSMST (Real Storage Management Steal lock)—Serializes the stealing of unchanged pages.

RSMCM (Real Storage Management Common lock)—Serializes RSM common area resources (such as page table entries).

RSMXM (Real Storage Management Cross Memory lock)—Serializes RSM control blocks on an address space level when serialization is needed to a second address space.

RSMAD (Real Storage Management Address Space lock)—Serializes RSM control blocks on an address space level.

RSM (Real Storage Management lock (shared/exclusive))—Serializes RSM resources during recovery and the processing of global functions (such as reading and writing RSM control blocks).

VSMPAG (Virtual Storage Management Pageable Subpools lock)—Serializes the allocation of pageable CSA. (This lock exists only in MVS/XA and MVS/ESA.)

DISP (Global Dispatcher lock)—Serializes the ASVT and the ASCB dispatching queue.

SALLOC (Space Allocation lock)—For MVS/370, serializes the allocation of SQA and CSA; for MVS/XA and MVS/ESA, serializes receiving routines that enable a processor for an emergency signal or malfunction alert.

IOSYNCH (I/O Supervisor Synchronization lock)—Serializes I/O global functions, using a table of lockwords and I/O resources.

IOSUCB (I/O Supervisor Unit Control Block lock)—Serializes access and updates to the UCB table. There is one IOSUCB lock for each UCB.

SRM (System Resources Management lock)—Serializes SRM control blocks and associated data.

TRACE (Trace lock(shared/ exclusive))—Serializes the reading and writing of the system trace buffer.

CPU (Processor lock)—A pseudo spin lock providing system-recognized disablement (logical, not physical). There is one CPU lock per processor, which is always available. May be used to cause the requesting program to execute disabled for I/O and external interruptions. (This lock exists only MVS/XA and MVS/ESA.)

CMSSMF (System Management Facilities Cross Memory Services lock)—Serializes SMF functions and control blocks.

CMSEQDQ (ENQ/DEQ Cross Memory Services lock)—SerializesENQ/DEQ functions and control blocks.

CMS (General Cross Memory Services lock)—Serializes on more than one address space where this serialization is not provided by one or more of the other global locks. The CMS lock provides global serialization when enablement is required.

CML (Cross Memory Local lock)—Serializes functions and the allocation of storage within an address space other than the home address space. There is one CML for each address space.

LOCAL (Local lock)—Serializes functions and the allocation of storage within an address space. There is one LOCAL lock for each address space.

Table 10.6.2

This table shows the hierarchy of locks and their characteristics.

Lock Name	Category	Type	Class
RSMGL	Global	Spin	M
VSMFIX	Global	Spin	S

(Table 10.6.2, continued)

Lock Name	Category	Type	Class
ASM	Global	Spin	M
ASMGL	Global	Spin	M
RSMDS	Global	Spin	M
RSMST	Global	Spin	M
RSMCM	Global	Spin	M
RSMXM	Global	Spin	M
RSMAD	Global	Spin	M
RSM	Global	Spin	S
VSMPAG	Global	Spin	S
DISP	Global	Spin	S
SALLOC	Global	Spin	S
IOSYNCH	Global	Spin	M
IOSUCB	Global	Spin	M
SRM	Global	Spin	S
TRACE	Global	Spin	S
CPU	Global	Spin	M
CMSSMF	Global	Suspend	S
CMSEQDQ	Global	Suspend	S
CMS	Global	Suspend	S
CML	Local	Suspend	M
LOCAL	Local	Suspend	M

NOTES:

- The hierarchy is shown in desending sequence with the RSMGL lock being the highest lock in the hierarchy.
- The CPU lock has no hierarchical position relative to the other spin type locks; however, it does have a hierarchical position relative to the suspend locks.
- The cross memory services locks (CMSSMF, CMSEQDQ, and CMS) are equal to each other in the hierarchy.
- The local locks (CML and LOCAL) are equal to each other in the hierarchy.

The SETLOCK macro instruction is used to obtain and release locks. Use of the SETLOCK macro instruction requires that the issuing program be in supervisor state and PSW protection key zero.

The format of the SETLOCK macro instruction is as follows.

```
[name] SETLOCK  {OBTAIN|RELEASE},TYPE={lock-id|SPIN|ALL}
                [,ADDR=(11)][,ASCB=ascb-addr]
                [,SCOPE={SHR|EXCL}][,MODE={COND|UNCOND}]
                [,DISABLED][,REGS={SAVE|USE}]
```

OBTAIN

Specifies that the specified lock is to be obtained.

RELEASE

Specifies that the specified lock is to be released.

TYPE=lock-name

Specifies which lock is to be obtained or released. The lock-names are listed and described in Table 10.6.1, In addition to the lock-names specified in Table 10.6.1, CMSALL may also be specified to indicate that all the global cross memory locks (CMS, CMSEQDQ, and CMSSMF) are to be obtained or released.

TYPE=SPIN
TYPE=ALL

These values of the TYPE parameter may be specified only with the RELEASE request.

SPIN	Indicates that all spin locks currently held by the processor are to be released.
ALL	Indicates that all locks currently held by the processor are to be released.

ADDR=(11) (Default: none)

Specifies that the address of the lockword is in register 11. Must be specified for multiple class spin locks (except the CPU lock). Table 10.6.2 indicates which locks are multiple class locks.

ASCB=(11) (Default: none)

Specifies that the address of the ASCB whose local lock is requested is contained in register 11. Must be specified for TYPE=CML.

SCOPE=SHR
SCOPE=EXCL (Default: none)

This parameter is valid only with the OBTAIN request for TYPE=RSM and TYPE=TRACE.

SHR	Specifies that the scope of the lock is share, which means that multiple processors may hold the lock concurrently.
EXCL	Specifies that the scope of the lock is exlusive, which means that the issuing processor requires exclusive use of the resource serialized by the lock.

MODE=COND
MODE=UNCOND (Default: UNCOND)

The parameter is valid only with the OBTAIN request.

COND	Specifies that the lock is to be conditionally obtained.
UNCOND	Specifies that the lock is to be unconditionally obtained.

DISABLED (Default: none)

This parameter is valid only with the RELEASE request. Specifies that control is to be returned to the calling program, with the processor physically disabled for I/O and external interruptions when a lock is successfully released. This parameter is not valid when the following lock-names are specified for TYPE: CPU, CMS, CMSEQDQ, CMSSMF, CMSALL, CML, and LOCAL.

REGS=SAVE
REGS=USE (Default: the contents of registers 11-14 are destoyed)

Specifies the use of registers 11-14. If this parameter is omitted, the return code is posted in register 13 instead of register 15.

SAVE	Specifies that the contents of registers 11-14 are saved in the savearea pointed to by register 13 and are restored when control is returned. Note: The savearea used for REGS=SAVE must be a different savearea from the standard linkage savearea used by the program.
USE	Specifies that registers 14, 15, 0, and 1 are available for use. Registers 11, 12, and 13 are saved in registers 15, 0, and 1, respectively, and are restored when control is returned.

When the SETLOCK macro instruction returns control from an OBTAIN request, register 15 (register 13 if the REGS parameter is omitted) is posted with one of the following return codes.

Return Code (Hex)	Meaning
00	The lock was successfully obtained.
04	The lock was already held by the processor on which the calling program is executing.
08	The conditional OBTAIN request was unsuccessful.
10	A level error was detected. A lock of a lower hierarchy was attempted to be obtained. The return code is not posted if MODE=UNCOND.

When the SETLOCK macro instruction returns control from a RELEASE request, register 15 (register 13 if the REGS parameter is omitted) is posted with one of the following return codes.

Return Code (Hex)	Meaning
00	The lock was successfully released.
04	The lock was not held by any processor.
08	The RELEASE request was unsuccessful because the specified lock is held by another processor.
0C	This return code applies only for the CML and LOCAL locks. The RELEASE request was unsuccessful because the specified lock is not held by the calling program.

Coding Example 10.6.1

This coding example illustrates how to conditionally obtain the DISP lock and preserve the contents of registers 11, 12, and 13.

```
SETLOCK OBTAIN,TYPE=DISP,MODE=COND,REGS=USE
LTR     R15,R15
...
```

Coding Example 10.6.2

This coding example illustrates how to release all the global spin locks currently held by the processor on which the requesting program executes.

```
SETLOCK RELEASE,TYPE=SPIN
```

The SETLOCK macro instruction is normally not used by user-written programs. When used, planning and caution must be exercised because the operating system's performance and integrity can be compromised if the macro instruction is misused. Chapters 12, 13 and 15 show some uses of the SETLOCK macro instruction.

10.7 THE SVCUPDTE MACRO INSTRUCTION

The SVCUPDTE macro instruction is used to dynamically alter the SVC Table. The SVC Table contains an entry for each of the available SVC routines. An SVC routine cannot be executed unless it has an entry in the SVC Table. Chapter 12 discusses SVC routines in detail.

The SVCUPDTE macro instruction is available in MVS/XA and MVS/ESA and requires that the caller be executing in supervisor state and PSW protection key zero, as well as providing the CVT DSECT. In MVS/XA and in MVS/ESA, the SVC Table is located in the page protected section of the MVS Nucleus. Page protection is implemented by turning on the page-protected bit in the page table entry of the page that is to be protected. Since virtual storage, which is page protected, cannot be modified by a program regardless of its PSW protection key, the SVCUPDTE macro instruction is provided to enable the user to alter the SVC Table.

The SVCUPDTE macro instruction provides a convenient way for developing and testing new SVCs or modifing existing ones, since the only other way to change the SVC Table is by IPLing the system.

The format of the SVCUPDTE macro instruction is as follows:

```
[name]    SVCUPDTE    SVC-number,{REPLACE|DELETE},TYPE=n,
                      {EP=addr|EPNAME=entry-name}[,LOCKS=(lock-id,...)]
                      [,APF={YES|NO}][,NPRMPT={YES|NO}]
```

`SVC-number`
Specifies the number of the SVC which is to be inserted into or deleted from the SVC table.

`REPLACE`
`DELETE`
Specifies which function is to be performed.

- `REPLACE` indicates that an SVC table entry is to be inserted into the SVC table. This may be a new SVC or a replacement for an existing one.
- `DELETE` indicates that the table entry corresponding to the specified SVC number is to be deleted from the SVC table. SVCUPDTE deletes an SVC entry by placing the address of the SVC error routine into the entry. This causes an X'Fxx' ABEND (xx is the number of the specified SVC) to occur when an SVC instruction specifying the deleted SVC number is executed.

`TYPE=n`
Specifies the SVC type. May be 1, 2, 3, 4, 5, or 6.

`EP=addr`
`EPNAME=entry-name`
Specifies the address of the SVC routine.

EP specified the entry point address of the SVC routine, and the SVC routine must be currently loaded in a common area of virtual storage (Nucleus, LPA, SQA, or CSA).

EPNAME specifies the entry name of the SVC routine. The entry name must be the name of a load module in the LPA or the entry name of a load module linkedited into the Nucleus.

The EP and the EPNAME parameters may not be used together.

`LOCKS=(lock-id,...) (Default: none)`

Specifies the locks required by the SVC routine when it receives control. The lock ids that may be specified, in any order, are CMS, DISP, SRM, LOCAL, and SALLOC. TYPE=1 must not specify LOCAL; TYPE=3 and TYPE=4 may specify CMS or LOCAL; TYPE=6 cannot specify any locks.

`APF=YES`
`APF=NO (Default: NO)`

Specifies whether the SVC routine requires an APF-authorized caller.

YES	Indicates that the caller of the SVC routine must be authorized.
NO	Indicates that the caller of the SVC routine is not required to be authorized.

`NPRMPT=YES`
`NPRMPT=NO (Default: NO)`

Specifies whether the SVC is a non-preemptive SVC, which indicates whether it can be preempted for I/O interruptions.

YES	Indicates that the SVC routine cannot be preempted for I/O interruptions.
NO	Indicates that the SVC routine can be preempted for I/O interruptions.

When the SVCUPDTE macro instruction returns control, register 15 is posted with a return code of X'00' to indicate successful completion. If register 15 is posted with a non-zero return code, it indicates that incorrect or conflicting parameters were specified. A return code of X'28' indicates that an error occurred while the SVC Table was being updated.

The major (qname) and minor (rname) resource names SYSZSVC and TABLE, respectively, are provided by MVS for the SVC Table. The ENQ macro instruction should be issued, specifying these names before the SVCUPDTE macro instruction is issued, to assure the integrity of the SVC Table. The DEQ macro instruction should be issued to release the resource after SVCUPDTE returns control.

Coding Example 10.7.1

This coding example illustrates how to code the SVCUPDTE macro instruction to add (or replace) the entry for SVC 250. The SVC is a type-3, does not require that its caller be authorized, holds no locks, can be preempted for I/O interruptions, and its routine is located in the Link Pack Area (LPA) with the name IGC0025A. The recommended ENQ and DEQ macro instructions are also illustrated.

```
         ENQ      (QNAME,RNAME,E,,SYSTEM)
         SVCUPDTE 250,REPLACE,TYPE=3,EPNAME=IGC0025A
         DEQ      (QNAME,RNAME,,SYSTEM)
         ...
QNAME    DC       CL8'SYSZSVC'
RNAME    DC       C'TABLE'
         ...
         CVT      DSECT=YES
```

Chapter 12 presents the code for a program that uses the SVCUPDTE macro instruction to dynamically change existing SVC routines and/or add new SVC routines to MVS.

BIBLIOGRAPHY FOR CHAPTER 10

The following IBM manuals contain reference material for the topics discussed in this chapter.

ID	TITLE
GC28-1046	*OS/VS2 SPL: Supervisor*
SY28-1133	*MVS Diagnostic Techniques*
GC28-1151	*MVS/XA SPL: System Macros and Facilities Volume 2*
LY28-1199	*MVS/XA Diagnostic Techniques*
GC28-1852	*MVS/ESA SPL: Application Development Guide*
GC28-1857	*MVS/ESA SPL: Application Development Macro Reference*
LY28-1011	*MVS/ESA Diagnosis: System Reference*

11

Introduction to Channel Programming

The purpose of this chapter is to introduce the reader to the basic elements of channel programming. No attempt is made to explore all avenues of channel programming, and advanced topics such as I/O appendages are not discussed. However, channel programming for DASD, since it is the most involved, is discussed in detail. Channel programming coding examples for DASD includes reading and writing data; track balance and capacity calculations; processing track, cylinder, and extent data-end conditions; and obtaining secondary allocation. Channel programming for Magnetic Tape Volumes is also discussed.

11.1 WHAT IS CHANNEL PROGRAMMING?

Channel programming is a facility for performing I/O operations without the use of the IBM-supplied access methods (BSAM, QSAM, etc.). It requires that the programmer code a device-dependant channel program to perform the desired operation, construct and initialize various control blocks, and direct the operating system to execute the channel program.

A channel program is a list (or chain) of channel command words (CCWs). Each CCW specifies a command to be executed, the address of a data buffer and its length (if applicable), and various bit settings to further describe the CCW's functions. The channel program is executed by means of the EXCP macro instruction.

Some of the uses of channel programming include the following:

- Providing additional I/O functions that are not included in the standard access methods;
- Providing support for I/O devices that are not supported by IBM;
- Writing one's own access method; and
- Processing nonstandard magnetic tape labels.

11.2 CONTROL BLOCKS AND INSTRUCTIONS USED IN CHANNEL PROGRAMMING

In order to perform channel programming, various control blocks must be defined and referenced, and certain Assembler instructions and macro instructions must be coded. Also, there are some optional macro instructions that may be used.

The operand of the macro instructions described in this section will not necessarily be completely described; only the parameters that are used in this chapter will be discussed. The parameters that specify an address may be specified as a name (A-type address) or as a register, enclosed in parentheses, containing the address. The registers that should normally be used to contain addresses or other values are 2-12.

THE DATA CONTROL BLOCK

The Data Control Block (DCB) may be generated by the DCB macro instruction. The DCB contains information about the characteristics and processing requirements of the dataset that is to be processed by the channel program. The DCB must be opened via the OPEN macro instruction and its address must be placed in the IOB before the channel program can be executed.

The DCB contains four parts: Foundation Block, EXCP Interface, Foundation Block Extention and Common Interface, and Device Dependant. The DCB parameters, which are specified, determine which parts of the DCB are generated. The Foundation Block is required and the other three parts are optional.

THE DATA EXTENT BLOCK

The Data Extent Block (DEB) contains information about the physical characteristics of the dataset (such as device location via UCB address and extents for a DASD dataset) and other control information used by the I/O Supervisor. The DEB is created by MVS when the OPEN macro instruction is issued and the address of the DEB is placed into the associated DCB. It may be used to obtain the actual DASD location (CCHHR) of the dataset that is to be referenced via the channel program.

THE EVENT CONTROL BLOCK

The Event Control Block (ECB) is used by the I/O Supervisor to post a completion code to indicate whether the channel program completed successfully or with errors. The address of the ECB must be placed into the IOB before the channel program can be executed. The ECB is a 4-byte area aligned on a fullword boundary and initialized to zeros. The ECB is defined as follows.

```
ecbname DC F'0'
```

The first two bits of the ECB are the Wait and Complete bits, respectively. When the WAIT macro instruction is issued, the Wait bit (bit 0) is set to one and the Complete bit (bit 1) remains set to zero while the channel program is executing. When the channel program terminates, the Wait bit is set to zero and the Complete bit is set to one.

The ECB should be initialized to zeros before each execution of the EXCP macro instruction, and then the ECB should be examined after the EXCP macro instruction is executed to determine the result of the operation.

Some of the more common completion codes are the following:

7F000000	The channel program has completed successfully.
41000000	The channel program was terminated with an error.
42000000	The channel program was terminated because a DASD extent address was violated.

THE INPUT/OUTPUT BLOCK

The Input/Output Block (IOB) is used for communication between the problem program and the I/O Supervisor component of MVS. The IOB contains the addresses of control blocks and other information required by the I/O Supervisor. In addition, certain fields of the IOB are posted by the I/O Supervisor when the requested I/O operation is complete. The programmer must define the IOB with consecutive Assembler DS and/or DC instructions. IBM provides the IEZIOB macro instruction to generate the DSECT for mapping the IOB. The contents and format of the IOB is illustrated in Figure 11.1.1.

The following describes the contents of the fields of the IOB. Some fields must be set by the programmer and some fields are set by the operating system. The fields that are set by the operating system may be examined by the programmer.

IOBFLAG1 (1 byte)

Programmer must set bits 0, 1, and 6. The bits, when set to one, indicate the following:

Bit 0 Specified channel program contains data chaining.

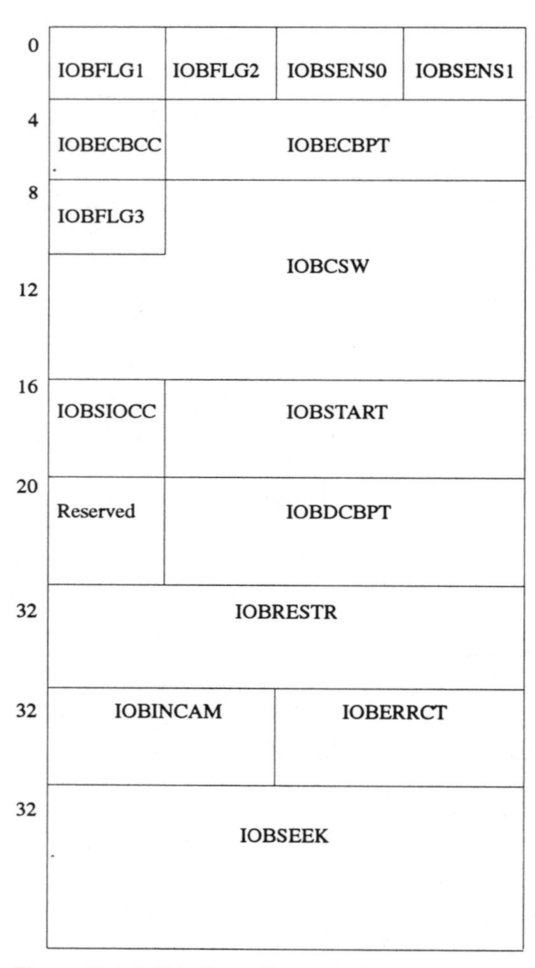

Figure 11.1.1 This figure illustrates the contents and format of the IOB. The names used for the fields are the same ones as in the DSECT.

`Bit 1`	Specified channel program contains command chaining. (Normally set to one.)
`Bit 6`	The specified channel program is not related to any other channel program. (Normally set to one.)

`IOBFLAG2 (1 byte)`

Programmer must set bits 2 and 3 if bit 6 was set to zero in IOBFLAG1. Related channel programs will not be discussed in this chapter.

`IOBSENS0 (1 byte)`
`IOBSENS1 (1 byte)`

When a unit check occurs, the operating system places sense bytes 0 and 1 into these fields. The sense bytes are defined in the hardware description manual for the particular device that is being programmed.

`IOBECBCC (1 byte)`

Operating system places the first byte of the completion code for the channel program into this field.

`IOBECBPT (3 bytes)`

Programmer-supplied address of the Event Control Block (ECB).

`IOBFLAG3 (1 byte)`

Used only by operating system.

`IOBCSW (7 bytes)`

The operating system places the last seven bytes of the Channel Status Word (CSW) into this field.

`IOBSIOCC (1 byte)`

Set by operating system. Bits 2 and 3 contain the condition code returned after the execution of the SIO instruction for this I/O operation.

`IOBSTART (3 bytes)`

Programmer-supplied address of Channel Program (CCW list) that is to be executed.

`IOBDCBPT (3 bytes)`

Programmer-supplied address of the Data Control Block (DCB).

`IOBRESTR (4 bytes)`

Used only by operating system.

`IOBINCAM (2 bytes)`

For magnetic tape only. Programmer-supplied amount by which the block count (DCBBLKCT) field in the DCB is to be incremented. This value may be changed between EXCPs. For forward operations, these bytes must contain a positive binary number (normally +1); for backward operations, these bytes must contain a negative binary number.

`IOBERRCT (2 bytes)`

Used only by operating system.

`IOBSEEK (8 bytes)`

For DASD only. Programmer-supplied address of required seek of supplied channel program in the format MBBCCHHR, where M is the extent number (starting with 0), BB is the bin number (set to 00 since current IBM DASD have no such architecture), CC is the cylinder number, HH is the head (track) number, and R is the record number.

THE CHANNEL STATUS WORD

The Channel Status Word (CSW) is located in real storage location X'40' and is updated after each I/O interruption and sometimes during the execution of certain I/O machine instructions. It provides an indication of how the I/O operation completed as well as the status of the I/O device that was involved in the operation. The CSW is eight bytes in length. The low-order seven bytes are placed into the IOB upon completion of the I/O operation requested by EXCP.

The only fields of the CSW that will be used in this chapter are the Unit Status and Residual Byte Count. The Unit Status field (label IOBUSTAT in the IOB) is used to determine if there was a unit exception (X'01'), which indicates end-of-data for a DASD dataset (zero-count-record), or a magnetic tape dataset (tape mark). The Residual Byte Count field (the IBM mapping macro, IEZIOB, does not provide a label for this field, but the programming examples in this chapter show how to provide one) contains the difference between the count specified in the last CCW to execute and the actual data transfer count.

THE CCW ASSEMBLER INSTRUCTION

The Assembler instruction CCW is used to generate a channel command word (CCW). The operand of the instruction has four parameters, and the format is as follows.

```
[name]   CCW    command-code,storage-area,flags,count
```

`command-code`

Specifies the channel command code to perform the desired operation. The channel commands are found in the appropriate hardware description manual for the specific device that is to be programmed.

`storage-area`

Specifies a label that indicates the beginning of a virtual storage location that is required by the command.

`flags`

`Bit 0 (X'80')` Chain Data (CD) flag. When set to one, it specifies that the data-area of the next sequential CCW is to be used with the current CCW. Data chaining will not be discussed in this chapter.

`Bit 1 (X'40')` Chain Command (CC) flag. When set to one and CD flag is zero, it specifies that the operation specified by the next CCW is to be performed when the operation specified by the current CCW completes normally. In a typical channel program, this bit is set for all the CCWs (except the ones that do not require it, such as the TIC (Transfer in Channel) CCW) except the last.

`Bit 2 (X'20')` Suppress Incorrect Length Indication (SILI) flag. When set to one and CD flag is zero, it specifies that the incorrect length indication is suppressed (if the count field is incorrect), and the channel program continues. An incorrect length indication causes the following: termination of the channel program, an X'41' in the first byte of the ECB, and a non-zero value in the Residual Byte Count field of the CSW.

`Bit 3 (X'10')` Skip (SKIP) flag. When set to one, it specifies that the transfer of information into main storage from a Read command or a Sense command is to be suppressed.

`Bit 4 (X'08')` Program-Controlled-Interruption (PCI) flag. When set to one, it causes the channel to generate an I/O interruption and set the PCI bit to one in the CSW when the CCW is executed. Control is then passed to the user-written PCI appendage while the channel program continues to execute. This facility will not be discussed in this chapter.

`Bit 5 (X'04')` Indirect Data Address (IDA) flag. When set to one, it specifies indirect data addressing. This enables virtual storage above the 16 Mb line to be used as CCW buffers. This facility will not be discussed in this chapter.

`count`

Specifies the number of bytes the command is to retrieve from or insert into the storage-area. If this value is incorrect (based upon the requirements of the command, the actual record length, etc.), then the operation is suppressed and an X'41' is posted in the first byte of the ECB. If the SILI bit is on, then the operation is performed and the residual byte count (difference between the specified length and the actual length) is posted in the CSW, IOBCSW+5(2).

THE DCB MACRO INSTRUCTION

The DCB macro instruction is used to generate the Data Control Block. The minimum DCB parameters that are required for channel programming are the following: MACRF=, and DDNAME= (the ddname may also be specified dynamically before the DCB is opened). These parameters cause only the foundation block of the DCB to be generated.

The following shows the minimum coding requirements for the DCB macro instruction:

```
dcbname    DCB    MACRF=E,DDNAME=ddname
```

`dcbname`

Specifies the name of the DCB.

`MACRF=E`

Indicates that the EXCP macro instruction will be used to process the dataset.

`DDNAME=`

Specifies the ddname of the JCL DD statement that points to the dataset that will be processed.

The foundation block also contains information provided by the the REPOS= parameter. This parameter is for datasets that reside on magnetic tape volumes and indicates whether the programmer is maintaining an accurate block count (REPOS=Y) or if the block count is not being maintained (REPOS=N, the default) and is therefore unreliable. The block count is maintained in the DCBBLKCT field of the DCB. This information is used by Dynamic Device Reconfiguration (DDR) for swapping. DDR will not attempt a swap if REPOS= has a value of "N".

THE OPEN MACRO INSTRUCTION

The OPEN macro instruction is used to initialize the DCB and to perform other processing before the channel program can be executed. Some of the processing performed by OPEN are the following:

- Creation of the DEB;
- DCB merge, which is the transfer of information from the JFCB and dataset label to the DCB;
- Verification or creation of standard labels; and
- Magnetic tape volume positioning.

The format of the OPEN macro instruction is as follows:

```
[name]      OPEN  dcb-address,options
```

`dcb-address`
Specifies the address of the DCB. The address may be specified as the name of the DCB macro instruction or specified in a register.

`options`
The only options that will be used in this chapter are INPUT and OUTPUT.

THE EXCP MACRO INSTRUCTION

The EXCP (EXecute Channel Program) macro instruction is used to request that the I/O Supervisor initiate the I/O operations defined by the user-specified channel program.

The format of the EXCP macro instruction is as follows:

```
[name]      EXCP  iob-address
```

`iob-address`
Specifies the address of the IOB. The address may be specified as the name of the IOB or specified in a register.

THE WAIT MACRO INSTRUCTION

The WAIT macro instruction is used to determine if the channel program has terminated by examining the ECB pointed to by the IOB used by the EXCP macro instruction. It should normally be issued immediately after the EXCP macro instruction. However, if the program is able to make use of the wait time (time required for the I/O to complete), then it may test the post bit of the ECB with a TM instruction as follows.

```
         TM    ECB,X'40'      CHK POST BIT
         BO    IOCOMPLT       IF ON, I/O COMPLETE
         B     PROCESS        IF OFF, DO OTHER PROCESSING
```

If the post bit is off, other useful processing may be performed. When there is no more work to perform, then the WAIT macro instruction must be issued. This notifies MVS to suspend execution of the program until the I/O is complete.

The format of the WAIT macro instruction is as follows:

```
[name]      WAIT  1,ECB=ecb-address
```

`ecb-address`

Specifies the address of the ECB. The address may be specified as the name of the ECB or specified in a register.

THE CLOSE MACRO INSTRUCTION

The CLOSE macro instruction is used to restore the DCB that was used by the channel program and to perform other processing. Some of the processing performed by CLOSE are the following:

- Release of the DEB that was created by OPEN;
- Removal of information transferred to the DCB by OPEN;
- Verification or creation of standard labels; and
- Magnetic tape volume disposition.

The format of the CLOSE macro instruction is as follows:

```
[name]    CLOSE    dcb-address,options
```

`dcb-address`

Specifies the address of the DCB. The address may be specified as the name of the DCB macro instruction or specified in a register.

`options`

None of the options are used in this chapter.

THE DEVTYPE MACRO INSTRUCTION

The DEVTYPE macro instruction is used to obtain various information about the characteristics of an I/O device. The description of the macro instruction will be limited to DASDs and only to the information used in this chapter.

The format of the DEVTYPE macro instruction is as follows:

```
[name]    DEVTYPE ddname,area-address[,DEVTAB][,RPS]
```

`ddname`

The ddname of the JCL DD statement that points to the device.

`area-address`

The address of the area in which the information is to be placed. The area must be on a fullword boundary and is six words for a DASD with RPS.

The format of the first three words is as follows:

`Word 0`	The UCBTYP field of the UCB.
`Word 1`	For DASD, the smaller of the maximum size of an unkeyed physical record or the maximum BLKSIZE allowed by MVS.
`Word 2`	Bytes 0–1—The number of cylinders (not counting spares) in the DASD.
	Bytes 2–3—The number of tracks per cylinder.

The information in Words 3, 4, and 5 are not used in this chapter.

DEVTAB
Specified for DASDs.

RPS
Indicates that the DASD has the Rotational Position Sensing feature.

THE EOV MACRO INSTRUCTION

The EOV macro instruction is meaningful only for DASD and magnetic tape datasets.

The EOV macro instruction is used to obtain secondary space allocation for DASD datasets that are opened for output. In order for EOV to obtain the additional DASD space, secondary space allocation must have been specified in the JCL DD statement (or specified via TSO/ISPF/PDF) when the dataset was allocated or specified via a modified JFCB. The EOV macro instruction does not issue any return codes that indicate unsuccessful completion. Issuing the EOV macro instruction for an opened (for output) DCB that points to a dataset that was not allocated with a secondary allocation quantity results in an SD37 ABEND. If the dataset was allocated with secondary allocation specified, then an SB37 ABEND will result if all 16 extents (or if 16 extents cannot be allocated) are used and only 1 DASD volume was requested. If EOV is successful, the DASD address of the new extent may be obtained by examining the DEB.

For magnetic tape datasets, the EOV macro instruction causes the operating system to issue a mount message for additional tape volumes for multi-volume datasets and to write the EOV1/EOV2 labels, if applicable. If additional volumes cannot be mounted (due to JCL volcount limit), then an SE37 ABEND will occur.

The format of the EOV macro instruction is as follows.

```
[name]     EOV        dcb-address
```

---

dcb-address
Specifies the address of the DCB for the DASD or the magnetic tape dataset that requires the EOV service. The DCB must be opened (for output) when the EOV macro instruction is issued. The address of the DCB may be specified as the name of the DCB macro instruction or in a register.

THE TRKCALC MACRO INSTRUCTION

The TRKCALC macro is used to perform track balance and capacity calculations for DASD datasets that are being created, updated, or extended.

The format of the TRKCALC macro instruction is as follows.

```
[name]     TRKCALC    FUNCTN={TRKBAL,|TRKCAP,}
                      {DEVTAB=addr|UCB=addr|TYPE=addr}
                      [,BALANCE=addr]
                      [,MAXSIZE={YES|NO}
                      [{,RKDD=addr|,R=addr,K=addr,DD=addr}]
                      [,REGSAVE={YES|NO}]
```

FUNCTN=TRKBAL
FUNCTN=TRKCAP
Specifies the function that is to be performed.

TRKBAL Requests the calculation of the new track balance (space available after the current record is written). Certain information is returned to the user, depending on one of the following conditions:

- If record fits on the track, register 0 contains the new track balance and register 15 contains a return code of zero.
- If the record does not fit on the track, register 15 contains a return code of 8. If MAXSIZE=YES is specified, the data length of the largest record that will fit into the remaining space of the track is returned in register 0.

TRKCAP Requests the calculation of the number of fixed length records that can be written on a whole track or the number of fixed length records that can be added to a partially filled track.

DEVTAB=addr
UCB=addr
TYPE=addr

One of the above keyword parameters must be specified to indicate the DASD type for which the calculations are to be performed.

For DEVTAB, the address of a fullword that contains the address of the Device Characteristics Table Entry (DCTE) is specified.

For UCB, the address of a fullword that contains the address of the UCB is specified.

For TYPE, the address of a fullword that contains the address of the UCB device type (UCBTBYT4) is specifed.

BALANCE=addr

Specifies the address of a halfword that contains the current track balance or a register, enclosed in parentheses, that contains the track balance in the low-order two bytes. The value specified is the value returned when TRKCALC FUNCTN=TRKBAL was last issued. The initial value of BALANCE may be obtained by issuing the DEVTYPE macro instruction and using the track size value, which is returned.

MAXSIZE=YES
MAXSIZE=NO (Default: NO)

This parameter is meaningful only for FUNCTION=TRKBAL and when the specified record does not fit in the remaining space on the track. If YES is specified, the data length of the largest record with the specified key that can fit is returned in register 0. If NO is specified, no length is returned.

RKDD=addr
R=addr,K=addr,DD=addr

The parameter RKDD= or parameters R=, K=, and DD= must be specified to describe the record that is intended to be written with the next EXCP macro instruction.

If RKDD is used, the address specifies a fullword or register that contains the record number (1 byte), key length (1 byte), and data length (2 bytes), respectively.

The values may also be specified separately if R, K, and DD are used. The address specifies a storage area of appropriate length to contain the information or a register to contain the information in the low-order byte(s).

REGSAVE=YES
REGSAVE=NO (Default: NO)

YES indicates that registers 1 through 14 are saved and restored (using the savearea pointed to by register 13) across the TRKCALC call. NO indicates that registers are not saved across the TRKCALC call.

11.3 CHANNEL PROGRAMING FOR DASD

This section will discuss the track and record format of DASD, describe the common CCWs that operate on DASD, discuss the programming considerations and techiques for creating DASD channel programs, and provide examples of channel programs that will read, create, and update DASD datasets.

11.3.1 DASD Track and Record Format

In order to write channel programs for a direct access storage device (DASD or also known as disk), an understanding of the track and record format is necessary. IBM DASDs may have count, key, data (CKD) format (3350, 3375, 3380, etc.), or fixed block architecture (FBA) format (3370). This section discusses only CKD format.

A DASD is comprised of many cylinders. Each cylinder contains some tracks, which have a maximum capacity of a fixed number of bytes. For example, a single density 3380 DASD (each access mechanism) is comprised of 885 cylinders for data use. Each cylinder contains 15 tracks, and each track has a maximum capacity of 47,476 bytes. The actual number of bytes that may be written to and stored on a track depends on the number of records contained on the track and whether keys are used. There are inter-record gaps (IRG) between records, and these IRGs use up some of the track's capacity. The more records, the more IRGs; therefore, that much less track capacity available for data. For example, the largest single record (data area without keys) that can fit on a track of a 3380 DASD is 47,476 bytes (IBM standard access methods (QSAM, BSAM, etc.) support a maximum block size of 32,760). If the same track contained two records, the maximum size of each record would be 23,476 (2 x 23,476 = 46,952 < 47,476).

The beginning of a track is indicated by an Index Point. The end of a track is indicated by the same (logically, but not necessarily physically) Index Point.

Following the Index Point is the Home Address record. This record is written when the DASD is formatted or initialized by the IBM Device Support Facilities program (ICKDSF) and contains the actual address of the track as defined by its cylinder number and head number (CCHH). This record also contains information describing the condition of the track and indicates whether the track is usable, defective, or being used as an alternate track.

Following the Home Address record is the R0 record (which is also called the Track Descriptor record). This record is also created when a DASD is formatted or initialized by DSF. The R0 record may be a standard or nonstandard record. If the dataset is created and/or maintained by IBM access methods, then the R0 record is standard and is reserved for operating system use and has a key length of zero and a data length of eight. If the dataset is not created or maintained by IBM access methods, then the R0 record is nonstandard and may be used as a normal data record with the key length and data length defined by the user.

Following the Track Descriptor record may be one or more user-data records (which may be referred to as records R1 through Rn). These records are referred to as physical records. Physical records contain up to three sections: the Count Area, the Key Area (which is optional), and the Data Area. These areas are separated by gaps (which are smaller than IRGs).

The Count Area is eight bytes and contains the location of the record, the length of the key (these are external keys known to the hardware and referenced by the software, not imbedded keys that are part of the actual data), and the length of the actual user-data. The location of the record is specified by its cylinder number, head number, and record number (CCHHR) and is contained in the first five bytes of the Count Area. The sixth byte of the Count Area is the key length (KL). The KL may be from 0 to 255 bytes. If external keys are not being used, then KL is specified as zero. If IBM access methods are being used, the KL is indicated by the KEYLEN parameter of the DCB macro instruction. The last two bytes of the Count Area is the data length (DL). The DL is the length of the actual user-data. A DL of zero indicates end-of-data. If IBM access methods are being used, DL is the block size that is indicated by the BLKSIZE parameter of the DCB macro instruction for fixed length records.

The Key Area contains the actual key (if KL is specified as greater than zero). This area is optional and, when used, identifies the entire physical record. Examples of IBM's use of external keys would be the directory of partitioned datasets (see Chapter 8) and the DSCBs of the VTOC.

The Data Area contains the actual user-data. IBM access methods support a maximum physical record length of 32,760 bytes. Larger records may be created and referenced only with the use of EXCP. The hardware knows only about physical records. If physical records are to be divided into logical records, then it is the responsibility of the software to accomplish this. In IBM access methods, the logical record length for fixed length records is indicated by the LRECL parameter of the DCB macro instruction. This information is stored in the datasets's format-1 DSCB of the VTOC.

Physical records may be referenced by their external key or by their sequential record number (R1, R2, etc.).

11.3.2 DASD Exception Conditions

When reading from (or writing to) a DASD dataset with EXCP, certain exception conditions may occur that are part of the normal processing of the dataset. These exception conditions are indicated after the channel program terminates. The following describes those exception conditions, how to recognize them; and how to process them when the dataset is being read sequentialy.

- *End-of-records on a track.* This condition is indicated by a X'41' posted in the first byte of the ECB and a X'08' (no record found) in IOBSENS1. The condition is handled by resetting the record number to one and by incrementing the track number by one. If incrementing the track number exceeds the number of tracks per cylinder, then the cylinder number is incremented by one and the track number is reset to zero. Then the EXCP macro instruction is reissued.
- *End-of-records in an extent.* This condition is indicated by a X'42' being posted in the first byte of the ECB. This condition is handled by scanning the DEB and obtaining the beginning location (CCHH) of the next extent and resetting the record number to one. Then the EXCP macro instruction is reissued. If this is the last extent, and a new record is be written, then the EOV macro instruction may be used to obtain an additional extent.
- *End-of-data.* This condition is indicated by a X'41' in the first byte of the ECB and the control unit setting the unit exception bit in the CSW, which is indicated by a X'01' in IOBUSTAT. When this occurs, all the records have been read (if they were being read sequentially), and the end-of-data processing should start. This condition may also be indicated when data have been read from all the extents. In this case, a X'42' is posted in the first byte of the ECB, and the dataset contains no more extents.

11.3.3 Reading Data from a DASD Dataset

In order to read a record from a DASD dataset, a number of operations must be performed. First, the access mechanism (read/write head) is required to be positioned to the track that contains the record that is to be read. Then, since DASD tracks may contain many records, a search for the specific record must be made. A record may be identified by its ID (record number of track) or key. Finally, when the record is located, then it may be read into virtual storage with one of the Read commands.

Records may be read from a DASD dataset sequentially or randomly. Records may be read sequentially by specifying the record ID, which is the DASD location (CCHHR) of the record. The R (record number) is incremented by one for each read operation until all the records of a track are read. The process is repeated for each track until all the records are read. Records may be read randomly by specifying a specific record ID or a specific record key.

The required channel program (in words) to read one physical record from a DASD dataset is the following:

```
Seek
Set File Mask
Set Sector
Search ID Equal or Search Key Equal
Transfer in Channel
Read CKD or Read KD or Read Data
Read Sector
```

SEEK CCW

The Seek command causes the DASD access mechanism to be positioned to the indicated cylinder and head (CCHH) location. This command is not required for EXCP because the Seek is done by the I/O Supervisor using the location in the IOBSEEK field of the IOB when an EXCP macro instruction is executed.

SET FILE MASK CCW (X'1F')

The Set File Mask command is used to indicate which write and seek commands are permitted. It is normally not used, since the default is appropriate for most uses of the channel program. The purpose of the command is to protect data integrity by inhibiting certain sensitive commands such as Write Home Address, Write R0, and so on.

SET SECTOR CCW (X'23')
READ SECTOR CCW (X'22')

These commands are optional. The Set Sector and Read Sector commands are used together to achieve rotational position sensing (RPS), which is a way of improving record searching efficiency. RPS is based on a division of the track into evenly spaced angular sectors. When a Search command is issued, the storage director starts the command at a random location on the track and starts the search (if the Search command is repeated) for the specified record (indicated by its CCHHR or key). If a Set Sector command is used before the Search command, the storage director causes the Search command to be delayed (the channel and storage director disconnect from the device) until just before the required record comes under the read/write head. While the track performs nonproductive rotating (rotational delay), certain other I/O operations can be overlapped.

The Set Sector command transfers a 1-byte sector number from virtual storage to the storage director. The Read Sector command transfers a 1-byte sector number of the last record processed from the storage director to virtual storage. Using the Set Sector command with the sector number obtained from the previous Read Sector command (the first sector number of a track is zero) will cause the storage director to start a subsequent search at the approximate location where the last record was processed. This is fine for a performance improvement for sequential processing, but will cause no performance improvement for random processing. However, a performance improvement can be realized for random processing by using the sector number, which may be obtained from an IBM-supplied program (IECOSCR1, pointed to by CVT) for a specific record location.

SEARCH ID EQUAL CCW (X'31')

SEARCH KEY EQUAL CCW (X'29')

The Search ID Equal command causes the specified record ID (CCHHR) to be compared to the record ID of the count area of the next record encountered on the track (the track is continually rotating past the read/write head location selected by the Seek command). The search is based on the physical sequence of the record (R1, R2, etc.).

The Search Key Equal command operates similar to the Search ID Equal command except that the comparison is with the key area of the record. There also exists Search Equal or High and Search High commands, but those commands will not be discussed or used in this chapter.

If the comparison is not satisfied, then the next sequential CCW in the chain is executed. If the comparison is satisfied, then the next sequential CCW in the chain is skipped (by the control unit), and the CCW, after the skipped one, is executed. If the Search command is repeated (within the same CCW chain), then each record encountered on the track is compared until the record is found or is determined not to be present. The control unit determines that the record is not found if the Index Point is encountered twice without the search being satisfied.

TRANSFER IN CHANNEL CCW (X'08')

The TIC CCW does not initiate any I/O operation. Instead it provides branching capability in a CCW chain. The storage-area field specifies the label of the CCW that is to be executed next. The TIC command usually follows a Search command to provide looping capability until a specific record is found. The TIC CCW has all flag bits set to zero and has a count of zero.

READ COUNT, KEY, AND DATA (CKD) CCW (X'1E')
READ KEY AND DATA (KD) CCW (X'0E')
READ DATA CCW (X'06')

These Read commands all cause the record that was located by the Search command to be read into the storage area specified by the CCW. The Read CKD will cause the count, key, and data areas to be read; the Read KD will cause only the key and data areas to be read; and the Read Data command will cause only the data area to be read. The storage area specified in the CCW must be large enough to accommodate the data portion of the record as well as any other areas that are requested.

A DASD READ CHANNEL PROGRAM

An actual DASD read channel program would be coded as follows:

```
READPGM  CCW    X'31',CCHHR,X'60',5
         CCW    X'08',READPGM,X'00',0
         CCW    X'06',USERDATA,X'20',244
```

NOTES:

- The initial Seek command is not specified because it is performed automatically by the I/O Supervisor from the information supplied in the IOBSEEK field of the IOB when the EXCP macro instruction is executed.
- The first CCW specifies a Search ID Equal command for a specific record on the track selected by the Seek command. The virtual storage area labeled CCHHR contains the DASD location of the record. The Search ID Equal CCW has the chaining bit that will cause the next CCW in the list to be executed.
- If the Search is not successful for the current record encountered, then the second CCW (TIC) causes a branch back to the Search ID Equal command, and a compare is performed on the next record that is encountered. The loop continues until either two Index Points are encountered (record not found) or the record is located.
- If the record is not located, the channel program is terminated and a X'41' is posted in the first byte of the ECB and a X'08' is posted in IOBSENS1.
- If the record is located, then the second CCW (TIC) is skipped and the next (in this example, last) CCW is executed. The last CCW contains a Read Data command, which causes the data portion of the record to be read and stored into the virtual storage location specified by the label USERDATA. The Read Data CCW contains a count of 244 bytes and the SILI flag is set to one. If this count does not agree with the DL field of the count area of the record and if the SILI flag is zero, then the channel program is terminated with an error. However, since the SILI flag is set to one, a maximum of 244 bytes are read into virtual storage, and if the DL field does not agree with the CCW count, then the Residual Byte Count field of the CSW is set to the difference; otherwise it is set to zero. The Read Data CCW also has the chaining bit off, which indicates the logical end of the channel program.
- If the records are to be read sequentially, then the Set Sector and Read Sector commands may be specified to improve record searching performance. If the records are to be read randomly, then only the Set Sector command should be specified to improve performance.

In order to test our read channel program, we require a DASD dataset with known contents and structure. We should create this dataset, using the conventional IBM access methods. A convenient way to do this is by using TSO/ISPF/PDF in Edit Mode or to write a program, using QSAM, that creates the test dataset. In order to test the program completely, the data in the dataset should span consecutive tracks that cross a cylinder boundary and be contained in multiple noncontiguous extents.

To assure consecutive tracks that cross a cylinder boundary, we will allocate the dataset to have a primary allocation of two cylinders, and to obtain multiple extents, we will allocate a secondary allocation of one cylinder. Then, we will create enough records to fill two cylinders and part of another one. For a 3380 DASD, we will use DCB attributes of BLKSIZE=244, LRECL=244 and RECFM=F because this will minimize the number of records that are required to fill a track and still remain within the range of the TSO/ISPF/PDF Edit requirements (LRECL=255 or less). A 3380 DASD track will accommodate 65 records of 244 bytes, so we will create 2000 records (65 x 15 = 975 for each cylinder). When creating the records, we will make the first few bytes unique, while the rest of the record may contain blanks.

Coding Example 11.3.1

This coding example illustrates how to sequentially read all the records of the test DASD dataset created above. In this example, the records are read by specifying the record ID

(CCHHR) and incrementing the record number for each read operation. When all the records of a track are read, the track number is incremented. The cylinder number is incremented when all the records contained on all the tracks of a cylinder are read. When all the records of an extent are read, the cylinder and track numbers of the next extent are obtained from the DEB. The read operation continues sequentially until a zero-count-record is encountered or until all extents are exhausted.

```
READDASD CSECT
*
*
*************************************************************************
*    INITIALIZATION
*************************************************************************
*
         INITL 3,4,EQU=R        INITIALIZE PROGRAM
         USING DEBBASIC,R10     DEFINE REG FOR BASIC-DEB DSECT
         USING IHADCB,R11       DEFINE REG FOR DCB DSECT
         USING IOBSTDRD,R12     DEFINE REG FOR IOB DSECT
*
*
*************************************************************************
*    MAINSTREAM OF PROGRAM
*************************************************************************
*
         BAL   R6,SETDSCTS      LOAD DSECT REGS
         BAL   R6,SETIOB        SET REQUIRED IOB FIELDS
         BAL   R6,GTRKINFO      GET CYL AND TRK CAPAC INFO
         BAL   R6,OPEN          OPEN DCBS
         BAL   R6,GET1EXTN      GET 1ST EXTENT OF DATASET
NEXTREC  BAL   R6,READREC       READ A PHYSICAL RECORD
         BAL   R6,PRINTREC      PRINT FIRST 10 BYTES OF RECORD
         B     NEXTREC          READ NEXT RECORD
ENDDATA  BAL   R6,CLOSE         END-OF-DATA, CLOSE DCBS
         B     RETURN           RETURN TO MVS OR CALLING PROG
*
*
*************************************************************************
*    THIS ROUTINE LOADS THE REGISTERS FOR THE DCB AND THE IOB DSECTS.
*************************************************************************
*
SETDSCTS LA    R11,READDCB      LOAD DCB ADR FOR DSECT ADRBLTY
         LA    R12,READIOB      LOAD IOB ADR FOR DSECT ADRBLTY
         BR    R6               RETURN TO CALLING RTN
*
*
*************************************************************************
*    THIS ROUTINE SETS THE REQUIRED FIELDS OF THE IOB.
*************************************************************************
*
SETIOB   MVI   IOBFLAG1,X'42'   IND CCW-CHAINING, NOT RELATED
         MVC   IOBSTART,CCWADR  LOAD BG ADR OF CCW-LIST
         MVC   IOBDCBPT,DCBADR  LOAD DCB ADR
         MVC   IOBECBPT,ECBADR  LOAD ECB ADR
         BR    R6               RETURN TO CALLING RTN
*
*
*************************************************************************
*    THIS ROUTINE USES THE DEVTYPE MACRO TO OBTAIN THE NUMBER OF TRACKS
*    PER CYLINDER FOR THE DASD DEVICE, WHICH CONTAINS THE DATASET THAT IS
*    TO BE READ.
*************************************************************************
*
GTRKINFO MVC   DDNAME,DCBDDNAM  EXTRACT DDNAME FROM DCB
```

```
         DEVTYPE DDNAME,DEVTAREA,DEVTAB
         LH   R10,CYLTRKS       LD NUMB OF TRKS PER CYL
         BCTR R10,0             DECR TO GET HI-TRK ADR (REL TO 0)
         STH  R10,HITRKADR      SAVE HI-TRK ADR
         BR   R6                RETURN TO CALLING RTN
*
*
***********************************************************************
*    THIS ROUTINE OPENS ALL THE DCBS.
***********************************************************************
*
OPEN     OPEN  (READDCB,,SYSPRINT,(OUTPUT))
         ...                    CHK FOR GOOD OPEN
         BR   R6                RETURN TO CALLING RTN
*
*
***********************************************************************
*    THIS ROUTINE OBTAINS THE ADDRESS OF THE FIRST EXTENT FIELD IN THE
*    DEB AND THEN BRANCHES AND LINKS TO THE GETNXEXT SUBROUTINE WHICH
*    EXTRACTS THE BEGINNING CCHH OF THE EXTENT.
***********************************************************************
*
GET1EXTN L     R10,DCBDEBAD      LD DEB ADR FOR DSECT ADRBLTY
         MVC   TOTEXTN,DEBNMEXT EXTRACT TOTAL NUMB OF EXTENTS
         DROP  R10               DROP REG FOR BASIC-DEB DSECT
         USING DEBDASD,R10       DEFINE SAME REG FOR DASD-DEB DSECT
         LA    R10,32(0,R10)     INCR TO BG OF EXTENTS AREA IN DEB
         ST    R10,EXTNADR       SAVE 1ST EXTENT ADR FOR GETNXEXT RTN
         XC    EXTNCTR,EXTNCTR   INIT EXTENT CTR TO ZERO
         BAL   R8,GETNXEXT       GET CC AND HH OF 1ST EXTENT
         BR    R6                RETURN TO CALLING RTN
*
*
***********************************************************************
*    THIS SUBROUTINE EXTRACTS THE BEGINNING CCHH OF THE NEXT EXTENT FOR
*    THE CALLING ROUTINE. IT ALSO CHECKS FOR LAST-EXTENT, INCREMENTS
*    TO THE NEXT EXTENT FIELD IN THE DEB AND SAVES THE EXTENT FIELD
*    ADDRESS IN THE FULLWORD EXTNADR. THIS SUBROUTINE RECEIVES THE
*    ADDRESS OF THE FIRST EXTENT FIELD IN THE DEB FROM THE ROUTINE
*    GET1EXTN.
***********************************************************************
*
GETNXEXT IC    R10,EXTNCTR       LD PREV EXTENT NUMB
         LA    R10,1(0,R10)      INCR TO IND THIS EXTENT
         STC   R10,EXTNCTR       SAVE THIS EXTENT NUMB
         CLC   EXTNCTR,TOTEXTN   COMP THIS EXT NUMB TO TOT EXTENTS
         BH    ENDDATA           IF HIGH, IND END-OF-DATA
         L     R10,EXTNADR       LD ADR OF NEXT EXTENT FIELD IN DEB
         MVC   CC,DEBSTRCC       PUT CC OF NEXT EXTENT INTO RECPTR
         MVC   HH,DEBSTRHH       PUT HH OF NEXT EXTENT INTO RECPTR
         LA    R10,16(0,R10)     INCR TO NEXT EXTENT FIELD IN DEB
         ST    R10,EXTNADR       SAVE ADR OF NEXT EXTENT FIELD
         BR    R8                RETURN TO CALLING RTN
*
*
***********************************************************************
*    THIS ROUTINE READS THE NEXT PHYSICAL RECORD FROM THE DASD DATASET.
*    IN ORDER TO PERFORM THAT TASK, THIS ROUTINE BRANCHES AND LINKS TO THE
*    SUBROUTINES THAT PERFORM THE FOLLOWING FUNCTIONS:
*    * INCREMENT THE RECORD POINTER TO POINT TO THE NEXT RECORD THAT
*      IS TO BE READ;
*    * ISSUE THE EXCP MACRO TO READ THE NEXT PHYSICAL RECORD OF THE
*      DASD DATASET.
***********************************************************************
```

```
*
READREC  BAL   R7,SETRCPTR       SET CCHHR OF NEXT RECORD
         BAL   R7,DOEXCP         ISSUE EXCP TO READ RECORD
         BR    R6                RETURN TO CALLING RTN
*
*
************************************************************************
*    THIS SUBROUTINE INCREMENTS THE RECORD POINTER TO POINT TO THE NEXT
*    RECORD THAT IS TO BE READ AND MOVES THE NEW RECORD POINTER INTO THE
*    IOB.
************************************************************************
*
SETRCPTR IC    R10,R             LOAD PREV REC NUMB
         LA    R10,1(0,R10)      INCR REC NUMB TO NEXT RECORD
         STC   R10,R             SAVE NEXT REC NUMB
         MVC   IOBSEEK,RECPTR    MOVE NEW MBBCCHHR INTO IOB
         BR    R7                RETURN TO CALLING RTN
*
*
************************************************************************
*    THIS SUBROUTINE ISSUES THE EXCP MACRO TO READ THE PHYSICAL RECORD OF
*    THE DASD DATASET POINTED TO BY RECPTR, CHECKS THE ECB COMPLETION CODE
*    AND PERFORMS THE APPROPRIATE ACTION INDICATED BY THE COMPLETION CODE.
************************************************************************
*
DOEXCP   XC    READECB,READECB   CLEAR ECB FOR EXCP MACRO
         EXCP  READIOB           ISSUE EXCP
         WAIT  1,ECB=READECB     WAIT FOR I/O COMPLETION
         TM    READECB,X'7F'     CHK FOR GOOD I/O
         BNO   CHKECB            IF NO, EXAM ECB
         BR    R7                IF I/O GOOD, RET TO CALLING RTN
*
CHKECB   TM    READECB,X'41'     CHK FOR EXCEPTION COND
         BO    CHKERR41          IF YES, EXAM ADDITIONAL INFO
         TM    READECB,X'42'     CHK FOR END-OF-EXTENT
         BO    SETNXEXT          IF YES, SET RECPTR FOR NEXT EXTENT
         B     EXCPERR           IF NO, I/O ERROR, DUMP DIAG INFO
*
CHKERR41 TM    IOBUSTAT,X'01'    CHK IF END-OF-DATA IND SET
         BO    ENDDATA           IF YES, GO TO END-OF-DATA RTN
         TM    IOBSENS1,X'08'    CHK IF END-OF-TRACK IND SET
         BO    SETNXTRK          IF YES, SET RECPTR FOR NEXT TRACK
         B     EXCPERR           IF NO, I/O ERROR, DUMP DIAG INFO
*
SETNXTRK MVI   SECTOR,X'00'      RESET SECTOR NUMB FOR BG OF TRACK
         MVI   R,X'01'           SET REC NUMB TO 1ST REC ON TRACK
         LA    R10,0             CLEAR R10 FOR INCR TRK NUMB
         LH    R10,HH            LD CUR TRK NUMB
         LA    R10,1(0,R10)      INCR TRK NUMB
         STH   R10,HH            PUT NEW TRK NUMB INTO RECPTR
         BAL   R8,CHKNXTRK       VAL TRK NUMB, INCR CYL NUMB IF NEC
         MVC   IOBSEEK,RECPTR    PUT NEW RECPTR INTO IOB
         B     DOEXCP            RE-ISSUE EXCP MACRO
*
SETNXEXT MVI   SECTOR,X'00'      SET SECTOR TO ZERO (BG OF TRK)
         MVI   R,X'01'           SET REC NUMB TO 1ST REC TO READ
         IC    R10,M             LOAD CUR EXTENT NUMB
         LA    R10,1(0,R10)      INCR EXTENT NUMB
         STC   R10,M             PUT NEW EXTENT NUMB INTO RECPTR
         BAL   R8,GETNXEXT       GET CCHH OF NEXT EXTENT
         MVC   IOBSEEK,RECPTR    PUT NEW MBBCCHHR INTO IOB
         B     DOEXCP            RE-ISSUE EXCP MACRO
*
*
```

```
************************************************************************
*    THIS SUBROUTINE VALIDATES THE NEW TRACK NUMBER AFTER THE TRACK NUMBER
*    IS INCREMENTED TO DETERMINE IF IT EXCEEDS THE HI-TRACK ADDRESS OF A
*    CYLINDER. IF IT DOES, THEN THE CYLINDER NUMBER IS INCREMENTED AND THE
*    TRACK NUMBER IS SET TO ZERO.
************************************************************************
*
CHKNXTRK CLC    HH,HITRKADR       COMP NEW TRK NUMB TO HI-TRK ADR
         BH     SETNXCYL          IF HIGH, INCR CYL NUMB
         BR     R8                IF NOT HIGH, RET TO CALLING RTN
SETNXCYL XC     HH,HH             SET TRK NUMB TO ZERO (BG OF CYL)
         LA     R10,0             CLEAR R10 FOR INCR CYL NUMB
         LH     R10,CC            LD CUR CYL NUMB
         LA     R10,1(0,R10)      INCR CYL NUMB
         STH    R10,CC            PUT NEW CYL NUMB INTO RECPTR
         BR     R8                RETURN TO CALLING RTN
*
*
************************************************************************
*    THIS ROUTINE PRINTS THE FIRST TEN BYTES OF EACH RECORD READ.
************************************************************************
*
PRINTREC MVC   LINE+1(10),RECORD MOVE 1ST 10 BYTES OF REC
         PUT   SYSPRINT,LINE     PRINT 1ST 10 BYTES TO VERIFY READ
         BR    R6                RETURN TO CALLING RTN
*
*
************************************************************************
*    THIS ROUTINE RECEIVES CONTROL IF THE ATTEMPTED I/O IS UNSUCCESSFUL.
*    THIS ROUTINE LOAD VARIOUS DIAGNOSTIC INFORMATION INTO REGISTERS
*    8, 9, 10, AND 11 AND THEN CAUSES AN ABEND WITH A DUMP.
************************************************************************
*
EXCPERR  L     R8,READECB        LOAD CONTENTS OF ECB INTO A REG
         MVC   ERRINFO(1),EXTNCTR    EXTENT NUMBER
         MVC   ERRINFO+1(1),IOBUSTAT UNIT STATUS FIELD OF CSW
         MVC   ERRINFO+2(1),IOBSENS0 BYTE-1 OF HARDWARE SENSE CODE
         MVC   ERRINFO+3(1),IOBSENS1 BYTE-2 OF HARDWARE SENSE CODE
         L     R9,ERRINFO        LOAD ERROR INFO WORD INTO A REG
         L     R10,RECPTR        LOAD 1ST 4 BYTES OF RECORD PTR
         L     R11,RECPTR+4      LOAD 2ND 4 BYTES OF RECORD PTR
         L     R12,ERRID         LOAD ID TO FIND REGS IN DUMP
         ABEND 900,DUMP          ISSUE ABEND MACRO WITH DUMP REQ
*
*
************************************************************************
*    THIS ROUTINE CLOSES ALL THE DCBS.
************************************************************************
*
CLOSE    CLOSE (READDCB,,SYSPRINT) CLOSE ALL DCBS
         BR    R6                RETURN TO CALLING RTN
*
*
************************************************************************
*    THIS ROUTINE RESTORES THE REGISTERS AND RETURNS CONTROL.
************************************************************************
*
RETURN   RCNTL RC=0              RETURN TO MVS OR CALLING PROG
*
*
************************************************************************
*    THIS LIST REQUIRED FOR THE DEVTYPE MACRO.
************************************************************************
*
```

```
DEVTAREA DS     0CL24
         DS     CL8
         DS     CL2
CYLTRKS  DS     CL2                NUMBER OF TRACKS PER CYLINDER
         DS     CL12
*
*
***************************************************************************
*    THIS AREA MAPS OUT THE RECORD-POINTER FOR THE NEXT RECORD THAT IS
*    TO BE READ.
***************************************************************************
*
         DS    0F                  FOR ALIGNMENT FOR EXCPERR ROUTINE
RECPTR   DS    0CL8
M        DS    X'00'               EXTENT NUMBER (STARTING WITH 0)
BB       DS    XL2'00'             BIN NUMBER (NO LONGER USED)
CCHHR    DS    0CL5
CCHH     DS    0CL4
CC       DS    CL2                 CYLINDER NUMBER
HH       DS    CL2                 HEAD (TRACK) NUMBER
R        DC    X'00'               RECORD NUMBER
*
*
***************************************************************************
*    THE CCW-LIST, IOB, AND ECB
***************************************************************************
*
READCCWS CCW   X'23',SECTOR,X'40',1   SET SECTOR CCW
SEARCH   CCW   X'31',CCHHR,X'60',5    SEARCH ID EQUAL CCW
         CCW   X'08',SEARCH,X'00',0   TIC CCW
         CCW   X'06',RECORD,X'60',244 READ DATA CCW (SILI-BIT ON)
         CCW   X'22',SECTOR,X'00',1   READ SECTOR CCW
*
READIOB  DC    10F'0'                 AREA FOR IOB
READECB  DC    F'0'                   FULLWORD FOR ECB
*
*
***************************************************************************
*    OTHER DC/DS STATEMENTS
***************************************************************************
*
SECTOR   DC    X'00'
DDNAME   DS    CL8
HITRKADR DS    H
TOTEXTN  DS    CL1
EXTNCTR  DS    CL1
EXTNADR  DS    F
RECORD   DS    CL244
LINE     DC    CL133' '
ERRINFO  DS    F
ERRID    DC    4XL1'FF'
*
CCWADR   DC    A(READCCWS)
DCBADR   DC    A(READDCB)
ECBADR   DC    A(READECB)
*
*
***************************************************************************
*    THE DCBS
***************************************************************************
*
READDCB  DCB   MACRF=E,DDNAME=TESTDATA
SYSPRINT DCB   DSORG=PS,MACRF=PM,BLKSIZE=1330,LRECL=133,RECFM=FB,        -
               DDNAME=SYSPRINT
```

```
*
*
***********************************************************************
*    THE DSECTS
***********************************************************************
*
         PRINT NOGEN
         DCBD DSORG=XE          GENERATES EXCP-DCB DSECT
         IEZDEB                 GENERATES DEB DSECT
         IEZIOB                 GENERATES IOB DSECT
         ORG   IOBCSTAT+1       POS TO RESIDUAL COUNT FIELD OF CSW
IOBCSWCT DS    CL2              PROVIDE LABEL FOR RES CT FIELD
*
*
***********************************************************************
*    END OF PROGRAM
***********************************************************************
*
*
         END
```

NOTES:

- The PRINTREC routine is for illustration purposes only and does not include any code to provide for a new page after so many lines.
- As an exercise, the reader might try to read multiple records with the execution of a single channel program. This can be accomplished by defining multiple consecutive groups of Search ID Equal, TIC, and Read Data CCWs (with the command-chaining bit on except for TIC) in the CCW-list. Each Read Data CCW must point to a different I/O buffer.

DETERMINING THE SECTOR NUMBER OF A RECORD

To improve search performance time for random searches, the sector number of the record that is to be read (or updated) should be specified. However, obtaining the sector number from the Read Sector command, as with sequential processing, would not suffice. For random processing, the sector number may be obtained by using an IBM-supplied program. The name of the program is IECOSCR1 and its entry point address is stored in the CVTOSCR1 field of the CVT. The sector number may be obtained in advance only if the records are to be located by record ID. If the records are to be located by key, then the entire track has to be searched since there is no way of knowing the sector location of those records (unless the sector number is obtained when a record is written and a table is maintained to contain the record key and corresponding sector number and stored in the dataset or somewhere else on a DASD).

When IECOSCR1 receives control, the following information must be provided in registers 0, 2, 14, and 15:

`Register 0` For fixed length records. A 4-byte value in the form DDKR, where DD is a 2-byte field containing the length of the data area, K is a 1-byte field containing the length of the key area, and R is a 1-byte field containing the number of the record for which the sector number is desired. The high order bit of register 0 must be set to zero to indicate that the information provided is for fixed length records.

For variable length records. A 4-byte value in the form BBIR, where BB is a 2-byte field containing the total number of key and data bytes on the track up to but not including the record whose sector number is desired, I is a 1-byte key indicator (1 for keyed records, 0 for non-keyed records), and R is a 1-byte field containing the number of the record for which the sector number is desired. The high order bit of register 0 must be set to one to indicate that the information provided is for variable length records.

A 4-byte value of the track balance. The track balance is for the space on the track starting with the record whose sector number is desired. This value can be calculated via the TRKCALC macro instruction by specifying the previous record. If track balance information is provided, then control is passed to IECOSCR1 at eight bytes past the entry point address obtained from the CVT. The instruction BAL R14,8(0,R15) could be used to call IECOSCR1.

`Register 2` Contains two fields. The high order byte contains the UCB device type code (UCBTBYT4), which can be obtained via the DEVTYPE macro instruction. The low order three bytes contain the address of a 1-byte area that is to receive the sector number.

`Register 14` Return address of calling program.

`Register 15` Entry point address of IECOSCR1.

In addition, registers 1, 3-8, 12, and 13 are not used by IECOSCR1; and registers 9-11 are used by IECOSCR1, but are not saved or restored.

When IECOSCR1 returns control to the calling program, register 15 is posted with a return code of zero if the conversion was successful. If successful, the area pointed to by register 2 contains the sector number.

11.3.4 Writing Data into a DASD Dataset

In order to write a record into a DASD dataset, a number of operations must be performed. The operations that must be performed are based upon the type of write function that is required. Records are written to a DASD for the following purposes:

- Creating a new dataset;
- Extending an existing dataset; and
- Updating existing records of a dataset.

This section will discuss the channel programming considerations and techniques for all the above mentioned write functions and provide programming examples.

Regardless of the function of the write operation, the same basic set of CCWs are used to perform a DASD write. The required channel program (in words) to write one physical record to a DASD dataset is the following:

```
Seek
Set File Mask
Set Sector
Search ID Equal or Search Key Equal
Transfer in Channel
Write CKD or Write KD or Write Data
Read Sector
```

All the commands mentioned above have the same meaning as the corresponding commands in the read DASD channel program as discussed in Section 11.3.3. The only new commands mentioned are the Write commands.

WRITE COUNT, KEY, AND DATA (CKD) CCW (X'1D')

The Write CKD command is used to create (format) new records. It will cause the count, key, and data areas contained in the storage area specified by the CCW to be written *after* the record located by the Search command and erase the remainder of the track. The count area of the record must be specified first in the storage area, followed by the key, area and then followed by the data area. The count specified in the CCW is equal to the total bytes of the three areas.

WRITE KEY AND DATA (KD) CCW (X'0D')

The Write KD command causes the key and data areas of a previously formatted DASD record that was located by the Search command to be replaced by the corresponding record areas contained in the storage area specified by the CCW. The key area of the record must be specified first in the storage area, followed by the data area of the record. The count specified in the CCW is equal to the total of both areas.

WRITE DATA CCW (X'05')

The Write Data command causes the data area of a previously formatted DASD record that was located by the Search command to be replaced by the data area contained in the storage area specified by the CCW.

A DASD WRITE CHANNEL PROGRAM

An actual DASD write channel program for the three write functions would be coded as follows:

```
WRTPGM1  CCW   X'31',CCHHR,X'60',5
         CCW   X'08',WRTPGM1,X'00',0
         CCW   X'1D',FULLREC,X'20',92

WRTPGM2  CCW   X'31',CCHHR,X'60',5
         CCW   X'08',WRTPGM2,X'00',0
         CCW   X'0D',KEYDATA,X'20',84

WRTPGM3  CCW   X'31',CCHHR,X'60',5
         CCW   X'08',WRTPGM3,X'00',0
         CCW   X'05',USERDATA,X'20',80
```

NOTES:

- The initial Seek command is not specified because it is performed automatically by the I/O Supervisor from the information supplied in the IOBSEEK field of the IOB when the EXCP macro instruction is executed.
- The first CCW in each example specifies a Search ID Equal command for a specific record on the track selected by the Seek command. The virtual storage area labeled CCHHR contains the DASD location of the record. WRTPGM1 will search for the previous record and then write the new record after the record that was found. WRTPGM2 and WRTPGM3 will search for the actual record that is to be updated.
- If the Search is not successful for the current record encountered, then the second CCW (TIC) causes a branch back to the Search ID Equal command and a compare is performed on the next record that is encountered. The loop continues until either two Index Points are encountered (record not found) or the record is located.
- If the record is not located, the channel program is terminated. A X'41' is posted in the first byte of the ECB and a X'08' is posted in IOBSENS1.
- If the record is located, then the second CCW (TIC) is skipped and the next (in this example, last) CCW is executed. The last CCW contains a Write command. WRTPGM1 contains a Write CKD command; WRTPGM2 contains a Write KD command; and WRTPGM3 contains a Write Data command. The count area is

assumed to be 8 bytes; the key area, 4 bytes; and the data area, 80 bytes. Notice that the size of the count field of the Write CCW in each channel program is set to account for the amount of data that is to be transferred from virtual storage to the storage director.

- If the dataset is being created or extended or if existing records are to be updated sequentially, then the Set Sector and Read Sector commands may be specified to improve record searching performance. If the records are to be updated randomly, then only the Set.Sector command should be used.

CREATING A NEW DASD DATASET

New records are written with the Write Count-Key-Data (CKD) command. The first operation that is required is to position the access mechanism (read/ write head) to the track that is to contain the record. Next, the position on the track that is to contain the new record must be selected. When a dataset is created, each new record is placed immediately (after the IRG) after the previous one, and the count, key, and data areas of the record must be written. When the Write CKD command is used, it causes the new record to be written immediately after the record that was found with the Search command. Therefore, a search of the previous record must precede the Write CKD command. The previous record number for the first record (R1), that is to be written as user-data would be the R0 record of the first track. Then the previous record of the next new record that is to be written would be the record that was just written, and so on. When the capacity of the track is exhausted, then the Search command would be for the R0 record of the next track, and so on, until the cylinder or extent is exhausted. Then the previous record would be the R0 record of the first track of the next cylinder or extent.

The initial starting point (CCHH) of the dataset is obtained from the DEB. The initial track capacity of the track may be obtained by using the DEVTYPE macro instruction. The initial track capacity may also be obtained from the DS1TRBAL field of the format-1 DSCB (read via the OBTAIN/CAMLST macro instructions) since the system initializes that field with the full track capacity when a dataset is allocated.

As records are being written to each track, the TRKCALC macro instruction is required to determine if the track has enough capacity to contain the next record.

After the last record is written, a zero-count-record (KL=0, DL=0 in count area) must be written to indicate end-of-data. After the creation of the dataset is complete, two fields in the DCB should be updated. The DASD location (MBBCCHHR) of the last record written (not the zero count record) should be placed into the DCBFDAD field of the DCB, and the remaining track balance (obtained via the TRKCALC macro instruction) should be put into DCBTRBAL field of the DCB. If the DCB macro instruction is coded with DSORG=PS, the CLOSE macro instruction will cause those fields to be written to the DS1LSTAR and DS1TRBAL fields, respectively, of the format-1 DSCB for the dataset just created. If the DCB is not updated with this information, the CLOSE will automatically place the proper values into the format-1 DSCB (if DSORG=PS is specified, the system is maintaining those fields). If these fields are not required by the access method that is being developed and if the dataset will not be accessed by IBM access methods, then DSORG=PS need not be specified. If these fields are not updated, DS1LSTAR will contain zeros and DS1TRBAL will contain the full track capacity; therefore, if an IBM sequential access method is used to read the dataset, it will indicate that the dataset is empty. The DCBFDAD and DCBTRBAL fields could also be used for other control purposes. The CLOSE routine causes those values that are specified in the DCB to be placed into the corresponding fields of the format-1 DSCB. If it is a requirement that the DS1LSTAR points to a record other than the last record of the dataset, then the programmer must put the actual DASD location of that record into DCBFDAD before CLOSE processing.

Coding Example 11.3.2

This coding example illustrates how to create a DASD dataset. In this example, the records that are to be written to the DASD dataset are contained in a card-image sequential dataset pointed to by the INRECS JCL DD statement. The output dataset will contain no keys and 80-byte physical records.

```
WRTDASD CSECT
*
*
***********************************************************************
*    INITIALIZATION
***********************************************************************
*
        INITL 3,EQU=R             INITIALIZE PROGRAM
        USING DEBBASIC,R9         DEFINE REG FOR BASIC-DEB DSECT
        USING DEBDASD,R10         DEFINE REG FOR DASD-DEB DSECT
        USING IHADCB,R11          DEFINE REG FOR DCB DSECT
        USING IOBSTDRD,R12        DEFINE REG FOR IOB DSECT
*
*
***********************************************************************
*     MAINSTREAM OF PROGRAM
***********************************************************************
*
        BAL   R6,SETDSCTS         LOAD DSECT REGS
        BAL   R6,SETIOB           SET REQUIRED IOB FIELDS
        BAL   R6,GTRKINFO         GET CYL/TRK CAPAC INFO
        BAL   R6,OPEN             OPEN DCBS
        BAL   R6,GET1EXTN         GET 1ST EXTENT OF DATASET
NEXTREC BAL   R6,GETREC           READ A CARD-IMAGE RECORD
        BAL   R6,WRTREC           WRITE THE RECORD TO DASD
        B     NEXTREC             READ NEXT RECORD
ENDDATA BAL   R6,WRTEND           END-OF-DATA, WRITE ZERO-CT REC
        BAL   R6,CLOSE            CLOSE DCBS
        B     RETURN              RETURN TO MVS OR CALLING PROG *
*
***********************************************************************
*    THIS ROUTINE LOADS THE REGISTERS FOR THE DCB AND THE IOB DSECTS.
***********************************************************************
*
SETDSCTS LA   R11,WRTDCB          LOAD DCB ADR FOR DSECT ADRBLTY
         LA   R12,WRTIOB          LOAD IOB ADR FOR DSECT ADRBLTY
         BR   R6                  RET TO CALLING RTN
*
*
***********************************************************************
*    THIS ROUTINE SETS THE REQUIRED FIELDS OF THE IOB.
***********************************************************************
*
SETIOB  MVI   IOBFLAG1,X'42'      IND CCW-CHAINING, NOT RELATED
        MVC   IOBSTART,CCWADR     LOAD BG ADR OF CCW-LIST
        MVC   IOBDCBPT,DCBADR     LOAD DCB ADR
        MVC   IOBECBPT,ECBADR     LOAD ECB ADR
        BR    R6                  RETURN TO CALLING RTN
*
*
***********************************************************************
*    THIS ROUTINE USES THE DEVTYPE MACRO TO OBTAIN THE NUMBER OF TRACKS
*    PER CYLINDER AND THE TRACK CAPACITY FOR THE DASD DEVICE, WHICH IS TO
*    CONTAIN THE DATASET THAT IS TO BE WRITTEN, AND USES THE TRKCALC
*    MACRO TO DETERMINE THE NUMBER OF 80-BYTE RECORDS THAT CAN BE WRITTEN
*    ON A TRACK OF THE SAME DEVICE TYPE.
```

```
************************************************************************
*
GTRKINFO MVC  DDNAME,DCBDDNAM    EXTRACT DDNAME FROM DCB
         DEVTYPE DDNAME,DEVTAREA,DEVTAB
         LH   R10,CYLTRKS        LD NUMB OF TRKS PER CYL
         BCTR R10,0              DECR TO GET HI-TRK ADR
         STH  R10,HITRKADR       SAVE HI-TRK ADR (REL TO 0)
         MVC  TRKBAL,TRKSIZE     SAVE TRK CAPAC
         TRKCALC FUNCTN=TRKCAP,TYPE=UCBTBYT4,RKDD=RKDD,REGSAVE=YES
         STC  R0,TRKRECS         SAVE NUMB OF 80-BYTE RECS/TRK
         BR   R6                 RETURN TO CALLING RTN
*
*
************************************************************************
*    THIS ROUTINE OPENS ALL THE DCBS.
************************************************************************
*
OPEN     OPEN (INRECS,,WRTDCB,(OUTPUT))
         BR   R6                 RETURN TO CALLIN RTN
*
*
************************************************************************
*    THIS ROUTINE OBTAINS THE ADDRESS OF THE FIRST EXTENT FIELD IN THE
*    DEB AND THEN BRANCHES AND LINKS TO THE GETNXEXT SUBROUTINE, WHICH
*    EXTRACTS THE BEGINNING CCHH OF THE EXTENT.
************************************************************************
*
GET1EXTN L    R9,DCBDEBAD        LD DEB ADR FROM DCB, DSECT ADRBLTY
         MVC  TOTEXTN,DEBNMEXT   EXTRACT TOTAL NUMB OF EXTENTS
         LA   R10,32(0,R9)       INCR TO BG OF EXTENTS AREA IN DEB
         ST   R10,EXTNADR        SAVE 1ST EXTENT ADR FOR GETNXEXT RTN
         XC   EXTNCTR,EXTNCTR    INIT EXTENT CTR TO ZERO
         BAL  R8,GETNXEXT        GET CC AND HH OF NEXT EXTENT
         BR   R6                 RETURN TO CALLING RTN
*
*
************************************************************************
*    THIS SUBROUTINE EXTRACTS THE BEGINNING CCHH OF THE NEXT EXTENT FOR
*    THE CALLING ROUTINE. IT ALSO CHECKS FOR LAST-EXTENT, INCREMENTS
*    TO THE NEXT EXTENT FIELD IN THE DEB AND SAVES THE EXTENT FIELD
*    ADDRESS IN THE FULLWORD EXTNADR. IF THERE ARE NO MORE EXTENTS, THIS
*    SUBROUTINE ATTEMPTS TO ALLOCATE ANOTHER ONE VIA THE EOV MACRO. THIS
*    SUBROUTINE RECEIVES THE ADDRESS OF THE FIRST EXTENT FIELD IN THE DEB
*    FROM THE ROUTINE GET1EXTN.
************************************************************************
*
GETNXEXT IC   R10,EXTNCTR        LD PREV EXTENT NUMB
         LA   R10,1(0,R10)       INCR TO IND THIS EXTENT
         STC  R10,EXTNCTR        SAVE THIS EXTENT NUMB
         CLC  EXTNCTR,TOTEXTN    COMP THIS EXT NUMB TO TOT EXTENTS
         BH   DOEOV              IF ALL ALLO EXTENTS USED, TRY TO
*                                ALLO ANOTHER EXTENT
LDNXEXT  L    R10,EXTNADR        LD ADR OF NEXT EXTENT FIELD IN DEB
         MVC  CC,DEBSTRCC        PUT CC OF NEXT EXTENT INTO RECPTR
         MVC  HH,DEBSTRHH        PUT HH OF NEXT EXTENT INTO RECPTR
         MVC  RCNTCCHH,CCHH      PUT CCHH INTO COUNT AREA
         LA   R10,16(0,R10)      INCR TO NEXT EXTENT FIELD IN DEB
         ST   R10,EXTNADR        SAVE ADR OF NEXT EXTENT FIELD
         BR   R8                 RETURN TO CALLING RTN
DOEOV    EOV  WRTDCB             ALLO ANOTHER EXTENT
         L    R9,DCBDEBAD        LD ADR OF DEB
         MVC  TOTEXTN,DEBNMEXT   EXTRACT TOTAL NUMB OF EXTENTS
         LA   R14,0              ZERO REG 14 FOR IC INSTR
         IC   R14,TOTEXTN        LD NEW TOT EXTENT NUMB
```

```
         BCTR R14,0                DECR TOT EXTENT NUMB FOR SLL INSTR
         SLL  R14,4                MULT TOT EXTENT NUMB MINUS 1 BY
*                                  16 (ENTENT ENTRY LEN) TO GET
*                                  NEW EXTENT OFFSET
         LA   R10,32(R14,R9)       LD ADR OF NEW EXTENT ALLOCATED
         ST   R10,EXTNADR          SAVE ADR OF NEW EXTENT FIELD
         B    LDNXEXT              PROCESS EXTENT
*
*
***********************************************************************
*     THIS ROUTINE READS THE RECORDS USED TO CREATE THE DASD DATASET.
***********************************************************************
*
GETREC  GET   INRECS,RECDATA       READ A CARD-IMAGE RECORD
        BR    R6                   RETURN TO CALLING RTN
*
*
***********************************************************************
*    THIS ROUTINE WRITES A NEW RECORD INTO THE DASD DATASET. IN ORDER TO
*    PERFORM THAT TASK, THIS ROUTINE BRANCHES AND LINKS TO THE SUBROUTINES
*    THAT PERFORM THE FOLLOWING FUNCTIONS:
*    * INCREMENT THE RECORD POINTER TO POINT TO THE NEXT RECORD LOCATION
*      FOR WHICH THE NEW RECORD IS TO BE WRITTEN;
*    * CHECK IF THE NEW RECORD FITS IN THE SPACE REMAINING ON THE TRACK;
*    * OBTAIN THE NEW TRACK BALANCE AFTER THE NEW RECORD IS WRITTEN;
*    * ISSUE THE EXCP MACRO TO WRITE THE NEXT PHYSICAL RECORD OF THE
*      DASD DATASET.
***********************************************************************
*
WRTREC  BAL   R7,SETRCPTR          SET RECPTR TO PREV RECORD
        BAL   R7,CHKFIT            CHK IF NEW REC WILL FIT ON TRK
        BAL   R7,GETRKBAL          GET TRK BAL AFTER REC WRITTEN
        BAL   R7,DOEXCP            ISSUE EXCP MACRO TO WRITE RECORD
        BR    R6                   RETURN TO CALLING RTN
*
*
***********************************************************************
*    THIS SUBROUTINE INCREMENTS THE RECORD POINTER TO POINT TO THE NEXT
*    RECORD LOCATION FOR WHICH THE NEW RECORD IS TO BE WRITTEN AND MOVES
*    THE NEW RECORD POINTER INTO THE IOB. SINCE A WHOLE (COUNT, KEY AND
*    DATA) NEW RECORD IS TO BE WRITTEN (FORMATTED), THE RECORD POINTER
*    ACTUALLY POINTS TO THE PREVIOUS RECORD.
***********************************************************************
*
SETRCPTR IC   R10,R                LOAD OLD PREV REC NUMB
         LA   R10,1(0,R10)         INCR REC NUMB TO NEW PREV REC NUMB
         STC  R10,R                SAVE NEW PREV REC NUMB
         MVC  IOBSEEK,RECPTR       MOVE BMMCCHHR OF PREV REC INTO IOB
         LA   R10,1(0,R10)         INCR TO CURRENT REC NUMB
         STC  R10,RCNTR            PUT CUR REC NUMB INTO COUNT AREA
         BR   R7                   RETURN TO CALLING RTN
*
*
***********************************************************************
*    THIS SUBROUTINE CHECKS IF THE NEW RECORD FITS IN THE SPACE REMAINING
*    ON THE TRACK. IF THE NEW RECORD WILL NOT FIT IN THE REMAINING SPACE
*    OF THE TRACK, THEN THE RECORD POINTER IS INCREMENTED TO THE NEXT
*    TRACK.
***********************************************************************
*
CHKFIT  CLC   RCNTR,TRKRECS        COMP CUR REC NUMB WITH MAX RECS/TRK
        BNHR  R7                   IF EQUAL/LOW, RET TO CALLING RTN
        BAL   R8,SETNXTRK          IF HIGH, GET NEXT TRK ADR
        B     WRTREC               WRITE RECORD TO NEXT TRK
```

```
*
*
***************************************************************************
*    THIS SUBROUTINE SETS THE RECORD POINTER TO POINT TO THE BEGINNING
*    OF THE NEXT TRACK FOR THE NEXT NEW RECORD TO BE WRITTEN, BRANCHES AND
*    LINKS TO THE CHKNXTRK ROUTINE TO VALIDATE THE TRACK NUMBER, AND
*    RESETS THE RECORD NUMBER AND TRACK BALANCE FOR THE NEW TRACK.
***************************************************************************
*
SETNXTRK DS    0H
         WTO   '*** NEXT TRACK ***',ROUTCDE=11 ***FOR TESTING ONLY ***
         MVI   SECTOR,X'00'       SET SECTOR NUMB TO BG OF TRK
         MVI   R,X'FF'            INIT REC NUMB FOR NEW TRK
         LH    R10,HH             LOAD CUR TRK NUMB
         LA    R10,1(0,R10)       INCR TRK NUMB
         STH   R10,HH             PUT NEW TRK NUMB INTO RECPTR
         BAL   R9,CHKNXTRK        VAL TRK NUMB, INCR CYL NUMB IF NEC
         MVC   TRKBAL,TRKSIZE     INIT TRK BALANCE FOR NEW TRK
         MVC   RCNTCCHH,CCHH      PUT CUR CYL/TRK NUMB INTO COUNT AREA
         BR    R8                 RETURN TO CALLING RTN
*
*
***************************************************************************
*    THIS SUBROUTINE VALIDATES THE NEW TRACK NUMBER AFTER THE TRACK NUMBER
*    IS INCREMENTED TO DETERMINE IF IT EXCEEDS THE HI-TRACK ADDRESS OF A
*    CYLINDER. IF IT DOES, THEN THE CYLINDER NUMBER IS INCREMENTED AND THE
*    TRACK NUMBER IS SET TO ZERO.
***************************************************************************
*
CHKNXTRK CLC   HH,HITRKADR        COMP NEW TRK NUMB TO HI-TRK ADR
         BH    SETNXCYL           IF HIGH, INCR CYL NUMB
         BR    R9                 IF NOT HIGH, RET TO CALLING RTN
SETNXCYL XC    HH,HH              SET TRK NUMB TO ZERO (BG OF CYL)
         LH    R10,CC             LOAD CUR CYL NUMB
         LA    R10,1(0,R10)       INCR CYL NUMB
         STH   R10,CC             PUT NEW CYL NUMB INTO RECPTR
         BR    R9                 RETURN TO CALLING RTN
*
*
***************************************************************************
*    THIS SUBROUTINE USES THE TRKCALC MACRO TO OBTAIN WHAT THE TRACK
*    BALANCE WILL BE AFTER THE RECORD IS WRITTEN. THIS VALUE IS USED TO
*    UPDATE THE DCBTRBAL FIELD OF THE DCB, WHICH IS USED TO UPDATE THE
*    FORMAT-1 DSCB, WHEN THE DATASET IS CLOSED.
***************************************************************************
*
GETRKBAL MVC   RKDD(1),RCNTR      SET CUR REC NUMB FOR TRKCALC MACRO
         TRKCALC FUNCTN=TRKBAL,TYPE=UCBTBYT4,RKDD=RKDD,REGSAVE=YES,       -
               BALANCE=TRKBAL
         STH   R0,TRKBAL          SAVE TRK BALANCE AFTER REC WRITTEN
         BR    R7                 RETURN TO CALLING RTN
*
*
***************************************************************************
*    THIS SUBROUTINE ISSUES THE EXCP MACRO TO WRITE THE NEXT PHYSICAL
*    RECORD OF THE DASD DATASET, CHECKS THE ECB COMPLETION CODE, AND
*    PERFORMS THE APPROPRIATE ACTION INDICATED BY THE COMPLETION CODE.
***************************************************************************
*
DOEXCP   XC    WRTECB,WRTECB      CLEAR ECB FOR EXCP MACRO
         EXCP  WRTIOB             ISSUE EXCP
         WAIT  1,ECB=WRTECB       WAIT FOR I/O COMPLETION
         TM    WRTECB,X'7F'       CHK FOR GOOD I/O
         BNO   CHKECB             IF NO, EXAM ECB
```

```
         BR    R7                    IF I/O GOOD, RET TO CALLING RTN
*
CHKECB   TM    WRTECB,X'41'          CHK FOR EXCEPTION COND
         BO    CHKEND                IF YES, CHK FOR INPUT END-OF-DATA
         TM    WRTECB,X'42'          CHK FOR END-OF-EXTENT
         BO    SETNXEXT              IF YES, ALLO NEW EXTENT
         B     EXCPERR               IF NO, I/O ERROR, DUMP DIAG INFO
*
CHKEND   CLI   WRTENDSW,C'1'         CHK IF END-OF-DATA ON INPUT
         BER   R7                    IF YES, RET TO CALLING RTN
         B     EXCPERR               IF NO, I/O ERROR, DUMP DIAG INFO
*
SETNXEXT DS    0H
         WTO   '*** NEXT EXTENT ***',ROUTCDE=11    *** FOR TESTING ONLY ***
         IC    R10,M                   LOAD CUR EXTENT NUMB
         LA    R10,1(0,R10)            INCR EXTENT NUMB
         STC   R10,M                   PUT NEW EXTENT NUMB INTO RECPTR
         BAL   R8,GETNXEXT             GET CCHH OF NEXT EXTENT
         MVI   SECTOR,X'00'            SET SECTOR TO ZERO (BG OF TRK)
         MVI   R,X'00'                 SET REC NUMB OF RECPTR TO REC PREV
*                                      OF 1ST REC TO WRITE
         MVI   RCNTR,X'01'             SET COUNT REC NUMB TO 1ST TO WRITE
         MVC   IOBSEEK,RECPTR          PUT NEW MBBCCHHR INTO IOB
         B     DOEXCP                  RE-ISSUE EXCP MACRO
*
*
***********************************************************************
*    THIS ROUTINE RECEIVES CONTROL WHEN ALL THE NEW DASD RECORDS ARE
*    WRITTEN. THIS ROUTINE BRANCHES AND LINKS TO THE SUBROUTINES THAT
*    PERFORM THE FOLLOWING FUNCTIONS:
*    * INCREMENT THE RECORD POINTER TO POINT TO THE LAST RECORD WRITTEN;
*    * WRITE A ZERO-COUNT-RECORD AFTER THE LAST RECORD TO INDICATE
*      END-OF DATA;
*    * UPDATE THE DCB WITH THE DASD LOCATION OF THE LAST RECORD AND
*      THE TRACK BALANCE (NUMBER OF BYTES REMAINING ON THE TRACK,
*      INCLUDING THE SPACE OCCUPIED BY THE ZERO-COUNT-RECORD).
***********************************************************************
*
WRTEND   BAL   R7,SETRCPTR           SET RECPTR TO LAST RECORD WRITTEN
         XC    RCNTDLEN,RCNTDLEN     SET COUNT DATA-LEN TO ZERO
         MVC   IOBSTART,CCWXADR      PUT ADR OF ZERO-CT-RECORD CCW-LIST
*                                    INTO IOB
         MVI   WRTENDSW,C'1'         IND INPUT END-OF-DATA
         BAL   R7,DOEXCP             WRITE ZERO-CT-RECORD
         BAL   R7,UPDTDCB            UPDATE DCB
         BR    R6                    RETURN TO CALLING RTN
*
*
***********************************************************************
*    THIS SUBROUTINE UPDATES THE DCB FIELDS DCBFDAD (POINTER TO LAST
*    RECORD WRITTEN) AND DCBTRBAL (TRACK BALANCE) BEFORE THE DATASET IS
*    CLOSED.
***********************************************************************
*
UPDTDCB  MVC   DCBFDAD,IOBSEEK       MOVE DASD ADR (MBBCCHHR) OF LAST
*                                    NON-ZERO CT RECORD WRITTEN INTO DCB
         MVC   DCBTRBAL,TRKBAL       MOVE BYTES REMAINING ON TRACK INTO
*                                    DCB
         BR    R7                    RETURN TO CALLING RTN
*
*
***********************************************************************
*    THIS ROUTINE CLOSES ALL THE DCBS. FOR THE DASD DATASET JUST CREATED,
*    THIS CLOSE CAUSES THE FIELDS DS1LSTAR AND DS1TRBAL OF THE FORMAT-1
```

```
*    DSCB TO BE UPDATED FROM THE CONTENTS OF THE CORRESPONDING FIELDS
*    DCBFDAD AND DCBTRBAL, RESPECTIVELY, OF THE DCB.
***********************************************************************
*
CLOSE    CLOSE (INRECS,,WRTDCB)
         BR    R6                  RETURN TO CALLING RTN
*
*
***********************************************************************
*    THIS ROUTINE RECEIVES CONTROL IF THE ATTEMPTED I/O IS UNSUCCESSFUL.
*    THIS ROUTINE LOADS VARIOUS DIAGNOSTIC INFORMATION INTO REGISTERS
*    8, 9, 10, 11, AND 12 AND THEN CAUSES AN ABEND WITH A DUMP.
***********************************************************************
*
EXCPERR L     R8,WRTECB            LOAD CONTENTS OF ECB INTO A REG
         MVC   ERRINFO(1),EXTNCTR       EXTENT NUMBER
         MVC   ERRINFO+1(1),IOBUSTAT    UNIT STATUS FIELD OF CSW
         MVC   ERRINFO+2(1),IOBSENS0    BYTE-1 OF HARDWARE SENSE CODE
         MVC   ERRINFO+3(1),IOBSENS1    BYTE-2 OF HARDWARE SENSE CODE
         L     R9,ERRINFO          LOAD ERROR INFO WORD INTO A REG
         L     R10,RECPTR          LOAD 1ST 4 BYTES OF REC-PTR
         L     R11,RECPTR+4        LOAD 2ND 4 BYTES OF REC-PTR
         L     R12,ERRID           LOAD ERR-ID TO FIND REGS IN DUMP
         IC    R12,RCNTR           INSERT REC-ID FROM COUNT AREA
         ABEND 900,DUMP            ISSUE ABEND MACRO AND REQ A DUMP
*
*
***********************************************************************
*    THIS ROUTINE RESTORES THE REGISTERS AND RETURNS CONTROL.
***********************************************************************
*
RETURN   RCNTL RC=0                RETURN TO MVS OR CALLING RTN
*
*
***********************************************************************
*    THIS LIST REQUIRED FOR THE DEVTYPE MACRO.
***********************************************************************
*
DEVTAREA DS    0CL24
UCBTYP   DS    0CL4
         DS    CL3
UCBTBYT4 DS    CL1
         DS    CL4
         DS    CL2
CYLTRKS  DS    CL2                 NUMBER OF TRACKS PER CYLINDER
TRKSIZE  DS    CL2                 TRACK CAPACITY IN BYTES
         DS    CL2
         DS    CL8
*
*
***********************************************************************
*    THIS AREA MAPS OUT THE RECORD-POINTER THAT IS USED TO POINT TO THE
*    RECORD AT WHICH THE NEW RECORD IS TO BE WRITTEN AFTER.
***********************************************************************
*
         DS    0F                  FOR ALIGNMENT FOR THE EXCPERR ROUTINE
RECPTR   DS    0CL8
M        DC    X'00'               EXTENT NUMBER (STARTING WITH ZERO)
BB       DC    XL2'00'             BIN NUMBER (NO LONGER USED)
CCHHR    DS    0CL5
CCHH     DS    0CL4
CC       DS    CL2                 CYLINDER NUMBER
HH       DS    CL2                 HEAD (TRACK) NUMBER
R        DC    X'FF'               RECORD NUMBER
```

```
*
*
***********************************************************************
*    THIS AREA MAPS OUT A COMPLETE (COUNT, KEY, AND DATA) DASD RECORD AND
*    IS USED TO WRITE (FORMAT) THE NEW DASD RECORDS.
***********************************************************************
*
RECORD   DS    0CL88              WHOLE RECORD (COUNT-KEY-DATA)
RECCOUNT DS    0CL8               COUNT AREA OF RECORD
RCNTCCHH DS    CL4                CCHH OF RECORD
RCNTR    DS    CL1                RECORD NUMBER OF RECORD
RCNTKLEN DC    X'00'              KEY LENGTH
RCNTDLEN DC    X'0050'            DATA LENGTH
RECDATA  DS    CL80               DATA AREA OF RECORD
*
*
***********************************************************************
*    OTHER DC/DS STATEMENTS
***********************************************************************
*
WRTENDSW DC   C'0'
DDNAME   DS   CL8
SECTOR   DC   X'00'
HITRKADR DS   H
TRKBAL   DS   H
TRKRECS  DS   CL1
CYLNUM   DC   F'0'
TRKNUM   DC   F'0'
RKDD     DC   X'01000050'        USED BY TRKCALC MACRO
TOTEXTN  DS   CL1
EXTNCTR  DS   CL1
EXTNADR  DS   F
ERRINFO  DS   F
ERRID    DC   4XL1'FF'
*
CCWADR   DC   A(WRTCCWS)
CCWXADR  DC   A(WRTXCCWS)
DCBADR   DC   A(WRTDCB)
ECBADR   DC   A(WRTECB)
*
*
***********************************************************************
*    THE CCW-LISTS, IOB AND ECB
***********************************************************************
*
WRTCCWS  CCW   X'23',SECTOR,X'40',1    SET SECTOR CCW
SEARCH   CCW   X'31',CCHHR,X'60',5     SEARCH ID EQUAL CCW
         CCW   X'08',SEARCH,X'00',0    TIC CCW
         CCW   X'1D',RECORD,X'60',88   WRITE CKD CCW
         CCW   X'22',SECTOR,X'00',1    READ SECTOR CCW
*
WRTXCCWS CCW   X'23',SECTOR,X'40',1    SET SECTOR CCW
SEARCHX  CCW   X'31',CCHHR,X'60',5     SEARCH ID EQUAL CCW
         CCW   X'08',SEARCHX,X'00',0   TIC CCW
         CCW   X'1D',RECORD,X'20',8    WRITE CKD (ZERO-CT) CCW
*
WRTIOB   DC    10F'0'                  AREA FOR IOB
WRTECB   DC    F'0'                    FULLWORD FOR ECB
*
*
***********************************************************************
*    THE DCBS
***********************************************************************
*
```

```
INRECS   DCB   DSORG=PS,MACRF=GM,LRECL=80,RECFM=FB,EODAD=ENDDATA,          -
               DDNAME=INRECS
WRTDCB   DCB   MACRF=E,DDNAME=TESTFILE,DSORG=PS
*
*
***********************************************************************
*     THE DSECTS
***********************************************************************
*
         PRINT NOGEN
         DCBD DSORG=XE          GENERATES EXCP-DCB DSECT
         IEZDEB                 GENERATES DEB DSECT
         IEZIOB                 GENERATES IOB DSECT
         ORG  IOBCSTAT+1        POS TO RESIDUAL COUNT FIELD OF CSW
IOBCSWCT DS   CL2               PROVIDE LABEL FOR RES CT FIELD
*
*
***********************************************************************
*     END OF PROGRAM
***********************************************************************
*
         END
```

NOTES:

- Since the DS1LSTAR and DS1TRBAL fields of the format-1 DSCB are updated, this dataset may be read by IBM-supplied access methods (QSAM and BSAM). Therefore, the contents of the dataset can be verified by reading it using the IBM utility program IEBGENER or by writing a program, using QSAM or BSAM to read the dataset. The appropriate DCB attributes (BLKSIZE=80, LRECL=80, RECFM=F) must be specified in the JCL for IEBGENER or in the JCL or in the DCB macro instruction for a user-written program since that information is not specified in an EXCP DCB and, therefore, was not stored in the VTOC. The contents (first ten bytes of each record) of the dataset can also be verified by using the READDASD EXCP program from Coding Example 11.3.1 to read (since the SILI-bit is on) the dataset.
- As an exercise, the reader might try to block the records. This can be accomplished by specifying an I/O buffer large enough to accommodate multiple records that are written by a single Write CKD CCW. Also, the count field in the CCW statement and the data length field in the count area would have to be increased to reflect the new physical record size. The new code should also contain logic to handle a short last block.

EXTENDING A DASD DATASET

Extending a dataset means writing new records starting after the last physical record of the dataset. Since new records are being written, the Write CKD command is required. The procedure is similar to creating a dataset, except that the initial starting point is obtained from the DS1LSTAR field of the format-1 DSCB instead of the DEB, and the initial track balance must be obtained from the DS1TRBAL field of the format-1 DSCB. The DS1LSTAR points to the last data record written. Therefore, that location is used for the first Search command since it points to the previous record (relative to the first new record). The first new record will be written after the one pointed to by DS1LSTAR, overlaying the zero-count-record. When all the new records are written, a zero-count-record must be rewritten to indicate the new end-of-data position. Then the DS1LSTAR and DS1TRBAL fields are updated with the new values by CLOSE (if MACRF=PS was specified in the DCB macro instruction).

The format of DS1LSTAR is in relative track and record format (same as the location information in a PDS directory). In order for the Search command to use this information, the TTR format must be converted into CCHHR format. IBM provides a conversion program to perform that task. The name of the program is IECPCNVT, and its entry point address is stored in field CVTPCNVT of the CVT.

When IECPCNVT receives control, the following information must be provided in registers 0, 1, 2, 14, and 15.

- `Register 0` The TTRN of the record. TTR comes from DS1LSTAR, and N is used only for BPAM and is set equal to zero for EXCP.
- `Register 1` Address of the DEB (obtained from the DCBDEBAD field of the opened DCB).
- `Register 2` Address of an 8-byte area that is to receive the DASD location. The format is MBBCCHHR.
- `Register 14` Return address of calling program.
- `Register 15` Entry point address of IECPCNVT.

In addition, registers 9-13 are used by IECPCNVT, but are not saved or restored.

When IECPCNVT returns control to the calling program, register 15 contains one of the following return codes:

Return Code (Hex)	Meaning
00	Successful completion.
04	The specified relative address converted to an actual address outside the extents defined in the DEB.

If the conversion is successful, the DASD location is placed into the area that was pointed to by register 2.

Coding Example 11.3.3

This coding example illustrates how to invoke IECPCNVT and use it to convert relative track and record format (TTR) into actual DASD location format (MBBCCHHR). In this example, the last block pointer, which is stored in TTR format in the format-1 DSCB of the VTOC, is obtained for a dataset allocated via JCL. Then this TTR is converted into MBBCCHHR format.

```
TTRCONV CSECT
*
*
***********************************************************************
*    INITIALIZATION
***********************************************************************
*
         INITL 3,EQU=R            INITIALIZE PROGRAM
         USING IECSDSF1,R10       DEFINE REG FOR DSCB DSECT
         USING IHADCB,R11         DEFINE REG FOR DCB DSECT
         USING CVT,R12            DEFINE REG FOR CVT DSECT
*
*
***********************************************************************
*    MAINSTREAM OF PROGRAM
***********************************************************************
```

```
*
         BAL   R6,OBTAIN           READ DSCB-1 OF DATASET
         BAL   R6,OPEN             OPEN DCB, CREATE DEB
         BAL   R6,GETTTR           GET LAST REC PTR (TTR) OF DATASET
         BAL   R6,GETDEB           GET DEB ADR
         BAL   R6,CONVERT          CONVERT TTR TO MBBCCHHR
         BAL   R6,LOADCCHH         LOAD MBBCCHHR INTO PARM REGS
         BAL   R6,DUMPCCHH         DUMP MBBCCHHR (FOR TESTING ONLY)
         B     RETURN              RETURN TO MVS OR CALLING PROG
*
*
***********************************************************************
*    THIS ROUTINE READS THE FORMAT-1 DSCB OF THE DATASET. THE DSCB IS
*    PLACED INTO THE AREA DSCB1.
***********************************************************************
*
OBTAIN   OBTAIN READDSCB           READ FORMAT-1 DSCB OF DATASET
         LTR   R15,R15             CHECK IF DATASET IN JCL
         BNZ   NODSNM              IF NO, INDICATE IT
         BR    R6                  RETURN TO CALLING RTN
*
*
***********************************************************************
*    THIS ROUTINE OPENS THE DCB OF THE DATASET IN ORDER TO CAUSE THE DEB
*    TO BE CREATED.
***********************************************************************
*
OPEN     OPEN  TESTFILE            OPEN DCB
         ...                       CHECK FOR GOOD OPEN
         BR    R6
*
*
***********************************************************************
*    THIS ROUTINE EXTRACTS THE LAST-RECORD-POINTER FIELD IN THE FORMAT-1
*    DSCB OF THE DATASET. THIS FIELD IS IN THE TTR FORMAT.
***********************************************************************
*
GETTTR   LA    R10,DSCB1           SET ADRBLTY FOR DSCB DSECT
         MVC   TTRN(3),DS1LSTAR    EXTRACT LAST-REC-PTR
         L     R0,TTRN             LOAD TTRN INTO REG FOR IECPCNVT
         BR    R6                  RETURN TO CALLING PROG
*
*
***********************************************************************
*    THIS ROUTINE EXTRACTS THE ADDRESS OF THE DEB FROM THE DCB. THE DEB
*    ADDRESS IS REQUIRED BY THE CONVERSION PROGRAM.
***********************************************************************
*
GETDEB   LA    R11,TESTFILE        SET ADRBLTY FOR DCB DSECT
         L     R1,DCBDEBAD         EXTRACT DEB ADR
         BR    R6                  RETURN TO CALLING RTN
*
*
***********************************************************************
*    THIS ROUTINE CONVERTS THE LAST-RECORD-POINTER FROM TTR FORMAT INTO
*    THE EQUIVALENT MBBCCHHR FORMAT.
***********************************************************************
*
CONVERT  L     R12,16              SET ADRBLTY FOR CVT DSECT
         LA    R2,MBBCCHHR         LD ADR OF RECEIVING AREA
         L     R15,CVTPCNVT        LD EPA OF IECPCNVT
         BALR  R14,R15             BRANCH AND LINK TO IECPCNVT
         BR    R6                  RETURN TO CALLING RTN
*
```

```
*
***********************************************************************
*    THIS ROUTINE LOADS THE RESULTING MBBCCHHR FROM THE CONVERSION INTO
*    THE PARAMETER REGISTERS 0 AND 1 FOR THE CALLING PROGRAM.
***********************************************************************
*
LOADCCHH L     R0,MBBCCHHR         LOAD 1ST 4 BYTES OF MBBCCHHR
         L     R1,MBBCCHHR+4       LOAD 2ND 4 BYTES OF MBBCCHHR
         BR    R6                  RETURN TO CALLING RTN
*
*
***********************************************************************
*    THIS SUBROUTINE IS USED ONLY DURING TESTING TO VERIFY THAT THE
*    CONVERSION PROGRAM IS BEING CALLED PROPERLY. THE MBBCCHHR IS LOCATED
*    INTO REGISTERS 8 AND 9 AND THEN THE ABEND MACRO IS ISSUED REQUESTING
*    A DUMP.
***********************************************************************
*
*
DUMPCCHH L     R8,MBBCCHHR         LOAD 1ST 4 BYTES OF MBBCCHHR
         L     R9,MBBCCHHR+4       LOAD 2ND 4 BYTES OF MBBCCHHR
         ABEND 900,DUMP            ISSUE ABEND MACRO WITH DUMP
*
***********************************************************************
*    THIS SUBROUTINE DISPLAYS AN ERROR MESSAGE IF THE DATASET IS NOT
*    SPECIFIED IN THE JCL AND THEN CAUSES AN ABEND.
***********************************************************************
*
NODSNM  WTO    '*** DATASET NOT FOUND ON SPECIFIED DASD VOLUME ***',      -
               ROUTCDE=11
        ABEND 901
*
*
***********************************************************************
*    THIS ROUTINE RESTORES THE REGISTERS (EXCEPT THE PARAMETER REGISTER
*    0 AND 1) OF THE CALLING PROGRAM AND RETURNS CONTROL.
***********************************************************************
*
RETURN  L      R13,4(0,R13)        RESTORE ADR OF PREV SA
        L      R14,12(0,R13)       RESTORE REG 14
        LA     R15,0               SET RC=0 INTO REG 15
        LM     R2,R12,28(R13)      RESTORE REGS 2 THRU 12
        BR     R14                 RETURN TO CALLING PROG
*
*
***********************************************************************
*    DC/DS STATEMENTS
***********************************************************************
*
TTRN     DC    F'0'
MBBCCHHR DS    D
*
*
***********************************************************************
*    THE CAMLST USED BY THE OBTAIN MACRO.
***********************************************************************
*
READDSCB CAMLST SEARCH,DSNAME,VOLSER,WORKAREA
VOLSER   DC    CL6'STRG01'
DSCB1    DS    0CL140
DSNAME   DC    CL44'USER.TESTDATA'
WORKAREA DS    CL140
*
*
```

```
*****************************************************************************
*    THE DCB
*****************************************************************************
*
TESTFILE DCB  DSORG=PS,MACRF=E,DDNAME=TESTFILE
*
*
*****************************************************************************
*    THE DSECTS
*****************************************************************************
*
         PRINT NOGEN
*
         DSECT
         IECSDSL1 1              GENERATES FORMAT-1 DSCB DSECT
*
         DSECT
         DCBD  DSORG=PS          GENERATES PS-DCB DSECT
*
         DSECT
         CVT   DSECT=YES         GENERATES CVT DSECT
*
*
*****************************************************************************
*    END OF PROGRAM
*****************************************************************************
*
           END
```

NOTES:

- In this example, the volser and dataset name are hard-coded in the program. This is for illustration purposes only. This information should be obtained by reading the JFCB (discussed in Chapter 7).
- The OBTAIN/CAMLST macro instructions are used to read the corresponding format-1 DSCB of the specified dataset from the VTOC of the DASD volume with the specified volser. After the OBTAIN macro instruction executes, the first 96 bytes in WORKAREA will contain bytes 44 to 139 of the format-1 DSCB. The structure of the VTOC was briefly discussed in Chapter 7.
- After the conversion, the actual DASD location (MBBCCHHR) is loaded into registers 8 and 9, and then an ABEND macro instruction is issued requesting a dump. During development, this is a means of determining if the calling program is functioning properly. Normally, this program would be called by a program, that is extending (adding new records to the end of) a DASD dataset using EXCP, to determine the DASD location, in MBBCCHHR format, of the last record. The resulting MBBCCHHR can be sent back to the calling program either by placing it into an area provided by the calling program or the MBBCCHHR can be placed into the parameter registers 0 and 1.

UPDATING RECORDS OF A DASD DATASET

Records of a dataset are updated when the key area, the key and the data areas, or the data area of previously formatted records (records written with the Write Count-Key-Data CCW) are changed. This is accomplished by using one of the Search commands to search for the record that is to be updated and then using the Write Key-Data command or the Write Data command to change the required areas of the record. When existing records are updated, the Search is for the actual record that is to be updated (as opposed to a Search for the previous record, which is required by the Write Count-Key-Data CCW). Records that are to be updated may be located by record ID or by record key. If the records are located by record ID, then to improve search performance, the Set Sector command and the Read Sector command should be specified before and after the Search command, respectively, if the records are read and updated sequentially. If the records are read and updated randomly, then only the Set Sector command should be specified, while the sector number is obtained from the IBM-supplied program IECOSCR1, which was described in Section 11.3.3 above.

11.4 CHANNEL PROGRAMMING FOR MAGNETIC TAPE DEVICES

Channel programming for magnetic tape is not as involved as DASD channel programming. This section will discuss the format of magnetic tape volumes and the required channel programs for reading and creating magnetic tape datasets that have no labels and that have standard labels.

11.4.1 Magnetic Tape Volume Format

The beginning of a magnetic tape volume (MTV) after the feed portion is indicated by a reflector strip known as the load-point. This is where the MTV is positioned after it is loaded and the tape drive is made ready. The logical end of the MTV also contains a reflector strip to indicate the end of the usable recording surface. The beginning and ending reflector strips are on the same surface side of the tape, but their widths are about half the width of the tape. The beginning and ending reflector strips are on different edges of the tape, thus enabling the tape drive to determine if a given reflector strip indicates load-point or logical end of the MTV. The format of the MTV after the load-point depends on which of the following conditions exist:

- The MTV has been initialized.
- The MTV contains one standard label dataset.
- The MTV contains multiple standard label datasets.
- A standard label dataset or datasets spans multiple MTVs.
- The MTV contains unlabeled datasets.
- The MTV contains user defined label datasets.

An MTV is initiaized by use of the IBM-supplied program IEHINITT. Initializing an MTV prepares it to be used to contain datasets that have standard labels.

After an MTV has been initialized, it has the following format.

```
(Load-Point)
VOL1 label
HDR1 label
  (TM)
```

The VOL1 and HDR1 labels (and all the other standard labels) are 80-byte unblocked records. The VOL1 and HDR1 labels (and all the other standard labels) contain the name of the label ("VOL1", etc.) in the first four positions of the label. The VOL1 label contains the volume serial id of the MTV and other information. After the MTV is initialized, the HDR1 is a dummy record and contains binary zeros. The (TM) is a tape mark. A tape mark is a special character that is written by the control unit (via a CCW). The tape drive recognizes a tape mark during read operations and signals the control unit, which sets the unit exception bit in the CSW. The tape mark indicates an end-of-data condition (similar to the zero-count-record in DASD). A unit exception is also indicated during write operations when the tape drive encounters the end reflector strip.

When the first standard label dataset is allocated, the HDR1 label is filled in with information about the dataset. This information includes dataset name (only last 17 bytes), creation and expiration dates, and other information. Also, an HDR2 label is created following the HDR1 label and contains other information about the dataset such as the DCB attributes. The actual data is written after the labels. The data is followed by an EOF1 and an EOF2 label. The EOF1 and EOF2 labels contain the same information as the HDR1 and HDR2 labels, respectively, except that the EOF1 label also contains the block count of the dataset (the HDR1 contains zeros for the block count field).

The MTV has the following format after the first dataset has been created.

```
(Load-Point)
VOL1 label
HDR1 label
HDR2 label
  (TM)
DATA RECORDS
  (TM)
EOF1 label
EOF2 label
  (TM)
  (TM)
```

The two consecutive tape marks at the end indicate that the previous dataset is the last one on the volume.

If the MTV contains multiple standard label datasets, then the other datasets are framed with the HDRx and EOFx labels, just like the first one.

The MTV has the following format when it contains two standard label datasets.

```
(Load-Point)
VOL1 label
HDR1 label for dataset-1
HDR2 label for dataset-1
  (TM)
DATA RECORDS FOR DATASET-1
  (TM)
EOF1 label for dataset-1
EOF2 label for dataset-1
  (TM)
HDR1 label for dataset-2
HDR2 label for dataset-2
  (TM)
DATA RECORDS FOR DATASET-2
  (TM)
EOF1 label for dataset-2
EOF2 label for dataset-2
  (TM)
  (TM)
```

If a dataset spans multiple MTVs, then the end of the portion of the dataset on the first and intermediate MTVs is followed by an EOV1 and an EOV2 label, instead of the EOF1 and EOF2 labels. The EOV1 and EOV2 labels contain the same information as the EOF1 and EOF2 labels, respectively. The last MTV of the dataset contains the EOF1/EOF2 labels after the dataset.

Magnetic tape volumes that contain unlabeled datasets are not required to be initialized, and contain only data records and tape marks. An initialized MTV can be made into an unlabeled MTV by specifying the LABEL=(1,BLP) parameter in the JCL DD statement for the first dataset that is created. This causes the data to overlay the VOL1 and any HDRx labels at the beginning of the MTV.

The format of an MTV that contains three unlabeled datasets is as follows.

```
(Load-Point)
DATA RECORDS FOR DATASET-1
  (TM)
DATA RECORDS FOR DATASET-2
  (TM)
DATA RECORDS FOR DATASET-3
  (TM)
  (TM)
```

Magnetic tape volumes, like DASDs, contain inter-record gaps (IRG). But, unlike DASDs, the IRGs of magnetic tape volumes are the same size (about 6/10 of an inch), regardless of the physical record size. Therefore, similar capacity considerations (minimizing the number of IRGs) exist for the determination of physical record sizes for datasets that reside on MTVs as they do for DASDs.

11.4.2 Magnetic Tape Device Exception Conditions

When reading from or writing to a magnetic tape dataset with EXCP, certain exception conditions may occur that are part of the normal processing of the dataset. These exception conditions are indicated after the channel program ends.

The only exception condition that will be discussed for magnetic tape is the unit exception condition. A unit exception condition is indicated by a X'41' in the first byte of the ECB and a X'01' in IOBUSTAT. This exception condition occurs when the tape drive encounters a tape mark during a read operation or the tape drive encounters the ending reflector strip during a write operation.

The following describes the meaning of the unit exception during a read operation and during a write operation, and how to process it for standard label datasets and unlabeled datasets.

For standard label datasets:

- Unit exception after read:
  - Occurs after the HDR2 label is read. This indicates end-of-header-label. It is handled by continuing the read operations to read the actual data of the dataset.
  - Occurs while the actual user-data is being read. This indicates end-of-data. It is handled by continuing the read operations to the read the trailer labels.
  - Occurs after the EOF2 label has been read. This indicates end-of-trailer-label. At this point, the end-of-data routine should receive control.
  - If two consecutive unit exceptions occur after the EOF2 label has been read, it indicates that the preceding dataset is the last dataset on the magnetic tape volume. This should occur only after the trailer label has been read.
  - If a unit exception occurs anywhere else, there is an error in the format of the magnetic tape volume.
- Unit exception after write:

- Indicates that the record has been written and the usable section of the MTV has been exhausted. It is handled by setting the DCBOFLWR bit in the DCBOFLGS byte of the DCB and then issuing the EOV macro instruction. This causes the EOV1 and EOV2 labels to be written, followed by two tape marks, and then causes the operating system to issue a mount message for the next MTV. The write operations then continue with the next record that is to be written.

For unlabeled datasets:

- Unit exception after read:
  - Indicates the end of the user-data of the dataset. At this point, the end-of-data routine should receive control.
  - If two consecutive unit exceptions occur, it indicates that the preceding dataset is the last dataset on the MTV.
- Unit exception after write:
  - Indicates that the record has been written and the MTV has been exhausted. It is handled by issuing the EOV macro instruction to cause the operating system to issue a mount message for the next tape. The write operations then continues with the next record that is to be written.

11.4.3 Reading Data from a Magnetic Tape Dataset

Records (physical records or blocks) are read from a magnetic tape dataset using the Read Forward CCW (X'02'). Records may be read from a magnetic tape dataset sequentially, forward or backward, only. To read consecutive records (no skipping) forward, set IOBINCAM to binary one (X'0001'); to read consecutive records backward, set IOBINCAM to binary minus one (X'FFFF') and use the Read Backward CCW (X'0C'). Only read forward operations will be discussed. The execution of each Read command causes the next record to be read into the storage area specified by the CCW. The length of the record is specified via the count field of the CCW. The specified storage area must be large enough to accomodate the record. If the record size is unknown, then the count field should be set to 32,760 and the SILI bit (X'20') turned on in the CCW flags field. The length of the record read could then be determined by subtracting the value in the Residual Byte Count field of the CSW (IOBCSW+5(2) or IOBCSWCT) from 32,760.

READING A STANDARD LABEL MAGNETIC TAPE DATASET

The appropriate dataset may be selected via the LABEL parameter of the JCL DD statement by specifying LABEL=(n,SL). After the dataset is opened, each record is read using a Read command until a unit exection occurs. If the program requires reading the standard labels or all of the data on the MTV, then the LABEL parameter must be specified as LABEL=(1,BLP). In this case, the program will read the label as data. After the unit exception, which indicates end-of-data of the label, the next Read command will read the first data record. Coding Example 11.4.1 shows how to read all the data records of a specific magnetic tape dataset when LABEL=(n,SL) is specified.

READING AN UNLABELED MAGNETIC TAPE DATASET

The appropriate dataset may be selected via the LABEL parameter of the JCL DD statement. After the dataset is opened, each record is read using a Read command until a unit exception occurs. Reading an unlabeled dataset requires the same code as reading a standard label dataset (if the labels are not read). Coding Example 11.4.1 shows how to read all the records of a magnetic tape dataset when LABEL=(n,NL) is specified.

Coding Example 11.4.1

This coding example illustrates how to read all the data records of a specific magnetic tape dataset. The dataset may contain standard labels or be unlabeled. The logic of the program is independent of the label since that information is specified by the JCL (or specified via a modified JFCB as described in Chapter 7). In this example, the physical records are assumed to be variable length with a maximum length of 120 bytes each. Each record is read and then printed after the length is determined.

```
READMTV CSECT
*
*
************************************************************************
*     INITIALIZATION
************************************************************************
*
         INITL 3,EQU=R              INITIALIZE PROGRAM
         USING IOBSTDRD,R12         DEFINE REG FOR IOB DSECT
*
*
************************************************************************
*     MAINSTREAM OF PROGRAM
************************************************************************
*
         BAL   R6,SETDSCTS          LOAD DSECT REGISTER
         BAL   R6,SETIOB            SET REQUIRED IOB FIELDS
         BAL   R6,OPEN              OPEN DCBS
NEXTREC  BAL   R6,READREC           READ A PHYSICAL RECORD
         BAL   R6,PRINTREC          PRINT THE RECORD
         B     NEXTREC              READ NEXT RECORD
ENDDATA  BAL   R6,REWIND            EOD, REWIND TAPE
         BAL   R6,CLOSE             CLOSE DCBS
         B     RETURN               RETURN TO MVS OR CALLING PROG
*
*
************************************************************************
*     THIS ROUTINE LOADS THE REGISTER FOR THE IOB DSECT.
************************************************************************
*
SETDSCTS LA    R12,READIOB          LOAD IOB ADR FOR DSECT ADRBLTY
          BR   R6                   RETURN TO CALLING RTN
*
*
************************************************************************
*     THIS ROUTINE SETS THE REQUIRED FIELDS OF THE IOB
************************************************************************
*
SETIOB   MVI   IOBFLAG1,X'42'       IND CCW-CHAINING, NOT RELATED
         MVC   IOBSTART,CCWADR      LOAD BG ADR OF CCW LIST
         MVC   IOBDCBPT,DCBADR      LOAD DCB ADR
         MVC   IOBECBPT,ECBADR      LOAD ECB ADR
         MVC   IOBINCAM,BINONE      READ FORWARD ONE BLOCK AT A TIME
```

```
         BR    R6                  RETURN TO CALLING RTN
*
*
***************************************************************************
*    THIS ROUTINE OPENS ALL THE DCBS.
***************************************************************************
*
OPEN     OPEN  (READDCB,,SYSPRINT,(OUTPUT))
         ...                       CHK FOR GOOD OPEN
         BR    R6                  RETURN TO CALLING RTN
*
*
***************************************************************************
*    THIS ROUTINE READS THE NEXT PHYSICAL RECORD FROM THE TAPE DATASET.
*    IN ORDER TO PERFORM THAT TASK, THIS ROUTINE BRANCHES AND LINKS TO THE
*    SUBROUTINES THAT PERFORM THE FOLLOWING FUNCTIONS:
*    * ISSUE THE EXCP MACRO TO READ THE NEXT PHYSICAL RECORD OF THE
*    TAPE DATASET.
*    * CALCULATE THE LENGTH OF THE RECORD READ.
***************************************************************************
*
READREC  BAL   R7,DOEXCP           ISSUE EXCP TO READ RECORD
         BAL   R7,GETLEN           CALCULATE LENGTH OF RECORD READ
         BR    R6                  RETURN CALLING RTN
*
*
***************************************************************************
*    THIS SUBROUTINE ISSUES THE EXCP MACRO TO READ A PHYSICAL RECORD OF
*    THE TAPE DATASET, CHECKS THE ECB COMPLETION CODE AND PERFORMS THE
*    APPROPRIATE ACTION INDICATED BY THE COMPLETION CODE.
***************************************************************************
*
DOEXCP    XC   READECB,READECB     CLEAR ECB FOR EXCP MACRO
          EXCP READIOB             ISSUE EXCP
          WAIT 1,ECB=READECB       WAIT FOR I/O COMPLETION
          TM   READECB,X'7F'       CHECK FOR GOOD I/O
          BNO  CHKECB              IF NO, EXAMINE ECB
          BR   R7                  IF I/O GOOD, RET TO CALLING RTN
CHKECB    TM   READECB,X'41'       CHK FOR EXCEPTION COND
          BO   CHKERR41            IF YES, CHK FOR END-OF-DATA
          B    EXCPERR             IF NO, I/O ERROR, DUMP DIAG INFO
CHKERR41  TM   IOBUSTAT,X'01'      CHK FOR TAPE MARK (END-OF-DATA)
          BO   ENDDATA             IF YES, GO TO END-OF-DATA RTN
          B    EXCPERR             IF NO, I/O ERROR, DUMP DIAG INFO
*
*
***************************************************************************
*    THIS SUBROUTINE CALCULATES THE LENGTH OF THE RECORD READ BY
*    SUBTRACTING THE RESIDUAL COUNT FROM THE MAXIMUM RECORD LENGTH.
***************************************************************************
*
GETLEN   LH    R10,IOBCSWCT        LOAD RESIDUAL COUNT FROM CSW
         LA    R11,MXRECLEN        LOAD MAXIMUM RECORD LENGTH
         SR    R11,R10             SUBTRACT RES CT FROM MAX LEN
         ST    R11,RECLEN          SAVE ACTUAL NUMB OF BYTES READ
         BR    R7                  RETURN TO CALLING RTN
*
*
***************************************************************************
*    THIS ROUTINE PRINTS THE VARIABLE LENGTH RECORD READ FROM THE TAPE
*    DATASET.
***************************************************************************
*
PRINTREC L     R10,RECLEN          LOAD REC LEN
```

```
         BCTR R10,0              DECR REC LEN FOR EX INSTR
         EX   R10,EXMVC          MOVE RECORD INTO PRINT LINE
         PUT  SYSPRINT,LINE      PRINT RECORD
         MVC  LINE,LINE-1        CLEAR PRINT LINE
         BR   R6                 RETURN TO CALLING RTN
EXMVC    MVC  LINE+1(0),RECORD   MVC FOR EX INSTR
*
*
***********************************************************************
*    THIS ROUTINE RECEIVES CONTROL IF THE ATTEMPTED I/O IS UNSUCCESSFUL.
*    THIS ROUTINE LOADS VARIOUS DIAGNOSTIC INFORMATION INTO REGISTERS 8
*    AND 9 AND THEN CAUSES AN ABEND WITH A DUMP.
***********************************************************************
*
EXCPERR L     R8,READECB          LOAD CONTENTS OF ECB INTO A REG
        MVC   ERRINFO+1(1),IOSUSTAT   UNIT STATUS FIELD OF CSW
        MVC   ERRINFO+2(1),IOBSENS0   BYTE-1 OF HARDWARE SENSE CODE
        MVC   ERRINFO+3(1),IOBSENS1   BYTE-2 OF HARDWARE SENSE CODE
        L     R9,ERRINFO              LOAD ERROR INFO WORD INTO A REG
        L     R10,ERRID               LOAD ID TO FIND REGS IN DUMP
        ABEND 900,DUMP                ISSUE ABEND MACRO WITH A DUMP
*
*
***********************************************************************
*    THIS ROUTINE CAUSES THE REWINDING OF THE TAPE VOLUME.
***********************************************************************
*
REWIND  MVC   IOBSTART,CCWADR2
        BAL   R7,DOEXCP
        BR    R6
*
*
***********************************************************************
*    THIS ROUTINE CLOSES ALL THE DCBS.
***********************************************************************
*
CLOSE   CLOSE (READDCB,,SYSPRINT)
        BR    R6                 RETURN TO CALLING RTN
*
*
***********************************************************************
*    THIS ROUTINE RESTORES THE REGISTERS AND RETURNS CONTROL.
***********************************************************************
*
RETURN  RCNTL RC=0
*
*
***********************************************************************
*    THE CCW, IOB, AND ECB
***********************************************************************
*
READCCW CCW   X'02',RECORD,X'20',MXRECLEN READ CCW
REWDCCW CCW   X'07',0,X'00',1            REWIND CCW
*
READIOB DC    10F'0'             AREA FOR IOB
READECB DC    F'0'               FULLWORD FOR ECB
*
*
***********************************************************************
*    OTHER DC/DS STATEMENTS
***********************************************************************
*
MXRECLEN EQU  120
BINONE   DC   H'1'
```

```
RECLEN   DS  F
RECORD   DS  CL(MXRECLEN)
         DC  C' '
LINE     DC  CL133' '
*
CCWADR   DC  A(READCCW)
CCWADR2  DC  A(REWDCCW)
DCBADR   DC  A(READDCB)
ECBADR   DC  A(READECB)
*
ERRINFO  DC  F'0'
ERRID    DC  4XL1'FF'
*
*
***************************************************************************
*    THE DCBS
***************************************************************************
*
READDCB  DCB   MACRF=E,DDNAME=TESTFILE
SYSPRINT DCB   DSORG=PS,MACRF=PM,BLKSIZE=1330,LRECL=133,RECFM=FB,          -
               DDNAME=SYSPRINT
*
*
***************************************************************************
*    THE DSECTS
***************************************************************************
*
         PRINT NOGEN
         IEZIOB                  GENERATES IOB DSECT
         ORG   IOBCSTAT+1        POS TO RESIDUAL COUNT FIELD OF CSW
IOBCSWCT DS    CL2               PROVIDE LABEL FOR RES CT FIELD
*
*
***************************************************************************
*    END OF PROGRAM
***************************************************************************
*
*
         END
```

NOTES:

- The REWIND routine is for illustration reasons only; it is not required for the magnetic tape volume to be rewound. The CLOSE macro instruction causes a REWIND operation if the JCL DISP parameter specifies KEEP.

11.4.4 Writing Data to a Magnetic Tape Dataset

Records (physical records or blocks) are written to an MTV, using the Write CCW (X'01'). The record length is specified via the count field of the CCW. Blocking logical records is the responsibility of the program. If the program is required to write tape marks, then the Write Tape Mark CCW (X'1F') is used.

CREATING A STANDARD LABEL MAGNETIC TAPE DATASET

The standard labels may be created by the operating system or by the program. It is easier to let the operating system do it. If the LABEL parameter is specified as LABEL=(n,SL), then the operating system creates the HDR1/HDR2 labels, writes a tape mark, and positions the MTV for the data. Each record of the user-data is written using the Write command.

When all the records have been written, bit DCBOFLWR of byte DCBOFLGS must be set before the CLOSE macro instruction is issued. This causes the operating system to write a tape mark at the end of the last data record written, write the EOF1/EOF2 trailer labels and write the two tape marks at the end of the trailer labels.

If the data being written exceeds the capacity of the MTV, which is indicated by a unit exception, then the program and operating system must perform additional processing. Bit DCBOFLWR of byte DCBOFLGS must be set, and then the EOV macro instruction must be issued. This causes the operating system to write a tape mark after the last data record written, create the EOV1/EOV2 trailer labels, write two tape marks, issue a mount message for another MTV and write the HDR1/HDR2 labels on the new MTV, write a tape mark, and position the new MTV for the additional data. Then the writing of records continues until all have been written. The CLOSE macro instruction is then issued.

If the programmer chooses to write the standard labels, then tape marks must be written in the appropriate places.

Coding Example 11.4.2 shows how the write the data records of a standard label magnetic tape dataset.

CREATING AN UNLABELED MT DATASET

The appropriate position on the MTV for the new dataset is selected by specifying LABEL=(n,NL) on the JCL DD statement. Each record is written with the Write command until the last record is written. When all the records have been written, a tape mark must be written (two, if this is the last dataset on the MTV) and then the CLOSE macro instruction issued. However, it is better programming to set the DCBOFLWR bit of the DCBOFLGS byte before issuing the CLOSE macro instruction. This will cause the operating system to write the tape mark(s) at the end of the last record written. If standard labels have not been requested via the JCL, then the operating system will not write any. However, if the JCL is changed to request standard labels, then having set the DCBOFLWR bit will cause the operating system to create the EOF1/EOF2 trailer labels. This will make the program independent of any JCL specifications regarding labels.

If the data being written exceeds the capacity of the MTV, then it is handled the same way as it is for a standard label dataset (except that the operating system does not write the EOV1/EOV2 or the HDR1/HDR2 label records).

Writing an unlabeled dataset requires the same code as writing a standard label dataset (if the labels are not written by the program).

Coding Example 11.4.2 shows how to write the records of an unlabeled magnetic tape dataset.

Coding Example 11.4.2

This coding example illustrates how to create a magnetic tape dataset. The dataset may contain standard labels or be unlabeled. The logic of the program is independent of the label since that information is specified by the JCL (or specified via a modified JFCB as described in Chapter 7). In this example, 80-byte card-image records are read and then written to the magnetic tape dataset.

```
WRTMTV CSECT
*
*
***********************************************************************
*    INITIALIZATION
```

```
***********************************************************************
*
         INITL 3,EQU=R            INITIALIZE PROGRAM
         USING IHADCB,R11         DEFINE REG FOR DCB DSECT
         USING IOBSTDRD,R12       DEFINE REG FOR IOB DSECT
*
*
***********************************************************************
*    MAINSTREAM OF PROGRAM
***********************************************************************
*
         BAL   R6,SETDSCTS        LOAD DSECT REGISTERS
         BAL   R6,SETIOB          SET REQUIRED IOB FIELDS
         BAL   R6,OPEN            OPEN DCBS
NEXTREC  BAL   R6,GETREC          READ A REC FOR THE TAPE DATASET
         BAL   R6,WRTREC          WRITE A PHYSICAL REC TO TAPE
         B     NEXTREC            PROCESS NEXT REC
ENDDATA  BAL   R6,WRTEND          EOD, INDICATE EOF1/EOF2 REQUIRED
         BAL   R6,CLOSE           CLOSE DCBS
         B     RETURN             RETURN TO MVS OR CALLING PROG
*
*
***********************************************************************
*    THIS ROUTINE LOADS THE REGISTERS FOR THE DCB AND THE IOB DSECTS
***********************************************************************
*
SETDSCTS LA    R11,WRTDCB         LOAD DCB ADR FOR DSECT ADRBLTY
         LA    R12,WRTIOB         LOAD IOB ADR FOR DSECT ADRBLTY
         BR    R6                 RETURN TO CALLING RTN
*
*
***********************************************************************
*    THIS ROUTINE SETS THE REQUIRED FIELDS OF THE IOB
***********************************************************************
*
SETIOB   MVI   IOBFLAG1,X'42'     IND CCW-CHAINING, NOT RELATED
         MVC   IOBSTART,CCWADR    LOAD BG ADR OF CCW-LIST
         MVC   IOBDCBPT,DCBADR    LOAD DCB ADR
         MVC   IOBECBPT,ECBADR    LOAD ECB ADR
         MVC   IOBINCAM,BINONE    WRITE FORWARD ONE BLOCK AT A TIME
         BR    R6                 RETURN TO CALLING RTN
*
*
***********************************************************************
*    THIS ROUTINE OPENS ALL THE DCBS.
***********************************************************************
*
OPEN     OPEN  (INRECS,,WRTDCB(OUTPUT))
         ...                      CHECK FOR GOOD OPEN
         BR    R6                 RETURN TO CALLING RTN
*
*
***********************************************************************
*    THIS ROUTINE READS THE RECORDS USED TO CREATE THE TAPE DATASET.
***********************************************************************
*
GETREC   GET   INRECS,RECORD      READ A RECORD
         BR    R6                 RETURN TO CALLING RTN
*
*
***********************************************************************
*    THIS ROUTINE WRITES THE NEXT PHYSICAL RECORD TO THE TAPE DATASET.
*    IN ORDER TO PERFORM THAT TASK, THIS ROUTINE BRANCHES AND LINKS TO THE
*    SUBROUTINE THAT PERFORMS THE FOLLOWING FUNCTION:
```

```
*     * ISSUE THE EXCP MACRO TO WRITE THE NEXT PHYSICAL RECORD OF THE
*       TAPE DATASET.
***********************************************************************
*
WRTREC   BAL   R7,DOEXCP           ISSUE EXCP MACRO TO WRITE REC
         BR    R6                  RETURN TO CALLING RTN
*
*
***********************************************************************
*    THIS SUBROUTINE ISSUES THE EXCP MACRO TO WRITE A PHYSICAL RECORD TO
*    THE TAPE DATASET, CHECKS THE ECB COMPLETION CODE, AND PERFORMS THE
*    APPROPRIATE ACTION INDICATED BY THE COMPLETION CODE.
***********************************************************************
*
DOEXCP   XC    WRTECB,WRTECB       CLEAR ECB FOR EXCP MACRO
         EXCP  WRTIOB              ISSUE EXCP MACRO
         WAIT  1,ECB=WRTECB        WAIT FOR I/O COMPLETION
         TM    WRTECB,X'7F'        CHECK FOR GOOD I/O
         BNO   CHKECB              IF NO, EXAMINE ECB
         BR    R7                  RETURN TO CALLING RTN
*
CHKECB   TM    WRTECB,X'41'        CHECK FOR EXCEPTION COND
         BO    CHKERR41            IF YES, CHK FOR END OF TAPE
         B     EXCPERR             IF NO, I/O ERROR, DUMP DIAG INFO
*
CHKERR41 TM    IOBUSTAT,X'01'      CHECK FOR END-OF-TAPE
         BO    DOEOV               IF YES, CAUSE ANOTHER TAPE MOUNT
         B     EXCPERR             IF NO, I/O ERROR, DUMP DIAG INFO
*
DOEOV    OI    DCBOFLGS,DCBOFLWR   IND EOV1/EOV2 LABELS, ETC. REQRD
         EOV   WRTDCB              DO END-OF-VOLUME PROCESSING
         BR    R7                  RETURN TO CALLING RTN
*
*
***********************************************************************
*    THIS ROUTINE RECEIVES CONTROL IF THE ATTEMPTED I/O IS UNSUCCESSFUL.
*    THIS ROUTINE LOADS VARIOUS DIAGNOSTIC INFORMATION INTO REGISTERS 8
*    AND 9 AND THEN CAUSES AN ABEND WITH A DUMP.
***********************************************************************
*
EXCPERR  L     R8,WRTECB           LOAD CONTENTS OF ECB INTO A REG
         MVC   ERRINFO+1(1),IOSUSTAT   UNIT STATUS FIELD OF CSW
         MVC   ERRINFO+2(1),IOBSENS0   BYTE-1 OF HARDWARE SENSE CODE
         MVC   ERRINFO+3(1),IOBSENS1   BYTE-2 OF HARDWARE SENSE CODE
         L     R9,ERRINFO          LOAD ERROR INFO WORD INTO A REG
         L     R10,ERRID           LOAD ID TO FIND REGS IN DUMP
         ABEND 900,DUMP            ISSUE ABEND MACRO AND REQ DUMP
*
*
***********************************************************************
*    THIS ROUTINE SETS THE DCBOFLGS FIELD TO INDICATE TO DATA MGMT TO DO
*    THE FOLLOWING AFTER THE DATASET IS CLOSED:
*    * WRITE A TAPE MARK AFTER THE LAST RECORD OF THE DATASET;
*    * WRITE THE EOF1/EOF2 LABELS IF THE JCL SPECIFIED STANDARD
*    LABELS FOR THE DATASET;
*    * WRITE A DOUBLE TAPE MARK AFTER THE EOF1/EOF2 LABELS (FOR A
*    STANDARD LABEL DATASET) OR AFTER THE LAST RECORD OF THE
*    DATASET (FOR AN UNLABELED DATASET) TO INDICATE THAT THE
*    DATASET IS THE LAST ONE ON THE TAPE VOLUME.
***********************************************************************
*
WRTEND   LA    R11,WRTDCB          SET ADRBLTY FOR DCB DSECT
         OI    DCBOFLGS,DCBOFLWR   IND TO DATAMGMT TO DO EOD PROC
         BR    R6                  RET TO CALLING RTN
```

```
*
*
***********************************************************************
*    THIS ROUTINE CLOSES ALL THE DCBS.
***********************************************************************
*
CLOSE    CLOSE (INRECS,,WRTDCB)
         BR    R6                   RETURN TO CALLING RTN
*
*
***********************************************************************
*    THIS ROUTINE RESTORES THE REGISTERS AND RETURNS CONTROL.
***********************************************************************
*
RETURN   RCNTL RC=0                 RETURN TO MVS OR THE CALLING PROG
*
*
***********************************************************************
*    CCW, IOB, AND ECB
***********************************************************************
*
WRTCCW   CCW   X'01',RECORD,X'20',80  WRITE CCW
*
WRTIOB   DC    10F'0'                 AREA FOR IOB
WRTECB   DC    F'0'                   FULLWORD FOR ECB
*
*
***********************************************************************
*    OTHER DC/DS STATEMENTS
***********************************************************************
*
BINONE   DC    H'1'
RECORD   DS    CL80
*
CCWADR   DC    A(WRTCCW)
DCBADR   DC    A(WRTDCB)
ECBADR   DC    A(WRTECB)
*
ERRINFO  DC    F'0'
ID       DC    4XL1'FF'
*
*
***********************************************************************
*    THE DCBS
***********************************************************************
*
INRECS   DCB   DSORG=PS,MACRF=GM,LRECL=80,RECFM=FB,EODAD=ENDDATA,        -
               DDNAME=INRECS
WRTDCB   DCB   MACRF=E,DDNAME=TESTFILE
*
*
***********************************************************************
*    THE DSECTS
***********************************************************************
*
         PRINT NOGEN
         DCBD  DSORG=XE             GENERATES EXCP-DCB DSECT
         IEZIOB                     GENERATES IOB DSECT
         ORG   IOBCSTAT+1           POS TO RESIDUAL COUNT FIELD OF CSW
IOBCSWCT DS    CL2                  PROVIDE LABEL FOR RES CT FIELD
*
*
***********************************************************************
*    END OF PROGRAM
```

```
***********************************************************************
*
         END
```

NOTES:

- As an exercise, the reader might try to block the records before writing them to the magnetic tape volume. The additional code should include logic to handle a short last block.

BIBLIOGRAPHY FOR CHAPTER 11

The following IBM manuals contain reference material for the topics discussed in this chapter.

ID	TITLE
GC26-3830	*OS/VS2 SPL: Data Management*
GC26-4010	*MVS/XA SPL: Data Management*
SC26-4515	*MVS/ESA System—Data Administration*
GA26-1661	*IBM 3880 Storage Control Models 1, 2 and 3 Description*
GA32-0021	*IBM 3803-2/3420 Magnetic Tape Subsystem Description*
GC26-4064	*MVS/370 Magnetic Tape Labels*
GC26-4003	*MVS/XA Magnetic Tape Labels and File Structure Administration*
SC26-4511	*MVS/ESA Magnetic Tape Labels and File Structure Administration*

12

Writing SVC Routines

IBM provides numerous SVC routines for system functions and user facilities. In addition, MVS provides the capability for the user to develop his/her own SVC routines to provide additional functions. This chapter discusses writing and implementating user-written SVC routines.

12.1 WHAT IS AN SVC ROUTINE?

An SVC routine is a reentrant program that executes in supervisor state and PSW storage protection key zero. SVC routines have the ID numbers 0–255 associated with them and are invoked by the SVC machine instruction with the desired SVC number specified as the operand. The SVC routine returns control to the calling program at the instruction following the SVC instruction.

Providing user-written SVC routines is a convenient and safe way of permitting user programs to request the use of special MVS facilities, which require that the requestor execute in supervisor state and/or PSW protection key zero. As a precaution, certain sensitive SVCs may have the requirement that the calling program be authorized.

A program executes in supervisor state when the Problem State bit (bit 15) in the current PSW is set to zero, and executes in storage protection key zero when the Protect Key bits (bits 8–11) in the current PSW are set to zeros.

Execution in supervisor state and PSW protection key zero have different meaning to hardware (CPU) and to software (MVS).

To the CPU, a program that executes in supervisor state is allowed to execute priviliged machine instructions (such as SIO, LPSW, SIGP, STIDP, etc.), and programs that execute with protection key zero are allowed to fetch from and/or store to any real storage location.

To MVS, it indicates that the use of certain facilities are allowed. Certain facilities (such as issuing the SETLOCK and SCHEDULE macros instructions, issuing a branch-entry GETMAIN macro instruction, etc.) in MVS are permitted to be used only by programs that execute in supervisor state and PSW protection key zero. Other facilities (such as GETMAINing virtual storage from the CSA and the SQA, OPENing the VTOC for UPDATE, issuing the MODESET macro instruction, etc.) are permitted to be performed only by authorized programs. A program is authorized if it is APF-authorized, or executing in supervisor state, or executing in PSW protection key 0–7.

Therefore, SVC routines may execute any machine instructions, fetch from and store to any real storage location or any virtual storage location (if it is not page-protected), and use any MVS facility.

The Problem State bit and Protection Key bits are set appropriately when an SVC machine instruction is executed. The execution of an SVC machine instruction causes a Supervisor-Call Interruption, which causes the CPU to store the current PSW into the SVC Old PSW location and load (activate) the SVC New PSW. The SVC New PSW (as well as the New PSWs for all the other interruption types) are loaded at IPL time into the appropriate real storage locations by MVS. The SVC Old PSW is located at real storage location X'20' and the SVC New PSW is located at real storage location X'60'.

The SVC New PSW has the Problem State bit off (indicating supervisor state) and has the Protection Key bits off (indicating key zero). That PSW becomes the current one (via a hardware initiated LPSW instruction) when the SVC machine instruction has completed execution. The instruction address in the SVC New PSW points to the MVS SVC First Level Interruption Handler (FLIH). The SVC FLIH receives control whenever an SVC instruction is executed and, among other things, determines which SVC routine is to be executed by examining the low order byte of the interruption-code field that the CPU uses to store the requested SVC number. The 2-byte interruption-code field used is located at offset 2 into the SVC Old PSW in BC mode or at real location X'8A' in EC mode. The high order byte of the interruption-code field is set to zeros.

12.2 TYPES AND CHARACTERISTICS OF SVC ROUTINES

In MVS, there are five type of SVCs: Type-1, Type-2, Type-3, Type-4 and Type-6. (The so-called type-5 SVC is not discussed or considered.) Each of the SVC types has a different set of execution characteristics; therefore, certain SVC types may be better suited to perform a particular task than other types.

The type and characteristics of each SVC are contained in the SVC Table, located in the MVS nucleus. There is an 8-byte entry for each SVC number. Each entry contains the SVC type, locks that are to be obtained before the SVC receives control, whether the caller of the SVC should be authorized, and the entry point address of the SVC routine. The entries in the SVC table are sequenced from SVC number 0 to SVC number 255. SVC numbers from 0-199 are reserved for IBM use, and SVC numbers 200-255 are reserved for user-written SVCs. It is the systems programmer's responsibility to define the characteristics of SVCs 200-255. For MVS/370 and MVS/XA (prior to version 2.2), the SVC Table is created during SYSGEN time and the entries for SVCs 200-255 are created from information specified in the SYSGEN SVCTABLE macro instruction. For MVS/XA (version 2.2 and later) and MVS/ESA, the SVC Table is created dynamically at IPL time, and the entries for SVCs 200-255 are created from information specified in the IEASVCxx member of SYS1.PARMLIB. All the information for each SVC (200-255) entry is specified (or defaulted) except for the entry point address of the actual SVC routine, which is inserted by MVS at IPL time.

12.3 NAMING SVC ROUTINES

All SVC types do not have the same naming convention.

SVC types 1, 2, and 6 are named IGCnnn, where nnn is the actual decimal number of the SVC. For example, a type-1 SVC with the number 225 would be named IGC225.

SVC types 3 and 4 are named IGC00ddd, where ddd is the signed number of the SVC. For example, a type-3 SVC with the number 251 would be named IGC0025A. To provide the required sign, the numbers 1-9 of the last character of the SVC name would be changed to the alpha characters A-I, respectively. Zero would be changed to the special character { (X'C0').

Table 12.2.1

This table summarizes the characteristics of each SVC type.

SVC Type	Characteristics
1	• Resident in MVS Nucleus. • FLIH does not built a SVRB; therefore, cannot issue other SVCs or call other routines. • Always receives control with LOCAL lock held. • Can obtain other locks dynamically via SETLOCK macro instruction.
2	• Resident in MVS Nucleus. • May issue other SVCs and call other routines. • Requires no locks, but may receive control with locks held and/or obtain them dynamically via SETLOCK.
3	• Located in Link Pack Area. • May issue other SVCs and call other routines. • Requires no locks but may receive control with locks held and/or obtain them dynamically via 'SETLOCK.
4	• Located in Link Pack Area. • May issue other SVCs and call other routines. • Requires no locks but may receive control with locks held and/or obtained them dynamically via SETLOCK.
6	• Resident in MVS Nucleus. • FLIH does not build an SVRB; therefore, cannot issue other SVCs or call other routines. • Executes disabled. • Cannot receive control with locks held. • Cannot obtain any locks dynamically.

By convention (but not enforced by MVS), for type-4 SVCs, the third and forth characters of the name may be incremented to 01, 02, and so on, to name other routines called or loaded by the base SVC routine.

12.4 GUIDELINES FOR SELECTING WHICH SVC TYPE

In most cases, a type-3 SVC will suffice. In MVS, a type-3 and a type-4 SVC are identical. The difference was in the MVT days (predecessor to MVS) when non-nucleus resident SVCs were loaded into a 2K-byte transient area when execution was required. If the size of the SVC was 2K bytes or less, then it was defined as a type-3 SVC. If the size of the SVC exceeded 2K bytes, then it was defined as a type-4 SVC and coded as multiple load modules of 2K bytes or less. Then each load module of the type-4 SVC received control from the previous load module via the XCTL macro instruction. Since non-nucleus resident

SVCs are now loaded into the LPA and have no size limitation, the original concept of a type-4 SVC is no longer required. Therefore, there is no need to define a type-4 SVC; all LPA resident SVCs may be defined as type-3 SVCs.

A type-3 (and a type-4) SVC has the advantage of not occupying any real storage until execution is required.

A type-1, type-2, and type-6 SVC have a performance advantage since they are resident in the nucleus and, therefore, are page fixed. However, if the optional Fixed LPA (FLPA) were defined, then specific type-3 (and type-4) SVCs could be loaded there at IPL time and then also be page fixed.

Type-6 SVCs receive control with the CPU disabled for interruptions; therefore, if that is a requirement, then a type-6 SVC should be selected. However, since a type-6 SVC executes disabled, its execution time should be short to minimize any degradation on overall system performance. A type-6 SVC (new with MVS, did not exist in MVT) has similar use as a type-1 SVC, but offers a performance advantage because the instruction path length for receiving and returning control (if the T6EXIT macro instruction is used) is shorter. A type-6 SVC also provides a more efficient way to change from TCB mode to SRB mode. This is accomplished by using the T6EXIT macro instruction as opposed to the normally used SCHEDULE macro instruction. Writing SRB routines is discussed in Chapter 15.

12.5 SVC PROGRAMMING REQUIREMENTS AND CONSIDERATIONS

The following itemizes the programming requirements and considerations for all SVC types:

- SVC routines must be reentrant. Type-3 and type-4 SVCs, which reside in the PLPA, must also be refreshable. The section "Writing Reusable Programs"in Chapter 5 discusses how to write reentrant programs and refreshable programs.
- Saving and restoring the caller's registers is not necessary because MVS performs this function.
- SVC routines must adhere to the restrictions for their types as summarized in Table 12.2.1.
- SVC routines must issue the appropriate ENQ/DEQ or SETLOCK macro instructions when accessing resources that require serialization to assure resource integrity.
- If the SVC routine provides sensitive services or provides multiple services (some of which are sensitive), then it should use the TESTAUTH macro instruction to determine if the caller has the proper level of authorization to use the provided services. The TESTAUTH macro instruction was discussed in Chapter 10. The SVC table entry could also indicate that the caller must be authorized in order to call a specific SVC routine, but that method is limited. The TESTAUTH method will allow a non-authorized caller entry to a sensitive SVC routine if a nonsensitive service is requested. The SVC table entry method will allow a caller entry to a sensitive SVC routine only if the caller is authorized (any type of authorization), regardless of the service requested. Also, the TESTAUTH macro instruction can distinguish among the various types of authorization (APF-authorized, supervisor state, PSW protection key 0–7). SVC routines could set up an authorization scheme to determine what services a caller is allowed access to depending upon the caller's level (or type) of authorization. For example, nonsensitive services can be accessed by any caller; sensitive services can be accessed by a caller having any type of authorization; and very sensitive services can be accessed only by callers who are in supervisor state (or both supervisor state and PSW protection key 0).

- SVC routines have no size limit.
- SVC routines may issue the ABEND macro instruction to perform abnormal termination.
- Type-2, type-3, and type-4 SVCs may set up a recovery environment by using the ESTAE or the SETFRR macro instructions. Type-1 and type-6 SVCs may use only the SETFRR macro instruction to set up a recovery environment.
- The calling program and the SVC routine may pass parameters to each other by using registers 0, 1, and 15, since those registers are left unchanged by MVS.
- User-written macros should be developed for generating the SVC instructions to invoke user-written SVCs. This is particularly true if the setup for the required parameters is involved.
- The address of the RB (usually a PRB or an SVRB) of the caller can be used to obtain various information about the calling program (or SVC routine) such as the contents of the registers at the time of interruption, the PSW at time of interruption, and so forth.

  For type-1 and type-6 SVC routines, the address of the RB is stored in register 5 upon entry into the SVC routine.

  For type-2, type-3, and type-4 SVC routines, an SVRB is created and its address is stored in register 5 upon entry into the SVC routine. The SVRB contains a 48-byte user area (field RBEXSAVE), which may be used by the SVC routine to store information. The address of the RB of the caller can be obtained from the RBLINKB field of the SVRB.
- Type-1, type-2, type-3, and type-4 SVCs must return control by branching to the address that was contained in register 14 when control was received. The type-6 SVC may also return control this way or by issuing the T6EXIT macro instruction.

The format of the T6EXIT macro instruction is as follows:

```
[name]    T6EXIT    [RETURN={CALLER|DISPATCH|SRB}
```

`RETURN (Default: CALLER)`

Specifies how the type-6 SVC routine is to return control.

`CALLER` indicates that control is to be returned to the caller (issuer of the SVC instruction) via the FLIH.

`DISPATCH` indicates that control is to be through the dispatcher. This type of return is for SVC routines that have suspended the current task.

`SRB` indicates that the FLIH is to immediately dispatch an SRB and return control to the caller. The type-6 SVC routine must perform the same initialization functions as required by the SCHEDULE macro instruction, which are the following:

- Build an SRB that has the same format as the one used with the SCHEDULE macro instruction.
- Load register 1 with the address of the SRB.

However, there is one restriction with dispatching an SRB in this manner. The SRB routine must execute in the same address space as the SVC routine as opposed to any specified address space as with the SCHEDULE macro instruction.

When the T6EXIT macro instruction specifies DISPATCH or SRB, the contents of the parameter registers (and the others) are not preserved; therefore, the caller cannot receive information back from the SVC routine via those registers.

When an SVC routine receives control, the contents of the registers are as follows:

`Register 0` The same information as when the SVC was called.
`Register 1` The same information as when the SVC was called.
`Register 3` The address of the CVT.

Register 4 The address of the TCB of the task that called the SVC.
Register 5 The address of the SVRB for a type-2, type-3, and type-4 SVC. The address of the last active RB for a type-1 and type-6 SVC.
Register 6 The entry point address of the SVC routine.
Register 7 The address of the ASCB that contains the task that called the SVC.
Register 13 Same information as when the SVC was called.
Register 14 The return address.
Register 15 The same information as when the SVC was called.

In addition, the contents of registers 2 and 8-12 are unpredictable. The contents of registers 2-14 are restored to that of the calling program when the SVC routine returns control.

12.6 SVC ROUTINE CODING EXAMPLES

This section contains the code for a number of sample SVC routines. The SVC routine presented in Coding Example 12.6.1 may be either a type-1, type-2, type-3, or type-4 SVC. The CSECT name used for that SVC routine indicates that it is for SVC number 252. If that SVC routine is used as a type-1 or type-2 SVC, then the CSECT name (and the load module name) must be changed to IGC252. The SVC routines presented in Coding Examples 12.6.2A, 12.6.3 and 12.6.4 may be either type-2, type-3, or type-4 SVCs. The CSECT names used for those SVC routines indicate that those SVC routines are for SVC numbers 253, 254, and 255, respectively. If they are used as type-2 SVCs, then the CSECT name (and the load module name) must be changed to IGC253, IGC254, and IGC255, respectively. Coding Example 12.6.2B is for a type-1 SVC. Coding Example 12.6.3 (SVC 254) could also qualify for a type-1 SVC if the WTO macro instructions were removed and the name changed to IGC254.

Coding Example 12.6.1

This coding example illustrates the code for an SVC routine that returns the addresses of the TCB and the ASCB of the calling program into the area provided.

For this SVC routine, the calling program uses register 1 as the parameter register. Register 1 contains the address of a parameter-list that contains two consecutive fullwords. The fullwords contain the addresses of the areas that are to receive the TCB address and the ASCB address, respectively.

```
IGC0025B CSECT
*
*
************************************************************************
*    INITIALIZATION
************************************************************************
*
         REGEQU EQU=R                DEFINE EQU'S FOR REGISTERS
         USING *,R6                  SETUP ADDRESSABILITY
*
*
************************************************************************
*    MAINSTREAM OF SVC ROUTINE
************************************************************************
*
         BAL   R8,SAVEREGS           SAVE REGISTERS
         BAL   R8,PUTADDRS           PUT TCB/ASCB ADRS INTO PARM AREA
         B     RETURN                RETURN TO CALLING PROG VIA FLIH
```

```
*
*
***********************************************************************
*    THIS ROUTINE SAVES THE CONTENTS OF ALL REGISTERS THAT CONTAIN
*    CONTROL INFORMATION.
***********************************************************************
*
SAVEREGS LR   R12,R14              SAVE RETURN ADDRESS
         LR   R11,R1               SAVE CALLERS PARM AREA ADDRESS
         BR   R8                   RETURN TO CALLING RTN
*
*
***********************************************************************
*    THIS ROUTINE RETURNS THE ADDRESSES OF THE CALLER'S TCB AND ASCB IN
*    THE PARM AREA PROVIDED BY THE CALLER. THE CALLER PASSES THE ADDRESS
*    OF ITS PARM-LIST IN REGISTER 1. THE PARM AREA CONTAINS TWO FULLWORDS.
*    THE FIRST FULLWORD CONTAINS THE ADDRESS OF THE AREA THAT IS TO
*    RECEIVE THE ADDRESS OF THE TCB, AND THE SECOND FULLWORD CONTAINS THE
*    ADDRESS OF THE AREA THAT IS TO RECEIVE THE ADDRESS OF THE ASCB. THE
*    SAVEREGS ROUTINE SAVES REGISTER 1 IN REGISTER 11.
***********************************************************************
*
PUTADDRS L    R10,0(0,R11)         LOAD ADR OF 1ST WORD OF PARM
         L    R12,4(0,R11)         LOAD ADR OF 2ND WORD OF PARM
         ST   R4,0(0,R10)          PUT TCB ADR INTO PROV AREA
         ST   R7,0(0,R12)          PUT ASCB ADR INTO PROV AREA
         BR   R8                   RETURN TO CALLING RTN
*
*
***********************************************************************
*    THIS ROUTINE LOADS THE PARAMETER REGISTERS, RESTORES THE RETURN
*    ADDRESS INTO REGISTER 14, AND RETURNS CONTROL TO THE FLIH.
***********************************************************************
*
RETURN   LR   R1,R11               RESTORE PARM AREA ADR
         LA   R15,0                LOAD RC IN A PARM REG
         LR   R14,R12              RESTORE RETURN ADDRESS
         BR   R14                  RETURN TO CALLING PROG VIA FLIH
*
*
***********************************************************************
*    END OF SVC ROUTINE
***********************************************************************
*
           END
```

NOTES:

- REGEQU is a macro instruction used to generate EQU symbols for all the registers. The operand EQU=R specifies the prefix for the numbers of the registers.

The following coding example shows how a program would call the SVC 252, defined in this example, to request the TCB and the ASCB addresses.

```
         ...
         LA   R1,PARMAREA          LOAD ADR OF PARM AREA
         SVC  252                  ISSUE SVC TO RET TCB/ASCB ADRS
         LTR  R15,R15              CHECK RC
         BNZ  NOADDRS              IF NOT 0, ADRS NOT RETURNED
         ...                       USE TCB/ASCB ADRS
PARMAREA DS   0F
         DC   A(TCBADR)
         DC   A(ASCBADR)
TCBADR   DS   F
ASCBADR  DS   F
```

Coding Example 12.6.2A

This coding example illustrates the code for an SVC routine that obtains virtual storage from the CSA for the calling program.

For this SVC routine, the calling program uses register 0 as a parameter register. Register 0 contains the requested CSA storage length. The SVC routine allocates storage from subpool 231 (CSA, fetch-protected). The allocated CSA storage is set to the same PSW protection key as the caller. This is necessary in order to permit the calling program access to the allocated storage. When the SVC routine returns control to the caller, register 1 contains the address of the allocated CSA storage and register 15 contains a return code. A zero return code indicates that the CSA storage was successfully allocated.

```
IGC0025C CSECT
*
*
***********************************************************************
*    INITIALIZATION
***********************************************************************
*
         REGEQU  EQU=R              DEFINE EQU'S FOR REGISTERS
         USING   *,R6               SETUP ADDRESSABILITY
*
*
***********************************************************************
*    MAINSTREAM OF SVC ROUTINE
***********************************************************************
*
         BAL  R8,SAVEREGS           SAVE REGISTERS
         BAL  R8,SETKEY             SET PSW KEY TO THAT OF CALLER
         BAL  R8,GETCSA             GET REQUESTED CSA STORAGE
         BAL  R8,RSTORKEY           RESTORE PSW KEY TO ZERO
         B    RETURN                RETURN TO CALLING PROG VIA FLIH
*
*
***********************************************************************
*    THIS ROUTINE SAVES THE CONTENTS OF ALL REGISTERS THAT CONTAIN
*    CONTROL INFORMATION.
***********************************************************************
*
SAVEREGS LR   R12,R14               SAVE RETURN ADDRESS
         LR   R10,R0                SAVE REQUESTED LENGTH OF CSA ALLO
         WTO  '*** 253 ENTERED ***',ROUTCDE=11 FOR TESTING ONLY
         BR   R8                    RETURN TO CALLING RTN
*
*
***********************************************************************
*    THIS ROUTINE CHANGES THE PSW STORAGE PROTECTION KEY TO THAT OF THE
*    CALLING PROGRAM. THIS IS DONE SO THAT THE ALLOCATED CSA STORAGE
*    IS SET TO THE PROTECTION KEY OF THAT OF THE CALLING PROGRAM INSTEAD
*    OF THE PROTECTION KEY OF THE SVC ROUTINE, WHICH IS KEY ZERO.
***********************************************************************
*
SETKEY   MODESET KEY=NZERO          SET KEY TO THAT OF CALLER
         BR    R8                   RETURN TO CALLING RTN
*
*
***********************************************************************
*    THIS ROUTINE ALLOCATES FETCH-PROTECTED VIRTUAL STORAGE FROM THE CSA.
*    THE LENGTH OF THE REQUESTED CSA STORAGE IS SPECIFIED VIA REGISTER 0
*    BY THE CALLER OF THE SVC. THE SAVEREGS ROUTINE SAVES REGISTER 0 IN
*    REGISTER 10.
```

```
***********************************************************************
*
GETCSA   GETMAIN RC,LV=(R10),SP=231 ALLO CSA STORAGE
         LR     R11,R1              SAVE ADDRESS OF CSA STORAGE
         LR     R9,R15              SAVE RC FROM GETMAIN
         BR     R8                  RETURN TO CALLING RTN
*
*
***********************************************************************
*    THIS ROUTINE RESTORES THE PSW STORAGE PROTECTION KEY BACK TO KEY
*    ZERO. THIS IS REQUIRED OR THE SVC ROUTINE WILL ABEND WHEN IT
*    RETURNS CONTROL:
***********************************************************************
*
RSTORKEY MODESET KEY=ZERO           RESTORE KEY VALUE OF SVC
         BR     R8                  RETURN TO CALLING RTN
*
*
***********************************************************************
*    THIS ROUTINE LOADS THE PARAMETER REGISTERS, RESTORES THE RETURN
*    ADDRESS INTO REGISTER 14, AND RETURNS CONTROL TO THE FLIH.
***********************************************************************
*
RETURN   LR     R1,R11              LOAD ALLO CSA ADR IN A PARM REG
         LR     R15,R9              LOAD RC IN A PARM REG
         LR     R14,R12             RESTORE RETURN ADDRESS
         BR     R14                 RETURN TO CALLING PROG VIA FLIH
*
*
***********************************************************************
*    END OF SVC ROUTINE
***********************************************************************
*
          END
```

NOTES:

- The GETMAIN assigns the PSW storage protection key of the caller (the SVC routine) to the allocated virtual storage. The first MODESET macro instruction sets the PSW protection key to that of the calling program. The information comes from the TCBPKF field of the TCB of the calling program. This is done so that the allocated CSA storage is assigned the protection key of the calling program instead of the SVC routine. This is necessary so that the calling program can access the requested CSA storage since that storage is fetch-protected.
- The PSW protection key of the allocated CSA storage can be set directly by using the KEY parameter of a branch-entry GETMAIN macro instruction (discussed in Chapter 13). This method eliminates the need to issue a MODESET macro instruction to change the PSW protection key to that of the calling program and then issue the MODESET macro instruction again to restore the PSW protection key to that of the SVC routine. This method is illustrated in Coding Example 12.6.1B.

The following coding example shows how a program would call the SVC 253, defined in this example, to request a CSA allocation of 100 bytes:

```
         ...
         LA     R0,100              SET LENGTH OF REQ CSA
         SVC    253                 ISSUE SVC TO ALLO CSA
         LTR    R15,R15             CHECK RC
         BNZ    NOCSA               IF BAD, NO CSA AVAIL
         MVC    0(100,R1),CSADATA   IF OK, MOVE DATA INTO CSA
         ...
```

Coding Example 12.6.2B

This coding example is a modification of Coding Example 12.6.2A. This coding example illustrates how to allocate virtual storage from the CSA and set that storage to the same PSW protection key as that of the caller of the SVC routine using the KEY parameter of a branch-entry GETMAIN macro instruction.

```
IGC253   CSECT
*
*
***************************************************************************
*     INITIALIZATION
***************************************************************************
*
         REGEQU EQU=R               DEFINE EQU'S FOR REGISTERS
         USING  *,R6                SETUP ADDRESSABILITY
         USING  TCB,R4              DEFINE REG FOR TCB DSECT
*
*
***************************************************************************
*     MAINSTREAM OF SVC ROUTINE
***************************************************************************
*
         BAL    R8,SAVEREGS         SAVE REGISTERS
         BAL    R8,GETCSA           GET REQUESTED CSA STORAGE
         B      RETURN              RETURN TO CALLING PROG VIA FLIH
*
*
***************************************************************************
*     THIS ROUTINE SAVES THE CONTENTS OF ALL REGISTERS THAT CONTAIN
*     CONTROL INFORMATION.
***************************************************************************
*
SAVEREGS LR     R12,R14             SAVE RETURN ADDRESS
         LR     R10,R0              SAVE REQUESTED LENGTH OF CSA ALLO
         BR     R8                  RETURN TO CALLING RTN
*
*
***************************************************************************
*     THIS ROUTINE ALLOCATES FETCH-PROTECTED VIRTUAL STORAGE FROM THE CSA
*     AND ASSIGNS IT THE PSW STORAGE PROTECTION KEY OF THE CALLER OF THE
*     SVC ROUTINE. THE LENGTH OF THE REQUESTED CSA STORAGE IS SPECIFIED
*     VIA REGISTER 0 BY THE CALLER OF THE SVC. THE SAVEREGS ROUTINE SAVES
*     REGISTER 0 IN REGISTER 10.
***************************************************************************
*
GETCSA   IC     R2,TCBPKF           GET PSW PROT KEY OF CALLER
         GETMAIN RC,LV=(R10),SP=231,BRANCH=YES,KEY=(R2)
         LR     R11,R1              SAVE ADDRESS OF CSA STORAGE
         LR     R9,R15              SAVE RC FROM GETMAIN
         BR     R8                  RETURN TO CALLING RTN
*
*
***************************************************************************
*     THIS ROUTINE LOADS THE PARAMETER REGISTERS, RESTORES THE RETURN
*     ADDRESS INTO REGISTER 14, AND RETURNS CONTROL TO THE FLIH.
***************************************************************************
*
RETURN   LR     R1,R11              LOAD ALLO CSA ADR IN A PARM REG
         LR     R15,R9              LOAD RC IN A PARM REG
         LR     R14,R12             RESTORE RETURN ADDRESS
         BR     R14                 RETURN TO CALLING PROG VIA FLIH
*
```

```
*
************************************************************************
*     THE DSECTS
************************************************************************
*
         IKJTCB                   GENERATES TCB DSECT
*                                 REQR BY BRANCH-ENTRY GETMAIN
*
*
************************************************************************
*     END OF SVC ROUTINE
************************************************************************
*
              END
```

NOTES:

- This coding example is for a type-1 SVC routine. This SVC routine can be converted to a type-2, type-3, or type-4 SVC routine by doing the following:
  - Obtain the LOCAL lock via the SETLOCK macro instruction before the GETMAIN macro instruction is executed. This use of the SETLOCK macro instruction is illustrated in Chapters 10, 13, and 15.
  - For a type-3 and type-4 SVC, change the CSECT name (and load module name) to IGC0025C.

Coding Example 12.6.3

This coding example illustrates the code for an SVC routine that sets the APF-authorization bit for the calling program. The authorization bit is in the Job Step Control Block (JSCB) of the task under which the program executes.

For this SVC routine, the calling program uses registers 0 and 1 as parameter registers. Register 0 contains the authorization on/off indicator: X'00' requests authorization, and X'04' requests that authorization is to be turned off. Since this is a sensitive function, the security used by this SVC routine requires that the calling program load register 1 with a 4-byte password that matches the password that the SVC routine requires before the request can be honored. When the SVC routine returns control, register 15 contains one of the following return codes: X'00' if the request was successful, X'04' if register 0 did not contain the proper authorization indicator, and X'08' if the program passed an invalid password.

```
IGC0025D CSECT
*
*
************************************************************************
*     INITIALIZATION
************************************************************************
*
         REGEQU EQU=R             GENERATE EQU'S FOR REGISTERS
         USING  *,R6              SETUP ADDRESSABILITY
         USING  TCB,R4            DEFINE DSECT REG FOR TCB
         USING  IEZJSCB,R5        DEFINE DSECT REG FOR JSCB
*
*
************************************************************************
*     MAINSTREAM OF SVC ROUTINE
************************************************************************
*
         BAL    R8,SAVEREGS       SAVE REGISTERS
```

```
         BAL   R8,GETJSCB           GET JSCB ADR
         BAL   R8,VERPW             VERIFY PASSWORD FROM CALLER
         BAL   R8,SETAPF            SET REQ APF INDICATOR
         B     RETURN               RETURN TO CALLING PROG VIA FLIH
*
*
***********************************************************************
*     THIS ROUTINE SAVES THE CONTENTS OF ALL REGISTERS THAT CONTAIN
*     CONTROL INFORMATION.
***********************************************************************
*
SAVEREGS LR    R12,R14              SAVE RETURN ADR
         LR    R10,R0               SAVE APF INDICATOR
         LR    R11,R1               SAVE USER SPECIFIED PW
         WTO   '*** SVC 254 ENTERED ***',ROUTCDE=11 FOR TESTING ONLY
         BR    R8                   RETURN TO CALLING RTN
*
*
***********************************************************************
*     THIS ROUTINE OBTAINS THE ADDRESS OF THE JSCB FROM THE TCB.
***********************************************************************
*
GETJSCB  L     R5,TCBJSCB           LOAD JSCB ADR FROM TCB
         BR    R8                   RETURN TO CALLING RTN
*
*
***********************************************************************
*     THIS ROUTINE VERIFIES THE PASSWORD RECEIVED FROM THE CALLER OF THIS
*     SVC ROUTINE. THE PASSWORD IS SPECIFIED IN REGISTER 1. THE SAVEREGS
*     ROUTINE SAVES REGISTER 1 IN REGISTER 11. IF THE PASSWORD IS OK, THEN
*     THE REQUESTED SERVICE IS PERFORMED. IF THE PASSWORD IS INVALID, THEN
*     A RC OF X'08' IS SET, AND CONTROL IS RETURNED TO THE CALLER WITHOUT
*     THE REQUESTED SERVICE BEING PERFORMED.
***********************************************************************
*
VERPW    C     R11,PASSWORD         CHECK CALLER'S PASSWORD
         BER   R8                   IF OK, RET TO CALLING RTN
         LA    R15,8                IF BAD, INDICATE IT
         B     RETURN               RETURN TO CALLING PROG VIA FLIH
*
*
***********************************************************************
*     THIS ROUTINE SETS THE APF BIT AS REQUESTED BY THE CALLER OF THIS SVC
*     ROUTINE. THE REQUESTED ACTION IS SPECIFIED IN REGISTER 0. THE
*     SAVEREGS ROUTINE SAVES REGISTER 0 IN REGISTER 10. A X'00' INDICATES
*     APF ON, A X'04' INDICATES APF OFF. IF THE CALLING PROGRAM SPECIFIES
*     AN INVALID INDICATOR, THEN A RC OF X'04' IS SET AND CONTROL IS
*     RETURNED TO THE CALLER WITHOUT THE REQUESTED SERVICE BEING PERFORMED.
***********************************************************************
*
SETAPF   C     R10,BIN0             CHK IF APF REQ IS FOR "ON"
         BE    SETAON               IF YES, DO IT
         C     R10,BIN4             CHK IF APF REQ IS FOR "OFF"
         BE    SETAOFF              IF YES, DO IT
         LA    R15,4                INDICATE BAD REQ
         BR    R8                   RETURN TO CALLING RTN
SETAON   OI    JSCBOPTS,X'01'       SET APF ON
         WTO   '*** AUTH ON ***',ROUTCDE=11 FOR TESTING ONLY
         LA    R15,0                SET GOOD RC
         BR    R8                   RETURN TO CALLING RTN
SETAOFF  NI    JSCBOPTS,X'FE'       SET APF OFF
         WTO   '*** AUTH OFF ***',ROUTCDE=11 FOR TESTING ONLY
         LA    R15,0                SET GOOD RC CODE
         BR    R8                   RETURN TO CALLING RTN
```

```
*
*
***************************************************************************
*    THIS ROUTINE RESTORES THE RETURN ADDRESS INTO REGISTER 14 AND
*    RETURNS CONTROL TO THE FLIH.
***************************************************************************
*
RETURN   LR   R14,R12              RESTORE RETURN ADR
         BR   R14                  RETURN TO CALLING PROG VIA FLIH
*
*
***************************************************************************
*    CONSTANTS
***************************************************************************
*
BINO     DC   F'0'                 SET APF-ON INDICATOR
BIN4     DC   F'4'                 SET APF-OFF INDICATOR
PASSWORD DC   C'....'              PASSWORD TO USE THIS SVC
*
*
***************************************************************************
*    THE DSECTS
***************************************************************************
*
         PRINT NOGEN
         IKJTCB            GENERATES TCB DSECT
         IEZJSCB           GENERATES JSCB DSECT
*
*
***************************************************************************
*    END OF SVC ROUTINE
***************************************************************************
*
           END
```

The following coding example shows how a program would call the SVC 254, defined in this example, to request authorization:

```
         ...
         LA   R0,0                 SET AUTH-ON REQUEST
         L    R1,PASSWORD          LOAD PW FOR SVC
         SVC  254                  ISSUE SVC TO SET AUTH
         C    R15,BINO             CHECK RC
         BE   AUTHON               IF 0, AUTH ON
         C    R15,BIN4             CHECK RC
         BE   INVAUTH              IF 4, BAD AUTH IND
         B    INVPSWD              IF 8, BAD PW
AUTHON   ...                        PERFORM AUTH FUNCTION
```

Coding Example 12.6.4

This coding example illustrates the code for an SVC routine that fixes/frees pages for the calling program.

For this SVC routine, the calling program uses registers 0 and 1 as parameter registers. Register 0 contains a fix/free indicator: X'00' requests that a specific area of virtual storage be page fixed, and X'04' requests that a specific area of virtual storage, which was previously page fixed by this task, be freed. Register 1 points to a fullword address, which points to two consecutive fullwords. The fullwords contain the starting and ending addresses, respectively, of the virtual storage area that is to be page fixed/freed.

```
IGC0025E CSECT
*
*
***********************************************************************
*    INITIALIZATION
***********************************************************************
*
         REGEQU EQU=R             GENERATE EQU'S FOR REGISTERS
         USING *,R6               SETUP ADDRESSABILITY
*
*
***********************************************************************
*    MAINSTREAM OF SVC ROUTINE
***********************************************************************
*
         BAL  R8,SAVEREGS         SAVE REGISTERS
         BAL  R8,DOREQ            DO PAGE FIX/FREE
         B    RETURN              RETURN TO CALLING PROG VIA FLIH
*
*
***********************************************************************
*    THIS ROUTINE SAVES THE CONTENTS OF ALL REGISTERS THAT CONTAIN
*    CONTROL INFORMATION.
***********************************************************************
*
SAVEREGS LR   R12,R14             SAVE RETURN ADR
         LR   R10,R0              SAVE PG FIX/FREE INDICATOR
         LR   R11,R1              SAVE PG FIX/FREE ADR LIST
         WTO  '*** SVC 255 ENTERED ***',ROUTCDE=11 FOR TESTING ONLY
         BR   R8                  RETURN TO CALLING RTN
*
*
***********************************************************************
*    THIS ROUTINE PERFORMS THE PAGE FIX/FREE AS REQUESTED BY THE CALLER
*    OF THIS SVC ROUTINE. THE REQUESTED ACTION IS SPECIFIED IN REGISTER 0.
*    THE SAVEREGS ROUTINE SAVES REGISTER 0 IN REGISTER 10. A X'00'
*    INDICATES A PAGE FIX, A X'04' INDICATES A PAGE FREE. IF THE CALLING
*    PROGRAM SPECIFIES AN INVALID INDICATOR, THEN A RC OF X'04' IS SET AND
*    CONTROL IS RETURNED TO THE CALLER WITHOUT THE REQUESTED SERVICE BEING
*    PERFORMED. THE BEGINNING AND ENDING ADDRESSES OF THE PAGE FIX/FREE
*    ARE SPECIFIED AS TWO CONSECUTIVE FULLWORDS POINTED TO BY REGISTER 1.
*    THE SAVEREGS ROUTINE SAVES REGISTER 1 IN REGISTER 11.
***********************************************************************
*
DOREQ    L     R2,0(0,R11)        LOAD BG ADR TO FIX/FREE
         L     R9,4(0,R11)        LOAD END ADR TO FIX/FREE
         C     R10,BIN0           CHK FIX/FREE IND
         BE    DOPGFIX            IF 0, DO PAGE FIX
         C     R10,BIN4           CHK FIX/FREE IND
         BE    DOPGFREE           IF 4, DO PAGE FREE
         LA    R15,4              IF NOT 0 OR 4, SET INV IND
         BR    R8                 RETURN TO CALLING RTN
DOPGFIX  PGFIX R,A=(R2),EA=(R9),ECB=0
         BR    R8                RETURN TO CALLING RTN
DOPGFREE PGFREE R,A=(R2),EA=(R9)
         BR    R8                RETURN TO CALLING RTN
*
*
***********************************************************************
*    THIS ROUTINE RESTORES THE RETURN ADDRESS INTO REGISTER 14 AND
*    RETURNS CONTROL TO THE FLIH.
***********************************************************************
*
RETURN   LR   R14,R12             RESTORE RETURN ADR
```

```
          BR    R14                    RETURN TO CALLING PROG VIA FLIH
*
*
**************************************************************************
*    CONSTANTS
**************************************************************************
*
BINO      DC    F'0'                   PAGE FIX INDICATOR
BIN4      DC    F'4'                   PAGE FREE INDICATOR
*
*
**************************************************************************
*    END OF SVC ROUTINE
**************************************************************************
*
             END
```

The following coding example shows how a program would call the SVC 255, defined in this example, to perform a page fix. Registers 10 and 11 contain the beginning and ending addresses, respectively, of the area that is to be page fixed.

```
          ...
          LA    R0,0                   SET PAGE-FIX REQUEST
          ST    R10,BGADDR             STOR BG ADR
          ST    R11,ENDADDR            STOR END ADR
          LA    R1,ADDRSPTR            LOAD ADR OF BG/END ADR-LIST
          SVC   255                    ISSUE SVC TO PAGE FIX
          LTR   R15,R15                CHECK RC
          BNZ   NOPGFIX                IF NON-ZERO, BAD PGFIX
          ...                          PROCESS
ADDRSPTR  DS    0F
BGADDR    DS    F
ENDADDR   DS    F
          ...
```

12.7 INSERTING SVC ROUTINES INTO THE OPERATING SYSTEM

In order for an SVC routine to be executed by MVS, there are two requirements, in addition to the SVC routine being called by a program.

- The SVC number must have a complete entry in the SVC Table. Section 12.2 briefly discussed the procedure for accomplishing this.
- The actual SVC routine must be included in MVS.

If the user-written SVC routines are available before SYSGEN time, then they may be included during the SYSGEN process with the DATASET macro instruction. If the user-written SVC routines are not available before SYSGEN time, then they may be included, when available, after MVS is generated.

Type-1, type-2, and type-6 SVCs are part of the MVS Nucleus (IEANUCxx located in SYS1.NUCLEUS). They may be inserted into the Nucleus, or existing SVC routines may be replaced after SYSGEN by relinkediting the Nucleus and including the required SVC routines. The following is a sample jobstream to include SVC routines 247 and 252 into the MVS Nucleus for an MVS/370 operating system. The required jobstreams for an MVS/XA and an MVS/ESA operating system are similar and can be determined by examining the jobstream used during the SYSGEN process. The JCL DD statements and linkedit IN-

CLUDE control statements, which point to the distribution libraries, are not required when the Nucleus is relinkedited.

```
//jobname   JOB  - - -
//LKEDNUC   EXEC PGM=IEWL,
//          PARM='LIST,XREF,NCAL,SCTR'
//SYSPRINT DD   SYSOUT=*
//SYSUT1    DD   UNIT=SYSDA,SPACE=(CYL,(3,1))
//SVCLIB    DD   DSN=SYS2.SVCLIB,DISP=OLD
//SYSLMOD   DD   DSN=SYS1.NUCLEUS,DISP=OLD,UNIT=SYSDA,VOL=SER=ssssss
//SYSLIN    DD   *
    INSERT IEAVNIPO
    INSERT IEAVFX00
    INCLUDE SVCLIB(IGC247)
    INCLUDE SVCLIB(IGC252)
    INCLUDE SYSLMOD(IEANUC01)
    NAME IEANUC01(R)
//
```

Type-3 and type-4 SVC routines are resident in the Pageable (or optionally Fixed or Modified) Link Pack Area. Load modules that are resident in the PLPA are stored in SYS1.LPALIB. The SVC routines may be placed into SYS1.LPALIB by assembling and linkediting them directly into that library or by linkediting them into a staging library and then, when required, copying them into SYS1.LPALIB. The copy may be performed by using the IBM batch utility program IEBCOPY or by using Option 3.3 of TSO/ISPF/PDF.

In order for MVS to recognize the new or replaced SVCs, MVS must be IPLed. In addition, for SVC types 3 and 4, the parameter CLPA must be specified in response to the IPL message IEA101A (SPECIFY SYSTEM PARAMETERS...).

During IPL time, the entry point addresses of the SVCs are placed in the appropriate SVC entries of the SVC Table.

12.8 DYNAMICALLY LOADING SVC ROUTINES

SVC routines must be incorporated into the operating system before they can be referenced for testing or use. This would normally require an IPL and possibly a rebuilding of the LPA (for type-3 and type-4 SVC routines). However, it is impractical to continually IPL the system while developing a new SVC routine or enhancing an existing one. Each time an error is discovered and corrected, a new version of the SVC routine would need to be incorporated into the system via an IPL before it can be tested again.

However, there is a method that will dynamically incorporate SVC routines into the operating system. This method requires no IPL and can be done as often as is required for testing.

The method involves loading the SVC routine into common addressable storage (CSA or SQA) and storing the address of its entry point into the appropriate location of the SVC Table. The secondary CVT points to the SVC Table. The SVC Table contains 256 8-byte entries. The entries correspond sequentially to SVC number 0 through SVC number 255. The first word of the entry contains the entry point address of the SVC routine, and the second word contains various bit settings, indicating the various SVC characteristics that were specified.

When the SVC routine development is complete, it can then be incorporated into the operating system in the conventional manner.

Coding Example 12.8.1

This coding example illustrates the code for a program that will dynamically load an SVC routine into the CSA and update the SVC Table. This program will function properly only for the MVS/370 operating system. The MVS/XA and MVS/ESA version of the program is presented in Coding Example 12.8.2.

The program references the JCL PARM data, which contains the SVC number, and the member name of the SVC routine, contained in the specified load library, that is to be dynamically loaded. The SVC routine is assumed to be a type-3.

```
LOADSVC CSECT
*
*
***********************************************************************
*     INITIALIZATION
***********************************************************************
*
         INITL 3,EQU=R               INITIALIZE PROGRAM
         USING CVT,R10               DEFINE REG FOR CVT DSECT
         USING SCVTSECT,R11          DEFINE REG FOR SEC CVT DSECT
         USING SVCENTRY,R12          DEFINE REG FOR SVC TBL ENTRY DSECT
*
*
***********************************************************************
*    MAINSTREAM OF PROGRAM
***********************************************************************
*
         BAL   R6,GETPARM            EXTRACT PARM DATA
         BAL   R6,VERSVCNO           VERIFY SVC NUMBER
         BAL   R6,CNVSVCNO           CONVERT SVC NUMBER TO BINARY
         BAL   R6,SETMODE            SET PROGRAM TO SUPV STATE, KEY ZERO
         BAL   R6,LDNEWSVC           LOAD NEW SVC INTO CSA
         BAL   R6,GETSVCTA           GET SVC TABLE ADR
         BAL   R6,SETNWSVC           STORE NEW SVC EPA INTO SVC TBL
         BAL   R6,WTOR               REQUEST OPER DELETE OF NEW SVC
         B     RETURN                RETURN TO MVS OR CALLING PROGRAM
*
*
***********************************************************************
*    THIS ROUTINE OBTAINS THE SPECIFIED SVC NUMBER AND SVC ROUTINE NAME
*    FROM THE PARM PARAMETER OF THE JCL EXEC STATEMENT.
***********************************************************************
*
GETPARM  L     R1,0(0,R1)            LOAD ADR OF JCL PARM AREA
         LH    R15,0(0,R1)           LOAD LEN OF SPECIFIED PARM
         LTR   R15,R15               CHK IF PARM SPECIFIED
         BZ    NOPARM                IF LEN=0, NO PARM SPECIFIED
         BCTR  R15,0                 DECR PARM LEN FOR EX INSTR
         EX    R15,MOVE              MOVE PARM INTO PROC AREA
         BR    R6                    RETURN TO CALLING RTN
MOVE     MVC   SVCINFO(0),2(R1)      MOVE INSTR FOR EX
NOPARM   WTO   '*** SVC NUMBER AND NAME NOT SPECIFIED—PROGRAM TERMINA-
               TED ***',ROUTCDE=11
         ABEND 901
*
*
***********************************************************************
*    THIS ROUTINE VERIFIES THAT THE SPECIFIED SVC NUMBER IS A DECIMAL
*    NUMBER FROM 200 THROUGH 255.
***********************************************************************
*
```

```
VERSVCNO LA   R0,3                SET NUMB OF DIGITS IN SVC NUMB
         LA   R10,DECSVCNO        LD ADR OF AREA WITH SVC NUMB
NXTSVCDG CLI  0(R10),C'0'         CHK IF A DIGIT IS LESS THAN 0
         BL   INVSVCNO            IF YES, INVALID SVC NUMB
         CLI  0(R10),C'9'         CHK IF A DIGIT IS MORE THAN 9
         BH   INVSVCNO            IF YES, INVALID SVC NUMB
         LA   R10,1(0,R10)        INCR TO NEXT SVC NUMB DIGIT
         BCT  R0,NXTSVCDG         CHK NEXT DIGIT UNTIL ALL 3 CHECKED
         CLC  DECSVCNO,=C'200'    CHK IF SVC NUMB IS LESS THAN 200
         BL   INVSVCNO            IF YES, INVALID SVC NUMB
         CLC  DECSVCNO,=C'255'    CHK IF SVC NUMB IS GREATER THAN 255
         BH   INVSVCNO            IF YES, INVALID SVC NUMB
         BR   R6                  RETURN TO CALLING RTN
INVSVCNO WTO  '*** INVALID SVC NUMBER SPECIFIED—PROGRAM TERMINATED *-
              **',ROUTCDE=11
         ABEND 902
*
*
***********************************************************************
*    THIS ROUTINE CONVERTS THE SPECIFIED DECIMAL SVC NUMBER INTO BINARY.
***********************************************************************
*
CNVSVCNO PACK PKSVCNO,DECSVCNO    PACK SPEC ZONED DEC SVC NUMB
         CVB  R10,PKSVCNO         CONV SVC NUMB INTO BINARY
         ST   R10,SVCNUM          STORE BIN SVC NUMB
         BR   R6                  RETURN TO CALLING RTN
*
*
***********************************************************************
*    THIS ROUTINE PUTS THE TASK INTO SUPERVISOR STATE AND PSW PROTECTION
*    KEY ZERO VIA THE MODESET MACRO. THIS IS REQUIRED TO MODIFY THE
*    SVC TABLE.
***********************************************************************
*
SETMODE  MODESET MODE=SUP,KEY=ZERO
         BR   R6                  RETURN TO CALLING RTN
*
*
***********************************************************************
*    THIS ROUTINE LOADS THE NEW SVC ROUTINE INTO CSA. THE LOAD MACRO
*    SPECIFIES THAT ONLY THE LIBRARY POINTED TO BY THE DDNAME SPECIFIED
*    IN THE SVCLIB DCB IS TO BE SEARCHED FOR THE NEW SVC ROUTINE.
***********************************************************************
*
LDNEWSVC BAL  R7,OPENLIB          OPEN LOADLIB FOR LOAD MACRO
         LOAD EPLOC=SVCNAME,GLOBAL=(YES,P),DCB=SVCLIB,LSEARCH=YES
         ST   R0,SVCEPA           SAVE EP ADR OF NEW SVC
         BAL  R7,CLOSELIB         CLOSE LOADLIB
         BR   R6                  RETURN TO CALLING RTN
*
*
***********************************************************************
*    THIS ROUTINE OPENS THE LIBRARY THAT CONTAINS THE NEW SVC ROUTINE.
***********************************************************************
*
OPENLIB  OPEN SVCLIB              OPEN PRIV LOADLIB THAT HAS SVC RTN
         BR   R7                  RETURN TO CALLING RTN
*
*
***********************************************************************
*    THIS ROUTINE CLOSES THE LIBRARY THAT CONTAINS THE NEW SVC ROUTINE.
***********************************************************************
*
CLOSELIB CLOSE SVCLIB             CLOSE PRIV LOADLIB
```

```
         BR    R7                    RETURN TO CALLING RTN
*
*
***********************************************************************
*     THIS ROUTINE OBTAINS THE ADDRESS OF THE SVCTABLE.
***********************************************************************
*
GETSVCTA L     R10,16·               LOAD CVT ADR INTO REG 10
         L     R11,CVTABEND          LOAD SEC CVT ADR INTO REG 11
         L     R10,SCVTSVCT          LOAD SVC TABLE ADR INTO REG 10
         BR    R6                    RETURN TO CALLING RTN
*
*
***********************************************************************
*     THIS ROUTINE PUTS THE ENTRY POINT ADDRESS OF THE NEW SVC ROUTINE
*     INTO THE PROPER ENTRY IN THE SVCTABLE AND INDICATES THAT THE SVC
*     ROUTINE IS A TYPE-3 SVC.
***********************************************************************
*
SETNWSVC L     R11,SVCNUM            LOAD BIN SVC NUM INTO REG 11
         SLL   R11,3                 MULT SVC NUM BY 8 (SVCTBL ENTRY LEN)
         LA    R12,0(R11,R10)        LOAD REG 12 WITH REQ SVC TBL ENTRY
         MVC   SVCEP,SVCEPA          LOAD NEW SVC EPA INTO SVC TBL ENTRY
         MVI   SVCATTR1,SVCTP34      FORCE TYPE-3 SVC INTO SVC TBL ENTRY
         BR    R6                    RETURN TO CALLING RTN
*
*
***********************************************************************
*     THIS ROUTINE CONTROLS THE DURATION IN WHICH THE NEW SVC ROUTINE IS
*     ACTIVE. THE NEW SVC ROUTINE REMAINS ACCESSIBLE UNTIL "D" IS REPLIED
*     TO THE OUTSTANDING WTOR MESSAGE.
***********************************************************************
*
WTOR     XC    ECB,ECB               CLEAR ECB FOR WTOR MACRO
         WTOR '*** REPLY "D" TO DELETE NEW SVC',REPLY,1,ECB
         WAIT 1,ECB=ECB              WAIT FOR REPLY
         CLI   REPLY,C'D'            CHK REPLY
         BER   R6                    IF OK, RETURN TO CALLING RTN
         WTO   '*** INVALID REPLY ***'
         B     WTOR                  REISSUE WTOR MACRO
*
*
***********************************************************************
*     THIS ROUTINE RESTORES THE REGISTERS AND RETURNS CONTROL.
***********************************************************************
*
RETURN   RCNTL RC=0                  RETURN TO MVS OR CALLING PROG
*
*
***********************************************************************
*     DC/DS STATEMENTS
***********************************************************************
*
PKSVCNO  DS    D
SVCNUM   DS    F
SVCEPA   DS    F
ECB      DS    F
SVCINFO  DS    0CL12
DECSVCNO DS    CL3
         DS    CL1
SVCNAME  DC    CL8' '
REPLY    DS    CL1
*
*
```

```
***********************************************************************
*    THE DCB FOR THE SVC ROUTINE LIBRARY USED BY THE LOAD MACRO
***********************************************************************
*
SVCLIB   DCB  DSORG=PO,MACRF=R,DDNAME=SVCLIB
*
*
***********************************************************************
*    THE DSECTS
***********************************************************************
*
         PRINT NOGEN
         CVT   DSECT=YES          GENERATES CVT DSECT
         IHASCVT                  GENERATES SECONDARY CVT DSECT
         IHASVC                   GENERATES SVC TBL ENTRY DSECT
*
*
***********************************************************************
*    END OF PROGRAM
***********************************************************************
*
               END
```

NOTES:

- The format of the JCL PARM data is:

  ```
  PARM='sss,nnnnnnnn'
  ```

  where: sss is the 3-digit SVC number, and nnnnnnnn is the 1- to 8-character name of the load library member containing the SVC routine. The member name need not adhere to the SVC naming convention.

  Example:

  ```
  //LOADSVC EXEC PGM=LOADSVC,PARM='255,IGC0025E'
  ```

- The above information should be documented in the prologue of the program.
- This program must be authorized.
- The DCB and the LSEARCH parameters of the LOAD macro instruction are used; therefore, only the library pointed to by the ddname SVCLIB is searched for the SVC routine. This library must be included in the JCL and must be authorized.
- The GLOBAL=(YES,P) parameter of the LOAD macro instruction indicates that the SVC routine is to be loaded into pageable storage of the CSA. Replacing P with F would load the SVC into fixed storage of the CSA.
- Since the SVC routine is loaded into the CSA via the LOAD macro instruction, the SVC routine is implicitly deleted (for MVS/370 only) and the occupied CSA storage is set to binary zeros when the LOADSVC program terminates. Any further attempts to execute the SVC instruction to call that SVC routine will result in a S0C1 ABEND. The WTOR macro instruction controls the duration that the SVC routine will be available for testing.

  If it is desirable to make the SVC routine available for the life of the IPL without an outstanding WTOR, then the following method can be used:

  - LOAD the SVC routine into the virtual storage of the address space of the executing load program (omit GLOBAL parameter).
  - GETMAIN CSA virtual storage equal to the size of the SVC routine (returned in register 1 from the LOAD macro instruction).
  - Use the MVCL instruction to copy the SVC routine from the Private Area into the CSA.

- Update the EPA field of the SVC table entry with the address of the allocated storage from the CSA (the first byte of the SVC routine must be the entry point).
- With this method, if the SVC routine is to be replaced with a different version during the same IPL, then it is the user's responsibility to explicitly release the CSA storage with the FREEMAIN macro instruction and reallocate CSA storage equal to the size of the replacing SVC routine.

- The message generated from the WTOR macro instruction could be more descriptive if the phrase "NEW SVC" is changed to "SVC-nnn", where nnn is the actual decimal number of the SVC routine.
- This program forces a type-3 SVC indication in the SVC table entry, but the execution logic for all SVC types can be tested. However, using this method does require special considerations for the testing of type-1 and type-6 SVCs. A type-1 SVC (since it is being tested as a type-3 SVC) will not receive control with the local lock held. If this condition is required for a successful test, then the SETLOCK macro instruction can be used to obtain that lock during the test. A type-6 SVC (since it is being tested as a type-3 SVC) will not receive control disabled and may not use the T6EXIT macro instruction to return control. If any or both of these conditions are required for a successful test, then this method cannot be used to test that particular SVC.

Coding Example 12.8.2

This coding example contains the program that was presented in Coding Example 12.8.1, with the required modifications to enable it to function under MVS/XA and MVS/ESA. In MVS/XA and MVS/ESA, the SVC Table is stored in the page protected section (which is located above the 16 Mb line) of the Nucleus. Page protection is implemented by turning on the page-protected bit in the Page Table entry of the page that is to be protected. Virtual storage, which is page protected, cannot be modified by a program regardless of its PSW protection key. In order to modify the SVC Table, the SVCUPDTE macro instruction is provided for both MVS/XA and MVS/ESA. The SVCUPDTE macro instruction was discussed in Chapter 10.

```
LOADSVC2 CSECT
*
*
***********************************************************************
*     INITIALIZATION
***********************************************************************
*
         INITL 3,EQU=R
*
*
***********************************************************************
*     MAINSTREAM OF PROGRAM
***********************************************************************
*
         BAL   R6,GETPARM          EXTRACT PARM DATA
         BAL   R6,VERSVCNO         VERIFY SVC NUMBER
         BAL   R6,CNVSVCNO         CONVERT SVC NUMBER TO BINARY
         BAL   R6,SETMODE          SET PROGRAM TO SUPV STATE, KEY ZERO
         BAL   R6,LDNEWSVC         LOAD NEW SVC INTO CSA
         BAL   R6,SETNWSVC         STORE NEW SVC EPA INTO SVC TBL
         B     RETURN              RETURN TO MVS OR CALLING PROGRAM
*
*
***********************************************************************
```

```
*    THIS ROUTINE OBTAINS THE SPECIFIED SVC NUMBER AND SVC ROUTINE NAME
*    FROM THE PARM PARAMETER OF THE JCL EXEC STATEMENT.
***********************************************************************
*
GETPARM  L     R1,0(0,R1)          LOAD ADR OF JCL PARM AREA
         LH    R15,0(0,R1)         LOAD LEN OF SPECIFIED PARM
         LTR   R15,R15             CHK IF PARM SPECIFIED
         BZ    NOPARM              IF LEN=0, NO PARM SPECIFIED
         BCTR  R15,0               DECR PARM LEN FOR EX INSTR
         EX    R15,MOVE            MOVE PARM INTO PROC AREA
         BR    R6                  RETURN TO CALLING RTN
MOVE     MVC   SVCINFO(0),2(R1)    MOVE INSTR FOR EX
NOPARM   WTO   '*** SVC NUMBER AND NAME NOT SPECIFIED---PROGRAM TERMINA-
               TED  ***',ROUTCDE=11
         ABEND 901
*
*
***********************************************************************
*    THIS ROUTINE VERIFIES THAT THE SPECIFIED SVC NUMBER IS A DECIMAL
*    NUMBER FROM 200 THROUGH 255.
***********************************************************************
*
VERSVCNO LA    R0,3                SET NUMB OF DIGITS IN SVC NUMB
         LA    R10,DECSVCNO        LD ADR OF AREA WITH SVC NUMB
NXTSVCDG CLI   0(R10),C'0'         CHK IF A DIGIT IS LESS THAN 0
         BL    INVSVCNO            IF YES, INVALID SVC NUMB
         CLI   0(R10),C'9'         CHK IF A DIGIT IS MORE THAN 9
         BH    INVSVCNO            IF YES, INVALID SVC NUMB
         LA    R10,1(0,R10)        INCR TO NEXT SVC NUMB DIGIT
         BCT   R0,NXTSVCDG         CHK NEXT DIGIT UNTIL ALL 3 CHECKED
         CLC   DECSVCNO,=C'200'    CHK IF SVC NUMB IS LESS THAN 200
         BL    INVSVCNO            IF YES, INVALID SVC NUMB
         CLC   DECSVCNO,=C'255'    CHK IF SVC NUMB IS GREATER THAN 255
         BH    INVSVCNO            IF YES, INVALID SVC NUMB
         BR    R6                  RETURN TO CALLING RTN
INVSVCNO WTO   '*** INVALID SVC NUMBER SPECIFIED---PROGRAM TERMINATED **  -
               *',ROUTCDE=11
         ABEND 902
*
*
***********************************************************************
*    THIS ROUTINE CONVERTS THE SPECIFIED DECIMAL SVC NUMBER INTO BINARY.
***********************************************************************
*
CNVSVCNO PACK  PKSVCNO,DECSVCNO    PACK SPECIFIED ZONED DEC SVC NUMB
         CVB   R10,PKSVCNO         CONV SVC NUMB INTO BINARY
         ST    R10,SVCNUM          SAVE BIN SVC NUMB
         BR    R6                  RETURN TO CALLING RTN
*
*
***********************************************************************
*    THIS ROUTINE PUTS THE TASK INTO SUPERVISOR STATE AND PSW PROTECTION
*    KEY ZERO VIA THE MODESET MACRO. THIS IS REQUIRED TO ISSUE THE
*    SVCUPDTE MACRO.
***********************************************************************
*
SETMODE  MODESET MODE=SUP,KEY=ZERO
         BR    R6                  RETURN TO CALLING RTN
*
*
***********************************************************************
*    THIS ROUTINE LOADS THE NEW SVC ROUTINE INTO CSA. THE LOAD MACRO
*    SPECIFIES THAT ONLY THE LIBRARY POINTED TO BY THE DDNAME SPECIFIED
*    IN THE SVCLIB DCB IS TO BE SEARCHED FOR THE NEW SVC ROUTINE.
```

```
***********************************************************************
*
LDNEWSVC BAL  R7,OPENLIB          OPEN LOADLIB FOR LOAD MACRO
         LOAD EPLOC=SVCNAME,GLOBAL=(YES,P),DCB=SVCLIB,LSEARCH=YES
         ST   R0,SVCEPA           SAVE EP ADR OF NEW SVC
         BAL  R7,CLOSELIB         CLOSE LOADLIB
         BR   R6                  RETURN TO CALLING RTN
*
*
***********************************************************************
*    THIS ROUTINE OPENS THE LIBRARY THAT CONTAINS THE NEW SVC ROUTINE.
***********************************************************************
*
OPENLIB  OPEN SVCLIB              OPEN PRIV LOADLIB THAT HAS SVC RTN
         BR   R7                  RETURN TO CALLING RTN
*
*
***********************************************************************
*    THIS ROUTINE CLOSES THE LIBRARY THAT CONTAINS THE NEW SVC ROUTINE.
***********************************************************************
*
CLOSELIB CLOSE SVCLIB             CLOSE PRIV LOADLIB
         BR    R7                 RETURN TO CALLING RTN
*
*
***********************************************************************
*    THIS ROUTINE ISSUES THE SVCUPDTE MACRO TO PUT THE ENTRY POINT ADDRESS
*    OF THE NEW SVC ROUTINE INTO THE PROPER ENTRY IN THE SVC TABLE AND TO
*    INDICATE THAT THE SVC ROUTINE IS A TYPE-3 SVC.
***********************************************************************
*
SETNWSVC L    R10,SVCEPA          LOAD EP ADR OF SVC RTN
         L    R11,SVCNUM          LOAD SVC NUMBER
         ENQ  (QNAME,RNAME,E,,SYSTEM)
         SVCUPDTE (R11),REPLACE,TYPE=3,EP=(R10)
         DEQ  (QNAME,RNAME,,SYSTEM)
         LTR  R15,R15             CHK IF SVC TBL UPDATE OK
         BZR  R6                  IF YES, RET TO CALLING RTN
         WTO  '*** ERROR UPDATING SVC TABLE---PROGRAM TERMINATED ***'
         ABEND 903,DUMP
*
*
***********************************************************************
*    THIS ROUTINE RESTORES THE REGISTERS AND RETURNS CONTROL.
***********************************************************************
*
RETURN   RCNTL RC=0               RETURN TO MVS OR CALLING PROG
*
*
***********************************************************************
*    DC/DS STATEMENTS
***********************************************************************
*
PKSVCNO  DS   D
SVCNUM   DS   F
SVCEPA   DS   F
SVCINFO  DS   0CL12
DECSVCNO DS   CL3
         DS   CL1
SVCNAME  DC   CL8' '
*
*
***********************************************************************
*    QNAME/RNAME FOR ENQ/DEQ FOR SVCUPDTE MACRO
```

```
***********************************************************************
*
QNAME    DC   CL8'SYSZSVC'
RNAME    DC   C'TABLE'
*
*
***********************************************************************
*    THE DCB FOR THE SVC ROUTINE LIBRARY USED BY THE LOAD MACRO
***********************************************************************
*
SVCLIB   DCB  DSORG=PO,MACRF=R,DDNAME=SVCLIB
*
*
***********************************************************************
*    THE DSECTS
***********************************************************************
*
         CVT  DSECT=YES          GENERATES CVT DSECT REQUIRED BY
*                                SVCUPDTE MACRO INSTRUCTION
*
*
***********************************************************************
*    END OF PROGRAM
***********************************************************************
*
           END
```

BIBLIOGRAPHY FOR CHAPTER 12

The following IBM manuals contain reference material for the topics discussed in this chapter.

ID	TITLE
GC28-1046	*OS/VS2 SPL: Supervisor*
GC28-1047	*OS/VS2 SPL: Debugging Handbook Volume 1*
GC28-1150	*MVS/XA SPL: System Macros and Facilities Volume 1*
GC28-1151	*MVS/XA SPL: System Macros and Facilities Volume 2*
LC28-1164	*MVS/XA Debugging Handbook Volume 1*
GC28-1852	*MVS/ESA SPL: Application Development Guide*
GC28-1857	*MVS/ESA SPL: Application Development Macro Reference*
LY28-1011	*MVS/ESA Diagnosis: System Reference*

13

Using the MVS Common Area

This chapter discusses the areas that comprise the MVS Common Area. The discussion includes the contents and uses of the individual areas of the Common Area and the required programming to gain access to these areas.

13.1 WHAT IS THE COMMON AREA?

In MVS/370, the Common Area is allocated from the top of virtual storage. From the top down they are the System Queue Area (SQA), the Pageable Link Pack Area (PLPA), and the Common Service Area (CSA). The Common Area may also optionally contain the Modified Link Pack Area (MLPA) and the Pageable BLDL Table; but those areas not discussed. Most of the discussion in this chapter will focus on the CSA.

In MVS/XA and MVS/ESA, the Common Area is comprised of the same areas. However, each of these areas has an additional part called an extended area. The Common Area straddles the 16 Mb line. The SQA, PLPA, and CSA are allocated below the 16 Mb line and the SQA/E, PLPA/E, and CSA/E are allocated above the 16 Mb line.

13.2 CONTENTS OF THE COMMON AREA

This section describes the contents of the System Queue Area, the Pageable Link Pack Area, and the Common Service Area.

THE SYSTEM QUEUE AREA

The SQA contains various MVS system control blocks, tables, and queues that are used by the entire system. Examples include the page tables that define the System Area and Common Area; the ASCBs of all address spaces; The TCCWs, which are used to perform CCW translation; the I/O control blocks IOQs and RQEs; the CSCBs and CIBs, which are used to process commands; and so on. All pages in the SQA are long-term fixed; therefore, the SQA is non-pageable. The SQA may also be used to contain user-defined data. Access to the SQA is limited to programs that execute in supervisor state and PSW storage protection key zero.

THE PAGEABLE LINK PACK AREA

he PLPA contains reentrant programs that are required to be executed by multiple tasks concurrently. Non-reentrant programs may not reside in the PLPA. The PLPA is pageable, but only page-ins are performed in this area. No page-outs are performed; therefore, any modifications made to programs residing in the PLPA will be lost. Programs that modify themselves can also cause integrity problems since they may be executed concurrently by other tasks. In MVS/XA and MVS/ESA, the PLPA is page-protected; if a program attempts to modify itself while resident there, the result will be an S0C4 ABEND. Optionally, the MLPA may not be page-protected. Examples of programs that reside in the PLPA are type-3 and type-4 SVC routines, access method routines, other system programs, and selected user programs.

THE COMMON SERVICE AREA

The CSA contains both system and user-data that may be fixed or pageable. The major use of CSA is to contain user-data that is required across address spaces; therefore, access to the CSA is less restrictive than it is for the SQA. Since the CSA is easily accessible by all address spaces, its primary use is for inter-address space communications. Subsystems and program products (both IBM and non-IBM) that are required to service multiple address spaces use CSA to store data. For example, VTAM uses CSA for its control blocks and buffers.

13.3 REQUIREMENTS TO USE THE COMMON AREA

This section decribes the requirements to use the Pageable Link Pack Area, and the CSA and SQA.

THE PAGEABLE LINK PACK AREA

Users may place nonsystem reentrant programs or type-3 and type-4 SVC routines into the PLPA by linkediting or copying them into the MVS system library SYS1.LPALIB and then IPLing MVS with the system parameter CLPA, specified in response to message IEA101A (SPECIFY SYSTEM PARAMETERS...).

Writing reentrant programs was discussed in Chapter 5 and writing SVC routines was discussed in Chapter 12.

Care should be taken as to which and how many user programs are placed into the PLPA. Programs that reside in the PLPA are accessible to all tasks, which may not be desirable if the functions of such programs are to be restricted to certain users. Also, an increase in the size of the PLPA causes a corresponding decrease in the size of the Private Area.

THE CSA AND THE SQA

In order to use the CSA or the SQA, a program must first allocate virtual storage in that area. This is accomplished by issuing the GETMAIN macro instruction (discussed in Chapter 4) with the appropriate subpool number specified and, optionally, other parameters that were not discussed in Chapter 4.

There are four subpool numbers associated with the CSA and five (only two for MVS/370) associated with the SQA. Table 13.3.1 lists those subpool numbers together with their characteristics.

Table 13.3.1

This table contains the subpool numbers and their characteristics for the CSA and the SQA.

CSA SUBPOOLS

Number	Protection	Storage	Storage Protection key
227	Fetch-protected	Fixed	PSW protection key of requesting program or user-assigned
228	Not fetch-protected	Fixed	PSW protection key of requesting program or user-assigned
231	Fetch-protected	Pageable	PSW protection key of requesting program or user-assigned
241	Not fetch-protected	Pageable	PSW protection key of requesting program or user-assigned

SQA SUBPOOLS

Number	Protection	Storage	Storage Protection key
226	Not fetch-protected	Fixed below 16 Mb	Always zero
239*	Read/write access only in Superviser State, PSW key zero	Fixed	Always zero
245	Not fetch-protected	Fixed	Always zero
247	Read/write access only in supervisor state, PSW key zero	Fixed above 16 Mb	Always zero
248	Not fetch-protected	Fixed above 16 Mb	Always zero

* This subpool is logically in the SQA, but is actually located in the CSA. This subpool is used when the SQA is full and additional SQA storage is required.

NOTES:

- The SQA subpool numbers 226, 247, and 248 are defined only for MVS/XA and MVS/ESA (they did not exist in MVS/370).
- The allocation of CSA storage above or below the 16 Mb line is determined by the LOC parameter (discussed in Chapter 14) of the GETMAIN macro instruction.
- The allocation of SQA storage above or below the 16 Mb line is determined by the LOC parameter of the GETMAIN macro instruction for subpools 239 and 245 (pre-MVS/XA subpools), and determined by the subpool number for the other subpools.

Fetch-protected means that the virtual storage in that particular subpool cannot be read unless the task is executing in the same protection key as the one that is assigned to the storage. If the virtual storage is not fetch-protected, then any task can read the data. In either case, a task cannot write to the CSA unless it is executing in the same protection key as that assigned to the storage.

Only authorized programs (APF-authorized or executing in PSW protection key 0–7 or executing in supervisor state) may allocate storage from the CSA or the SQA.

Storage allocated from the CSA or the SQA will remain allocated for the life of the IPL. When the storage is no longer required, it should be explicitly released via the FREEMAIN macro instruction.

The CSA is a better choice than the SQA for allocating storage for user-data that is to be accessed by other user or application programs. This is true because the SQA is non-pageable, access to it is restricted only to programs that execute in supervisor state and PSW protection key zero, and the SQA contains sensitive MVS control information. Most user-data may be pageable; therefore, using SQA for pageable data is an inefficient use of real storage frames. Since access to SQA is permitted only to supervisor state and PSW protection key zero programs, then any user program that requires to access that data must execute in supervisor state and PSW protection key zero. This is impractical and may cause serious integrity and security problems due to the sensitive MVS control information that is stored in the SQA and due to the freedom that such programs have. The only requirement for a user task to read/write CSA storage is to execute in the same protection key as that assigned to the storage. If a particular allocation of CSA storage is to be read-only, then the CSA storage could be allocated from a non-fetch-protected subpool (228 or 241) and set to key zero.

There are two types of entries into GETMAIN/FREEMAIN processing. One is the normal SVC-entry and the other is the branch-entry. The branch-entry requires some additional setup by the user but saves system overhead and, therefore, is more efficient. The branch-entry GETMAIN/FREEMAIN may be used by programs only if they are executing in supervisor state and PSW key zero, and the branch-entry must be used by programs that cannot issue an SVC instructions such as type-1 and type-6 SVC routines and programs executing in SRB mode. The branch-entry GETMAIN may also be used to set the protection key of the allocated storage to a number other than that of the PSW protection key of the issuing program.

The branch-entry provides two entry points into Virtual Storage Management (VSM). One of the entries is requested by specifying the BRANCH=YES parameter in the operand of the GETMAIN macro instruction. This branch-entry requires that the issuing program hold the LOCAL lock, register 4 be loaded with the address of the TCB, and register 7 be loaded with the address of the ASCB. Any subpool number may be requested with this branch-entry. Also, if storage is requested via the RC, RU, VRC, or VRU specification of the GETMAIN macro instruction, then the contents of register 3 are destroyed by the macro expansion. This branch-entry is well suited for SVC routines since they receive control with registers 4 and 7 preloaded with the addresses of the TCB and the ASCB, respectively, of the calling program. Type-1 SVC routines also receive control with the LOCAL lock held. If a problem program (or a type-2, type-3, or type-4 SVC routine) desires to use this branch-entry, then it must issue the SETLOCK macro instruction to obtain the LOCAL lock. Chapter 5 shows some methods by which a problem program can obtain the addresses of its TCB and its ASCB.

The other branch-entry is for allocating storage only in the CSA and the SQA and is requested by specifying the BRANCH=(YES,GLOBAL) parameter in the operand of the GETMAIN macro instruction. This branch-entry does not require that the LOCAL lock be held or that registers 4 and 7 be preloaded with the addresses of the TCB and the ASCB, but it does require that the issuing program execute while the CPU is disabled for interruptions. This form of the GETMAIN macro instruction must be specified with an RC, RU, VRC, or VRU request, and the macro expansion destroys the contents of registers 3 and 4. This branch-entry is suited for type-6 SVC routines, which receive control with the CPU disabled for interruptions. If a problem program desires to use this branch-entry (not recommended), then it must run disabled and issue the SETLOCK macro instruction to obtain the CPU lock.

Since the CSA and the SQA is common across address spaces, the allocation of it must be serialized among all requestors. The serialization is accomplished with the use of the system locking mechanism. When the storage is allocated via an SVC-entry GETMAIN or branch-entry GETMAIN, Virtual Storage Management (VSM) automatically obtains the appropriate lock. In MVS/370 and MVS/XA, the SALLOC lock is obtained. In MVS/ESA, the VSMFIX lock is obtained for SQA and fixed CSA, and the VSMPAG lock is obtained for pagable CSA.

After the storage is allocated from the CSA, some convention must be developed to provide the address of the allocated storage to all the users who are to reference that storage. One method is to make use of the CVTUSER field in the CVT. This is a 4-byte field that is available to the user. The address of the allocated storage can be placed into this field. Since the CVT is not fetch-protected, the field may be read by any task. However, if there is more than one storage area allocated from the CSA, then CVTUSER must be set up to accommodate all of them. This can be accomplished by setting CVTUSER to point to a list in the CSA. The recommendation is to define each entry in the list as two fullwords. The first word contains some type of ID or description code, indicating the contents or use of the allocated area of the CSA. The second word contains the actual address of allocated CSA storage for that particular use. The list contains one entry for each allocated area, followed by an entry of binary zeros (or ones) to indicate the end of the list. Figure 13.3.1 illustrates the suggested contents of the list pointed to by CVTUSER.

The address is usually placed into the CVTUSER field by a user-written program that allocates virtual storage from the CSA large enough to accommodate all the required entries in the list (and perhaps a few spare entries). This program executes after each IPL (and on demand after that). The individual users allocate an area from the CSA and place that address into the second word of the appropriate list-entry. The reference ID of that area is placed into the first word of that list-entry. When the list is being modified, the ENQ/DEQ mechanism

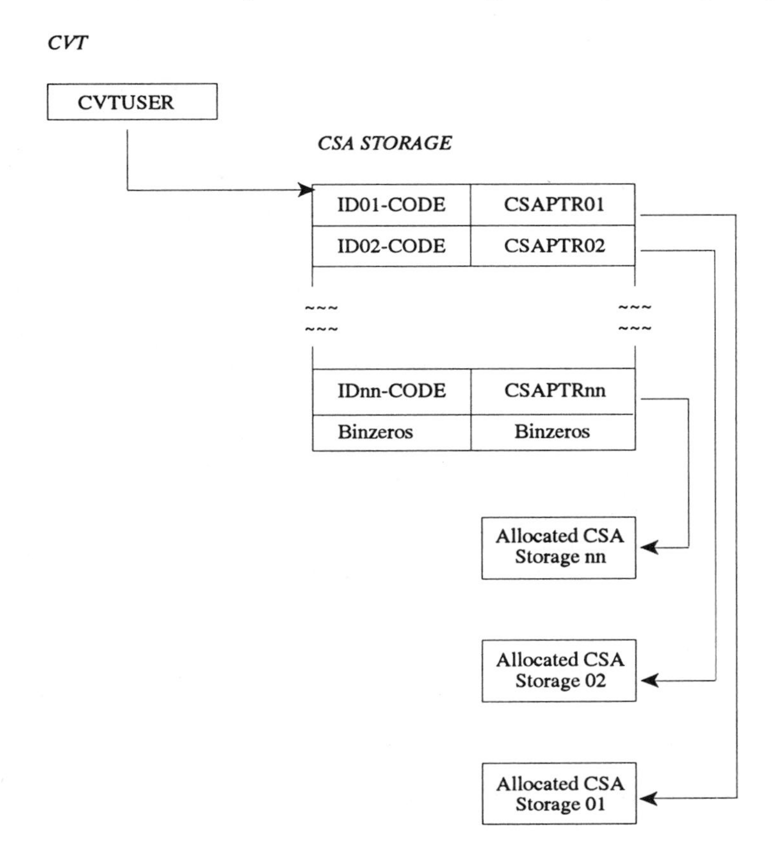

Figure 13.3.1. This figure illustrates the suggested contents of the CSA-use list pointed to by CVTUSER.

should be used to maintain the integrity of the list. Each user can be assigned a fixed position in the list or can scan the list and use the first available entry in the list (the better method).

13.4 CODING EXAMPLES OF USING THE CSA

The following coding examples illustrates how to allocate virtual storage from the Common Service Area using the SVC-entry and the branch-entry forms of the GETMAIN macro instruction.

Coding Example 13.4.1

This coding example illustrates how to allocate virtual storage from the CSA, using the SVC-entry form of the GETMAIN macro instruction.

```
ALLOCSA1 CSECT
*
*
***********************************************************************
*    INITIALIZATION
***********************************************************************
*
         INITL 3,EQU=R               INITIALIZE PROGRAM
         USING R10,CVT               DEFINE REG FOR CVT DSECT
*
*
***********************************************************************
*    MAINSTREAM OF PROGRAM
***********************************************************************
*
         BAL   R6,GETCSA             ALLOC STORAGE FROM CSA
         BAL   R6,SETMODE            SET PROG INTO SUPV STATE, KEY ZERO
         BAL   R6,SETCVT             PUT CSA STRG ADR INTO CVT USER FLD
         B     RETURN                RETURN TO MVS OR CALLING PROG
*
*
***********************************************************************
*    THIS ROUTINE ALLOCATES NON-FETCH-PROTECTED VIRTUAL STORAGE FROM THE
*    CSA AND ASSIGNS IT THE SAME PSW PROTECTION KEY AS THE ISSUING TASK.
***********************************************************************
*
GETCSA   GETMAIN EC,LV=2048,SP=241,A=CSAADR
         LTR   R15,R15               CHECK FOR SUCCESSFUL GETMAIN
         BNZ   NOCSA                 IF NON-ZERO, CSA STRG NOT AVAIL
         BR    R6                    RETURN TO CALLING RTN
NOCSA    WTO   '*** CSA STORAGE NOT AVAILABLE ***',ROUTCDE=11
         LA    R15,4                 SET UNSUCCESSFUL RC INDICATION
         B     RETURNX               RETURN TO MVS WITH BAD RC
*
*
***********************************************************************
*    THIS ROUTINE PUTS THE TASK INTO SUPERVISOR STATE AND PSW PROTECTION
*    KEY ZERO VIA THE MODESET MACRO. THIS IS REQUIRED TO MOVE THE
*    ADDRESS OF THE ALLOCATED CSA INTO THE CVT USER-FIELD.
***********************************************************************
*
SETMODE  MODESET MODE=SUP,KEY=ZERO
         BR    R6                    RETURN TO CALLING RTN
*
*
***********************************************************************
*    THIS ROUTINE PLACES THE ADDRESS OF THE ALLOCATED CSA INTO THE
```

```
*    CVT USER-FIELD.
***************************************************************************
*
SETCVT   L     R10,16              LOAD REG 10 WITH CVT ADR
         MVC   CVTUSER,CSAADR      MOVE CSA STRG ADR INTO CVT USER FLD
         BR    R6                  RETURN TO CALLING RTN
*
*
***************************************************************************
*    THIS ROUTINE RESTORES THE REGISTERS AND RETURNS CONTROL.
***************************************************************************
*
RETURN   LA    R15,0               SET RC=0
RETURNX  LA    R13,4(0,R13)        RESTORE PREV SA ADR
         L     R14,12(0,R13)       RESTORE REG 14
         LM    R0,R12,20(R13)      RESTORE REGS 0-12, R15 HAS RC
         BR    R14                 RETURN TO MVS OR CALLING PROG
*
*
***************************************************************************
*    DC/DS STATEMENTS
***************************************************************************
*
CSAADR   DS    F
*
*
***************************************************************************
*    THE DSECTS
***************************************************************************
*
         PRINT NOGEN
         CVT   DSECT=YES           GENERATES CVT DSECT
*
*
***************************************************************************
*    END OF PROGRAM
***************************************************************************
*
         END
```

NOTES:

- The program must be authorized in order to issue a GETMAIN macro instruction for subpool 241 (CSA) and to issue the MODESET macro instruction. Authorizing a program is discussed in Chapter 10.
- Supervisor state and key zero are required to write into the CVTUSER field.
- It may be necessary to serialize the writing into the CVTUSER field via the ENQ/DEQ macro instructions.
- The storage protection key of the allocated CSA storage is implicitly set to 8 (key of executing program). This will provide all problem programs that executue in virtual storage (V=V programs normally execute in key 8) with read/write access to that storage. All unauthorized programs that execute in a protection key other than 8 will have only read access (since subpool 241 is not fetch-protected) to that storage.
- If write access is to be denied to all unauthorized programs, then the GETMAIN macro instruction should be executed after the MODESET macro instruction. This will set the protection key of the allocated CSA storage to zero.

Coding Example 13.4.2

This coding example illustrates how to allocate virtual storage from the CSA, using the branch-entry form of the GETMAIN macro instruction.

```
ALLOCSA2 CSECT
*
*
***********************************************************************
*    INITIALIZATION
***********************************************************************
*
         INITL 5,EQU=R              INITIALIZE PROGRAM
         USING R10,CVT              DEFINE REG FOR CVT DSECT
*
*
***********************************************************************
*    MAINSTREAM OF PROGRAM
***********************************************************************
*
         BAL   R6,SETMODE           SET PROG INTO KEY ZERO, SUPV STATE
         BAL   R6,SETLOCK           OBTAIN LOCAL LOCK
         BAL   R6,GETCSA            ALLOC STORAGE FROM CSA
         BAL   R6,RELLOCK           RELEASE LOCAL LOCK
         BAL   R6,SETCVT            PUT CSA STRG ADR INTO CVT USER FLD
         B     RETURN               RETURN TO MVS OR CALLING PROG
*
*
***********************************************************************
*    THIS ROUTINE PUTS THE TASK INTO SUPERVISOR STATE AND PSW PROTECTION
*    KEY ZERO VIA THE MODESET MACRO. THIS IS REQUIRED TO MOVE THE
*    ADDRESS OF THE ALLOCATED CSA INTO THE CVT USER-FIELD.
***********************************************************************
*
SETMODE  MODESET MODE=SUP,KEY=ZERO
         BR    R6                   RETURN TO CALLING RTN
*
*
***********************************************************************
*    THIS ROUTINE ISSUES THE SETLOCK MACRO TO OBTAIN THE LOCAL LOCK,
*    WHICH IS REQUIRED FOR A BRANCH-ENTRY GETMAIN MACRO.
***********************************************************************
*
SETLOCK  SETLOCK OBTAIN,TYPE=LOCAL,MODE=UNCOND,REGS=USE,               -
               RELATED=(GETMAIN,CSA,RELLOCK)
         BR    R6                   RETURN TO CALLING RTN
*
*
***********************************************************************
*    THIS ROUTINE ALLOCATES VIRTUAL STORAGE FROM THE CSA AND ASSIGNS
*    PSW PROTECTION KEY=8 (NORMAL V=V JOBS) TO IT.
***********************************************************************
*
GETCSA   GETMAIN RC,LV=4096,SP=231,BNDRY=PAGE,BRANCH=YES               -
               KEY=8
         LTR   R15,R15              CHECK FOR SUCCESSFUL GETMAIN
         BNZ   NOCSA                IF NON-ZERO, CSA STRG NOT AVAIL
         LR    R11,R1               SAVE ADR OF CSA AREA IN REG 11
         BR    R6                   RETURN TO CALLING RTN
NOCSA    LA    R15,4                SET UNSUCCESSFUL RC INDICATION
         B     RETURNX              RETURN TO MVS WITH BAD RC
*
*
***********************************************************************
*    THIS ROUTINE RELEASES THE LOCAL LOCK.
***********************************************************************
*
RELLOCK  SETLOCK RELEASE,TYPE=LOCAL,REGS=USE,                          -
```

```
               RELATED=(GETMAIN,CSA,SETLOCK)
          BR   R6                    RETURN TO CALLING RTN
*
*
***************************************************************************
*    THIS ROUTINE PLACES THE ADDRESS OF THE ALLOCATED CSA INTO THE
*    CVT USER-FIELD.
***************************************************************************
*
SETCVT    L    R10,16                LOAD REG 10 WITH CVT ADR
          ST   R11,CVTUSER           STORE CSA STRG ADR INTO CVT USER FLD
          BR   R6                    RETURN TO CALLING RTN
*
*
***************************************************************************
*    THIS ROUTINE RESTORES THE REGISTERS AND RETURNS CONTROL.
***************************************************************************
*
RETURN    LA   R15,0                 SET RC=0
RETURNX   LA   R13,4(0,R13)          RESTORE PREV SA ADR
          L    R14,12(0,R13)         RESTORE REG 14
          LM   R0,R12,20(R13)        RESTORE REGS 0-12, R15 HAS RC
          BR   R14                   RETURN TO MVS OR CALLING PROG
*
*
***************************************************************************
*    THE DSECTS
***************************************************************************
*
          PRINT NOGEN
          CVT   DSECT=YES            GENERATES CVT DSECT
          IHAPSA                     GENERATES PSA DSECT
*                                    REQUIRED FOR SETLOCK MACRO
*
*
***************************************************************************
*    END OF PROGRAM
***************************************************************************
*
              END
```

NOTES:

- The program is reentrant and refreshable.
- Notice: This program uses register 5 as the base register instead of the normally selected register 3. This is because the branch-entry GETMAIN macro instruction with an RC type request destroys register 3, and register 4 contains the address of the TCB.
- The program must be authorized in order to issue the MODESET macro instruction. If the program is an SVC routine or an SRB routine, then the MODESET macro instruction is not required.
- Supervisor state and key zero are required to issue the SETLOCK macro instruction, issue a branch-type GETMAIN macro instruction, and write into the CVTUSER field.
- If this code is for a type-1 SVC routine, then the issuing of the SETLOCK macro instruction for obtaining the LOCAL lock is not required.
- The PSW protection key of the allocated CSA storage is set to 8, with the KEY= parameter of the GETMAIN macro instruction. This will provide all normal problem programs (those that executue in virtual storage (V=V, key 8)), with read/write access to that storage. All unauthorized programs that execute in a PSW protection

key other than 8 will not have any access to that storage (since subpool 231 is fetch-protected). If the KEY parameter is not specified when a branch-entry GETMAIN macro instruction is issued, then the default is key zero.

- Notice that the WTO macro instruction is not used to issue an error message if CSA storage is not available. Routines (type-1 and type-6 SVC routines and SRB routines) that are not allowed to issue an SVC instruction may request GETMAIN services only via the branch entry. Assuming that this code is used by such a routine, then the WTO macro instruction cannot be used because its expansion includes an SVC instruction. Also, if this code is used by other type SVC routines (other than type-1 or type-6), then the WTO macro instruction still cannot be used because SVC routines cannot call other SVC routines while a lock is held.
- If this code is not being executed by an SVC routine, then register 4 must be loaded with the address of the TCB, and register 7 must be loaded with the address of the ASCB before the GETMAIN macro instruction is executed. This is not required for SVC routines because SVC routines receive control with register 4 and register 7 preloaded with the TCB and the ASCB addresses, respectively. Writing SVC routines was discussed in Chapter 12.

13.5 USES OF THE CSA

Some of the uses of the Common Service Area include the following:

- For inter-address space communications, by using it as an intermediate holding area for data that is to be transferred between address spaces. Inter-address space communications in discussed in Chapter 15;
- To store global tables (such as accounting tables and security tables) used by multiple address spaces; and
- To contain dynamically loaded new and/or updated SVC routines. This technique was discussed in Chapter 12.

BIBLIOGRAPHY FOR CHAPTER 13

The following IBM manuals contain reference material for the topics discussed in this chapter.

ID	TITLE
GC28-0984	*OS/VS2 MVS Overview*
GC28-1046	*OS/VS2 SPL: Supervisor*
GC28-1047	*OS/VS2 SPL: Debugging Handbook Volume 1*
GC28-1348	*MVS/XA Overview*
GC28-1150	*MVS/XA SPL: System Macros and Facilities Volume 1*
GC28-1151	*MVS/XA SPL: System Macros and Facilities Volume 2*
LC28-1164	*MVS/XA Debugging Handbook Volume 1*
GC28-1852	*MVS/ESA SPL: Application Development Guide*
GC28-1857	*MVS/ESA SPL: Application Development Macro Reference*
LY28-1011	*MVS/ESA Diagnosis: System Reference*

14

Programming Using 31-Bit Addressing

In the middle 1960s, IBM introduced the System 360 series of computers. The size of the general registers was (and is today) 32 bits, but only the low order 24 bits were used for addressing. This provided addressability for 16 megabytes (16 million, actually $16 \times 1024^2 = 16{,}777{,}216$) of main storage locations. The major operating systems of those days—DOS, PCP (similar to a one partition MFT and used as a transition tool for the conversion from DOS to OS (MFT/MVT)), MFT, and MVT—did not support virtual storage; main storage consisted of only real storage. The System 360 hardware supported substantially less than 16 megabytes of real storage; therefore, even though the addressing scheme could support a maximum of 16M bytes, the actual amount of main storage (real storage) available to a program was much less. Programming techniques such as overlays were required for very large programs and when work space, tables, queues, and so forth, were too large to be entirely resident in main storage, auxiliary storage (DASD or magnetic tape) was used.

In the early 1970s, IBM introduced the System 370 series of computers. The System 370 computers used the same instruction set as the System 360, with a few new instructions added (MVCL, CLCL, LRA, etc.). Most of the System 370 CPU models supported virtual storage. DOS was enhanced to become DOS/VSE; PCP was dropped (actually, before System 370 was announced); MFT was enhanced to become VS1; MVT was enhanced to become VS2 (initially SVS, then MVS); and main storage became virtual storage.

Virtual storage is divided into segments, and segments are divided into pages (2048 bytes for VS1 and 4096 bytes for SVS/MVS). Virtual storage (like main storage from System 360) may contain program code and data. Pages are moved (paged) between real storage and auxiliary storage (DASD), as required. When the CPU needs to reference the contents of a page, it is paged into a real storage frame (same size as page). When the contents of a page are changed, it is paged (saved) into a page dataset located on auxiliary storage if the real storage frame that it occupies is required for another page. The size of virtual storage at that time was 16M bytes which is the entire range of addressability provided by 24 bits. Paging makes it possible for the effective size of virtual storage to exceed the size of the real storage which backs it up. Chapter 9 provided more information about paging.

VS1 and SVS (version 1, release 1 of VS2) provided 16M bytes of virtual storage that was shared by the operating system and the users. Each user had his/her own partition (VS1) or region (SVS). MVS (version 1, release 2, and later of VS2) provided each user with his/her own entire 16M bytes (less system overhead) of virtual storage called an address space.

In the late 1970s, IBM introduced the 303x series of computers (also System 370 architecture). The maximum amount of real storage available in this series of computers exceeded 16M bytes, but the System 370 hardware and software addressing scheme (24 bits) provided only 16M bytes of virtual storage to programs.

As MVS evolved, it and its associated system overhead could require more than half of the available 16M bytes of virtual storage allocated to each user. Also, after virtual storage was introduced, IBM subsystems (JES2, CICS, etc.) and user programs became larger, the technique of using virtual storage instead of DASDs for work space, data, tables, queues, and so on, become very popular, and the full capacity of 16M bytes of virtual storage started to become inadequate.

In the early 1980s, IBM introduced the 308x series of computers and the MVS Extended Architecture (MVS/XA, version 2 of MVS/SP) operating system. The 308x series of computers also supported real storage sizes in excess of 16M bytes and also used the System 370 instruction set with a few new instructions added (BASSM, BSM, etc.). The 308x series of computers (including the 4381) operate in 370 mode or 370-XA mode (the mode is selected at IMPL time). In 370 mode, the CPU functions like the older CPUs; when in 370-XA mode, the CPU provides the additional function and support required for the MVS/XA Operating System. Some of the machine instructions function differently between 370 mode and 370-XA mode, and the new instructions are available only in 370-XA mode.

In 370-XA mode, the low order 31 bits of the available 32 bits are used for addressing. This provides an addressing scheme that provides addressability for 2 gigabytes (2 billion, actually 2 x 1024^3 = 2,147,483,648) of virtual storage. For compatibility reasons, 370-XA mode also supports 24-bit addressing mode.

In the late 1980s, IBM introduced the 3090 series of computers and the MVS/ESA (version 3 of MVS/SP) operating system. Like MVS/XA, MVS/ESA supports 31-bit addressing and also provides for the use of additional virtual storage by providing Data Spaces and Hiperspaces (both of which are address spaces used for data only).

The 3090 series of computers uses the same instruction set as the 308x series of computers. In addition, when in ESA/370 mode, access registers (used for inter-address space communications) and some additional instruction (BAKR, PR, LAM, STAM, etc.) are provided.

This chapter discusses the programming techniques, including the new operating system facilities, required for 31 bit-addressing mode. This chapter also discusses the new machine instructions used with 31-bit addressing mode, the old machine instructions that function differently in 370-XA mode, and communications and compatability between programs executing in 24-bit addressing mode and programs executing in 31-bit addressing mode.

The information presented in this chapter concerning 31-bit addressing mode and the programming techniques involved applies to MVS/XA and MVS/ESA; however, only the term MVS/XA is used except when there is some difference.

14.1 INTRODUCTION TO 31-BIT ADDRESSING MODE

MVS/XA functions with the CPU in 370-XA mode (MVS/ESA functions with the CPU in ESA/370 mode) and supports 31-bit addressing for both real and virtual storage. In 31-bit addressing, the addresses range from 0 to 2,147,483,647 (X'7FFFFFFF'). MVS/XA also supports 24-bit addressing in order to provide compatibility for existing programs developed prior to MVS/XA. Programs with 24-bit addressing and programs with 31-bit addressing may execute concurrently, and MVS/XA allows programs with different addressing modes to communicate with each other.

In order to support both addressing modes concurrently, MVS/XA has defined the 16 megabyte (16 Mb) line, which is located between virtual storage addresses X'00FFFFFF' and X'01000000'. Programs that use 24-bit addressing must reside below the 16 Mb line because they cannot access virtual storage addresses greater that X'00FFFFFF'. Programs that use 31-bit addressing may reside below or above the 16 Mb line.

When a program is assembled or link edited, a specification is made (via AMODE and RMODE) as to what addressing mode the program is expected to use and where (relative to the 16 Mb line) the program is expected to reside. The default is 24-bit addressing and residence below the 16 Mb line for compatibility with existing programs. The addressing mode may remain the same or may be changed while a program is executing.

Certain machine instructions execute differently between 370 mode and 370-XA mode. In addition, the two new machine instructions, BASSM and BSM, are provided to assist in the linkage between programs with different addressing modes.

The PSW is formatted differently between 370 mode and 370-XA mode. In 370-XA mode, the last 31 bits (33–63) of the PSW is the 31-bit instruction address. Bit 32 is used to indicate the current addressing mode. A value of 0 indicates 24-bit addressing and a value of 1 indicates 31-bit addressing.

The GETMAIN macro instruction for later releases of MVS/370 and for MVS/XA has an additional keyword parameter (LOC=) that will (among other options) permit 24-bit addressing programs to request virtual storage above the 16 Mb line, and permit 31-bit addressing programs to request virtual storage below the 16 Mb line.

14.2 REQUIREMENTS, RULES, AND CONVENTIONS OF 31-BIT ADDRESSING MODE

There are some requirements for a program to execute in 31-bit addressing mode on an MVS/XA system. This does not happen automatically since the default is 24-bit addressing mode in order to remain transparent to previously developed programs. Besides executing on an MVS/XA system, the requirements for a program to execute in 31-bit addressing mode are the following:

- Be assembled using Assembler H Version 2 (or later) with the MVS/XA macro library.
- Be linkedited or loaded using the Linkage Editor or Loader supplied with Data Facility Product (DFP).
- Specify an AMODE of 31 via the Assembler, Linkage Editor, or Loader, or change to 31-bit addressing mode during execution. See Section 14.4.7 for methods of dynamically changing the addressing mode.

When a program is executing in 31-bit addressing mode, it must observe the following rules:

- Any addresses passed to a 24-bit addressing mode program must reside below the 16 Mb line because such programs cannot access data that resides above the 16 Mb line. Virtual storage below the 16 Mb line may be obtained via the GETMAIN macro instruction, using the LOC=BELOW parameter. If this is not done, then unpredictable results will occur since the called 24-bit addressing mode program will not use the seven high order bits of the 31-bit address of the data.
- Some instructions such as BAL, BALR, LA, and LRA function differently in 31-bit addressing mode and must be used accordingly. See Section 14.3.1 for details on the differences.

When a program is executing in 24-bit addressing mode, it must observe the following rule:

- Any 24-bit addresses passed to a 31-bit addressing mode program must be extented to a valid 31-bit address by setting the seven high order bits to zero.

The following convention should be observed by all programs that execute under MVS/XA:

- Programs should return control in the same addressing mode as that of the calling program. If this is not done, it may cause addressability errors in the calling program or cause a machine instruction to function differently than expected in the calling program. This is a concern of the called program only if it receives control without system intervention and if the addressing mode of the called program is different from that of the calling program. If control is received with system intervention (the LINK macro instruction, etc.), then the operating system assures addressing mode integrity. However, since it is unknown how a program will receive control, it should always return control with the BSM 0,R14 instruction instead of the BR R14 instruction. Sections 14.6 and 14.7 discuss this in more detail.

14.3 MACHINE INSTRUCTION CONSIDERATIONS

When the CPU is in 370-XA mode, it may support 24-bit and 31-bit addressing modes. The setting of the PSW A-mode bit (bit 32) indicates the current addressing mode.

When the CPU is set to 24-bit addressing mode (PSW A-mode bit = 0), the machine instructions function the same as they do in 370 mode with the MVS/370 operating system, and the instruction address field of the PSW contains a 24-bit address.

When the CPU is set to 31-bit addressing mode (PSW A-mode bit = 1), some instructions function differently and the instruction address field of the PSW contains a 31-bit address. The instructions that use an address (MVC, CLC, MVCL, B, etc.) and the instructions that develop an address (BAL, LA, etc.) will have a 31-bit address. The instructions that do not use or develop an address (AR, AP, CVB, etc.) will function as in 370 mode.

14.3.1 Instructions Sensitive to Addressing Mode

The machine instructions BAL, BALR, LA, and LRA are called mode sensitive instructions because they function differently in 31-bit addressing mode as compared to 24-bit addressing mode (or 370 mode).

BAL AND BALR INSTRUCTIONS

When executing in 24-bit addressing mode, the BAL (Branch And Link) and the BALR (Branch And Link, Register) instructions put link information (instruction length code, condition code, and program mask) in the high order byte of the first register of the operand (R_1), and put the 24-bit return address in the low order three bytes of R_1.

When executing in 31-bit addressing mode, the BAL and BALR instructions do not save the link information in the high order byte of R_1. Instead, the high order bit is used to save the current addressing mode (always 1 to indicate 31-bit addressing mode), and the remaining 31 bits are used to save the 31-bit return address.

If the logic of the program does not require that the link information be saved and restored, then using the BAL and the BALR instructions in 31-bit addressing mode do not present a problem. However, if the condition code and program mask are required to be saved and restored, then a new 370-XA mode instruction, IPM (Insert Program Mask), may be used to save this information in a register.

THE LA INSTRUCTION

When executing in 24-bit addressing mode (and in 370 mode), the LA (Load Address) instruction clears the high order byte of R_1 and loads a 24-bit address (or value) in the low order three bytes.

When executing in 31-bit addressing mode, the LA instruction clears the high order bit of R_1 and loads a 31-bit address (or value) into the remaining 31 bits.

If the high order byte of R_1 is not being used to contain flags or indicators, then using this instruction in either 24-bit or 31-bit addressing mode does not present a problem. However, if the high order byte is set with information after the LA instruction executes, then unpredictable results will occur because the high order seven bits of the 31-bit address will be overlayed. In this case, an alternate means must be developed for saving th is information before the program is converted from 24-bit addressing mode to 31-bit addressing mode.

THE LRA INSTRUCTION

The LRA (Load Real Address) instruction functions the same as in 370 mode. It always provides the corresponding real address of the specified virtual address as a 31-bit address regardless of the addressing mode of the issuing program. The high order bit of the real address is always set to zero. If the corresponding real address is below the 16 Mb line, then the high order seven bits of the address are set to zeros.

The meaning of condition code 1 from the LRA instruction may be different between 370 mode and 370-XA mode. Since some page tables for the address space located above the 16 Mb line are themselves pageable in MVS/XA, a condition code of 1 may have either one of the following meanings:

- The page table does not exist because the virtual storage has not been allocated.
- The page table is paged out or has not yet been built.

The specific meaning of condition code 1 can be determined by accessing the virtual address, which will cause an S0C4 ABEND or a segment fault/page fault resolution (virtual address successfully accessed) to occur.

14.3.2 Instructions that Manipulate Addressing Mode

The machine instructions BASSM and BSM perform branching operations and also manipulate the PSW A-mode bit. These instructions are available only when the CPU is in 370-XA mode. An attempt to execute these instructions when the CPU is in 370 mode will result in an S0C1 ABEND. Both instructions are RR format instructions.

THE BASSM INSTRUCTION

The BASSM (Branch And Save and Set Mode) instruction causes a branch to the address specified in the second register of the operand (R_2) and sets the addressing mode as indicated in the high order bit of R_2 (0 for 24-bit addressing, 1 for 31-bit addressing). The address of the next sequential instruction is placed into the first register of the operand (R_1) and the current addressing mode indicator (from the A-mode bit of the current PSW) is saved in the high order bit of R_1. When R_2 is zero, no branching or addressing mode setting is performed, but the operation on R_1 is still performed. The operation associated with R_1 is not suppressed when it is specified as zero.

THE BSM INSTRUCTION

The BSM instruction (Branch and Set Mode) causes a branch to the address specified in R_2 and sets the addressing mode as indicated in the high order bit of R_2. The current addressing mode indicator (from the A-bit of the currect PSW) is saved in the high order bit of R_1, and the remainder of R_1 is unchanged. If either operand register is specified as zero, then the operation associated with that register is suppressed.

14.4 ADDRESSING MODE AND RESIDENCY MODE

In MVS/XA, two new program attributes are introduced. They are addressing mode (AMODE) and residency mode (RMODE). This section will discuss their meaning, assignment, and how they are used.

14.4.1 Meaning of AMODE/RMODE Attributes

The AMODE attribute indicates the addressing mode in which the program is expected to receive control. The RMODE attribute indicates where the program is expected to reside (relative to the 16 Mb line) in virtual storage. These program attributes are important to assure that the addressing mode and the location of the program, when it receives control, is consistent with the addressability mode of the coding that is being used in the program. After the program receives control, it may change its addressing mode.

These attributes may be specified by the programmer via the Assembler or via the Linkage Editor/Loader. When AMODE and RMODE are specified via the Assembler, they are at the CSECT level. When AMODE and RMODE are specified via the Linkage Editor, they override any specification made via the Assembler. In addition, the Linkage Editor assigns (for multiple CSECT load modules) a single AMODE attribute and a single RMODE attribute for the entire load module. This is the AMODE and the RMODE that a load module has when it receives control (under most conditions, see Section 14.4.6). If the CSECTs of a multiple CSECT load module have different AMODE requirements, then it is the responsibility of the program to dynamically switch the AMODE accordingly, when the various CSECTs receive control. Section 14.6 discusses some techniques that may be used to accomplish this.

When the Linkage Editor creates a load module, its AMODE and RMODE attributes are stored in the load module's PDS directory entry (along with other information about the load module that is supplied by the Linkage Editor) of the load library.

14.4.2 Values and Valid Combinations of AMODE/RMODE

The value of AMODE may be one of the following:

24 The program is designed to receive control in 24-bit addressing mode.

31 The program is designed to receive control in 31-bit addressing mode.

ANY The program is designed to receive control in either 24-bit or or 31-bit addressing mode. In this case, the actual addressing mode in which the program receives control is determined by the MVS/XA service that is passing control. See Section 14.4.6 for additional information.

The value of RMODE may be one of the following:

24 The program is designed to reside below the 16 Mb line. When the program is invoked, MVS/XA loads the program below the 16 Mb line.

ANY The program is designed to reside at any virtual storage location. When the program is invoked, MVS/XA attempts to load the program above the 16 Mb line. If it is unable to do so, then it will load the program below the 16 Mb line.

The following AMODE/RMODE combinations are valid:

```
AMODE 24,   RMODE 24 (Default)
AMODE 31,   RMODE 24
AMODE 31,   RMODE ANY
AMODE ANY,  RMODE 24
AMODE ANY,  RMODE ANY (Changed to AMODE 31, RMODE ANY by linkage editor)
```

14.4.3 Assignment of AMODE/RMODE Via the Assembler

The AMODE and the RMODE attributes may be set by the Assembler by using the AMODE and the RMODE Assembler statements, respectively. The AMODE and the RMODE attributes may be set the same or different for each CSECT in the assembly. The following is the syntax of the AMODE and RMODE Assembler statements:

```
name        AMODE x
name        RMODE x
```

where: name represents the label of the corresponding CSECT; and x represents the value of the attribute.

The AMODE and the RMODE Assembler statements may be placed anywhere in the assembly; however, the label in the name field must match the name of the CSECT to which the AMODE and the RMODE Assembler statements refer. For readability and documentation purposes, it is good practice to place the AMODE and RMODE Assembler statements next to the CSECT Assembler statement to which they refer.

Coding Example 14.4.1

This coding example illustrates how the AMODE and RMODE Assembler statements are used in an assembly. In this example, the program contains two CSECTs, MAINPGM and SUBRTN1, which have different AMODE and RMODE requirements.

```
MAINPGM     CSECT
MAINPGM     AMODE 24
MAINPGM     RMODE 24
            ...
SUBRTN1     CSECT
SUBRTN1     AMODE 31
SUBRTN1     RMODE ANY
            ...
            END
```

NOTES:

- When a program is link edited, the resulting load module receives a single AMODE and a single RMODE attribute. Section 14.4.4 explains how the Linkage Editor makes that determination. If different CSECTs of the same load module have different AMODE requirements, then it is the program's responsibility to set the appropriate AMODE before calling the CSECT. Coding Example 14.6.2 shows a coding technique that can be used to accomplish this requirement.

14.4.4 Assignment of AMODE/RMODE Via the Linkage Editor

The AMODE and RMODE attributes may be set by the Linkage Editor via the PARM parameter of the JCL EXEC statement or via the Linkage Editor MODE control statement.

The syntax for the PARM parameter is as follows:

```
//LKED EXEC PGM=IEWL,PARM='AMODE=x,RMODE=x'
```

where: x represents the value of the attribute.

The syntax for the MODE control statement is as follows:

```
MODE AMODE(x),RMODE(x)
```

where: x represents the value of the attribute.

The Linkage Editor accepts the AMODE/RMODE values specified by the Assembler via the ESD entries in the object module and from previously created load modules via the CESD entries. If AMODE/RMODE values are specified via the PARM parameter of the Linkage Editor, then these values will override the specifications of the ESD and CESD entries. If AMODE/RMODE values are specified via the MODE control statement, then these values will override all other specifications.

The Linkage Editor assigns a single AMODE attribute and a single RMODE attribute for the entire load module and stores them in the PDS directory entry of that load module. If an AMODE/RMODE attribute is not specified via the PARM parameter or the MODE control statement and multiple AMODE/RMODE values are encountered via ESD and/or CESD entries, then the Linkage Editor will use the most restrictive value. For example, if the Linkage Editor encounters an RMODE of 24 and an RMODE of ANY, then it will use the RMODE of 24.

14.4.5 Assignment of AMODE/RMODE Via the Loader

The Loader will process the AMODE/RMODE specifications similar to the Linkage Editor except that it does not accept the MODE control statement from the SYSLIN dataset. The AMODE and RMODE values that the Loader assigns will be used when the load module is loaded into virtual storage and receives control.

14.4.6 MVS/XA Services Support of AMODE/RMODE Attributes

When a program is being developed for MVS/XA or migrated from MVS/370 to MVS/XA, it is necessary to know how the various services of MVS/XA handle the AMODE/RMODE attributes in order to assure that the program will function as intended.

Among the services (not every one will be discussed) that MVS/XA provides for loading a program into virtual storage, giving it control, or both are program Fetch (IEWFETCH), the Loader; the ATTACH, LINK, XCTL, SYNCH, LOAD, and CALL macro instructions, the SVC First Level Interruption Handler (FLIH), and the SRB dispatcher. All services that are responsible for loading a program into virtual storage honor the RMODE attribute as described in section 14.4.2. The following describes how the MVS/XA services handle the AMODE attribute of the load module.

PROGRAM FETCH

When a program is invoked via JCL, Program Fetch causes control to be passed to the program in the addressing mode associated with it. If an AMODE value of ANY was specified, then control is received in 31-bit addressing mode.

THE ATTACH, LINK, AND XCTL MACRO INSTRUCTIONS

The ATTACH, LINK, and XCTL macro instructions cause control to be passed to the program (whose entry point is specified) in the addressing mode indicated by the AMODE attribute associated with the called program. If the AMODE attribute is ANY, then control is passed using the same addressing mode as the issuer of the macro instruction. In addition, for the LINK macro instruction, the addressing mode of the calling program is saved by MVS/XA and restored when control is returned to the calling program.

THE LOAD MACRO INSTRUCTION

The LOAD macro instruction causes the program (whose entry point is specified) to be loaded (if a usable copy does not already exist) into virtual storage. The address of the entry point is placed into register 0, and the high order bit is set to indicate if the AMODE attibute of the program is 24 (bit 0 set to 0) or 31 (bit 0 set to 1). If the AMODE attribute is ANY, then the high order bit is set to match the addressing mode of the issuer of the LOAD macro instruction. If control is passed to the LOADed program via a branch instruction, then it is the user's responsibility to set the proper addressing mode before passing control to the called program. This can be accomplished by using the BASSM machine instruction. The called program must return control in the addressing mode of the calling program. This can be accomplished via the the BSM machine instruction (if control was passed via the BASSM machine instruction). Section 14.6.1 contains a coding example that illustrates the required code to assure addressing mode integrity when the combination of a LOAD macro instruction and a branch instruction is used to pass control to another load module.

THE CALL MACRO INSTRUCTION

The CALL macro instruction causes control to be passed to a specified entry point via a BALR machine instruction. Therefore, the entry point receives control in the same addressing mode of the issuer of the macro instruction since the addressing mode cannot be changed via BALR.

THE SYNCH MACRO INSTRUCTION

The SYNCH macro instruction has a new keyword parameter (AMODE=) in MVS/XA. The called program receives control in the addressing mode specified by the AMODE parameter. If the AMODE parameter is not specified, the called program receives control in the same addressing mode as the issuer of the macro instruction. The AMODE attribute associated with the called program is not used.

SUPERVISOR CALL ROUTINE

MVS/XA saves the addressing mode of the issuer of an SVC machine instruction. The SVC routine receives control in the addressing mode specified in its SVC table entry. The AMODE attribute associated with the program (SVC routine) is not used. The addressing mode is restored, by MVS/XA, when the issuing program receives control back from the SVC routine.

SERVICE REQUEST BLOCK ROUTINE

The program that receives control when an SRB is dispatched receives control in the addressing mode indicated in the high order bit (0 for 24-bit addressing, 1 for 31-bit addressing) of the SRBEP field of the SRB. The AMODE attribute associated with the called program is not used.

14.4.7 Dynamically Setting AMODE

In Section 14.4.6, we saw that the addressing mode of a task could be changed by using various MVS/XA services to pass control to another load module. However, in these cases, the addressing mode was constant across a load module. The addressing mode can also be dynamically changed within a load module without using any MVS/XA services.

Dynamically changing the addressing mode within a load module can be accomplished by using the BASSM and BSM machine instructions. It can also be performed with the LPSW machine instruction, but this method is not recommended and will not be discussed.

Some reasons for dynamically changing the addressing mode of a program would be the following:

- To permit a 24-bit addressing mode program to access data located above the 16 Mb line, such as user-data or certain MVS/XA control blocks;
- To permit a 31-bit addressing mode program to perform certain MVS/XA services that require an AMODE/RMODE of 24 (such as non-VSAM I/O or using the EXTRACT macro instruction); and
- To assure that a called (via a branch instead of MVS/XA services) program or routine receives control in the proper addressing mode.

The BASSM and the BSM instructions set the addressing mode to that indicated by the high order bit of the second register of the operand and then cause a branch to the address specified in that register. Section 14.3.2 described the complete operation of the BASSM and the BSM instructions. Section 14.6.1 shows how to use the BASSM and the BSM instructions to dynamically change the addressing mode.

14.5 ALLOCATING VIRTUAL STORAGE VIA GETMAIN

Since programs may use either 24-bit addressing or 31-bit addressing (or both) in MVS/XA, sometimes it may be required for a 24-bit addressing program to request virtual storage above the 16 Mb line and for a 31-bit addressing program to request virtual storage below the 16 Mb line. Some reasons why this may be necessary are the following:

- A 24-bit addressing program may require virtual storage above the 16 Mb line when a large area of virtual storage is required for work space or to contain huge amounts of data and there is insufficient virtual storage available below the 16 Mb line.
- A 31-bit addressing program requires virtual storage below the 16 Mb line when it is passing a parameter-list to a called 24-bit addressing program.

A potential addressing problem may arise when a 24-bit addressing program allocates, via the GETMAIN macro instruction, virtual storage above the 16 Mb line. When this is done, the virtual storage above the 16 Mb line must be referenced via 31-bit addressing, or unpredictable results will occur. This necessitates that the 24-bit addressing program change its addressing mode to 31-bit addressing when referencing the virtual storage that is located above the 16 Mb line. Section 14.8 discusses how this can be accomplished.

If a GETMAIN macro instruction is issued and no request is made for the location of virtual storage, then the default (LOC=RES) will be used to allocate virtual storage. The default is based upon the location of the issuing program. If the program resides below the 16 Mb line, then the virtual storage and real storage frames are allocated below the 16 Mb line. If the program resides above the 16 Mb line, then the virtual storage and real storage frames are allocated anywhere (above or below the 16 Mb line). The program need not be concerned about addressability problems (if AMODE remains constant) when allocating virtual storage, using the default LOC= value.

The keyword parameter LOC= of the GETMAIN macro instruction is used to request the location of the virtual storage and real storage frames. Virtual storage addresses above the 16 Mb line can be obtained only if the RC, RU, VRC, and VRU forms of the GETMAIN macro instruction are used.

Below is a list of the possible values of the LOC= parameter and their meaning:

`LOC=BELOW`

Specifies that the virtaul storage and real storage frames are to be located below the 16 Mb line.

`LOC=(BELOW,ANY)`

Specifies that the virtaul storage is to be located below the 16 Mb line and the real storage frames may be located anywhere.

`LOC=ANY`
`LOC=(ANY,ANY)`

Specifies that virtual storage and the real storage frames may be allocated anywhere.

NOTES:

- GETMAIN attempts to allocate the virtual storage and real storage frames above the 16 Mb line. If this is not possible (RC, RU, VRC, or VRU request is not specified, or virtual storage above the 16 Mb line is not available), then GETMAIN will allocate below the 16 Mb line.
- A 24-bit addressing program will use this parameter to request virtual storage above the 16 Mb line.
- GETMAIN provides no return code to indicate if storage was allocated below or above the 16 Mb line. A 24-bit addressing mode program should assume that virtual storage was allocated above the line and set up addressability accordingly. This technique will assure that the program will function properly, regardless of where the virtual storage was allocated.
- The location of the real storage frames is transparent to addressability requirements of the program, unless the program has special requirements to know the actual real address that corresponds to a specific virtual address.

`LOC=RES`

The default and defined above.

`LOC=(RES,ANY)`

The same as LOC=RES except that the real storage frames may be allocated anywhere.

14.6 ESTABLISHING LINKAGE BETWEEN PROGRAMS WITH DIFFERENT ADDRESSING MODES

The term "existing 24-bit addressing mode program" is used in this section and in Section 14.7. That term is defined as programs developed before MVS/XA or programs developed under MVS/XA but using MVS/370 program linkage (BALR and BR instructions).

Establishing linkage between 24-bit and 31-bit addressing mode programs can be accomplished by one of the following methods:

- Using the BASSM and the BSM machine instructions;
- Supervisor-Assisted linkage;
- Pointer-Defined linkage;
- Linkage Assist routines; and
- Capping (Prologue and Epilogue).

14.6.1 Using the BASSM and the BSM Machine Instructions

The BASSM and the BSM instructions should be used instead of the BALR and the BR instructions when control is passed between load modules without system intervention. If the load modules have different addressing modes, then the BASSM and the BSM instructions will assure addressing mode integrity. The BASSM instruction will normally be used to pass control to another load module, which was loaded into virtual storage via the LOAD macro instruction. The entry point address returned by the LOAD macro instruction is actually a pointer-defined value. The high order bit of the entry point address indicates the addressing mode of the LOADed program and is used by the BASSM instruction to dynamically set the appropriate addressing mode. The BSM instruction should always be used to return control in all new programs developed that execute exclusively under MVS/XA, regardless of the AMODE/RMODE attributes of the programs. This assures that the program returns control in the correct addressing mode if it receives control via a combination of a LOAD macro instruction and a BASSM instruction.

The BASSM and the BSM instructions may also be used to pass and return control between CSECTs and routines having different AMODEs within the same program. In this case, the user defines his/her own pointer-defined values. Pointer-defined linkage is discussed in Section 14.6.3.

Coding Example 14.6.1

This coding example illustrates the use of the BASSM and the BSM machine instructions to establish linkage between programs of different addressing modes. In this example, the BASSM instruction sets the addressing mode to that of the called program, saves the addressing mode of the calling program, and performs a branch to the called program. The BSM instruction sets the addressing mode to that of the calling program and performs a branch back to the calling program.

The calling program

```
PROG01   CSECT
         ...
         LOAD  EP=PROG02         LOAD PROGRAM WHICH IS TO RECV CONTROL
         LR    R15,R0            SAVE EP ADR AND AMODE OF CALLED PROGRAM
         BASSM R14,R15           SET ADR MODE OF CALLED PGM, SAVE AMODE
*                                OF CALLING PGM, BRANCH TO CALLED PROG
         ...
         END
```

The called program

```
PROG02   CSECT
         ...
         BSM   0,R14             SET AMODE OF CALLING PROG, RETURN
*                                CONTROL TO CALLING PROG
         ...
         END
```

14.6.2 Supervisor-Assisted Linkage

Two programs with unlike addressing modes can communicate with each other via the LINK macro instruction without an addressing integrity problem. The operating system will assure that the called program receives control in the proper addressing mode and when control is returned, the operating system will also assure that the calling program receives control in the proper addressing mode. The operating system will perform this function whether or not the BASSM and the BSM instructions are used to provide linkage. However, it is the user's responsibility to assure that any parameters passed to the called program reside in the proper location in virtual storage relative to the 16 Mb line. If the addressing mode of the called program is 24-bit or unknown, then the passed parameters should occupy virtual storage below the 16 Mb line, which may be allocated via the GETMAIN macro instruction by specifying LOC=BELOW.

14.6.3 Pointer-Defined Linkage

Pointer-defined linkage uses a pointer-defined value, which is a 4-byte address that points to the routine (a separate load module or a CSECT/routine in the same load module) which is to receive control. The high order bit of the address is set to indicate the addressing mode (0 for 24-bit, 1 for 31-bit) of the called routine. A pointer-defined value is returned by the LOAD macro instruction when it is used to load a program into virtual storage. A pointer-defined value may also be defined by the user. A pointer-defined value is in the proper format to be loaded into the branch register (R_2) used by the BASSM and the BSM instructions to pass control and return control, respectively, to a routine with a different addressing mode (or the same one), and set the addressing mode accordingly.

Coding Example 14.6.2 shows how to use pointer-defined linkage to pass control between CSECTs, which have different or unknown AMODEs, located in the same load module. Coding Example 14.6.3 shows how to use pointer-defined linkage with the pointer-defined value returned from the LOAD macro instruction. Coding Example 14.8.1 shows how to use pointer-defined linkage to call a subroutine that has a different AMODE from the calling routine located in the same program.

Coding Example 14.6.2

This coding example illustrates how pointer-defined values can be used to pass control between CSECTs, having different or the same AMODEs, in the same load module. In this example, the CSECT MAINRTN passes control to the CSECTs SUBRTN01 and SUBRTN02 and receives control back from them. MAINRTN passes control to the CSECTs via the BASSM instruction, using the pointer-defined values defined in the respective CSECTs.

Code for CSECT MAINRTN

```
MAINRTN  CSECT
MAINRTN  AMODE 31
MAINRTN  RMODE 24
         EXTRN SR01ADR
         EXTRN SR02ADR
*
         INITL 3,EQU=R
         ...
         BAL   R6,DOSRTN01
         ...
         BAL   R6,DOSRTN02
         ...
DOSRTN01 L     R15,=A(SR01ADR)
         L     R15,0(0,R15)
         BASSM R14,R15
         BR    R6
*
```

```
DOSRTN02 L     R15,=A(SR02ADR)
         L     R15,0(0,R15)
         BASSM R14,R15
         BR    R6
         ...
         END
```

Code for CSECT SUBRTN01

```
SUBRTN01 CSECT
SUBRTN01 AMODE 24
SUBRTN01 RMODE 24
ENTRY    SR01ADR
*
INITL    3,EQU=R
         ...
         ...                     AMODE 24 DEPENDENT CODE
         ...
RETURN   L     R13,4(0,R13)
         LM    R14,R12,12(R13)
         BSM   0,R14
         ...
SR01ADR  DC    A(SUBRTN01)       POINTER-DEFINED VALUE FOR THIS CSECT
         ...
         END
```

Code for CSECT SUBRTN02

```
SUBRTN02 CSECT
SUBRTN02 AMODE 31
SUBRTN02 RMODE ANY
         ENTRY SR02ADR
*
         INITL 3,EQU=R
         ...
         ...                     AMODE 31 DEPENDENT CODE
         ...
RETURN   L     R13,4(0,R13)
         LM    R14,R12,12(R13)
         BSM   0,R14
         ...
A31      EQU   X'80000000'
SR02ADR  DC    A(A31+SUBRTN02) POINTER-DEFINED VALUE FOR THIS CSECT
         ...
         END
```

Link Editor Control Statements

```
INCLUDE OBJLIB(MAINRTN)
INCLUDE OBJLIB(SUBRTN01)
INCLUDE OBJLIB(SUBRTN02)
MODE AMODE(31) RMODE(24)
ENTRY MAINRTN
NAME MAINRTN
```

NOTES:

- In this example, the three CSECTs are assembled separately to create an object module for each CSECT and are combined into one load module at linkedit time, using the linkedit control statements shown. The three CSECTs may also be contained in a single program. If a single program is used, then the labels must be unique across CSECTs.

- The EXTRN statements in MAINRTN may be omitted if the routines DOSRTN01 and DOSRTN02 load a VCON (=V(SR01ADR) and =V(SR02ADR), respectively) instead of an ADCON (=A(SR01ADR) and =A(SR02ADR), respectively) into register 15.
- Using this technique, the calling CSECT is not required to know the AMODE requirement of the called CSECT. The same coding technique is used to call each CSECT (regardless of its AMODE requirement) and the called CSECT will receive control in the proper AMODE if it defined its pointer-defined value correctly.

14.6.4 Linkage Assist Routines

A linkage assist routine is relatively simple to code. Its function is to isolate the calling/called programs, which have different addressing modes, from the need to be concerned about the addressing mode changes required to assure proper addressability. A linkage assist routine is useful when an existing 24-bit addressing mode program calls or is called by another program having a different AMODE, using a combination of a LOAD macro instruction and a branch.

The linkage assist routine is transparent to the calling and called programs. The calling and called programs continue to execute as though they are making a direct branch and return to each other, except that the linkage assist routine intercepts the calls. This is accomplished by providing the linkage assist routine with the name of the called program and renaming the called program to another name that is used by the linkage assist routine to call the called program.

The linkage assist routine has the following considerations and performs the following operations:

- Designed to receive control in any addressing mode.
- Saves the registers of the calling program.
- Saves the AMODE of the calling program.
- Allocates a savearea for use by the called program.
- If the call is from a 24-bit addressing mode program to a 31-bit addressing mode program, then the high order byte of register 1 is set to zeros to develop a valid 31-bit address. This is necessary because register 1 may be pointing to a parameter-list intended for the called 31-bit addressing mode program. Since the calling program is executing in 24-bit addressing mode, the high order byte of register 1 may contain flags, indicators, etc. which would be used as part of the address.

  If the call is from a 31-bit addressing mode program to a 24-bit addressing mode program, then the high order byte of register 1 is not required to be set to zeros. It is the responsibility of the calling 31-bit addressing mode program to allocate 24-bit addressable virtual storage to contain any parameters which are passed to the called program. The linkage assist routine should not verify that the high order byte of register 1 contains zeros because the calling program may not be passing a parameter-list address to the called program.
- Uses the LOAD macro instruction to load the called program into virtual storage (if a usable copy does not already exist) and passes control to it via the BASSM R14,R15 instruction. This can also be accomplished by the LINK macro instruction, in which case the operating system assures addressing mode integrity. However, since the LOAD macro instruction was used in the calling program, it should also be used in the linkage assist routine. If used properly, the LOAD macro instruction is also more efficient, which

may be the objective of the calling program. See the section entitled "Program Management" in Chapter 4 for an explanation of why the LOAD macro instruction may be more efficient.

- When control is returned from the called program:
  - Restores the registers of the calling program except register 15 since register 15 may contain a return code from the called program.
  - Restores the AMODE of the calling program and returns control.

Coding Example 14.6.3

This coding example illustrates how to code a linkage assist program. In this example, PROG01 has the requirement to call PROG02. The two programs have different AMODEs and neither one is to be modified. To make the linkage assist program transparent to the two programs, the linkage assist program is named PROG02 and the called program is renamed PROG02X.

```
*
*
        TITLE 'EXAMPLE OF A LINKAGE ASSIST PROGRAM' *
*
**********************************************************************
*     THIS PROGRAM IS·A LINKAGE ASSIST PROGRAM. IT RECEIVES CONTROL IN
*     THE AMODE OF THE CALLING PROGRAM. IT CHECKS THE AMODE OF THE
*     CALLING PROGRAM. IF THE AMODE IS 24-BIT, THEN THE HIGH ORDER BYTE
*     OF REGISTER ONE (THE PARAMETER REGISTER) IS SET TO BINARY ZEROS
*     TO CREATE A VALID 31-BIT ADDRESS FOR THE CALLED PROGRAM. THIS
*     PROGRAM THEN LOADS THE CALLED PROGRAM, CHANGES THE AMODE TO THAT
*     REQUIRED BY THE CALLED PROGRAM AND BRANCHES TO IT. WHEN CONTROL
*     IS RETURNED, THIS PROGRAM RESTORES THE REGISTERS (EXCEPT 15) AND
*     AMODE TO THAT OF THE CALLING PROGRAM AND RETURNS CONTROL.
**********************************************************************
*
*
PROG03  CSECT
PROG03  AMODE ANY                 RECV CNTL IN AMODE OF CALLING PROG
PROG03  RMODE 24                  RESIDE BELOW 16 MB LINE TO
*                                 ACCOMMODATE AMODE OF 24 OR 31
*
*
**********************************************************************
*     INITIALIZATION
**********************************************************************
*
        INITL 3,EQU=R             INITIALIZE PROGRAM
*
*
**********************************************************************
*     MAIN STREAM OF PROGRAM
**********************************************************************
*
         BAL   R6,VALIDATE         CHK IF REG 1 NEEDS ADJUSTMENT
         BAL   R6,LOAD             LOAD CALLED PROG
         BAL   R6,BRANCH           BRANCH TO CALLED PROG
         B     RETURN              RETURN TO CALLING PROG
*
*
**********************************************************************
*     THIS ROUTINE SAVES THE AMODE OF THE CALLING PROGRAM AND PASSES
*     CONTROL TO THE SUBROUTINE, WHICH DETERMINES IF REGISTER ONE
```

```
*    NEEDS TO BE ADJUSTED.
***********************************************************************
*
VALIDATE LA    R7,CHKAMODE          LD ADR OF CALLED RTN
         BASSM R8,R7                SAVE AMODE OF CALLING PROG,
*                                   BRANCH AND LINK TO CALLED RTN
         BR    R6                   RETURN TO CALLING RTN
*
*
***********************************************************************
*    THIS SUBROUTINE CHECKS THE AMODE OF THE CALLING PROGRAM. IF THE
*    AMODE IS 24, THEN THE HIGH ORDER BYTE OF REGISTER ONE IS SET
*    TO ZEROS.
***********************************************************************
*
CHKAMODE ST    R8,AMODE             STORE AMODE FOR TM INSTR
         TM    AMODE,X'80'          CHK AMODE OF CALLING PROG
         BZ    FIXREG1              IF AMODE=24 (BIT0=0), FIX REG 1
         ST    R1,PARMADR           STORE PARM ADR
         BR    R8                   AMODE=31,RET TO CALLING RTN
FIXREG1  ICM   R1,B'1000',=X'00'    SET BITS 0-7 OF PARM ADR TO ZEROS
         ST    R1,PARMADR           STORE FIXED PARM ADR
         BR    R8                   RETURN TO CALLING RTN
*
*
***********************************************************************
*    THIS ROUTINE LOADS THE CALLED PROGRAM AND SAVES THE
*    POINTER-DEFINED VALUE RETURNED FROM THE LOAD MACRO.
***********************************************************************
*
LOAD     LOAD  EP=PROG02X           LOAD CALLED PROG
         ST    R0,EPADR             SAVE POINTER-DEFINED VALUE
         BR    R6                   RETURN TO CALLING RTN
*
*
***********************************************************************
*    THIS ROUTINE CHANGES THE AMODE TO THAT OF THE CALLED PROGRAM
*    AND BRANCHES AND LINKS TO THE CALLED PROGRAM.
***********************************************************************
*
BRANCH   L     R1,PARMADR           LOAD PARM ADR FROM CALLING PROG
         L     R15,EPADR            LOAD EP ADR AND AMODE OF CALLED PROG
         BASSM R14,R15              SET AMODE AND BR AND LK TO CALLED PROG
         BR    R6                   RETURN TO CALLING RTN
*
*
***********************************************************************
*    THIS ROUTINE RESTORES THE REGISTERS AND THE AMODE TO THAT OF THE
*    CALLING PROGRAM AND RETURNS CONTROL.
***********************************************************************
*
RETURN   L     R13,4(0,R13)         RESTORE SA ADR OF CALLING PROG
         L     R14,12(0,R13)        RESTORE REG 14 OF CALLING PROG
         LM    R0,R12,20(R13)       RESTORE REGS 0-12 OF CALLING PROG
         BSM   0,R14                RSTR AMODE OF CALLING PROG AND RETURN
*
*
***********************************************************************
*    THE STORAGE AREAS USED BY THIS PROGRAM.
***********************************************************************
*
AMODE    DS    F
PARMADR  DS    F
EPADR    DS    F
```

```
*
*
***********************************************************************
*    END OF PROGRAM
***********************************************************************
*
*
         END
```

NOTES:

- The CHKMODE subroutine receives control via the BASSM instruction but returns control via the BR instruction. This is okay because the CHKMODE subroutine and the calling routine have the same addressing mode. The BASSM instruction is used to isolate the AMODE bit for the TM instruction.
- The linkage assist program returns control via the BSM 0,R14 instruction to assure that the calling program receives control back in the appropriate addressing mode. If the calling program uses the BALR R14,R15 instruction instead of the BASSM R14,R15 instruction to pass control, the BSM instruction will still function properly. This is because the link information in the high order byte of R_1 (register 14) due to the calling program executing in 24-bit addressing mode results in a value of zero in the high order bit for a BALR instruction. If the calling program is executing in 31-bit addressing mode, then the high order bit of R_1 (register 14) is always set to one for a BALR instruction.
- The link assist program, illustrated in this example, is written in a generic manner. It may be used by any 24-bit AMODE program to call (without system intervention) any 31-bit AMODE program or it may be used by any 31-bit AMODE program to call (without system intervention) any 24-bit AMODE program. The only customization required to use this linkage assist program for another set of calling/called programs is the following:
  - Change the name of the linkage assist program to that of the called program;
  - Change the name of the called program to another name; and
  - Change the program name specified in the LOAD macro instruction (in the linkage assist program) to that of the new name of the called program.

14.6.5 Capping (Prologue and Epilogue)

Capping can be used in lieu of a linkage assist routine to provide linkage between programs of different AMODEs. Capping is more efficient than a linkage assist routine, but requires source changes to the called program. Also, the capping method cannot be used on programs that reside above the 16 Mb line.

Capping is accomplished by adding prologue and epilogue code to an existing program to enable it to receive control in any AMODE and return control in the AMODE of the calling program. However, programs that reside above the 16 Mb line cannot receive control in 24-bit addressing mode because they will be unable to address their storage. This is why capping must not be used on programs that reside above the 16 Mb line.

When the prologue/epilogue code is written, the assumption must be that the calling program is not using supervisor intervention or the BASSM instruction for linkage. Therefore, the called program must determine the AMODE of the calling program and then restore the AMODE before returning control. If a capped program receives control via supervisor intervention or the BASSM instruction, then the prologue/epilogue code will not interfere with the linkage.

Coding Example 14.6.4

This coding example illustrates how an existing program can be capped to maintain addressing mode integrity during program linkage.

Called program before capping

```
PROGO4 CSECT
*
************************************************************************
*    INITIALIZATION
************************************************************************
*
         INITL 3,EQU=R
*
*
************************************************************************
*    MAINSTREAM OF PROGRAM
************************************************************************
*
         BAL   R6,RTNO1
         BAL   R6,RTNO2
         BAL   R6,RTNO3
         B     RETURN
*
*
************************************************************************
*    THIS ROUTINE RESTORES THE REGISTERS AND RETURNS CONTROL.
************************************************************************
*
RETURN   RCNTL RC=0
*
*
************************************************************************
*    END OF PROGRAM
************************************************************************
*
   END
```

Called program after capping code added

```
PROGO4 CSECT
*
*
************************************************************************
*    INITIALIZATION
************************************************************************
*
         INITL 3,EQU=R
*
*
************************************************************************
*    CAPPING PROLOGUE. THIS ROUTINE PERFORMS THE FOLLOWING:
*         * RECEIVES CONTROL IN AMODE OF CALLING PROGRAM;
*         * SAVES AMODE OF CALLING PROGRAM;
*         * CHANGES AMODE TO OWN AMODE.
************************************************************************
*
PROGO4   AMODE ANY
PROGO4   RMODE 24
*
PROLOG   LA    R10,RETURN          LOAD ADR OF RETURN RTN
```

```
         L     R11,OWNAMODE          LOAD OWN AMODE/PROLOGX RTN ADR
         BSM   R10,R11               GET CALLERS AMODE/BRANCH TO PROLOGX
PROLOGX  ST    R10,XAMODE            SAVE CALLERS AMODE/RETURN RTN ADR
         B     MAINSTRM              BRANCH TO MAINSTREAM OF PROG
OWNAMODE DC    A(PROLOGX)            OWN AMODE/PROLOGX RTN ADR
XAMODE   DS    F                     SAVE AREA FOR CALLERS AMODE AND
*                                    RETURN RTN ADR
*
*
***********************************************************************
*    MAINSTREAM OF PROGRAM
***********************************************************************
*
MAINSTRM BAL   R6,RTN01              *** LABEL ADDED ***
         BAL   R6,RTN02
         BAL   R6,RTN03
         B     EPILOG                *** CHANGED ***
*
*
***********************************************************************
*    CAPPING EPILOGUE. THIS ROUTINE PERFORMS THE FOLLOWING:
*         * RESTORES THE AMODE TO THAT OF THE CALLING PROGRAM;
*         * BRANCHES TO THE ORIGINAL RETURN ROUTINE.
***********************************************************************
*
EPILOG   L     R10,XAMODE            LOAD CALLING PROG AMODE/RETURN RTN ADR
         BSM   0,R10                 CHANGE AMODE, BRANCH TO RETURN RTN
*
*
***********************************************************************
*    THIS ROUTINE RESTORES THE REGISTERS AND RETURNS CONTROL.
***********************************************************************
*
RETURN   RCNTL RC=0                  RETURN TO MVS OR CALLING PROG
*
*
***********************************************************************
*    END OF PROGRAM
***********************************************************************
*
         END
```

NOTES:

- In the coding example, the called program is a 24-bit addressing mode program. The existing PROLOGUE code can support a 31-bit addressing mode program (which resides below the 16 Mb line), by making the following changes:

  - Removing the existing AMODE/RMODE statements of the program.
  - Adding the following instruction to the beginning of the PROLOGUE routine:

    ```
    ICM Rx,B'1000',=X'00'
    ```

    where: x is the number of the first base register.

  - This is necessary because if the 31-bit addressing mode program is called by a 24-bit addressing mode program, then the BALR instruction (functioning like in 370 mode) used for loading the first base register will insert link information in the high order byte of that register. When the PROLOGUE routine changes the AMODE to 31-bit addressing, then the link information will be used as part of the address. Since the program resides below the 16 Mb line, bits 1-7 of the high order byte of the base registers must be zero.

This instruction is not necessary in the PROLOGUE routine of a 24-bit addressing mode program because if the program receives control in 31-bit addressing mode, then the BALR instruction (functioning in 370-XA mode) will not insert link information in the high order byte of the first base register.

- Changing the contents of OWNAMODE as follows:

```
A31       EQU X'80000000'
OWNAMODE DC  A(A31+PROLOGX)
```

- Notice how the PROLOGUE and the EPILOGUE code is designed to be self-contained and cause minimal change to the existing program code.

14.7 TYPICAL PROGRAM LINKAGE SITUATIONS

When programs of unlike addressing modes call each other, certain planning and techniques are required. The following lists the typical combinations of calls. The assumption is made that existing 24-bit addressing programs are not to be modified:

- An existing 24-bit addressing mode program calls a new 31-bit addressing program.
- A new 31-bit addressing program calls an existing 24-bit addressing program.
- A new 31-bit addressing mode program calls a new 24-bit addressing mode program.
- A new 24-bit addressing mode program calls a new 31-bit addressing mode program.

AN EXISTING 24-AMODE PROGRAM CALLS A NEW 31-AMODE PROGRAM

If the 31-bit addressing mode program is called via the LINK, XCTL, or the ATTACH macro instruction, then there is no problem since these macro instructions cause the called program to receive control in the addressing mode associated with it. In addition, the LINK macro instruction causes the addressing mode of the calling program to be restored when control is returned. If the program is called via a combination of a LOAD macro instruction and a branch, then this may create a problem since the existing 24-bit addressing mode program will probably be using the BALR R14,R15 instruction to call the program instead of the BASSM R14,R15 instruction. The BALR instruction will not cause the addressing mode to be changed to that associated with the called 31-bit addressing mode program. Therefore, either a linkage assist routine would be required, or the 31-bit addressing mode program would be required to be "capped." Both solutions were described in Section 14.6.

A NEW 31-AMODE PROGRAM CALLS AN EXISTING 24-AMODE PROGRAM

If the 24-bit addressing mode program is called via the LINK, XCTL, or ATTACH macro instruction, then there is no problem since these macro instructions cause the called program to receive control in the addressing mode associated with it. In addition, the LINK macro instruction causes the addressing mode of the calling program to be restored when control is returned. If the LOAD macro instruction is used, then a pointer-defined value (see Section 14.6) is provided, and the 24-bit addressing mode program can be called via the BASSM R14,R15 instruction. However, the existing 24-bit addressing mode program will probably return control via the BR R14 instruction instead of via the BSM 0,R14 instruction, in which case the addressing mode of the calling 31-bit addressing mode program will not be restored. Therefore, a linkage assist routine would be required for a 31-bit addressing mode program to call an existing 24-bit addressing mode program via the combination of a LOAD macro instruction and a branch. In addition, if the 31-bit addressing mode program is passing any parameters to the 24-bit addressing mode program, then those parameters must reside below the 16 Mb line.

A NEW 24-AMODE PROGRAM CALLS A NEW 31-AMODE PROGRAM

This situation presents no problem. If the LINK, XCTL, or ATTACH macro instruction is used to call the program, then the operating system assures that the addressing mode is changed to that associated with the called program, and that the addressing mode is restored to that of the calling program when control is returned, if the LINK macro instruction was used to call the program. If a combination of a LOAD macro instruction and a branch is used to call the program, then the new 24-bit addressing mode program should be coded to use the BASSM R14,R15 instruction instead of the BALR R14,R15. This causes the addressing mode to be changed to that associated with the calling program. The 31-bit addressing mode program should be coded to use the BSM 0,R14 instruction to return control which causes the addressing mode of the calling program to be restored.

A NEW 31-AMODE PROGRAM CALLS A NEW 24-AMODE PROGRAM

This situation presents no problem. If the LINK, XCTL, or ATTACH macro instruction is used to call the program, then the operating system assures that the addressing mode is changed to that associated with the called program, and that the addressing mode is restored to that of the calling program when control is returned, if the LINK macro instruction was used to call the program. If a combination of a LOAD macro instruction and a branch is used to call the program, then the new 31-bit addressing mode program should be coded to use the BASSM R14,R15. This causes the addressing mode to be changed to that associated with the calling program. The 24-bit addressing mode program should be coded to use the BSM 0,R14 instruction instead of the BR R14 instruction to return control which causes the addressing mode of the calling program to be restored. The only potential problem is if parameters are being passed to the called program, in which case those parameters must reside below the 16 Mb line.

14.8 USING VIRTUAL STORAGE ABOVE THE 16 MB LINE BY 24-BIT ADDRESSING MODE PROGRAMS

Exploiting the huge amount of virtual storage available above the 16 Mb line presents no addressability problem for 31-bit addressing mode programs. However, this is not the situation for 24-bit addressing mode programs. If there are no plans to convert the 24-bit addressing mode programs to 31-bit addressing mode or if the 24-bit addressing mode programs cannot be converted due to various 24-bit addressing mode constraints such as the performance of I/O, then certain coding techniques are required to make use of the virtual storage located above the 16 Mb line.

The subroutine of the 24-bit addressing mode program, which references the virtual storage above the 16 Mb line, must execute in 31-bit addressing mode. This can be accomplished by dynamically changing the AMODE, via the BASSM instruction, from 24-bit to 31-bit and then passing control to the subroutine. When the subroutine completes processing, then the AMODE must be changed back to 24-bit before control is returned to the calling routine. This can be accomplished via the BASSM and the BSM instructions. Coding Example 14.8.1 shows the required code to accomplish this.

Coding Example 14.8.1

This coding example illustrates how a 24-bit addressing mode program can address virtual storage located above the 16 Mb line. In this example, the GETMAIN macro instruction is used to allocate virtual storage above the 16 Mb line, and card-image records are read from a sequential dataset and moved into that virtual storage.

```
*
*
         TITLE 'DEMO PROGRAM TO ILLUSTRATE HOW A 24-BIT AMODE PROGRAM -
               USES 31-BIT AMODE STORAGE'
*
*
***********************************************************************
*    THIS PROGRAM RECEIVES CONTROL IN 24-BIT ADDRESSING MODE. IT
*    READS DATA RECORDS FROM A SEQUENTIAL DATASET. THE DATA RECORDS
*    ARE MOVED INTO A VIRTUAL STORAGE TABLE LOCATED ABOVE THE 16 MB
*    LINE. WHEN ALL THE DATA RECORDS ARE READ, THE DATA IS PROCESSED
*    FROM THE TABLE. THE ROUTINE THAT CREATES THE TABLE EXECUTES IN
*    31-BIT ADDRESSING MODE.
***********************************************************************
*
*
XABLDTBL CSECT
*
*
***********************************************************************
*    INITIALIZATION
***********************************************************************
*
         INITL 3,EQU=R              INITIALIZE PROGRAM
         ICM   R3,B'1000',=X'00'    ZERO BITS 0-7 OF 1ST BASE REG
*
*
***********************************************************************
*    MAIN STREAM OF PROGRAM
***********************************************************************
*
         BAL   R6,OPEN              OPEN INPUT DCB
         BAL   R6,GETVS31           ALLO VS ABOVE 16 MB LINE
NEXTREC  BAL   R6,GETDATA           READ A DATA REC
         BAL   R6,PUTTBL            PUT DATA REC INTO TBL
         B     NEXTREC              READ NEXT REC
DATAEND  BAL   R6,DOTBLEND          EOD, IND END OF TBL
         BAL   R6,CLOSE             CLOSE INPUT DCB
         BAL   R6,PROCTBL           PROCESS DATA IN TABLE
         B     RETURN               RETURN TO MVS OR CALLING PGM
*
*
***********************************************************************
*    THIS ROUTINE OPENS THE INPUT DCB.
***********************************************************************
*
OPEN     OPEN  SYSIN                OPEN INPUT DCB
         ...                        CHK FOR GOOD OPEN
         BR    R6                   RETURN TO CALLING RTN
*
*
```

```
***********************************************************************
*    THIS ROUTINE ALLOCATES VIRTUAL STORAGE ABOVE THE 16 MB LINE.
***********************************************************************
*
GETVS31  GETMAIN RU,LV=4096,LOC=ANY,SP=10
         ST    R1,TBLADR31         SAVE BG-OF-TBL ADR
         ST    R1,TBLPTR31         SET TBL ENTRY PTR TO BG
         BR    R6                  RETURN TO CALLING RTN
*
*
***********************************************************************
*    THIS ROUTINE READS A DATA RECORD.
***********************************************************************
*
GETDATA  GET   SYSIN               READ A DATA REC
         ST    R1,DATAADR          SAVE ADR OF DATA REC
         BR    R6                  RETURN TO CALLING RTN
*
*
***********************************************************************
*    THIS ROUTINE CHANGES THE AMODE TO 31 AND PASSES CONTROL TO THE
*    SUBROUTINE, WHICH BUILDS THE TABLE IN VIRTUAL STORAGE ABOVE THE
*    16 MB LINE.
***********************************************************************
*
PUTTBL   L     R7,PTBL31X          LOAD ADR OF 31-BIT AMODE RTN TO
*                                  BUILD TABLE
         BASSM R8,R7               CHANGE AMODE TO 31, BRANCH AND LINK
*                                  TO PTBL31 RTN
         BR    R6                  RETURN TO CALLING RTN
*
*
***********************************************************************
*    THIS SUBROUTINE COPIES THE RECORD READ FROM THE INPUT DATASET
*    INTO THE TABLE ABOVE THE 16 MB LINE AND THEN CHANGES THE AMODE
*    BACK TO 24.
***********************************************************************
*
PTBL31   L     R10,TBLPTR31        LOAD ADR OF NEXT TBL SLOT
         L     R11,DATAADR         LOAD ADR OF DATA REC
         MVC   0(ENTLEN,R10),0(R11) MOVE DATA REC INTO TBL
         LA    R10,ENTLEN(0,R10)   INCR TO NEXT TBL SLOT
         ST    R10,TBLPTR31        SAVE ADR OF NEXT TBL SLOT
         BSM   0,R8                CHANGE AMODE TO 24, RET TO CALLING RTN
PTBL31X  DC    A(A31+PTBL31)       POINTER-DEFINED VALUE OF PTBL31 RTN
*
*
***********************************************************************
*    THIS ROUTINE CLOSES THE INPUT DATASET.
***********************************************************************
*
CLOSE    CLOSE SYSIN               CLOSE INPUT DCB
         BR    R6                  RETURN TO CALLING RTN
*
*
***********************************************************************
*    THIS ROUTINE CHANGES THE AMODE TO 31 AND PASSES CONTROL TO THE
*    SUBROUTINE, WHICH PUTS AN END-OF-TABLE INDICATOR AFTER THE LAST
*    ENTRY OF THE TABLE.
***********************************************************************
*
DOTBLEND L     R7,SETENDX          LOAD ADR OF 31-BIT AMODE RTN TO
*                                  SET TBL-END INDICATOR
         BASSM R8,R7               CHANGE AMODE TO 31, BRANCH AND LINK
```

```
*                                        TO SETEND RTN
         BR    R6                        RETURN TO CALLING RTN
*
*
*********************************************************************
*    THIS SUBROUTINE PUTS AN END-OF-TABLE INDICATOR AT THE LOGICAL
*    END OF THE TABLE AND THEN CHANGES THE AMODE BACK TO 24.
*********************************************************************
*
SETEND   L     R10,TBLPTR31              LOAD ADR OF NEXT TBL SLOT
         MVC   0(L'TBLENDID,R10),TBLENDID MOVE TBL-END IND INTO TBL
         MVC   TBLPTR31,TBLADR31         SET TBL PTR TO BG
         BSM   0,R8                      CHANGE AMODE TO 24, RET TO CALLING RTN
SETENDX  DC    A(A31+SETEND)             POINTER-DEFINED VALUE OF SETEND RTN
*
*
*********************************************************************
*    THIS ROUTINE PROCESSES THE DATA IN THE TABLE.
*********************************************************************
*
PROCTBL  ...                             PROCESS DATA IN TABLE
         BR    R6                        RETURN TO CALLING RTN
*
*
*********************************************************************
*    THIS ROUTINE RETURNS CONTROL TO MVS OR THE CALLING PROGRAM.
*********************************************************************
*
RETURN   RCNTL  RC=0
*
*
*********************************************************************
*    THE CONSTANTS AND WORK AREAS USED IN THIS PROGRAM.
*********************************************************************
*
A31      EQU   X'80000000'               31-BIT AMODE INDICATOR
ENTLEN   EQU   80                        LENGTH OF ENTRIES PUT INTO TABLE
TBLADR31 DS    F
TBLPTR31 DS    F
DATAADR  DS    F
TBLENDID DC    4XL1'FF'                  TBL-END INDICATOR
*
*
*********************************************************************
*     INPUT DCB
*********************************************************************
*
SYSIN    DCB   DSORG=PS,MACRF=GL,LRECL=80,RECFM=FB,EODAD=DATAEND,  -
               DDNAME=SYSIN
*
*
*********************************************************************
*    END OF PROGRAM
*********************************************************************
*
*
           END
```

NOTES:

- In this coding example, a fixed amount of virtual storage is obtained to store a variable amount of data. This is for illustration purposes only, to demostrate how virtual storage above the 16 Mb line can be referenced by a 24-bit addressing mode program. The virtual storage allocated for the table should actually be coded as an expandable table as discussed in Chapter 5.

- In order for the 31-bit addressing mode subroutine to reference the labels in the 24-bit addressing mode program, the addresses represented by these labels must be valid 31-bit addresses. The addresses represented by the labels are generated by adding the contents of the appropriate base register to the displacements associated with the labels. If the labels, which are referenced, are addressed by the first base register, then an addressability problem may exist. Since the first base register of a program is usually loaded with the BALR instruction and the program is executing in 24-bit addressing mode, then the high order byte of that register contains link information. When that base register is used to develop a 31-bit address, the link information in the high order byte is used as part of the address and will cause unpredictable results when referenced (usually an S0C4). To remedy this problem, the high order byte of the first base register must be set to zeros after the base register is loaded. This can be accomplished via the ICM machine instruction as demostrated in the coding example. The other base registers are normally loaded with LA or L instructions, which does not present a problem. If the contents of the previous base register are used as an index value to load the next base register (as the INITL macro instruction does), then there is still no problem because only the low order 24 bits are used from the index register since the program is executing in 24-bit addressing mode.

14.9 PERFORMING I/O IN 31-BIT ADDRESSING MODE PROGRAMS

Most I/O must be performed by programs that execute in 24-bit addressing mode. Certain VSAM services accept callers in either 24-bit or 31-bit addressing modes, but in either case the required I/O control blocks must reside below the 16 Mb line.

Programs that execute in 31-bit addressing mode have two options of performing I/O. One is to contain a subroutine that dynamically changes AMODE to 24-bit to perform the I/O and then changes AMODE back to 31-bit before returning control to the calling routine. The other option is to call a separate program, which executes in 24-bit addressing mode, to perform the actual I/O.

Coding Example 14.9.1 shows a 31-bit addressing mode program and the called 24-bit addressing mode program that performs the I/O.

The 24-bit addressing mode I/O program can be designed in one of two ways. One way is for it to be customized to the actual requirements of a specific calling 31-bit addressing mode program. In this case, the I/O program defines the DCBs specifying the required access methods and the LRECLs, any other required control blocks, and receives, via a parameter-list, a request for the required I/O operation (input, output, etc.).

The other way is for the 24-bit addressing mode I/O program to be generic, in which case, the calling 31-bit addressing mode program defines all required control blocks (below the 16 Mb line) and passes those addresses to the I/O program via a parameter-list, together with a request as to which Data Management macro instruction is to be issued (OPEN, READ, GET, etc). In this case, the called I/O program would be required to have the code to support all the possible Data Management macro instructions that can be requested by the callers of this program. However, with this design, processing of the end-of-data (EOD) routine can present a problem. If the input DCB is defined in the calling 31-bit addressing mode program, then the assumption would be that the EOD routine is also defined there. This can present an addressing mode integrity problem since Data Management expects the EOD routine to be located in a 24-bit addressing mode program such as the one that is executing the Data Management macro instructions. This problem can be remedied by placing the EOD routine in a section of the 31-bit addressing mode program that is set up for 24-bit addressing mode. But this would require additional work and defeat the presumed objective of the 31-bit addressing mode program of executing exclusively in 31-bit addressing mode. A better solution would be for the 31-bit addressing mode program to define the input DCB without specifying an EOD address (which would cause an MNOTE that can be ignored). In this case, the I/O program contains the EOD routine, and its address is inserted into the input DCB before any input Data Management macro instructions are executed. Upon EOD, the I/O program sends the calling 31-bit addressing mode program an indication of EOD, and the calling program can process the EOD condition in a 31-bit addressing mode routine.

Coding Example 14.9.1

This coding example illustrates how a 31-bit addressing mode program calls a 24-bit addressing mode program to perform I/O. In this example, the called I/O program is customized for the specific requirements of the calling 31-bit addressing mode program.

The calling 31-bit AMODE Program

```
*
*
         TITLE 'EXAMPLE OF A 31-BIT AMODE PROGRAM THAT CALLS A 24-BIT -
               AMODE PROGRAM TO PERFORM I/O'
*
*
**********************************************************************
*     THIS IS A 31-BIT AMODE PROGRAM THAT PERFORMS I/O BY CALLING A
*     24-BIT AMODE PROGRAM TO PERFORM THE ACTUAL I/O OPERATIONS.
*     THE TWO PROGRAMS COMMUNICATE VIA A USER-DEFINED COMMUNICATIONS
*     PARAMETER AREA (CPA) LOCATED BELOW THE 16 MB LINE. THIS PROGRAM
*     PLACES THE FUNCTION-CODE OF THE DESIRED I/O OPERATION AND THE
*     RECORD, IF APPLICABLE, INTO THE CPA AND CALLS THE I/O PROGRAM.
**********************************************************************
*
*
XAPROG01 CSECT
XAPROG01 AMODE 31                   EXECUTES IN 31-BIT AMODE
XAPROG01 RMODE ANY                  MAY RESIDE ANYWHERE IN VS
*
*
**********************************************************************
*     INITIALIZATION
**********************************************************************
*
         INITL 3,EQU=R               INITIALIZE PROG
         USING IOAREA,R1             DEF REG FOR PARM AREA DSECT
*
*
**********************************************************************
*     MAINSTREAM OF PROGRAM
**********************************************************************
*
         BAL   R6,LOAD               LOAD I/O PROG
         BAL   R6,GETMAIN            ALLO PARM AREA BELOW 16 MB LINE
         BAL   R6,OPEN               REQ I/O PROG TO OPEN DCBS
NEXTREC  BAL   R6,GETREC             REQ I/O PROG TO READ A RECORD
         BAL   R6,UPDTREC            UPDATE RECORD
         BAL   R6,PUTREC             REQ I/O PROG TO WRITE UPDATED REC
         B     NEXTREC               READ NEXT RECORD
```

```
DATAEND  BAL   R6,CLOSE            REQ I/O PROG TO CLOSE DCBS
         B     RETURN              RETURN TO MVS OR CALLING PROGM
*
*
***********************************************************************
*    THIS ROUTINE LOADS THE 24-BIT AMODE I/O PROGRAM AND SAVES THE
*    POINTER-DEFINED VALUE RETURNED FROM THE LOAD MACRO.
***********************************************************************
*
LOAD     LOAD  EP=IOPROG01
         ST    R0,IOPGMEPA         SAVE POINTER-DEFINED VALUE
         BR    R6                  RETURN TO CALLING RTN
*
*
***********************************************************************
*    THIS ROUTINE ALLOCATES VIRTUAL STORAGE BELOW THE 16 MB LINE
*    FOR THE COMMUNICATIONS PARAMETER AREA (CPA) FOR THE I/O PROGRAM.
***********************************************************************
*
GETMAIN  GETMAIN RU,LV=84,LOC=BELOW
         ST    R1,PARMADR          SAVE ADR OF VS FOR I/O PROG
         BR    R6                  RETURN TO CALLING RTN
*
*
***********************************************************************
*    THIS ROUTINE CALLS THE I/O PROGRAM AND REQUESTS AN OPEN OPERATION.
*    THE I/O PROGRAM OPENS THE INPUT AND THE OUTPUT DCBS.
***********************************************************************
*
OPEN     L     R1,PARMADR          LD PARM ADR FOR I/O PROG
         MVI   IOFUNC,OPENIND      SET OPEN FUNC-CODE
         L     R15,IOPGMEPA        LD PTR-DEF VALUE OF I/O PROG
         BASSM R14,R15             CHANGE AMODE, BR AND LK TO I/O PROG
         BAL   R7,CHECKRC          CHK RETURN CODE FORM I/O PROG
         BR    R6                  RETURN TO CALLING RTN
*
*
***********************************************************************
*    THIS ROUTINE CALLS THE I/O PROGRAM AND REQUESTS THAT A RECORD
*    BE READ.
***********************************************************************
*
GETREC   L     R1,PARMADR          LD PARM ADR FOR I/O PROG
         MVI   IOFUNC,GETIND       SET GET FUNC-CODE
         L     R15,IOPGMEPA        LD PTR-DEF VALUE OF I/O PROG
         BASSM R14,R15             CHANGE AMODE, BR AND LK TO I/O PROG
         BAL   R7,CHECKRC          CHK RETURN CODE FROM I/O PROG
         BR    R6                  RETURN TO CALLING RTN
*
*
***********************************************************************
*    THIS ROUTINE UPDATES THE RECORD READ BY THE I/O PROGRAM.
***********************************************************************
*
UPDTREC  ...                       UPDATE RECORD
         BR   R6                   RETURN TO CALLING RTN
*
*
***********************************************************************
*    THIS ROUTINE CALLS THE I/O PROGRAM AND REQUESTS THAT IT WRITE
*    THE SPECIFIED RECORD (THE RECORD JUST UPDATED).
***********************************************************************
*
PUTREC   L     R1,PARMADR          LD PARM ADR FOR I/O PROG
```

```
         MVI   IOFUNC,PUTIND      SET PUT FUNC-CODE
         L     R15,IOPGMEPA       LD PTR-DEF VALUE OF I/O PROG
         BASSM R14,R15            CHANGE AMODE, BR AND LK TO I/O PROG
         BAL   R7,CHECKRC         CHK RETURN CODE FROM I/O PROG
         BR    R6                 RETURN TO CALLING RTN
*
*
***********************************************************************
*    THIS ROUTINE CALLS I/O PROGRAM AND REQUESTS A CLOSE OPERATION.
*    THE I/O PROGRAM CLOSES THE INPUT AND THE OUTPUT DCBS.
***********************************************************************
*
CLOSE    L     R1,PARMADR         LD PARM ADR FOR I/O PROG
         MVI   IOFUNC,CLOSEIND    SET CLOSE FUNC-CODE
         L     R15,IOPGMEPA       LD PTR-DEF VALUE OF I/O PROG
         BASSM R14,R15            CHANGE AMODE, BR AND LK TO I/O PROG
         BAL   R7,CHECKRC         CHK RETURN CODE FROM I/O PROG
         BR    R6                 RETURN TO CALLING RTN
*
*
***********************************************************************
*    THIS ROUTINE CHECKS THE I/O COMPLETION INDICATOR RETURNED BY THE
*    I/O PROGRAM.
***********************************************************************
*
CHECKRC  L     R1,PARMADR         SET ADRBLTY FOR PARM DSECT
         CLI   IORC,OKIND         CHK IF OPERATION WAS OK
         BER   R7                 IF YES, RET TO CALLING RTN
         CLI   IORC,EODIND        CHK IF END-OF-DATA
         BE    DATAEND            IF YES, BR TO E-O-D RTN
         CLI   IORC,OPNERIND      CHK IF OPEN ERROR
         BE    OPENERR            IF YES, BR TO OPEN-ERROR RTN
         CLI   IORC,IOERRIND      CHK IF I/O ERROR
         BE    IOERR              IF YES, BR TO I/O-ERROR RTN
         B     INVFUNC            IF NO, INVALID FUNC CODE SPECIFIED
*
*
***********************************************************************
*    THESE SUBROUTINES PROCESS THE VARIOUS ERROR INDICATIONS RETURNED
*    BY THE I/O PROGRAM.
***********************************************************************
*
OPENERR  ...                      OPEN ERROR
*
IOERR    ...                      I/O ERROR
*
INVFUNC  ...                      INV FUNC CODE SPECIFIED
*
*
***********************************************************************
*    THIS ROUTINE RETURNS CONTROL TO MVS OR THE CALLING PROGRAM.
***********************************************************************
*
RETURN   RCNTL RC=0
*
*
***********************************************************************
*     THE STORAGE AREAS USED IN THIS PROGRAM.
***********************************************************************
*
IOPGMEPA DS    F
PARMADR  DS    F
*
*
```

```
***********************************************************************
*    THE EQUS FOR THE FUNCTION CODES AND ERROR INDICATORS.
***********************************************************************
*
OPENIND  EQU   01
GETIND   EQU   02
PUTIND   EQU   03
CLOSEIND EQU   04
OKIND    EQU   00
EODIND   EQU   04
OPNERIND EQU   08
IOERRIND EQU   12
INVIND   EQU   16
*
*
***********************************************************************
*    THIS DSECT IS USED TO MAP THE COMMUNICATIONS PARAMETER AREA.
***********************************************************************
*
IOAREA   DSECT
IOFUNC   DS    CL1                SPECIFIED FUNC-CODE FOR REQ
IORC     DS    CL1                RC RETURNED FROM I/O PROG
         DS    CL2
IORECORD DS    CL80 .             RECORD RET FROM I/O PROG FOR GET
*                                 RECORD PASSED TO I/O PROG FOR PUT
*
*
***********************************************************************
*    END OF PROGRAM
***********************************************************************
*
*
           END
```

The called 24-bit AMODE I/O Program

```
*
*
         TITLE 'I/O PROGRAM FOR CALLING PROGRAM XAPROG01'
*
*
***********************************************************************
*    THIS 24-BIT AMODE PROGRAM PERFORMS THE I/O FOR THE CALLING 31-BIT
*    AMODE PROGRAM XAPROG01. THE TWO PROGRAMS COMMUNICATE VIA A
*    COMMUNICATIONS PARAMETER AREA (CPA) LOCATED BELOW THE 16 MB LINE.
*    A FUNCTION-CODE IS RECEIVED FROM THE CALLING PROGRAM, VIA THE CPA,
*    AND THIS PROGRAM PERFORMS THE REQUESTED OPERATION. THIS PROGRAM
*    RETURNS THE RECORD, IF APPLICABLE, AND THE RETURN CODE, VIA THE
*    CPA, TO THE CALLING PROGRAM.
***********************************************************************
*
*
IOPROG01 CSECT
IOPROG01 AMODE 24                 AMODE=24 (DEFAULT) REQUIRED FOR I/O
IOPROG01 RMODE 24                 RMODE=24 (DEFAULT) REQUIRED FOR I/O
*
*
***********************************************************************
*    INITIALIZATION
***********************************************************************
*
         INITL 3,EQU=R            INITIALIZE PROGRAM
```

```
         USING IOAREA,R10        DEF REG FOR IOAREA DSECT
         USING IHADCB,R11        DEF REG FOR DCB DSECT
         LR    R10,R1            SET ADRBLTY FOR IOAREA DSECT
*
*
***********************************************************************
*    MAINSTREAM OF PROGRAM
***********************************************************************
*
         BAL   R6,ROUTFUNC       PERFORM REQUESTED FUNC
         B     RETURN            RETURN TO CALLING PROG
*
*
***********************************************************************
*    THE ROUTINE CHECKS THE FUNCTION-CODE RECEIVED FROM THE CALLING
*    PROGRAM AND ROUTES CONTROL TO THE APPROPRIATE SUBROUTINE.
***********************************************************************
*
ROUTFUNC CLI   IOFUNC,OPENIND    CHK FOR OPEN REQ
         BE    OPEN              IF YES, DO OPEN
         CLI   IOFUNC,GETIND     CHK FOR GET REQ
         BE    GETREC            IF YES, DO GET
         CLI   IOFUNC,PUTIND     CHK FOR PUT REQ
         BE    PUTREC            IF YES, DO PUT
         CLI   IOFUNC,CLOSEIND   CHK FOR CLOSE REQ
         BE    CLOSE             IF YES, DO CLOSE
         MVI   IORC,INVIND       IF NO, IND INVALID FUNC-CODE
         LA    R15,4             IND REQ WAS UNSUCCESSFUL
         BR    R6                RETURN TO CALLING RTN
*
*
***********************************************************************
*    THIS SUBROUTINE OPENS THE INPUT AND THE OUTPUT DCBS.
***********************************************************************
*
OPEN     OPEN  (RECIN,,RECOUT,(OUTPUT)) OPEN DCBS
         LA    R11,RECIN         SET DSECT ADRBLTY FOR INPUT DCB
         TM    DCBOFLGS,DCBOFOPN CHK IF OPEN OK
         BNO   OPENERR           IF NO, IND IT
         LA    R11,RECOUT        SET DSECT ADRBLTY FOR OUTPUT DCB
         TM    DCBOFLGS,DCBOFOPN CHK IF OPEN OK
         BNO   OPENERR           IF NO, IND IT
         MVI   IORC,OKIND        IF YES, IND OPEN OK
         LA    R15,0             IND REQ WAS SUCCESSFUL
         BR    R6                RETURN TO CALLING RTN
OPENERR  MVI   IORC,OPNERIND     IND OPEN ERROR
         LA    R15,4             IND REQ WAS UNSUCCESSFUL
         BR    R6                RETURN TO CALLING RTN
*
*
***********************************************************************
*    THIS SUBROUTINE PERFORMS A QSAM READ OF A RECORD AND RETURNS IT
*    TO THE CALLING PROGRAM. IT ALSO RECEIVES CONTROL AT END-OF-DATA
*    AND INDICATES THIS TO THE CALLING PROGRAM.
***********************************************************************
*
GETREC   GET   RECIN,IORECORD    READ A RECORD
         MVI   IORC,OKIND        IND GET OK
         LA    R15,0             IND REQUEST WAS SUCCESSFUL
         BR    R6                RETURN TO CALLING RTN
DATAEND  MVI   IORC,EODIND       IND EOD
         LA    R15,4             IND REQ WAS UNSUCCESSFUL
         BR    R6                RETURN TO CALLING RTN
*
```

```
*
***********************************************************************
*     THIS SUBROUTINE PERFORMS A QSAM WRITE OF THE RECORD RECEIVED FROM
*     THE CALLING PROGRAM.
***********************************************************************
*
PUTREC PUT   RECOUT,IORECORD   WRITE A RECORD
         MVI   IORC,OKIND         IND PUT OK
         LA    R15,0              IND REQUEST WAS SUCCESSFUL
         BR    R6                 RETURN TO CALLING RTN
*
*
***********************************************************************
*     THIS SUBROUTINE CLOSES THE INPUT AND THE OUTPUT DCBS.
***********************************************************************
*
CLOSE    CLOSE (RECIN,,RECOUT)    CLOSE DCBS
         MVI   IORC,OKIND         IND CLOSE OK
         LA    R15,0              IND REQUEST WAS SUCCESSFUL
         BR    R6                 RETURN TO CALLING RTN
*
*
***********************************************************************
*     THIS IS THE I/O ERROR ANALYSIS ROUTINE DEFINED BY SYNAD AND
*     RECEIVES CONTROL WHEN AN UNCORRECTABLE I/O ERROR OCCURS. IT USES
*     THE SYNADAF MACRO TO ANALYZE THE I/O ERROR AND DISPLAYS VIA WTO
*     THE ERROR MESSAGE GENERATED BY SYNADAF.
***********************************************************************
*
IOERR  SYNADAF ACSMETH=QSAM    ALLO SA, ANALYZE I/O ERROR
         MVI   IORC,IOERRIND      IND I/O ERROR
         MVC   IOERRMSG,50(R1)    EXTRACT I/O ERROR MSG FROM SYNADAF
         SYNADRLS                 RELEASE SYNADAF SA AND MSG BUFFER
         LA    R1,WTOLST          LD LIST-ADR FOR EXEC-FORM OF WTO
         WTO   MF=(E,(R1))        ISSUE EXEC-FORM OF WTO
         LA    R15,4              IND REQ WAS UNSUCCESSFUL
         BR    R6                 RETURN TO CALLING RTN
*
*
***********************************************************************
*     THIS ROUTINE RESTORES THE REGISTERS AND THE AMODE OF THE CALLING
*     PROGRAM AND RETURNS CONTROL.
***********************************************************************
*
RETURN L     R13,4(0,R13)      RESTORE SA ADR OF CALLING PROG
         L     R14,12(0,R13)      RESTORE REG 14 OF CALLING PROG
         LM    R0,R12,20(R13)     RESTORE REGS 0-12 OF CALLING PROG
         BSM   0,R14              CHANGE AMODE TO 31, RETURN TO
*                                 CALLING PROG
*
***********************************************************************
*     THE WTO-LIST FOR I/O ERROR MESSAGE RECEIVED FROM SYNADAF MACRO.
***********************************************************************
*
         CNOP  0,4
WTOLST   DC    AL2(WTOLSTX-WTOLST)
         DC    X'8000'            INDICATE DESC/ROUTCDE INCLUDED
IOERRMSG DS    CL78
WTOLSTX  EQU   *
         DC    X'0000'            DESC DEFAULT
         DC    X'0020'            ROUTCDE=11
*
*
***********************************************************************
*    THE INPUT AND THE OUTPUT DCBS.
***********************************************************************
*
```

```
RECIN    DCB   DSORG=PS,MACRF=GM,LRECL=80,RECFM=FB,EODAD=DATAEND,       -
-              SYNAD=IOERR,DDNAME=RECINDD
RECOUT   DCB   DSORG=PS,MACRF=PM,BLKSIZE=80,LRECL=80,RECFM=F,          -
-              SYNAD=IOERR,DDNAME=RECOUTDD
*
*
***********************************************************************
*    THE EQUS FOR THE FUNCTION CODES AND ERROR INDICATORS.
***********************************************************************
*
OPENIND  EQU   01
GETIND   EQU   02
PUTIND   EQU   03
CLOSEIND EQU   04
OKIND    EQU   00
EODIND   EQU   04
OPNERIND EQU   08
IOERRIND EQU   12
INVIND   EQU   16
*
*
***********************************************************************
*    THE DSECTS USED BY THIS PROGRAM.
***********************************************************************
*
***********************************************************************
*    THE DSECT USED TO MAP THE COMMUNICATIONS PARAMETER AREA.
***********************************************************************
*
IOAREA   DSECT
IOFUNC   DS    CL1                SPECIFIED FUNC-CODE FOR REQ
IORC     DS    CL1                RC RETURNED FROM I/O PROG
         DS    CL2
IORECORD DS    CL80               RECORD RET FROM I/O PROG FOR GET
*                                 RECORD PASSED TO I/O PROG FOR PUT
*
*
***********************************************************************
*    THE DSECT TO MAP OUT THE DCBS.
***********************************************************************
*
         PRINT NOGEN
         DCBD  DSORG=PS
*
*
***********************************************************************
*    END OF PROGRAM
***********************************************************************
*
*
         END
```

NOTES:

- The RCNTL macro instruction, presented in Chapter 3, should be modified to use the BSM 0,R14 instruction instead of the BR R14 instruction to return control.
- The IOAREA DSECT and the EQUs for the I/O function-codes and for the error indicators are coded for illustration purposes. They should actually be invoked via macro instructions or COPY statements.
- As an exercise, the reader might try to design and code a generic I/O program.

14.10 THE PGSER MACRO INSTRUCTION

The PGRLSE, PGLOAD, and PGOUT macro instructions were discussed in Chapter 9 and the PGFIX and PGFREE macro instructions were discussed in Chapter 10. These macro instructions perform services only for pages whose virtual storage addresses are below the 16 Mb line. The PGSER macro instruction performs the same services as all of the paging control macro instructions mentioned above for pages that are located below or above the 16 Mb line.

The format of the PGSER macro instruction is as follows:

```
[name]    PGSER    {R|L},{RELEASE|LOAD|OUT|FIX|FREE},A=start-addr
                   [,EA=end-addr][,ECB={ecb-addr|0}][,LONG={Y|N}]
                   [,RELEASE={Y|N}][,KEEPREL={Y|N}]
                   [,BACKOUT={Y|N}]
```

`R`

Indicates that no parameter-list is being supplied with this request.

`L`

Indicates that a parameter-list is being supplied with this request. This option will not be discussed.

`RELEASE`

Requests the same services as the PGRLSE macro instruction except that the specified virtual storage addresses may also be above the 16 Mb line.

`LOAD`

Requests the same services as the PGLOAD macro instruction except that the specified virtual storage addresses may also be above the 16 Mb line.

`OUT`

Requests the same services as the PGOUT macro instruction except that the specified virtual storage addresses may also be above the 16 Mb line.

`FIX`

Requests the same services as the PGFIX macro instruction except that the specified virtual storage addresses may also be above the 16 Mb line. This service is available only to authorized programs.

`FREE`

Requests the same services as the PGFREE macro instruction except that the specified virtual storage addresses may also be above the 16 Mb line. This service is available only to authorized programs.

`A=start-addr`

Specifies the address of the start of the virtual storage area for R requests.

`EA=end-addr (Default: start-addr)`

Specifies the address of the end of the virtual storage area for R requests. Note: Unlike other paging control macro instructions, this address is specified as the actual end address as opposed to the end address + 1.

ECB=ecb-addr
ECB=0 (Default: ECB=0, synchronous processing)

This parameter is used with the LOAD and FIX requests to indicate an asynchronous LOAD or FIX request. Specifies the address of the ECB that is to be posted when the LOAD or FIX request is complete.

Unlike the PGLOAD and PGFIX macro instructions, the return code must also be checked if an ECB address is specified because the ECB will not be posted if the return code is zero.

The ECB parameter may also be specified with the FREE request, but must specify the address of an ECB previously specified with a FIX request. If specified, any pages specified in the previous FIX request that are not yet fixed will not be fixed. Also, the ECB for the FIX request will not be posted if it was not yet posted at the time of the FREE request.

If the ECB address is specified as 0 or is omitted, then control is returned when the LOAD or FIX request is completely and successfully satisfied and the return code need not be checked. If the request is unsuccessful, then MVS will cause an ABEND. If the ECB address is not specified for a FREE request, then only the pages that are already fixed are released and the remaining page fixing activity and ECB processing of the corresponding FIX request are not affected.

LONG=Y
LONG=N (Default: Y)

This parameter may be specified only with the FIX request.
Specifies the relative real time duration for the page fix. Y indicates long and N indicates short. The convention is that Y implies a second or more. The value Y should normally be specified (or defaulted). If N is specified, then the page is fixed in the V=R or non-preferred storage areas. If that page fix actually has a long duration, then V=R functions and CONFIG STORAGE commands may be delayed.

RELEASE=Y
RELEASE=N (Default: N)

This parameter may be specified only with the LOAD, FIX, or FREE request.

- Y Specifies that the contents of the virtual pages, which are completely within the specified address range, are to be discarded.
- N Specifies that the contents of the virtual pages within the specified address range are to remain intact.

The sections"The PGLOAD Macro Instruction" and "Using the PGLOAD Macro Instruction" in Chapter 9 discussed the meaning and use of the RELEASE parameter in more detail.

KEEPREL=Y
KEEPREL=N (Default: N)

This parameter may be specified only with the OUT request.

- Y Specifies that, after the page-out, the virtual storage pages also remain in real storage.
- N Specifies that, after the page-out, the real storage frames are released.

BACKOUT=Y
BACKOUT=N (Default: Y)

Specifies the procedure to follow when a non-allocated page is encountered during the processing of a FIX request.

- Y specifies that all pages fixed as part of the request are freed before before returning to the caller.
- N specifies that the pages previously fixed as part of the request are not freed and no futher processing is done before returning to the caller.

When the PGSER macro instruction returns control, register 15 is posted with a return code of X'00' to indicate successful completion. The non-zero return codes for the specific requests (LOAD, FIX, etc.) have the same meaning as the corresponding macro instructions (PGLOAD, PGFIX, etc.) presented in Chapters 9 and 10.

Coding Example 14.10.1

This coding example illustrates how to code the PGSER macro instruction to request the loading (page-in) of the pages that contain any portion of the address range specified. In this example, registers 10 and 11 contain the beginning and ending addresses, respectively, of the virtual storage pages that are to be loaded.

```
         PGSER R,LOAD,A=(R10),EA=(R11)
```

Coding Example 14.10.2

This coding example illustrates how to code the PGSER macro instruction to request the page fixing of the pages that contain any portion of the address range specified. In this example, registers 10 and 11 contain the beginning and ending addresses, respectively, of the virtual storage pages that are to be page fixed, and the ECB labeled FIXECB will be posted when the request is complete.

```
         PGSER R,FIX,A=(R10),EA=(R11),ECB=FIXECB
         ...
FIXECB   DC F'0'
```

14.11 CONVERTING EXISTING PROGRAMS INTO 31-BIT ADDRESSING MODE

Before converting existing programs to 31-bit addressing mode, one must determine if it is really necessary. Existing programs execute correctly (with very few exceptions, which are discussed in the *IBM MVS/XA Conversion Notebook*) in MVS/XA. If the programs do not require any MVS/XA facilities that require 31-bit addressing mode and are small enough to reside below the 16 Mb line, then there is no need to convert the programs. If an existing program calls a 31-bit addressing mode program or is called by a 31-bit addressing program, then there are various techniques (some of which require no source change to the existing program) that can be used to maintain addressing mode integrity. These techniques were discussed in Section 14.6.

If there is a legitimate need to convert an existing 24-bit addressing mode program to 31-bit addressing mode, then there are two ways of converting. One way is to keep the value of RMODE the same at 24, in which case the 31-bit addressing mode program resides below the 16 Mb line. The other way is to change the value of RMODE to ANY, in which case the 31-bit addressing mode program resides (usually) above the 16 Mb line.

Forcing a 31-bit addressing mode program to reside below the 16 Mb line would be useful for the following reasons.

- To facilitate calls to 24-bit addressing mode programs which require a parameter-list. This would eliminate the need to issue a GETMAIN macro instruction (specifying LOC=BELOW) to obtain virtual storage below the 16 Mb line for the parameters.
- To facilitate the performance of non-VSAM I/O and the use of certain macro instructions, such as EXTRACT. Since the program resides below the 16 Mb line, all that is required is to dynamically change the AMODE to 24 before the service is invoked. This would eliminate the need to call a separate 24-bit addressing mode program to invoke the required service.

- To facilitate the performance of VSAM I/O. VSAM I/O may be performed by a 31-bit addressing mode program, but the control blocks must reside below the 16 Mb line.

The following are the requirements for converting an existing 24-bit addressing mode program to 31-bit addressing mode.

- Assemble or linkedit the program with an AMODE value of 31 and an RMODE value of 24 or ANY.
- Assemble the program using the Assembler H version 2 (or later) with the MVS/XA macro library.
- Linkedit the program with the Linkage Editor supplied with DFP.

The following are the suggestions and the major considerations for converting an existing 24-bit addressing mode program to a 31-bit addressing mode program.

- In order to maintain addressing mode integrity when performing program linkage without system intervention, change all BALR R14,R15 instructions, which are used to call programs, to BASSM R14,R15 instructions and change the BR R14 instruction, which is used to return control, to the BSM 0,R14 instruction.
- The LA instruction cannot be used to clear the high order byte of a register. In 31-bit addressing mode, the LA instruction clears the high order bit of the high order byte and sets bits 1–7 to the seven high order bits of the 31-bit address. If the program resides below the 16 Mb line, then the LA instruction will clear the high order byte, but this is poor programming and potentially risky because it places an RMODE restriction on the program. If the RMODE is changed at a later date, the logic of the program would require modification, or the program will not function as intended. The ICM (Insert Character under Mask) instruction may be used to clear the high order byte of a register as follows:

```
         ICM   R10,B'1000',=X'00'
```

- Convert all 3-byte areas containing addresses to 4-byte areas and set the high order byte to zero, and change all 3-byte ADCONs to 4-byte ADCONs (except the existing ones used by Data Management).
- All 4-byte areas that contain indicators in the high order byte and an address in the low order three bytes (except the ones used by Data Management) may be handled in one of the following ways:
  - Zero the high order byte and find some other means of storing the indicator bits. Then use the L instruction to load the address into a register.
  - Leave the 4-byte area alone, but load the address into a register with the following sequence of instructions.

```
         LA    R10,0
         ICM   R10,B'0111',ADCON+1
or
         SR    R10,R10
         ICM   R10,B'0111',ADCON+1
```

where: register 10 is used as the receiving register and ADCON is a 4-byte area containing indicators in the bits of the high order byte and an address in the low order three bytes.

The LA or SR instruction zeros the register which fulfills the requirement of clearing the high order byte. The ICM instruction with the specified mask loads the low order three bytes of ADCON into the low order three bytes of the specified register.

- Since the high order byte of a register containing an address may no longer be used to contain various indicator bits, check if the program is setting that byte. Since the ICM instruction may be used to set bits in the high order byte of a register, scan the program for ICM instructions and determine how those instructions are being used.

- The BAL and the BALR instructions function differently in 31-bit addressing mode. In 24-bit addressing mode, these instructions save the instruction length, condition code, and program mask in the high order byte of the return address register (this information is not saved in 31-bit addressing mode). Examine the program to determine if it requires this information. One way to determine some of the places in the program that may require the information is to scan the program for SPM (Set Program Mask) instructions. The SPM instructions may indicate places in the program where the BAL/BALR instructions were used to save the old program mask, which SPM may have reset. If this information is required, then the IPM (Insert Program Mask) instruction may be used to save the condition code and program mask.
- The SPIE and the STAE macro instructions and the STAI parameter of the ATTACH macro instruction are not supported in 31-bit addressing mode. Therefore, if ABEND recovery is being performed, then the SPIE and the STAE macro instructions must be converted to the ESPIE and the ESTAE macro instructions, respectively, and the STAI parameter of the ATTACH macro instruction must be converted to the ESTAI parameter. The SPIE, ESPIE, and ESTAE macro instructions are discussed in Chapter 6.
- The PGLOAD, PGOUT, PGRLSE, PGANY, PGFIX, and the PGFREE macro instructions may be used in 31-bit addressing mode but perform services only for pages whose addresses are below the 16 Mb line, Also, 24-bit addresses must be specified. If paging above the 16 Mb line is required to be controlled, then those macro instructions must be converted to the PGSER macro instruction (discussed above) that performs the functions of all those macro instructions for pages located either below or above the 16 Mb line.
- Non-VSAM I/O cannot be performed directly by a 31-bit addressing mode program. The program must either call a 24-bit addressing mode program to perform the I/O or dynamically change the AMODE to 24-bit (while residing below the 16 Mb line) and perform the I/O. VSAM services may be invoked by a 31-bit addressing mode program, but the control blocks and parameter-lists must reside below the 16 Mb line. Coding Example 14.9 shows a called 24-bit addressing mode program used to perform I/O for a calling 31-bit addressing mode program.
- Examine the program to determine which MVS services (via macro instructions) are being used. Then consult the *IBM MVS/XA Conversion Notebook* to determine if these macros are still supported, have replacements, or have special considerations in order to be used under MVS/XA.
- Examine the program linkage requirements. If it receives control from or calls a 24-bit addressing mode program without system intervention, then some means must be employed to assure addressing mode integrity between the programs. Section 14.6 discussed some techniques for establishing linkage between programs having different addressing modes. If the program calls a 24-bit addressing mode program, then any parameters passed to the called program must reside below the 16 Mb line.
- In addition, if the program has any known peculiarities, is using nonstandard interfaces, or is using standard interfaces other than macro instructions (such as system exits), then those should be examined.

14.12 DESIGNING PROGRAMS TO EXECUTE ON BOTH MVS/370 AND MVS/XA

A single program could be designed to execute correctly in either MVS/370 or MVS/XA mode. If no facilities that are new or unique to MVS/XA are required and published interfaces are used, then the simplest way to accomplish this is to assemble the program with the MVS/370 Assembler and macro library and then use the MVS/370 Linkage Editor to create the load module. The resulting load module will execute correctly (with very few exceptions, which are discussed in the *IBM MVS/XA Conversion Notebook Manual*) on either the MVS/370 or the MVS/XA operating systems. If the MVS/370 Assembler and macro library, are not available, then that program may be assembled using the MVS/XA Assembler and macro library and the MVS/XA Linkage Editor may be used to create the load module, but not all MVS/XA macro expansions are downward compatible. When using the MVS/XA Assembler and macro library, in order to assure compatability across both operating systems, the SPLEVEL macro instruction must be used. The SPLEVEL macro instruction uses one keyword parameter (SET=) to indicate to the MVS/XA macro definitions which macro expansion should be generated. The values may be SET=1 (for MVS/370 macro expansion) or SET=2 (for MVS/XA macro expansion, the default). (Note: for MVS/ESA, SET=3 is the default.) In this particular case, the SPLEVEL macro instruction should specify SET=1 and be specified before any other macro instructions are specified in the source code. This specification is compatible to MVS/370 and MVS/XA (with AMODE/RMODE 24). The SPLEVEL macro instruction communicates only with the MVS/XA macro definitions that support both expansions and accomplishes this by setting a global SET symbol.

Coding Example 14.12.1

This coding example illustrates how to code a program, using the MVS/XA Assembler and macro library, to have macro expansions that will function correctly under MVS/370 and MVS/XA (with AMODE/RMODE 24):

```
NEWPROG   CSECT
          SPLEVEL   SET=1           IND THAT MVS/370 MACRO EXPAND REQR
          ...                       MACROS AND OTHER ASSEMBLER STATEMENTS
          END
```

If the program needs to use MVS/XA facilities when executing under MVS/XA, then the design of the program is more involved. The technique involves using multiple coding paths and multiple specifications of the SPLEVEL macro instruction in the program. The *IBM MVS/XA Conversion Notebook Manual* (see Bibliography in the back of this chapter) contains two lists of macro instructions. One list contains the macro instructions that are new for MVS/XA or existing ones that contain new options. The other list contains existing macros whose MVS/XA expansions are not downward compatible. The new macro instructions or existing macro instructions with new options (except GETMAIN, which is downward compatible) will function only in MVS/XA. The existing macro instructions that have different expansions in MVS/XA will function in both operating systems if they are assembled using SPLEVEL SET=1, but they will not function correctly (with a few exceptions) in 31-bit addressing mode unless they are assembled with the MVS/XA expansion.

The technique involves designing the program with a common path, which will contain code that will function under both operating systems, and dual paths with equivalent function (if possible or desirable) that will contain operating system dependant code. The program would be required to receive control in 24-bit addressing mode. The program would then need to determine on which operating system it is executing and pass control to the appropriate path when required. The program can determine the host operating system by examining the CVTDCB field of the CVT. The high order bit (bit 0) indicates whether or not MVS/XA is the operating system. A value of 0 indicates MVS/370 and a value of 1 indicates MVS/XA (or MVS/ESA). In the CVT DSECT, the EQU symbol CVTMVSE is provided (only for MVS/370 SP 1.3 and later) for the test.

Coding Example 14.12.2

This coding example illustrates how to test for the host operating system.

```
         USING  CVT,R10
CHKSYS   L      R10,16              SET ADRBLTY FOR CVT DSECT
         TM     CVTDCB,CVTMVSE      CHK HOST OPER SYS
         BO     MVSXA               IF BIT ON, MVS/XA
         B      MVS370              IF BIT OFF, MVS/370
         ...
         CVT    DSECT=YES           GENERATES CVT DSECT
```

Coding Example 14.12.3

This coding example illustrates how to code a program that may execute in either the MVS/370 or the MVS/XA operating systems. The use of the the SPLEVEL macro instruction is illustrated in each of the operating system's dependent paths.

```
         USING  CVT,R10             DEFINE REG FOR CVT DSECT
         ...
************************************************************************
*    MAINSTREAM OF PROGRAM
************************************************************************
*
         BAL    R6,DOCOMMON         EXECUTE COMMON CODE
         ...
         BAL    R6,DOSYSDEP         EXECUTE SYSTEM DEPENDENT CODE
         ...
************************************************************************
*    THIS ROUTINE EXECUTES THE CODE THAT IS COMMON TO BOTH MVS/370 AND
*    AND MVS/XA.
************************************************************************
*
DOCOMMON ...                        EXECUTE COMMON CODE
         BR     R6                  RETURN TO CALLING RTN
*
*
************************************************************************
*    THIS ROUTINE DETERMINES THE OPERATING SYSTEM UNDER WHICH THE PROGRAM
*    IS EXECUTING AND ROUTES CONTROL TO THE APPROPRIATE SYSTEM DEPENDENT
*    SUBROUTINE.
************************************************************************
*
DOSYSDEP L      R10,16              SET ADRBLTY FOR CVT DSECT
         TM     CVTDCB,CVTMVSE      CHK HOST OPER SYS
         BO     MVSXA               IF BIT ON, MVS/XA
         B      MVS370              IF BIT OFF, MVS/370
*
*
************************************************************************
*    THIS SUBROUTINE EXECUTES MVS/370 DEPENDENT CODE.
************************************************************************
*
MVS370   SPLEVEL SET=1              IND THAT MVS/370 MACRO EXPAND REQR
         ...
         ...                        MACROS THAT REQR MVS/370 EXPAND
         ...                        OTHER ASSEMBLER STATEMENTS AND ONLY
         ...                        MVS/370 MACHINE INSTRUCTIONS
         BR     R6                  RETURN TO CALLING RTN
```

```
         ...
*
*
***********************************************************************
*    THIS SUBROUTINE EXECUTES MVS/XA DEPENDENT CODE.
***********************************************************************
*
MVSXA    SPLEVEL SET=2           IND THAT MVS/XA MACRO EXPAND REQR
         ...
         ...                     MACROS THAT REQR MVS/XA EXPAND
         ...                     OTHER ASSEMBLER STATEMENTS AND MVS/370
         ...                     AND/OR MVS/XA MACHINE INSTRUCTIONS
         BR    R6                RETURN TO CALLING RTN
         ...
*
*
***********************************************************************
*    REQUIRED DSECT
***********************************************************************
*
         CVT   DSECT=YES         GENERATES CVT DSECT
```

NOTES:

- Remember, the Assembler processes the Assembler statements sequentially (unless directed differently by Conditional Assembler at pre-assembly time) not logically (based upon instruction execution); therefore, the SPLEVEL macro instruction must be specified accordingly to obtain the desired macro expansions in the proper places in the program at assembly time.

14.13 WRITING NEW PROGRAMS FOR MVS/XA

When a program is being developed to execute under the MVS/XA operating system, certain decisions must be made, such as whether the program should execute in 24-bit or 31-bit addressing mode and whether or not the program should reside below the 16 Mb line. This section presents some considerations and suggestions for making these decisions.

14.13.1 Writing New Programs in 24-Bit Addressing Mode

Any new programs written in 24-bit addressing mode to execute under MVS/XA, which do not require any new MVS/XA facilities, may be written in the same way as in MVS/370. The only exception is that the BASSM and the BSM instructions should be used for program linkage to assure addressing mode integrity when program calls are performed without system intervention. The BASSM instruction should be used for any program calls performed with a combination of a LOAD macro instruction and a branch. The BSM instruction should be used to return control because if the program is called by another program (without supervisor intervention), then the BSM instruction assures that the calling program receives control back in the required addressing mode (if the call was made via the BALR or the BASSM instruction). If the program is invoked via JCL or called by another program using system intervention, then the BSM instruction will function just like the BR instruction. It would also be a good idea to define all (where possible) addresses as four bytes, instead of three, with the high order byte set to zero.

In general, the types of programs that should be coded in 24-bit addressing mode are the following:

- Programs that obtain no benefit from executing in 31-bit addressing mode;
- Programs that are small enough to reside below the 16 Mb line;

- Programs that have a requirement to execute in both the MVS/370 and the MVS/XA operating systems; and
- Programs that have 24-bit addressing mode dependencies, such as the performance of non-VSAM I/O.

14.13.2 Writing New Programs in 31-Bit Addressing Mode

New programs that are written to execute in MVS/XA in 31-bit addressing mode have the advantage of being able to use the new facilities offered by MVS/XA that are not available in 24-bit addressing mode. Also 31-bit addressing mode programs are able to exploit the huge amount of virtual storage available above the 16 Mb line without the requirement of a special routine that performs dynamic AMODE changes (as in 24-bit addressing mode programs). However, there are also some disadvantages. For example, a 31-bit addressing mode program cannot perform non-VSAM I/O directly when executing in 31-bit AMODE.

In general, the types of programs that should be coded in 31-bit addressing mode are the following:

- Programs that are too large to reside below the 16 Mb line; and
- Programs that require new MVS/XA facilities, which require 31-bit addressing mode.

BIBLIOGRAPHY FOR CHAPTER 14

The following IBM manuals contain reference material for the topics discussed in this chapter.

ID	TITLE
GC28-1143	*MVS/XA Conversion Notebook*
GC28-1143	*MVS/XA Conversion Notebook Volume 1* (for MVS/XA 2.2 only)
GC28-1411	*MVS/XA Conversion Notebook Volume 2* (for MVS/XA 2.2 only)
GC28-1158	*MVS/XA SPL: 31-Bit Addressing*
GG22-9305	*MVS/XA SPL: 31-Bit Assembler Programming*
GC28-1151	*MVS/XA SPL: System Macros and Facilities Volume 2*
GC28-1154	*MVS/XA Supervisor Services and Macro Instructions*
GC28-1820	*MVS/ESA SPL: Application Development 31-Bit Addressing*
GC28-1822	*MVS/ESA Application Development Macro Reference*
GC28-1857	*MVS/ESA SPL: Application Development Macro Reference*

15

Inter-Address Space Communications

The predecessor operating systems to MVS (MVT and SVS) used a single address space, which was shared among the operating system and the users. Each user was assigned a region whose address range was carved out of the single address space. Since only one set of addresses existed, communications between users in other regions was relatively straightforward.

MVS assigns a separate address space for each user. Therefore, the address range for each user is from 0 to 16M-1 for MVS/370 and from 0 to 2G-1 for MVS/XA and for MVS/ESA. Since each user has the same set of virtual addresses, but in separate address spaces, direct communication between address spaces is not possible just by specifying an address of an area contained within each address space.

There are a number of ways to communicate between address spaces. The methods include the use of a dataset on a shared DASD volume, the use of the common area to contain buffers used as intermediate storage areas, the scheduling of SRBs into the other address spaces, and cross memory services. Some of these methods are crude and inefficient, and other methods are sophisticated and efficient. This chapter explores all the methods mentioned above.

15.1 INTER-ADDRESS SPACE COMMUNICATIONS VIA SHARED DASD

Two tasks in different address spaces can communicate via a dataset located on a shared DASD volume. The dataset must be allocated to each of the jobs, which invoke the tasks that are to communicate, and the DISP of the dataset must be specified as SHR. Some mechanism must be set up to serialize the use of the dataset, such as ENQ/DEQ (discussed in Chapter 4) and an indicator must be defined in the dataset or in another dataset on a shared DASD volume to indicate if the dataset contains data that is to be accessed.

This method is crude and inefficient, but works fine if performance is not an issue. The advantages are that it can be set up quickly and easily and does not require any special program authorization.

15.2 INTER-ADDRESS SPACE COMMUNICATIONS VIA THE COMMON AREA

Tasks from different address spaces can also communicate by using an allocated virtual storage area in the common area (preferably the Common Service Area (CSA)) as an intermediate storage area. The allocated virtual storage of the CSA can be pointed to by the CVTUSER field of the CVT. The technique of using the CVTUSER field to point to an address-list of areas allocated in the CSA was discussed in Chapter 13. Like the shared DASD method, access to the buffer area in the CSA must be serialized with the ENQ/DEQ or similar mechanism and an indicator in the CSA is required to indicate when the buffer contains data that is to be accessed.

This method is more efficient than the shared DASD method since no I/O is done. But the program that allocates the area in the CSA must execute in supervisor mode and PSW storage protection key 0–7. That program must execute in supervisor state and PSW storage protection key zero to modify the contents of CVTUSER. Also, if the size of the CSA is required to be larger to accommodate an excessive number of buffers, then the sizes of all private areas available to each user become proportionately smaller. In MVS/ESA, inter-address space communications can also be accomplished via Data Spaces.

15.3 INTER-ADDRESS SPACE COMMUNICATIONS VIA SRBS

The use of Service Request Blocks (SRBs) and SRB routines can provide an asynchronous method of communications between address spaces. SRB routines communicate with other address spaces by actually executing in that address space. Unlike the shared DASD or the CSA method of inter-address space communications, the issuing program has direct access to the data and the control blocks located in the target address space since the SRB routine executes in that address space. However, any data that is passed back to the issuing address space must be done via the CSA (or the SQA, which is not recommended).

An SRB is similar to a TCB in the sense that it represents a unit of work. The TCB is the normal way of representing units of work (usually problem state programs) that are to be dispatched. The Address Space Extention Blook (ASXB), which is pointed to by the Address Space Control Block (ASCB), contains a pointer to the beginning of the TCB queue in dispatching sequence which contains the addresses of the TCBs that are to be dispatched. The ASXB also contains a pointer to the SRB chain in FIFO sequence, which contains the addresses of the SRBs that are to be dispatched. The dispatcher services the SRB queue before the TCB queue. The dispatching priority of an SRB can optionally be set to a dispatching priority higher than any address space in the system (SCOPE=GLOBAL). This implies that the SRB is the next unit of work to be dispatched. If this option is not specified in the SCHEDULE macro instruction, then the SRB is dispatched when the address space is dispatched and before any of the TCBs in the address space (SCOPE=LOCAL).

SRB routines should be small and efficient because once an SRB is dispatched, it does not lose control due to an I/O interruption. When an I/O interruption occurs, it is handled by the I/O interruption handler, but the I/O interruption handler returns control to the interrupted SRB instead of passing control to the dispatcher to select the highest priority ready unit of work.

15.3.1 Requirements for Using SRBs

In order to use the SRB method for inter-address space communications, the programmer must define an SRB and write an SRB routine. The SRB is then scheduled via the

SCHEDULE macro instruction in the address space with which communications is required (target address space). SRBs can also be scheduled in the same address space as the issuer of the SCHEDULE macro instruction, but that situation will not be discussed.

The SRB Control Block

The SRB is a 44-byte control block that is defined by the programmer. The SRB must reside in fixed, commonly-addressable storage in any PSW storage protection key. Table 15.3.1. describes the fields of the SRB that are normally set by the programmer. IBM provides the IHASRB macro instruction to map the SRB. Fixed, fetch-protected CSA in key zero is used in the coding examples to contain the SRB. When CSA is allocated, the length used should be the SRBSIZE equate symbol provided by the DSECT.

Table 15.3.1

This table contains a description of the fields of the SRB that are normally set by the programmer. The required fields must be set in the SRB before the SCHEDULE macro instruction is issued.

`SRBID (4 bytes)`	Contains the SRB identification. It may contain any 4-byte character string. The contents of this field are useful in locating the SRB in a dump. The setting of this field is optional.
`SRBASCB (4 bytes)`	Contains the address of the ASCB of the address space in which the SRB routine is to execute.
`SRBCPAFF (1 byte)`	Used in multi-processor configurations. All bits set to zeros or to ones indicate no processor affinity. Otherwise, the bit mask indicates on which processors the SRB routine is allowed to be dispatched. Bit n set to a one value indicates affinity for the processor with physical address n.
`SRBPTCB (4 bytes)`	Contains the address of the TCB associated with the SRB routine. If the SRB routine ABENDs and no recovery has been defined or if the recovery routine also ABENDs, then the TCB whose address is specified in this field is also ABENDed. If the TCB whose address is specified in this field ABENDs, then the RTM component of MVS purges all SRBs scheduled by this TCB. This address is also used as a reference by the PURGEDQ macro instruction to determine which SRBs are to be dequeued. If this SRB is not related to any task or if purging is not necessary, then this field may be specified as zero.
`SRBPASID (4 bytes)`	Contains the ASID of the address space associated with the SRB. This field is used with the SRBPTCB field. If the SRBPTCB was specified as non-zero, then this field must also be specified.
`SRBEP (4 bytes)`	Contains the address of the entry point of the SRB routine. If the SRB routine is to execute in 31-bit addressing mode, then the high order bit must be set to one.
`SRBPARM (4 bytes)`	The contents of this field is passed to the SRB routine via register 1. This field can be used to pass the address of a parameter-list. The setting of this field is optional.
`SRBPKF (1 byte)`	Contains the PSW storage protection key in which the SRB

routine receives control. The format is xxxx0000, where the high order 4-bits indicate the value of the key. The SRB routine can change the key after it receives control via the MODESET macro instruction.

SRBPRIOR (1 bit) Contains the priority level with which the SRB is dispatched. This field is set by the SCOPE parameter of the SCHEDULE macro instruction.

SRBRMTR (4 bytes) Contains the address of the entry point of a resource manager termination routine. This routine is responsible for cleaning up an SRB that has been scheduled but not dispatched. This usually involves releasing the allocated commonly addressable virtual storage, which contains the SRB (since it is not released automatically). An SRB can be dequeued by the issuing task via the PURGEDQ macro instruction, or by the system if the associated task (specified via SRBPTCB) ABENDs or if the address space in which the SRB is scheduled is terminated. This address is also used as a reference by the PURGEDQ macro instruction to determine which SRBs are to be dequeued. This routine must be located in commonly addressable storage. If the SRB routine is to execute in 31-bit addressing mode, then the high order bit must be set to one. At the very minimum, this address should point to a BR R14 instruction, which would return control back to the dispatcher.

THE SCHEDULE MACRO INSTRUCTION

The SCHEDULE macro instruction is used to schedule an SRB in the same address space as the issuing program or in another address space. The program issuing this macro instruction must be executing in supervisor state and PSW storage protection key zero.

The format of the SCHEDULE macro instruction is as follows.

```
[name]   SCHEDULE SRB=srb-addr[,SCOPE={GLOBAL|LOCAL}]
         [,LLOCK={YES|NO}]
```

srb-addr

Specifies the address of the SRB defined by the user.

SCOPE=GLOBAL
SCOPE=LOCAL (Default: LOCAL)

Specifies whether the SRB is to be scheduled at a global or local priority.

GLOBAL Indicates that the SRB is to receive a dispatching priority higher than any address space.

LOCAL Indicates that the SRB receives the highest priority in the address space in which it is scheduled.

LLOCK=YES
LLOCK=NO (Default: NO)

Specifies whether or not the SRB routine is to receive control with the LOCAL lock held

YES Indicates that the SRB routine is to receive control with the LOCAL lock held.

NO Indicates that the SRB routine is to receive control without the LOCAL lock held.

CHARACTERISTICS OF SRBS

The characteristics of SRBs must be considered when using them. These characteristics are the following:

- The SRB control block must be allocated in fixed, commonly addressable virtual storage. This includes the Nucleus, the SQA, or the CSA. The CSA is recommended. The virtual storage containing the SRB should be released before the SRB routine returns control if the storage was allocated from the SQA or the CSA.
- SRB routines execute enabled, in supervisor state and the PSW storage protection key specified by the programmer via the SRBPKF field of the SRB.
- SRB routines may issue the MODESET macro instruction to switch their assigned PSW storage protection key.
- SRB routines may not issue an SVC instruction (or any macro instructions whose expansion includes an SVC instruction). Therefore, supervisor services that depend on the issuing of an SVC instruction are not available. However, certain superviser services which provide a branch-entry interface (such as GETMAIN, FREEMAIN, and POST) may be invoked. The ABEND macro instruction (SVC 13) may be issued directly.
- SRB routines may obtain any lock via the SETLOCK macro instruction. Held locks must be released before the SRB routine returns control.
- SRB routines may schedule another SRB via the SCHEDULE macro instruction.
- SRB routines return control to the dispatcher by branching to the address that was contained in register 14 when control was received.
- Upon entry to an SRB routine, the registers contain the following.

Register	Contents
0	Address of the SRB control block.
1	The contents of SRBPARM.
14	Return address to the dispatcher.
15	Entry point address of the SRB routine.

The contents of the other registers are not significant to the SRB routine.

- An SRB routine may set up a recovery environment via the SETFRR macro instruction.

15.3.2 Using SRB Routines

The SRB method of inter-address space communications can be used when the issuing program does not require synchronous communication, which implies that the issuing program can perform other processing while the SRB is waiting to be dispatched and while the SRB routine is executing. An SRB routine can be used to obtain data from another address space or simply monitor another address space.

When an SRB routine is used to obtain user-data from the target address space, the target address space must perform some processing in order to communicate with the SRB routine. In this book, the address space that schedules the initial SRB is referred to as the originating address space. The following scenario describes the processing required to obtain user-data from another address space.

- The target address space allocates virtual storage from its own address space and places the address of that area into the TCB user field (field TCBUSER).
- The target address space writes the data, which is to be sent to the originating address space, into that area.
- The target address space places the address of its ASCB into a predeterminated location in the CSA and indicates that it has data to send.
- The originating address space periodically examines the CSA to determine if any address spaces are ready to send data.
- When it is determined that an address space has data to send, a program from the originating address space allocates virtual storage from its own address space for a work area, places the address of that work area into TCBUSER, and then schedules an SRB in the target address space. The work area contains an ECB and a field for the data from the target address space. The ECB is posted when the user-data from the target address space has been copied into the work area. Since the SCHEDULE macro instruction must be issued by a program executing in supervisor state and PSW storage protection key zero, an SVC routine is usually provided for the problem program to schedule the SRB. The SVC routine can also be used to place the address of the work area into TCBUSER.
- The SVC routine called by the originating address space allocates virtual storage from the CSA for the SRB control block and for a work area. The work area is used to pass information between the address spaces. The address of the work area is passed to the SRB routine via the SRBPARM field of the SRB. The SVC routine can also allocate the work area for the calling problem program (in the caller's address space and PSW storage protection key) and return that address in one of the parameter registers.
- The SRB routine, which executes in the target address space, performs the following processing:

  - Obtains the address of the data area from TCBUSER and copies the data into the work area allocated from the CSA; and
  - Schedules an SRB in the originating address space.

- The SRB routine, which executes in the originating address space, performs the following processing:

  - Obtains the address of the work area of the originating address space from TCBUSER:
  - Copies the data from the CSA into that work area;
  - Frees the allocated CSA storage (SRB control block and work area); and
  - Posts the ECB to indicate that the data from the target address space is in the work area of the originating address space.

- The program in the originating address space periodically checks the ECB to determine when the data from the target address space has been received. The TM instruction should be used to test the ECB for completion. This enables the program to perform other processing while the SRBs are waiting to be dispatched and while the SRB routines are executing. If the WAIT macro instruction is used to test the ECB for completion, then the communication becomes, in effect, synchronous communication.

Coding Example 15.3.1 shows the code for the SVC routine that schedules the initial SRB and the code for all the SRB routines that perform the asynchronous inter-address space communications as described above. Coding Example 15.3.2 shows the code for the problem program that calls the SVC routine that schedules the initial SRB. Coding Example 15.3.3 shows the code for the problem program that executes in the target address space and the code for the SVC routine that it calls to set the CVTUSER and the TCBUSER fields.

An SRB can also be scheduled in the target address space without any required setup processing from that address space. Therefore, SRBs can be used with a monitor program to extract various information about one or more address spaces by interrogating the various control blocks in that address space and sending back the information to the originating address space. The address spaces that are to be monitored can be indicated to the monitor program by specifying the jobnames associated with those address spaces. The addresses of the ASCBs can be obtained from the ASCB queue (pointed to by the CVTASCBH field of the CVT). Then, an SRB is scheduled in each address space, and the SRB routines examine the jobnames associated with these address spaces to determine which of these address spaces are to be monitored. The writing of the monitor program and the required SRB routines are left as an exercise for the reader. Some of the information that can be sent back to the monitor program are the following:

- The name of the job.
- The name of the last active program (CDENAME).
- The entry point of that program (CDENTPT).
- The resume address of that program (RBOPSW).

NOTES:

- TCBRBP points to the current Request Block (RB).
- The name of the RB mapping DSECT macro instruction is IHARB.
- RBCDE points to the Contents Directory Entry (CDE).
- The name of the CDE mapping DSECT macro instruction is IHACDE.

By periodically scheduling (controlled by the STIMER macro instruction) an SRB in a particular address space, the monitor program can obtain a sampling of statistics to determine the approximate percentage of time each program is executing in a particular address space and which instructions of these programs are executing.

Coding Example 15.3.1

This coding example illustrates how to schedule an SRB in another address space. The SRB routine invoked extracts the jobname associated with the target address space and reads the user-provided data located in that address space. The target address space provides the address of the data in the TCBUSER field of the TCB. The jobname and the data are placed in the CSA, and then another SRB is scheduled in the originating address space to move the data from the CSA into that address space. Since the SCHEDULE macro instruction can be issued only by programs executing in supervisor state and PSW storage protection key zero, this coding example is actually an SVC routine (253) that is invoked by the originating address space. The SVC routine also contains the code for all the SRB routines that are scheduled. The code for the problem program, which invokes this SVC routine, is shown in Coding Example 15.3.2.

```
IGC0025C CSECT
*
*************************************************************************
*    INITIALIZATION
*************************************************************************
*
         REGEQU EQU=R              GENERATE EQU'S FOR REGS
         USING  *,R6               DEFINE BASE REG
         USING  CVT,R3             DEFINE REG FOR CVT DSECT
         USING  TCB,R4             DEFINE REG FOR TCB DSECT
```

```
         USING  SRB,R10            DEFINE REG FOR SRB DSECT
         USING  CSACOMAR,R11       DEFINE REG FOR CSACOMAR DSECT
         USING  WORKAREA,R12       DEFINE REG FOR WORK AREA DESCT
*
*
***********************************************************************
*    MAINSTREAM OF SVC ROUTINE
***********************************************************************
*
         BAL    R8,SAVREGS1        SAVE CONTENTS OF CONTROL REGS
         BAL    R8,GETWKAR         ALLO WORK AREA FOR CALLING PROG
         BAL    R8,GETCSA          ALLO CSA FOR WKAR AND SRB'S
         BAL    R8,SAVEADRS        SAVE PROCESSING ADRS
         BAL    R8,INITSRB1        SET UP SRB CONTROL BLOCK
         BAL    R8,SCHDSRB1        SCHEDULE SRB IN TARGET A.S.
         B      RETURN1            RETURN TO CALLING PROG VIA SVC FLIH
*
*
***********************************************************************
*    THIS ROUTINE SAVES THE CONTENTS OF ALL REGISTERS THAT CONTAIN
*    CONTROL INFORMATION.
***********************************************************************
*
SAVREGS1 LR     R2,R14             SAVE RETURN ADR
         BR     R8                 RETURN TO CALLING ROUTINE
*
*
***********************************************************************
*    THIS ROUTINE ALLOCATES A WORK AREA FROM THIS ADDRESS SPACE FOR THE
*    CALLING PROGRAM IN THE PSW STOR PROT KEY OF THE CALLING PROGRAM.
***********************************************************************
*
GETWKAR  MODESET KEY=NZERO         SET PSW KEY TO THAT OF CALLER
         GETMAIN RU,LV=WKARLEN,SP=0  ALLOC STOR FOR CALLER
         LR     R12,R1             SET ADBLTY OF WKAR DSECT
         ST     R12,WGMADR         SAVE WKAR ADR IN WORK AREA
         MODESET KEY=ZERO          SET PSW KEY BACK TO ZERO
         BR     R8                 RETURN TO CALLING PROG
*
*
***********************************************************************
*    THIS ROUTINE ALLOCATES VIRTUAL STORAGE FROM FIXED, FETCH-PROTECTED
*    CSA FOR USE BY THE SRB ROUTINES. THIS AREA IS USED TO CONTAIN THE
*    SRB CONTROL BLOCK AND A WORK AREA. THE NAME OF THE DSECT FOR THE
*    WORK AREA SECTION OF THIS STORAGE IS CALLED CSACOMAR.
***********************************************************************
*
GETCSA   GETMAIN RU,LV=CSALEN,SP=227
         LR     R10,R1             SET ADBLTY FOR SRB
         LA     R11,SRBSIZE(0,R10) SET ADBLTY FOR CSA WKAR
         ST     R10,CCSAADR        SAVE ADR OF ALLO CSA
         BR     R8                 RETURN TO CALLING ROUTINE
*
*
***********************************************************************
*    THIS ROUTINE SAVES THE REQUIRED ADDRESSES FOR PROCESSING.
***********************************************************************
*
SAVEADRS ST     R4,CTCB1ADR        SAVE ADR OF TCB OF ISSUING A.S.
         ST     R7,CASCB1AD        SAVE ADR OF ASCB OF ISSUING A.S.
         ST     R12,TCBUSER        SAVE ADR OF CALLER'S WKAR IN TCB
         BR     R8                 RETURN TO CALLING ROUTINE
*
*
```

```
***********************************************************************
*    THIS ROUTINE SETS UP THE SRB FOR THE SRB ROUTINE THAT IS TO
*    EXECUTE IN THE TARGET ADDRESS SPACE.
***********************************************************************
*
INITSRB1 MVC  SRBID,SRB1          SET SRB ID
         MVC  SRBCPAFF,BINONES    IND SRB OK TO EXEC IN ALL CPU'S
         MVC  SRBPKF,BINZEROS     SET PSW KEY OF SRB RTN TO ZERO
         MVC  SRBASCB,CVTUSER     SET ADR OF TARGET ASCB
         LA   R5,DATASRB          LOAD EPA OF SRB ROUTINE
         ST   R5,SRBEP            SET EPA OF SRB ROUTINE
         LA   R5,DUMYRMTR         LOAD EPA OF DUMMY RECV RTN
         ST   R5,SRBRMTR          SET ADR OF RECV RTN
         ST   R11,SRBPARM         LOAD ADR OF CSA WKAR
         BR   R8                  RETURN TO CALLING ROUTINE
*
*
***********************************************************************
*    THIS ROUTINE SCHEDULES THE SRB IN THE TARGET ADDRESS SPACE.
***********************************************************************
*
SCHDSRB1 SCHEDULE SRB=(R10),SCOPE=LOCAL
         BR   R8                  RETURN TO CALLING ROUTINE
*
*
***********************************************************************
*    THIS ROUTINE RETURNS CONTROL TO THE CALLER VIA THE SVC FLIH.
***********************************************************************
*
RETURN1  LR   R14,R2              RESTORE RETURN ADDRESS
         LA   R15,0               SET RC=0
         LR   R1,R12              RETURN ADR OF CALLER'S WKAR
         BR   R14                 RETURN TO CALLING PROG VIA FLIH
*
*
***********************************************************************
*    DUMMY RECOVERY ROUTINE
***********************************************************************
*
DUMYRMTR BR   R14
*
*
***********************************************************************
*    CONSTANTS
***********************************************************************
*
BINZEROS DC   F'0'
BINONES  DC   4XL1'FF'
SRB1     DC   C'SRB1'             ID OF SRB THAT EXEC IN TARGET A.S.
*
*
         LTORG                    FORCE LITERALS TO ASM HERE FOR ADRBLTY
         DROP                     RELEASE ALL REGS USED WITH USING STMTS
*
*
*
*
***********************************************************************
*    THE FOLLOWING CONTAINS THE CODE FOR THE SRB ROUTINE THAT EXECUTES
*    IN THE TARGET ADDRESS SPACE. ITS FUNCTIONS ARE THE FOLLOWING:
*
*        * MOVE THE DATA FROM THE TARGET A.S. TO THE CSA WKAR;
*        * SCHEDULE AN SRB IN THE ORIGINATING A.S.
*
```

```
**********************************************************************
*
*
DATASRB  DS   0H
*
*
**********************************************************************
*    INITIALIZATION
**********************************************************************
*
         USING *,R6                DEFINE BASE REG
         USING SRB,R10             DEFINE REG FOR SRB DSECT
         USING CSACOMAR,R11        DEFINE REG FOR CSACOMAR DSECT
         LR    R6,R15              LOAD BASE REGISTER
*
*
**********************************************************************
*    MAINSTREAM OF SRB ROUTINE
**********************************************************************
*
         BAL   R8,SAVREGS2         SAVE CONTENTS OF CONTROL REGS
         BAL   R8,GETJNAME         GET JOBNAME OF TARGET A.S.
         BAL   R8,GETDATA          GET DATA FROM TARGET A.S.
         BAL   R8,INITSRB2         INIT SRB FOR ORIG A.S.
         BAL   R8,SCHDSRB2         SCHEDULE SRB FOR ORIG A.S.
         B     RETURN2             RETURN TO DISPATCHER
*
*
**********************************************************************
*    THIS ROUTINE SAVES THE CONTENTS OF THE CONTROL REGISTERS AND SETS
*    ADDRESSABILITY FOR THE VARIOUS DSECTS.
**********************************************************************
*
SAVEREG2 LR    R2,R14              SAVE RETURN ADDRESS
         LR    R10,R0              SET ADBLTY FOR SRB DSECT
         LR    R11,R1              SET ADBLTY FOR CSACOMAR DSECT
         BR    R8                  RETURN TO CALLING ROUTINE
*
*
**********************************************************************
*    THIS ROUTINE EXTRACTS THE JOBNAME ASSOCIATED WITH THE TARGET
*    ADDRESS SPACE.
**********************************************************************
*
GETJNAME L     R9,SRBASCB          LD ADR OF ASCB OF TARGET A.S.
         L     R9,ASCBXTCB-ASCBEGIN(R9)    LOAD ADR OF TCB
         L     R9,TCBTIO-TCB(R9)           LOAD ADR OF TIOT
         MVC   CJOBNAME,0(R9)              MOVE JOBNAME INTO CSA WKAR
         BR    R8                          RETURN TO CALLING ROUTINE
*
*
**********************************************************************
*    THIS ROUTINE MOVES THE DATA FROM THE TARGET ADDRESS SPACE INTO THE
*    CSA WORKAREA.
**********************************************************************
*
GETDATA  L     R9,SRBASCB          LD ADR OF ASCB OF TARGET A.S.
         L     R9,ASCBXTCB-ASCBEGIN(R9)    GET ADR OF TCB
         L     R9,TCBUSER-TCB(R9)          GET ADR OF DATA BUFFER
         MVC   CJOBDATA,0(R9)              MOVE DATA INTO CSA WKAR
         BR    R8                          RETURN TO CALLING ROUTINE
*
*
**********************************************************************
```

```
*    THIS ROUTINE SETS UP THE SRB FOR THE SRB ROUTINE THAT IS TO
*    EXECUTE IN THE ORIGINATING ADDRESS SPACE. THE PREVIOUS SRB IS USED,
*    AND SELECTED FIELDS ARE UPDATED.
***********************************************************************
*
INITSRB2 MVC    SRBID,SRB2          SET SRB ID
         MVC    SRBASCB,CASCB1AD    SET ADR OF ORIG ASCB
         LA     R5,POSTSRB          LD EPA OF SRB ROUTINE
         ST     R5,SRBEP            SET EPA OF SRB ROUTINE
         BR     R8                  RETURN TO CALLING ROUTINE
*
*
***********************************************************************
*    THIS ROUTINE SCHEDULES THE SRB IN THE ORIGINATING ADDRESS SPACE.
***********************************************************************
*
SCHDSRB2 SCHEDULE SRB=(R10),SCOPE=LOCAL
         BR     R8
*
*
***********************************************************************
*    THIS ROUTINE RETURNS CONTROL TO THE DISPATCHER.
***********************************************************************
*
RETURN2  LR     R14,R2              RESTORE RETURN ADDRESS
         LA     R15,0               SET RC=0
         BR     R14                 RETURN CONTROL TO DISPATCHER
*
*
***********************************************************************
*    CONSTANTS
***********************************************************************
*
SRB2     DC     C'SRB2'             ID OF SRB THAT EXEC IN ORIG A.S.
*
*
         LTORG                      FORCE LITERALS TO ASM HERE FOR ADRBLTY
         DROP                       RELEASE ALL REGS USED WITH USING STMTS
*
*
*
*
***********************************************************************
*    THE FOLLOWING CONTAINS THE CODE FOR THE SRB ROUTINE THAT EXECUTES
*    IN THE ORIGINATING ADDRESS SPACE. ITS FUNCTIONS ARE THE FOLLOWING:
*
*          * MOVE THE DATA FROM THE CSA WKAR TO THE WKAR OF THE ORIG A.S.;
*          * POST THE ECB TO INDICATE THAT THE DATA MOVEMENT IS COMPLETE;
*          * RELEASE THE ALLOCATED CSA VIRTUAL STORAGE.
*
***********************************************************************
*
*
POSTSRB  DS     0H
*
*
***********************************************************************
*    INITIALIZATION
***********************************************************************
*
         USING *,R6                 DEFINE BASE REGISTER
         USING CVT,R3               DEFINE REG FOR CVT DSECT
         USING TCB,R4               DEFINE REG FOR TCB DSECT
         USING SRB,R10              DEFINE REG FOR SRB DSECT
```

```
         USING CSACOMAR,R11       DEFINE REG FOR CSACOMAR DSECT
         USING WORKAREA,R12       DEFINE REG FOR ORIG A.S. WKAR DSECT
         LR    R6,R15             LOAD BASE REGISTER
*
*
***********************************************************************
*    MAINSTREAM OF SRB ROUTINE
***********************************************************************
*
         BAL   R8,SAVREGS3        SAVE CONTENTS OF CONTROL REGS
         BAL   R8,LOADADRS        LOAD PROCESSING ADDRESSES
         BAL   R8,MOVEINFO        MOVE INFO FROM CSA TO ORIG A.S.
         BAL   R8,SETLLOCK        OBTAIN LOCAL LOCK FOR POST MACRO
         BAL   R8,POSTAS1         POST ECB TO IND INFO MOVED
         BAL   R8,RELLLOCK        RELEASE LOCAL LOCK
         BAL   R8,FREECSA         RELEASE ALLO CSA STORAGE
         B     RETURN3            RETURN TO DISPATCHER
*
*
***********************************************************************
*    THIS ROUTINE SAVES THE CONTENTS OF THE CONTROL REGISTERS AND SETS
*    ADDRESSABILITY FOR THE VARIOUS DSECTS.
***********************************************************************
*
SAVREGS3 LR    R2,R14             SAVE RETURN ADDRESS
         LR    R10,R0             SET ADBLTY FOR SRB DSECT
         LR    R11,R1             SET ADBLTY FOR CSACOMAR DSECT
         BR    R8                 RETURN TO CALLING ROUTINE
*
*
***********************************************************************
*    THIS ROUTINE LOADS THE REQUIRED ADDRESSES FOR PROCESSING.
***********************************************************************
*
LOADADRS L     R4,CTCB1ADR        SET ADBLTY FOR TCB DSECT
         L     R12,TCBUSER        LD ADR FOR WKAR OF ORIG A.S.
         BR    R8                 RETURN TO CALLING ROUTINE
*
*
***********************************************************************
*    THIS ROUTINE MOVES THE JOBNAME AND DATA OF THE TARGET A.S. FROM
*    THE CSA TO THE WORK AREA IN THE ORIGINATING A.S.
***********************************************************************
*
MOVEINFO MVC   WJOBNAME,CJOBNAME  MOVE JOBNAME FROM CSA TO ORIG A.S.
         MVC   WJOBDATA,CJOBDATA  MOVE DATA FROM CSA TO ORIG A.S.
         BR    R8                 RETURN TO CALLING ROUTINE
*
*
***********************************************************************
*    THIS ROUTINE OBTAINS THE LOCAL LOCK. THIS IS REQUIRED WHEN A
*    BRANCH-ENTRY POST MACRO IS ISSUED.
***********************************************************************
*
SETLLOCK SETLOCK OBTAIN,TYPE=LOCAL,MODE=UNCOND,REGS=USE,               -
               RELATED=(POSTAS1,RELLLOCK)
         BR    R8                 RETURN TO CALLING ROUTINE
*
*
***********************************************************************
*    THIS ROUTINE POSTS THE ECB LOCATED IN THE WKAR OF THE ORIGINATING
*    A.S. TO INDICATE THAT THE DATA MOVEMENT FROM THE TARGET A.S. TO THE
*    WORK AREA IN THE ORIGINATING A.S. VIA THE CSA IS COMPLETE.
***********************************************************************
```

```
*
POSTAS1   LA    R5,WECB             LOAD ADR OF ECB
          POST  (R5),X'00',BRANCH=YES,RELATED=(WAIT-IN-ASCB1)
          BR    R8                  RETURN TO CALLING ROUTINE
*
*
**************************************************************************
*    THIS ROUTINE RELEASES THE LOCAL LOCK.
**************************************************************************
*
RELLLOCK  SETLOCK RELEASE,TYPE=LOCAL,REGS=USE,  -
                RELATED=(POSTAS1,SETLLOCK)
          BR    R8                  RETURN TO CALLING ROUTINE
*
*
**************************************************************************
*    THIS ROUTINE RELEASES THE CSA STORAGE ALLOCATED BY THE SVC ROUTINE
*    INVOKED BY THE ORIGINATING A.S.
**************************************************************************
*
FREECSA   LA    R10,CCSAADR         LD ADR OF CSA POINTER
          FREEMAIN RU,LV=CSALEN,SP=227,A=(R10)
*         L     R3,16               LOAD ADR OF CVT
*         XC    CVTUSER,CVTUSER     CLEAR CVTUSER TO IND DATA COPIED
          BR    R8                  RETURN TO CALLING ROUTINE
*
*
**************************************************************************
*    THIS ROUTINE RETURNS CONTROL TO THE DISPATCHER.
**************************************************************************
*
RETURN3   LR    R14,R2              RESTORE RETURN ADDRESS
          LA    R15,0               SET RC=0
          BR    R14                 RETURN CONTROL TO DISPATCHER
*
*
**************************************************************************
*    THE DSECTS
**************************************************************************
*
WORKAREA  DSECT
WGMADR    DS    F
WECB      DS    F
WJOBNAME  DS    CL8
WJOBDATA  DS    CL100
WKARLEN   EQU   *-WORKAREA
*
CSACOMAR  DSECT
CCSAADR   DS    F
CTCB1ADR  DS    F
CASCB1AD  DS    F
CJOBNAME  DS    CL8
CJOBDATA  DS    CL100
COMARLEN  EQU   *-CSACOMAR
*
CSALEN    EQU   COMARLEN+SRBSIZE
*
          PRINT NOGEN
          IHAASCB                   GENERATES ASCB DSECT
          IHASRB                    GENERATES SRB DSECT
          CVT   DSECT=YES           GENERATES CVT DSECT
          IHAPSA                    GENERATES PSA DSECT (REQD BY SETLOCK)
          IKJTCB                    GENERATES TCB DSECT
*
```

```
*
***********************************************************************
*     END OF SVC ROUTINE
***********************************************************************
*
         END
```

NOTES:

- Remember from Chapter 12, when an SVC routine receives control: register 6 contains the entry point address, register 3 points to the CVT, register 4 points to the TCB of the calling program, and register 7 points to the ASCB of the calling program.
- If the target address space is using multi-tasking (has more than one TCB), then some method must be developed to determine which TCB points to the user-data area. One method can be to have only one TCB send data to the issuing address space. This TCB can be located by scanning the TCB queue and examining the TCBUSER field of each TCB. All the TCBs will have binzeros in that field except the one that is sending data. The beginning of the TCB queue is pointed to by the ASXBFTCB field of the ASXB, and the ASXB is pointed to by the ASCBASXB field of the ASCB. IBM provides the IHAASXB macro instruction to map the ASXB. The TCBTCB field of the TCB points to the next TCB on the queue.
- The CVTUSER field is used to contain the address of the ASCB. This is for illustration reasons only. In a normal production environment, the CVTUSER field should contain the address of a list of addresses located in the CSA. Each address in the list points to an allocated area in the CSA required by individual users. This enables multiple users to use the single CVTUSER field. This was discussed in more detail in Chapter 13.
- The instruction in the routine FREECSA of the POSTSRB SRB routine that clears CVTUSER is commented out. See the notes at the end of Coding Example 15.3.2 for more details. When the instruction is activated, the appropriate ENQ/DEQ macro instructions are required.
- The WORKAREA DSECT is hard-coded in both the SVC routine and the problem program. This is for illustration reasons only. In a normal production environment, this DSECT should be invoked via a macro instruction or a COPY statement.

Coding Example 15.3.2

This coding example illustrates the code for the problem program (which executes in the originating address space) that invokes the SVC routine presented in Coding Example 15.3.1.

```
AS1PROG CSECT
*
*
***********************************************************************
*     INITIALIZATION
***********************************************************************
*
         INITL 3,EQU=R            INITIALIZE PROGRAM
         USING CVT,R10            DEFINE REG FOR CVT DSECT
         USING WORKAREA,R12       DEFINE REG FOR WORK AREA DSECT
*
*
***********************************************************************
*     MAINSTREAM OF PROGRAM
***********************************************************************
*
```

```
GETDATA  BAL   R6,CHKDATA                  CHECK IF ANY A.S. HAS DATA TO SEND
         BAL   R6,SCHLDSRB                 IF YES, SCHEDULE AN SRB
         BAL   R6,PROCESS                  PROCESS DATA FROM SRB + NORM PROC
         BAL   R6,FREEMAIN                 RELEASE WORK AREA ALLO BY SVC
         B     GETDATA                     GET MORE DATA FROM ANY A.S.
*
*
***********************************************************************
*    THIS ROUTINE CHECKS THE CVTUSER FIELD TO DETERMINE IF ANY ADDRESS
*    SPACES HAVE DATA TO SEND TO THIS ADDRESS SPACE. IF THERE ARE NONE,
*    THEN THIS ROUTINE PERFORMS A CYCLE OF NORMAL PROCESSING AND THEN
*    CHECKS THE CVTUSER FIELD AGAIN. WHEN THE CVTUSER INDICATES THAT AN
*    ADDRESS SPACE HAS DATA TO SEND, THIS ROUTINE TURNS ON DATASW AND
*    RETURNS CONTROL TO THE CALLING ROUTINE.
***********************************************************************
*
CHKDATA  BAL   R7,ENQ                      SERIALIZE ACCESS TO CVTUSER
         L     R10,16                      LOAD ADR OF CVT
         CLC   CVTUSER,BINZEROS            CHECK IF CVTUSER HAS ADR OF A.S.
         BE    NODATA                      IF NO, NO DATA TO BE RECEIVED
         MVI   DATASW,C'1'                 IF YES, TURN ON DATASW
         BAL   R7,DEQ                      RELEASE CVTUSER ENQ
         BR    R6                          RETURN TO CALLING ROUTINE
NODATA   MVI   DATASW,C'0'                 IND NO DATA TO BE RECEIVED
         BAL   R7,DEQ                      RELEASE CVTUSER ENQ
         WTO   '*** NO DATA ***'           *** FOR INITIAL TESTING ONLY ***
         ABEND 901                         *** FOR INITIAL TESTING ONLY ***
         BAL   R7,PROCESS1                 DO A CYCLE OF NORM PROC
         B     CHKDATA                     CHK AGAIN IF ANY A.S. HAVE DATA
*
*
***********************************************************************
*    THIS SUBROUTINE ISSUES AN EXCLUSIVE ENQ TO SERIALIZE THE ACCESS
*    TO CVTUSER.
***********************************************************************
*
ENQ      ENQ   (QNAME,RNAME,E,,SYSTEM)     DO ENQ
         BR    R7                          RETURN TO CALLING ROUTINE
*
*
***********************************************************************
*    THIS SUBROUTINE ISSUES A DEQ TO RELEASE EXCLUSIVE ACCESS TO CVTUSER.
***********************************************************************
*
DEQ      DEQ   (QNAME,RNAME,,SYSTEM)       DO DEQ
         BR    R7                          RETURN TO CALLING ROUTINE
*
*
***********************************************************************
*    THIS ROUTINE INVOKES THE APPROPRIATE SVC ROUTINE TO SCHEDULE AN SRB
*    IN THE ADDRESS SPACE WHOSE ASCB ADDRESS IS STORED IN CVTUSER.
***********************************************************************
*
SCHLDSRB SVC   253                         IF YES, ISSUE SVC TO SCHEDULE SRB
         LR    R12,R1                      SET ADBLTY FOR WORK AREA ALLO BY SVC
         BR    R6                          RETURN TO CALLING ROUTINE
*
*
***********************************************************************
*    THIS ROUTINE PERIODICALLY CHECKS IF ANY OUTSTANDING SRB'S HAVE
*    COMPLETED MOVING THE DATA FROM ANOTHER ADDRESS SPACE TO THIS ONE.
*    NORMAL PROGRAM PROCESSING IS PERFORMED BETWEEN CHECKS.
***********************************************************************
*
```

```
PROCESS  BAL   R7,CHKSRB          CHECK IF DATA MOVEMENT COMPLETE
         BAL   R7,PROCESS1        DO A CYCLE OF NORM PROC
         CLI   DATASW,C'1'        CHECK IF SRB OUTSTANDING
         BE    PROCESS            IF YES, CHECK AGAIN FOR COMPLETION
         BR    R6                 IF NO, RETURN TO CALLING ROUTINE
*
*
***********************************************************************
*    THIS SUBROUTINE CHECKS THE ECB TO DETERMINE IF THE DATA MOVEMENT
*    FROM THE TARGET ADDRESS SPACE TO THIS ADDRESS SPACE HAS BEEN
*    COMPLETED.
***********************************************************************
*
CHKSRB   TM    WECB,X'40'         IF YES, CHK ECB FOR COMPLETION
         BO    PROCDATA           IF COMPLETE, PROC DATA FROM OTHER A.S.
         BR    R7                 IF NOT, RET TO CALLING ROUTINE
PROCDATA MVI   DATASW,C'0'        TURN OFF OUTSTANDING SRB SWITCH
         BAL   R8,PROCESS2        PROC DATA RECEIVED FROM OTHER A.S.
         BR    R7                 RETURN TO CALLING ROUTINE
*
*
***********************************************************************
*    THIS SUBROUTINE SIMULATES PROGRAM PROCESSING BY GOING INTO A
*    FINITE I/O LOOP.
***********************************************************************
*
PROCESS1 LA    R10,10
OPEN     OPEN  (DCB,(OUTPUT))
         PUT   DCB,RECORD
         CLOSE DCB
         BCT   R10,OPEN
         BR    R7
*
*
***********************************************************************
*    THIS SUBROUTINE PROCESSES THE DATA RECEIVED FROM THE OTHER ADDRESS
*    SPACE. DURING TESTING, THIS ROUTINE DISPLAYS THE JOBNAME OF THE
*    OTHER ADDRESS SPACE AND THE FIRST 8 BYTES OF THE DATA RECEIVED.
***********************************************************************
*
PROCESS2 MVC   WTOJBNM,WJOBNAME   MOVE JOBNAME INTO WTO-LIST
         MVC   WTODATA,WJOBDATA   MOVE FIRST 8 BYTES OF DATA RECEIVED
         LA    R1,WTOLST1         LD ADR OF WTO-LIST
         WTO   MF=(E,(R1))        ISSUE EXEC-FORM OF WTO
         BR    R8                 RETURN TO CALLING ROUTINE
*
*
***********************************************************************
*    THIS ROUTINE RELEASES THE WORK AREA ALLOCATED BY THE SVC ROUTINE.
***********************************************************************
*
FREEMAIN LA    R10,WGMADR          LOAD ADR OF GETMAIN AREA POINTER
         FREEMAIN EU,LV=WKARLEN,A=(R10)
         ABEND 902                *** FOR INITIAL TESTING ONLY ***
         BR    R6                 RETURN TO CALLING ROUTINE
*
*
***********************************************************************
*    THIS ROUTINE RESTORES THE REGISTERS AND RETURNS CONTROL TO MVS OR
*    THE CALLING PROGRAM.
***********************************************************************
*
RETURN   RCNTL RC=0               RETURN TO MVS OR CALLING PROG
*
```

```
*
*************************************************************************
*    THE WTO-LIST FOR THE EXECUTE FORM OF THE WTO MACRO
*************************************************************************
*
         DS    0F
WTOLST1  DC    AL2(WTOLST1X-WTOLST1)
         DC    H'0'
         DC    C'*** JOBNAME: '
WTOJBNM  DS    CL8
         DC    C' DATA: '
WTODATA  DS    CL8
WTOLST1X EQU *
*
*
*************************************************************************
*    DC/DS STATEMENTS
*************************************************************************
*
BINZEROS DC    F'0'
DATASW   DC    C'0'
QNAME    DC    CL8'USER'
RNAME    DC    C'CVTUSER'
*
*
*************************************************************************
*    DATA RECORD AND DCB USED TO SIMULATE PROCESSING
*************************************************************************
*
RECORD  DC     80CL1'A'
DCB     DCB    DSORG=PS,MACRF=PM,BLKSIZE=80,LRECL=80,RECFM=F,           -
               DDNAME=WORK
*
*
*************************************************************************
*    THE DSECTS
*************************************************************************
*
WORKAREA DSECT
WGMADR   DS    F
WECB     DS    F
WJOBNAME DS    CL8
WJOBDATA DS    CL100
WKARLEN  EQU   *-WORKAREA
*
         PRINT NOGEN
         CVT   DSECT=YES         GENERATES THE CVT DSECT
*
*
*************************************************************************
*    END OF PROGRAM
*************************************************************************
*           END
```

NOTES:

- The subroutine PROCESS1 performs a finite I/O loop. This routine is used to simulate asynchronous processing (before the actual routine is developed) in order to test the SRB routines. Processing should not be simulated with a B * instruction. The JCL DD statement for that I/O can be coded as follows:

```
//WORK DD UNIT=SYSDA,SPACE=(TRK,1)
```

- This program has ABEND macro instructions in strategic places. The SVC routine invoked by this program (illustrated in Coding Example 15.3.1) and the SVC routine invoked by the target address space (illustrated in Coding Example 15.3.3) have certain instructions commented out. This will cause data to be copied from the target address space to the originating address space only once. The initial asynchronous inter-address space communications demonstration begins by initiating the target address space first. After CVTUSER is set by the target address space (within a few seconds after it starts), the originating address space is initiated. The subroutine PROCESS2 displays the first eight bytes of the data received, and after the GETMAINed WORKAREA is released, a U902 ABEND occurs.
- As an exercise, the reader is invited to activate the commented out instructions and make the required enhancements to the SVC routine and problem program that execute in the target address space to cause data to be sent to the originating address space more than once.

Coding Example 15.3.3

This coding example illustrates how the target address space communicates with the SRB scheduled in that address space by placing the address of the data that is to be accessed in the TCBUSER field of the TCB. Since a problem state program cannot modify the TCB, an SVC routine is provided to perform this function. The SVC routine also places the address of the ASCB in CVTUSER to indicate to the originating address space that this address space has data to send.

The Code for the SVC (254) routine

```
IGC0025D CSECT
*
*
***********************************************************************
*    INITIALIZATION
***********************************************************************
*
         REGEQU EQU=R                 GENERATE EQU'S FOR REGS
         USING  *,R6                  DEFINE BASE REGISTER
         USING  CVT,R3                DEFINE REG FOR CVT DSECT
         USING  TCB,R4                DEFINE REG FOR TCB DSECT
*
*
***********************************************************************
*    MAINSTREAM OF SVC ROUTINE
***********************************************************************
*
         BAL    R8,SAVEREGS           SAVE CONTENTS OF CONTROL REGS
         BAL    R8,SETASCB            PUT ASCB ADR INTO CVTUSER
         BAL    R8,SETTCBU            PUT BUFFER ADR INTO TCBUSER
         B      RETURN                RETURN TO CALLING PROG VIA SVC FLIH
*
*
***********************************************************************
*    THIS ROUTINE SAVES THE CONTENTS OF ALL REGISTERS THAT CONTAIN
*    CONTROL INFORMATION.
***********************************************************************
*
SAVEREGS LR     R2,R14                SAVE RETURN ADDRESS
         LR     R11,R1                SAVE BUFFER ADDRESS
         BR     R8                    RETURN TO CALLING ROUTINE
*
*
```

```
************************************************************************
*     THIS ROUTINE CHECKS THE CVTUSER FIELD OF THE CVT. IF IT CONTAINS
*     ZEROS, THEN THE ADDRESS OF THE ASCB, WHICH HAS DATA TO SEND, IS
*     STORED. IF THE CVTUSER CONTAINS NON-ZEROS, THEN NO PROCESSING IS
*     DONE AND RC=4 IS RETURNED TO THE CALLING PROGRAM.
************************************************************************
*
SETASCB  BAL   R9,ENQ               SERIALIZE ACCESS TO CVTUSER
*        CLC   CVTUSER,BINZEROS     CHECK IF CVTUSER AVAILABLE
*        BNE   INUSE                IF NO, INDICATE IN-USE
         ST    R7,CVTUSER           IF YES, SET ASCB ADR IN CVTUSER
         BAL   R9,DEQ               RELEASE CVTUSER ENQ
         LA    R15,0                INDICATE ASCB ADR SET
         BR    R8                   RETURN TO CALLING ROUTINE
INUSE    BAL   R9,DEQ               RELEASE CVTUSER ENQ
         LA    15,4                 IND CVTUSER HAS OUTSTANDING REQUEST
         BR    R8                   RETURN TO CALLING ROUTINE
*
*
************************************************************************
*     THIS SUBROUTINE ISSUES AN EXCLUSIVE ENQ TO SERIALIZE THE ACCESS
*     TO CVTUSER.
************************************************************************
*
ENQ      ENQ   (QNAME,RNAME,E,,SYSTEM)
         BR    R9                   RETURN TO CALLING ROUTINE
*
*
************************************************************************
*     THIS SUBROUTINE ISSUES A DEQ TO RELEASE EXCLUSIVE ACCESS TO CVTUSER.
************************************************************************
*
DEQ      DEQ   (QNAME,RNAME,,SYSTEM)
         BR    R9                   RETURN TO CALLING ROUTINE
*
*
************************************************************************
*     THIS ROUTINE STORES THE BUFFER ADRRESS SPECIFIED BY THE CALLER
*     INTO THE TCBUSER FIELD OF THE TCB IF THE ASCB ADDRESS WAS SET.
************************************************************************
*
SETTCBU  LTR   R15,R15              CHK IF ASCB ADR SET
         BNZR  R8                   IF NO, RET TO CALLING ROUTINE
         ST    R11,TCBUSER          IF YES, STORE BUFF ADR INTO TCBUSER
         BR    R8                   RETURN TO CALLING ROUTINE
*
*
************************************************************************
*     THIS ROUTINE RETURNS CONTROL TO THE CALLER VIA THE SVC FLIH.
************************************************************************
*
RETURN   LR    R14,R2               RESTORE RETURN ADDRESS
         BR    R14                  RETURN TO CALLING PROG VIA FLIH
*
*
************************************************************************
*     THE CONSTANTS
************************************************************************ *
*
BINZEROS DC    F'0'
QNAME    DC    CL8'USER'
RNAME    DC    C'CVTUSER'
*
*
```

```
***********************************************************************
*    THE DSECTS
***********************************************************************
*
         CVT   DSECT=YES               GENERATES CVT DSECT
         IKJTCB                        GENERATES TCB DSECT
*
*
***********************************************************************
*    END OF SVC ROUTINE
***********************************************************************
*
              END
```

The code for the problem program that executes in the target address space

```
AS2PROG CSECT
*
*
***********************************************************************
*    INITIALIZATION
***********************************************************************
*
         INITL 3,EQU=R                 INITIALIZE PROGRAM
*
*
***********************************************************************
*    MAINSTREAM OF PROGRAM
***********************************************************************
*
         BAL   R6,GETMAIN              ALLO STOR FOR DATA TO SEND
         BAL   R6,GETDATA              OBTAIN DATA FOR OTHER A.S.
         BAL   R6,MOVEDATA             MOVE DATA INTO GM STOR FOR OTHER A.S.
         BAL   R6,SETADRS              SET UP ADRS FOR SRB COMMUNICATION
         BAL   R6,PROCESS              PERFORM NORMAL PROG PROCESSING
         B     RETURN                  RETURN TO MVS OR CALLING PROG
*
*
***********************************************************************
*    THIS ROUTINE ALLOCATES VIRTUAL STORAGE, WHICH IS TO CONTAIN THE DATA
*    THAT IS TO BE SENT TO THE OTHER ADDRESS SPACE.
***********************************************************************
*
GETMAIN  GETMAIN EU,LV=BUFFLEN,A=BUFFADR
         BR    R6                      RETURN TO CALLING ROUTINE
*
*
***********************************************************************
*    THIS ROUTINE OBTAINS THE DATA THAT IS TO BE SENT TO THE OTHER
*    ADDRESS SPACE.
***********************************************************************
*
GETDATA  DS    OH
         ...                           OBTAIN DATA
         BR    R6
*
*
***********************************************************************
*    THIS ROUTINE MOVES THE DATA THAT IS TO BE SENT TO THE OTHER
*    ADDRESS SPACE INTO THE BUFFER, WHICH WILL BE POINTED TO BY TCBUSER.
***********************************************************************
*
MOVEDATA L     R10,BUFFADR             LD ADR OF BUFFER
         MVC   O(BUFFLEN,R10),BUFFDATA MOVE DATA INTO BUFFER
```

```
         BR    R6                   RETURN TO CALLING ROUTINE
*
*
***********************************************************************
*    THIS ROUTINE INVOKES THE SVC ROUTINE THAT COMMUNICATES WITH THE SRB
*    ROUTINE BY PUTTING THE ADDRESS OF THE ASCB OF THIS ADDRESS SPACE INTO
*    CVTUSER AND BY PUTTING THE ADDRESS OF THE DATA BUFFER INTO TCBUSER.
***********************************************************************
*
SETADRS  L     R1,BUFFADR           LD BUFFER ADR FOR SVC
         SVC   254                  ISSUE SVC TO COMM WITH OTHER A.S.
         BR    R6                   RETURN TO CALLING ROUTINE
*
*
***********************************************************************
*    THIS ROUTINE SIMULATES PROCESSING OF THIS ADDRESS SPACE WHILE THE
*    SRB'S ARE SCHEDULED AND COPY THE DATA FROM THIS A.S. TO THE
*    ORIGINATING A.S.
***********************************************************************
*
PROCESS  OPEN  (DCB,(OUTPUT))
         PUT   DCB,RECORD
         CLOSE DCB
         B     PROCESS
*
*
***********************************************************************
*    THIS ROUTINE RESTORES THE REGISTERS AND RETURNS CONTROL TO MVS OR
*    THE CALLING PROGRAM
***********************************************************************
*
RETURN   RCNTL RC=0                 RETURN TO MVS OR CALLING PROG
*
*
***********************************************************************
*    THE DC/DS STATEMENTS
***********************************************************************
*
BUFFADR  DS    F
BUFFDATA DC    100CL1'D'            TEST DATA TO SEND TO OTHER A.S.
BUFFLEN  EQU   *-BUFFDATA
*
*
***********************************************************************
*     THE RECORD AND THE DCB USED FOR THE I/O LOOP FOR TESTING
***********************************************************************
*
RECORD   DC    80CL1'A'
DCB      DCB   DSORG=PS,MACRF=PM,BLKSIZE=80,LRECL=80,RECFM=F,          -
               DDNAME=WORK
*
*
***********************************************************************
*    END OF PROGRAM
***********************************************************************
*
               END
```

NOTES:

- The routine PROCESS in the program AS2PROG performs an endless I/O loop. This routine simulates processing while the originating address space schedules an SRB to retrieve the data from this address space.

- Certain instructions are commented out in this SVC routine and in the SVC routine that is invoked by the problem program, which executes in the originating address space. (Coding Examples 15.3.1 and 15.3.2 illustrate the code for the SVC and problem program which execute in the originating address space, respectively.) See the notes at the end of Coding Example 15.3.2 for more details.
- As an exercise, the reader might try to modify AS2PROG and the SVC routine that it invokes to send additional data to the originating address space. Some of the considerations are the following:

  - The routine PROCESS must be modified to be a finite loop.
  - Origin of the data that is sent to the originating address space.
  - When a return code of X'04' is received from the SVC routine (CVTUSER not zero, which implies that the data transfer has not been completed), a retry is required.
  - Some mechanism is required to terminate the programs in both address spaces other than an MVS CANCEL command or an ABEND macro instruction.

15.3.3 Advantages of Using SRBs

The following are some of the advantages of using SRBs:

- Due to the asynchronous processing nature of SRBs, they are suited for parallel processing. This can be exploited if a job step is able to divide its processing requirements into units of work that can execute concurrently. This can also be accomplished via the ATTACH macro instruction, but SRBs have the additional advantage and flexibility of being able to perform the parallel processing in another address space.
- Since an SRB can be scheduled in other address spaces without any required intervention by those address spaces, SRB routines can be used to monitor the activity of address spaces.
- Since SRB routines execute in supervisor state and the specified PSW storage protection key, they can be used to perform certain sensitive functions that the issuing problem state program cannot perform. This improves system integrity by isolating that code away from the issuing program.

15.4 INTER-ADDRESS SPACE COMMUNICATIONS VIA CMS

Cross Memory Services (CMS) provides a synchronous method of communications between address spaces. With CMS, programs can pass control directly to programs residing in other address spaces and can move data directly from one address space to another address space. The use of the CSA is not required as an intermediate storage area for the transfer of data between address spaces as it is when SRBs are used. During execution, a program has associated with it a primary address space and a secondary address space, which may be different address spaces or may be the same one. CMS provides services between these two address spaces.

In MVS/ESA, data can also be moved between address spaces without the requirement that the address spaces be designated as the primary and the secondary address spaces. This can be done with the use of access registers (new with 3090 computers in ESA/370 mode and used by MVS/ESA) and AR ASC (access register–address space control) mode. However, this facility will not be discussed.

The calling and called programs may be in the same or different address spaces. Only the situation when the calling and called programs are in different address spaces will be discussed. This chapter refers to the called programs and their address spaces as the service-providers, and the calling programs and their address spaces as the users. The service-providers can provide service for only one user or for many users.

CMS is implemented with a combination of macro instructions and machine instructions. In order to use CMS, certian data structures and tables must be set up. MVS provides macro instructions to accomplish this. Also, certain programming conventions must be used in order to save and restore the contents of registers and other status information and to pass control between programs in different address spaces.

15.4.1 CMS Terminology

There are a number of terms introduced by CMS with which the reader may not be familiar. The understanding of these terms is helpful in understanding the rest of this chapter. The following contains an explanation of the more important terms used in CMS:

Cross Memory Environment — The environment in which synchronous inter-address space communications occurs. It occurs between a primary address space and a secondary address space and requires authorization, linkage, and entry tables.

Home Address Space — The address space to which a unit of work is associated and whose address is pointed to by the PSA field PSAAOLD when the unit of work is executing. The home address space contains the local control blocks (TCBs, RBs, etc.) that describe the unit of work to MVS. The called program (PC routine) executes under the TCB of the calling program from the home address. When the job step is initially dispatched, the home address space, the primary address space, and the secondary address space are the same. The ASID of the home address space is called the HASID.

Primary Address Space — The address space whose segment table (pointed to by control register 1) is used to access instructions and data when the CPU is in primary mode. The PC and PT instructions may be issued only from the primary address space. When the PC and PT instructions are executed, the target address space becomes the primary address space. When the job step is initially dispatched, the home address space and the primary address space are the same. The ASID of the primary address space is called the PASID.

Secondary Address Space — The address space whose segment table (pointed to by control register 7) is used to access data when the CPU is in secondary mode. The secondary address space may be set explicitly to the desired address space by specifying its ASID as the operand of the SSAR instruction or will be set implicitly to the ASID of the address space that issues the PC or PT instruction. Placing the CPU into secondary mode is not required to move data between address spaces. This can be accomplished with the MVCP and the MVCS instructions while executing in primary mode. When the job step is initially dispatched, the home address space and the secondary address space are the same. The ASID of the secondary address space is called the SASID.

Home Mode	A unit of work is in home mode if the HASID and the PASID are the same.
Primary Mode	The CPU is in primary mode when the S-bit (bit 16) of the current PSW is set to 0. In ESA/370 mode, this is indicated when the AS-bits (bits 16–17) are set to 00.
Secondary Mode	The CPU is in secondary mode when the S-bit (bit 16) of the current PSW is set to 1. In ESA/370 mode, this is indicated when the AS-bits (bits 16–17) are set to 10. When code is executing with the CPU in secondary mode, the instructions must be located in commonly addressable virtual storage because it is unpredictable whether the instructions will be fetched from either the primary or the secondary address space.
Currently Addressable Address Space	The address space whose segment table is used to fetch data.
CML Address Space	The address space other than the home address space whose local lock is held as a Cross Memory Local (CML) lock. When a program attempts to obtain the CML lock via the SETLOCK macro instruction (discussed in Chapter 10), it must have established the CML address space as either the primary or secondary address space (one way is via the PC instruction). After the CML lock is obtained, the CML address space does not have to remain the primary or secondary address space. A user may hold only one lock at the local level, either the LOCAL lock of the home address space or one CML lock. Owning the CML lock creates an "active bind" between the CML address space and the address space that owns the lock (usually the home address space). This prevents either address space from being swapped-out. Owning the CML lock also permits synchronization at the address space level. One way in which this can be accomplished is for the service-providing address space to obtain its local lock (as a CML lock) on entry to the called program and release the CML lock just before returning control. This has the effect of preventing multiple user address spaces from obtaining services from the service-providing address space concurrently.
PC routine (Service Program)	The generic name of the program that receives control via a PC instruction.

In addition, control registers and general purpose registers are discussed throughout the remainder of this chapter. When a reference is made to a control register, the term control register is used; however, when a reference is made to a general purpose register, either the single word register is used (as is the practice throughout this book) or the term general purpose register is used.

15.4.2 Macro and Machine Instructions Used With CMS

In order to set up and use a cross memory environment, certain macro and machine instructions are used. Some are required and some are optional. The macro instructions described must be issued from programs executing in either supervisor state or PSW storage protection keys 0–7 and be enabled and unlocked with the CPU in primary mode. The machine instructions described are semi-privileged, which means that the issuing program must be executing in either supervisor state or in problem state, with certain authority requirements met. For example, for a PC instruction, the authorized key mask (AKM) in the entry-table entry (ETE) must match at least one of the PSW storage protection keys indicated in the PSW key mask (PKM) of the executing program.

MACRO INSTRUCTIONS USED WITH CMS

The following are macro instructions used with CMS:

- The AXRES macro instruction is used to reserve an authorization index (AX) in the authorization table.
- The AXFRE macro instruction is used to return an AX for reuse.
- The AXEXT macro instruction is used to extract the AX value of an address space.
- The AXSET macro instruction is used to set the AX value for an address space.
- The ATSET macro instruction is used to set PT and the SSAR authority in an authorization table entry (referenced by the AX).
- The LXRES macro instruction is used to reserve a linkage index (LX) in the linkage table.
- The LXFRE macro instruction is used to return an LX for reuse.
- The ETCRE macro instruction is used to create an entry table. An entry table contains the description of one or more programs which receive control via a PC instruction.
- The ETDEF macro instruction is used to define a program in the entry table. This macro instruction is available only in MVS/ESA.
- The ETDES macro instruction is used to destroy an entry table.
- The ETCON macro instruction is used to connect an entry table to a linkage table at the specified LX.
- The ETDIS macro instruction is used to disconnect an entry table from a linkage table.
- The PCLINK macro instruction is used by PC routines to save linkage information from the calling program and to restore the linkage information before returning control to the calling program. To issue this macro instruction, the caller must be executing in supervisor state with the CPU in primary mode.

MACHINE INSTRUCTIONS USED WITH CMS

The following are machine instructions used with CMS:

- The PC machine instruction causes a program in another address space (or the same address space) to receive control.
- The PT machine instruction causes control to be returned from a program that was called via a PC instruction.
- The SSAR machine instruction is used to set a specified address space to the secondary address space.
- The MVCP machine instruction is used to move data from the secondary address space to the primary address space.
- The MVCS machine instruction is used to move data from the primary address space to the secondary address space.
- The MVCK machine instruction is used to move data between storage areas that have different protection keys.
- The SAC machine instruction is used to explicitly set either the primary or the secondary mode. In ESA/370 mode, it is also used to set AR (access register) mode.

- The IAC machine instruction is used to indicate in a register whether primary mode or secondary mode is in effect. In ESA/370 mode, it also indicates if AR mode is in effect.
- The EPAR machine instruction is used to place the primary ASID into a register.
- The ESAR machine instruction is used to place the secondary ASID into a register.

15.4.3 Requirements to Set Up a Cross Memory Environment

A cross memory environment uses a set of data structures, tables, and programming conventions. These requirements can be divided into three areas.

`Cross Memory Authorization` defines how address spaces and programs are authorized to use the PC, SSAR, and PT instructions to communicate with other address spaces and programs, and defines how the user can request that the operating system provide this authorization.

`Cross Memory Linkage` defines the data structures and tables used by the PC instruction to call programs in other address spaces, and defines how a user can request that the operating system create these data structures and tables and connect them to a particular address space(s).

`Linkage Conventions` defines a set of programming conventions that must be used to save and restore the contents registers and other status information and to pass control between programs in different address spaces.

15.4.3A Cross Memory Authorization

CMS provides a multi-level authorization facility, which permits programs executing in either supervisor state or problem state to have access to the programs and data residing in selected address spaces, and to restrict programs executing in problem state from having access to certain programs residing in selected address spaces. Cross memory authorization consists of program authorization and address space authorization.

PROGRAM AUTHORIZATION

Each unit of work (defined by a TCB or an SRB) has associated with it a PSW key mask (PKM) value. The PKM is a 16-bit value (located in bits 0–15 of control register 3) that represents the PSW storage protection keys that are valid for programs to use. Initially, the PKM is equal to the value in the TCBPKF field (for TCBs) or the SRBPKF field (for SRBs). For TCBs, this value is usually X'0080', which represents key 8. The PKM value can be changed by using the PC and PT machine instructions or by using the MODESET macro instruction.

The PKM value is used to authorize problem state programs to use cross memory services; supervisor state programs do not require PKM authorization. The PKM value is checked for the following reasons:

- To determine if a problem state program is allowed to issue a PC instruction for a particular program (defined by an ETE). The PKM value is checked against the authorization key mask (AKM) value (located in the ETE) associated with the called program. There must be at least one key (corresponding bit on) in common between the PKM and the AKM or the issuer of the PC instruction ABENDs with an S0C2 (program interruption-privileged operation).
- To determine if a problem state program is allowed to access the secondary address space via MVCP, MVCS, or MVCK instructions.

The setting in the AKM is used to permit access to the service-provider's address space by the user's address space. Coding Example 15.4.3 shows how to define the AKM associated with a PC routine.

ADDRESS SPACE AUTHORIZATION

There is a system authorization table (SAT) located in the PC/AUTH address space (the address space for CMS). Each entry in the authorization table is indexed by an authorization index (AX). The AX entries indicate whether an address space is authorized to access other address spaces.

The first two AX entries are permanently reserved. The AX entry at location 0 (AX value of 0) indicates an unauthorized address space (p and s bits are both zero) and the AX entry at location 1 (AX value of 1) indicates a completely authorized address space (p and s bits are both one).

When an address space is initialized, it is associated with the SAT and is assigned an AX value of 0, but certain system address spaces (PC/AUTH, GRS, etc.) that functionally serve all address spaces are assigned an AX value of 1.

Each address space remains associated with the SAT until a program of the address space alters an SAT entry corresponding to a non-permanent AX. At this time, the invoked system service creates an authorization table (AT) for the address space and copies the SAT into the AT.

The AX entry indicates whether the address space associated with it can access other address spaces by the setting of two bits: the p-bit and the s-bit. The p-bit indicates that the program is authorized to access the AT owner's address space as a primary address space (via the PT instruction), and the s-bit indicates that the program is authorized to access the AT owner's address space as a secondary address space (via the SSAR instruction).

When an address space, such as a subsystem (service-provider), is to provide cross memory services to other address spaces, it is required to obtain an AX value other than 0. This is accomplished by the service-provider's address space requesting the use of (reserving) a non-permanent AX value via the AXRES macro instruction. When the AXRES macro instruction is issued, the reserved AX value is owned by the home address space (in this case, the service-provider's address space). The AX values are unique across the system. The PC/AUTH address space maintains an Authorization Index Allocation Table (AXAT) to keep track of which address spaces owns which AXs. Remember that the AX is just an index into the AT.

In order for the service-provider's address space (SP-AS) to obtain authorization to access a user's address space (U-AS), the entry in the AT of the U-AS associated with (indexed by) the AX reserved by the SP-AS must indicate the appropriate authorization (usually both the p-bit and the s-bit on). This is accomplished by the user's address space issuing the ATSET macro instruction and referencing the AX value of the SP-AS. Figure 15.4.1 shows the relationship of the AX value of the service provider to the AT of the user. Coding Example 15.4.1 shows the code that is required for both the service-provider and the user in order to set up the authorization to permit access to the U-AS by the SP-AS.

Coding Example 15.4.1

This coding example illustrates the required macro instructions used by the SP-AS and the U-AS to authorize the SP-AS access to the U-AS.

The code for the service-provider's address space

```
         AXRES AXLIST=AXLIST       REQUEST TO RESERVE AN AX FOR SP-AS
```

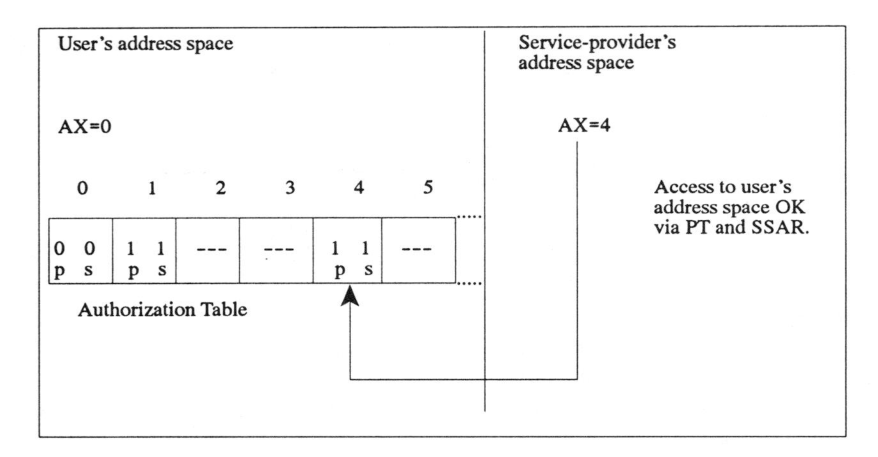

FIGURE 15.4.1. This figure shows the relationship between the AX value owned by the SP-AS and the corresponding entry into the AT of the U-AS. In this figure, the AX value of the service-provider is 4. This AX value is used as an index into the user's AT. At this entry, the p-bit and the s-bit are both set to one, which indicates that the SP-AS may access the U-AS via the PT and the SSAR instructions.

Coding Example 15.4.1 (Continued)

```
         AXSET AX=AXVALUE          SET NEW AX VALUE FOR SP-AS
         ...
AXLIST   DS    0F
AXCOUNT  DC    H'1'                RESERVE ONE AX
AXVALUE  DS    H                   VALUE OF RESERVED AX
```

The code for the user's address space

```
         ATSET AX=AXVALUE,PT=YES,SSAR=YES   PROV SP-AS WITH ACCESS TO U-AS
         ...
AXVALUE  DS    H
```

NOTES:

- The value of the requested AX is returned in AXVALUE by the AXRES macro instruction. When the SP-AS is initiated, it receives an AX value of 0. The AXSET macro instruction changes the AX value associated with the SP-AS to the new AX value reserved by the AXRES macro instruction.
- Each U-AS that requires the services provided by the SP-AS must issue the ATSET macro instruction to provide the SP-AS access (via the PT and the SSAR instructions) to the U-AS.
- The U-AS must use the AX value reserved by the SP-AS. This information can be passed to the U-AS via the CSA.
- The ATSET macro instruction must be issued by a program executing in supervisor mode or PSW storage protection key 0–7. Since the programs in the U-AS normally execute in problem state, there must be some means for the U-AS to issue the macro instruction. This is normally accomplished by providing the problem program with the use of an SVC routine.

15.4.3B Cross Memory Linkage

The PC and PT instructions are used to pass and return control, respectively, between programs via CMS. The operand of the PC instruction is a PC number associated with the program (PC routine) that is to be called. The PC number is composed of two concatenated index values: the linkage index (LX) and the entry index (EX).

There is a system linkage table and a linkage table associated with each address space. The system linkage table defines the set of cross memory services available to all address spaces, and the linkage table associated with each individual address space defines the set of cross memory services available only to that address space. Each entry (slot) in the linkage table is referenced via a linkage index (LX). The LXRES macro instruction is used by the SP-AS to reserve an LX. When the LXRES macro instruction is issued, the reserved LX value is owned by the home address space (in this case, the SP-AS). The LX values are unique across the system. The LX may be reserved in the system linkage table or in the linkage table associated with an address space. Coding Example 15.4.2 shows how to use the LXRES macro instruction to reserve an LX for a nonsystem linkage table.

Coding Example 15.4.2

This coding example illustrates how to code the LXRES macro instruction to reserve an LX value for the SP-AS.

```
         LXRES LXLIST=LXLIST       REQUEST TO RESERVE AN LX FOR SP-AS
         ...
LXLIST   DS    0F
LXCOUNT  DC    F'1'                RESERVE ONE LX
LXVALUE  DS    F                   VALUE OF RESERVED LX
```

NOTES:

- The value of the requested LX is returned in LXVALUE. This value is required by the ETCON macro instruction to connect the entry table defined by the SP-AS to the linkage table of the U-AS at the slot indexed by LX.

Each LX that is in use points to an entry table. Each entry table contains the descriptions of one or more of the services (progams that are to be called via the PC instruction) offered by the SP-AS. Each program description is assigned an entry index (EX). The first entry (EX value of X'00') of an entry table describes the first program defined, the second entry (EX value of X'01') of an entry table describes the second program defined, and so on. The entry table is created by the SP-AS via the ETCRE macro instruction. The programs are defined in a parameter-list that consists of a series of DC instructions. IBM provides the IHAETD macro instruction to map the parameter-list. Coding Example 15.4.3 shows how the SP-AS creates an entry table by setting up the parameter-list and issuing the ETCRE macro instruction. The ETCRE macro instruction creates one entry-table entry (ETE) for each program description that is located via the appropriate EX. The PC instruction references an ETE. Figure 15.4.2 shows the format of an ETE. Figure 15.4.3 shows the relationship between the linkage table and the entry table.

Coding Example 15.4.3

This coding example illustrates how the SP-AS sets up the parameter-list and issues the ETCRE macro instruction to create the entry table that describes the service programs that

AKM	ASID	A	IA	P	PARM	EKM	////////////

0 16 32 64 96 112 127

AKM — The authorized key mask (bits 0-15). If the program that issues the PC instruction is executing in problem mode, then the AKM in the ETE and PKM of the executing program are ANDed together. If the result is non-zero, then the program is authorized to execute the PC instruction to reference that ETE.

ASID — The ASID of the address space that contains the PC routine. If the value is zero, then the PC routine is located in the same address space as the calling program.

A — The addressing mode bit of the PC routine.

IA — The instruction address (entry point address) of the PC routine.

P — The problem state bit of the PC routine.

PARM — The entry parameter (bits 64–95). The contents of this field are loaded into register 4 and passed to the PC routine.

EKM — The execution key mask (bits 96–111). The EKM is ORed with the PKM of the executing program to become the new PKM of the PC routine.

Figure 15.4.2. This figure illustrates the format of an entry-table entry (ETE).

are available to the users. In this example, the SP-AS defines two programs: SERV01 and SERV02.

SERV01 receives control in supervisor state, can cause an address space switch, allows the caller to be executing in any PSW storage protection key, and can access virtual storage in PSW protection key zero and any other protection keys in callers's PKM (if the PC routine was executing in problem state). The code for SERV01 is in the program that issues the CMS macro instructions.

SERV02 receives control in supervisor state, can cause an address space switch, allows the caller to be executing in only PSW storage protection key 0 or 8, and can access virtual storage in all PSW storage protection keys (if the PC routine were executing in either supervisor state or problem state). SERV02 is loaded into the SP-AS via a LOAD macro instruction.

```
BLDETBL BAL   R8,SETET01           SET UP ENTRY TABLE PARAMETER-LIST
        ETCRE ENTRIES=ET01PGMS     CREATE ENTRY TABLE
        ST    R0,ET01TKEN          SAVE RETURNED TOKEN
        BR    R7                   RETURN TO CALLING RTN
*
*
***********************************************************************
*    THIS SUBROUTINE CREATES THE EX=0 AND THE EX=1 ENTRIES IN THE ENTRY
*    TABLE PARAMETER-LIST, WHICH DEFINES THE PROGRAMS SERV01 AND SERV02.
***********************************************************************
*
        USING ETD,R10              DEFINE REG FOR ENT-TBL HEADER DSECT
```

```
SETET01 LA     R10,ETDHDR          POINT TO AREA FOR ENT-TBL HDR
        MVC    ETDNUM,=H'2'        IND TWO PGMS ARE DEFINED IN PARM-LIST
*
        DROP   R10                 RELEASE REG 10 FOR REUSE
        USING  ETDELE,R10          DEFINE REG FOR E.T. ELEMENT DSECT
*
* DEFINITION FOR PC ROUTINE SERV01
*
        LA     R10,ET01S01         POINT TO PARM AREA FOR SERV-PROG-1
        MVI    ETDEX,X'00'         INDICATE EX=0
        OI     ETDFLG,ETDSUP+ETDXM  IND SUPV MODE AND ADR SPACE SWITCH
        MVC    ETDAKM,=X'FFFF'     IND CALLING PGM CAN HAVE ANY KEY
        MVC    ETDEKM,=X'8000'     IND PC RTN CAN ACCESS STORAGE THAT
*                                  HAS KEY 0 AND CALLING PROG KEYS
        MVC    ETDPAR,=C'OPT2'     SPECIFY PARM TO BE PASSED TO SERV01
        XC     ETDPRO1,ETDPRO1     ZERO FIELD TO IND EPA SPECIFIED
        MVC    ETDPRO2,EPAPC01     LOAD EPA OF SERV-PGM-1
*
* DEFINITION FOR PC ROUTINE SERV02
*
        LA     R10,ETD01S02        POINT TO PARM AREA FOR SERV-PROG-2
        MVI    ETDEX,X'01'         INDICATE EX=1
        OI     ETDFLG,ETDSUP+ETDXM  IND SUPV MODE AND ADR SPACE SWITCH
        MVC    ETDAKM,=X'8080'     IND CALLING PROG MUST HAVE KEY 0 OR 8
        MVC    ETDEKM,=X'FFFF'     IND PC RTN CAN ACCESS STORAGE THAT
*                                  HAS ANY KEY
        MVC    ETDPAR,=C'SW=5'     SPECIFY PARM TO BE PASSED TO SERV02
        MVC    ETDPRO1(8),=CL8'SERV02'   MOVE NAME OF SERV-PGM-2
*
        BR     R8                  RETURN TO CALLING RTN
*
*
***********************************************************************
*    THE AREA FOR THE ENTRY TABLE AND THE SAVEAREA FOR THE RETURNED
*    TOKEN FROM THE ETCRE MACRO
***********************************************************************
*
ET01PGMS DS    0F
ETD01HDR DS    CL(ETDLEN)          ENTRY TABLE HEADER
ETD01S01 DS    CL(ETDELEN)         EX=0 ENTRY FOR PGM SERV01
ETD01S02 DS    CL(ETDELEN)         EX=1 ENTRY FOR PGM SERV02
*
ET01TKEN DS    F
*
*
***********************************************************************
*    THE DSECTS FOR THE ENTRY TABLE
***********************************************************************
*
        IHAETD                     GENERATES DSECTS FOR ENTRY TABLE
```

NOTES:

- When the ETCRE macro instruction returns control, a token is returned in register 0. This token must be saved because it is required by the ETCON macro instruction to connect the entry table to the linkage table.
- The setting of the ETDAKM field (authorized key mask) is used to permit access to the services provided by the SP-AS by the problem programs of the U-AS via the PC instruction.
- The setting of the ETDEKM (execution kay mask) field is meaningful only if the PC routine does not execute in supervisor state.
- The ETDPAR field is used to define a parameter to be passed to the PC routine. The specified value is stored in commonly addressable virtual storage area by the

ETCON macro instruction, and the pointer to that area is stored in the ETE. When the PC routine receives control, register 4 is loaded with the pointer to the specified parameter.

In order for the U-AS to have access (via the PC instruction) to the service programs of the SP-AS, the entry table created by the SP-AS must be connected to the linkage table owned by the U-AS. The slot in the linkage table used is the slot indexed by the LX value owned by the SP-AS. This is accomplished by the U-AS issuing the ETCON macro instruction as illustrated in Coding Example 15.4.4. This must be done by each U-AS that requires the use of those services.

Coding Example 15.4.4

This coding example illustrates how a U-AS connects to its linkage table the SP-AS's entry table.

```
         ETCON LXLIST=LXLIST,TKLIST=ET01LIST
         ...
LXLIST   DS    0F
LXCOUNT  DS    F'1'                    NUMB OF LX'S IN LIST
LXVALUE  DS    F                       LX VALUE RESERVED BY SP-AS
*
ET01LIST DS    0F
ET01CNT  DC    F'1'                    NUMB OF ENT-TBL TOKENS IN LIST
ET01TKEN DS    F                       TOKEN OF ENTRY TABLE OF SP-AS
```

NOTES:

- The LX value and the token required by the ETCON macro instruction are the values returned from the LXRES and ETCRE macro instructions, respectively, which were issued in the SP-AS. These values can be passed to the U-AS via the CSA.

If the services are to be provided to all address spaces, then the SP-AS can make its services available to all address spaces by assigning the AX value of 1 to itself and by reserving a system LX. In this case, the U-ASs are not required to issue any CMS's macros instructions to set up any authorization and linkage. Coding Example 15.4.5 shows the code required for an SP-AS to make its services available to all U-ASs.

Unlike the LXs for linkage tables associated with address spaces, the LXs for the system linkage table cannot be freed for reuse. When an address space that owns a system LX terminates, the LX becomes dormant and may be reconnected to an address space different from the original owning address space. Since there are only a limited number of system LXs available for users, if an SP-AS is required to come down and be restarted between IPLs, then the SP-AS should provide some method of saving the LX value. If a dormant LX is reused, then the LXRES macro instruction is not required to be issued.

Coding Example 15.4.5

This coding example illustrates how an SP-AS makes its services available to all U-ASs. The entry table that was created in Coding Example 15.4.3 is used.

```
PROVSERV LA    R2,1                       LOAD 1 FOR AXSET MACRO
         AXSET AX=(R2)                    ASSIGN AX VALUE OF 1 SELF
         LXRES LXLIST=LXLIST,SYSTEM=YES   RESERVE A SYSTEM LX
         ETCON LXLIST=LXLIST,TKLIST=ET01LIST CONNECT ET TO SYSTEM LT
         BR    R7                         RETURN TO CALLING RTN
```

```
          ...
LXLIST    DS    0F
LXCOUNT   DS    F'1'                              NUMB OF LX'S IN LIST
LXVALUE   DS    F                                 SYS LX VALUE RESERVED BY SP-AS
*
ET01LIST  DS    0F
ET01CNT   DC    F'1'                              NUMB OF ENT-TBL TOKENS IN LIST
ET01TKEN  DS    F                                 TOKEN OF ENTRY TABLE OF SP-AS
```

15.4.3C Linkage Conventions

There are a number of conventions that must be followed when a program is called from another address space via the PC instruction. This is necessary to assure that the calling program's status is saved and that the called program returns control properly. There are linkage conventions for both the calling program and the called program.

- Just before the calling program issues the PC instruction, it must do the following:
  - Save registers 2-12 in their normal places (words 8-18) in a standard save area pointed to by register 13 (the PC instruction modifies registers 3, 4, and 14);
  - Save the current SASID in bits 16-31 of word 5 (where register 15 is normally saved) of the standard savearea;
  - Optionally load registers 0, 1, and 15 with parameter information; and
  - Load register 2 with the PC number.
- The program that receives control as a result of the PC instruction issues the PCLINK macro instruction with the STACK option. The PCLINK macro instruction creates a stack element (STKE) that contains the following:
  - Caller's savearea address (from caller's register 13);
  - The AMODE, return address and PSW problem state bit (from caller's register 14);
  - Parameter registers 0, 1, and 15;
  - Caller's PKM and the PASID (from the caller's register 3);
  - Entry parameter (from the caller's register 4);
  - The caller's PSW key and bits 8-31 from the caller's register 2; and
  - The address in the caller's program just after the PC instruction.
- After the PCLINK macro instruction is issued, the base registers (if required) are loaded and the called program starts execution. Register 14 must be saved because it contains the address of the STKE.
- When the execution is complete, register 14 is restored and the PCLINK macro instruction with the UNSTACK THRU(R14) option is issued. This restores the status of the calling program.
- Control is returned to the calling program at the point after the PC instruction, with the PT instruction using the contents of register 3 and register 14 (after they are restored with the PCLINK macro instruction) as follows.

```
PT R3,R14
```

- Register 3 contains the PKM and the PASID of the program that issued the PC instruction, and register 14 contains the AMODE, return address, and problem state bit of the program that issued the PC instruction.
- The following are considerations for a PC routine:
  - The SP-AS should be non-swappable. MVS does not support cross memory services to a swapped-out address space. Chapter 10 discusses how this program property can be

defined. When the U-AS calls a program located in the SP-AS, an S0D5-021 ABEND will occur if the SP-AS is swapped-out.

- The U-AS can be made non-swappable while it is communicating with the SP-AS. This can be accomplished by the called PC routine issuing the SETLOCK macro instruction to obtain the CML lock for the SP-AS address space. Since the PC routine executes under the TCB of the calling program from the home address, it must issue the EPAR instruction to obtain the PASID (the address space of the SP-AS when it receives control via the PC instruction). The LOCASCB macro instruction can be used to obtain the address of the ASCB of the PASID. The ASCB address is required by the SETLOCK macro instruction to obtain the CML lock. The CML lock was discussed in the section entitled "CMS Terminology."

  If the SP-AS cannot be made non-swappable due to real storage constraints, then the program executing in the U-AS that issues the PC instruction should set up an ESTAE recovery environment to intercept the S0D5-021 ABEND. The recovery action is to simply reissue the PC instruction.
- PC routines may be reentrant, but this is not required. The PC routine can serialize calls to itself by the U-ASs by holding the CML lock. This was discussed in the section entitled "CMS Terminology."
- PC routines may not issue any SVC instructions (or macro instructions whose expansion includes an SVC instruction). Therefore, system services that depend on the issuing of an SVC instruction are not available. However, certain supervisor services that provide a branch-entry interface (such as GETMAIN, FREEMAIN, and POST) may be invoked. The ABEND macro instruction (SVC 13) may be invoked directly.

15.4.3D Releasing the Cross Memory Environment

When the U-AS no longer requires the use of the cross memory services, it can remove access to/from the SP-AS by removing the SP-AS's PT and SSAR authority and by disconnecting the SP-AS's entry table from the U-AS's linkage table. This is illustrated in Coding Example 15.4.6.

When the cross memory services are no longer offered by the SP-AS or just before the SP-AS terminates, the cross memory environment should be removed. This involves destroying the entry table(s) and releasing any cross memory resources that it owns (LX and AX). The LX (nonsystem only) and AX are released so that they are available for another SP-AS to use, and the AX of the SP-AS is reset to its original value (usually 0). The U-AS must disconnect the entry table from the linkage table before the SP-AS can destry the entry table. However, the SP-AS can specify PURGE=YES on the ETDES macro instruction in order to destroy the entry table if the U-AS has not or is unable to disconnect it. Coding Example 15.4.7 shows how the SP-AS removes the cross memory environment. If the task, that set up the cross memory environmemnt ABENDs, then the cross memory environment is released by MVS.

Coding Example 15.4.6

This coding example illustrates how the U-AS removes access to/from the SP-AS.

```
         ATSET AX=AXVALUE,PT=NO,SSAR=NO      RELEASE ACCESS FROM SP-AS
         ETDIS TKLIST=ET01TKEN               DISCONNECT ENTRY TBL FROM LT
         ...
ET01LIST DS    0F
ET01CNT  DC    F'1'                  NUMB OF ENT-TBL TOKENS IN LIST
ET01TKEN DS    F                     TOKEN OF ENTRY TABLE OF SP-AS
```

Coding Example 15.4.7

This coding example illustrates how the SP-AS removes the cross memory environment.

```
REMOVEXM  BAL   R7,DESTRYET          DESTROY ENTRY TABLE
          BAL   R7,FREELX            RELEASE RESERVED LX
          BAL   R7,RSETAUTH          RESET ORIG AX VALUE AND REL RESV AX
          BR    R6                   RETURN TO CALLING ROUTINE
          ...
DESTRYET  ETDES TOKEN=ET01TKEN,PURGE=YES   DESTROY/PURGE ENTRY TBL
          BR    R7                   RETURN TO CALLING ROUTINE
*
FREELX    LXFRE LXLIST=LXLIST        RELEASE RESERVED LX BACK TO MVS
          BR    R7                   RETURN TO CALLING ROUTINE
*
RSETAUTH  LA    R10,0                LD ZERO FOR AXSET MACRO
          AXSET AX=(R10)             RESET AX VALUE BACK TO ZERO
          AXFRE AXLIST=AXLIST        RELEASE RESERVED AX BACK TO MVS
          BR    R7                   RETURN TO CALLING ROUTINE
          ...
AXLIST    DS    0F
AXCOUNT   DC    H'1'                 NUMB OF AX'S IN LIST
AXVALUE   DS    H                    VALUE OF RESERVED AX
*
LXLIST    DS    0F
LXCOUNT   DS    F'1'                 NUMB OF LX'S IN LIST
LXVALUE   DS    F                    LX VALUE RESERVED BY SP-AS
*
ET01LIST  DS    0F
ET01CNT   DC    F'1'                 NUMB OF ENT-TBL TOKENS IN LIST
ET01TKEN  DS    F                    TOKEN OF ENTRY TABLE OF SP-AS
```

15.4.4 Using Cross Memory Services

In Section 15.4.3, the requirements for setting up a cross memory environment were discussed, and coding examples were provided. This section shows how to actually use CMS. Two facilities of CMS are discussed: calling programs in another address space and passing data directly between address spaces.

The coding examples in this section include the code executed by the SP-AS to set up the cross memory environment, the code for the SVC routine invoked by the U-AS to set up the authorization and linkage to the SP-AS, and the code for some PC routines.

15.4.4A Calling a Program in Another Address Space

This section discusses how a program in one address can pass control to a program in another address space.

In section 15.4.3, we saw that the programs that receive control via the PC machine instruction are defined in an entry table. One or more of the entries in the linkage table associated with a particular U-AS contains pointers to the entry tables. Each entry in the linkage table is assigned an LX value (the LX values are unique across the system) that is associated with an entry table. Each entry table defines one or more programs. Each program description within an entry table is assigned an EX value (starting with X'00'). The PC instruction calls a program by specifying its PC number. The PC number is composed of two concatenated index values: the linkage index (LX) and the entry index (EX).

The PC Machine Instruction

The format of the PC instruction is as follows

```
PC D2(B2)
```

The address of the specified operand is not used to address data; instead, the 20 low order bits (right-most) are used to define a program call (PC) number. The 12 high order bits of the address are ignored. The format of the PC number is as follows:

////////////	LX	EX
0	12	24 31

LX — Linkage Table Index. Bits 12–23 of the specified address specifies the LX value. When an address space is dispatched, the Linkage Table Designation Control Register (control register 5) points to the linkage table associated with that address space. The value of the LX is used as an index into the linkage table to locate an entry. This linkage table entry points to the entry table that contains the definitions for the programs (PC routines).

EX — Entry Table Index. Bits 24–31 of the specified address specifies the EX. The value of the EX is used as an index to locate an entry (ETE) in the entry table. The PC instruction causes the program described by this ETE to receive control.

The PC number associated with a particular PC routine can be obtained by inserting the 1-byte EX value into bits 24–31 (last byte) of the LX value (the right-most 8-bits of the LX value are always zero). This value is then set to an address for use with the PC instruction. Coding Example 15.4.8 shows the code that accomplishes this.

Coding Example 15.4.8

This coding example illustrates how to create a PC number and call the PC routine associated with this number.

```
L     R2,LXVALUE        LOAD LX VALUE
IC    R2,EXVALUE        INSERT EX VALUE INTO LAST BYTE
PC    0(R2)             ISSUE PC INSTRUCTION
```

The PC instruction causes a two-level table lookup to be performed to locate the specified entry-table entry (ETE). The format of the ETE was shown in Figure 15.4.2 and Figure 15.4.3 shows the structure of the tables used by the PC instruction to locate the ETE. If the issuing program is executing in problem state, then the authorization key mask (AKM) in the ETE is checked against the PKM of the issuing program to determine if the program is authorized to issue the PC instruction for that ETE. At least one corresponding bit in the AKM and PKM must be set to one, or the issuing program ABENDs with a S0C2 (program interruption-privileged operation). If the issuing program is executing in supervisor state or if the problem program authorization is OK, then the operation continues.

The execution key mask (EKM) in the ETE is ORed with the PKM of the issuing program, and the result is placed into bits 0–15 of control register 3 to become the new

PKM of the PC routine. The original contents of bits 0-15 of control register 3 are placed into the same bit locations in general purpose register 3. The entry parameter in the ETE is loaded into general purpose register 4. The AMODE bit is saved in bit 0, the high order 30 bits of the return address is saved in bits 1-30, and the problem bit is placed in bit 31 of general purpose register 14. Since an instruction must be aligned on a half-word boundary, the low order bit of the return address is always zero; therefore, this bit can be used to store other information.

If the ETE contains an ASID of non-zero, then the PC instruction causes a program in another address space to receive control, sets the address space of the issuing program to the current secondary address space, and sets the address space (whose ASID is set in the ETE) that contains the PC routine to the current primary address space. The PC instruction performs the following operations to set the new primary/secondary address space designations:

- The current PASID from bits 16-31 of control register 4 are placed (saved) in bits 16-31 of general purpose register 3 and are also placed into bits 16-31 of control register 3 to become the new current SASID.
- The current primary segment table address in control register 1 is placed in control register 7 to become the new current secondary segment table.
- The ASID from the ETE is used to locate the Address Space Second Table Entry (ASTE) of that address space. From the ASTE, the values of the segment table address, AX value, and linkage table address are obtained and loaded into control registers 1, 4 (bits 0-15) and 5 (bits 1-24), respectively, to cause that ASID to become the new current PASID.

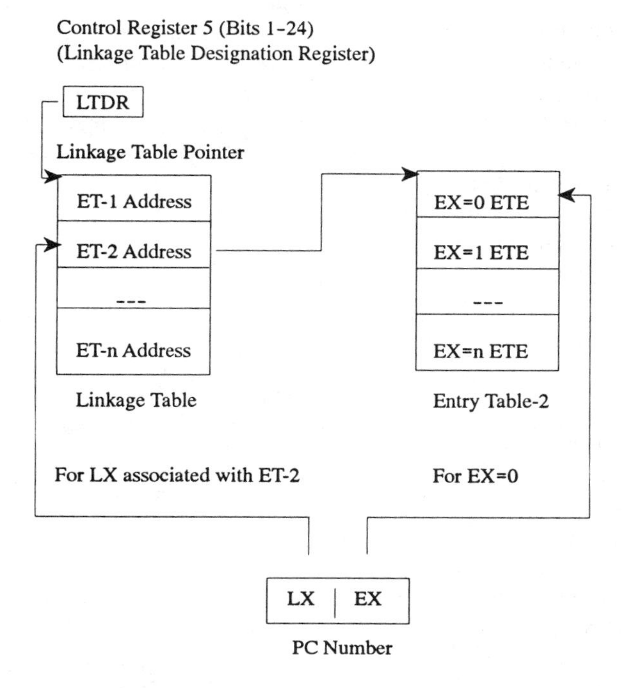

Figure 15.4.3. This figure illustrates the structure of the tables used by the PC instruction.

PC numbers are not permanently associated with a particular service (the called program). The LX value is assigned by MVS and varies from IPL to IPL and by the number of current cross memory users. The EX values are defined by the creator (the SP-AS) of the entry table and may be permanently assigned to specific programs, but this is not a requirement and may be impractical. Since the PC numbers vary and are not known until the SP-AS sets up the cross memory environment, there must be some means to determine the current PC number for a particular service. One way that this can be done is for the SP-AS to assign predetermined ID numbers (or names) to each service provided and then create a cross-reference table in commonly addressable virtual storage, containing the service ID with its associated PC number. The service ID numbers are constant and are known to the users.

Coding Example 15.4.9 shows the SP-AS program that sets up a cross memory environment and contains the code for two simple PC routines that pass information back to the calling program in a parameter register. This coding example also shows how to create a service ID/PC number cross-reference table in the CSA. Coding Example 15.4.10 shows the code for the SVC routine invoked by the U-AS to set up the required authorization and linkage and to invoke the requested PC routine.

Coding Example 15.4.9

This coding example illustrates how a program that is executing in the SP-AS sets up the CMS environment. The code of the program also contains two PC routines (entries EX=0 and EX=1 in the entry table).

The name of the program is SRVPROV1. After it sets up the cross memory environment, it copies the AXLIST, ETLIST, and LXLIST into the CSA for the U-AS. In addition, SRVPROV1 creates a cross-reference table in the CSA that equates the service ID numbers with the PC numbers associated with the corresponding service programs. This program also contains the code for two service programs: PCSERV01 and PCSERV02.

PCSERV01 (Service ID-1) returns in parameter register 1 the value X'11111111', which it obtains from the parameter field of its definition entry in the entry table.

PCSERV02 (Service ID-2) returns in parameter register 1 the value X'22222222', which it obtains from the parameter field of its definition entry in the entry table.

The program from the U-AS that calls the PC routines defined by SRVPROV1 is illustrated in Coding Example 15.4.10

```
SRVPROV1 CSECT
*
*
***************************************************************************
*    INITIALIZATION
*************************************************************************** *
         INITL 3,EQU=R              INITIALIZE PROGRAM
         USING CVT,R10              DEFINE REG FOR CVT DESCT
*
*
***************************************************************************
*    MAINSTREAM OF PROGRAM
***************************************************************************
*
         BAL   R6,SETMODE           SET PROG INTO SUPV STATE, KEY ZERO
         BAL   R6,GETCSA            ALLO CSA FOR STORING CONTROL INFO
         BAL   R6,SETUPXM           SET UP CROSS MEMORY ENVIR
         BAL   R6,PUTCSA            PUT CONTROL INFO INTO CSA FOR U-AS
         BAL   R6,PROCESS           PERFORM MAIN PROC OF PROG
         BAL   R6,REMOVEXM          REMOVE CROSS MEMORY ENVIR
         B     RETURN               RETURN TO MVS OR CALLING PROG
```

```
*
*
***********************************************************************
*    THIS ROUTINE PUTS THE PROGRAM INTO SUPERVISOR STATE AND PSW STORAGE
*    PROTECTION KEY ZERO VIA THE MODESET MACRO. THIS IS REQUIRED TO ISSUE
*    THE CROSS MEMORY MACROS AND TO MODIFY THE CVTUSER FIELD OF THE CVT.
***********************************************************************
*
SETMODE MODESET MODE=SUP,KEY=ZERO
        BR    R6                    RETURN TO CALLING PROG
*
*
***********************************************************************
*    THIS ROUTINE ALLOCATES FIXED, FETCH-PROTECTED CSA VIRTUAL STORAGE
*    AND PLACES THE ADDRESS IN CVTUSER. THIS STORAGE IS USED TO CONTAIN
*    A COPY OF THE AX-LIST, LX-LIST, AND ENTRY TABLE TOKEN-LIST AND TO
*    CONTAIN THE CREATION OF THE SERVICE-ID/PC NUMBER CROSS-REFERENCE
*    TABLE.
***********************************************************************
*
GETCSA  GETMAIN EU,LV=CSALEN,SP=227,A=CSAADR
        L     R10,16                LOAD ADR OF CVT
        MVC   CVTUSER,CSAADR        PUT CSA ADR INTO CVTUSER
        BR    R6                    RETURN TO CALLING ROUTINE
*
*
***********************************************************************
*    THIS ROUTINE SETS UP THE CROSS MEMORY ENVIRONMENT.
***********************************************************************
*
SETUPXM BAL   R7,SETAUTH            RESERVE AN AX AND ASSIGN IT TO SELF
        BAL   R7,GETLX              RESERVE AN LX
        BAL   R7,BLDETBL            CREATE ENTRY TABLE
        BR    R6                    RETURN TO CALLING ROUTINE
*
*
***********************************************************************
*    THIS SUBROUTINE RESERVES AN AX VALUE AND ASSIGNS IT TO THIS A.S.
***********************************************************************
*
SETAUTH AXRES AXLIST=AXLIST         RESERVE AN AX VALUE
        AXSET AX=AXVALUE            ASSIGN AX VALUE TO SELF
        BR    R7                    RETURN TO CALLING ROUTINE
*
*
***********************************************************************
*    THIS SUBROUTINE RESERVES AN LX VALUE FROM A NON-SYSTEM LINKAGE TABLE.
***********************************************************************
*
GETLX   LXRES LXLIST=LXLIST         RESERVE AN LX VALUE
        BR    R7                    RETURN TO CALLING ROUTINE
*
*
***********************************************************************
*    THIS SUBROUTINE CREATES THE ENTRY TABLE TO DESCRIBE THE PC ROUTINES
*    CONTAINED IN THIS PROGRAM.
***********************************************************************
*
BLDETBL BAL   R8,SETETBL            BUILT PARM-LIST FOR ETCRE MACRO
        ETCRE ENTRIES=PCRTNS        CREATE ENTRY TABLE
        ST    R0,ETTOKEN            SAVE TOKEN OF ENTRY TABLE
        BR    R7                    RETURN TO CALLING ROUTINE
*
*
```

```
***********************************************************************
*    THIS SUBROUTINE SETS UP THE PARAMETER-LIST USED BY THE ETCRE MACRO
*    TO CREATE THE ENTRY TABLE.
***********************************************************************
*
         DROP  R10                  REL REG FOR REUSE
         USING ETD,R10              DEFINE REG FOR ENT-TBL HDR DSECT
*
* ENTRY TABLE HEADER
*
SETETBL  LA    R10,ETDHDR           POINT TO AREA FOR ENT-TBL HDR
         MVC   ETDNUM,=H'2'         IND TWO PGMS ARE DEFINED IN PARM-LIST
         DROP  R10                  REL REG FOR REUSE
         USING ETDELE,R10           DEFINE REG FOR E.T. ELEMENT DSECT
*
* DEFINITION FOR SERVICE-1
*
         LA    R10,ETDSERV1         POINT TO PARM AREA FOR SERV-PROG-1
         MVI   ETDEX,X'00'          INDICATE EX=0
         OI    ETDFLG,ETDSUP+ETDXM  IND SUPV MODE AND ADR SPACE SWITCH
         MVC   ETDAKM,=X'FFFF'      IND CALLING PROG CAN HAVE ANY KEY
         MVC   ETDEKM,=X'8000'      IND PC RTN CAN ACCESS STORAGE THAT
*                                   HAS KEY 0 OR CALLING PROG KEYS
         MVC   ETDPAR,=4XL1'11'     ENTRY PARM
         XC    ETDPRO1,ETDPRO1      ZERO FIELD TO IND EPA SPECIFIED
         MVC   ETDPRO2,=A(PCSERV01)    LOAD EPA OF PC ROUTINE
*
* DEFINITION FOR SERVICE-2
*
         LA    R10,ETDSERV2         POINT TO PARM AREA FOR SERV-PROG-2
         MVI   ETDEX,X'01'          INDICATE EX=1
         OI    ETDFLG,ETDSUP+ETDXM    IND SUPV MODE AND ADR SPACE SWITCH
         MVC   ETDAKM,=X'8080'      IND CALLING PROG CAN HAVE KEY 0 AND 8
         MVC   ETDEKM,=X'FFFF'      IND PC RTN CAN ACCESS STORAGE THAT
*                                   HAS ANY KEY
         MVC   ETDPAR,=4XL1'22'     ENTRY PARM
         XC    ETDPRO1,ETDPRO1      ZERO FIELD TO IND EPA SPECIFIED
         MVC   ETDPRO2,=A(PCSERV02)   LOAD EPA OF PC ROUTINE
         BR    R8                   RETURN TO CALLING ROUTINE
*
*
***********************************************************************
*    THIS ROUTINE PUTS CONTROL INFORMATION INTO THE CSA FOR USE BY THE
*    USER ADDRESS SPACES, WHICH ARE REQUIRED TO CALL THE PC ROUTINES
*    CONTAINED IN THIS PROGRAM.
***********************************************************************
*
         DROP  R10                  RELEASE REG FOR REUSE
         USING CSAMAP,R10           DEFINE REG FOR CSAMAP DSECT
PUTCSA   L     R10,CSAADR           LD ADR OF ALLO CSA
         BAL   R7,PUTLISTS          COPY CONTROL LISTS INTO CSA
         BAL   R7,PUTXTBL           CREATE CROSS-REF TBL IN CSA
         BR    R6                   RETURN TO CALLING ROUTINE
*
*
***********************************************************************
*    THIS SUBROUTINE COPIES THE AX-LIST, LX-LIST, AND ENTRY TABLE
*    TOKEN-LIST INTO THE CSA FOR USE BY THE USER ADDRESS SPACES, WHICH
*    ARE REQUIRED TO CALL THE PC ROUTINES.
***********************************************************************
*
PUTLISTS MVC   $AXCOUNT,AXCOUNT
         MVC   $AXVALUE,AXVALUE
         MVC   $LXCOUNT,LXCOUNT
```

```
         MVC   $LXVALUE,LXVALUE
         MVC   $ETCOUNT,ETCOUNT
         MVC   $ETTOKEN,ETTOKEN
         BR    R7                  RETURN TO CALLING ROUTINE
*
*
***********************************************************************
*    THIS SUBROUTINE CREATES IN THE CSA THE CROSS-REFERENCE TABLE
*    EQUATING THE SERVICE-IDS TO THE CORRESPONDING PC NUMBERS OF THE
*    PC ROUTINES. THIS TABLE IS USED BY THE USER ADDRESS SPACES, WHICH
*    ARE REQUIRED TO CALL THE PC ROUTINES.
***********************************************************************
*
* FOR SERVICE ID=1
*
PUTXTBL XC     $SRV01ID,$SRV01ID  ZERO SERVICE ID
        MVI    $SRV01ID+3,X'01'   SET SERVICE ID=1
        MVC    $PCNUM01,LXVALUE   SET LX VALUE PART OF PC NUMB
        MVI    $PCNUM01+3,X'00'   SET EX VALUE PART OF PC NUMB
*
* FOR SERVICE ID=2
*
        XC     $SRV02ID,$SRV02ID  ZERO SERVICE ID
        MVI    $SRV02ID+3,X'02'   SET SERVICE ID=2
        MVC    $PCNUM02,LXVALUE   SET LX VALUE PART OF PC NUMB
        MVI    $PCNUM02+3,X'01'   SET EX VALUE PART OF PC NUMB
*
* END-OF-TABLE
*
        MVC    $XREFEND,BINONES   INDICATE END OF CROSS-REF TBL
        BR     R7                 RETURN TO CALLING ROUTINE
*
*
***********************************************************************
*    THIS ROUTINE IS USED FOR TESTING ONLY. IT SIMULATES ADDRESS SPACE
*    PROCESSING UNTIL THE ACTUAL PROCESSING ROUTINE IS WRITTEN.
***********************************************************************
*
PROCESS OPEN   (DCB,(OUTPUT))
        PUT    DCB,RECORD
        CLOSE DCB
        B      PROCESS
*
*
***********************************************************************
*    THIS ROUTINE REMOVES THE CROSS MEMORY ENVIRONMENT.
***********************************************************************
*
         DROP  R10                RELEASE REG FOR REUSE
         USING CVT,R10            DEFINE REG FOR CVT DSECT
REMOVEXM L     R10,16             LOAD ADR OF CVT
         XC    CVTUSER,CVTUSER    CLEAR CVTUSER
         BAL   R7,DESTRYET        DESTROY/PURGE ENTRY TABLE
         BAL   R7,FREELX          RELEASE RESERVED LX VALUE
         BAL   R7,RSETAUTH        RESET ORIG AX VALUE AND REL RESV AX
         BAL   R7,FREECSA         RELEASE ALLO CSA
         BR    R6                 RETURN TO CALLING ROUTINE
*
*
***********************************************************************
*    THIS SUBROUTINE DESTROYS THE ENTRY TABLE AND USES THE PURGE OPTION
*    IN CASE THE USER ADDRESS SPACE HAS NOT DISCONNECTED IT FROM ITS
*    LINKAGE TABLE.
***********************************************************************
```

```
*
DESTRYET ETDES TOKEN=ETTOKEN,PURGE=YES   DESTROY/PURGE ENTRY TABLE
        BR    R7                    RETURN TO CALLING ROUTINE
*
*
***********************************************************************
*    THIS SUBROUTINE RELEASES THE RESERVED LX VALUE.
***********************************************************************
*
FREELX  LXFRE LXLIST=LXLIST         RELEASE RESERVED LX VALUE
        BR    R7                    RETURN TO CALLING ROUTINE
*
*
***********************************************************************
*    THIS SUBROUTINE RESETS THE AX VALUE OF THE ADDRESS SPACE BACK TO
*    ITS ORIGINAL VALUE AND RELEASES THE RESERVED AX VALUE.
***********************************************************************
*
RSETAUTH LA    R10,0                LD ZERO FOR AXSET MACRO
         AXSET AX=(R10)             RESET AX VALUE BACK TO ORIG ZERO
         AXFRE AXLIST=AXLIST        RELEASE RESERVED AX VALUE
         BR    R7                   RETURN TO CALLING ROUTINE
*
*
***********************************************************************
*    THIS SUBROUTINE RELEASES THE CSA STORAGE.
***********************************************************************
*
FREECSA FREEMAIN EU,LV=CSALEN,SP=227,A=CSAADR
        BR    R7
*
*
***********************************************************************
*    THIS ROUTINE RESTORES THE REGISTERS AND RETURNS CONTROL TO MVS
*    OR THE CALLING PROGRAM.
***********************************************************************
*
RETURN  RCNTL RC=0                  RETURN TO MVS OR CALLING PROG
*
*
***********************************************************************
*     THE DC/DS STATEMENTS
***********************************************************************
*
CSAADR  DS    F
BINONES DC    4XL1'FF'
*
***********************************************************************
*    THE AUTHORIZATION-VALUE (AX) LIST
***********************************************************************
*
AXLIST  DS    0F
AXCOUNT DC    H'1'
AXVALUE DS    H
*
*
***********************************************************************
*    THE LINKAGE-VALUE (LX) LIST
***********************************************************************
*
LXLIST  DS    0F
LXCOUNT DC    F'1'
LXVALUE DS    F
*
```

```
*
*************************************************************************
*    THE ENTRY-TABLE TOKEN LIST
*************************************************************************
*
ETLIST  DS    0F
ETCOUNT DC    F'1'
ETTOKEN DS    F
*
*
*************************************************************************
*    THE AREAS USED TO CREATE THE ENTRY TABLE PARAMETER-LIST
*************************************************************************
*
PCRTNS    DS   0F
ETDHDR    DS   CL(ETDLEN)
ETDSERV1  DS   CL(ETDELEN)
ETDSERV2  DS   CL(ETDELEN)
*
*
*************************************************************************
*    THE RECORD AND THE DCB USED FOR THE I/O LOOP FOR TESTING
*************************************************************************
*
RECORD    DC   80CL1'A'
DCB       DCB  DSORG=PS,MACRF=PM,BLKSIZE=80,LRECL=80,RECFM=F,           -
               DDNAME=WORK
*
*
*
*
*************************************************************************
*************************************************************************
*    THE CODE FOR THE PCSERV01 PC ROUTINE
*************************************************************************
*************************************************************************
*
*
PCSERV01 PCLINK STACK,SAVE=NO     SAVE STATUS
         L    R1,0(0,R4)          LD PARM FROM E.T. INTO REG 1
         PCLINK UNSTACK,THRU=(R14),SAVE=NO     RESTORE STATUS
         PT   R3,R14              RETURN TO CALLING PROG
*
*
*
*
*************************************************************************
*************************************************************************
*    THE CODE FOR THE PCSERV02 PC ROUTINE
*************************************************************************
*************************************************************************
*
*
PCSERV02 PCLINK STACK,SAVE=NO     SAVE STATUS
         L    R1,0(0,R4)          LD PARM FROM E.T. INTO REG 1
         PCLINK UNSTACK,THRU=(R14),SAVE=NO     RESTORE STATUS
         PT   R3,R14              RETURN TO CALLER
*
*
*************************************************************************
*    THE DSECTS
*************************************************************************
*
CSAMAP   DSECT
```

```
*
* AX-LIST IN CSA
*
$AXLIST   DS    0F
$AXCOUNT  DS    H
$AXVALUE  DS    H
*
* LX-LIST IN CSA
*
$LXLIST   DS    0F
$LXCOUNT  DS    F
$LXVALUE  DS    F
*
* ENTRY TABLE TOKEN-LIST IN CSA
*
$ETLIST   DS    0F
$ETCOUNT  DS    F
$ETTOKEN  DS    F
*
* SERVICE ID/PC NUMBER CROSS-REFERENCE TABLE IN CSA
*
$XREFTBL  DS    0F
$SRV01ID  DS    F
$PCNUM01  DS    F
$SRV02ID  DS    F
$PCNUM02  DS    F
$XREFEND  DS    F
*
CSALEN    EQU   *-CSAMAP
*
          CVT   DSECT=YES          GENERATES THE CVT DSECT
*
          IHAETD                   GENERATES THE ENTRY TABLE DSECTS
*
*
**************************************************************************
*    END OF PROGRAM
**************************************************************************
*
          END
```

NOTES:

- The program must be APF authorized in order to issue the MODESET macro instruction. Chapter 10 discusses how to APF authorize a program.
- The service programs are for illustration purposes only. They just demostrate how to code a PC routine using the required linkage. Coding Example 15.4.11 shows a practical use of a PC routine.
- The CSAMAP DSECT is hard-coded in this program, in the SVC routine in Coding Example 15.4.10 and in the program SRVPROV2 in Coding Example 15.4.11. This is for illustration purposes only. In a normal production environment, this DSECT should be invoked via a macro instruction or a COPY statement.
- When the test is complete, an MVS CANCEL command is required to terminate this program until the PROCESS routine is coded.

Coding Example 15.4.10

This coding example illustrates how a program that executes in the U-AS sets up the required authorization and linkage for the SP-AS and invokes the required service. This program invokes the services defined by the SP-AS in Coding Example 15.4.9.

Since the CMS macro instructions are required to be issued by a program executing in supervisor state or PSW storage protection key 0–7, an SVC routine is provided to perform this function.

The name of the program is USER01. It invokes SVC-255 and passes it (in parameter register 0) the ID number of the service to be performed.

SVC-255 provides the following services for the caller:

- Sets up the cross memory authorization and linkage for the SP-AS. (Requested by user specifying X'00' in register 0.)
- Scans the service ID/PC number cross-reference table in the CSA to locate the PC number associated with the specified service ID and calls this PC routine via the PC instruction. (Requested by user specifying a valid service ID; in this example, they are X'01' and X'02'.)

When SVC-255 returns control, it posts X'FF' in register 15 if an invalid request ID was specified in register 0. If the call to the PC routine is successful, then register 1 and register 15 contain the values loaded by the PC routine.

The code for the SVC (255) routine

```
IGC0025E CSECT
*
*
***************************************************************************
*    INITIALIZATION
***************************************************************************
*
         REGEQU EQU=R               GENERATE EQU'S FOR REGS
         USING  *,R6                DEFINE BASE REGISTER
         USING  CVT,R3              DEFINE REG FOR CVT DSECT
         USING  CSAMAP,R10          DEFINE REG FOR CSAMAP DSECT
*
*
***************************************************************************
*    MAINSTREAM OF SVC ROUTINE
***************************************************************************
*
         BAL    R7,SAVEREGS         SAVE CONTENTS OF CONTROL REGS
         BAL    R7,GETPARMS         GET ADR OF CONTROL INFO IN CSA
         BAL    R7,SETAUTH          SET AUTH FOR SP-AS
         BAL    R7,CONNECT          CONNECT ENTRY TBL TO LINKAGE TBL
         BAL    R7,GETPCNUM         FIND PC NUMB FOR SPEC SERV-ID
         BAL    R7,DOPC             SAVE STATUS, ISSUE PC
         B      RETURN              RETURN TO CALLING PROG VIA SVC FLIH
*
*
***************************************************************************
*    THIS ROUTINE SAVES THE CONTENTS OF ALL REGISTERS THAT CONTAIN
*    CONTROL INFORMATION.
***************************************************************************
*
SAVEREGS LR     R2,R14              SAVE RETURN ADDRESS
         LR     R5,R0               SAVE SPECIFIED SERVICE-ID
         LR     R8,R1               SAVE PARM REG 1
         LR     R9,R15              SAVE PARM REG 15
         BR     R7                  RETURN TO CALLING ROUTINE
*
*
***************************************************************************
```

```
*    THIS ROUTINE OBTAINS THE ADDRESS OF THE ALLO CSA AREA THAT
*    CONTAINS THE AX-LIST, LX-LIST, ENTRY TABLE TOKEN-LIST, AND THE
*    SERVICE ID/PC NUMBER CROSS-REFERENCE TABLE.
***********************************************************************
*
GETPARMS L    R10,CVTUSER          LD CSA ADR FORM CVTUSER
         BR   R7                   RETURN TO CALLING ROUTINE
*
*
***********************************************************************
*    THIS ROUTINE CHECKS THE SERVICE-ID. IF ID=0 IS SPECIFIED, THEN THIS
*    ROUTINE PROVIDES THE SP-AS WITH ACCESS TO THE U-AS.
***********************************************************************
*
SETAUTH LTR   R5,R5                CHK IF SP-AS ACCESS REQUESTED
        BNZR  R7                   IF NO, RETURN TO CALLING RTN
        LH    R11,$AXVALUE         LD AX OF SP-AS FOR ATSET MACRO
        ATSET AX=(R11),PT=YES,SSAR=YES   SET AUTH FOR SP-AS
        BR    R7                   RETURN TO CALLING ROUTINE
*
*
***********************************************************************
*    THIS ROUTINE CHECKS THE SPECIFIED SERVICE-ID. IF ID=0 IS SPECIFIED,
*    THEN THIS ROUTINE CONNECTS THE ENTRY TABLE OF THE SP-AS TO THE
*    LINKAGE TABLE OF THE U-AS.
***********************************************************************
*
CONNECT LTR   R5,R5                CHK IF CONNECTION REQUESTED
        BNZR  R7                   IF NO, RETURN TO CALLING ROUTINE
        LA    R11,$LXLIST          LD ADR OF LX-LIST FROM CSA
        LA    R12,$ETLIST          LD ADR OF ET TOKEN-LIST FROM CSA
        ETCON LXLIST=(R11),TKLIST=(R12)   CONNECT ET TO LT
        BR    R7                   RETURN TO CALLING ROUTINE
*
*
***********************************************************************
*    THIS ROUTINE CHECKS THE SPECIFIED SERVICE-ID. IF THE ID IS NOT
*    EQUAL TO ZERO, THEN THIS ROUTINE SCANS THE SERVICE ID/PC NUMBER
*    CROSS-REFERENCE TABLE IN THE CSA TO OBTAIN THE REQUIRED PC NUMBER.
*    IF THE SERVICE-ID CANNOT BE FOUND IN THE TABLE, THEN RC=4 IS SET IN
*    REG 15. IF SERVICE-ID IS FOUND, THEN RC=0 IS SET IN REG 15 AND
*    REG 10 POINTS TO THE PC NUMBER.
***********************************************************************
*
GETPCNUM LTR  R5,R5                CHECK IF SPECIFIED SERV ID=0
         BZR  R7                   IF YES, RET TO CALLING ROUTINE
         LA   R10,$XREFTBL         LD ADR OF SERV-ID/PC-NUMB X-REF TBL
NEXTSERV CLC  0(4,R10),BINONES     CHK IF END-OF-TBL
         BE   INVPCNUM             IF YES, INV SERV-ID SPECIFIED
         C    R5,0(R10)            COMP SPEC SERV-ID WITH SERV-ID IN TBL
         BE   SETPCNUM             IF EQUAL, GET CORRES PC NUMB
         LA   R10,8(0,R10)         IF NOT, INCR TO NEXT ENTRY IN TBL
         B    NEXTSERV             CHECK NEXT ENTRY
SETPCNUM LA   R10,4(0,R10)         INCR PAST SERV-ID TO PC NUMB
         LA   R15,0                IND PC NUMB FOUND
         BR   R7                   RETURN TO CALLING ROUTINE
INVPCNUM LA   R15,255              IND INVALID SERV-ID SPECIFIED
         BR   R7                   RETURN TO CALLING ROUTINE
*
*
***********************************************************************
*    THIS ROUTINE CHECKS THE SPECIFIED SERVICE-ID. IF THE ID IS NOT EQUAL
*    TO ZERO, THEN THIS ROUTINE SAVES THE REGISTERS AND THE SASID AND
*    THEN ISSUES THE PC INSTRUCTION TO CALL THE REQUESTED PC ROUTINE.
```

```
***********************************************************************
*
DOPC     LTR   R5,R5              CHECK IF SPECIFIED SERV ID=0
         BZR   R7                 IF YES, RET TO CALLING ROUTINE
         LTR   R15,R15            CHECK IF VALID SERV-ID SPECIFIED
         BNZR  R7                 IF NO, RET TO CALLING ROUTINE
         STM   R2,R12,28(R13)     SAVE REGS 2-12 IN CALLERS S.A.
         ESAR  R2                 OBTAIN SASID
         ST    R2,16(0,R13)       SAVE SASID
         L     R2,0(0,R10)        LOAD PC NUMBER
         LR    R1,R8              RESTORE PARM REG 1
         LR    R15,R9             RESTORE PARM REG 15
         PC    0(R2)              ISSUE PC INSTR
         L     R2,16(0,R13)       LOAD SASID
         SSAR  R2                 RESET SECONDARY A.S.
         LM    R2,R12,28(R13)     RESTORE REGS 2-12
         BR    R7                 RETURN TO CALLING ROUTINE
*
*
***********************************************************************
*    THIS ROUTINE RETURNS CONTROL TO THE CALLING PROGRAM VIA THE SVC FLIH.
*    THE PARAMETER REGISTERS 1 AND 15 AS SET BY THE PC ROUTINE ARE
*    RETURNED TO THE CALLING PROGRAM.
***********************************************************************
*
RETURN   LR    R14,R2             RESTORE THE RETURN ADDRESS
         BR    R14                RETURN TO CALLING PROG VIA FLIH
*
*
***********************************************************************
*     CONSTANTS
***********************************************************************
*
         DS    0F
BINONES  DC    4XL1'FF'
*
*
***********************************************************************
* THE DSECTS
***********************************************************************
*
CSAMAP   DSECT
*
* AX-LIST IN CSA
*
$AXLIST  DS    0F
$AXCOUNT DS    H
$AXVALUE DS    H
*
* LX-LIST IN CSA
*
$LXLIST  DS    0F
$LXCOUNT DS    F
$LXVALUE DS    F
*
* ENTRY TABLE TOKEN-LIST IN CSA
*
$ETLIST  DS    0F
$ETCOUNT DS    F
$ETTOKEN DS    F
*
* SERVICE ID/PC NUMBER CROSS-REFERENCE TABLE IN CSA
*
$XREFTBL DS    0F
```

```
$SRV01ID DS    F
$PCNUM01 DS    F
$SRV02ID DS    F
$PCNUM02 DS    F
$XREFEND DS    F
*
CSALEN   EQU   *-CSAMAP
*
         CVT   DSECT=YES
*
*
***********************************************************************
*     END OF SVC ROUTINE
***********************************************************************
*
         END
```

The code for the problem program

```
USER01 CSECT
*
*
***********************************************************************
*     INITIALIZATION
***********************************************************************
*
        INITL 3,EQU=R              INITIALIZE PROGRAM
*
*
***********************************************************************
*     MAINSTREAM OF PROGRAM
***********************************************************************
*
        BAL    R6,SETUP             SET UP AUTH AND LINKAGE FOR SP-AS
        BAL    R6,CALLSRV1          CALL SERVICE ID-1
        BAL    R6,CALLSRV2          CALL SERVICE ID-2
        BAL    R6,CHKDATA           DUMP RETURNED DATA TO VERIFY
        B      RETURN               RETURN TO MVS OR CALLING PROG
*
*
***********************************************************************
*     THIS ROUTINE INVOKES THE APPROPRIATE SVC ROUTINE AND REQUESTS THAT
*     IT SETS UP THE AUTHORIZATION AND LINKAGE FOR ACCESS TO/FROM THE
*     SP-AS.
***********************************************************************
*
SETUP   LA     R0,0                 REQUEST AUTH/LINKAGE FOR SP-AS
        SVC    255                  ISSUE SVC TO SET UP AUTH/LINKAGE
        BR     R6                   RETURN TO CALLING ROUTINE
*
*
***********************************************************************
*     THIS ROUTINE INVOKES THE APPROPRIATE SVC ROUTINE AND REQUESTS THAT
*     IT FINDS THE CORRESPONDING PC NUMBER FOR SERVICE-ID=1 AND THEN
*     CALLS THAT PC ROUTINE.
***********************************************************************
*
CALLSRV1 LA    R0,1                 REQUEST CALL TO SERVICE ID-1
         SVC   255                  ISSUE SVC TO SAVE STATUS, CALL PC RTN
         ST    R1,SRV1DATA          SAVE RETURNED DATA
         BR    R6                   RETURN TO CALLING ROUTINE
```

```
*
*
***********************************************************************
*    THIS ROUTINE INVOKES THE APPROPRIATE SVC ROUTINE AND REQUESTS THAT
*    IT FINDS THE CORRESPONDING PC NUMBER FOR SERVICE-ID=2 AND THEN
*    CALLS THAT PC ROUTINE.
***********************************************************************
*
CALLSRV2 LA   R0,2                REQUEST CALL TO SERVICE ID-2
         SVC  255                 ISSUE SVC TO SAVE STATUS, CALL PC RTN
         ST   R1,SRV2DATA         SAVE RETURNED DATA
         BR   R6                  RETURN TO CALLING ROUTINE
*
*
***********************************************************************
*    THIS ROUTINE IS USED DURING TESTING ONLY. IT DUMPS THE RETURNED DATA
*    FROM THE TWO CALLED PC ROUTINES.
***********************************************************************
*
CHKDATA  L    R8,SRV1DATA         LD RETURNED DATA FROM SERV ID-1
         L    R9,SRV2DATA         LD RETURNED DATA FROM SERV ID-2
         ABEND 901,DUMP           DUMP RETURNED DATA
*
*
***********************************************************************
*    THIS ROUTINE RESTORES THE REGISTERS AND RETURNS CONTROL TO MVS OR
*    THE CALLING PROGRAM.
***********************************************************************
*
RETURN   RCNTL RC=0
*
*
***********************************************************************
*    THE DC/DS STATEMENTS
***********************************************************************
*
SRV1DATA DS   F
SRV2DATA DS   F
*
*
***********************************************************************
*    END OF PROGRAM
***********************************************************************
*
         END
```

NOTES:

- USER01 is authorized to issue the PC instruction (the ETE specifies that the caller can be executing in PSW storage protection key 8 and others). The SVC routine is not required for this function. But for USER01 to issue the PC instruction, it would require the appropriate PC number. The service ID/PC number cross-reference table is created in a fetch-protected area of the CSA with a protection key of zero assigned for security reasons. Since the SVC routine is required to obtain the required PC number for the requested service, it is convenient to let the SVC routine also save the status (registers, SASID) of the calling program and issue the PC instruction. However, if additional security is required for specific PC routines, then the problem program should issue the PC instruction. This causes the AKM of the ETE for the called PC routine to be checked to verify if the problem program is authorized to call the PC routine.

- Since the problem program issues an SVC instruction to issue the PC instruction, the SVC FLIH saves the registers of the program.
- If it is desirable for the problem program to issue the PC instruction (instead of the SVC routine), then a macro definition can be developed to perform that task. As an exercise, the reader might try to write a macro definition to perform the following:
  - Accept the requested service ID from the caller;
  - Invoke the SVC routine to set up the authorization and linkage for the SP-AS (for ID=0) or obtain the corresponding PC number (for ID equal to a non-zero value);
  - Save the registers and SASID in the savearea; and
  - Pass the PC number to the caller in register 2.

  When the calling program receives control, it issues the PC instruction, using the PC number loaded into register 2 by the macro instruction.

15.4.4B Passing Data Directly Between Address Spaces

In MVS/370, MVS/XA, and MVS/ESA, data can be moved between address spaces, using the MVCP (move to primary address space) and the MVCS (move to secondary address space) machine instructions. Either instruction may be issued from either the primary address space or the secondary address space. In addition, in MVS/ESA, data can also be moved between address spaces (without regard to primary/secondary designation), using a combination of access registers and general purpose registers with the processor in AR ASC (access register–address space control) mode, but this method will not be discussed.

The MVCP and MVCS machine instructions

The formats of the MVCP and the MVCS instructions are as follows:

```
MVCP D1(R1,B1),D2(B2),R3
MVCS D1(R1,B1),D2(B2),R3
```

The data pointed to by the second address of the operand is copied into the area pointed to by the first address of the operand. The specified contents in bits 0–31 in register R_1 is referred to as the true length. The amount of data copied is equal to the true length or 256, whichever is less. The specified contents in bits 24–27 of R_3 is used as the secondary address space access PSW key; however, the standard fetch and store protection mechanism (current PSW key) apply for the primary address space access. Data movement is performed by ignoring the currently active addressing mode (the PSW s-bit).

The MVCP and MVCS instructions may be executed in either problem state or supervisor state. When executed in problem state, the access PSW key (specified by R_3) is checked for validity. The access key is valid only if at least one of the specified keys matches one of the keys indicated in the PKM (PSW key mask located in control register 3). If not, an S0C2 ABEND occurs (program interruption–privileged operation). The contents of R_3 is, in effect, a mechanism to authorize a problem program to issue the MVCP/MVCS instructions similar to the AKM field in the ETE for a PC instruction.

For the MVCP instruction, the virtual address specified by the first address of the operand points to an area in the primary address space and is translated by using the primary segment table (pointed to by control register 1). The virtual address specified by the second address of the operand points to an area in the secondary address space and is translated by using the secondary segment table (pointed to by control register 7).

For the MVCS instruction, the virtual address specified by the first address of the operand points to an area in the secondary address space and is translated by using the secondary segment table The virtual address specified by the second address of the operand points to an area in the primary address space and is translated by using the primary segment table.

Coding Example 15.4.11

This coding example illustrates how to move data between a primary address space and a secondary address space, using the MVCP and the MVCS instructions. This coding example is a modification of Coding Example 15.4.9. Only the SETETBL subroutine is changed. The PC routines PCSERV01 and PCSERV02 are removed, and a new PC routine called PCSERV03 is added. This program contains a table of data. Each entry in the table is associated with a unique key. The U-AS calls PCSERV03 to retrieve an entry in the table. The U-AS specifies in register 1 the address of an area that contains a key and specifies in register 15 the address of an area that is to receive the data portion of the table entry corresponding to the specified key. PCSERV03 copies the key into its own address space, scans the table for the corresponding table entry, and sends the data back to the calling program. Coding Example 15.4.12 shows the program from the U-AS, which calls PCSERV03.

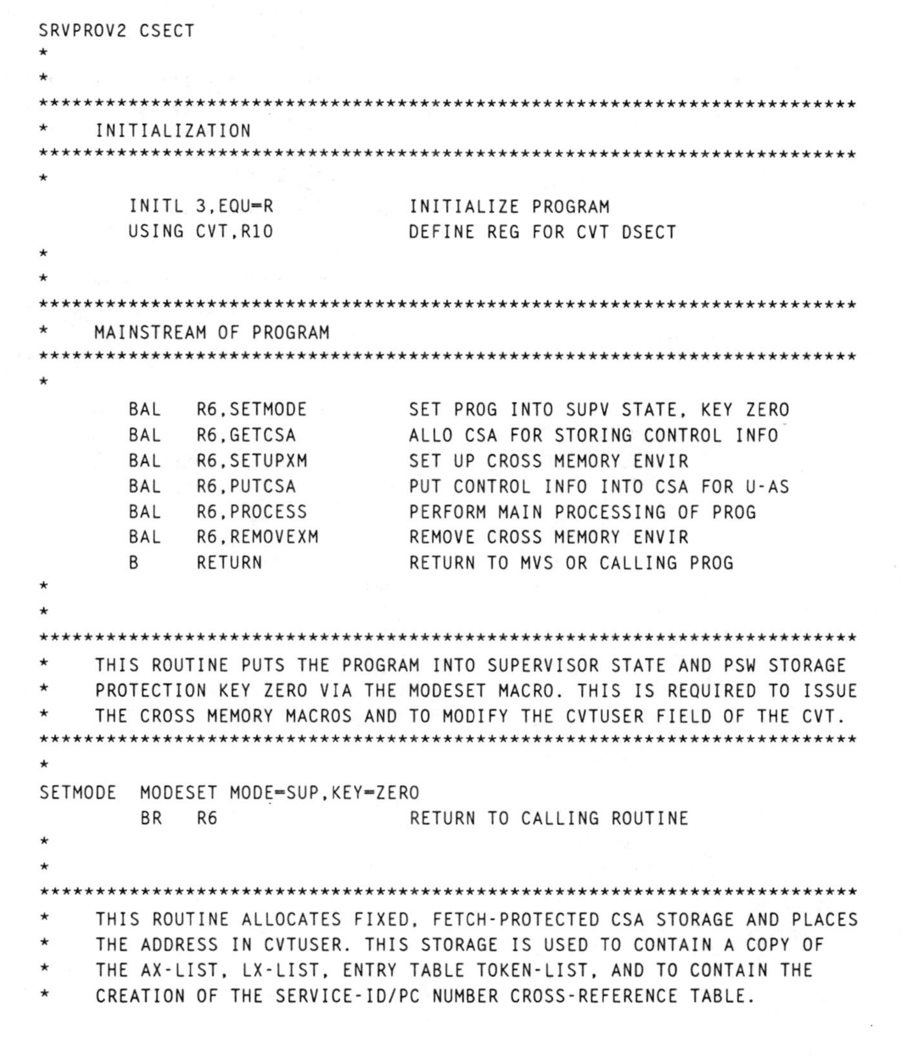

```
SRVPROV2 CSECT
*
*
*************************************************************************
*    INITIALIZATION
*************************************************************************
*
         INITL 3,EQU=R            INITIALIZE PROGRAM
         USING CVT,R10            DEFINE REG FOR CVT DSECT
*
*
*************************************************************************
*    MAINSTREAM OF PROGRAM
*************************************************************************
*
         BAL   R6,SETMODE         SET PROG INTO SUPV STATE, KEY ZERO
         BAL   R6,GETCSA          ALLO CSA FOR STORING CONTROL INFO
         BAL   R6,SETUPXM         SET UP CROSS MEMORY ENVIR
         BAL   R6,PUTCSA          PUT CONTROL INFO INTO CSA FOR U-AS
         BAL   R6,PROCESS         PERFORM MAIN PROCESSING OF PROG
         BAL   R6,REMOVEXM        REMOVE CROSS MEMORY ENVIR
         B     RETURN             RETURN TO MVS OR CALLING PROG
*
*
*************************************************************************
*    THIS ROUTINE PUTS THE PROGRAM INTO SUPERVISOR STATE AND PSW STORAGE
*    PROTECTION KEY ZERO VIA THE MODESET MACRO. THIS IS REQUIRED TO ISSUE
*    THE CROSS MEMORY MACROS AND TO MODIFY THE CVTUSER FIELD OF THE CVT.
*************************************************************************
*
SETMODE  MODESET MODE=SUP,KEY=ZERO
         BR    R6                 RETURN TO CALLING ROUTINE
*
*
*************************************************************************
*    THIS ROUTINE ALLOCATES FIXED, FETCH-PROTECTED CSA STORAGE AND PLACES
*    THE ADDRESS IN CVTUSER. THIS STORAGE IS USED TO CONTAIN A COPY OF
*    THE AX-LIST, LX-LIST, ENTRY TABLE TOKEN-LIST, AND TO CONTAIN THE
*    CREATION OF THE SERVICE-ID/PC NUMBER CROSS-REFERENCE TABLE.
```

```
*************************************************************************
*
GETCSA  GETMAIN EU,LV=CSALEN,SP=227,A=CSAADR
        L     R10,16                LOAD ADR OF CVT
        MVC   CVTUSER,CSAADR        PUT CSA ADR IN CVTUSER
        BR    R6                    RETURN TO CALLING ROUTINE
*
*
*************************************************************************
*    THIS ROUTINE SETS UP THE CROSS MEMORY ENVIRONMENT.
*************************************************************************
*
SETUPXM BAL   R7,SETAUTH            RESERVE AN AX AND ASSIGN IT TO SELF
        BAL   R7,GETLX              RESERVE AN LX
        BAL   R7,BLDETBL            CREATE ENTRY TABLE
        BR    R6                    RETURN TO CALLING ROUTINE
*
*
*************************************************************************
*    THIS SUBROUTINE RESERVES AN AX VALUE AND ASSIGNS IT TO THIS A.S.
*************************************************************************
*
SETAUTH  AXRES AXLIST=AXLIST        RESERVE AN AX VALUE
         AXSET AX=AXVALUE           ASSIGN THAT AX TO SELF
         BR    R7                   RETURN TO CALLING ROUTINE
*
*
*************************************************************************
*    THIS SUBROUTINE RESERVES AN LX VALUE FROM A NONSYSTEM LINKAGE TABLE.
*************************************************************************
*
GETLX   LXRES LXLIST=LXLIST         RESERVE AN LX VALUE
        BR    R7                    RETURN TO CALLING ROUTINE
*
*
*************************************************************************
*    THIS SUBROUTINE CREATES THE ENTRY TABLE TO DESCRIBE THE PC ROUTINE
*    CONTAINED IN THIS PROGRAM.
*************************************************************************
*
BLDETBL BAL   R8,SETETBL            BUILD PARM-LIST FOR ETCRE MACRO
        ETCRE ENTRIES=PCRTNS        CREATE ENTRY TABLE
        ST    R0,ETTOKEN            SAVE TOKEN OF ENTRY TABLE
        BR    R7                    RETURN TO CALLING ROUTINE
*
*
*************************************************************************
*    THIS SUBROUTINE SETS UP THE PARAMETER-LIST USED BY THE ETCRE MACRO
*    TO CREATE THE ENTRY TABLE.
*************************************************************************
*
        DROP  R10                   RELEASE REG FOR REUSE
        USING ETD,R10               DEFINE REG FOR ENT-TBL HDR DSECT
*
* ENTRY TABLE HEADER
*
SETETBL LA    R10,ETDHDR            POINT TO AREA FOR ENT-TBL HDR
        MVC   ETDNUM,=H'1'          INDICATE ONE PC ROUTINE IS DEFINED
        DROP  R10                   REL REG FOR REUSE
        USING ETDELE,R10            DEFINE REG FOR E.T. ELEMENT DSECT
*
* DEFINITION FOR SERVICE PROGRAM
*
       LA     R10,ETDSERV1          POINT TO PARM AREA FOR SERV-PROG
```

```
         MVI     ETDEX,X'00'          INDICATE EX=0
         OI      ETDFLG,ETDSUP+ETDXM   IND SUPV MODE AND ADR SPACE SWITCH
         MVC     ETDAKM,=X'FFFF'      IND CALLING PROG CAN HAVE ANY KEY
         MVC     ETDEKM,=X'8000'      IND PC RTN CAN ACCESS STORAGE THAT
*                                     HAS KEY 0 OR CALLING PROG KEYS
         XC      ETDPRO1,ETDPRO1      ZERO FIELD TO IND EPA SPECIFIED
         MVC     ETDPRO2,=A(PCSERV03)   LOAD EPA OF PC ROUTINE
         BR      R8                   RETURN TO CALLING PROG
*
*
***********************************************************************
*    THIS ROUTINE PUTS CONTROL INFORMATION INTO THE CSA FOR USE BY THE
*    USER ADDRESS SPACES, WHICH ARE REQUIRED TO CALL THE PC ROUTINE
*    CONTAINED IN THIS PROGRAM.
***********************************************************************
*
         DROP    R10                  RELEASE REG FOR REUSE
         USING   CSAMAP,R10           DEFINE REG FOR CSAMAP DSECT
PUTCSA   L       R10,CSAADR           LD ADR OF ALLO CSA
         BAL     R7,PUTLISTS          COPY CONTROL LISTS INTO CSA
         BAL     R7,PUTXTBL           CREATE CROSS-REF TBL IN CSA
         BR      R6                   RETURN TO CALLING ROUTINE
*
*
***********************************************************************
*    THIS SUBROUTINE COPIES THE AX-LIST, LX-LIST, AND ENTRY TABLE
*    TOKEN-LIST INTO THE CSA FOR USE BY THE USER ADDRESS SPACES, WHICH
*    ARE REQUIRED TO CALL THE PC ROUTINE.
***********************************************************************
*
PUTLISTS MVC     $AXCOUNT,AXCOUNT
         MVC     $AXVALUE,AXVALUE
         MVC     $LXCOUNT,LXCOUNT
         MVC     $LXVALUE,LXVALUE
         MVC     $ETCOUNT,ETCOUNT
         MVC     $ETTOKEN,ETTOKEN
         BR      R7                   RETURN TO CALLING ROUTINE
*
*
***********************************************************************
*    THIS SUBROUTINE CREATES IN THE CSA THE CROSS-REFERENCE TABLE,
*    EQUATING THE SERVICE-IDS TO THE CORRESPONDING PC NUMBERS OF THE PC
*    ROUTINES. THIS TABLE IS USED BY THE USER ADDRESS SPACES, WHICH
*    ARE REQUIRED TO CALL THE PC ROUTINE.
***********************************************************************
*
PUTXTBL  XC      $SRV01ID,$SRV01ID    ZERO SERVICE ID
         MVI     $SRV01ID+3,X'03'     SET SERVICE ID=3
         MVC     $PCNUM01,LXVALUE     SET LX VALUE PART OF PC NUMB
         MVI     $PCNUM01+3,X'00'     SET EX VALUE PART OF PC NUMB
         MVC     $XREFEND,BINONES     INDICATE END OF CROSS-REF TBL
         BR      R7                   RETURN TO CALLING ROUTINE
*
*
***********************************************************************
*    THIS ROUTINE IS USED FOR TESTING ONLY. IT SIMULATES ADDRESS SPACE
*    PROCESSING UNTIL THE ACTUAL PROCESSING ROUTINE IS WRITTEN.
***********************************************************************
*
PROCESS  OPEN    (DCB,(OUTPUT))
         PUT     DCB,RECORD
         CLOSE   DCB
         B       PROCESS
*
```

```
*
***********************************************************************
*    THIS ROUTINE REMOVES THE CROSS MEMORY ENVIRONMENT.
***********************************************************************
*
         DROP  R10                  RELEASE REG FOR REUSE
         USING CVT,R10              DEFINE REG FOR CVT DSECT
REMOVEXM L     R10,16               LOAD ADR OF CVT
         XC    CVTUSER,CVTUSER      CLEAR CVTUSER
         BAL   R7,DESTRYET          DESTROY/PURGE ENTRY TABLE
         BAL   R7,FREELX            RELEASE RESERVED LX VALUE
         BAL   R7,RSETAUTH          RESET ORIG AX VALUE AND REL RESV AX
         BAL   R7,FREECSA           RELEASE ALLOC CSA
         BR    R6                   RETURN TO CALLING ROUTINE
*
*
***********************************************************************
*    THIS SUBROUTINE DESTROYS THE ENTRY TABLE AND USES THE PURGE OPTION
*    IN CASE THE USER ADDRESS SPACE HAS NOT DISCONNECTED IT FROM ITS
*    LINKAGE TABLE.
***********************************************************************
*
DESTRYET ETDES TOKEN=ETTOKEN,PURGE=YES    DESTROY/PURGE ENTRY TABLE
         BR    R7                   RETURN TO CALLING ROUTINE
*
*
***********************************************************************
*    THIS SUBROUTINE RELEASES THE RESERVED LX VALUE.
***********************************************************************
*
FREELX   LXFRE LXLIST=LXLIST        RELEASE RESERVED LX VALUE
         BR    R7                   RETURN TO CALLING ROUTINE
*
*
***********************************************************************
*    THIS SUBROUTINE RESETS THE AX VALUE OF THE ADDRESS SPACE BACK TO
*    ITS ORIGINAL VALUE AND RELEASES THE RESERVED AX VALUE.
***********************************************************************
*
RSETAUTH LA    R10,0
         AXSET AX=(R10)
         AXFRE AXLIST=AXLIST
         BR    R7
*
*
***********************************************************************
*    THIS SUBROUTINE RELEASES THE CSA STORAGE.
***********************************************************************
*
FREECSA  FREEMAIN EU,LV=CSALEN,SP=227,A=CSAADR
         BR    R7
*
*
***********************************************************************
*    THIS ROUTINE RESTORES THE REGISTERS AND RETURNS CONTROL TO MVS OR
*    THE CALLING PROGRAM.
***********************************************************************
*
RETURN   RCNTL RC=0                 RETURN TO MVS OR CALLING PROG
*
*
***********************************************************************
*    THE DC/DS STATEMENTS
***********************************************************************
```

```
*
BINONES  DC    4XL1'FF'
CSAADR   DS    F
*
*
***************************************************************************
*    THE AUTHORIZATION-VALUE (AX) LIST
***************************************************************************
*
AXLIST   DS     0F
AXCOUNT  DC     H'1'
AXVALUE  DS     H
*
*
***************************************************************************
*    THE LINKAGE-VALUE (LX) LIST
***************************************************************************
*
LXLIST   DS     0F
LXCOUNT  DC     F'1'
LXVALUE  DS     F
*
*
***************************************************************************
*    THE ENTRY-TABLE TOKEN LIST
***************************************************************************
*
ETLIST   DS     0F
ETCOUNT  DC     F'1'
ETTOKEN  DS     F
*
*
***************************************************************************
*    THE AREAS USED TO CREATE THE ENTRY TABLE PARAMETER-LIST
***************************************************************************
*
PCRTNS   DS     0F
ETDHDR   DS     CL(ETDLEN)
ETDSERV1 DS     CL(ETDELEN)
*
*
***************************************************************************
*    THE RECORD AND DCB USED FOR THE I/O LOOP FOR TESTING
***************************************************************************
*
RECORD   DC     80CL1'A'
DCB      DCB    DSORG=PS,MACRF=PM,BLKSIZE=80,LRECL=80,RECFM=F,               -
                DDNAME=WORK
*
*
*
*
***************************************************************************
***************************************************************************
*    THE CODE FOR THE PCSERV03 PC ROUTINE
***************************************************************************
***************************************************************************
*
*
***************************************************************************
*    INITIALIZATION
***************************************************************************
*
         DROP  R3                    RELEASE REG FOR REUSE
```

```
PCSERV03 PCLINK STACK,SAVE=NO     SAVE STATUS OF CALLING PROG
         BALR  R3,0               LOAD BASE REGISTER
         USING *,R3               DEFINE BASE REGISTER
*
*
***********************************************************************
*    MAINSTREAM OF PC ROUTINE
***********************************************************************
*
         BAL   R6,SAVEREGS        SAVE CONTENTS OF CONTROL REGS
         BAL   R6,GETPASCB        GET ADR OF ASCB OF PASID
         BAL   R6,SETCMLOK        OBTAIN CML LOCK
         BAL   R6,GETKEY          GET KEY FROM U-AS
         BAL   R6,FINDDATA        GET CORRES DATA FROM TBL IN SP-AS
         BAL   R6,MOVEDATA        MOVE DATA TO U-AS
         BAL   R6,RELCMLOK        RELEASE CML LOCK
         B     RETCALL            RETURN TO CALLING PROG IN U-AS
*
*
***********************************************************************
*    THIS ROUTINE SAVES THE CONTENTS OF ALL REGISTERS THAT CONTAIN
*    CONTROL INFORMATION.
***********************************************************************
*
SAVEREGS ST    R14,SAVR14         SAVE STACK-ENTRY ADR
         ST    R1,SKEYADR         SAVE ADR OF KEY IN U-AS
         ST    R15,SBUFFADR       SAVE ADR OF REVC BUFF IN U-AS
         BR    R6                 RETURN TO CALLING ROUTINE
*
*
***********************************************************************
*    THIS ROUTINE OBTAINS THE ADDRESS OF THE ASCB FOR THE PRIMARY
*    ADDRESS SPACE.
***********************************************************************
*
GETPASCB EPAR R1                  LD REG 1 WITH PASID
         LOCASCB ASID=(R1)        GET ASCB ADR OF PASID
         ST      R1,PASCBADR      SAVE ADR OF ASCB OF PRIM A.S.
         BR      R6               RETURN TO CALLING ROUTINE
*
*
***********************************************************************
*    THIS ROUTINE OBTAINS THE CML LOCK TO MAKE THE U-AS NON-SWAPPABLE
*    DURING THE SYNCHRONOUS COMMUNICATION AND TO SERIALIZE THE USE OF
*    THE PC ROUTINES IN THIS ADDRESS SPACE.
***********************************************************************
*
SETCMLOK LA      R1,0                LD ZERO FOR SPKA INSTR
         SPKA    0(R1)               SET PSW STOR PROT KEY TO ZERO
         L       R11,PASCBADR        LD ADR OF ASCB OF PASID
         SETLOCK OBTAIN,TYPE=CML,ASCB=(11),RELATED=(RELCMLOK),MODE=COND
         BR      R6                  RETURN TO CALLING ROUTINE
*
*
***********************************************************************
*    THIS ROUTINE COPIES THE SPECIFIED TABLE KEY FROM THE SECONDARY A.S.
*    (THE INVOKING A.S.) TO THE PRIMARY A.S. (THIS A.S.).
***********************************************************************
*
GETKEY   LA   R9,KEYLEN          LD LENGTH OF KEY AREA IN SP-AS
         LA   R10,KEY            LD ADR OF KEY AREA IN SP-AS
         L    R11,SKEYADR        LD ADR OF KEY AREA IN U-AS
         LA   R12,X'80'          LD ACCESS PSW STOR PROT KEY
         MVCP 0(R9,R10),0(R11),R12   MOVE KEY FROM U-AS TO SP-AS
```

```
         BR   R6                  RETURN TO CALLING ROUTINE
*
*
**********************************************************************
*    THIS ROUTINE SCANS THE TABLE LOCATED IN THE SP-AS TO LOCATE THE
*    TABLE DATA ENTRY THAT CORRESPONDS TO THE KEY SPECIFIED BY THE U-AS.
*    IF THE KEY IS NOT LOCATED IN THE TABLE, THEN RC=4 IN SET IN REGISTER
*    15 AND CONTROL IS RETURNED TO THE CALLING PROGRAM. IF THE SPECIFIED
*    KEY IS FOUND IN THE TABLE, THEN RC=0 IN SET IN REGISTER 15, AND
*    REGISTER 11 POINTS TO THE CORRESPONDING DATA ENTRY OF THE TABLE.
**********************************************************************
*
FINDDATA LA   R11,TABLE           LOAD ADR OF TABLE
NEXTENTY CLI  0(R11),X'FF'        CHECK FOR END-OF-TABLE
         BE   INVKEY              IF YES, IND INVALID KEY
         CLC  0(KEYLEN,R11),KEY      COMP SPEC KEY TO KEY IN TBL
         BE   KEYOK                  IF EQUAL, LD ADR OF DATA
         LA   R11,ENTRYLEN(0,R11)    IF NOT, INCR TO NEXT TBL ENTRY
         B    NEXTENTY               CHECK NEXT TBL ENTRY
KEYOK    LA   R11,KEYLEN(0,R11)   LD ADR OF CORRES DATA
         LA   R15,0                  IND KEY OK, DATA ADR LOADED
         BR   R6                  RETURN TO CALLING ROUTINE
INVKEY   LA   R15,4               IND INVALID KEY
         BR   R6                  RETURN TO CALLING ROUTINE
*
*
**********************************************************************
*    THIS ROUTINE COPIES THE DATA ENTRY FROM THE TABLE THAT CORRESPONDS
*    TO THE SPECIFIED KEY TO THE SECONDARY A.S. (THE INVOKING A.S.).
*    THE TABLE IS LOCATED IN THE PRIMARY A.S. (THIS A.S.). WHEN THIS
*    ROUTINE RECEIVES CONTROL, IT FIRST EXAMINES THE RC IN REGISTER 15.
*    IF THE RC IS NON-ZERO, NO DATA IS COPIED TO THE U-AS. IF THE RC IN
*    REGISTER 15 IS ZERO, THEN REGISTER 11 POINTS TO THE DATA THAT IS
*    TO BE COPIED TO THE U-AS.
**********************************************************************
*
MOVEDATA LTR  R15,R15             CHECK IF DATA FOUND
         BNZR R6                  IF NO, RET TO CALLING ROUTINE
         LA   R9,DATALEN          LD LENGTH OF DATA ENTRY IN TBL
         L    R10,SBUFFADR        LD ADR OF RECV BUFF IN U-AS
         LA   R12,X'80'           LD ACCESS PSW STOR PROT KEY
         MVCS 0(R9,R10),0(R11),R12   MOVE DATA FROM SP-AS TO U-AS
         BR   R6                  RETURN TO CALLING ROUTINE
*
*
**********************************************************************
*    THIS ROUTINE RELEASES THE CML LOCK.
**********************************************************************
*
RELCMLOK L    R11,PASCBADR        LD ADR OF ASCB OF PASID
         ST   R15,SAVR15          SAVE RC
         SETLOCK RELEASE,TYPE=CML,ASCB=(11),RELATED=(SETCMLOK)
         L    R15,SAVR15          RESTORE RC
         BR   R6                  RETURN TO CALLING ROUTINE
*
*
**********************************************************************
*    THIS ROUTINE RESTORES THE STATUS OF THE CALLING PROGRAM AND RETURNS
*    CONTROL.
**********************************************************************
*
RETCALL  L    R14,SAVR14          RESTORE ADR OF STACK ENTRY
         PCLINK UNSTACK,THRU=(R14),SAVE=NO   RESTORE STATUS
         PT   R3,R14              RETURN CONTROL TO CALLING PROG
```

```
*
*
***********************************************************************
*    DC/DS STATEMENTS
***********************************************************************
*
SAVR14   DS   F
SAVR15   DS   F
SKEYADR  DS   F
SBUFFADR DS   F
PASCBADR DS   F
*
*
***********************************************************************
*    INFORMATION TABLE
***********************************************************************
*
TABLE    DC   C'CODE01'
KEYX     EQU  *
         DC   CL20'INFO-01'
ENTRYX   EQU  *
         DC   C'CODE02',CL20'INFO-02'
         DC   C'CODE03',CL20'INFO-03'
         DC   C'CODE04',CL20'INFO-04'
         ...                        ADDITIONAL DATA ENTRIES
         DC   X'FF'
KEYLEN   EQU  KEYX-TABLE
DATALEN  EQU  ENTRYLEN-KEYLEN
ENTRYLEN EQU  ENTRYX-TABLE
*
KEY      DS   CL(KEYLEN)
*
*
***********************************************************************
*    THE DSECTS
***********************************************************************
*
CSAMAP   DSECT
$AXLIST  DS   0F
$AXCOUNT DS   H
$AXVALUE DS   H
*
$LXLIST  DS   0F
$LXCOUNT DS   F
$LXVALUE DS   F
*
$ETLIST  DS   0F
$ETCOUNT DS   F
$ETTOKEN DS   F
*
$XREFTBL DS   0F
$SRV01ID DS   F
$PCNUM01 DS   F
$XREFEND DS   F
*
CSALEN   EQU  *-CSAMAP
*
         CVT  DSECT=YES            GENERATES CVT DSECT
         IHAETD                    GENERATES ENTRY TABLE DSECTS
         IHAPSA                    GENERATES PSA DSECT (REQD BY SETLOCK)
*
*
***********************************************************************
*    END OF PROGRAM
```

```
************************************************************************
*
         END
```

NOTES:

- The program must be APF authorized in order to issue the MODESET macro instruction.

Coding Example 15.4.12

This coding example illustrates the code for the program from the U-AS, which calls the PC routine PCSERV03 from Coding Example 15.4.11.

```
USER02 CSECT
*
*
************************************************************************
*    INITIALIZATION
************************************************************************
*
         INITL 3,EQU=R            INITIALIZE PROGRAM
*
*
************************************************************************
*    MAINSTREAM OF PROGRAM
************************************************************************
*
         BAL  R6,SETUP            SET UP AUTH AND LINKAGE FOR SP-AS
         BAL  R6,SRCHTBL          SEARCH TBL FOR SPECIFIC DATA ENTRY
         BAL  R6,CHKDATA          VERIFY DATA BY DUMPING IT
         BAL  R6,PROCESS          PROCESS DATA FROM TBL
         B    RETURN              RETURN TO MVS OR CALLING PROG
*
*
************************************************************************
*    THIS ROUTINE INVOKES THE APPROPRIATE SVC ROUTINE AND REQUESTS THAT
*    IT SETS UP THE REQUIRED AUTHORITY AND LINKAGE FOR ACCESS TO/FROM
*    THE SP-AS.
************************************************************************
*
SETUP    LA   R0,0                REQUEST AUTH/LINKAGE FOR SP-AS
         SVC  255                 INVOKE SVC TO SET UP AUTH/LINKAGE
         BR   R6                  RETURN TO CALLING ROUTINE
*
*
************************************************************************
*    THIS ROUTINE INVOKES THE APPROPRIATE SVC ROUTINE TO CALL A SPECIFIC
*    PC ROUTINE TO SEARCH A TABLE LOCATED IN THAT ADDRESS SPACE AND
*    RETURN THE SPECIFIC DATA ENTRY THAT CORRESPONDS TO THE SPECIFIED
*    KEY.
************************************************************************
*
SRCHTBL  LA   R0,3                SPEC SERV-ID
         LA   R1,KEY              LD ADR OF KEY FOR SVC
         LA   R15,DATA            LD ADR OF RECV DATA AREA FOR SVC
         SVC  255                 INVOKE SVC TO GET DATA
         LTR  R15,R15             TEST FOR GOOD RC
         BZR  R6                  IF OK, RET TO CALLING ROUTINE
         WTO  '*** INVALID ID SPECIFIED ***',ROUTCDE=11
         LA   R15,4               IND INVALID ID SPECIFIED
         BR   R6                  RETURN TO CALLING ROUTINE
```

```
*
*
***********************************************************************
*    THIS ROUTINE IS USED FOR TESTING ONLY. IT VERIFIES THAT THE CORRECT
*    DATA FROM THE TABLE WAS RECEIVED FOR THE SPECIFIED KEY FROM THE
*    CALLED PC ROUTINE.
***********************************************************************
*
CHKDATA  L     R8,DATA             LOAD 1ST FOUR BYTES OF RECV DATA
         L     R9,DATA+4           LOAD 2ND FOUR BYTES OF RECV DATA
         ABEND 900,DUMP            DUMP REGS
*
*
***********************************************************************
*    THIS ROUTINE PERFORMS THE MAIN PROCESSING OF THE PROGRAM.
***********************************************************************
*
PROCESS  LTR  R15,R15              CHK IF DATA RECEIVED FROM PC ROUTINE
         BNZ  R6                   IF NO, RET TO CALLING ROUTINE
*        ...                       IF YES, PROCESS DATA
         BR   R6                   RETURN TO CALLING ROUTINE
*
*
***********************************************************************
*    THIS ROUTINE RESTORES THE REGISTERS AND RETURNS CONTROL TO MVS OR
*    THE CALLING PROGRAM.
***********************************************************************
*
RETURN   RCNTL RC=0                RETURN TO MVS OR CALLING PROG
*
*
***********************************************************************
*    THE DC/DS STATEMENTS
***********************************************************************
*
         DS   0F
KEY      DC   C'CODE02'            SPECIFIED ARGUMENT KEY
DATA     DS   CL20                 RECEIVING FIELD FOR DATA FROM SP-AS
*
*
***********************************************************************
*    END OF PROGRAM
***********************************************************************
*
         END
```

NOTES:

- Since the code in PCSERV03 receives control via a PC instruction, it executes with the CPU in primary mode; therefore, it is not required to be located in commonly addressable virtual storage.
- The usual way to pass addresses to a called program is to provide a parameter-list containing a list of ADCONs with register 1 pointing to the beginning of the list, such as the following:

```
         LA   R1,PARMLIST
         ...
PARMLIST DC   A(KEY)
         DC   A(DATA)
```

This technique will not work between program calls accross different address spaces. When a parameter-list is passed to a called program, the individual addresses are extracted as follows:

```
         L     R10,0(0,R1)          LOAD KEY ADR
         L     R11,4(0,R1)          LOAD DATA ADR
```

Since the address in register 1 points to an area located in the calling address space (U-AS), the L instruction cannot be used in the way shown above to extract the addresses contained in the parameter-list (located in the U-AS) because the address in register 1 is being used (erroneously) to point to an area in the called address space (SP-AS). If a parameter-list must be used to pass a series of addresses, then the entire parameter-list must be moved as data into the called address space. Then, each entry (address) contained in the parameter-list (the copy in the SP-AS) can be loaded into a register and used in the MVCP and/or MVCS instructions.

The SVC-255 used in this coding example is the same one as used in Coding Example 15.4.10.

15.4.5 Advantages of Using CMS

The following are some of the advantages of using cross memory services.

- Of the methods discussed in this chapter, CMS provides the most efficient way to transfer data between address spaces.
- Since called programs (which are located in an address space) can be accessible to multiple other address spaces, virtual storage is saved since only one copy of each called program is required in virtual storage. These programs are not required to be resident in the common area, such as the Link Pack Area. Performance is also improved since the called programs reside in virtual storage instead of being invoked from a load library.
- Since large amounts of data can be stored in another address space, more virtual storage is available, and performance is also improved since the data stored in the address space can be accessed without performing I/O. MVS/ESA also provides Data Spaces and Hiperspaces, which have a similar function.
- Since the called PC routines may execute at a higher authority level (supervisor state and/or additional PSW storage protection keys), they can perform certain sensitive functions that cannot be performed by the calling problem state program. This improves system integrity by isolating that code away from the calling program.

BIBLIOGRAPHY FOR CHAPTER 15

The following IBM manuals contain reference material for the topics discussed in this chapter.

ID	TITLE
GC28-1046	*OS/VS2 SPL: Supervisor*
GC28-1150	*MVS/XA SPL: System Macros and Facilities Volume 1*
GC28-1151	*MVS/XA SPL: System Macros and Facilities Volume 2*
GC28-1852	*MVS/ESA SPL: Application Development Guide*
GC28-1854	*MVS/ESA SPL: Application Development–Extended Addressability*
GC28-1857	*MVS/ESA SPL: Application Development Macro Reference*
GG22-9231	*Cross Memory Services User's Guide*

Bibliography

This Bibliography contains the titles of books and of IBM manuals which contain prerequisite material for this book. In addition, the names of the IBM manuals which contain the descriptions of the DSECTs used throughout this book are included.

The names of the IBM manuals which contain reference material specific to each chapter are included at the end of those chapters.

Where applicable and possible, the MVS/370, MVS/XA and MVS/ESA versions of the manuals are listed.

Books for MVS and Assembler Language Programming:

MVS Concepts and Facilities;
McGraw Hill; Robert H. Johnson

Assembler Language Programming for IBM and IBM Compatible Computers;
Wiley & Sons; Stern & Stern.

Principles of Assembler Language Programming for the IBM 370;
McGraw Hill; Spotswood D. Stoddard.

Introduction to Machine and Assembler Language: Systems/360/370;
Holt, Rinehart and Winston; Frank D. Vickers.

IBM manuals which contain prerequiste and other reference material relevent to all chapters:

ID	TITLE
GA22-7000	*IBM System/370 Principles of Operation*
SA22-7085	*IBM System/370 XA Principles of Operation*
SA22-7000	*IBM ESA/370 Principles of Operation*
GC33-4010	*OS/VS - DOS/VSE - VM/370 Assembler Language*
GC33-4021	*OS/VS - VM/370 Assembler Programmer's Guide*
SC26-4036	*Assembler H Version 2 Application Programming: Guide*
SC26-4037	*Assembler H Version 2 Application Programming: Language Reference*
GC26-4061	*MVS/370 Linkage Editor and Loader User's Guide*
GC26-4011	*MVS/XA Linkage Editor and Loader User's Guide*
SC26-4510	*MVS/ESA Linkage Editor and Loader User's Guide*

IBM manuals which contain the descriptions of the DSECTs used in this book:

For MVS/370:

ID	TITLE
GC28-1048 OS/VS2	*SPL: Debugging Handbook Volume 2*
GC28-1049 OS/VS2	*SPL: Debugging Handbook Volume 3*

For MVS/XA:

ID	TITLE
LC28-1165	*MVS/XA Debugging Handbook Volume 2*
LC28-1166	*MVS/XA Debugging Handbook Volume 3*
LC28-1167	*MVS/XA Debugging Handbook Volume 4*
LC28-1168	*MVS/XA Debugging Handbook Volume 5*
LC28-1169	*MVS/XA Debugging Handbook Volume 6 (For MVS/XA 2.2 only)*

For MVS/ESA:

ID	TITLE
LY28-1043	*MVS/ESA Diagnosis: Data Areas Volume 1*
LY28-1044	*MVS/ESA Diagnosis: Data Areas Volume 2*
LY28-1045	*MVS/ESA Diagnosis: Data Areas Volume 3*
LY28-1046	*MVS/ESA Diagnosis: Data Areas Volume 4*
LY28-1047	*MVS/ESA Diagnosis: Data Areas Volume 5*

Index

FLPA, (*see* Fixed Link Pack Area)
FLPA, (*see* Fixed Link Pack Area)

Coding Examples Available on PC Diskettes

The coding examples (over 150) in this book are available on PC diskettes. The contents can be uploaded to a mainfarame computer.

ORDERING INFORMATION:

Name: ______________________________

Company: ______________________________

Address: ______________________________

City/State/Zip code: ______________________________

Country: ______________________________

Diskette Size: ❑ 5¼″ ❑ 3½″

SEND CHECK OR MONEY ORDER TO:

CAC, Inc.
JAF Station
P.O. Box 8585
New York, NY 10116

COST: $50.00 in U.S. Dollars. (International mailings, add $10.00 for shipping and handling)

Allow 2 to 4 weeks for delivery after receipt of order.